TEACHING ENGLISH THROUGH PRINCIPLED PRACTICE

Peter Smagorinsky
University of Georgia

Merrill
Prentice Hall

Upper Saddle River, New Jersey
Columbus, Ohio

Library of Congress Cataloging-in-Publication Data

Smagorinsky, Peter.
  Teaching English through principled practice / Peter Smagorinsky.
    p. cm.
  Includes bibliographical references and index.
  ISBN 0-13-025840-7
  1. English philology—Study and teaching. I. Title.

PE65 .S63 2002
428'.0071'2—dc21

                                    00-050011

Vice President and Publisher: Jeffery W. Johnston
Editor: Linda Ashe Montgomery
Production Editor: Mary M. Irvin
Design Coordinator: Diane C. Lorenzo
Project Coordination and Text Design: Carlisle Publishers Services
Cover Design: Linda Fares
Cover Art: SuperStock
Production Manager: Pamela D. Bennett
Director of Marketing: Kevin Flanagan
Marketing Manager: Krista Groshong
Marketing Coordinator: Barbara Koontz

This book was set in Garamond by Carlisle Communications, Ltd., and was printed
and bound by R. R. Donnelley & Sons Company. The cover was printed by The Lehigh
Press, Inc.

All photos supplied by the author.

Prentice-Hall International (UK) Limited, *London*
Prentice-Hall of Australia Pty. Limited, *Sydney*
Prentice-Hall Canada, Inc., *Toronto*
Prentice-Hall Hispanoamericana, S.A., *Mexico*
Prentice-Hall of India Private Limited, *New Delhi*
Prentice-Hall of Japan, Inc., *Tokyo*
Prentice-Hall Singapore Pte. Ltd.
Editora Prentice-Hall do Brasil, Ltda., *Rio de Janeiro*

10 9 8 7 6 5 4 3 2
ISBN 0-13-025840-7

Dedicated to my first and most important teachers,
Margaret and Joseph Smagorinsky

"Choose a job you love and you will never work a day in your life."
—Confucius

PREFACE

This book is about teaching middle and high school English. Teaching English is a complicated business, so I can't tell you everything about being an English teacher in one book. What I do try to do, however, is *outline a way to plan instruction* that you can apply to many different situations, whether you teach seventh grade or twelfth, in the city or in the country, with unmotivated or autonomous learners.

There's no magic formula for teaching English. But, it is wise to consider that the context of where you teach is important to making decisions about how you teach and so part of the method is to understand where you teach, whom you teach, and the purpose of schooling in that setting. You also create a context within your classroom in terms of the way you arrange the furniture, the way you arrange the tone, and the way you arrange learning experiences. Within these contexts, you plan your instruction. How you teach also helps to construct the context of your work— you and your students help to produce your own environment. It's important to remember this so that you don't feel that you are a pawn in somebody else's game. You might play on a board that limits the things you can do, but you also have opportunities to change the rules, change the roles of the players, affect the purpose of the action, change how you move about the board, and occasionally alter the board itself. You can see that as a teacher, you will make many instructional decisions that ultimately affect your students' learning.

General Instructional Planning

Throughout this text I approach instructional planning on four levels: the *whole course,* the *unit,* individual *lessons* within the unit, and the *daily plan.* I first ask you to think about your larger purposes in teaching a whole course, such as sophomore English, American Literature, and the like. Any teaching fits within a set of larger goals and practices. Thinking about your larger purposes will help you plan instruction that is coherent to students at the incremental levels of planning: units, lessons, and daily plans.

When I talk about units, I refer to what I'll call *conceptual units of instruction.* These are four- to six-week blocks of time that you devote to a particular topic: a *theme,* such as progress, an *author,* such as Toni Morrison, a *period,* such as American naturalism, a *region,* such as the area that produced the British Lake poets, a *movement,* such as transcendentalism, a *reading strategy,* such as understanding irony, or a *genre,* such as the detective novel. I devote much of this text to planning at the unit level. If you learn how to plan instruction in four- to six-week blocks of time, your teaching will have continuity and purpose for students. You will also relieve yourself of the burden of planning day to day. This skill is particularly important early in your career when you can be overwhelmed by the stresses of starting a new teaching life: moving, learning a new political environment, managing your income, making new friends, and so on. You can also be overwhelmed by the parts of teaching that are difficult to treat in a book, particularly interpersonal dynamics with both individual students and whole classrooms (or individual colleagues and whole faculties). But if your lessons are well planned, you will have one less major responsibility to face each day and can focus on other aspects of your teaching.

When you first begin to teach, you may also be overwhelmed by the number of **preparations**—that is, different teaching assignments—you have. You may be assigned to teach two sections of freshmen, two sections of sophomores, and one section of juniors. That means three different preparations for each day. If you do not plan ahead, each night will require you to think of something new to do for three different sets of classes. This is not my idea of a good time, nor do I suspect, yours.

Further, within parts of this text I show you how to plan units to incorporate each minute of every class. You will learn that your daily plan is a guide rather than a script and that anticipating roughly how much time to budget for each activity will help make you more successful. Careful unit planning can help provide you with some security in your classroom preparation, especially at the beginning of your teaching career.

As you continue reading, carefully review the following aspects of this text.

- the book's general organization
- the metaphor I use for discussing teaching and learning
- the kinds of work you can do in response to the book
- the source of the vignettes I relate throughout the book

General Text Organization

The text begins with a general introduction. In this Introduction I define a conceptual unit, define other key terms used in the book, provide a rationale for organizing your teaching according to units, and outline the principles of practice that are behind the primary instructional approach.

Part I is devoted to principles of planning. Within this section, I review theories of teaching and learning, all of which suggest the need for teaching that is purposeful, flexible, and constructive. I then lay out a set of procedures for designing a course curriculum based on these theories and then I provide procedures for creating individual units that compose this course curriculum. These units consist of both lessons (instruction in how to do one thing within the unit that often takes several days) and daily plans. If I've done my job well, you'll be able to apply these procedures to the design of units you teach with your own students. The idea, then, is for you to learn a planning process that you will use hereafter in your own English teaching.

Part II describes life in classrooms, including ideas for setting up both the physical layout and classroom routines. I use illustrations taken from classrooms I have observed over the years to show how students interact and learn in classrooms that follow the design principles outlined in this book. All discussion excerpts come from discussions tape-recorded in real classrooms; all names are pseudonyms.

Part III includes essays about rethinking the curriculum. In these chapters I raise questions about how the content and process of the curriculum can affect students. The essays consider three topics: how to plan a curriculum with attention to diversity, how to think about character education, and how to think about educational standards. They have been written in large part as a way for me to think about vexing questions I have faced in my own teaching. They also reflect issues that are frequently debated in the field.

The text closes with three appendices. Appendix A includes outlines of dozens of instructional units. Each includes a list of possible texts, key questions, and problems to consider for the unit's focus. You may find these to be useful when designing your own units, at least as a starting place in identifying appropriate texts for your students. Appendix B contains an example of a classroom activity based on a court case, with the purpose of teaching students extended definitions as well as how to argue with appropriate evidence. Appendix C illustrates how to teach students to critique one another's writing as well as teaching them ways to critique their own. Each appendix is linked to particular issues raised in the book.

The chapters in Part I are indexed to a set of model units, found at *http://www.coe.uga.edu/~smago/VirtualLibrary/index.html.* These units have been written by preservice teachers at the University of Georgia and are examples of the kinds of units I advocate in this book. You will find periodic references to these units while you're reading, with suggestions to consult them while you're writing your own unit of instruction.

General Focus and Features of the Text

The Greeks had a word, *tektonikos,* which means "of a builder." You might call the approach I outline in this book *tectonic teaching,* that is, teaching as a process of construction. This construction occurs simultaneously at two levels. At the teaching level, you will be a builder of curriculum, of a classroom community, of instructional units. Building requires tools, materials, plans, and methods of building. Your unit design, then, will be described as a process of construction that engages you in purposeful—and at times collaborative—activity.

Similarly, your students will be builders. One of my premises about being a teacher is that *people learn by making, and reflecting on, things that they find useful and important.* Your unit design should involve students in the production of things they find useful. These things are called *texts.* Texts are usually written, but can also be spoken or nonverbal (art or dance, for instance). When designing units of instruction, consider the tools, materials, plans, and methods of construction your students will need to use as they work. Like other kinds of builders, your students will work in a social environment where they get frequent feedback on their texts as they construct them.

Think of yourself, then, as a builder of curriculum and as one who helps students learn to build their own texts. This approach is known as *constructivist* teaching. As you might know from your experiences as a student, schools are more likely to rely on what I call *authoritative* teaching. In this approach, the teacher is presumed to be an expert who fills students with knowledge. In asking you to use a different metaphor for teaching, then, I'm asking you to rethink what it means to be a teacher. I'm asking you to be reflective as you consider more meaningful ways to teach.

Reflective Writing Prompts: I often use some variation on the term *reflection* in this book. By *reflection* I mean a process in which you pause to think back on something you've done and ruminate on it in some way. There's no single form a reflection might take. Often the act of describing a situation serves as an occasion for thinking about it. I ask you to reflect on your own experiences with teaching and learning and meditate on their impact on you. I also urge you to teach reflectively, so that you are always thinking about the processes and effects of your teaching.

A number of Reflective Writing Prompts ask you to reflect on issues related to those arising in the book. Often, these prompts are designed to get you to think about your own beliefs and assumptions about teaching, to consider how you developed those beliefs, and to think about them in light of issues raised in this book. The purpose of such reflection is to help you understand why you believe what you believe. This understanding is particularly important when you find the ideas I present to be at odds with what you assume to be true.

Discussion Topics: Periodically, I include possible discussion topics. Discussions might take place with your whole class or in small groups, which provide you with the opportunity to speak more freely, to take more risks with what you say, and to feel less inhibited than you might feel in addressing the whole class and the professor. I devote much of this book to the use of small groups in unit design and the use of exploratory talk as a way of learning. These discussion topics may help you see the potential of strategically using small groups to facilitate learning. Discussion topics follow from issues covered in the text.

Field Observations: For those whose course includes a practicum or field experience component, these prompts are designed to help relate field observations to what I discuss in the book. It's possible that you won't get an opportunity to use some of them, depending on how your field experience is structured. Some teachers in the field, for instance, will allow you to visit, but will restrict you to observations. Others will invite you to dinner, become your lifelong friends, and let you plan and teach lessons. Still others will put you to work grading student papers or laminating materials for them. Your field experiences will likely fall somewhere along this continuum.

Vignettes: Most chapters include vignettes of teaching that I've collected over the years. The purpose of the vignettes is to provide real illustrations of what it's like to be a teacher. Many of them come from my own work in the classroom: as a substitute teacher, primarily in the New Jersey and Chicago public school systems, and as a classroom teacher for thirteen more years in three suburban high schools in the

Chicago area. From these forty different schools, in most subject areas and at all grade levels, I've seen the good, the bad, and the ugly of public education.

I have drawn on these experiences to write about instructional planning as well as provide vignettes relevant to points raised in this book.

Onward

One note before moving along: I've just provided you with an explanation of how the book is structured and what you can expect. As you'll see, I recommend that any time you teach something complex, it's helpful to provide some kind of map for students so they know where they're headed. As with any other journey, the destination may change and detours may entice you off the path—but traveling is much easier on the nerves when you have some idea of where you're headed and which paths you'll follow to arrive there.

One more note on the presentation of the text: I have tried to make the book as readable as possible. In considering how to do this, I made a decision that violates one rule of scholarly writing, which is to provide references in the text to published scholarship to support claims made in the text. In most scholarly writing, this convention makes a sentence look like this: "Cognitive psychologists have found that people use knowledge networks, called *schemata,* to organize their thinking (Arbib & Conklin, 1987; Bransford, 1979; Kintsch, 1977; Kitao, 1989; Mandler, 1984; Tierney & Pearson, 1986)." Much of my own writing looks like this. For this book, I thought that using in-text citation lists would interfere with, rather than assist, reading. I therefore have included citation lists in proximity to claims that require references, rather than within the text itself. (I do use in-text citations when they are brief and do not break the flow of reading.) A master list of references at the end of the book includes each citation listed in the book. Readers are welcome to consult these sources if they wish to do further reading or check the basis for my claims about teaching and learning.

ACKNOWLEDGMENTS

This book is the result of my career as an educator: to this point, fourteen years of teaching in public high schools and ten years of teaching English education in universities. Anything written from such extensive experience is greatly indebted to many friends, colleagues, students, and teachers. Recognizing them all would take up more than my allotted pages for the whole project. I will try, then, to thank a few people who've been particularly instrumental in helping me understand something about teaching.

First I should thank all of the students I taught in the Pilot Enrichment/Upward Bound Program and at Martin Luther King High School, both in Chicago, while earning my teaching credentials in 1976–1977. From then until 1990 I taught in the Chicago suburbs of Westmont, Barrington, and Oak Park-River Forest, where my students never hesitated to let me know what was working and especially what wasn't. I imagine that each and every one of the roughly 1,500 students I taught in these schools has influenced my teaching in some way, and that each of them is responsible for something in this book.

I also worked with many gifted and dynamic teachers at these schools, a number of whom remain friends. Not only did they contribute to my thinking about teaching, they also helped to create environments where good teaching was possible. Creating a supportive teaching environment both in and around the classroom is vital to finding fulfillment in a teaching career. I'm thankful for having had the opportunity to work in schools that not only enabled me to do my best work, but created the expectation that I could always be better. I'm especially grateful for the latitude and support that Dale Griffith provided for me at Barrington High School during my critical formative years of teaching. I could never publish this book without tipping my hat to some of my BHS colleagues for their support and friendship during my years there: Jane Christino, Tim Hull, Art Hutchinson, Carol Mayer, Pat Millen, Bernie Phelan, Charles White, and Joe Wolnski. It's very important for early-career teachers to have such support if they are to teach happily beyond the teacher's manual and prescribed curriculum.

My own schooling as an educator has been fundamental to my understanding of how to teach. All my formal education for teaching came at the University of Chicago under the guidance of George Hillocks, whose ideas permeate this book and have influenced a few generations of teachers who have come through his M.A.T. and Ph.D. programs. George is the architect of the basic approach to unit design I describe in this book, though I'm sure that he would in turn credit it to his own mentors. In addition to providing the conception for this unit design, George created a remarkable community among his students over the years, one that established his program as what I call the *conceptual home base* for those who go through it. That community has provided me with some of the best friends and colleagues I'll ever have in this profession, some of whom deserve attention here. I've co-authored with Steve Gevinson, Steve Kern, Carol Lee, Tom McCann, and my long-time partner in various projects, Michael W. Smith. I have also been privileged to have the friendship and support of Betsy Kahn and Larry Johannessen for many years; though I've never written with them, their work has inspired much of my own. Larry and Betsy were especially supportive of me when I was making my first attempts at writing about education in the 1980s. I feel a kinship with anyone associated with the Chicago program; the sense of community among its graduates would be the envy of any professional group that seeks affective and conceptual unity over time.

I have also worked in two university departments. At the University of Oklahoma I would particularly like to thank the undergraduate, master's, and doctoral students I worked with. I was particularly privileged to work closely with several graduate students including John Coppock and Cindy O'Donnell-Allen who were especially gracious in opening their classroom doors and excellent collaborators in studying the learning processes that took place among their students. I also extend my gratitude to their students for granting me permission to record and share their conversations and schoolwork. You'll read about these students in Part II of this book.

At the University of Georgia my work has been enhanced by the support of my colleagues and the response of my students, with whom I piloted the first draft of this book. My colleagues in English Education—Mark Faust, Peg Graham, Sally Hudson-Ross, and Bettie St. Pierre—have supported my work and contributed to my thinking. Mark and Bettie—along with Alecia Jackson, Tara Johnson, and Diane Sekeres, our assistants and colleagues in the *Teaching as Principled Practice Project*—have been stimulating partners in our work with preservice English teachers. The students who participated in the piloting of this book in 1999–2000 provided feedback that informed my revisions. These students, now teachers in Georgia, were Mary Catherine Begnaud, Tommy Behr, Quiana Camp, Jenny Cockrill, Matt Davis, Jeff Deroshia, Lee Evans, Stephanie Hall, Chellee Harris, Eric Hasty, Todd Hedden, Charlie Hollingshead, Jobie Johnson, Rebecca Long, Shane Orr, Jamie Reece, Allison Shroyer, Dana Siegmund, Jonathan Stroud, Julie Waters, Angie Watkins, and Sandra Wood. I would be most remiss in not also extending thanks to Joel Taxel, my friend and department chair, for his appreciation of faculty diversity and support of my work in writing this book. When not talking about Georgia football or gardening, Joel and I have been working on a study of character education programs; Joel's influence appears throughout Chapter 14.

Several people were kind enough to read early drafts of this book and offer useful feedback: Mark Faust, Peg Graham, George Hillocks, Larry Johannessen, Betsy Kahn, George Newell, and Bettie St. Pierre. George Hillocks and George Newell piloted the book with their preservice teachers and I am grateful to both them and their students for their responses to the manuscript. George Newell brought my attention to the phrase *principled practice* that I use in the title of this book.

Other people contributed to parts of the book. The reading lists in Appendix A were originally compiled with Steve Gevinson, with considerable input from Cynthia Maziarka at Oak Park and River Forest High School, and have been updated with suggestions from Stacy Appel, Bill Connolly, Judy Ellsesser, Mai Kiigemagi, Linde Knighton, Tom McCann, and Jean Petrovs.

My production of this book came while I was affiliated with the Center on English Learning and Achievement, headed by Arthur Applebee, Judith Langer, and Marty Nystrand. I greatly benefited from being involved with the Center and being in touch with the ideas emerging from its work. My particular strand of the CELA research was on teachers' early-career development, with a focus on their experiences as they moved from their university education programs into their first jobs. My work on this project was important in thinking about the contexts of teaching that I emphasize often in this book. Thanks to Jane Agee, Leslie Cook, Pam Fry, Pam Grossman, Alecia Jackson, Bonnie Konopak, Cynthia Moore, Cindy O'Donnell-Allen, and Sheila Valencia for their contributions to my thinking about the ways in which the settings of teaching affect the ways in which people learn to think about teaching. Thanks are due as well to the teachers I visited during this research and their generous contribution of time to my work.

I would like to thank Linda McElhiney at Prentice-Hall/Merrill for encouraging this project and providing feedback as I wrote it, and to Sue Canavan for originally passing the prospectus along to her. Thanks are due as well to the reviewers enlisted by Prentice Hall/Merrill: Peggy Albers, Georgia State University; Anna Bolling, California State University–Stanislaus; Todd Goodson, Kansas State University; Patricia M. Haworth, The University of Texas–Dallas; and Patricia P. Kelly, Virginia Tech. All provided extensive commentary that led to revisions.

I save my most profound gratitude for last, that being my thanks to my family for giving me the time, love, and support to complete this project: my wife, Jane, my daughter, Alysha, and my son, David.

P. S.

CONTENTS

CHAPTER 1   **PRINCIPLES OF PRACTICE**   **2**

Beginnings: Learning to Question What's Normal   2

Conceptual Units of Instruction: A Way to Integrate Learning   5

The Conceptual Unit: What It Is   5
Seven Types of Units   10
Benefits of the Unit Approach   15
A Drawback of the Unit Approach   16

A Rationale for Conceptual Units   16

The Need for Integrated Knowledge   16
Schemas and Scripts   18
Scaffolding Learning   19
Transactional Learning   22
Principles of Practice   25
Discussion Topic   32

PART 1   **PRINCIPLES OF PLANNING**   **33**

CHAPTER 2   **GETTING STARTED: BASICS OF UNIT DESIGN**   **34**

Who Decides on the Topic?   34

The Curriculum Says   35
Teacher Decides   35
Students Choose within Limits   36
Students Choose   36

Identifying Unit Topics   36

Curriculum   37

Discussion Topic   39

Students   41

Community   46

Teacher   47

Selecting Materials   48

Who Gets to Choose?   48

Considerations in Selecting Materials   51

Rationales   57

Psychology/Human Development   58

Cultural Significance   60

Literary Significance   60

Civic Awareness   61

Relevance to Current Social Problems   61

Preparation for Future Needs   61

Writing a Rationale   62

CHAPTER 3 **WHAT STUDENTS KNOW
AND WHAT SCHOOLS ASSESS**   **66**

**Two Theories of Communication: Transmission and
Constructivism   69**

Transmission   70

Constructivism   71

**Two Views of Speech and Writing: Final Draft and
Exploratory   73**

Final Draft Speech   73

Exploratory Talk   73

Paradigmatic and Narrative Ways of Knowing   75

Paradigmatic Knowledge   75

Narrative Knowledge   76

Gendered Ways of Knowing   77

Authoritative Ways of Relating   78

Connected Ways of Knowing   78

Types of Intelligence   80

Final Thoughts   83

Discussion Topic   83

CHAPTER 4   **PLANNING BACKWARDS: HOW ENDPOINTS SUGGEST PATHWAYS**   **84**

Sophomore Year English Curriculum   85

The Year-Long Curriculum: Overarching Concepts and Assessments   86

Considerations in Curriculum Planning   87

Types of Overarching Concepts   87

One Possible Theme: Negotiating Thresholds   88

Other Possibilities for Overarching Concepts   90

Discussion Topic   94

Assessing Students for a Whole Course   94

Portfolio   96

Extended Definition of Good Literature   98

Multimedia Project   99

Analytic Essay   101

Assessment Developed by Students   102

Culminating Texts for Teachers   103

Work That Parallels Student Work   103

Ethnographic Experiments   104

Frame Experiments   105

Studies of Classroom Relationships   105

Electronic Conversations   105

Final Thoughts   107

CHAPTER 5   **SETTING AND ASSESSING UNIT GOALS**   **108**

Preliminaries   108

Constructing Units, Constructing Texts   108

Conceptualizing Your Unit Focus   109

Setting Goals   110

Conventions and Alternatives   111

Unit Goals as Assessments   114

Discussion Topic   115

Conventional Assessments   115

Alternative Assessments   121

Assessing Culminating Projects   134

Final Thoughts   137

CHAPTER 6 **REFINING THE UNIT FOCUS** **140**

Whole-Course Considerations 140

Conceptual Unit on Coming of Age 141

Materials 142
Unit Goals 142
Discussion Topic 147

Final Thoughts 151

CHAPTER 7 **INTRODUCTORY ACTIVITIES: GATEWAY TO THE UNIT CONCEPTS** **152**

Writing About Personal Experiences 156

Opinionnaire/Survey 158

Scenarios/Case Studies 159

Writing about Related Problems 161

Discussion Topic 162

Final Thoughts 162

CHAPTER 8 **THE CONSTRUCTION ZONE: BUILDING TOWARD UNIT GOALS** **164**

Thinking of Your Class as a Construction Zone 164

My Approach in This Chapter 165

Preliminaries 167

Teaching Language 167
Getting Started: Outlining the Unit 170

Contexts of Teaching 172

The School and Community Context 172
Time Considerations 173
Back to School 174

Setting up Shop: Getting Started with Students 174

Starting the Unit 177

Discussion Topic 178

Week 2   183

Week 3   191

Week 4   195

Week 5   205

Week 6   209

Final Thoughts   211

PART 2   LIFE IN CLASSROOMS   **213**

CHAPTER 9   SETTING UP YOUR CLASSROOM   **216**

Seating Arrangement   217

Learning Students' Names   218

Student-Designed Environments   219

Discussion-Leading Techniques   220

Small Groups   221

Setting Up   221
Setting Up and Operating Groups   223

Classroom Management   226

Final Thoughts   229

Discussion Topic   229

CHAPTER 10   HOW WAYS OF TALKING AFFECT WAYS OF LEARNING   **230**

A Contrast of Two Approaches to Discussion   232

Prompting Students to Generate a Context for Their
Interpretation   233
Prompting Students to Elaborate on Their Responses   237
Building on Student Contributions to Generate
Questions   238

Making the Process of Analysis Explicit   239

Discussion Topic   240

Final Thoughts   240

CHAPTER 11   **MULTIMEDIA COMPOSING WITH A BIG TOOL KIT   242**

A Rationale for an Expanded Tool Kit   242

Composing Across the Curriculum   244

Multimedia Composing in English   249

Discussion Topic   255

Final Thoughts   255

CHAPTER 12   **BUILDING BODY BIOGRAPHIES   258**

Reflecting on My Own Teaching   258

Multimedia Composing in a Mainstream School   259

The Classroom   261

The Hamlet Unit   262

The Body Biography Assignment   264

What Students Learned through Their Composing of Body Biographies   266

Composing Processes for Body Biographies   266
Establishing Working Relationships   274

Final Thoughts   280

Discussion Topic   283

PART 3   **RETHINKING THE CURRICULUM   285**

CHAPTER 13   **RETHINKING THE CURRICULUM FROM A MULTICULTURAL PERSPECTIVE   288**

The Adventures of Teaching *Huckleberry Finn*   292

Using Multicultural Education to Broaden Students' Minds   295

Texts Selected to Represent a Particular Group of People   297

Final Thoughts   300

Discussion Topic   301

CHAPTER 14   RETHINKING CHARACTER EDUCATION   302

What Do We Talk about When We Talk about Character?   303

What Character Is   303
Where Character Is Located   304

How Students Learn   305

Didactic Approach   306
Reflective Approach   306

Teaching Character through Thematic Units   308

A Unit on Success   308
Unit on Peer Groups, Cliques, and Gangs   310
Discussion Topic   315

Final Thoughts   315

CHAPTER 15   RETHINKING STANDARDS FOR TEACHING ENGLISH   318

What Do We Talk about When We Talk about Standards?   321

Meaning 1: Making Things the Same for All Students   321
Meaning 2: Minimum Level of Performance   322
Meaning 3: Typology of Experiences   322

Standards for Whom?   322

Standards for Students   323
Discussion Topic   324
Standards for Teachers   325

Developing Standards: Issues to Consider   330

What Is English?   330
Whose Standards?   331
Discussion Topic   334

Goals for Schooling and Students and Notions of the Ideal Adult   334

Metaphors for Schooling   335

Using Standards to Develop Standards   **337**

Discussion Topic   338

AFTERWORD: **THEORY IN PRACTICE** **340**

REFERENCES **345**

APPENDIX A: **TEXTS FOR THEMATIC UNITS** **361**

APPENDIX B: **COURTROOM CASE STUDY** **423**

APPENDIX C: **ROLE-PLAYING PEER-RESPONSE GROUPS** **435**

INDEX **443**

ABOUT THE AUTHOR **459**

TEACHING ENGLISH THROUGH PRINCIPLED PRACTICE

Principles of Practice

This book as a whole teaches you how to design *conceptual units of instruction*. In this chapter I explain what a conceptual unit is, describe its primary components, review seven types of conceptual units, and provide a rationale for using a unit approach for your teaching. Finally, I outline the *principles of practice* that are behind the approach to teaching that I endorse throughout this book.

> The things taught in school are not an education but the means to an education.
>
> —Ralph Waldo Emerson

BEGINNINGS: LEARNING TO QUESTION WHAT'S NORMAL

In this book I borrow Arthur Applebee's (1986) notion of *principled practice* to describe an approach to instructional planning. In this approach, I emphasize the need to develop principles that guide your decisions about how to teach effectively in particular situations. In so doing, I reject the idea that any single teaching method—journal writing, five-paragraph themes, readers' theater, lectures, whatever—will always work. Rather, I challenge you to think about what is appropriate given the unique crossroads your classroom provides for your many and varied students, your own beliefs about teaching and learning, the materials available for you to use, and the public, professional, and policy contexts in which you teach.

In other words, this book is not designed to provide you with a collection of methods to use with your students, regardless of who or where they might be—although you'll read about plenty of methods as the book unfolds. The notion of principled practice focuses instead on the *why* of teaching: why teaching tools work in particular ways in particular settings. This approach invests a great deal of authority and responsibility in you, the teacher, because the decisions you make have great implications for the kinds of learning your students experience.

I will review principles of practice specifically as they pertain to the design of conceptual units of instruction. My faith in conceptual units comes in large part from my personal experiences during my career as a high school English teacher, from 1976 to 1990, and particularly from my first few years in the classroom. I learned principles of unit design from George Hillocks in the master of arts in teaching program at the University of Chicago. Prior to attending his program, I had taken a few semesters of education courses at another university and had found them dreary and ineffectual. The courses there presented the practice of teaching as a chaotic array of unconnected theories and teaching tips. The other students and I had a hard time seeing how all of these tidbits fit together into a whole, purposeful, principled approach to teaching. We all felt we were just going through the motions to get our credentials so that we could get into the classroom, where we thought our real teacher education would begin.

Fortunately, however, I abandoned this program and enrolled in the Chicago M.A.T. program. I was initially shocked to see that education courses could be intellectually challenging and rigorous, and at the same time highly practical in terms of learning how to plan instruction. My previous experiences had led me to share the general conviction that education classes are a waste of time. You read this opinion often in the newspapers. You hear it in teachers' lounges across the country. It's become a truism among university faculty. And, unfortunately, it's a well-enough earned reputation on too many campuses. The courses I took in that first education program did not contradict the stereotype: They had no practical value, no coherent theoretical grounding, no dynamic classroom quality, no life whatsoever.

But it doesn't have to be that way. George made it clear immediately that teaching was complex and difficult and required careful preparation. He also made it clear that his program would be demanding and challenging, that we needed to have a strong work ethic if we were to get through with his certification. His view of a teaching career was that it was among the most complex, challenging, difficult, and ultimately satisfying things that a person could do. To do it well, we needed a disposition that would lead us to continually inquire into the purposes, procedures, and effects of our teaching.

From the start, we were challenged to defend every decision we made. In particular, we were asked to examine the assumptions we had about what it means to teach and learn. We asked, among other things,

- What is English? Does it include the traditional three strands of literature, writing, and language, or should other strands (media, technology, arts, etc.) be included too?
- Does the teaching of literature come first, with language and writing covered in service of literature, or should all three (or more) strands be given equal priority and emphasis?
- Why teach English? Why require it throughout middle and high school for all students?
- What is a curriculum? Why should a curriculum include one set of materials, but not others? For example, do film, art, music, and student writing belong in a literature curriculum? Why read Shakespeare instead of Stephen King? Why require courses in American and British literature, but not the literature of other nations?
- Should the strands of the English curriculum be taught in separate courses as is done in many schools, or all together in a single class?

- How do different ways of organizing and sequencing materials affect the ways in which students learn and what they learn?
- What do students learn when assessed in particular ways?
- How do you know when a student has learned something?
- Where does meaning reside, in texts, in readers, or somewhere in between . . . or in the environments in which readers learn how to make meaning?
- How do different classroom arrangements affect the opportunities students have for learning? How are learning processes different when learning opportunities are provided through lectures, whole-class discussions, small-group discussions, project-oriented learning, drama, and other vehicles?
- When students are given responsibilities for directing their learning, are teachers really teaching—and if so, what are they teaching?
- To what extent should students choose what they learn about and choose the form in which they represent their learning?
- What principles should guide the assessment of student work? Should all work be assessed? Should all students be assessed according to the same criteria?

> **Reflective Writing Prompt**
> Choose any of these sets of questions and write informally in response. As part of your reflection, write about the basis for the beliefs you hold.

These questions, and many more like them, quickly became constant preoccupations for all of us in the program. Previously, we had assumed that teaching should follow the customs that typically prevail in school. Students should read canonical works, that is, the same "great books" from British and American literature that we had read as students. Teachers should shepherd discussions toward particular interpretations of literature. Students should demonstrate their knowledge on content exams, or with an occasional analytic essay that reiterates the meaning of texts that the teacher-led discussions had inevitably produced.

George, troublemaker that he was, provoked us to trouble these assumptions and consider whether other alternatives to teaching and learning might be available. Ed-ucation courses, I was finding, weren't for dummies after all, in contrast to what I read in the newspaper. At least, they didn't need to be. Rather, the education courses I was taking were far more stimulating than any other courses I'd taken in my undergraduate and graduate degree programs. The reason had nothing to do with a lack of challenge from these other courses, and everything to do with the quality and rigor of the education courses.

> I have often wondered about two things. First, why high school kids almost invariably hate the books they are assigned to read by their English teachers, and second, why English teachers almost invariably hate the books students read in their spare time. Something seems very wrong with such a situation. There is a bridge out here, and the ferry service is uncertain at best.
>
> —Stephen King

Teaching literature, I was learning, involved more than simply learning conventional interpretations and making sure that students got them. Teaching writing meant more than giving hard assignments and then grading them. Teaching language meant more than doing exercises in the grammar textbook. Teaching English often meant more than attending to the three traditional strands; it meant attending to whatever other medium—art, architecture, music, dance, performance, technology—could contribute to students' learning.

And learning to teach meant more than getting classroom experience. Being a teacher involved the consideration of perplexing questions about what it means to learn, particularly through the vehicles of language and its texts, and about what it means to teach. Simply considering those questions, however, wasn't enough. Finding answers that could be translated into effective teaching proved to be even more difficult—and more rewarding—than learning how to question our assumptions.

CONCEPTUAL UNITS OF INSTRUCTION: A WAY TO INTEGRATE LEARNING

Through our exploration of these questions we came to believe that the domain of English could become accessible to students through an approach involving *sustained attention to a related set of ideas*. These ideas could be pursued through a variety of texts, both those read (usually literary) and those produced (usually written). Sustained attention would allow students—and, given a provocative topic, the teacher—to consider a related set of issues from a variety of perspectives and with increasing understanding.

This consideration could ultimately provide opportunities for each student to construct a personal interpretation or perspective, ideally, one that takes into account and synthesizes the various ideas explored through the unit texts and discussions. By considering the same topic, the class could work toward a sense of community, in which students would appreciate and critique the ideas their classmates produced in response to the unit texts. By considering student texts in conjunction with published works, the class could work toward a contemporary vision of how a particular topic might be imagined in society.

The Conceptual Unit: What It Is

What I have just described is an approach to teaching that emerges from the design of conceptual units of instruction. I borrow the term *conceptual unit* from David Anderson, the chair of the English department at Hinsdale South High School in Darien, Illinois. As the name implies, a conceptual unit is designed to organize students' learning around a particular emphasis. Literature and related artistic texts provide the stimulus for student inquiry into the unit topic. The texts, it's important to remember, include those produced outside the class (typically in published form) and those produced by students. Students do not simply react to texts and consume knowledge. Rather, they have an active role in constructing new knowledge through their engagement with the unit concepts. They produce texts of their own that contribute to the class's exploration of the key unit questions and raise new questions.

A conceptual unit is not simply a collection of texts that share a topic. One key characteristic of a conceptual unit, as opposed to a unit that is simply about a topic, is that it involves students in a conversation that deepens as they progress through the texts, activities, and discussions. A conceptual unit must focus on a set of key concepts that students engage with over time. This extended consideration is designed to

- help students come to a better personal understanding of the topic and their related experiences

- provide students with tools that will enable them to read and produce new texts
- furnish students with a social context through which they can develop this new knowledge to the best of their potential

A conceptual unit typically consists of all or most of the following:

- Inventory
- Goals
- Assessment
- Lessons
- Activities
- Discussions
- Texts
- Tools
- Composing

Inventory

An inventory is a vehicle that helps you learn about your students. Most school text-books are written for a generic student, yet in the classroom, you will have all kinds of students. If you view your role as one of teaching students as well as teaching a subject, it's a good idea to know something about them and who they are, including;

- what they're interested in
- what their goals are for this class
- what they know about certain topics
- what they've already read
- how they use language and how they write
- what other skills they have on which you can build in the classroom

Such information can help you design more appropriate instruction. You won't make the mistake of trying to teach them things they already do well, or pitching instruction too far beyond what they know, or teaching in ways that have nothing to do with their own purposes. Remember that you will always teach within constraints, and it's possible that you will teach in a district that restricts your decision making in these areas. Even so, teachers can develop ways to meet their own goals and their students' goals while satisfying other people's requirements.

Inventories can be taken in a variety of ways. You can learn a lot about students, for instance, by having them write an introductory letter about themselves—you will not only learn about their interests, you will get a sense of their writing fluency. Another option is to develop a questionnaire that asks specific questions about their background in education, their interests in school, their interests outside school, their reading experiences and preferences, their attitudes toward writing, and other information you can use in planning your teaching. Or, you may want to provide students with literature of different degrees of difficulty and ask them to respond to it—their responses will help you identify appropriate reading material for the class.

You should be prepared for a broad range of performance on these inventories. Knowing this range can help you make good decisions about your teaching, such as whether you will need to use different materials within a single class.

Goals

Instructional goals refer to the unit's destination. This destination is the ultimate learning you anticipate for students as a result of their experiences during the unit. Their ultimate learning comes about through their production of a *culminating text*—something they produce that synthesizes their learning. Most commonly these texts are some kind of extended writing, such as an essay, a narrative, a research report, and so on. However, students should have opportunities to learn through the production of other kinds of texts as well, particularly those I would call artistic.

The goals you set imply a path for the instruction to follow. Identifying worthwhile goals, then, is a key facet of planning worthwhile instruction.

Assessment

Goals are tied to the inevitable question of assessment. Whether you like it or not, whether you have philosophical objections to grading or not, you will almost certainly have to issue a grade for each student. Ideally, these grades will correspond to the students' learning. If your students are enabled to produce culminating texts that they find worthwhile, it is likely that you will assess them in what some call *authentic* ways. Earlier in this book, I made the point that people learn by making and reflecting upon things they find useful and important. I urge you to set unit goals that will provide students the opportunity to produce things—culminating texts—that you can assess and that you and your students believe reflect their learning during the unit.

When knowledge is reduced to right and wrong answers, assessment is fairly straightforward and simple. When knowledge is open-ended and constructed, as I advocate in this book, assessment becomes much more problematic. I will recommend that you use a tool called a *rubric* to help you distinguish among different levels of student performance when assessing the texts they produce.

Lessons

I use the term *lesson* somewhat hesitantly because, for many, it connotes the kind of authoritarian teaching I argue against in this book. For most, a lesson connotes a top-down learning relationship, in which the student does what the teacher says. Furthermore, there's a connotation of being punished, as in "being taught a lesson"; one dictionary definition for *lesson* is "reprimand," and that's not what I'm encouraging here. In an ideal world I'd use a different term, but as *lesson* is still a commonly used word in schools, I'll use it here so that you can communicate more easily with the folks you meet in your teaching.

If you view your unit of instruction as addressing a concept, then a lesson is a shorter unit of instruction within the larger unit. If, for instance, you are teaching a unit on animals as symbols and have a goal of enabling students to see how symbolic animals can represent human characteristics, you might include a lesson in which students are introduced to the idea that literary animals can symbolize people and their (often negative) tendencies. This lesson might include different parts of the unit that I describe here: *discussion* of *texts,* such as a set of fables; an *activity,* in which they *compose* a fable of their own using the *tool* of writing, and an *assessment* of their fable.

It's important to remember that, although lessons are identifiable as pieces of the larger unit, they should be integrated and sequenced, rather than discrete. You are designing a unit, which means that the lessons need to be related to one another and to the overall conceptual knowledge that students construct.

Activities

An activity is a hands-on experience, often taking place within a lesson. It is related to the unit concepts and helps prepare students for reaching the unit goals. An activity typically involves

- interaction with other people
- the manipulation of ideas, or objects, or both
- the production of an idea, a text, or both
- the inductive development of strategies for learning
- an open-ended task

Activities are, not surprisingly, active. Let's say, for instance, that you would like to teach students a lesson on how to make inferences in their reading. One way to introduce this idea in an accessible way is through an activity such as a spy game (see Hillocks, 1972). In this game, small groups of students are told that a spy has been captured and they are presented with the contents of the spy's pockets: coins from foreign countries, a rabbit's foot, a scrap of paper with code on it, a set of paper clips strung together, a ticket to the opera, and any other items you wish to provide. Each group makes inferences about the spy's personality, characteristics, and mission. The students then discuss their inferences with the class, comparing and critiquing one another's ideas.

Following this activity, the class may examine characters from literature, making inferences that may help them construct a response to the literature. Small groups working on an analysis of the narrator of a poem would be engaging in another activity, but with a more complex text. These activities could lead students to individual efforts to analyze literature in terms of the inferences they can make about narrators or other characters.

Discussions

By discussion I mean talk in which participants exchange ideas, in contrast to a lecture, in which one person provides information for others to record. Many teachers regard their classes as discussion oriented even though input from students is limited. To count as a discussion, an exchange needs to be

- open-ended (not having a specific or correct answer or destination)
- authentic (concerned with the purposes and interests of all participants, not only a few)

- democratic (open to all and involving the greatest possible number of willing participants)

Most classroom discussions take place as whole-class or small-group efforts. Typically, whole-class discussions are led by teachers. In this book I will also consider the benefits of teaching students how to lead whole-class discussions.

People involved in discussions tend to have one of two different dispositions. One disposition is that of *arguing to win.* Lawyers do this: Right or wrong, their goal is to win the argument. Participants who take this stance typically do not view themselves as learners in the discussion; rather, they see themselves as contestants.

The other disposition is that of *arguing to learn.* Participants who take this stance typically view discussions as opportunities to think through ideas and learn from the others involved. For them there are not winners and losers. These participants cannot help but benefit from the discussion, even if they ultimately change their minds about the ideas they express.

For now, I'll simply introduce these dispositions. You will have opportunities throughout the book to decide which disposition you'd like to promote in your own classroom.

Texts

A text is any meaning-laden product or artifact. You are probably familiar with literature as a text. In addition, we will consider art, dance, film, and other artifacts that have a potential for meaning. In most cases a text is tangible (e.g., a poem, a sculpture, a film), but we will also include those artifacts that are fleeting: a song, an expression, and so on. Our consideration of texts will include both those that students read (also referred to as *materials*) and those that they produce.

Tools

A tool is any instrument through which you act on your environment. Tools are important to all builders, including teachers and students.

Students who construct knowledge use tools. Through the tool of language, they can communicate, explore ideas, and impose order on their worlds. Like other tools, language can have more specific constructive purposes. Students can use language to argue, to tell stories, to classify, to amuse. Students can also use nonverbal artistic devices to construct meaning-laden texts. They can draw, for instance, to signify relationships they see in literature. They can communicate through body language. The key to all these actions is that they must be used in service of the construction of meaning.

Teachers, too, use tools. These may include conceptual tools that serve as umbrellas. An educational theory, such as constructivism, for instance, may be applied to reading, writing, math, science—to any learning situation that emphasizes constructing knowledge rather than receiving it. Teachers also use practical tools. These tools include any methods used to enact teaching: lesson plans, small-group activities, handouts, and so on. Different tools help achieve different ends. In this book,

I'll advocate the development of a big and versatile tool kit to help you carry out your teaching.

Composing

I use the term *composing* to describe the act by which people make things that have meaning or use for them. In school, these things are what I have previously called texts: essays, drawings, dramas, and so on. The emphasis of teaching and learning ought to be to engage students in acts of composition that produce meaningful texts. These acts of composition involve

- the use of an appropriate tool or set of tools
- an understanding of the conventions and genres within which one is working and an understanding of the effects of breaking these conventions
- an extended process that usually includes planning, drafting, feedback, reflection, and revising
- building on prior knowledge and understanding as a basis for the construction of new ideas and a new text
- new learning that takes place through the process of composing
- regarding both the process of composing and the ultimate texts as sources of meaning

In school, *writing* is typically considered to be synonymous with *composing*. As you can see, however, much school writing would not meet the criteria for my definition (e.g., writing factual short answers on an exam). Other kinds of production (writing a musical score, choreographing an interpretation of a story) do meet these criteria. When I refer to composition, I am talking about a way of producing texts, rather than a way of producing a particular kind of text.

Seven Types of Units

Here I'll describe seven kinds of organization for conceptual units. These are not the only possible ways to organize instruction; indeed, I encourage you to think about other ways of unifying instruction around a concept.

Whichever type of conceptual unit you design, it is important that it ought to lead class members (including the teacher) into new understandings. The unit needs to be complex enough to generate thoughtful consideration about whatever thread ties the texts and lessons together. Simply considering a topic does not make a four- to six-week block of time a conceptual unit. Rather, the topic needs to help students develop frameworks for thinking about issues so that they can think about new situations (including new texts) through that framework.

A unit on friendship, for example, ought to involve more than simply reading stories about friends; it should approach these texts in a way that enables students to develop frameworks for thinking about new situations that develop in their friendships or in their reading about friendship. One of a teacher's responsibilities in designing a unit, then, is to think about how different sequences of activities and readings will contribute to students' ability to develop these generative frameworks for thinking about the unit concept. The conceptual growth of students during a unit was aptly described by Hillocks, McCabe, and McCampbell in *The Dynamics of English Instruction, Grades 7–12:* "One of the most important things that any literature unit can do is to provide a conceptual matrix against which the student can examine each new work he reads. Insights into any given work are partly the result of experience in reading others because concepts grow by comparison and contrast" (p. 254).

The kinds of units I outline are described in terms of the kinds of texts students read. Keep in mind that I use the terms *text* and *read* broadly to include any production that represents something else. Most English majors, when hearing the phrase "read a text," think about reading a poem, a story, or the like. And in English classes, that's mostly what you do. I also include, however, images on computer screens, film, art, music, architecture, dance, and other forms of representation when I speak of texts. All of these can contribute to the texts that students read during a conceptual unit.

I also view student texts as critical parts of any conceptual unit. In some ways, these are the unit's most important texts, because they distill what students have learned through their engagement with the unit. These texts are significant not only for assessment purposes, but also as texts from which all students in the class may learn. Whenever possible, students should have opportunities to read and think about what their classmates have produced in terms of the unit concepts.

Table 1.1 provides examples of different types of conceptual units found at the Virtual Library of Conceptual Units at http://www.coe.uga.edu/~smago/Virtual Library/index.html. In the left column under "Unit" are listed the authors of the units in the Virtual Library; note that most units are coauthored. The type of unit is indicated by an x in the appropriate column.

Theme

A theme is an idea or motif that ties together the texts, activities, and discussions of a unit. A theme often refers to a set of experiences, ideas, concepts, or emotions shared by people within and often across cultures. Themes include presumably universal experiences, such as rites of passage, dealing with peer groups, coping with loss, social responsibility, and other topics that are frequently the subject of art and literature.

Such archetypal experiences provide a compelling way to organize an English curriculum, one that is responsive both to recurring patterns in all art forms and to students' authentic interests in learning. Students are engaged in integrated inquiry into topics that parallel their social development or that help lead their development. In other words, the themes they study can

> The teaching life is the life of the explorer, the creator, constructing the classroom for free exploration. It is about engagement. It takes courage. It is about ruthlessly excising what is flawed, what no longer fits, no matter how difficult it was to achieve. It is about recognizing teaching as a medium that can do some things exquisitely but cannot do everything.
>
> —Christa L. Walck

- help students consider pivotal experiences in their lives, such as their relationships with their friends or families
- introduce students to issues not previously considered, such as what it means to be a responsible citizen

Studying thematic units gives students the potential to see literature and related texts as useful tools and touchstones in their own development as people.

TABLE 1.1 Virtual Library Types of Conceptual Units

Unit	Unit Type						
	Theme	Period	Movement	Region	Genre	Author	Strategy
Askari	X						
Barrett Endres Stinchcomb	X						
Begnaud Evans	X X						
Behr Reece Watkins	X						
Bryan Skorupski	X						
Camp Davis Harris	X						
Cockrill Hall Long	X						
Deroshia	X						
Hedden Orr Shroyer					X		
Hollingshead Wood	X						
Johnson					X		
Loggins Taggart Thomas	X				X	X	
Rachmuth Shuler	X				X		
Siegmund Stroud Hasty					X		
Swann Williams							X

Period

A period can serve as the basis for a conceptual unit, particularly when authors from that period write from a cultural perspective that gives them a common set of themes. For example, the literature of the Victorian period, which encompassed the sixty-three-year reign of Queen Victoria of Great Britain, reveals the sentiments, beliefs, tastes, and accomplishments of the British people of that time. Victorian literature was often staged around the class struggle that followed from the Industrial Revolution, creating tensions among the working class, the new industrial middle class, and the old aristocracy. The literature of Dickens typifies the Victorian period, with sympathy extended to the poor, the working class, and their children.

Shorter periods can also provide the basis for a conceptual unit, such as American colonial rhetoric, Beat literature of the '50s, and the Vietnam era.

Movement

A movement is a belief system that is expressed through a variety of media and is embedded in a broader philosophy. Romanticism, for instance, had a coherent set of principles, including an emphasis on the imagination and emotions over intellect and reason, a belief in the innate goodness of people in their natural state, a reverence for nature, a philosophical idealism, a belief in individualism, rejection of political authority and social convention, affirmation of the human passions, and appreciation of religious mysticism. A movement, unlike a literary period, extends across nations and time periods. Romanticism, for instance, had large followings in Germany, France, Great Britain, and the United States, although at different times and for different durations.

Because it represents a coherent worldview, a movement can provide the basis for a conceptual unit. Other movements are the Enlightenment, naturalism, transcendentalism, neoclassicism, surrealism, and realism. Designing a unit around a movement enables the inclusion of historical and philosophical writing as well as art, architecture, and other artifacts that embody the movement's beliefs.

Region

Often, a geographic region can serve as the means for organizing a conceptual unit. Authors and artists from a particular region may share common outlooks, themes, and styles. The British Lake poets, Southern fiction, and Harlem Renaissance are examples of regional influences. My university students have designed conceptual units featuring the authors of the state in which they lived (e.g., Oklahoma authors, Georgia authors). At times these units have come under the heading "A Sense of Place," in which a sense of place was a function of a region's history, geography, culture, and so on.

Genre

Another possible organizing principle is literary *genre*. I use this term to refer to works that share codes: Westerns, heroic journeys, detective stories, comedies of manners, and so on. These genres are often produced through a variety of media: short story, drama, novel, and so on, which themselves are referred to as genres.

Possible Texts for the Study of Satire

Don Juan, epic poem by Lord Byron
"The Piano," short story by Anibal Monteiro
    Machado
The Importance of Being Earnest, play by
    Oscar Wilde
Moo, novel by Jane Smiley
The Boondocks, cartoon by Aaron McGruder

"Fight Fiercely Harvard," song by Tom Lehrer
Nothin' but Good Times Ahead, essays by
    Molly Ivins
Hollywood Shuffle, film by Robert Townsend
"The Tortoise and the Hare," fable by Aesop
"The Golf Links Lie So Near the Mill," poem by
    Sarah Cleghorn

Many textbooks group literature according to these other kinds of genres, a practice not conducive to sustained study. The short story, for instance, is so varied in form and theme that it seems an odd basis for grouping literature for study. Typically, students are asked to recognize such elements as plot, setting, character, rising action, and so on. Yet plot seems to be a hopelessly diverse trait given the myriad ways in which a story can unfold. "The Secret Life of Walter Mitty" jumps between Walter's real and imaginary worlds. "The Short Happy Life of Francis Macomber" feeds bits of the past into the present. "The Bear" takes place in several eras that are not presented sequentially—and it's an awfully long short story that's organized into chapters—how do we explain that? (Answer: We avoid the question.) In other words, the genre of the short story is a questionable organizing principle because reading one short story rarely helps a student read the next. All they have in common is that they are (more or less) short and that they are stories.

When genre means texts that share a set of codes, however, it does provide an organizing principle. Authors of satire, for instance, typically employ a set of devices, such as exaggeration, voicing opinions different from their own, creating foolish characters, and so on, that are designed to invite particular responses. Jonathan Swift's "A Modest Proposal" argues that society can solve both its hunger problem and its persistent problem of having a social underclass if its comfortable classes eat the babies of the poor. Taken literally, this suggestion is horrifying. An astute reader, however, knows how to recognize Swift's use of irony and understand that he is criticizing attitudes toward the poor rather than introducing a culinary solution to a social problem. In this conception, a genre is not confined to a single medium, but includes multimedia texts that rely on common interpretive codes.

Works by a Single Author

If an author has produced a body of work that is highly compelling or holds a significant place in literary history, that work can provide the basis for a unit of instruction. The work of a single author is amenable to a unit approach because it tends to rely on a set of themes and techniques that students can follow across texts. The main question you should ask when considering this means of organization is, With all of the literature ever written at my disposal, and with 180 or so school days available, how do I justify committing 20 of those days to just one writer?

In other words, you need to consider the impact on the rest of what you teach of dedicating 10 percent of your instructional time to one author. You are not likely to have much choice in the matter when it comes to Shakespeare, whose works are typically required reading at all high school grade levels—including the junior year American literature course.

Learning a Key Strategy

Literature is a very particular kind of text. You don't read it in the same way in which you read a scientific report. When reading a scientific report, you assume that the speaker is seeking accuracy, precision, and logic. Often, however, the speaker in literature is a highly flawed character whose worldview, diction, and so on are different from those of the author. The author relies on readers to recognize the character's flaws and disagree with the narrative perspective. Huck Finn's narration in *The Adventures of Huckleberry Finn,* for instance, assumes the inferiority of Jim; yet other evidence presented by Twain suggests that Jim is the book's most noble character. Knowing how to read an ironic narration is a key strategy that is useful in becoming an informed reader of literature.

A unit, then, can be organized around learning strategies for recognizing and interpreting literary codes. By this I do *not* mean memorizing lists of literary terms. I refer instead to knowing how authors use literary techniques. A unit built around this approach would have students analyze a specific technique through a series of increasingly sophisticated texts. Michael W. Smith (1991), for instance, has written an extended unit, *Understanding Unreliable Narrators,* in which students begin by reading Calvin and Hobbes comics and then move through more sophisticated literature. Having formal strategies for recognizing and interpreting literary codes can be very useful for students in their subsequent reading.

Benefits of the Unit Approach

Learning design principles based on unit organization provided my career with a very satisfying start. Most of the other beginning teachers I knew entered the profession with a bag of instructional tricks, but little preparation in how to incorporate them into long-term, integrated instruction. I remember being surprised to hear them complaining that they were always up past midnight trying to figure out what to do the next day in class.

Although I thought obsessively about my teaching and constantly tinkered with my plans, I was not plagued by daily uncertainty, because I had learned to plan ahead and design conceptual units. I found teaching less stressful than did most of my new colleagues because I was not always struggling to figure out what to do next. I was also happier with my teaching because my students saw continuity in what we did from day to day and week to week, and saw it within the context of questions that mattered to them. In various units, we considered such questions as

- What does it mean to be a success?
- What does one do in the face of peer pressure?
- How does discrimination affect society and its individuals?

- What is a social conscience, and at what point and in what form does one register a protest against a social wrong?
- How does it feel to be an outcast?

Taking this approach made my classes far more interesting to me also, because the answers were different for each class. Rather than explaining the same interpretation to students class after class, year after year, and having them repeat it to me on tests, I had the opportunity to be involved in discussions that were as varied as the students themselves. My classes were places where I did a lot of learning as I listened to my students construct for themselves an awareness of how they understood and acted within their worlds.

A Drawback of the Unit Approach

One drawback to the unit approach is that it has the potential for leading students to pigeonhole the texts they read. Let's say, for instance, that you teach Charles Dickens's *Hard Times*. You could include this text in a unit on Victorian literature, grouping it with other texts from this period to illustrate the conditions and perspectives of that time. You could include it in a unit on satire, teaching it along with other satiric works to help students understand the conventions of the genre. You could include it in a unit on the theme of progress, using Dickens's portrayal to question whether increased industrialism represents social progress.

Field Observation

In a school you are visiting, find out how teachers organize instruction. What is the basis for this organization? What reasons are given for organizing in this way? How do students appear to respond to and learn from this means of organization? How do teachers appear to feel about it? What are the benefits and drawbacks to this means of organization?

Any of these approaches could enable students to have fruitful experiences with the novel. The drawback is that by emphasizing one aspect of the novel, you might preclude other ways of viewing it. It's important to remember that your unit approach will be beneficial in that it will, in a sense, narrow students' vision and help them focus on the unit concepts. But this more narrow vision also has the potential for preventing them from seeing other worthwhile ways to approach the individual texts of the unit. One way to resolve this problem is to provide opportunities for open-ended thinking, such as journals and student-led discussions. I review such approaches in Chapter 3.

A RATIONALE FOR CONCEPTUAL UNITS

As will be evident in the next section of this book, I believe that if you can't defend something, you shouldn't teach it. The study of literature by means of conceptual units may be justified in a number of ways, which I'll review next.

The Need for Integrated Knowledge

Many curriculum theorists argue that effective instruction seeks to help students make connections that cohere around principles. Arthur Applebee (1993), for instance, conceives of curriculum "as a domain for culturally significant conversations"

Books on Integrated Knowledge

Applebee, A. N. (1993). *Literature in the secondary school* (NCTE Research Report No. 25). Urbana, IL: National Council of Teachers of English.

Applebee, A. N. (1996). *Curriculum as conversation: Transforming traditions of teaching and learning.* Chicago: University of Chicago Press.

Barnes, D. R. (1992). *From communication to curriculum* (2nd ed.). Portsmouth, NH: Heinemann.

Bruner, J. (1996). *The culture of education.* Cambridge, MA: Harvard University Press.

Csikszentmihalyi, M., & Larson, R. (1984). *Being adolescent: Growth and conflict in the teenage years.* New York: Basic Books.

Dewey, J. (1964). *John Dewey on education: Selected writings* (R. Archambault, Ed.). Chicago: University of Chicago Press.

Wells, G., & Chang-Wells, G. L. (1992). *Constructing knowledge together: Classrooms as centers of inquiry and literacy.* Portsmouth, NH: Heinemann.

(p. 200) that take place across space and time, suggesting the need to explore a set of questions across a series of related texts. Conceptual units are well-suited for integrated learning, enabling students to explore a topic over time through the lens offered by a variety of texts. Such an approach avoids the problem of fragmentation that Applebee (1996) sees as characterizing much of the English curriculum and that works against students' ability to integrate knowledge and experience the domain coherently.

A well-designed conceptual unit can promote the kind of integration and continuity that Applebee sees as essential to an effective curriculum, one that students actively participate in and help to construct with their own contributions and compositions. Furthermore, Applebee argues for the importance of extending this sense of coherence to the curriculum as a whole. Adapting Applebee's ideas to the language in this text, I argue that learning for the whole year should contribute to the development of an *overarching concept.* An overarching concept helps connect class discussions and student productions from unit to unit, giving students an overall sense of direction and continuity for their learning. Whereas most curricula emphasize a series of facts and skills to be mastered, this conception of curriculum focuses on ideas, particularly as students enter and transform the subject of English and grow through the process of their inquiry.

The notions of overarching concepts and human growth also fit well with Csikszentmihalyi and Larson's (1984) views on human happiness. Their study of adolescents focused on identifying the kinds of experiences that put them *in the flow,* a state in which they were so heavily involved in what they were doing that they lost all track of time. It will surprise few that these experiences rarely occur during mainstream school classes, particularly during that most common classroom practice: listening to a teacher talk. Ultimately, Csikszentmihalyi and Larson identify happy people—that is, those whose life work most frequently provides for flow experiences—as those who develop overarching concepts for their activity.

A literature curriculum that students experience and contribute to, that provides them with a domain for developing themes to guide their life's actions and decisions, can make two key, related contributions to students' education. First, through transactions with provocative texts, it can provide them with a strong literary education and thus enable them to participate in and contribute to a major tradition in arts and letters. Second, it can enable them to experience this tradition in a way that allows them to understand the social conditions, life experiences, and literary conventions that guide the production of literature and other texts—including those they produce themselves—and help these texts serve as vehicles for students' growth into happy, productive citizens.

Schemas and Scripts

Another rationale for conceptual units comes from cognitive psychologists' *schema theory*. A schema is a network of knowledge that includes both elements and processes. Having schematic knowledge enables a person to understand situations that are new, yet are related to ones already known. This should sound familiar. As I said previously, an effectively designed conceptual unit will help students understand new material that is related to familiar material. This approach to schooling is quite different from the approach in which assessment is based on tests of students' recall of what they have already read and discussed.

You probably have schemas for many familiar routines in life. Let's say, for instance, that you enter a restaurant. If you have eaten out before, you likely have a general schema for how the evening will proceed. You will be seated at a table, a waiter will come and take your order, you will wait for a period of time, the food will come in a particular order (appetizers, soup or salad, main course), you will eat it, be offered an opportunity to order dessert, be given a check, and then pay either the waiter or the cashier and leave (leaving a tip of roughly 15 to 20 percent).

Your knowledge of how the script will unfold will help you conduct yourself in an appropriate manner. You will not, for instance, juggle flaming torches or play the bagpipes while waiting for your food, unless the restaurant has a very special theme. You will also be alert to signals that indicate a variation in the script. At an Ethiopian restaurant, for instance, you will eat your food with your hands instead of with silverware. If the expectations of your script are violated—for instance, if your waiter brings the main course before the soup—you have a way of recognizing the discrepancy and likely a means for resolving it (complaining to the manager). Your schema for dining out, then, enables you to anticipate the rules of propriety, the sequence of events, and the elements of the setting so that you can understand, appreciate, and enjoy your meal.

Organizing instruction by conceptual units fits well with schema theory. If prior knowledge helps anticipate new situations, then studying texts that are conceptually unified makes sense. Often students already have prior knowledge that can help them engage with the unit concepts. Coming-of-age experiences, for instance, appear to be archetypal among young people. Anyone who has had a coming-of-age experience has a script for such events, just as people who have dined in restaurants have scripts for eating out. And, just as people tend to eat in restaurants repeatedly over time and refine their restaurant scripts through exposure to new restaurant ex-

Books on Schemas and Scripts

Arbib, M. A., Conklin, E. J., & Hill, J. A. C. (1987). *From schema theory to language.* New York: Oxford University Press.

Bransford, J. D. (1979). *Human cognition: Learning, understanding and remembering.* Belmont, CA: Wadsworth.

Kintsch, W. (1977). *Memory and cognition* (2nd ed.). New York: Wiley.

Kitao, S. (1989). *Reading, schema theory, and second language learners.* Tokyo: Eichosha Shinsha.

Mandler, J. M. (1984). *Stories, scripts, and scenes: Aspects of schema theory.* Hillsdale, NJ: Erlbaum.

Tierney, R., & Pearson, P. D. (1986). *Schema theory and implications for teaching reading: A conversation.* Champaign, IL: University of Illinois at Urbana-Champaign.

periences, people have many coming-of-age experiences rather than just one. The prior knowledge from personal experience (and likely from prior reading and media viewing) can form the basis for understanding how the theme works in newly encountered literature, film, and art. In a reciprocal process, these newly encountered texts can provide the basis for reflection on the prior experiences.

Furthermore, each text can serve to develop a schema that in turn helps a reader to understand the experiences that are at the heart of the theme as well as the textual conventions that authors use to help convey a theme. For instance, a coming-of-age story typically involves a character who exhibits immature behavior at the outset, has a transforming experience, and gains greater wisdom or maturity at the end. This script presumably parallels the kinds of experiences that young readers have as they negotiate adolescence. By organizing literature according to conceptual units, teachers can help students refine their schemas for both their own unfolding experiences and their knowledge of narrative conventions.

Scaffolding Learning

The notion of an *instructional scaffold,* developed by Jerome Bruner from Vygotsky's views on human development, also supports teaching through conceptual units. Scaffolding refers to the way in which experienced and capable people assist others in learning new knowledge and skills. An example would be the way in which an experienced carpenter teaches a novice how to build a cabinet.

The carpenter might use a variety of methods to teach the skills of cabinetmaking: providing information verbally (e.g., explaining why it's important to use safety goggles), modeling (e.g., demonstrating how to strike a nail without bending it), showing how to find resources (e.g., doing comparative shopping by phone), and so on. As the learner grasps the concepts and learns to use the tools properly, the carpenter begins handing over responsibilities to the novice. This process might involve providing feedback and support while the novice begins to apply the concepts (corners should be square) and use the tools (using a T square to prepare for a right-angle cut). As the novice demonstrates increasing competency, the carpenter allows more autonomy and intervenes only as needed. Ultimately, the novice grasps how to build a cabinet and can work independently.

In learning complex new knowledge, a person benefits from an extended process of using concepts and tools across a variety of contexts: building a china cabinet, making built-in kitchen cabinets, fashioning cabinets from different materials, and so on. The novice might learn from the initial building experience how to construct a level, freestanding cabinet from oak, but might struggle with how to use softer wood in a confined kitchen space without denting it. The novice might struggle again when building kitchen cabinets in a house set on a steep incline. Knowledge learned from the first experience might require modification and refinement when applied to the next. Multiple experiences would be necessary in order for the novice to be considered a skilled builder of cabinets. When encountering new circumstances, the novice would benefit from additional support from the carpenter so as to recognize how to adjust knowledge of concepts and tools to new circumstances.

Here is where the scaffolding metaphor becomes useful in thinking about instructional planning. Because a unifying concept plays out differently under different circumstances, it is helpful to engage in sustained exploration of the concept across a variety of texts. A thematic unit on loyalty, for instance, might begin with some relatively clear-cut texts that emphasize the need for loyalty to a higher authority. Biblical tales, such as the story of Cain and Abel or of Moses and Aaron, for example, show people who are torn between obeying their god or taking matters into their own hands, with punishment meted out to those who break their faith. Loyalty oaths, including the U. S. Pledge of Allegiance or agreements signed by state employees to uphold state laws, also fall in this category. These initial explorations could then lead to consideration of more problematic texts.

Thoreau's "Civil Disobedience," for instance, advocates the breaking of unjust laws, as does Martin Luther King Jr.'s "Letter from a Birmingham Jail." In addition to looking at loyalty issues involving allegiance to higher authorities, students could examine loyalty in local and voluntary relationships. Chaim Potok's *The Chosen* involves a series of relationships that call for loyalty. Two boys from different Jewish traditions become friends, and it turns out that their fathers are rivals. One father favors the establishment of a Jewish state and the other believes that it is God's will to wait for divine intervention for deliverance to the promised land.

When I taught this novel, I often paired it with the biblical story of Moses and Aaron because of the parallels between the fathers' conflicts and similar dilemmas faced by Moses (who has faith in God's will) and Aaron (who grows impatient and fashions a golden calf as an idol). The boys in *The Chosen* are caught amidst these competing loyalties and must choose between their friendship and the beliefs of their fathers and their faiths. By examining these issues of loyalty across situations and texts, students, like the novice carpenter, can have the opportunity to work through their understanding and application of knowledge about loyalty. They can then understand it in both future works of art and literature and future crises of loyalty in their own lives.

The scaffolding comes into the teacher's design of the unit and decisions about when to provide support once students have begun to grasp the principles. Through

Books Involving Scaffolding

Bruner, J. (1983). *Child's talk: Learning to use language.* New York: Norton.

Cazden, C. B. (1992). *Whole language plus: Essays on literacy in the United States and New Zealand.* New York: Teachers College Press.

Hillocks, G. (1995). *Teaching writing as reflective practice.* New York: Teachers College Press.

Langer, J. A., & Applebee, A. N. (1987). *How writing shapes thinking: A study of teaching and learning* (NCTE Research Report No. 22). Urbana, IL: National Council of Teachers of English.

Lee, C. D. (1993). *Signifying as a scaffold for literary interpretation: The pedagogical implications of an African American discourse genre* (NCTE Research Report No. 26). Urbana, IL: National Council of Teachers of English.

Rogoff, B., & Lave, J. (Eds.). (1984). *Everyday cognition: Its development in social context.* Cambridge, MA: Harvard University Press.

Rogoff, B., & Wertsch, J. V. (Eds.). (1984). *Children's learning in the "zone of proximal development."* San Francisco: Jossey-Bass.

Tharp, R. G., & Gallimore, R. (1988). *Rousing minds to life: Teaching, learning, and schooling in social context.* New York: Cambridge University Press.

skillful planning and assistance, the teacher can plan a conceptual unit so that, ultimately, the students can understand the complexity of the theme and construct their own understanding of the role it plays in their lives.

The scaffolding metaphor has its critics, and their reservations are worth noting. Dennis Searle (1984) posed the important question, "Who's building whose building?" In other words, the scaffolding metaphor suggests that the person providing the support will lead the learner toward the best possible construction. Searle questions the extent to which a teacher's decisions are always in the students' best interests—that is, it's possible that students might have entirely different needs and purposes than are served by the kinds of constructions the teacher imposes. This question also implies a criticism about the conventional notion of the teacher as someone who teaches rather than learns. Critics of authoritarian approaches to schooling maintain that teachers ought to learn through the process of teaching. Their notion of a building potentially can change through their engagement with learners and their ideas about what needs to be constructed.

This criticism is important to keep in mind when teaching. You should always ask yourself, Whose building is being constructed here? Whose needs will it serve? Who is learning what through this kind of construction? Are there other possible ways to envision and build this text?

You should also keep in mind that sometimes people need to learn things they don't think they need to learn. I remember teaching in high school when AIDS was declared an epidemic and students were required to attend informational assemblies. Many students resisted going. One student in my homeroom even wailed that nobody from our town would ever get AIDS, so why should she have to waste her afternoon at an assembly? It's very important to give students a strong role in their own learning, but placing an absolute faith in their knowledge of their own needs is unfounded and unwise. At times, the things they think they don't need can be critical to their survival.

Transactional Learning

Additional support for using conceptual units within an integrated curriculum comes from Louise Rosenblatt's *transactional theory* of response to literature, outlined primarily in two books: *Literature as Exploration* (1996; originally published in 1938), and *The Reader, the Text, the Poem: The Transactional Theory of the Literary Work,* (1978). She based her ideas on the educational philosophy of John Dewey, who outlined a transactional theory of human development in *Art as Experience.*

Rosenblatt proposed her theory at a time when university literary theorists were concerned with developing text-centered approaches to literary criticism that minimized the value of a reader's affective response or personal constructions of meaning. Rosenblatt argued instead for a democratic view that gave the ordinary reader as much authority in determining a literary work's meaning as that accorded to a professional literary critic.

It took some time for her ideas to gain widespread acceptance, and various reasons have been proposed for this delay. One suggested reason was that accepting this democratic view meant that students could conceivably understand a work better than a teacher, an idea that few English professors were willing to embrace. Another was that a certain aesthetic snobbery prevailed among English professors, holding that the idiosyncratic, often emotional responses of ordinary readers were inherently inferior to the reasoned criteria by which professional critics separated the great books from the rest. Yet another factor may have been the effort of professors of literary criticism to achieve greater status for their discipline and their use of scientific methods of analysis to elevate their stature among their colleagues—again, making ordinary, unscientific response less legitimate in their eyes. Or, the delay in acceptance of these ideas may have been related to the fact that university faculties at the time were primarily male in makeup. The minority status of women created obstacles to an individual woman's acceptance and obstacles to fair consideration of a woman's outlook. Rosenblatt's difficulties in gaining acceptance were not unusual for a woman of her time.

As time passed, however, her ideas attracted a following, particularly after James Britton and colleagues argued persuasively in the 1960s for a "growth model" of education that shifted attention from texts to students. Rosenblatt's acceptance also coincided with the Civil Rights and Women's Rights movements of the 1960s in which such efforts as affirmative action created new opportunities for women within the academy. With more women taking faculty positions and asserting authority through their new avenues of influence, the likelihood that a woman's stature would rise in the world of ideas greatly increased.

Rosenblatt asserts clearly that readers need to attend carefully to the words a writer uses to craft a work of literature. What those words might mean, however, is a matter of personal construction. This construction is based on

- a reader's personal experiences
- the cultural factors that shape both readers and texts

- the social environment of a classroom and its effects on a reader's response
- the psychological makeup of individual readers that provides a particular frame of mind for interpreting events in particular ways

The same text, then, might be read quite differently by two readers in the same class who bring different cultural expectations to the experience, or who have different personal experiences, or whose psychological makeups provide different frameworks for interpreting events.

Let me give an example of an occasion when students interpreted a story in a way that initially struck me as naïve, but ultimately made sense when I recognized the reason for their interpretation. At the time I was the cooperating teacher for a student teacher, Ann Jordahl. For her master's thesis Ann was doing a study of how to teach students to write generalization and support in their persuasive essays. She wanted to see if working in small groups promoted students' ability to support their generalizations.

For the study, she taught two of her classes in similar ways, with one variation. Prior to instruction she had both classes read some stories and make generalizations about the authors, which they supported with evidence. Instruction then began, with Ann leading a discussion on how to read several stories by the same author (Hemingway), make generalizations about their style, and support the generalizations with evidence from the texts.

The variation came in the next stage of instruction. For one class, Ann led another discussion reinforcing the process of supporting generalizations; for the other class, small groups of students supported their own generalizations. For the final evaluation, Ann considered students' ability to make generalizations from a set of stories they read on their own. For the purposes of the study, she contrasted the gains made by one class with the gains made by the other, using the preinstruction and postinstruction essay scores as her measurements.

I would like to focus on the responses of a group of boys who read the final set of stories, all from Hemingway's *In Our Time*. In particular, the boys' responses to "The Three Day Blow" were illuminating. In this story a three-day storm maroons Nick Adams and his companion Bill in a cabin, where they drink steadily and talk about their lives. In their essays, the boys argued that the story was a cautionary tale against excessive alcohol use. This interpretation initially gave us concerns, both about our teaching and about the boys' reading. After all, Ann and I had both been college English majors. In graduate school, we had both been required to satisfy the English department's master's degree requirements as well as those of our education program. Furthermore, the high school where we were teaching was the alma mater of Hemingway himself, a source of great pride within the English department—and as a consequence, there was considerable knowledge about Hemingway among faculty members. We knew that his life and literature did not suggest a didactic reading of his work when it came to alcohol abuse.

As we thought about these boys and their responses and tried to make sense of them, I realized that all of them were football players. I also remembered that athletes in the school were put through regular and extensive programs on substance abuse, one of which they had recently attended. Returning to Rosenblatt, we can see that these students had likely

Books on Transactional Learning

Beach, R. W. (1993). *A teacher's introduction to reader-response theories.* Urbana, IL: National Council of Teachers of English.

Beach, R. W., & Marshall, J. D. (1991). *Teaching literature in the secondary school.* San Diego: Harcourt Brace Jovanovich.

Clifford, J. (Ed.). (1991). *The experience of reading: Louise Rosenblatt and reader-response theory.* Portsmouth, NH: Heinemann.

Dewey, J. (1934). *Art as experience.* New York: Berkeley Publishing Group.

Hynds, S. (1997). *On the brink: Negotiating literature and life with adolescents.* New York: Teachers College Press.

Marshall, J. D., Smagorinsky, P., & Smith, M. W. (1995). *The language of interpretation: Patterns of discourse in discussions of literature* (NCTE Research Report No. 27). Urbana, IL: National Council of Teachers of English.

Moffett, J., & Wagner, B. J. (1992). *Student-centered language arts, K–12* (4th ed.). Portsmouth, NH: Heinemann.

Nelms, B. F. (Ed.). (1988). *Literature in the classroom.* Urbana, IL: National Council of Teachers of English.

Probst, R. E. (1988). *Response and analysis: Teaching literature in junior and senior high school.* Portsmouth, NH: Heinemann.

Purves, A., Rogers, T., & Soter, A. (1995). *How porcupines make love III: Readers, texts, cultures in the response-based literature classroom.* New York: Longman.

Rosenblatt, L. M. (1978). *The reader, the text, the poem: The transactional theory of literary response.* Carbondale, IL: Southern Illinois University Press.

Rosenblatt, L. M. (1996). *Literature as exploration* (5th ed.). New York: Modern Language Association.

Tchudi, S. (1991). *Planning and assessing the curriculum in English language arts.* Alexandria, VA: Association for Supervision and Curriculum Development.

Vine, H., & Faust, M. (1993). *Situating readers: Students making meaning of literature.* Urbana, IL: National Council of Teachers of English.

- witnessed other teenagers who had problems with drugs and alcohol (personal experiences)
- been taught to view alcohol consumption as unhealthy and destructive (cultural orientation to reading)
- developed a framework for interpreting the behavior of drunkards (psychological framework)

When Ann and I considered what the boys brought to the text, it seemed more reasonable that they would interpret a pair of besotten characters as symbols of the ravages of alcohol. The lesson we learned was that what students bring to stories is often quite different from what college literature majors bring to stories. We decided that, when teaching Hemingway in the future, we should provide some background on his life and values to help inform students' responses to the stories.

Some people might find this a heavy-handed intervention that interferes with students' personal efforts to construct meaning from literature. Many educators feel that teachers should honor all readers' responses to literature, particularly first readings. They believe that it's more important for students to be allowed the latitude to interpret the story on their own terms than for a teacher to introduce information that might affect those interpretations. One of the people who reviewed this book wrote, "Even if some students don't come to the 'right' answer then, I believe it's better to hold to the principle of reading literature as a transactional process where students construct their understandings than to try to predict where they are going to go wrong and give them the information that will fix it."

Rather than trying to settle this issue—about which there is considerable disagreement—I'll leave it to you as a topic for thought and discussion: Should students have the opportunity to construct whichever understandings they arrive at, or should a teacher provide what he or she feels is useful information that could help inform the students' understandings?

However you interpret Rosenblatt's transactional theory, its emphasis on what readers bring to texts and in turn construct from them contributes to a rationale for organizing literature according to concepts. If, for instance, themes represent archetypal experiences, then they can serve students well in two ways. First, students will bring critical prior knowledge to their reading, giving them authority as knowledgeable readers of literature. If students have had experience with justice, or Puritan values, or satire, or whatever topic is covered, then those experiences provide them with knowledge about the topic that deserves acknowledgment and respect in the classroom.

Second, their consideration of the concept through literary study ought to provide them with opportunities to reflect on their experience and construct new knowledge. They can thus develop a relationship with literature and classmates that potentially enriches their understanding of themselves, the literature, and one another. This approach does not promote an "anything goes" classroom, where any interpretation by a student is acceptable. It does, however, honor the ways in which students can find meaning that has a basis in the actual language of the text, whether that meaning matches the teacher's reading or not.

Principles of Practice

The rationale I have given for teaching according to conceptual units implies the following principles of practice:

- Instruction is defensible
- Instruction is purposeful
- Students show their learning in different ways
- Students should learn through being assessed
- Teachers should have high expectations for students
- Never dumb down instruction
- Teachers scaffold students' learning
- Instruction is sequenced
- Learning proceeds from what students know
- The context of learning is critical
- There's a time and place for everything
- Teachers should grow through the process of teaching
- Assessing students is assessing teaching

1. *Instruction is defensible.* Often it seems as though teachers teach something because it's in the textbook or in the curriculum. This does not strike me as a compelling reason for students to read particular texts, to read them in particular combinations, to read them with a particular emphasis, or to produce certain kinds of texts in response to them. Everything a teacher does ought to be defensible; that is, a teacher should be able to provide a rationale for whatever and however he or she teaches, as I have tried to do to support this approach to teaching.

2. *Instruction is purposeful.* At one time, teachers were encouraged to teach toward behavioral objectives, which were the things students would do to show that they had learned something (see Bloom, 1956). Objectives went out of fashion because they were perceived to be too rigid. Many teachers felt that by identifying objectives, they were narrowing their flexibility during the course of instruction and overspecifying how students were to perform. In addition, some thought that objectives implied that only one type of performance could demonstrate that learning had taken place. In general, those who objected to objectives worried that they allowed for too little diversity: Students all had to do the same thing regardless of where they came from and what they'd learned, and teachers were discouraged from creatively acting on situations as they arose.

Then along came *outcomes,* in the guise of *outcomes-based education* (OBE), which also conceived of teaching as leading to particular endpoints, albeit different ones. OBE was short-lived, however, because many people believed that the outcomes being sought were the development of a particular kind of person. Whereas objectives had required that students produce a particular kind of artifact of their learning, outcomes described a particular kind of person who would emerge from an education. Many parents rebelled against the idea that schools should decide how their kids would turn out. Outcomes were accused of encouraging satanism, promoting secular humanism, and engaging in social engineering. Powerful opposition arose, motivated by the belief that homes should produce people and schools should produce knowledgeable students.

I'll sidestep the question for now of whether it's possible to separate the two kinds of development. Instead, I'll emphasize the ways in which the decline in objectives quickly gave way to the advent of outcomes. Both assumed that teachers should teach with an endpoint in mind. This belief has recurred throughout educational history in one form or another. It is a belief that you'll find alive and well in schools. It is a belief that I hold as well, and it will be a central idea in the principles of planning that I describe in this book.

Yet it has also been a problematic belief, for the reasons I have outlined. I would like to retain the idea that teaching should begin with a destination in mind without having that idea get bogged down in old disagreements. To do so, I will need to change the terminology and in the process change the particular ideas that go with it. The central point here is: When teachers teach, they should do so with an idea of what students will produce for purposes of assessment. I'll refer to this culminating activity or text as a *goal* and assert that instruction should be purposeful in helping students achieve this goal. In other words, instruction ought to help students to produce the culminating text that will serve as the assessment of their learning. Although it's possible (and often desirable) that some instruction will be tangential to this goal, by and large students should know what it is and learn how to do it.

3. *Students show their learning in different ways*. This principle is related to the previous one and refers to the kinds of goals toward which students work. Schools tend to evaluate students in narrow ways. Howard Gardner (1983) has argued that schools focus on linguistic and mathematical knowledge, so that students with other intelligences (musical, interpersonal, kinesthetic, intrapersonal, spatial, naturalistic) appear to have learned poorly according to school assessments.

Even within the privileged school intelligences, a narrow range of assessment is allowed. In English classes, for instance, students are primarily evaluated on their analytic writing, with affective, expressive, and reflective writing overlooked as indicators of what students have learned. In this book I will argue that the goals of instruction ought to accommodate students with a variety of ways of knowing.

4. *Students should learn through being assessed*. I have always maintained that any assessment of students ought to be the occasion for new learning. If an assessment tests students only on their ability to recall facts, there seems little point in doing the assessment. In such cases students' preparation for the test has likely been designed for immediate recall and not for what cognitive psychologists call deep processing or what cultural psychologists call appropriation. In other words, students do not view test preparation as authentic activity in which they grasp knowledge and adopt it for their own purposes. Instead, they view test preparation as serving the short-term goal of passing a test. And, as Ralph Tyler (1949) reported long ago, people forget 80 percent of memorized information within two years. That hardly seems like a worthwhile basis for assessing what students have learned.

Rather, assessment should not only test students' knowledge, but in doing so should offer a new and worthwhile problem to solve. The process of solving this problem should lead to the construction of new knowledge that students find useful. In other words, assessment should not only assess students' knowledge of content, but should also allow them to use the assessment process as a tool to serve their growth.

5. *Teachers should have high expectations for students*. One of the great debates in education involves the question of extrinsic motivation and intrinsic motivation. Most educators feel that students should do things in school because those things are worth doing, rather than because an adult is saying they must do them. I certainly agree that what students do in school ought to be of interest to them and ought to help them grow into thoughtful and productive citizens.

Yet I also believe that efforts to locate motivation solely within the individual do not take into account what Vygotsky views as the social nature of human development. People's goals do not spring spontaneously from them, but are made available to them through interaction with other people. If books did not exist, for instance, I would not be motivated to write one. And if people did not have expectations for what might be in a book, I would not know what to put in one. In other words, expectations provide goals with definition and standards. It is a truism in education that students perform at the level of expectations their schools provide. In my view, students get more out of an education if their teachers set high expectations for them.

I've done some work with the Southern Regional Education Board, which has interviewed many students shortly after high school graduation. One consistent statement students have made is that they wished that their teachers had asked more of them. This retrospective lament often stands in contrast to what students plead for while in school, which is less work. When all is said and done, students end up respecting the teachers who set the bar high and do not wilt under student pressure to lower it.

6. *Never dumb down instruction.* When I talk about high expectations, I think they should apply to everyone. One of the most distressing things about schooling is the way in which some students are relegated to a "skills" curriculum in which they spend day after day doing workbook exercises designed to teach them "basics," such as proper spelling, how to label adjectives, how to choose among homonyms, and so on. Although these issues should be given attention, I find it alarming that for some students, that's all they ever get. And the presentation of the material is so tedious and disconnected from any authentic activity that the students benefit little from the drills.

One of the virtues of teaching in conceptual units is that there is potential for every student to engage with the issues on some level. Students who speak nonstandard dialects, who are slow learners, and who historically have done poorly in school still participate in friendship, rites of passage, conflicts with authority, and other experiences that can serve as organizing principles for their literary reading and writing.

Some of the most poignant writing I've ever read was produced by students in "remedial" or "basic" classes. I still remember Vietnamese refugees writing of setting out to sea in boats, waving good-bye for the last time to their families, and watching them shrink into nothing on the shoreline. The writing lacked conventional precision, yet was very moving. To assume that students who lack "skills" should receive a skills-only curriculum underestimates their potential for engagement with substantive issues and reinforces the idea that going to school is a form of punishment for lack of conventional fluency.

Indeed, many stories from research on schooling illustrate the ways in which expectations can affect students with supposed low ability levels. Often these stories involve students who are mistakenly placed in the wrong ability track and end up doing quite well in the more demanding curriculum. Although all students will not necessarily respond to higher challenges, as a teacher you should make every effort to expect that your students can benefit from a curriculum that engages them and challenges them to grow intellectually.

7. *Teachers scaffold students' learning.* I previously described the metaphor of the instructional scaffold, in which teachers provide appropriate levels of support for students' learning with the goal of having students eventually take over responsibility for their learning. Classrooms can include many teachers—that is, students as well as teachers can teach—and in scaffolding learning, teachers should find opportunities for students to assist one another's learning. And, as noted, teachers should always be sensitive to whose building is being built, and how.

8. *Instruction is sequenced.* If teaching is purposeful and leads toward goals for students, then teachers should be responsible for teaching so that students have the greatest potential for reaching those goals. If instructional design follows prin-

ciples of scaffolding, then the sequence of instruction ought to begin with the most highly supported learning and move to learning that involves the students' ultimate grasp of the material.

Sequencing is key to an instructional scaffold. Sequencing takes into account both the relationships of class members and the kinds of materials studied. A sequence based on relationships might involve teacher-led activities at the beginning of a unit, move to teacher-supported small-group applications of the unit concepts, and ultimately assess students on their individual grasp and application of those concepts. A sequence based on materials might involve a progression, from relatively accessible materials in which the concepts are clearly outlined through engagement with increasingly challenging materials as students gain understanding of the unit concepts.

9. *Learning proceeds from what students know.* In many cases, people have relevant knowledge that could help them with new learning, but they don't see the connections and don't apply their prior knowledge to new situations. Students might have personal experience with ostracism, for instance, yet not realize that this knowledge could help them understand *The Scarlet Letter*. Some kind of activity that would help them consider relevant personal knowledge before reading could enable such students to understand Hester Prynn and Puritan society in terms of what they already know. Instruction ought to make links between what students know and what they learn.

A more controversial question concerns what a teacher should do when students lack personal knowledge that would help them understand literature. A modern teenager growing up after the fall of the Soviet Union, for instance, might not understand the appeal that communism held for African American intellectuals of the 1930s, such as Richard Wright. Some would believe that students should proceed with their reading transaction and construct whatever meaning they find in the text. Others would believe that the students' transaction would benefit if they were provided with a brief social history prior to reading *Native Son*. Given the disagreement on this point in the field, I'll leave it to you to think about which approach you will take.

10. *The context of learning is critical.* Most high school textbooks and anthologies are written for a generic student and school setting. No matter who the students are, no matter what the values of the community are, the textbook provides a single way of teaching. In my view, teachers ought to be attentive to the context in which teaching and learning take place. States typically set the larger policy context for instruction, mandating that certain skills be taught, certain tests passed, and certain books read (or *not* read). Districts also provide constraints, often adding layers of assessment and further restrictions on what students may and may not read. Schools have their own curricula (often written to match textbook outlines) that dictate certain requirements and limitations. In some districts students are required to write in journals, for instance, whereas in others they are prohibited from doing so.

Within this set of official constraints, teachers need to be attentive to any factors that might affect teaching and learning.

- Who are the students?
- Do social circumstances make it difficult for them to do homework?
- Does the racial or ethnic makeup influence any decisions about what to read or not read?

- Does the percentage of students who historically have attended college suggest the degree to which instruction should focus on college preparation?
- Do the income levels of the community allow for certain expectations with regard to students' familiarity with technology and other resources?
- Do the religious values of the community suggest the appropriateness or inappropriateness of particular modes of instruction?

In other words, few teachers have classes composed entirely of the generic, usually middle-class students anticipated by textbooks and anthologies. Teachers need to know who their students are in order to make appropriate decisions about how to design instruction.

11. *There's a time and place for everything.* One idea frequently recommended in educational publications is that a teacher should be a *facilitator* of students' learning. Rather than standing in front of students and lecturing on content knowledge, the teacher should serve as a medium between students and texts, with students being the ultimate constructors of all knowledge. Furthermore, the teacher should be a *coach,* which in this conception is a benevolent leader who encourages greater effort, instructs with care, and allows for enthusiastic participation among students.

For now I'll set aside the question of whether or not coaches are benevolent (I say this as a former high school athlete in three sports, a one-year college basketball player, a high school coach of track and basketball, and a coach of youth baseball, softball, and basketball). What I would like to do instead is contest the idea that a teacher should always be a facilitator and instead argue that teachers should play whatever role is necessary to promote student learning.

This role is likely to change during the course of the unit, depending on what students need. At times, you might decide that students will benefit from being presented with content knowledge, as Ann and I concluded about the boys who interpreted Hemingway as a substance-abuse moralist. At times teachers need to be taskmasters because students are not taking their work seriously. When all is well, teachers can serve the facilitating role so frequently advocated by progressive educators. My point here is that teachers should not assume that facilitating is appropriate for all students on all occasions. Rather, teachers need to be alert to students' learning and make decisions on which role to play in each situation.

12. *Teachers should grow through the process of teaching.* On various occasions I have made the argument that teaching and social science research share much in common. I strongly believe that the process of inquiry is central to any notion of expertise, and is among the defining characteristics of good teaching. And I believe that the same thing is true of research; that is, good research is a process of inquiry, one that both generates knowledge and promotes changes in the researcher. And so I present my case that good teachers are also teacher-researchers.

Although teachers and educational researchers are often thought to be distinct species vying for survival on the same territory, when engaged in a process of inquiry, they share much in common. First, both work under the assumption that there is an ideal way for students to turn out. A teacher usually has instructional goals in mind that serve as the basis for choices of materials and activities in the classroom and lead students toward the teacher's sense of what constitutes a desirable developmental

Vignette

My son, David, has been involved in martial arts (first kung fu, now tae kwon do) since he was five years old. Now, at age eleven, he is a black belt. (So sue me, I'm a proud papa.) Getting there has taken a lot of hard work. I've found it very interesting to watch his instructors and how they teach within the context of martial arts. The environment is highly structured, and as a result the students are able to get through rigorous workouts very efficiently, even with large numbers of students in a single class. The students must be respectful to all within the studio: bowing when entering, addressing the teachers as sir or ma'am, bowing to one another before and after competing, and being extremely obedient to the word of any instructor. The teachers have absolute authority. They are the ones who know the discipline and how to achieve proficiency.

The most advanced teachers are known as Master or Grand Master and are treated with a certain reverence. The teachers, though generally supportive and encouraging, are punitive when necessary. My son, who is on the frisky side, has run laps, done push-ups, and so on, for fooling around during workouts. Some students have been threatened with demotion to a lower belt level for not acting respectfully during workouts.

My point is that there is no one teaching style that works in all contexts. (I don't recommend that your students do push-ups for misbehaving.) Martial arts teachers work within traditions that are highly authoritarian and their methods are extremely effective in achieving the goals of the discipline. All teachers need to consider their circumstances in deciding what role to play in the classroom.

path. Similarly, researchers have a sense of optimal outcome that leads them to make judgments about the processes and products they observe in classrooms.

Second, both teaching and research involve change through the means of instruction and assessment. Teachers promote these changes deliberately, using specific instructional tools to lead students toward outcomes they believe to be positive and beneficial, and using assessments that not only measure change, but promote it as well. Researchers, too, promote change through their interventions, although often they don't admit it. I feel that one of the reasons that people accept the distinction between teachers and researchers is that they don't recognize the ways in which researchers affect the people and situations they observe. Researchers are not neutral and objective, but instead introduce something new into the classroom, often in the form of the teaching methods they're studying. They, like teachers, affect the experiences that students have; ideally, they do so in ways that benefit students.

Finally, both teaching and research use some sort of evidence to gauge how people are progressing toward desired ends. Teachers use students' performance on assignments as evidence of change; researchers might rely on student work in conjunction with observational notes, interviews, and other interventions. Without evidence of some sort, neither one could make any kind of informed judgment about the effectiveness of the teaching.

Through this process of inquiry, teachers grow in their understanding of what it means to teach well and what it means to learn. Such inquiry requires careful attention to students and how they respond to instruction. Teachers who believe that they teach a subject, rather than teach students, are not so likely to reflect on why some students grasp the material more than others. They will be more likely to locate the problem in the student alone rather than in the transaction between student and instruction. Teachers who make an effort to understand the effects of their teaching therefore have the opportunity to grow over the course of their careers and view teaching as the kind of flow activity described by Csikszentmihalyi and Larson.

13. *Assessing students is assessing teaching.* Assessment is often thought of as a way to evaluate students' learning. Darling-Hammond, Ancess, and Falk (1995), however, argue that any assessment that is authentic allows a teacher to reflect on the effectiveness of the instruction. In other words, by assessing students a teacher should evaluate the quality of his or her teaching. This tendency is part of what is known as *reflective practice,* teaching that is characterized by reflection on the processes involved and the learning that occurs.

The notion of principled practice refers to a way of thinking about teaching that is derived from theories of teaching and learning. There are, of course, other ways to think about teaching. But my purpose here is to provide a detailed account of one approach, rather than to provide a tour of teaching methods. The chapters that follow outline a way for you to conceive of teaching according to these principles.

Discussion Topic

In a small group, discuss the best teachers you've ever had, and the worst.

- What characteristics do the exceptionally good teachers have? Is there a set of traits that characterizes all good teachers?
- What characteristics do the exceptionally bad teachers have? Is there a set of traits that characterizes all bad teachers?
- How do your conceptions of good and bad teachers compare to the principles of practice outlined in this chapter?

PART 1

PRINCIPLES OF PLANNING

Part I of this book is devoted to teaching you how to design four- to six-week units of instruction within the overall goals and purposes of a whole curriculum. This design takes into account a host of considerations that I call the context of instruction: the particular students you have, the values and needs of the community as a whole, the mandates imposed by district and state, the values and politics of your school and department, and the environment you create within your classroom. I make an effort to acquaint you with the ways in which the context of your teaching affects the decisions you make.

The kind of unit design I describe considers what students know and tries to build on that knowledge to reach new goals. These goals suggest what you should teach and how you should teach it. There's no single set of goals that are best to pursue, nor is there a single path to follow to reach a particular goal. What I try to do is provide you with a way of thinking about instructional planning that you can thoughtfully apply when facing new teaching situations.

2 Getting Started: Basics of Unit Design

In this chapter I outline the first steps of planning a conceptual unit of instruction. I consider the question of who gets to choose the topic for a unit: you alone, a curriculum designer from outside your class, or you in conjunction with others. I review what's involved in identifying appropriate units for your students and how choosing units is affected by the context of teaching. I address the materials that go into the unit—the literature and other texts that present the unit topic to students—and finally, describe the writing of a rationale for the unit, that is, a justification for teaching it. The process of unit design is not linear, but often involves going back and forth between topic and materials and continual refinement throughout the process of planning, teaching, and post-teaching reflection.

This chapter describes a process for beginning to plan a conceptual unit. Although I'm suggesting an order, you will not necessarily stick to this order in designing your own unit. Rather than plan a unit strictly in stages, you are likely to jump around. You will consider good books to teach, think of how they'd fit together into a unit of instruction, devise good reasons to teach them, come up with additional texts to include, refine the topic of the unit, and so on. However, if I were to make spontaneous leaps the way your mind will while planning a unit, it would be confusing. Here, then, I will address each area separately with the understanding that each will be done in conjunction with others in whatever sequence works for you.

WHO DECIDES ON THE TOPIC?

Before considering the separate steps that constitute designing a unit, I want to address a fundamental question, Who decides what topics students will explore during the year? The answer ranges from the curriculum itself as arbiter of topics to students as curriculum makers. The approach I outline in this book can be adjusted to fit into either a teacher- or a student-determined curriculum. Because it requires thoughtful decisions and actions on the teacher's part, however, it will be harder to implement in schools where teachers are required to follow a script.

I next review different approaches to curriculum development, moving from the least flexible to the most flexible.

The Curriculum Says

In some schools, the curriculum serves as a fairly rigid guideline for what teachers teach. Of course, the curriculum doesn't write itself. Rather, it's the work of people, often teachers themselves. Sometimes the curriculum follows the table of contents of the anthology series they buy. The curriculum usually reflects the values of the people who write it. A curriculum can be prescribed or mandated from several locations. A school or school district may have a single curriculum that all teachers are expected to follow, or a state may have a centralized curriculum that all schools must follow. Often, a prescribed curriculum is tied to some form of assessment. In other words, a centralized curriculum is often accompanied by a prescribed examination that students must pass in order to be promoted to the next grade. Sometimes a teacher's annual evaluation is based on his or her students' performance on such exams.

The rationale behind this approach is to ensure that all students, no matter which school they attend or which teacher they are assigned, whether they are from poorer or wealthier districts, get the same education. In this sense, the curriculum is viewed as democratic. A centralized curriculum also presumably helps compensate for unevenness in the overall teaching force, as students will get the same curriculum whether their teachers are more or less effective. Another stated advantage to a centralized curriculum is that students who transfer from one class or school to another will not be penalized, because their new class will be at the same point in the curriculum where their old class was.

The disadvantage to this approach is that it takes decision making out of the hands of teachers and students, making the school environment less dynamic for everyone. A school in which the curriculum rules is a school that underestimates and shortchanges students as well as teachers. Making this point aggressively too early in your career, when you have the least job security and authority, would probably work against your goals, but once you build security and respect, you might consider introducing this idea into discussions of curriculum.

Teacher Decides

In the most likely scenario, a teacher takes a given curriculum into consideration and makes decisions about what to teach before the year begins. The teacher has little choice about some things—if you teach American literature, for instance, you will likely be restricted to literature written by Americans (though it's not always clear who counts as an American). However, within such limitations, the teacher may be able to choose the particular units to teach, the texts used within those units, the order in which to present the units, and the methods to use in teaching.

The advantage of this approach is that the teacher has a sense of order and comfort about the stability of the curriculum and security in knowing how to plan. The students can also benefit from this clear sense of order.

The disadvantage is that students have no choice in what they read or do, which might make them feel less invested in their work. In addition, with this approach, because each teacher provides a different curriculum, all students in all classes are not learning the same thing at the same pace, which some consider a disadvantage.

Students Choose within Limits

In this approach to choosing a curriculum, the teacher sets up a menu of possible topics, allowing the students to select eight or so for their year's study. The menu should be organized so that students are not likely to confine their selections to a single time period, set of issues, or other principle. This approach has the advantage of giving the students choices in their learning while operating within a framework of topics that the teacher considers culturally and educationally important.

A disadvantage to this approach is that students in different classes are likely to make different choices. The teacher, then, would end up teaching many different combinations of topics, and having to prepare for so many different topics could make teaching stressful and exhausting. It is often a good idea to wait a few years before taking this approach so that you will have several units prepared, rather than having to write many new units from scratch in your first or second year on the job. Allowing students this level of choice is viewed as disadvantageous by people who prefer a curriculum to be uniform across classes and schools.

Students Choose

Reflective Writing Prompt

In your experiences as a student, on which occasions have you been consulted in the development of the curriculum? How do you feel your involvement, or lack of involvement, affected your motivation and engagement with the course? To what degree do you think students ought to be involved in deciding what they will study?

To turn the responsibility for choosing the curriculum over to the students, allowing them to decide what they will study for the year, the teacher first needs to teach them how to think about curriculum and instruction. I'd recommend this approach for students who find literature and composition tremendously fulfilling and who are mature enough to make choices about what they will find both immediately engaging and ultimately educational.

It is difficult to use this approach in school systems that allow students to make schedule changes for the first few weeks of the school year because enrollments often shift and the students who plan the curriculum might not end up in the class.

IDENTIFYING UNIT TOPICS

Identifying a unit topic is a complex process that involves the consideration of a variety of factors. In the best of all possible worlds, you—perhaps in conjunction with your students—would pick topics and teach them. However, if you work in a typical school, every decision you make comes within the context of a range of factors that constrain your choices.

Although you can still make a lot of choices, it's wise to teach in ways that are considerate of your students and their parents, members of the broader taxpaying community, your individual colleagues and your department, the English curriculum, the domain of English/language arts, and any broader policy structures imposed by school, district, and state. I'm not saying that you should follow the crowd. I am saying that you should know how your actions will be viewed by the crowd. That way, if your actions contradict the crowd's preferences, you'll know what you're getting into.

You need to walk a delicate line, to be a good citizen of your school and community and to do what you think is right. The two don't always mix so well. One component of good citizenship, however, is to exercise one's constitutional right to free speech, which means, in this context, trying to introduce different ideas into the discussion when appropriate. And so in this chapter I'd like to offer some resolution to the tensions you may feel when working in a community school system. One is a sense of the context in which you'll be teaching and how it sets up limitations on what you can do. The other is a set of tools that will enable you to work effectively within those limitations or to change them so that your environment suits you and your students better.

Curriculum

I will next discuss a number of constraints that should enter into your consideration of what topics will work well for you and your students. The order in which I present them does not reflect their importance, as the order of importance might vary from setting to setting. This discussion applies to any curricular planning, no matter how it is shared or divided between teachers and students.

A *constraint* is not necessarily bad, although it can be a problem. Often constraints are useful boundaries that help you act decisively and confidently according to agreed-upon rules. So don't regard the following constraints as necessarily negative, even though some can be a nuisance at times.

Restrictions

One constraint most teachers face is the confines of the curriculum. For instance, most U.S. high schools dedicate the senior year to British literature. It would be hard to justify teaching a unit on the Harlem Renaissance in a class on British literature. Understanding the confines of a curriculum, then, is an important step in determining what is and what is not available to teach to particular groups of students.

A related constraint is limited materials available for teaching, usually because of budgetary concerns. Most schools provide English faculty with some combination of a literature anthology (and its many ancillary materials), a grammar and composition textbook, and a small set of novels. In most districts, these texts have passed through some sort of adoption procedure, beginning at the state level and ending with reviews at the school level. All mass-produced textbooks undergo a process whereby they are examined for offensive material, accuracy, and other concerns before they can be adopted within a state. Because they provide such large markets for textbook publishers, California and Texas set the terms for textbook adoption for the rest of the nation. Individual teachers have little control over the adoption process, which provides initial screening for most of the textbooks a district will ultimately adopt. By and large, this process screens out anything that might offend anybody, resulting in books that many teachers and students find rather bland.

Vignette

Darlene Brown, a teacher at a highly regarded high school, decided that she wanted to teach Alice Walker's *The Color Purple,* a book she'd read and thought high school students would find compelling. The book, however, was not on her district's approved book list. She talked it over with many of her colleagues. Some said that she was crazy to want to teach the book because the lesbian relationship would bring in a storm of angry parents. Others said that they were behind her 100 percent and that if she got the book approved and taught it without incident, they'd teach it too. She decided to go through the complex process of getting the book added to the curriculum.

First, she needed to write a detailed proposal, one that provided a rationale for teaching the book that would be defensible in both scholarly and political ways. She then submitted the proposal to the first layer of approval, a departmental curriculum committee. Once approved at this level, the proposal had to go through committees at the school and district level, and finally be discussed and voted on at

a public school board meeting. She was ultimately successful in getting the book approved, though with much aggravation and some strain on relationships with colleagues who questioned her motives in wanting to teach the novel (they accused her of being a politically correct feminist).

After a year of working through the system to gain approval, she was finally able to teach the novel. It did not create quite the controversy people had anticipated, with either students or parents. Darlene kept detailed notes of her experiences throughout the approval process and her teaching of the novel, and ultimately used her experience as the basis for her master's thesis, which she wrote as a teacher-research study. Her thesis remains one of the best examples of teacher research I've come across. In the end, she had to go through a great struggle to make a relatively small change in her school. Yet without question, her quest paid off: She, her students, and her school were much better off because she had the courage and strength to follow through on her challenge.

At the school level, books then typically pass through a two- or three-step adoption process. First, departmental faculty members look through the textbook series that are commercially available and come to an agreement on the one they wish to use. In some schools, a faculty curriculum committee must then approve of the selection. Finally, books are officially adopted by the board of education.

If you teach from an anthology, you are likely on safe territory with regard to the topics and texts you and your students read because the anthology has been approved at so many levels. If you teach beyond the anthology, things can get more interesting, because individual works of literature can include themes or actions that may be controversial in some communities. One annual source of contention is J. D. Salinger's *The Catcher in the Rye,* which is often taught in schools because of its engaging portrayal of teen angst. Holden Caulfield's narration is, however, profane, causing some boards of education to ban the book.

You need to know which books are acceptable to teach in your community and which are not. If you want to teach a book apart from the approved anthology, you need to check with authorities in your school to learn whether the book has board approval. Many districts have procedures that enable faculty to propose new books

A Sampler of Banned and Protested Books

1984 by George Orwell
The Adventures of Huckleberry Finn by Mark
  Twain
All the King's Men by Robert Penn Warren
An American Tragedy by Theodore Dreiser
Appointment in Samarra by John O'Hara
The Arabian Nights
As I Lay Dying by William Faulkner
Brave New World by Aldous Huxley
The Call of the Wild by Jack London
Can Such Things Be? by Ambrose Bierce
Candide by Voltaire
Canterbury Tales by Chaucer
Catch-22 by Joseph Heller
The Catcher in the Rye by J. D. Salinger
A Clockwork Orange by Anthony Burgess
Confessions by Jean-Jacques Rousseau
Decameron by Boccaccio
Deliverance by James Dickey
A Farewell to Arms by Ernest Hemingway
From Here to Eternity by James Jones
Go Tell It on the Mountain by James Baldwin
The Grapes of Wrath by John Steinbeck
The Great Gatsby by F. Scott Fitzgerald
I. Claudius by Robert Graves
Invisible Man by Ralph Ellison
Leaves of Grass by Walt Whitman
Little Red Riding Hood

Lolita by Vladimir Nabokov
The Lorax by Dr. Seuss
Lord of the Flies by William Golding
Lysistrata by Aristophanes
The Merchant of Venice by William
  Shakespeare
Moll Flanders by Daniel Defoe
The Naked and the Dead by Norman Mailer
Native Son by Richard Wright
Origin of Species by Charles Darwin
Point Counter Point by Aldous Huxley
Portnoy's Complaint by Philip Roth
The Rainbow by D. H. Lawrence
Silas Marner by George Elliot
Sister Carrie by Theodore Dreiser
Slaughterhouse Five by Kurt Vonnegut
Sons and Lovers by D. H. Lawrence
Sophie's Choice by William Styron
State and Revolution by A. I. Lenin
Studs Lonigan by James T. Farrell
The Sun Also Rises by Ernest Hemingway
The Three Little Pigs
Tom Sawyer by Mark Twain
Tropic of Cancer by Henry Miller
Twelfth Night by William Shakespeare
Ulysses by James Joyce
Uncle Tom's Cabin by Harriet Beecher Stowe
Women in Love by D. H. Lawrence

for approval. It's in your interests to know how your system works and to operate responsibly within it.

Discussion Topic

Under what conditions do you think a book should be banned from a school curriculum and/or library?

Requirements

In addition to providing restrictions, a curriculum can provide requirements. Some freshman curricula require *Romeo and Juliet,* for example. Some curricula have topics

Vignette

Throughout this chapter, I'll advise some caution in starting a new job with a highly critical stance toward your school. Your early years are your most vulnerable in terms of job security. If you lose your job, you won't have an opportunity to do any teaching at all. So you'll want to develop some political savvy in knowing how and when to mount a challenge.

I give this advice because I've seen some good teachers self-destruct at the beginnings of their careers by starting noisy crusades in their first years on the job. I was almost one of them. My first job was in a school that I felt was not well run. I made my opinions known, and immediately ran into difficulties with the school

administration. Fortunately, I was able to leave this school after one year because I applied for and was offered a job in a district more suited to my beliefs.

By and large, my handling of the situation was not very productive. Because of my confrontational approach, people were resistant to making any changes and I didn't make any headway. In addition, I suffered personal anguish because the administration gave my job performance negative evaluations.

I'm not telling you to avoid making waves. But I am saying that if you make tidal waves too early in your career, you may end up drowning yourself.

and sequences built in. I've always found that I could adapt such curricula to my own preference for unit organization.

You need to know what your curriculum requires so that you are a good citizen of your department. Also keep in mind, though, that one important element of citizenship is speaking freely on matters of conscience. If you believe the requirements do not serve students well, then you need to raise this point with your colleagues. Doing so in a confrontational and condescending manner may do your cause more harm than good. Doing so before you have job security may do your career more harm than good. But not doing so at all may do your students more harm than good.

Overarching Concept

One consideration in planning units is the overarching concept that unifies the curriculum over the whole course. You should ask, to borrow Applebee's (1996) language, What larger conversation should students be engaged in that in turn suggests good topics to build units around?

I'll suggest a few possibilities. An American literature curriculum might ask, What does it mean to be an American? Students might explore this question through a variety of units, possibly including the following (each of which is fleshed out in Appendix A):

> *Protest literature,* beginning with the colonial rhetoric that helped launch the American Revolution and inscribe American values in the Constitution and including key protest literature from other eras, such as the women's suffrage and civil rights movements.

The Puritan ethic, which would seek to understand what this ethic is and how it has endured throughout U.S. history and helped shape the American character.

Success, which would consider what makes a person successful, whether one person's notion of success will work for others, and whether the same actions would be considered successful in different situations.

Frontier literature, including both literature that gives the pioneers' perspective on western expansion and literature that provides the indigenous peoples' views.

The works of Mark Twain, whose characters (particularly Huckleberry Finn) are often thought to be quintessentially American.

Cultural conflict, which would help illuminate the issues involved when (a) a country is inhabited by natives whose society is threatened by the arrival of explorers from radically different cultures, and (b) the ensuing nation is designed to embrace immigrants who bring new ways that can conflict with established customs.

Gender roles, which might look at how those roles have changed over time and examine how a conception of gender plays a role in fulfilling the American dream.

The authors and artists of [*your state*], which would help students see how their own state fits in with broader themes and perspectives of American society and help acquaint them with significant authors and artists from their own part of the country.

These are only some of the unit topics available within this overarching concept. I imagine that a teacher would provide variety from year to year, or possibly even with different classes within the same year. If, for instance, you are assigned five classes of American literature, you might consider the benefits of dividing your assignment into two preparations so that you don't get burned out or bored from teaching the same thing five times in one day.

Furthermore, if you design the curriculum through negotiation with your students, their choice of topics would undoubtedly vary from what I offer here, and would probably vary from class to class. The point is that when picking a unit topic, you don't make your choice in isolation. Instead, you need to consider its role within the overall goals and themes of the course curriculum.

> Engaged pedagogy not only compels me to be constantly creative in the classroom, it also sanctions involvement with students beyond that setting. I journey with students as they progress in their lives beyond our classroom experience. In many ways, I continue to teach them, even as they become more capable of teaching me. The important lesson that we learn together, the lesson that allows us to move together within and beyond the classroom, is one of mutual engagement.
>
> —bell hooks

Students

When asked, "What do you teach?" some teachers answer, "Students." Rather than viewing themselves as subject-area specialists, they see themselves first as teachers of the people who are in their care. Taking this approach will make you different from some people in the teaching profession. Some teachers feel that they teach a

> The students teach me. We don't give kids enough credit. We give up on them too soon. We box them in too much. . . . I think of myself as preparing them for life. School is about more than books.
>
> —Willene Agnew, Stephens County Middle School, Eastanollee, Georgia

subject, rather than students. Teaching a subject releases the teacher from much of the responsibility of making sure that the students are learning. It's the students' job to learn the subject. As long as the teacher knows the subject well and presents it effectively, the characteristics and needs of particular students do not come into play.

Where you fall on the continuum of teaching students versus teaching the subject is a personal matter. If you find this book useful, you probably think it's important to teach both. In determining what units to teach, considering who your students are can help you make good choices. I'll next review some factors that I think ought to enter into your thinking.

Culture

As a teacher you will be caught amid many tensions. One that you will likely feel every day is the tension between viewing everyone as being equal, or the same, and viewing everyone as unique. For example, if you teach students of different races you will be encouraged on the one hand to be color blind, to try to view your students as being the same regardless of race. On the other hand, you will be encouraged to be aware of cultural differences so that you can understand the perspectives and behaviors of students whose cultural upbringing has been different from yours.

Understanding cultural differences can be both illuminating and dangerous. Let me give an example provided by my friend and colleague Carol Lee, an African American educator from Chicago. The widely believed notion that African Americans come from an oral culture is grounded in the historical fact that slaves were typically prohibited from learning to read and write, forcing them to develop highly refined oral communication. There is strong evidence to support this belief and to use it to interpret modern circumstances.

Carol has argued persuasively, however, that this belief has had a negative impact in schools. Often, white teachers believe that because African American students come from an oral culture, they should not be expected to read and write with the same fluency as white students. The effort to understand culture, then, results in a very limiting set of expectations that underestimates the potential of African American students.

Understanding culture is important, but it can be dangerous if it results in limiting stereotypes. Of course, race is only one aspect of culture. Ethnicity, region, religion, gender, and countless other factors are a part of culture. Understanding these factors can help you understand your students, but also brings the potential for you to operate according to limiting stereotypes.

> A little learning is a dang'rous thing;
> Drink deep, or taste not the Pierian spring;
> There shallow draughts intoxicate the brain,
> And drinking largely sobers us again.
>
> —Alexander Pope

Luis Moll has recommended that teachers conduct community ethnographies, which he calls ethnographic experiments, to learn about students and how their cultures contribute to their worldviews and behaviors. Rather than relying on books, he suggests getting out into the community, visiting homes, and making other efforts to understand students' cultural backgrounds. I

Books on Culture and Education

Cazden, C. B. (1988). *Classroom discourse.* Portsmouth, NH: Heinemann.

Cazden, C. B., John, V. P., & Hymes, D. (Eds.). (1972). *Functions of language in the classroom.* New York: Teachers College Press.

Delpit, L. (1995). *Other people's children: Cultural conflict in the classroom.* New York: The New Press.

Eckert, P. (1989). *Jocks and burnouts: Social categories and identity in the high school.* New York: Teachers College Press.

Finders, M. J. (1997). *Just girls: Hidden literacies and life in junior high.* New York: Teachers College Press; Urbana, IL: National Council of Teachers of English.

Gee, J. (1990). *Social linguistics and literacies: Ideology in discourses.* New York: Falmer.

Heath, S. B. (1983). *Ways with words.* New York: Cambridge University Press.

Hollins, E. R. (1996). *Culture in school learning: Revealing the deep meaning.* Mahwah, NJ: Erlbaum.

Lee, C. D. (1993). *Signifying as a scaffold for literary interpretation: The pedagogical implications of an African American discourse genre* (NCTE Research Report No. 26). Urbana, IL: National Council of Teachers of English.

Lee, C. D., & Smagorinsky, P. (Eds.). (2000). *Vygotskian perspectives on literacy research: Constructing meaning through collaborative inquiry.* New York: Cambridge University Press.

Mahiri, J. (1998). *Shooting for excellence: African American and youth culture in new century schools.* New York: Teachers College Press.

Moll, L. C. (Ed.). (1990) *Vygotsky and education: Instructional implications and applications of sociohistorical psychology.* New York: Cambridge University Press.

Rose, M. (1989). *Lives on the boundary: The struggles and achievements of America's underprepared.* New York: Penguin.

Smitherman, G. (1977). *Talkin and testifyin: The language of black America.* Boston: Houghton Mifflin. (Reprint, Detroit: Wayne University Press, 1986).

do not mention this trivially. Conducting a community ethnography is quite an undertaking. If you have trouble understanding the needs, outlooks, values, and behaviors of your students, and if their grades do not correspond to your sense of their capabilities, you might consider conducting community ethnographies as a way to teach in more culturally appropriate ways.

Developmental Level

Although your students' age or grade level is not an absolute indicator of what they should study, it does provide some broad guidelines for what is appropriate to teach at different stages of schooling. Of course, a class at one grade level will include students of differing ages, levels of maturity, levels of knowledge, and so on. This variation makes it hard to say that something is an especially ripe topic for students at a particular grade. However, some things probably are more appropriate than others for particular groups.

Let's say, for instance, that you are teaching seventh grade students in a typical suburban community. Most of your students will be twelve or thirteen years old.

Would you teach them a unit on transcendentalism? Probably not. The language would be too forbidding, the concepts too abstract. Ideally, you would choose a topic that is appropriate for their adolescent interests and provides literary codes suitable for their reading experiences.

Developmental psychologists have described some tendencies that could help make decisions about what is developmentally appropriate. Over the course of adolescence, children move in thought, feeling, and action

- from simple to complex
- from concrete to abstract
- from personal orientation to impersonal or multipersonal orientation
- from activity without thought to thought with less activity
- from conception of objects themselves to conception of their properties
- from literal to symbolic
- from absolute to relative

In general, they develop an ability to step back and see the big picture, what Irving Sigel calls "distancing" oneself from experience to view it in less egocentric ways. As they grow older, students are able to grapple with problems of greater abstraction and are increasingly able to stand back and view themselves as participants in a larger society. Topics for young adolescents, then, might center on the immediate worlds of young protagonists: peer pressure, friendship, new kid on the block, and so on. Toward the end of high school, topics might consider the individual in relation to the broader society, using more abstract themes: success, justice, progress, changing times, and the like.

In considering students' developmental levels, keep in mind Vygotsky's belief that *teaching leads development*. In other words, if you think students are at a particular level, don't teach *to* that level; instruction should lead students to a higher level of development. With this principle in mind, attention to students' developmental levels does not lead to a static curriculum targeted at presumed levels, but instead calls for teachers to be attentive to where students are and where instruction might take them.

Interests

Another factor to consider when choosing unit topics is students' interests. I am not saying that you ought to pander to students' more trivial pursuits. Instead, I'm saying that if one of our goals is to make school learning something that students view with anticipation, then we should consider what they find interesting when evaluating possible topics of inquiry.

Simply finding out student interests and building a curriculum around them is not sufficient. Some student interests do not make for appropriate English class topics. I recall teaching high school sophomore boys who were quite interested in the misogynist humor of the stand-up comic Andrew Dyce Clay. I had to provide a stern lecture on respect when they incorporated this interest into a class project that they performed before the class to the obvious discomfort of many girls. Although I usually advocate remaining open-minded about how students interpret things and express themselves, some kinds of expression should be prohibited.

Knowing students' interests can be useful when those interests coincide with topics related to unit concepts. One way to get to know what students are interested

Books About Human Development

Belenky, M. F., Clinchy, B. M., Goldberger, N. R., & Tarule, J. M. (1986). *Women's ways of knowing: The development of self, voice, and mind.* New York: Basic Books.

Csikszentmihalyi, M., & Larson, R. (1984). *Being adolescent: Conflict and growth in the teenage years.* New York: Basic Books.

Erikson, E. (1950). *Childhood and society.* New York: Norton.

Erikson, E. (1980). *Identity and the life cycle.* New York: Norton.

Gilligan, C. (1982). *In a different voice: Psychological theory and women's development.* Cambridge, MA: Harvard University Press.

Kagan, J., & Coles, R. (Eds.). (1971). *12 to 16: Early adolescence.* New York: Norton.

Kohlberg, L. (1981). *The philosophy of moral development.* San Francisco: Harper & Row.

Piaget, J. (1995). *The essential Piaget* (H. E. Gruber & J. J. Voneche, Eds.). Northvale, NJ: Jason Aronson.

Pipher, M. (1994). *Reviving Ophelia: Saving the selves of adolescent girls.* New York: Putnam's.

Sigel, I. E., & Brody, G. H. (Eds.). (1990). *Methods of family research: Biographies of research projects: Vol. 1 Normal families.* Hillsdale, NJ: Erlbaum.

Taylor, J. M., Gilligan, C., & Sullivan, A. M. (1995). *Between voice and silence: Women and girls, race and relationship.* Cambridge, MA: Harvard University Press.

Vygotsky, L. S. (1978). *Mind in society: The development of higher psychological processes* (M. Cole, V. John-Steiner, S. Scribner, & E. Souberman, Eds.). Cambridge, MA: Harvard University Press.

in is to listen to them talk. Another is to see what kinds of icons they wear on their clothing (or draw on their desks). You can invite more formal accounts of their interests, by having them write an introduction to themselves or a user's manual for themselves or by having their parents or guardians write you a letter about them. You need to be careful to phrase your inquiry so that it is not invasive, as parents in some communities may oppose any efforts to require confessional or personally revealing writing from their children. I'll return to this issue later when discussing consideration of the students' community.

If you include students in the planning of the curriculum, you'll learn their interests quickly enough. Your main concern when turning choice over to students is that you need to help them stretch beyond what they are aware of, rather than having them read and study only what they already know and like. To repeat Vygotsky's view of schooling, *instruction should lead development, rather than follow it.* If you accept this proposition, then you need to take responsibility as a teacher for introducing themes, strategies, perspectives, and so on that help move students' thinking into new areas and into new complexity.

Needs

Needs are different from interests. Interests are those things that students want to learn about. Needs refer to deeper psychological issues. Some of these are developmental and shared by just about everyone passing through a certain point in life, whereas others are created by circumstances. I'll treat each in turn.

Common needs result from predictable experiences. I've already referred to the coming-of-age experience as an archetypal experience that can provide the basis for a good, developmentally appropriate unit of instruction. Other units might be based on conflict with authority, the trickster, peer pressure, the outcast, rites of passage, or any other social rite or character type that most students are likely to be dealing with in their lives.

Needs created by circumstances might be tied to archetypal experiences, but have a more local impact because of events affecting the community. Let's say that a community is experiencing a rise in gang involvement among its youth. It might be appropriate to teach a unit that deals with gangs, cliques, and peer pressure. Or perhaps bullying and violence in school are increasing. Students might be helped to think through the causes and effects of such behavior by studying a topic such as discrimination or alienation and discussing the literature in terms of events in school.

Unless you are trained as a psychologist or counselor, you should be very careful about how you deal with students' needs and equally careful about how you solicit and respond to their thoughts and feelings on sensitive topics. You also need to be prepared to allow students to resist efforts to have them reveal their feelings. I strongly believe that literature and writing can serve as vehicles for people to reflect on and understand better the experiences of their lives. I believe just as strongly that teachers have no right to require personal revelations from students who don't want to share them. All students have the right to keep to themselves and that right should be respected, no matter how much a teacher believes in the power of spoken and written reflection.

At the same time, though, teachers have an obligation to ensure a healthy environment for their students. If you think that a student's withdrawal has its roots in depression, drug use, suicidal thoughts, or another threat to his or her well-being, you should share your concern with a counselor or school psychologist who can intervene in knowledgeable and appropriate ways.

Community

One important piece of the transition from university education programs to schools is the difference in what counts as a good idea. University faculty members are, relative to the rest of the population, radical in their thinking. Many university faculty see themselves as agents of change. They urge (and often require) students to deconstruct the status quo, interrogate issues of class privilege, question conservative ideologies, and in general create upheaval with belief systems. They often urge aspiring teachers to do the same when they reach the classroom.

Yet teachers usually find that the public school setting is quite different from what they were used to at the university. Most parents don't want their parenting questioned. Nor do they want their values attacked, or their family and career goals deconstructed. They consider university professors an odd and meddlesome breed, who live in ivory towers, sequestered from the concerns of ordinary working people. They see teachers as people who have knowledge in their chosen fields and the ability to lead children toward proficiency in those fields. Deconstructing the community doesn't fit in with parents' expectations for good teaching.

My purpose here is to criticize neither the professors nor the citizens, but to make you aware that teaching to promote an ideology is much more robustly en-

Vignette

I supervised a first-year teacher in a small Bible Belt town who, during the troop buildup prior to the Gulf War, refused to put her hand over her heart during the daily Pledge of Allegiance. When her students asked why, she said that it was because she opposed conformity, and pledging the flag could lead to the kind of conformist state that Hitler had established in Germany. The students shared her beliefs with their parents. The parents shared her beliefs with the principal. She had a very short career as a teacher.

couraged and rewarded in universities than it is in public schools. Understanding your community will help you make choices about what to teach and what not to teach. Citizens are not always right, but they are the ones funding local education and they are the ones raising their kids. Teachers need to respect the rights and values of their constituency when making decisions about what to teach. This is not to say that you must give in to the status quo of your community, simply that you should understand how parents feel about their children. I say this as a parent who doesn't believe that his own children's teachers have always been right.

Consider the following example. Many communities south of the Mason-Dixon line are known to be patriotic—disproportionate numbers of their citizens enlist in the military during times of war, community members believe strongly in military service to their country, and war veterans are among the most respected citizens. Let's say you decide to teach a unit on the Vietnam War era and include texts that take primarily an antiwar stance. This would be a political decision on your part, imposing your opposition to war on the unit. Doing so could conceivably be offensive to many community members who believe that without militarism, we would have no United States. In their view, you would be overstepping your duties as an English teacher by politicizing the curriculum in this way.

I agree with the view that any act is a political act. You cannot be neutral on any issue nor should you always seek parental approval with your choices. But when you deliberately teach in ways that turn students against their homes and communities, you had better be prepared with a very convincing rationale in order to persuade your colleagues, students, and community that you are teaching responsibly.

Field Observation

In the school you're visiting, pay careful attention to the students. What are they like? Where do they come from? Does the school regard them as all having the same needs, or as having needs that vary according to their individual and cultural differences? In what ways are the students' home and community values taken into consideration in providing them with an education? To what degree are school policies and operations based on an understanding of the particular students enrolled in the school? What are the consequences of the school's approach for the education of the students?

Teacher

Teachers ought to consider their own interests and needs when deciding what topics to teach and to recognize the value of their judgment in knowing what students might benefit from studying, even if the students haven't identified it as an interest. I'll briefly cover considerations that teachers can make about meeting their own needs.

Interests

Just as classes should be interesting to students, so should they be interesting to the teacher. Students know when teachers are going through the motions. Many student evaluations of teachers that I've read over the years have stressed the importance of teachers' being enthusiastic and passionate about their work. Nothing kills enthusiasm like teaching topics and books you don't like.

The corollary of this is that you should not teach something *because* you find it interesting. Millions of students have been punished because teachers persistently teach their favorite books, year after year, no matter what students think. Consider your interests, yes; but consider them in the context of other factors. Perhaps it's a good idea to think of it this way: Part of your pleasure from teaching a book comes from the response it gets from students. If your favorite literature is painful for students, then view their suffering as a part of your overall experience.

Knowledge

A second factor for teachers to consider is their own knowledge. What do you know about? Presumably, your certification program mandates certain courses to prepare you to teach canonical American and British literature, and perhaps world literature as well. Such courses should provide you with the background you need to teach a topic knowledgeably.

Some teachers teach a topic or a work *as a way to learn about it*. Some suggest that it's a good idea for all teachers periodically to teach a book that they are reading for the first time, so as to share the students' experience of reading without knowing the outcome. This approach is quite different from that of the standard image of the English teacher, who knows in advance where all the foreshadowing and rising action and alliteration are and is eager to point out these instances and require students to identify them on a quiz.

Reading a book for the first time with students is a good way to stay in tune with students' experiences with literature and to model a different conception of what it means to know something. It shows the teacher in the role of reading tentatively and provisionally, as readers do the first time around, instead of in the role of knowing the book as a concrete whole, as most teachers are accustomed to doing.

SELECTING MATERIALS

Who Gets to Choose?

Before reviewing the factors you should take into account when selecting materials for your unit, I would again like to raise the question of the role of student choice in deciding what to read. Just as it's possible to organize your class so that students can select topics from a menu of choices you provide, it's possible to provide some range of choice within each unit. Following are several ways to decide on materials, ranging from the curriculum itself determining the materials to students making the choice.

Any method that involves thoughtful deliberation can work, depending on your sense of your own authority, the relative expediency of different approaches, stu-

Pick Topics

Either individually or in groups, imagine a community in which you would like to teach.

- Characterize its people in terms of their careers, values, aspirations, and views of schooling.
- Describe the school, including its size, its curriculum, its English department, its approach to grouping (if and how it tracks students), and its overall mission.
- Think of a particular grade level you would be teaching and describe the kinds of students you'd have in your class. If the school tracks students, describe the track you would be teaching. If it does not, describe the range of students you'd find in a typical class.
- Think of an overarching concept that would guide the curriculum as a whole for the grade level or course you're envisioning.
- Within this overarching concept, identify a set of topics that could serve as the basis for instructional units.
- Exchange your community profile, school profile, grade-level description, overarching concept, and list of unit topics with that of another student or group of students and share feedback on the appropriateness of the topics for the context.

dents' maturity and responsibility in making choices, and the flexibility of the curriculum within which you are teaching. Of course, many possibilities are not available when the curriculum itself rules.

The Curriculum Decides

Just as a curriculum can specify the topics of study, it can specify the texts students read. The advantages and disadvantages are similar to those described in relation to the identification of unit topics: On the one hand, a prescribed curriculum promotes uniformity and democracy; on the other hand, it works against creativity and generative thinking.

Teacher Selection

In systems that trust the judgment of teachers and allow for flexible interpretation of a curriculum, probably the easiest and most expedient approach is for the teacher to decide ahead of time what students will read and in what order. This approach has the advantages of being efficient and allowing teachers to draw on their expertise in knowing which texts work well with particular groups of students and which texts ultimately might benefit students. The primary disadvantage of this approach is that students have no say in what they read, which may affect their engagement with and commitment to their reading.

Books on Book Clubs and Literature Circles

Daniels, H. (1994). *Literature circles: Voice and choice in the student-centered classroom.* York, ME: Stenhouse.

Jacobsohn, R. W. (1998). *The reading group handbook: Everything you need to know to start your own book club.* New York: Hyperion.

Hill, B. C., Johnson, N. J., & Noe, K. (1995). *Literature circles and response.* Norwood, MA: Christopher-Gordon.

Marshall, J. D., Smagorinsky, P., & Smith, M. W. (1995). *The language of interpretation: Patterns of discourse in discussions of literature* (NCTE Research Report No. 27). Urbana, IL: National Council of Teachers of English.

McMahon, S. I., Raphael, T. E., & Goatley, V. J. (Eds.). (1997). *The book club connection: Literacy learning and classroom talk.* New York: Teachers College Press.

Students Choose from a Menu

With this approach the teacher makes available a set of texts and lets students go through a selection process to decide which ones they will read. Through negotiation or vote, students select the texts that the whole class will read and discuss together. The process allows students a sense of control and authority over what they read. The discussions leading to the selection can be interesting and beneficial in that they can help students develop and articulate their own criteria for determining the quality of literature.

Book Clubs and Literature Circles

With book clubs and literature circles, the teacher also provides a menu of texts. Rather than having the students arrive at a common text for the class to read, however, subgroups of students select a book of their choice and use class time for small-group discussion and analysis. For several weeks the whole class might read preparatory texts together, after which the major works would be read in the small groups.

Literature circles are small, temporary discussion groups consisting of students who have chosen to read the same work of literature. Each member of the group is responsible for something that will help the discussion of the text (e.g., discussion director, summarizer, vocabulary enricher, illustrator). These responsibilities rotate for each meeting. After they have discussed the text or group of texts (e.g., a set of short stories by a particular author), students plan some way of sharing their reading and discussion experiences with the class. At the end of this cycle, groups change membership and begin a new cycle. The ultimate goal is for literature circles to replace teacher-led discussions as a way of examining literature in class.

Student Choice

For students to brainstorm entirely on their own for texts to read relative to the unit topic, they need knowledge of a range of texts and good judgment regarding what's appropriate for school. This method of selecting materials also assumes that students have the resources to get the texts they choose, since it's likely that at least some would not be available in the school anthology or book room.

Books About Reading Workshops and Independent Reading

Atwell, N. (Ed.). (1989). *Workshop 1 by and for teachers: Writing and literature.* Portsmouth, NH: Heinemann.

Hynds, S. (1997). *On the brink: Negotiating literature and life with adolescents.* New York: Teachers College Press.

Keene, E. O., & Zimmermann, S. (1997). *Mosaic of thought: Teaching comprehension in a reader's workshop.* Portsmouth, NH: Heinemann.

The major advantage of this approach is that students take control of their learning in important ways and presumably choose texts of high interest to them. Students may read texts together following whole-class negotiations, read in small-group book clubs or literature circles, or read individually if each student chooses a different set of texts.

Considerations in Selecting Materials

If you view teaching as primarily concerned with the content of your discipline, then the traditions of that discipline will provide you with a canon of literary works that students should read. Although the traditional canon can provide excellent reading for secondary school students, it should be only one of several factors in settling on the materials for your unit. Other considerations come from the students themselves, the community and its values, and your teaching in relation to that of your colleagues.

In this section I will assume that you will play some role in selecting the materials for the unit. Your involvement may range from assembling menus for students to use as the basis of their own choices to choosing each text students will read.

I'm assuming that this approach will require you to teach to some extent outside the canon of works that have traditionally made up the literature curriculum. The issue of broadening the canon raises an old conundrum for teachers of literature. The problem concerns the long-standing tension between the idea that certain works are required reading for all educated people and the idea that the canon meets the needs of professional literary critics more than it does the needs of the general reading public.

Teachers are caught in this tension. Typically, they have earned degrees in English and so have taken part in traditional literary study as a kind of formal scholarship. Most of their students, however, will not view literature as a field of scholarship, and instead read for pleasure, escape, fulfillment, knowledge, connection, or other personal reasons. How teachers manage this tension will influence the choices they make about the content of the literature curriculum.

The following factors are important to take into account when selecting materials.

Tracking

Many schools group students according to their perceived ability or level of performance. A typical school will have two or three tracks. The most academically successful students might be in honors classes; the next track usually includes students who have varying degrees of academic success and is often called regular, but may go by one of a variety of other names; the third track, often known as the basic track, comprises students who struggle with school. There are many different ways to refer to tracks. Over the years, I have come across the names advanced placement, aegis, high ability, college bound, average, high average, low average, vocational, essential, remedial, and developmental, as well as color codes that students quickly translate into some level of ability or performance.

Although it is the target of much criticism in universities, tracking is near-ubiquitous in schools throughout the United States, for several reasons. Tracking sorts students into groups based on some combination of perceived achievement, competence, and performance. Having relatively homogeneous groups of students makes life easier for teachers because it lets them move at one pace, use a uniform set of texts, and otherwise tailor instruction to the needs of particular groups of learners. Many parents also like tracking. When the English Coalition Conference recommended that tracking be abolished (see Lloyd-Jones & Lunsford, 1989), my high school department chair said that we could never untrack classes in our community because the parents wouldn't allow it to happen.

In my very first year of teaching, I taught in an untracked school. I had a very difficult time providing instruction that kept all students consistently engaged and challenged. I hope that if I'd continued teaching in untracked schools I'd have found ways to serve the whole range of students better. During that first year, however, I was frequently frustrated because I was moving too fast for some and too slowly for others and serving too few students well.

Tracking is frowned upon in universities for several reasons. Although now justified as a way to provide appropriate instruction for the diverse students who attend schools, tracking was initially tied to intelligence testing (and sometimes still is). Intelligence tests have been critiqued for their cultural bias, that is, the way in which the test items are more familiar and accessible to members of some cultures than to members of others. Given that immigrants and racial minorities consistently scored lower than whites on intelligence tests, and were thus placed in lower tracks, there is reason to believe that tracking had at least some basis in an effort to provide a de facto segregation system within schools.

This kind of segregation is still apparent in tracked schools, with white students superabundant in the higher tracks and minority students dominating the lower. Tracking can thus create a social class system within the school, whose boundaries grow more impermeable with each year. Once students are placed in a lower track, their upward mobility decreases each year because they tend to fall farther and farther behind. In the economic metaphor, tracking allows the rich to get richer and the poor to get relatively poorer.

Race is but one factor used to segregate students. A good friend of mine—who went on to earn a Ph.D. in English education—grew up on the wrong side of the tracks in a white, working-class part of his city. When he registered for high school, the counselor looked at his residential address and automatically assigned him to the school's vocational track. Disgusted with the limited academic coursework he was provided, he ended up dropping out of high school and joining the military.

Books on Tracking

Apple, M. W. (1982). *Education and power.* Boston: Routledge & Kegan Paul.

Cohen, E. (1994). *Designing groupwork: Strategies for the heterogeneous classroom.* New York: Teachers College Press.

Loveless, T. (1999). *The tracking wars: State reform meets school policy.* Washington, DC: Brookings Institution Press.

Lucas, S. (1999). *Tracking inequality: Stratification and mobility in American high schools.* New York: Teachers College Press.

Mehan, H., Villanueva, I., Hubbard, L., & Lintz, A. (1996). *Constructing school success: The consequences of untracking low-achieving students.* New York: Cambridge University Press.

Moore, D., & Davenport, S. (1988). *The new improved sorting machine.* Madison, WI: National Center on Effective Secondary Schools.

Oakes, J. (1985). *Keeping track: How schools structure inequality.* New Haven, CT: Yale University Press.

Oakes, J., Quartz, K. H., Ryan, S., & Lipton, M. (2000). *Becoming good American schools: The struggle for civic virtue in school reform.* San Francisco: Jossey-Bass.

Rosenbaum, J. (1976). *Making inequality: The hidden curricula of high school tracking.* New York: John Wiley & Sons.

Schurr, S. L. (1995). *Prescriptions for success in heterogeneous classrooms.* Columbus, OH: National Middle School Association.

Slavin, R. (1990). *Achievement effects of ability grouping in secondary schools: A best-evidence synthesis.* Madison, WI: Wisconsin Center for Educational Research.

Spring, J. (1976). *The sorting machine: National educational policy since 1945.* New York: David McKay.

Welner, K. G., & Oakes, J. (2000). *Navigating the politics of detracking.* Arlington Heights, IL: Skylight Publications.

Wheelock, A. (1992). *Crossing the tracks: How "untracking" can save America's schools.* New York: The Free Press.

My purpose is not to say which system, tracking or not tracking, is better. Each is problematic in its own way—in a sense, it's a matter of choosing which problems you'd rather live with. I've taught in both kinds of systems and know that resolving the problems of one approach only creates new problems. I've also taught in both high schools and universities and know that the logic that prevails in one is not always persuasive when argued within the other.

Rather, I want to alert you to the fact that the presence or absence of tracking should influence your decisions about teaching. If your school is untracked, you need to be prepared to meet the needs of the whole range of students in your school, suggesting the need for differentiated materials within single classes. If your school uses tracking, your decisions about materials should be responsive to the reading abilities and interests of your students, and you should be alert to the ways in which racial and class-based discrimination can account for the different populations you find in different tracks. (Thanks to Jack Morse for providing information on the history of tracking.)

Literary Value

Educators disagree about the extent to which certain texts are sufficiently scholarly to serve as educational texts. The very existence of a literary canon and of a Great Books program suggests that at least some people differentiate between literature of high quality and literature of lesser value. What makes something literary is a question that all teachers should consider. Furthermore, it is a question that all students should consider. Having students establish criteria for identifying works of literary merit can be a central aim of a literature curriculum.

This book is not designed to answer the question of what distinguishes literature that is great from literature that is not. Rather, it is designed to get you to think about how and why you make decisions. In reflection on literary value, you might consider the following questions:

- To what extent should one rely on the wisdom of literary critics in identifying works of literary merit, that is, is relying on the traditional canon sufficient?
- Are the criteria for excellence the same for adolescents and for adults? For mainstream adolescents and for college English majors? For members of one cultural group and for members of another? If they are different, whose criteria should prevail in decisions about what to read for school?
- What is important in having a satisfying experience with reading? How can one distinguish the traits that result in such satisfying experiences? Are these traits the same for all people? If they are different, how do teachers and students make decisions about which texts are appropriate for reading in school?

Variety of Textual Forms

When selecting materials, take advantage of the range of textual forms available to illuminate the themes of the literature. Unless your unit topic is restricted to an author who specializes in a particular medium (e.g., Emily Dickinson's exclusive use of poetry) or focuses on reading a particular type of literature (e.g., detective novels), you should consider what is available in short story, novel, poetry, drama, film, song, fable, biblical story, myth, essay, and other artistic forms.

Appropriateness

By appropriateness I mean the extent to which texts meet the rules of propriety that govern life in your school and community. I'll give an example of why this factor is important. A preservice teacher I taught in Oklahoma grew up in a small, conservative, rural community in the 1970s. In high school, he was caught reading Eldridge Cleaver's *Soul on Ice,* a book of essays recounting Cleaver's experiences as a Black Panther, civil rights activist, and rapist, and was suspended from school. The next year, he moved to a community in a metropolitan area with a more diverse population and liberal mind-set. He was surprised to see *Soul on Ice* on the required reading list for his senior year.

You'll need to differentiate between what you think is a good text and what people in your community will find objectionable. This distinction is particularly important as you move from college to schools. These arenas are different in at least two critical ways: (1) the college environment is likely to be far more liberal than the community environment, and (2) in the college environment adult norms prevail, whereas in a school community children's sensibilities (and their parents' proprietary views of those sensibilities) prevail.

The texts you personally find riveting may include sex, violence, profanity, and ideologies that may create problems between you and your students' parents. Especially at the beginning of your career, use caution in choosing texts with potentially objectionable content and discretion in making sure that the materials you choose are on your school's approved list. Consider the following poem, for instance, which has always been among my favorites:

i sing of Olaf glad and big by e. e. cummings

i sing of Olaf glad and big
whose warmest heart recoiled at war:
a conscientious object-or

his wellbeloved colonel (trig
westpointer most succinctly bred)
took erring Olaf soon in hand;
but-though an host of overjoyed
noncoms (first knocking on the head
him) do through icy waters roll
that helplessness which others stroke
with brushes recently employed
anent this muddy toiletbowl,
while kindred intellects evoke
allegiance par blunt instruments—
Olaf (being to all intents
a corpse and wanting any rag
upon what God unto him gave)
responds, without getting annoyed
"I will not kiss your fucking flag"
straightaway the silver bird looked grave
(departing hurriedly to shave)
but-though all kinds of officers
(a yearning nation's blueeyed pride)
their passive prey did kick and curse
until for wear their clarion
voices and boots were much the worse,
and egged the firstclass privates on
his rectum wickedly to tease
by means of skilfully applied
bayonets roasted hot with heat—
Olaf (upon what were once knees)
does almost ceaselessly repeat
"there is some shit I will not eat"

our president, being of which
assertions duly notified
threw the yellowsonofabitch
into a dungeon, where he died

Christ (of His mercy infinite)
i pray to see; and Olaf too

preponderatingly because
unless statistics lie he was
more brave than me: more blond than you.

> Here in eastern Kentucky, most students put people ahead of their educations. Absenteeism is high because they are expected to go to every funeral and wedding of even their most distant kin. They leave school to visit friends and relatives in the hospital, to keep someone company at a doctor's visit or in traffic court, or to help out on the family farm or business. These students make me realize what I have missed over the years by not taking an interest in my extended family.
>
> —Lynne Taetzsch

In a university English class, you would probably be assigned this poem without a second thought about its language or content. Would you teach it in a public middle or high school? Would it be riskier in some communities than in others? Could you use it with selective editing?

Believe it or not, I've actually taught this poem in a public school. Call me chicken, but I did substitute *s . . .* and *f . . . ing* for two of the words in the original. It's possible that even this modification would put me in the hot seat in some communities. What would you do in the school where you anticipate doing your student teaching?

Variety of Authorship

Studies of high school literature curricula (see Applebee, 1993) have shown that most books taught in public high schools in the United States have been written by so-called DWMs (dead white males) or PSMs (pale stale males). There's a good economic reason that literature anthologies feature works by the deceased: Dead men collect no royalties. The preponderance of white males troubles many, however. In the traditional literary canon, both white culture and masculine outlooks inform the worldview presented through literature. This worldview then becomes the norm through which other perspectives are judged to be deficient. Women and minorities are less likely to see themselves and their worlds reflected in the curriculum and thus are less likely to feel a part of the educational enterprise. There are exceptions, but these objections are frequently made to the content of the traditional canon.

With this in mind, I suggest looking for variety in authorship, particularly variety that provides different points of view. When selecting materials, make an effort to include both canonical works and works from underrepresented traditions and cultures. Items from your broadened list may not always be available, but if you teach so that students have options for their reading, you may find that those who want different kinds of experiences will find the books on their own.

Turf

The final consideration is a somewhat touchy issue—the tendency people have to view something as part of their territory, never to be usurped or transgressed. Here

Select Materials

From the list of topics you identified in the previous section, select two. For each, think of a set of possible materials to include in the unit, keeping in mind the constraints that exist in the setting you're envisioning. Try to include several selections from each of the categories listed.

It is possible that a topic won't allow for choices in all areas. A unit on William Faulkner, for instance, will be limited to novels, short stories, and essays. In most cases, however, you will be able to find selections for each category.

Poetry
Short story
Novel
Drama
Fable/Myth/Parable
Song
Film
Essay/Nonfiction
Art

is a composite of a situation I've seen all too often: A teacher decides to teach a particular work, only to be confronted later by an irate colleague who teaches at the next grade level and *always* teaches that book, but now *can't* because the students have *already read it*. The whole year is now *ruined* because of this thoughtless decision.

My advice to early-career teachers is never to view your work as taking place in isolation from that of your colleagues; learn the territory you work within and how you need to occupy it. You should not always accede to the wishes and priorities of others, but you should understand the consequences of your actions on your colleagues. Keep in mind that on occasion their priorities will be open to question and that you should argue your own conscience in response. I do not advocate silence when you believe a wrong is being committed, but I advise you to choose your political battles carefully so as to invest your energy where it counts and to expend your political capital prudently.

Reflective Writing Prompt

When you were in middle school and high school, did your teachers tend to teach the subject, or teach the students? How did the teachers' emphasis affect your success in school? How did it affect the success of other students? In general, how did the teachers' emphasis affect students' engagement with school and their learning?

RATIONALES

In the introduction to this book, I wrote a rationale for a constructivist, unit-based approach to teaching. To teach this way, you need to be able to explain your reasons for teaching the way you do. These reasons come in the form of a *rationale* for each unit you design. A rationale is a persuasive essay in which you explain why, of all the things on earth you could possibly teach, you've decided to teach this.

There will be occasions during your career when your ability to develop a compelling rationale will change how things are done in your school. Earlier, for instance, I referred to Darlene Brown's fight to include *The Color Purple* in her school's list of approved novels. Her ability to provide a rationale for including this novel accomplished what several people told her was impossible to achieve.

In selecting your unit topic, you've already gone through an informal process of providing a rationale for your unit. You've thought about the community you teach in and how that might suggest topics. You've thought about the students' developmental needs and the topics that might help meet them. You've thought about the merit of the works you've considered and what students might learn from them. You've given a lot of thought to the concepts that the unit texts will involve. In this section I'll go over some other factors that might help you provide a justification for your teaching.

Think of your rationale as serving rhetorical needs. If someone were to challenge your teaching, how would you defend it? Teachers come under attack from various quarters. The media criticize schools for one reason or another. Irate parents voice their displeasure with this or that. University faculty blame secondary school teachers for any shortcomings of college students. Taxpayers claim that schools are overfunded (even though teachers are paid disproportionally low for their level of education). Students complain about irrelevant or tedious instruction. Teachers even snipe at one another's methods on occasion.

If you were asked by any of these people to defend your teaching, what would you say? "It's in the curriculum," "It's always been done this way," or "Everyone should read *The Faerie Queene*" are not satisfactory or persuasive answers. Your rationale is your ticket to teaching in ways you believe in. It's important to write a good one.

You also need to persuade yourself. If you don't teach with conviction, students will be the first to know. You have to have thought through your teaching decisions as carefully as possible so that students can see that you are acting in principled ways.

I'll next review a series of justifications to consider when writing a rationale. The rationale you write may focus on one of them, or include attention to several. Table 2.1 provides examples of different types of rationales found at the Virtual Library of Conceptual Units at http://www.coe.uga.edu/~smago/VirtualLibrary/index.html. In the left column under "Unit" are listed the authors of the units in the Virtual Library; note that most units are coauthored. The type of rationale is indicated by an x in the appropriate column.

Psychology/Human Development

Many units can be justified because they respond to the psychological needs of students. Literature often deals with common human experiences about the pressures, changes, dilemmas, aspirations, conflicts, and so on that make growing up (and being grown up) such a challenge. Adolescent literature in particular often features youthful protagonists dealing with the kinds of problems your students are likely experiencing, both those that have endured across the ages and those that are more topical. The field of developmental psychology has provided abundant descriptions of the stages that most people go through during their maturation and

TABLE 2.1   Virtual Library: Types of Rationales

Unit	Rationale					
	Psychology/ Human Development	Cultural Significance	Literary Significance	Civic Awareness	Current Problem	Future Needs
Askari	x	x	x		x	
Barrett Endres Stinchcomb	x	x		x	x	x
Begnaud Evans	x			x	x	
Behr Reece Watkins				x	x	x
Bryan Skorupski		x		c		
Camp Davis Harris	x			x	x	x
Cockrill Hall Long	x			x		
Deroshia	x				x	x
Hedden Orr Shroyer	x					x
Hollingshead Wood	x	x		x		x
Johnson			x	x		
Loggins Taggart Thomas	x				x	
Rachmuth Schuler	x	x	x	x		
Siegmund Stroud Hasty	x		x			
Swann Williams		x		x	x	x

can help provide a rationale for a number of units that deal with youth culture and the challenges of growing through it.

Cultural Significance

Some units are worth teaching because they are culturally significant. The materials they use contain themes that are central to an understanding of a particular culture—national, local, or distant. Let me give a few examples of culturally significant topics from each of these three categories.

National

Some topics involve themes that are central to national concerns. Puritan literature, for instance, can be justified because the Puritans were among the first Europeans to establish a stable society in North America and operated according to values that are still pervasive in modern American society. Consider, for instance, how Americans are scandalized by the private lives of their public figures, compared with the reactions of Italians to similar behaviors.

Local

Learning about a local culture can instill in students a sense of pride and of identity with their community. A unit on *a sense of place* or local authors (e.g., Texas authors, prairie literature) can feature local authors and help students engage with themes that have historically been important to their region and culture.

Distant

Schools should do more than help students know their own cultures; it should also help acquaint them with others. These cultures needn't be situated across the globe; they can be "distant" even in close proximity. For instance, by reading a body of literature by members of a race other than their own, students can learn about how life is viewed and experienced differently even within the same general setting. In high school, I read books by African American writers (e.g., Richard Wright's *Native Son,* Claude Brown's *Manchild in the Promised Land*) that were culturally distant from me and opened my eyes to worlds that, although remote from my own experiences, were important for me to understand in order to be a good citizen in a pluralistic society.

> Books were my pass to personal freedom. I learned to read at age three, and soon discovered there was a whole world to conquer that went beyond our farm in Mississippi.
>
> —Oprah Winfrey

Literary Significance

A unit topic may have literary significance that makes it essential to any kind of cultural literacy. The works of Shakespeare, for instance, have been performed for nearly four centuries on stages throughout the world. You might mount a convincing argument that studying Shakespeare is central to understanding the themes of Western culture and the metaphors that are invoked to explain it.

You could also argue that certain periods or regions have produced literature of historical and cultural significance. The Harlem renaissance, for instance, served to establish African American writers as a significant group in American letters, the first minority group to achieve this stature in the United States. Southern fiction helped establish the identity of the antebellum South (primarily from a white perspective) and illustrate its tensions in rebuilding its economy and culture in the twentieth century. Constructing these arguments would require some research into the genres and likely the reading of some cultural or literary criticism that establishes their significance.

Civic Awareness

Some units of study help students understand their roles as citizens in their communities, states, and nation. In Appendix A you'll find unit outlines for topics such as justice, social responsibility, self-reliance, protest literature, and others in which students consider the role of the individual in society. In justifying such units, you might consider the importance of developing a citizenry that knows its history, laws, customs, rights, and responsibilities and uses that knowledge to act responsibly for a more equitable, democratic, and dynamic society. Your rationale might argue that throughout American history, citizens have taken action to achieve what they feel is just and that these actions have been driven by different social goals, different types of conscience, and different understandings of law.

Examples abound: native peoples who resisted European explorers, patriots who defied the British, abolitionists who defied slave owners, slave owners who defied the Union, slaves who escaped via the Underground Railroad, war protesters of various degrees of legality and violence, civil rights demonstrators, women fighting for the right to vote, women fighting for workplace equity—the list goes on and on. A unit focusing on one of these topics can find its justification in the historical background that students gain through the unit texts and in the code of civic ethics they develop through their engagement with the problems they read about.

Relevance to Current Social Problems

Some units of study find their justification in their effort to help adolescents understand and make choices about problems they face in their lives. A unit on peer pressure, for instance, would be justified in a community where teen smoking, drinking, drug abuse, and other behaviors are a threat to the security and health of teens. A unit on problem resolution could be justified in a community in which students are increasingly violent toward one another. In a community that has experienced a devastating loss, a unit on coping with loss might help students find the tools they need to work toward an understanding of their loss.

Preparation for Future Needs

Teaching is a future-oriented career. Most of what we do in the classroom is in preparation for what we think students need next. Teaching students what they will likely need later on is therefore a good justification for a unit.

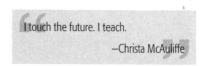

I touch the future. I teach.

—Christa McAuliffe

College

One reason teachers often cite for teaching something is that it will help students succeed in college. I do not find this reason terribly compelling. For one thing, it doesn't help students who don't go to college. Also, this reasoning suggests if students learn something before they go to college and they are then required to study it there, they're ahead of the game for already having learned it. This assumption defines knowledge a little too narrowly for my taste.

Nonetheless, it's conceivable that you could justify teaching some things on the basis that students will need them later in college, particularly if what students get is tools rather than simply facts. For instance, a unit on satire could focus on teaching students how to recognize and interpret satires; then, when they read *Gulliver's Travels* in college, they will recognize the literary techniques used by Swift and understand the ways in which he is criticizing society.

Social Needs

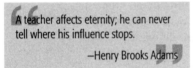
A teacher affects eternity; he can never tell where his influence stops.

—Henry Brooks Adams

Teachers might teach a topic because they feel that it will prepare students to help construct a better society in the future. A unit on the outcast or effects of discrimination, for instance, might raise students' awareness of the general lack of tolerance for those who are different or less fortunate and pave the way for students to help create a more compassionate society.

Writing a Rationale

A rationale is a type of argument, a genre that typically includes a number of key elements. In writing your rationale, consider the following related questions:

- What concepts are central to the topic of this unit?
- Why am I teaching this unit and its concepts?
- What *type(s) of justification(s)* am I primarily relying on to support my rationale (psychology/human development, cultural significance, etc.)?
- Within each justification, what are the main *claims* that can be made about its relevance to the unit I'm proposing (e.g., studying protest literature is important because it helps students understand the role of conscience in social action)?
- For each claim, what kinds of *evidence* can I provide that would be persuasive to others, and how can I provide a *warrant* that explains the ways in which that evidence supports my claim?
- What *counterarguments* can I anticipate against my rationale, and how can I provide a *rebuttal* for them?
- How can I provide a rationale for each of the texts that my students read in conjunction with the unit focus?

With these criteria in mind, you can begin to provide a rationale for your own proposed unit. There is no set procedure for writing a rationale, but there are several planning steps you might want to try. Keep in mind that ultimately you will be

Look at Rationales

Select three units from the list of model units and read the rationale for each. Think about the following questions:

- Which *justifications* does the rationale rely on and how appropriate are they?
- What are the teacher's main claims?
- How effectively does the teacher support each claim with persuasive evidence?
- How effectively are the evidence and claims *warranted* (i.e., how is the evidence argued in service of the claim)?
- Could the teacher have provided different, more persuasive reasons for teaching the unit?
- Does the teacher anticipate disagreements (*counterarguments*) with the rationale and provide a *rebuttal* for them?
- If you were a skeptical school board member or other stakeholder, would you be persuaded that this is a good unit to teach?
- On the whole, what are the strengths and weaknesses of the rationale, and how could it be written to be more persuasive? In other words, generate a set of criteria for deciding what is included in a persuasive rationale.

producing a persuasive piece of writing, so however you proceed, you should think in terms of coordinating a set of related claims that support a general thesis, each based on some kind of evidence.

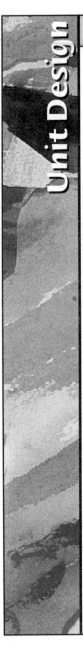

Plan a Rationale

1. One way to start is by informally generating ideas. You might do this by
   - discussing ideas in a small group, taking notes as needed
   - freewriting (writing down ideas quickly without concern for how your writing looks or sounds; the purpose is to use the process of writing as a way to think, rather than to produce a formal piece of writing that someone else will judge)
   - taking notes, either in categorical form (outline, cluster) or in random form
2. Once your ideas are on paper, you can begin to organize them in some way, by yourself or with the aid of your peers. This step might include
   - exploring whether any themes logically emerge from what you've written down
   - identifying which kinds of justifications you have produced
   - associating particular claims with particular kinds of justifications
   - looking for a pattern or relationship among the claims
   - discussing or thinking further about inconsistencies or gaps in your initial effort and revising your ideas accordingly
   - creating a new outline in which you organize your ideas
3. With your justification(s) and claims established, you should then think of how to support your claims, considering
   - what type of evidence (research, anecdote, personal experience, statistics, etc.) is available
   - how persuasive these different kinds of evidence will be to different constituents
   - where you might find evidence that effectively supports your claims
   - what particular evidence will support your claims
4. At this point, you would need to take some time to find the evidence necessary for supporting your claims. If you have taken courses in educational foundations or educational psychology, among others, you might know of research that would support your arguments. English courses may provide information on the cultural or literary significance of certain topics. You may need to gather other supporting evidence from new sources.
5. While gathering evidence, think of ways in which people could disagree with your argument and how you could counter these disagreements. By addressing these concerns in your rationale, you can short-circuit possible challenges to your teaching decisions.

Writing Your Rationale

Remember that you are writing a persuasive essay, something you probably have had years of experience doing as a student. Keep in mind your audience for your rationale: an irate parent, a skeptical department chair or principal, the president of the board of education, who has received a complaint. Your rationale should provide a defense of your teaching that will make it clear that you've thought through the issues, know what you're doing, and know why you're doing it.

You should have a lot of information assembled to inform your rationale. You should also have a set of criteria for a good rationale that you developed from analyzing those in the Virtual Library of Instructional Units. Make sure that you apply these criteria when using this information as the basis for your rationale.

You may wish to ask another person to read and respond to your rationale so that you can see how somebody else constructs meaning from your prose. Readers can take the perspective of a skeptical parent or school board member and provide rebuttals that can help you strengthen your argument. For ideas on how to provide this kind of feedback for your students, see Appendix C.

What Students Know and What Schools Assess

T his chapter looks at the ways in which schools most frequently evaluate students' competency and knowledge and contrasts them with the many ways people do things intelligently outside school. For the most part, schools rely on *authoritative* views of knowledge that teachers explain to students for purposes of testing. I propose a number of other ways in which schooling might be conducted to take advantage of what students know and can do. This approach generally falls under the name of *constructivism* because it assumes that knowledge is always reconstructed by people for their own purposes. I argue in this chapter that constructivist, exploratory, narrative, and connected ways of knowing should be coupled with students' use of multiple intelligences to allow for different approaches to teaching English than is typically found in schools.

> I didn't enjoy teaching at first. In retrospect, the reason is clear. I had adopted the "banker model" of teaching. The students were merely receptacles—empty vessels into which I must deposit a certain sum of knowledge. . . . I didn't view my students as individuals, partly because as I lectured to them, they looked uniformly bored.
>
> —Margaret Matlin

Something happened when I was teaching in high school that I'll never forget, although to the other people involved it seemed to be a routine, passing moment that was entirely unremarkable. I was standing in the hallway between classes talking to the English teacher who taught next door. We engaged in the typical brief banter that teachers exchange amidst the currents of students going to class, talking, laughing, rummaging through their lockers, and catching their breath before the next class begins. Another English teacher walked by and, seeing my colleague, called across the clamor, "Hey, I'm just finishing up *Death of a Salesman,* and somebody told me that you have a really great test to use with it. Could you lend me a copy?" "Sure," answered the other, and as the bell approached we scattered along with the students to start the next class.

The incident seemed so casual that I'm sure neither one of them thought anything odd about it at all. To me, though, the idea of teaching something for several weeks and then using an assessment developed by another teacher for other students was fundamentally at odds with everything I understood about evaluation. Testing students in this way involves the following assumptions:

- There's such a thing as a "good test" that can be given to everybody studying a text to see how well they've understood it. This assumption carries further assumptions:

- The play itself stands as a concrete work with a meaning that is stable across readers and groups of readers. I refer to this presumed stable meaning as the work's *official meaning*.
- Anyone teaching the text will inevitably emphasize the official meaning.
- The test itself stands as an objective measure of students' understanding of the official meaning, which is invariant.
- Whatever knowledge students construct from the literature beyond the official interpretation is irrelevant in terms of their grade on the assessment.
- It's fine for teachers to teach without any sense of how they will assess the students when they are done. This assumption carries the following assumptions:
  - Instruction is about the texts, which have a particular meaning that can ultimately be assessed by an exam designed by a person who has never seen any of the teaching or learning.
  - There is not necessarily a relationship between actual classroom processes and assessment.
  - Assessment does not necessarily need to be related to the unique exchanges that take place among groups of students and teachers when discussing works of literature or unit concepts.

Perhaps the utter casualness of the exchange I witnessed, its very mundane character, is what made it so striking to me. The assumptions behind it were so deeply embedded in their conception of teaching that the loan could be uncritically secured through a chance meeting in the hallway. And so the exam moved from one file cabinet to another, perhaps still being administered to this day, the meaning of the play stable no matter who teaches the class or enrolls in it.

My account of this exchange undoubtedly seems harsh. You might be surprised to learn that I liked both of these teachers a great deal and that both had extremely good reputations in the school. And perhaps that's what makes it all so remarkable—that two highly regarded teachers in a highly reputable school would view assessment in what struck me as a thoughtless and cavalier manner.

I tell this story to open this chapter because this chapter and the two that follow are about assessment. I will consider what it means to know something, as a prelude to the more specific focus in Chapters 4 and 5 on how to plan assessments. Schools tend to have a well-established conception of what counts as knowledge. You will recognize this conception when I describe it, for you have undoubtedly been assessed according to it in most classes you have taken.

I don't want to suggest that I think that the dominant values of school are always off the mark or unimportant, even if in significant ways they often are. I will, however, try to persuade you that you should also assess other ways students have of knowing things. As I review them, you will probably recognize these other conceptions of knowledge, although you may not have considered their role in formal education.

Some ways of knowing things are inborn; for example, some of us are born better able to configure space than others. Some ways of knowing come from the culture;

for example, some cultures promote collaboration, whereas others promote competition. In some cases, the source of difference is not so clear; for example, although most people agree that men and women tend to see the world differently, whether the difference is innate or the result of socialization has never been established.

Regardless of the source of difference, you will be teaching classes in which your students will exhibit a broad range of capacities. Throughout much of their schooling, these diverse students will have been forced to fit the Procrustean bed of conventional assumptions about knowledge and assessment. By including assessments that take other ways of knowing things into account, you will be teaching in ways responsive to the range of diversity your students bring to class. I will try to persuade you instead to allow for flexibility in the ways in which students can express themselves and come to know the discipline of English so that you'll be assessing students more on their own terms and through vehicles that suit their strengths.

Let's take something relatively simple, a bicycle, and see how you might know it.

- You might have memorized its different parts and be able to answer questions about them.
- You might know how to ride the bicycle across a variety of terrains.
- You might associate the bicycle with your dear grandparent who fixed it for you, and know it through sentiment and love.
- You might know the history of bicycles and this particular type of bicycle's place in that history.
- You may know the rhythms generated by riding the bicycle at different speeds and know its potential for producing percussive sounds.
- You may have had significant experiences while riding it and view those stories as central to your identity.

There are undoubtedly many other ways in which you could know a bicycle. As you probably know from having been a student for many years, in schools there are relatively few ways in which your knowledge is assessed. If you were to study the bicycle in school, it's likely that you would be tested on your knowledge by your ability to identify its parts and their correct functions. It wouldn't matter much if you could actually ride a bicycle; you might know how to shift gears appropriately to ride the bike up any incline, but if you forgot the names of the gear mechanisms you were asked to identify, you would be deemed unknowledgeable about bicycles.

In this chapter I will ask you to open your mind with regard to thinking about what it means to know something. This consideration should take into account a few key points:

- Achievement is a function of what you measure. By this I mean that students are judged to be good or bad, knowledgeable or unknowledgeable, A students or D students, according to some means and focus of measurement. Far too often, those measurements are restricted to their memory of official or factual knowledge. Any other knowledge they have, particularly knowledge that departs from the conventional, is not considered noteworthy when achievement is measured through an assessment.

Vignette

I read a cartoon once that I thought was quite a hoot. It pictured a girl sitting at a desk taking an exam, with question marks coming out of her head and beads of perspiration leaping from her brow. The caption read, "If religion were taught in the schools." The exam questions were something like these:

1. Who was the pope in 1853?
2. How many shekels of gold went into each of King Solomon's large shields?
3. In what years did Mas'ud bin Mahmud bin Sebuktegin serve as a Ghaznavid sultan?

- What you test is what you get. By this I mean that assessment tends to set the terms for what is emphasized in instruction. And so when students will be assessed according to their memory of official knowledge, classes will likely be conducted to impress that knowledge on them.

I next review ways of thinking about knowledge that are much broader than what is typically assessed in school. For each conception of knowledge I review, I will suggest possibilities for instructional goals. My purposes in doing so are

- to illustrate the relationship between a conception of knowledge and an assessment of that knowledge in school
- to show the range of what is possible, if rarely practiced, in school
- to argue that this range ought to be provided to account for the diversity of students in a class, rather than restricting assessment and in the process making some very bright and insightful students appear to be unknowledgeable

In Chapters 4 and 5, I will look at ways to create specific kinds of assessments to take into account this broader conception of knowledge.

TWO THEORIES OF COMMUNICATION: TRANSMISSION AND CONSTRUCTIVISM

I next review two theories of communication that will provide a vocabulary for further discussions of assessment. The argument I make here is not new, yet the problem I discuss is remarkably persistent. The problem concerns a paradox of schooling: that the most pervasive assumption about knowledge is the *transmission* view that conceives of knowledge and communication in superficial ways; whereas the relatively rich *constructivist* assumptions rarely influence curriculum, instruction, and assessment.

> When . . . I started to panic and walk out of exams, the school counselor diagnosed my stress level around tests and papers as so high that I could literally not hear myself think. My teachers, Miss Stevenson and later Miss St. Pierre, found the solution in allowing me to write "creatively" about what I was learning, essays, poems, stories, journals, which I could work on in my room and hand in without the dreaded clock incapacitating me.
>
> —Julia Alvarez

Transmission

As a student for sixteen years or so, you have probably taken quite a few tests of your knowledge, and based on these tests, you have received grades that categorized your prowess as a student on a scale of A through F. It's likely that on a number of occasions you felt that what you knew was not measured by the assessment. I still remember the exam for a college course I took in classics. After reading all sorts of interesting history and literature from early Mediterranean culture and having a reasonable understanding of how these civilizations shaped subsequent history, I found a question on the final exam asking me to identify a classical figure named Bucephalus. Perhaps you don't recognize this name, as I didn't when taking the test. Yet the professor believed that identifying Bucephalus was so significant that it should serve as a measure of my knowledge of classical history. It turned out to be the name of Alexander the Great's horse. Fortunately, we were not asked to identify his cat, or I might still be in college.

Such is the way knowledge has typically been conceived and measured in schools. Rather than focusing on important concepts, schools fixate on labeling their parts. Another example: Not long ago, the certification exam for English teachers in one state asked candidates to identify the name of the frog in Mark Twain's "The Celebrated Jumping Frog of Calaveras County." In case you've forgotten, it's Dan'l Webster—fortunately for you, your future as a teacher probably does not depend on knowing this nugget of information, as it did for the teachers taking that exam. When test makers pose questions of this sort, they assume that knowledge is objective and static and capable of being handed down intact from one person to another, from text to student, from lecture to notebook, and back again to the teacher on a test. When the questions concern the names of horses and frogs, rather than their significance, the test makers appear to believe that any detail will do for testing purposes.

This view of knowledge has been called the *transmission* view. Knowledge is thought to be a stable entity that can be transmitted like a baseball, thrown from one person to another and arriving in the same condition in which it began. And thus a teacher can say in a lecture that in Emily Dickinson's "A Narrow Fellow in the Grass," the narrow fellow is a snake, and students can write this fact down. Later, the students can be tested as knowledgeable readers by affirming the serpentine nature of the narrow fellow. Woe unto the student who believes that it is something else and has the poor judgment to say so on the official assessment.

Schools in general support a transmission view of knowledge because they tend to follow a top-down model of authority. Administrators make decisions that teachers put into practice. Teachers, though they usually lack schoolwide authority, are the authorities in their classrooms and so transmit their knowledge of facts to students. Students have the option of "doing school" in ways that lead to success, or resisting those ways and being labeled troublemakers or bad students. To be a success, students must show that they have mastered the knowledge that their teachers have provided for them, no matter how useful they find that knowledge or whether they even believe it. Indeed, James W. Loewen, in *Lies My Teacher Told Me: Everything Your American History Textbook Got Wrong*, argues that school textbooks frequently suppress historical facts in order to promote a sanitized version of U.S. history. It's also quite common for one commercial textbook to present facts different from the facts provided in another. The students' job is to memorize the particular version of history presented in the textbook they study—even though this version might be contradicted in a different textbook and viewed with skepticism by many historians—and report it correctly on exams.

Students' ability to replicate official knowledge intact is reflected in their grades, a sorting process appreciated by colleges that need ways to discriminate among applicants. The flow of transmission is invariably from teacher and text to student. Students have little say in deciding what is good or bad, right or wrong, meaningful or not meaningful. Their role is to show that they've received the information and can throw it back in the same form. Cynics have used such unseemly analogies as "regurgitation" or mindless metaphors as "parroting" to describe the expectations for students under a transmission pedagogy.

Constructivism

Even though schools are widely operated according to transmission assumptions, there are plenty of ways to think about what it means to know something other than to know it according to its official facts, right or wrong. Another view of knowledge falls under the umbrella term *constructivism.* As the word suggests, this refers to the idea that knowledge is constructed rather than received through a transmission. Learners draw on a variety of sources for the knowledge they construct.

> [You] mentioned the book *Lies My Teacher Told Me.* I recently finished this pearl, WOW! . . . I believe that this *very* interesting and entertaining book will help to promote future teachers to conduct research on the characters that they are teaching to students. Hopefully, this book will encourage future teachers to view their teacher's textbook with skepticism. I vividly recall the [large school district] sophomore book discussing how Malcolm X reneged his stance on Black militancy. I have recently learned otherwise (Mumia-Abu Jamal's *Live from Death Row*—however, I have yet to read *The Autobiography of Malcolm X*). How many other erroneous myths do we teach our students because we take the textbook at face value?
>
> —Tommy Behr,
> Hidden Lake Academy,
> Dahlonega, Georgia

1. One is their reading of the codes provided by whatever text they are studying. If, for instance, a student reads or writes a science report on the dissection of a frog (not, presumably, Dan'l Webster), the expectation of the genre would suggest that a material frog existed and was duly parsed as described in the report. If, however, the same student were to read Swift's *Gulliver's Travels* and come across talking horses (not Bucephalus), the literary codes would suggest that they not be viewed literally. If a student included an account of a talking frog in a lab report for a science class, the teacher would likely assume it was either an unfaithful science report or a work of fiction and if the latter, assign it a low grade because it did not include the proper codes for science reports.

2. A second source of constructed knowledge is the learner's personal experiences. While reading *Gulliver's Travels,* someone with personal experience in human avarice might evoke images of avaricious people. Doing so would infuse the literary characters with a particular and probably idiosyncratic meaning. In contrast, a transmission view would frown on an idiosyncratic reading of literature as a departure from the official meaning and would in all likelihood dismiss the interpretation as irrelevant or incorrect.

3. A learner's attributions of meaning can also be a function of the social context of reading. If *Gulliver's Travels* were being read in preparation for the Advanced Placement exam, the teacher's instruction might focus students' readings

on AP values. The AP scoring rubrics would provide the guidelines for learning how to read and think about the novel. In contrast, if it were being read by adult readers as part of a book club, its reading might be accompanied by wine and snacks, the conversation might include much laughter, the discussion might digress to consider personal experiences with avaricious people, and open emotions, such as crying, would be viewed as appropriate responses. Readers would give little attention to how to write a high-scoring essay that would please AP judges and more attention to what they did and didn't get from the book. The conversation might include a lot of storytelling, rather than a lot of analysis. Similarly, it would be highly inappropriate to respond to Swift's satire in an AP class by bursting into tears. In both cases, the social context helps determine what kinds of responses are appropriate.

4. Finally, the cultural backgrounds of the learners can influence their construction of meaning. Margaret Mitchell's *Gone with the Wind,* for instance, for many years was among the twentieth century's most beloved novels, at least among white readers. Toward the end of the century, however, its depiction of Southern gentility came under criticism because of its unproblematic view of slaves. In both novel and film, the slaves are devotedly subservient and regret the fall of the South. This portrayal was accepted for many years by the text's devoted fans. The modern poststructural climate, with its emphasis on deconstructing power relationships, has fostered more critical views of this depiction of contented slaves. *Gone with the Wind* is now read as racist by those who view its representation of Southern gentility as a valorization of oppression. The different reading afforded by poststructuralism reveals the ways in which a cultural worldview can provide the framework for a different kind of meaning.

> It is better to know some of the questions than to know all the answers.
>
> —James Thurber

Knowledge construction, therefore, comes as part of a transaction among a variety of factors: the text the student reads or produces; the personal experiences the student brings to the situation that contribute to understanding and interpretation; the influences of the environment that suggest appropriate ways to be literate; and the cultural history that provides the values for both the immediate environment and the individual's experiences.

You might recall that in the introduction to this book, one of the principles I identified was that any assessment ought to provide the occasion for new learning. It is possible that transmission-oriented assessments can provide occasions for new learning, although most such assessments I've seen do not (my enduring knowledge of Bucephalus's identity notwithstanding). Rather, many assessments of this type reduce some pretty splendid literature to a tedious job of memorizing information that's forgotten before long. Most taxonomies of cognition place simple memorization fairly low on the hierarchy, and inference and generating new knowledge fairly high. Yet school assessment concentrates on rote memorization and location of facts, even in the decidedly ambiguous and symbolic world of literature.

TWO VIEWS OF SPEECH AND WRITING: FINAL DRAFT AND EXPLORATORY

Field Observation
In the school you are visiting, where does teaching generally fall on the continuum from transmission to constructivism? What are the consequences for students of the approach you've observed?

Related to the transmission and constructivist views of communication are Douglas Barnes's (1992) descriptions of classroom speech. I will next outline his descriptions of two kinds of speech:

- *Final draft* speech, which often occurs in conjunction with transmission pedagogies
- *Exploratory* speech, which can serve to achieve constructivist ends

Final Draft Speech

In his studies of classroom interactions Barnes found that assumptions about knowledge affect the ways in which students speak and write in school. Most readers of this book will understand Barnes's metaphor of final draft speech. A final draft is the one in which all the kinks have been worked out, all the bad ideas rejected, all of the language smoothed over. It has a certainty about it that reflects an authoritative view of the topic. The product is complete and presented for the teacher's approval.

Barnes argues that in too many classrooms, discussions are conducted so that final draft speech is rewarded. That is, students are only encouraged to participate when they have arrived at a fairly well thought out idea that they can present to the teacher for approval. Under these circumstances, a lot of students don't say much at all because they are thinking through their ideas and never quite reach that final draft state at which their thoughts can be offered for the teacher to approve. Rather, the teacher—who has often taught the book or the class a number of times and can provide an authoritative interpretation in reasonably polished form—occupies much of the floor.

This conception of speech is compatible with a transmission view of communication because only finished, authoritative ideas are considered legitimate, and for the most part the teacher is the one who has them. The teacher's role in this case is to provide official knowledge for the students, who demonstrate their expertise by repeating the knowledge as faithfully as possible on assessments.

Exploratory Talk

Barnes argues that classrooms ought to encourage more exploratory talk in which students think aloud as they work through their ideas. Such talk is tentative, spontaneous, provisional, and constructive as students discover what they have to say by voicing their emerging thoughts.

Allowing such talk changes much about classrooms. First of all, it changes the purpose of discussion from transmitting official knowledge to constructing new

Books about Writing and Speech as Exploratory Tools

Applebee, A. N. (1981). *Writing in the secondary school.* Urbana, IL: National Council of Teachers of English.

Barnes, D. R. (1992). *From communication to curriculum* (2nd ed.). Portsmouth, NH: Heinemann.

Barnes, D. R., Britton, J., & Torbe, M. (1990). *Language, the learner and the school* (4th ed.). Portsmouth, NH: Heinemann.

Britton, J., Burgess, T., Martin, N., McLeod, A., & Rosen, H. (1975). *The development of writing abilities (11–18).* London: Macmillan Education Ltd. for the Schools Council.

Cazden, C. B. (1988). *Classroom discourse: The language of teaching and learning.* Portsmouth, NH: Heineman.

Dewey, J. (1960). *The quest for certainty.* New York: Putnam.

Marshall, J. D., Smagorinsky, P., & Smith, M. W. (1995). *The language of interpretation: Patterns of discourse in discussions of literature* (NCTE Research Report No. 27). Urbana, IL: National Council of Teachers of English.

Newman, D., Griffin, P., & Cole, M. (1989). *The construction zone: Working for cognitive change in school.* New York: Cambridge University Press.

Wells, G., & Chang-Wells, G. L. (1992). *Constructing knowledge together: Classrooms as centers of inquiry and literacy.* Portsmouth, NH: Heinemann.

knowledge. This change in turn alters the dynamics of discussions. The teacher no longer exclusively holds the floor, but instead orchestrates students' efforts to realize new ideas through exploratory talk. The contributions of speakers needn't be formal and authoritative, but can be partial and experimental. Since ideas are not being offered as finished products for final approval, they can be half-baked and provisional. These conditions apply not only to the students, but to the teacher as well, who also has the opportunity to realize new thoughts and insights through the process of discussion.

The idea of exploratory talk also extends to writing. Although schools now pay more attention to writing process than they used to, writing is still not typically viewed as an opportunity to discover ideas through exploratory, tentative expression. A constructivist approach would include informal opportunities for students to write freely as a way to find what they have to say without concern for submitting the finished product for approval. Used in this way, writing would serve as a *tool* for thinking, part of the student's tool kit for constructivist thinking.

This conception of writing and speech contributes to what James Britton and his colleagues called a *growth model* of education. In this view, the emphasis of school is on students as well as on subjects. An English teacher's primary focus is on students of English, rather than on the subject of English. The purpose of the class then shifts from teaching the subject—lecturing on the

> ### Reflective Writing Prompt
>
> Think about your own experiences with writing and/or speaking. In school, have you been encouraged to use writing or speaking as a tool for exploring ideas? What have you learned from your experiences of writing or speaking in school?
>
> What of your experiences with writing or speaking outside school? How does your use of writing or speaking outside school compare with your use of them in school? Are there differences in the kinds of learning that have resulted from the writing and speaking you've done in and out of school?

Victorians, explaining the significance of literary symbols, and so on—to considering how engagement with a domain will contribute to the personal growth of learners. Such an emphasis relies on language as a psychological tool for exploring ideas and constructing new knowledge and is less concerned with the knowledge displays inherent to transmission pedagogies that rely on final draft speech.

> In the traditional method the child must say something that he has merely learned. There is all the difference in the world between having something to say, and having to say something.
>
> —John Dewey

PARADIGMATIC AND NARRATIVE WAYS OF KNOWING

Psychologist Jerome Bruner (1985) has argued that there are primarily two ways of knowing, *paradigmatic* and *narrative,* which I will describe in turn. These ways of knowing are not necessarily tied to transmission and constructivist assumptions about learning. Both paradigmatic and narrative knowledge can be constructed or can rely on presumably transmitted facts. Schools tend to rely on paradigmatic knowledge more than on narrative knowledge, and, unfortunately, paradigmatic knowledge is often reduced to displays of knowledge for teachers, robbing students of the opportunity to construct new knowledge. But, as I will argue, it needn't be that way.

Paradigmatic Knowledge

Paradigmatic knowledge is the most widely emphasized way of knowing in U.S. schools. It involves rational problem solving and scientific procedures of investigation using formal verification and empirical proof. The scientific report is an obvious example of how a paradigmatic approach is used in schools.

In an English class, however, we also see an emphasis on paradigmatic knowledge. The approach to literary criticism known as New Criticism (not so new any more—it was introduced in the 1930s) was founded on principles of scientific analysis. New Criticism has become ingrained in U.S. schools and the textbook industry. Although falling out of favor in universities, it is still the dominant approach to teaching literature in secondary schools.

Paradigmatic approaches to literature involve any of the kinds of analytic essays typically required in English classes:

Compare/contrast papers, which compare one author to another, one period to another, one novel to another, and so on.

Extended definition essays, which generate a set of criteria that define a term and attempt to classify various items according to that definition. Examples include defining realistic literature and determining whether a particular author's work meets the definition; and defining an abstract term, such as *progress,* and judging various actions (e.g., the frontier society in Thomas Berger's *Little Big Man*) in terms of the criteria of the definition.

Analytic essays, which require the analysis of some aspect of a literary work that follows the conventions of argumentation. Such essays usually involve a major thesis, a set of claims (in school, usually three), and supporting evidence for each claim, often adding up to what is known as the five-paragraph theme. An example might be to analyze Twain's *The Adventures of Huckleberry Finn* and identify the human vices that are being exposed through the action in the novel. (I should add that I do not see the five-paragraph theme as the only or best means of writing analytically, and will offer alternatives in Chapter 4.)

The paradigmatic mode accounts for the bulk of writing done in U.S. secondary schools (Applebee, 1981). Because of the emphasis placed on paradigmatic thinking throughout school, it is not surprising or inappropriate for students to get considerable experience with paradigmatic writing about literature. Argumentation and analysis are skills one would expect students to learn in school. The case I would like to make here is that there should be opportunities for other ways to think in English classes as well. I will next review what Bruner means by the *narrative* mode of thought, which gets surprisingly less attention in a field so heavily concerned with stories.

Narrative Knowledge

Narrative knowledge refers to our effort to make sense of things by rendering them in story. Narrative does not rely on the paradigmatic elements of logic, verification, and rational proof. Rather, it is concerned with verisimilitude, the likeness of truth, the creation of characters and events that represent emotional and social truths but need not replicate them. Believability is the hallmark of well-formed narratives, even while they contain falsehoods.

Narratives might be evaluated according to the degree of emotional resonance they prompt in readers. To return to one of my previous examples, it would be plausible for a student to write a narrative about a talking frog in the dissection tray. The evaluation of the quality of the writing would not be based on whether such a thing was really possible, but instead on the extent to which the frog was able to articulate or represent some truth about the human (or possibly the ranine) condition.

The world of knowledge revealed by narratives is often different from that revealed paradigmatically. Dwayne Huebner (1985) describes this world as one involving *spiritual* knowledge:

> What are these histories, stories, myths, and poems? They are symbols of moreness, of otherness, of the transcendent—symbols that life as lived can be different. The otherness, moreness, the transcendent is demonstrated in creativity. It shows forth in insight and new understanding, and is anticipated in hope for the future. The symbols may be stories of relationships—of struggle, conflict, forgiveness, love—during which something new is produced: new life, new relationships, new understandings, new forms of power and political control. There are symbols of wholeness and unity: of the body and mind, of self and others, of the human and natural world, of past, present, and future. There are symbols of at-one-ness when the inchoate and disturbing cohere in new meanings. There are symbols of liberation, of exodus from various forms of enslavement and domination: personal, interpersonal, or social. They are symbols of more than

the present, more than current forms for life. These are the symbols of the spirit and the spiritual and how life as lived is, and can be, informed, reformed, and transformed. (pp. 164–165)

I have gone on at greater length with narrative modes of thought than paradigmatic because I do not need to justify the role of paradigmatic thinking in education, given that it is already part of the furniture of schooling. Again, I do not dispute the importance of learning to think logically and analytically in school. This book is primarily a rational (I hope) argument, as is much of my own writing. Most of what I know about this kind of thinking I learned in school. My goal in justifying narrative thinking is to argue for an increased role for other ways of thinking and making sense of the world, ways that psychologists have found have been central to sense making throughout history. Even in a discipline as devoted to stories as English, narrative ways of knowing are rarely allowed as ways *for students* to express themselves.

> As the midwife/teacher image dramatically conveys, education is relational—a relationship that involves knowledge, attentiveness, and care; care directed not only at disciplinary material but to who students are and what they can become. It involves responsiveness and a stance of hopefulness.
>
> —Ann Stanton

GENDERED WAYS OF KNOWING

Do traditional school practices favor boys, girls, both, or neither? It depends on whom you ask. Some observers of schools have argued that, as the American Association of University Women claims, schools shortchange girls. As evidence, they point to the ways in which schools operate according to masculine conceptions of knowledge. Feminist critics point out that the predominant emphasis in school is on paradigmatic knowledge taught primarily through transmission assumptions involving final draft uses of language. Girls, according to this argument, benefit more from constructivist knowing facilitated by exploratory speech and narrative ways of knowing. Boys, because of their more aggressive and competitive behavior, are more likely to get noticed and called on and are treated more favorably.

On the other hand, there's much evidence to support the view that girls do better in schools than boys. Christina Hoff Sommers (2000) reports that in comparison to boys, girls get higher grades, are more likely to go to college, take more rigorous academic programs, enroll in AP classes at higher rates, enroll in more high-level math and science courses, read more books, score higher on tests for artistic and musical ability, are more engaged academically, do more homework, and participate more frequently in student government, honor societies, debate clubs, and school newspapers. More frequently than girls, boys are suspended from school, are held back, drop out, are diagnosed as having attention deficit/hyperactivity disorder, commit crimes, get involved with drugs and alcohol, and commit suicide.

There appears to be no easy resolution to the disagreement over whether school benefits one sex or the other. There does seem to be some agreement, however, that boys and girls experience school differently. I think it's worthwhile, then, to think about gendered ways of knowing to bring an informed perspective to the discussion.

I will next review the basic terms of gendered views of psychology, making one small but significant change. In much of the literature, ways of knowing are distinguished as either masculine or feminine, as the province of men and boys or of women and girls. Although I agree that women and men are often different from one another in consistent ways, I hesitate to apply these terms so that they suggest absolute differences between the two (or, for that matter, that gender is neatly divided into two types).

I will therefore use the terms *authoritative* and *connected* in place of men's and women's psychological makeups. These terms allow for a discussion of the issues without so strictly dividing the world into two distinct, gender-based groups. I'm sure that any reader of this book can think of plenty of examples of people who do not act in accordance with their gender profiles, while at the same time seeing that these two ways of relating exist, even if they don't always coexist so well. I present these two types as points on a continuum, rather than as absolute categories. Most people, I suspect, fall somewhere in between these two extremes.

> I am always ready to learn although I do not always like being taught.
>
> —Winston Churchill

Authoritative Ways of Relating

People who take an authoritative view of the world tend to take a competitive and aggressive stance toward other people. In a discussion their goal is to win and so assert their greater authority, rather than to compromise, co-construct new knowledge, or learn more about the other people involved. Their competitive stance suggests a need for autonomy, therefore making collaboration both unnecessary and perhaps even counterproductive. The need for autonomy reduces attention to other people and their needs and feelings, resulting in a lack of connection to others who, after all, are competitors.

This de-emphasis on personal connections leads away from empathic and emotional language and toward the language of analysis and abstraction. The point of schooling then becomes to work toward the creation of taxonomies and hierarchies that establish rules that resist contextual considerations. Classroom time is devoted to analysis of literature, emotional responses are discouraged, and the strongest arguments prevail (with strength at times determined by force as much as by logic).

Connected Ways of Knowing

Connected knowing refers to ways of relating to other people and constructing knowledge that are more collaborative, less competitive, and more likely concerned with the personal relationships of the people involved. Talk that characterizes connected knowing is often

- *tentative*, indicated by hesitations, false starts, qualifiers, politeness, intensifiers, repetition, slow rate of speech, deferential remarks, and tag questions

Books about Gender and Talk

American Association of University Women. (1995). *The AAUW Report: How schools shortchange girls.* New York: Marlowe.

Belenky, M. F., Clinchy, B. M., Goldberger, N. R., & Tarule, J. M. (1986). *Women's ways of knowing: The development of self, voice, and mind.* New York: Basic Books.

Coates, J. (1993). *Women, men and language* (2nd ed.). New York: Longman.

Finders, M. J. (1997). *Just girls: Hidden literacies and life in junior high.* New York: Teachers College Press; Urbana, IL: National Council of Teachers of English.

Gilligan, C. (1982). *In a different voice: Psychological theory and women's development.* Cambridge, MA: Harvard University Press.

Josselson, R. (1996). *Revising herself.* New York: Oxford University Press.

Lakoff, R. (1975). *Language and woman's place.* New York: Harper & Row.

Llewelyn, S., & Osborne, K. (1990). *Women's lives.* New York: Routledge.

Maher, F., & Tetreault, M. (1994). *The feminist classroom.* New York: Basic Books.

McCormick, T. M. (1994). *Creating the nonsexist classroom: A multicultural approach.* New York: Teachers College Press.

Miller, J. B. (1986). *Toward a new psychology of women* (2nd ed.). Boston: Beacon Press.

Mills, S. (1995). *Feministic stylistics.* New York: Routledge.

Ng, S., & Bradac, J. (1993). *Power in language: Verbal communication and social influence.* Newbury Park, CA: Sage.

Noddings, N. (1992). *The challenge to care in schools: An alternative approach to education.* New York: Teachers College Press.

Orenstein, P. (1994). *SchoolGirls.* New York: Doubleday.

Pipher, M. (1994). *Reviving Ophelia: Saving the selves of adolescent girls.* New York: Putnam's.

Sadker, M., & Sadker, D. (1994). *Failing at fairness: How America's schools cheat girls.* New York: Scribner's.

Smith, P. M. (1985). *Language, the sexes and society.* New York: Basil Blackwell.

Sommers, C. H. (2000). *The war against boys: How misguided feminism is harming our young men.* New York: Simon & Schuster.

St. Pierre, E., & Pillow, W. (Eds.). (2000). *Working the ruins: Feminist poststructural theory and methods in education.* New York: Routledge.

Tannen, D. (1989). *Talking voices.* New York: Cambridge University Press.

Taylor, J. M., Gilligan, C., & Sullivan, A. M. (1995). *Between silence and voice: Women and girls, race and relationship.* Cambridge, MA: Harvard University Press.

Thorne, B., Kramarae, C., & Henley, N. (1983). *Language, gender, and society.* Rowley, MA: Newbury House.

Todd, A. D., & Fisher, S. (Eds.). (1988). *Gender and discourse: The power of talk.* Norwood, NJ: Ablex.

Walkerdine, V. (1990). *Schoolgirl fictions.* New York: Verso.

Many schools provide some kind of team-teaching opportunities. You'll often see English and history teachers team-teach a course called American Studies, which makes an effort to study American history and American literature together. Doing so gives students a potentially enriched understanding of America through the combined lenses of the two disciplines.

In Barrington High School, where I taught from 1978 to 1985, members of the English and art departments—Joe Wolnski, Charles White, and David Engle—have team-taught a course called Interrelated Arts, in which litera-ture, language, and writing are taught in conjunction with the abundant arts available in the Chicago area. Students go on a number of expeditions to look at Chicago architecture, attend the symphony or opera, visit art galleries, and take in other cultural opportunities. They produce not only writing, but artistic, musical, and other renditions of their ideas. They also read literature that fits with whatever themes guided their studies and thinking. Not only has the course been quite provocative for students, it has energized the faculty who teach it, and it has done so for nearly twenty years and counting.

- *nurturing,* demonstrated by efforts to encourage the contributions of other speakers
- *connected* with other speakers, indicated by the way in which discussions are cohesive and collaborative
- *indirect,* allowing speakers to establish a rapport and requiring listeners to make inferences

Because of concern for the emotional well-being of others, connected knowers are less aggressive in group discussions and more likely to support others or co-construct knowledge with them. Because they are less concerned with autonomy, they are less emphatic about developing universal rules and more interested in understanding how situational factors affect behavior. The acceptance of the tentative possibilities for language is consistent with Barnes's characterization of exploratory speech.

TYPES OF INTELLIGENCE

Howard Gardner has proposed that people have *multiple intelligences* through which they make sense of the world. Gardner's views on intelligence overlap in many ways with the issues I have covered thus far, in particular in his account of how schools take a narrow view of student performance. Gardner takes exception to the ways in which schools stress two types of intelligence. The first is what he calls *linguistic* intelligence, the ability to express oneself through language. English teachers, to no one's surprise, share this emphasis on language in most aspects of teaching and learning. The second is what Gardner calls *logical/mathematical* intelligence. Emphasis on this type of intelligence is most obvious in math classes, but is also evident in the analytic focus of most writing and problem solving. As I have already described, English classes focus on analytic thinking and writing, often to the exclusion of other ways of knowing the domain (e.g., through emotions, narratives, etc.).

Gardner, who has worked as a neurologist and has read extensively on cultural history, has argued that people across time and cultures have drawn on eight types of intelligence to know and act on their worlds. His theory originally identified seven intelligences and it continues to evolve as Gardner further explores the question of human intelligence.

Historically, the linguistic and mathematical/logical intelligences so exclusively valued by modern U.S. schools have figured peripherally in the essential work of other cultures. Among Gardner's favorite examples is the ancient sailor who spent much of life at sea. The sailor had to know how to navigate ships according to stellar patterns, forecast weather, size up waves, repair and maintain the ship facility, catch fish and preserve foods attained through trade, and barter effectively once on land. The operation of the ship required sailors to employ *spatial* intelligence, which Gardner identifies as the ability to configure space in order to pose and solve problems. Spatial intelligence was fundamental to the survival of sailors and was their most important means of problem solving.

Spatial intelligence is not simply an artifact of an ancient culture, however, but vital to life for many in the modern world. Many people, for instance, still fish for a living, requiring the skills of the ancient navigators described by Gardner. Tailors, landscape architects, football coaches, engineers, artists, and others whose work requires the order of space all rely on spatial intelligence to make their way successfully in the world. With the explosion of the telecommunications and computer industry and the resultant emphasis on producing and comprehending images, spatial intelligence will undoubtedly become increasingly important in society.

Gardner identified other kinds of intelligence through which people have historically understood their worlds and solved problems. *Musical* intelligence is the ability to produce or appreciate music. Musicians, music critics, dancers, figure skaters, and others who must understand the use of rhythm, tone, melody, and other aspects of musical expression are blessed with musical intelligence.

Bodily/kinesthetic intelligence is the ability to use the body effectively in order to solve problems. Gardner distinguishes between having athletic skills and having bodily/kinesthetic intelligence; a strong and fast athlete does not necessarily use that physical giftedness in intelligent ways. Rather, a player who can "read" a playing field well and make the appropriate moves; a thespian who can suggest pathos with the arch of an eyebrow; a massage therapist who has an understanding of the body's needs and an ability to apply appropriate pressure—these and others who use their bodies to solve problems possess bodily/kinesthetic intelligence.

The ability to read and respond to the needs of others is *interpersonal* intelligence. Good teachers, therapists, salespeople, politicians, and others who deal effectively with the public often demonstrate interpersonal intelligence in their

Books on Multiple Intelligences

Christenbury, L. (Ed.). (1995). Multiple intelligences. Special theme issue of *English Journal, 84*(8).

Gardner, H. (1983). *Frames of mind: The theory of multiple intelligences.* New York: Basic Books.

Gardner, H. (1993). *Multiple intelligences: The theory into practice.* New York: Basic Books.

Gardner, H. (1999). *Intelligence reframed: Multiple intelligences for the 21st century.* New York: Basic Books.

Lazear, D. G., & Ray, H. (1999). *Eight ways of knowing: Teaching for multiple intelligences.* Arlington Heights, IL: Skylight Training.

Smagorinsky, P. (1991). *Expressions: Multiple intelligences in the English class.* Urbana, IL: National Council of Teachers of English.

communion with people. The whole notion of collaboration is predicated on the idea that people can interact successfully, requiring interpersonal intelligence.

Intrapersonal intelligence is the ability to look within oneself for self-knowledge and understanding. People who are highly reflective have intrapersonal intelligence, including those who seek and benefit from therapy, those who learn from their mistakes, those who practice yoga, and others who have the ability to come to a greater understanding of themselves.

Naturalistic intelligence allows people to distinguish among, classify, and use features of the environment. Charles Darwin is an obvious example. A teacher who reflects on the consequences of his or her teaching through careful selection and analysis of evidence would also qualify, as would students who conduct primary-source research.

Most activities in life require some combination of these intelligences. A building remodeler must have spatial intelligence to know how to reconfigure the space of a household and also interpersonal intelligence to deal effectively with customers, mathematical intelligence to operate a budget, and bodily/kinesthetic intelligence to manipulate tools properly.

As noted, however, it's possible to get through school without being assessed through most of these intelligences. When schools are set up to promote autonomy, they provide few opportunities to employ interpersonal intelligence. When schools focus on analytic thinking, they tend not to provide chances to reflect on personal issues. When budgets are cut, art and music are often sacrificed. When students are expected to sit quietly all day, they rarely have opportunities for kinesthetic performance.

FINAL THOUGHTS

In Chapters 4 and 5, I will provide illustrations of how to broaden assessment to allow for multiple intelligences to play a role in English classes. For now I simply ask you to think about how you know and do things in school and out and whether conventional approaches to schooling meet the needs of the diverse students you will be teaching.

Discussion Topic

In this chapter you've reviewed a number of different perspectives on the kinds of knowledge that schools assess and the kinds of knowledge that students have. What do you feel is appropriate for schools to assess? On what do you base this opinion?

> "I'm no longer a banker, whose primary goal is to talk and to worry about whether she can insert two more paragraphs of a lecture into students' minds before the end of class. Instead, I can become more of a midwife, who listens to students' ideas. As a midwife, I can encourage them when their ideas are not yet fully formed, and I can respond enthusiastically when they supply innovative answers. My goal is to help students develop the cognitive skills to think on their own.
>
> —Margaret Matlin"

4 Planning Backwards: How Endpoints Suggest Pathways

In this chapter I propose that it's wise to think in terms of assessment at the very earliest stages of course and unit design. If you know where students are headed, you'll have a better idea of how to teach them appropriately. As a result, students will proceed through the course and unit more confidently and purposefully because the instruction will be relevant to the work they're graded on. I illustrate this process with a hypothetical sophomore curriculum that follows the principles of planning outlined in previous chapters. In this chapter I focus on how to think in terms of a whole course and its overarching concepts, with special attention to the final assessments through which students will show their understanding of the whole course. I also discuss ways for you to produce work in conjunction with the class to show what you are learning through your engagement of the concepts with your students.

Recall the story with which I opened Chapter 3: After several weeks of discussing a play, the teacher borrowed another teacher's exam to administer. I will try to persuade you that if you plan your assessment *before* teaching rather than after, you will reduce the likelihood of disjunctures between what your students learn and what you grade. You will establish a clear, tangible goal for your teaching and for students' learning and in the process will identify what you need to be responsible for in your teaching.

In a sense, you are planning backwards—that is, you are thinking about the endpoint first and then using that goal to plan the path of instruction. To me, this is an excellent way to ensure that your teaching and assessment will be well aligned and that students will find your classes purposeful and helpful in accomplishing the unit goals.

In writing this book I am trying to practice what I preach. My ultimate goal is for you to learn how to produce a particular kind of text: a unit of instruction designed according to a set of principles. Once I set this goal for what *you* will do, I set for myself a number of teaching challenges. I need to teach you how to

- identify a topic
- choose appropriate materials
- write a rationale
- think about and choose appropriate assessments
- introduce students to the unit concepts

- write lessons that teach students how to do the things they'll be assessed on
- evaluate the texts students produce that represent what they've learned

As a teacher my task is to teach as appropriately and effectively as possible so that you can produce this culminating text to the best of your ability. Note that even though the text is specified—the task is to produce a unit of instruction—the goal is still open-ended because there are infinitely variable ways in which to write the unit. That's a balance I think you can achieve in assessing your secondary school English students. You can identify instructional goals that specify an endpoint yet allow for considerable interpretation, reconstruction, and divergent thinking by students.

In this chapter and in Chapter 5, I will illustrate how to identify appropriate, open-ended culminating texts that can serve as assessments of students' learning. My method will be to view a unit as part of a year's work that is unified by an overarching concept.

My task in this chapter is to

- conceive of a course curriculum as a related set of units that contribute to a group of ongoing, related conversations
- identify one possible curriculum and a set of instructional units that would help students work productively within it
- think about assessment for a whole course, sketching out some culminating projects for the year's (or semester's) work

SOPHOMORE YEAR ENGLISH CURRICULUM

For the purposes of illustrating curriculum development, I will design a hypothetical curriculum for the sophomore year in high school. One of the design features I would like to stress is that *the culminating projects can be produced by any student, regardless of perceived ability,* because the students are using prior knowledge as the basis for constructing new knowledge. The projects allow students to reconstruct the material they transact with in class so that they learn something new. All students, except perhaps those with severe learning disabilities, are capable of doing this.

You will recall that one of the principles of this book is that you should never, never dumb down instruction, that you should always have high expectations for your students. Although the texts of some students might impress you more than

Field Observation

Look at the curriculum for a whole course in the school you are visiting. What is the overarching concept of the curriculum as a whole? In what ways does it promote a conversation that connects and extends each unit within the curriculum? What are the consequences of using this concept as the guiding issue for the course of study? If there is no identifiable overarching concept, what unifying principles can you identify in the curriculum as a whole? What are the benefits of learning English through this unifying principle?

> I set really high expectations for my emotionally and behaviorially disordered students, and they always rise to the challenge.
>
> —Cindy Lou Peebles, Shiloh Middle School, Lithonia, Gwinnett County, Georgia

those of others, all mainstreamed students are capable of engaging with the unit as outlined in these chapters.

The Year-Long Curriculum: Overarching Concepts and Assessments

I will first consider what might serve as overarching concepts for the whole year. These themes are often suggested by the title of the course you are teaching. If you teach British literature to high school seniors, for instance, your identification of an overarching concept will be limited by the range of literature afforded by the curriculum. Often the overarching purpose for English classes in grades 7–10 is less clearly specified than it is in grades 11 and 12. In grades 7–10, the curriculum often consists of a set of skills to be learned.

In other words, the year's study is not defined by the range of literature you will read (e.g., American literature, British literature, world literature), or by any literary focus. Rather, the curriculum is governed by an anthology, and the goals are identified according to performance levels within strands. The strands typically are writing, literature, and language, and the goals identify skills that students should master within each strand (e.g., writing complete sentences, distinguishing homonyms, writing paragraphs with thesis statements, etc.). Because the curriculum in grades 7–12 typically lacks a thematic focus, you often have the latitude to identify one yourself. Keep in mind that your decisions will likely be constrained by the content of the literature anthology your school has selected.

For the purposes of this chapter, I will try to identify overarching concepts for the sophomore year that are feasible in terms of the kinds of options I typically see in schools. Even if my choices are not possible everywhere, they should illustrate the design processes I'm advocating. The question you should ask yourself is, After a year of engaging with literature and related arts, producing writing and other texts, and learning about uses of language and other forms of communication, what kinds of culminating texts can my students produce to show what they've learned? In particular, how is this learning related to a set of concepts that have recurred in our engagement with the year's materials?

In thinking about what your students will produce for this culminating assessment, you might also think about what *you* could produce that would help you understand your own learning during the year. Some teachers produce their own version of the texts required of students as a way of synthesizing their own learning during the year. In other words, you might want to demonstrate to your students that you, too, are in the process of learning by producing a culminating text to share with them.

Such a stance would reinforce a constructivist perspective because it would mean that texts, including literary texts, are continually open to reinterpretation and do not have a static, official meaning. You would also show that your engagement with them and the literature has caused you to change and learn, reinforcing the idea that educational processes should promote the construction of new meaning for both teachers and students. If you take this stance, you will likely surprise your students, who are probably accustomed to authoritative teaching in which teachers serve as experts of a stable knowledge base. In school, there are not nearly enough of these surprises.

Considerations in Curriculum Planning

Because the sophomore year does not usually have an official guiding theme, it is up to the teacher to establish one, possibly through negotiation with students, colleagues, or both. For the sophomore curriculum, the literature anthology—in conjunction with whatever mandates are issued by the state, county, district, school, and department—will constrain your choices. In all like-lihood, your anthology will be organized according to literary forms: poems, short stories, drama, nonfiction prose, and possibly a short novel.

> **Reflective Writing Prompt**
>
> When you were a middle and high school student, how often did you see an overarching purpose for the English classes you took? To what degree did your classes involve you in conversations that developed across the units of study? What were the consequences of the degree of continuity you found in the English classes you took as a student?

I have already explained why this means of organization works against the principles of planning that guide the approach of this book. You'll probably have to develop a set of overarching concepts beyond what's offered through your anthology. In addition, you'll probably end up teaching the selections in an order quite different from their order in the anthology. Such is the life of the maverick.

Types of Overarching Concepts

I am using the term *overarching concept* to describe related sets of ideas that unify a whole curriculum. The overarching concept may include, but is not limited to, the following types:

- *Theme:* A theme provides a recurring idea, question, or topic to be developed across a series of units. For an American literature curriculum, an example would be, *Whose perspective provides the American outlook?*
- *Strategy:* A strategy reinforces a particular way of approaching reading and/or writing. Broadly speaking, a strategy could encompass *attention to learning processes;* more specifically, it could focus on a particular strategy, such as *understanding narrative perspective* in texts that students both read and produce.
- *Stance:* A stance is a perspective taken toward living and learning. Some educators view schooling as an arena in which to foster a stance toward life, such as being imaginative, caring, thoughtful, inquiring, critical, tolerant, and so on.
- *Aesthetic awareness:* This type of concept focuses students' attention on questions of evaluating the quality of experiences and of artistic forms. An overarching concept in this category might be, What is beauty?
- *Body of knowledge:* A body of knowledge emphasizes a specified set of facts, such as Western heritage, as the foundation of learning.

I will elaborate on one overarching concept that could unify the sophomore curriculum, then outline other overarching concepts that might provide additional conversational threads for the course. Students might find it tiresome to have a single emphasis for a whole course, so it's wise to provide a set of overarching concepts rather than just one.

One Possible Theme: Negotiating Thresholds

When you look at what high school sophomores tend to read, you'll notice that much of it concerns some kind of transforming experience, often emerging from a conflict. This emphasis can serve as the basis for an overarching theme, such as negotiating thresholds, which explores the border between adolescence and adulthood, peer-group values and home values, and other critical junctures in the lives of tenth graders that require a decision about which direction to take.

A rationale for this overarching theme could come from the findings of developmental psychology, which sees this age as one of identity formation. If the school or community is experiencing problems with inappropriate negotiations of these thresholds—bullying, discrimination, harassment, fighting, gang involvement, and so on—then these factors could also figure into the rationale.

The theme of negotiating thresholds could suggest a series of units through which students read and produce texts dealing with some of the key conflicts they face in their midteen years. For our hypothetical curriculum, the following thematic units would serve this purpose well:

- Coming of age
- Conflict with authority
- Gangs, cliques, and peer pressure
- Discrimination

Keep in mind that thematic units are only one of several types of units you can develop. For our hypothetical curriculum, I'll suggest four other units for the year's activities. These units represent some of the other types of conceptual units I outlined in Chapter 1 and also include the open-ended approach to instruction known as a *workshop*.

- Shakespeare: *Julius Caesar* (works of a single author)
- Heroic journey (genre)
- Writing workshop
- Reading workshop

A Shakespeare unit is often required in the sophomore curriculum, and *Julius Caesar* is often included in the literature anthology. The Shakespeare unit is therefore a somewhat pragmatic choice, although it is also highly defensible from other perspectives. A unit on the heroic journey is compatible with the theme of negotiating thresholds because the genre involves the hero's overcoming of a series of obstacles in the course of the quest.

The writing or reading workshop is an open-ended block of time in which students have the opportunity to write or read about topics and genres of their choice, with the teacher serving as resource; the teacher writes or reads along with the students. Because workshops involve a complex set of managerial skills, I will not devote extensive space to them, but instead refer you to other books that explain workshops in detail. Workshops can fit well with the other overarching concepts you

Books about Workshops

Atwell, N. (Ed.). (1989). *Workshop 1 by and for teachers: Writing and literature.* Portsmouth, NH: Heinemann.

Atwell, N. (1998). *In the middle: New understandings about writing, reading, and learning* (2nd ed.). Portsmouth, NH: Heinemann.

Barbieri, M. (1994). *Workshop 6: The teacher as writer.* Portsmouth, NH: Heinemann.

Bomer, R. (1995). *Time for meaning: Crafting literate lives in middle and high school.* Portsmouth, NH: Heinemann.

Calkins, L. M. (1994). *The art of teaching writing.* Portsmouth, NH: Heinemann.

Capossela, T. L. (1993). *The critical writing workshop: Designing writing assignments to foster critical thinking.* Portsmouth, NH: Heinemann.

Hynds, S. (1997). *On the brink: Negotiating literature and life with adolescents.* New York: Teachers College Press.

Keene, E. O., & Zimmermann, S. (1997). *Mosaic of thought: Teaching comprehension in a reader's workshop.* Portsmouth, NH: Heinemann.

Krogness, M. M. (1995). *Just teach me, Mrs. K: Talking, reading, and writing with resistant adolescent learners.* Portsmouth, NH: Heinemann.

Lensmire, T. J. (1994). *When children write: Critical re-visions of the writing workshop.* New York: Teachers College Press.

Lensmire, T. J. (2000). *Powerful writing, responsible teaching.* New York: Teachers College Press.

Rief, L. (1992). *Seeking diversity: Language arts and adolescents.* Portsmouth, NH: Heinemann.

might identify for your whole course. Later I'll suggest how they might be used when emphasizing the stance of self-determination.

To provide students with varied formats and focuses, the units might be distributed and sequenced across the year as follows:

First Semester

Coming of age

Writing workshop

Heroic journey

Discrimination

Second Semester

Gangs, cliques, and peer pressure

Reading workshop

Conflict with authority

Shakespeare: *Julius Caesar*

This distribution places one workshop, two units on negotiating thresholds, and one unit from a different type of concept in each semester. Shakespeare is at the end of the year—a good location given the play's likely difficulty for many students, as it allows them to gain maturity as readers over the course of the year. This variation

Books on Narrative Perspective

Booth, W. (1974). *A rhetoric of irony.* Chicago: University of Chicago Press.

Rabinowitz, P., & Smith, M. W. (1997). *Authorizing readers: Resistance and respect in the teaching of literature.* New York: Teachers College Press.

Smith, M. W. (1991). *Understanding unreliable narrators: Reading between the lines in the literature classroom.* Urbana, IL: National Council of Teachers of English.

in focus and format should help keep students stimulated, even while they explore recurring ideas.

Other Possibilities for Overarching Concepts

I will next review overarching concepts in the other categories that could conceivably complement the negotiating thresholds theme in the sophomore English course. You would *never* use all these focuses for a single course; rather, you would identify a few that could provide conversational continuity for your class.

Strategy

Understanding Narrative Perspective.   When he taught high school English, Michael W. Smith made narrative perspective a recurring issue in students' engagement with literature (Smith, 1991). He believed that understanding literature was dependent on understanding who told the story. Central to this knowledge was the ability to recognize a narrator's limitations and how those limitations affected the narrator's reliability. Holden Caulfield in *The Catcher in the Rye,* for instance, has a uniquely jaundiced view of his world that prevents him from seeing many of his own flaws. Smith identified a set of questions that recurred in each unit of instruction, providing his classes with an overarching strategic approach, regardless of the topics covered in the units.

Cultural Modeling.   Carol Lee has argued that teachers can build on students' cultural resources when teaching them to become literate in a particular domain. For many students, school is already well aligned with their cultural resources. As many critics have pointed out, school is conducted according to the norms of the white middle class. As a result, white, middle-class students tend to be well matched to the expectations that schools have for successful performance.

Lee has argued that students from other backgrounds also bring plentiful cultural resources to school. Because the curriculum focuses on Western history and literature and on middle-class speech patterns, these resources often go untapped. Her primary interest is in African American students and their rich uses of figurative language in their daily speech. Lee has argued that teachers can do two things to help African American students have more fulfilling experiences in school:

Books about Culturally Appropriate Teaching

Delpit, L. (1995). *Other people's children: Cultural conflict in the classroom.* New York: The New Press.

Hollins, E. R. (1996). *Culture in school learning: Revealing the deep meaning.* Mahwah, NJ: Erlbaum.

Ladson-Billings, G. (1997). *The dream-keepers: Successful teachers of African-American children.* San Francisco: Jossey-Bass.

Lee, C. D. (1993). *Signifying as a scaffold for literary interpretation: The pedagogical implications of an African American discourse genre* (NCTE Research Report No. 26). Urbana, IL: National Council of Teachers of English.

Mahiri, J. (1998). *Shooting for excellence: African American and youth culture in new century schools.* New York: Teachers College Press.

- Include more literature by African American writers to allow for clearer connections to the speech and experiences of African American students
- Explicitly draw attention to figurative properties of African American English to provide students with strategies for understanding literature, not just by African American writers but by any writers who use figurative devices for making social commentary

A teacher who uses cultural modeling as an overarching strategy would routinely find ways for students to reflect on and analyze their own cultural practices, particularly their uses of language. Formal knowledge of these language practices would then serve as essential knowledge in students' experiences with literature that employs similar devices.

Dramatic Images.   Another approach that could govern a whole course would be to teach students a range of strategies for helping them visualize literature. Jeffrey Wilhelm and Brian Edmiston (1998) have described a number of strategies through which students can enact sections of stories in order to help them visualize how characters might interact and to help them make inferences about why characters think and act as they do. Others have identified various approaches to using art and drama to help students both represent their understandings of literature and develop new understandings through the process of interpretation.

Wilhelm (1997) has argued that these approaches are particularly helpful for students who resist reading. He believes that their resistance comes largely from frustration over how to make sense of texts because they have difficulty evoking those texts through images.

Stance

Critical Literacy.   Some observers of school advocate what they call *critical literacy* taught through *critical pedagogy*. Critical literacy teaches students about power relationships, particularly those involving one group or class of people that has advantages over another. Critical pedagogues have their students reflect on their own

Books about Dramatic and Artistic Responses to Literature

Smagorinsky, P. (1991). *Expressions: Multiple intelligences in the English class.* Urbana, IL: National Council of Teachers of English.

Wagner, B. J. (Ed.). (1999). *Building moral communities through educational drama.* Stamford, CT: Ablex.

Wilhelm, J. D. (1997). *You gotta BE the book.* New York: Teachers College Press; Urbana, IL: National Council of Teachers of English.

Wilhelm, J. D., & Edmiston, B. (1998). *Imagining to learn: Inquiry, ethics, and integration through drama.* Portsmouth, NH: Heinemann.

status and examine how their communities and nation favor some groups of people over others. If you were to emphasize critical literacy as an overarching stance, you would routinely have students ask questions about who has power and why. These questions can be directed toward any kind of human relationship:

- School (e.g., What kinds of people make decisions? Who serves in menial positions?)
- Classroom (e.g., Which students speak about what? Whose opinions are likely to be favorably rewarded?)
- Characters in literature (e.g., How are characters of different classes, genders, and races portrayed by writers of different classes, genders, and races?)
- Traditional literary canon (e.g., Which authors have privileged status? Which topics and themes have privileged status?)
- Society as a whole (e.g., How are class, gender, and race implicated in power relationships in society?)

Self-Determination.   Some teachers believe that education should be geared toward helping students determine who they are and what their purposes are and that the role of the teacher is to provide the environment in which students work, without specifying what that work is or which standards it should meet. Teachers who embrace this belief would employ the most student oriented approaches designed in this book: negotiating the curriculum with students, using book clubs or literature circles to discuss novels, establishing writing workshops, and so on.

Multicultural Awareness.   As I write this book, the term *multiculturalism* is quite the rage. I use the term *rage* in two senses: It is a fiercely advocated trend in colleges of education and many school curricula, and it has caused outcry and equally fierce opposition among traditionalists, who wish to preserve the status quo in schools. Whereas a traditionalist would advocate preserving the literary canon, a multiculturalist would want to diversify it to include more women; authors of color; gay, lesbian, bisexual, or transsexual authors, and authors from traditionally underrepresented nations and cultures. A multicultural stance would perhaps include a heavy dose of critical literacy, critiquing established norms and questioning why things are as they are, as well as a concerted effort to read authors from diverse backgrounds and to consider the ways in which cultural practices contribute to different worldviews.

Books about Critical Literacy

Freire, P. (1995). *Pedagogy of the oppressed.* New York: Continuum.

Giroux, H. (Ed.). (1997). *Counternarratives: Cultural studies and critical pedagogies in postmodern spaces.* New York: Routledge.

hooks, b. (1994). *Teaching to transgress: Education as the practice of freedom.* New York: Routledge.

Luke, A. (1988). *Literacy, textbooks and ideology.* New York: Falmer.

McLaren, P. (1997). *Life in schools: An introduction to critical pedagogy in the foundations of education.* Boston: Addison-Wesley.

Shor, I. (1996). *When students have power: Negotiating authority in a critical pedagogy.* Chicago: University of Chicago Press.

Aesthetic Awareness

Beauty, Truth, Goodness.   Howard Gardner, in *The Disciplined Mind,* argues that education ought to be concerned with the ancient considerations of inquiring into what is beautiful, true, and good. If a teacher were to adopt this as an overarching concept, students would continually ask a set of questions when considering literature: By what criteria do I distinguish the aesthetic quality of a text? What eternal truths does the literature suggest? What notion of virtue does the author promote? What does it mean to be good, true, and beautiful?

Body of Knowledge

Cultural Literacy.   Earlier I referred to multicultural awareness. On the opposite end of this spectrum is what E. D. Hirsch (1987) calls "cultural literacy." To Hirsch, education ought to reinforce the history and cultural practices of the West—societies that have roots in western Europe, including the United States. Rather than focusing on pluralism, Hirsch argues that students need to be well versed in the history and cultural icons that formed the middle-class norms that a critical pedagogue would question. He advocates a transmission approach to conveying this cultural knowledge, which he feels is central to successful participation in U.S. society.

> "The schools ain't what they used to be and never was.
>
> —Will Rogers

Summary

My review here is hardly complete. A number of other worthwhile goals for schooling have been identified by others that could serve as overarching concepts. The goals that you identify for a whole course will be a consequence of a variety of factors. I will not advocate any one over any other, but instead will encourage you to think about the importance of having a limited set of overarching concepts to serve as the conversational thread across a whole course of study. How you arrive at them (e.g., through your own choice, through negotiation with colleagues, through negotiation with students) and how you put them into practice are questions that deserve considerable thought. Next,

Books about Multicultural Approaches to Education

Ada, A. F., Harris, V. J., & Hopkins, L. B. (1993). *A chorus of cultures: Developing literacy through multicultural poetry.* Carmel, CA: Hampton-Brown.

Banks, J. A. (1998). *An introduction to multicultural education* (2nd ed.). Boston: Allyn & Bacon.

Goldberg, M. R. (1997). *Arts and learning: An integrated approach to teaching and learning in multicultural and multilingual settings.* New York: Longman.

Grant, C. (Ed.). (1997). *Dictionary of multicultural education.* Phoenix, AZ: Oryx Press.

Harris, V. J. (Ed.). (1993). *Teaching multicultural literature in grades K–8.* Norwood, MA: Christopher-Gordon.

Tiedt, P. L., & Tiedt, I. M. (1999). *Multicultural teaching: A handbook of activities, information, and resources* (5th ed.) Boston: Allyn & Bacon.

I will illustrate how you might think of assessments through which students synthesize ideas from the whole course that are related to particular themes.

Discussion Topic

What are the consequences of using different overarching concepts to unify a whole course? Which combinations of overarching concepts might work well together? In addition to the overarching concepts identified here, what might be worthwhile ways to unify a whole course curriculum?

ASSESSING STUDENTS FOR A WHOLE COURSE

One overarching concept for the sophomore course I am designing will be the theme of negotiating thresholds. I have already provided a brief rationale for this theme.

Books about Emphasizing Western Culture

Adler, M. J. (1999). *The great ideas: A lexicon of Western thought.* New York: Scribner.

Bloom, A. (1987). *The closing of the American mind.* New York: Simon & Schuster.

Ellis, J. M. (1997). *Literature lost: Social agendas and the corruption of the humanities.* New Haven, CT: Yale University Press.

Hirsch, E. D. (1987). *Cultural literacy: What every American should know.* Boston: Houghton Mifflin.

Ravitch, D. (1991). *The American reader: Words that moved a nation.* New York: HarperCollins.

Stotsky, S. (1999). *Losing our language: How multicultural classroom instruction is undermining our children's ability to read, write, and reason.* New York: The Free Press.

Webster, Y. O. (1997). *Against the multicultural agenda.* Westport, CT: Praeger.

With this overarching concept serving to provide continuity across these units, I next consider what students might do at the end of the year to synthesize their understanding of the year's work. It is possible that you will need to think in terms of semesters rather than years, depending on how your curriculum is set up and on how many students change courses at the semester break. My reference to a year's final exam might need adjustment depending on how your school is organized and conducted. A school that has adopted block scheduling, for instance, might have students take each course for one semester only, attending each class for 80–90 minutes a day.

I will identify a set of possible culminating texts for a whole course of study. You are not likely to use all these texts for a single course. My goal here is to identify a variety of *types of assessments* that can help students *synthesize their knowledge* from the year and *construct new knowledge* through the process of producing them. I will review the following:

- Assessment of the students' own learning about learning through a *portfolio.* This kind of assessment fits well with an overarching stance of self-determination, as the portfolio helps students determine what they have learned and what they have learned it from.
- Assessment of the students' understanding and evaluation of literary form through an *extended definition of good literature.* This kind of assessment suits Gardner's emphasis on aesthetic awareness and his belief that students should consider what is beautiful, true, and good. Students would apply Gardner's considerations to the question of what counts as quality literature.
- Assessment of the students' learning about the year's overarching concept through a *multimedia project,* synthesizing knowledge gained from the year's engagement with texts and classroom activities. This kind of assessment combines the course's attention to negotiating thresholds with its emphasis on the strategy of generating dramatic images.
- Assessment of the students' understanding of the literary texts through an *essay analyzing literary characters' changes* in relation to the overarching concept. This type of assessment takes a paradigmatic approach to understanding the theme of negotiating thresholds.
- *Assessment developed by students* based on their own construction of the purpose of the course. This type of assessment fits the stance of self-determination.

Each of these types of assessments provides an opportunity for students to learn something new in a different arena. Through the portfolio they can learn about how and what they have learned. Through the extended definition they can learn how they evaluate literature. Through the multimedia project they can generate an image that both shows their learning and enables them to learn something new about the year's work. Through the analytic essay they can learn about the literature they have studied.

Again, doing all of these projects for a single course—particularly if students do them earnestly and in detail—would probably be more than they could manage without shortchanging some. Rather, this discussion is meant to illustrate possible ways in which a course final exam can enable students to construct new meaning through engagement with the course's overarching concepts and the materials and activities through which they have explored them.

In Chapter 5, I will review how to develop *assessment rubrics* to evaluate culminating projects. For now, I will outline the projects themselves.

Portfolio

A portfolio is a culminating project that serves any curriculum well. Portfolio assessment is borrowed from the world of the arts, where artists use a collection of representative works as a way of showing their prowess to galleries, customers, art
schools, and other venues for their work. The idea is that rather than having each
and every effort evaluated, an artist (or student) works at a variety of projects—some
of which are abandoned or turn out poorly, others of which turn out well—and then
chooses the best products for evaluation. This conception of assessment assumes
that not all work is intended to be graded and that evaluation should focus on the
work that best represents the person's ability.

In education, the idea of a portfolio has been adapted rather than adopted
wholesale. Indeed, a portfolio can be assembled in a variety of ways. For the culminating project for the sophomore curriculum, I will focus on a kind of portfolio
called the *process portfolio*. This type of portfolio is unique in that its purpose is to
encourage students to reflect on their learning processes rather than to feature their
best work (which is the artist's approach, known as a *showcase portfolio*). A process
portfolio gives students the opportunity to go through their year's work and select
artifacts that demonstrate key learning experiences. A key learning experience is not
necessarily reflected in a polished, final product. In a process portfolio, the artifacts
(referred to also as *exhibits*) may include

- something that received a poor grade, yet through which the student learned
  something about the topic, the importance of good work habits, and so on
- a rough draft for a piece of writing, rather than the final draft, if the rough
  draft served as an occasion for significant learning or if the rough draft
  received feedback that contributed to new understanding
- an abandoned effort, if the abandonment came about through an important
  realization
- a text produced by someone else, if through reading that text the student
  gained critical new insights

In other words, the purpose of a process portfolio is to trace and reflect on significant learning through the exhibition of key learning experiences, regardless of
whether those experiences are reflected in rough, unfinished, or polished texts. A
showcase portfolio, in contrast, would feature the student's "best" work as a way of
demonstrating the most successful *products* of learning.

The process portfolio assignment might look like this:

Throughout the year you have had a lot of experiences with literature and other
art forms. In response to these texts, you have produced a variety of pieces of
writing, art, and other forms of expression. Presumably you have learned something about yourself, the literature, how to write, how to read, and other things.

Your culminating project for the year is to prepare a portfolio in which you
present things you've produced that have resulted in your most valuable learning. We will call these things *exhibits*. The exhibits you present do not need to

Books about Portfolio Assessment

Belanoff, P., & Dickson, M. (Eds.). (1991). *Portfolios: Process and product.* Portsmouth, NH: Heinemann.

Black, L., Daiker, D., Sommers, J., & Stygall, G. (Eds.). (1994). *New directions in portfolio assessment: Reflective practice, critical theory, and large-scale scoring.* Portsmouth, NH: Heinemann.

Calfee R., & Perfumo, P. (1996). *Writing portfolios in the classroom.* Hillsdale, NJ: Erlbaum.

Darling-Hammond, L., Ancess, J., & Falk, B. (1995). *Authentic assessment in action: Studies of schools and students at work.* New York: Teachers College Press.

Graves, D., & Sunstein, B. (1992). *Portfolio portraits.* Portsmouth, NH: Heinemann.

Hewitt, G. (1995). *A portfolio primer: Teaching, collecting, and assessing student writing.* Portsmouth, NH: Heinemann.

Tierney, R., Carter, M., & Desai, L. (1991). *Portfolio assessment in the reading-writing classroom.* Norwood, MA: Christopher-Gordon.

Yancey, K. B. (Ed.). (1992). *Portfolios in the writing classroom: An introduction.* Urbana, IL: National Council of Teachers of English.

Yancey, K. B., & Weiser, I. (Eds.). (1997). *Situating portfolios: Four perspectives.* Urbana, IL: National Council of Teachers of English.

be your best work. Often we learn the most from our rough drafts, our frustrated efforts, and other experiences that do not yield our best products. *You will not be graded on the quality of the exhibits that you include.* Rather, you will be graded on how carefully you reflect on what you learned from producing them.

Your portfolio should include:

- title page with name and date.
- a minimum of eight items that serve as your exhibits. You must include a minimum of one exhibit for each of the eight units we studied. Your portfolio may include additional exhibits if you wish, including things from outside this class.
- a written statement that identifies and discusses significant learning based on each exhibit, consisting of a minimum of 200 words.
- a longer *synthesis paper,* in which you discuss how these artifacts as a whole reveal what you've learned this year both about yourself and about the material we have studied, consisting of a minimum of 1,000 words (roughly four typed pages).

If you plan to use a portfolio assessment of any kind, *students need to know this at the beginning of the year* so that they know to save their work. Students need to know that if they don't save their work, they may do poorly on the final evaluation for the course, which will require them to reflect on something from each unit studied. You might need to weave instruction in reflective thinking into each unit, stressing to students that they need to save at least one exhibit from that unit for their portfolios. You might want to provide models of successful portfolios, particularly if students are not required to produce them elsewhere in your school. You could use these models throughout the year to help students assemble their portfolio materials as they work on each unit. Doing so would also reinforce the constructivist, reflective emphasis of your teaching during the process of each unit.

Extended Definition of Good Literature

Elliot Eisner (1985) has argued that one way to know something is through an understanding and appreciation of its form, which he calls *aesthetic knowledge.* To Eisner, it's important to understand how things are made, how their ultimate form suggests meaning, and how the aesthetics of art enhance the quality of life.

Eisner's attention to aesthetic knowledge can be taken several ways. To a transmission-oriented teacher, it might imply a duty to explain to students the aesthetic aspects of literature—Shakespeare's metaphors, the rhyme scheme he employs in particular kinds of verse, and other aspects of form—and then assess students' knowledge of them on a test. As you can imagine, I would recommend minimizing this kind of attention to literary form, limiting it to whatever formal knowledge students find useful in making sense of literature. If you simply lecture students about the difference between synecdoche and metonymy without engaging them in literary reading in which they find this distinction useful, and then give them a test in which they match terms to definitions without using them in some productive way, they will likely forget the distinction soon after the exam.

My preferred alternative would be for aesthetic knowledge to serve as one of the overarching concepts for a course of study. Rather than taking the typical textbook approach of memorizing a technical vocabulary and adopting the values of literary critics in evaluating literature, imagine telling students that their task for the year is to develop criteria for evaluating the quality of literature. If this were a goal of instruction, classroom time would need to be devoted to discussing the relative merits of different literary works. Students are rather quick to express their opinions on whether they like a text or not. Rare is the teacher who hasn't heard, "This book's boring!" or "What a stupid story" or some similar point of view in response to a text. Such comments are rarely treated as legitimate in classrooms, where the typical response from the teacher is to ignore or suppress negative evaluations of literature and simply to continue to discuss it.

Yet such comments could serve as the starting point for helping students articulate what they see as quality in literature (and the lack thereof). Why is a story boring? What makes literature interesting? Is it possible for a boring story to be a good work of literature? Can literature that someone finds personally offensive still be quality literature? Is it possible for different people to have different conceptions of what counts as good literature?

If these questions are routinely asked during literary discussions, and if you as a teacher consistently help students formulate their opinions into criteria for a definition of quality literature, then you are helping them develop a formal understanding of what they think good literature is. You need to provide instruction in how to write extended definitions as well. If you are effective in both these areas, you might be able to ask students to do the following on a final exam:

> Throughout the year you have read a variety of texts: poems, short stories, plays, novels, essays, songs, and more. You have undoubtedly liked some of these better than others. For your final exam, write an essay in which you ex-

plain what distinguishes quality literature from other literature. To do so, provide the following:

- A set of *criteria* or rules that state clearly what each literary quality is
- For each criterion, an *example* from literature we have read this year (including literature you have read on your own) that illustrates the rule at work
- For each criterion, a *counterexample* from literature we have read this year (including literature you have read on your own) that illustrates literature that comes close to meeting the conditions of the rule, but falls short in some way
- For each example and counterexample, a *warrant* that clearly explains why the criterion is or is not being met
- For your whole argument, a *counterargument* expressing the viewpoint of someone who might disagree with you
- For the counterargument, a *rebuttal* in which you defend your position

This final exam suggests the need for a constructivist classroom with an aesthetic focus and reliance on exploratory talk. The final evaluation is primarily logical/analytic—that is, paradigmatic—yet the year's activities can include a variety of approaches to thinking about what makes good literature. The purpose of the class is established from the outset, allowing students to work confidently toward a worthwhile goal. They are engaging in a practice central to their domain, the construction of criteria for evaluating literature.

Those criteria might vary from student to student. One student may decide that literature ought to be primarily entertaining, another might feel it should ring true emotionally, still another might feel it should make a statement about the human condition, and so on. The assessment of their knowledge will be based on how effectively they construct their argument, rather than on how close their opinion is to the teacher's or to that of professional literary critics.

This kind of assessment would be fitting for the approaches to curriculum outlined in Chapter 1 in which students contribute to the selection of the texts they read, providing an appropriate dialectic between the discussions about text selection and the development of criteria for text selection.

Multimedia Project

A third kind of culminating project would enable students to reflect on how they have changed personally through their engagement with the year's reading and activities, with special attention to the overarching concept (negotiating thresholds). The year's activities should include reflection on the themes of each unit, contributing to the conversation surrounding this overarching concept. For instance, students might have kept a journal in which they reflected on their own conflicts with authority, experiences with peer groups, coming-of-age experiences, and so on. They might have written personal narratives describing such experiences. They might have produced art, music, or drama depict-

> " I try to make my students life-long learners. If you can make learning fun and they can enjoy what they're doing, they'll want to continue learning. "
>
> –Carol Hall,
> Hilsman Middle School,
> Clarke County, Georgia

ing their experiences. In other words, if this theme has consistently served as the conversational thread running through the units, students should be conversant in thinking about how their own lives have changed in relation to the changes they have seen in literary characters.

These reflections can be brought together in a culminating project, produced in a form of the student's choice. It might be a personal narrative in which students recount and reflect on key experiences through which they have negotiated thresholds. The narrative could be a conventional written story or it could rely on other artistic tools, including the capabilities offered by computer software. It could be a song that depicts threshold experiences, perhaps performed and/or recorded. It could be a drama, written and/or performed. It could be sculpture, painting, or other rendition. And, of course, it could combine a range of media and genres chosen by the student (see, e.g., Romano, 1995).

Such an assignment might look like this:

> Throughout the year we have read a series of texts that concerned the theme of *negotiating thresholds.* Undoubtedly, like the literary characters, you have negotiated thresholds yourself in the last year or so. You entered the class fresh out of ninth grade and now are prepared to become a high school junior. During this time you have gone from being among the youngest students in the school to being among the older half, bringing about changes in expectations, peer groups, relationships with adults, cultural groups, and many other things.
>
> For your culminating project for the year, your assignment is to produce a text that in some way depicts how you have personally negotiated significant thresholds during the year. You have had many opportunities to reflect on such experiences during previous units of study. For your culminating project, select one significant experience, or one set of related experiences, and use your project to depict how you have changed.
>
> Your project can take any form you choose. Possible forms include:
>
> - A written narrative about a significant experience or set of experiences
> - A narrative about a significant experience or set of experiences produced in a different form (song, computer graphics, cartoon series, drama, or other medium)
> - A work of art that depicts the experience and how you have changed; be prepared to explain how the work of art accomplishes your goals
> - A text that combines any of these forms and others to depict your changes

This project could enable students to reflect on how their schooling has helped them realize personal growth. The major disadvantage is that it is not easy to assess; many teachers avoid projects of this sort because they feel it's hard to grade them objectively. My recommendation would be to grade it as you would a portfolio, focusing on the extent to which the student accounts for change (or lack thereof). In order to do this, you might find it helpful for some projects (e.g., a sculpture) to be accompanied by an oral or written explanation.

Analytic Essay

The assessments thus far have focused on the students and how they have learned about their own learning, their development of aesthetic criteria, and their personal changes in relation to the year's overarching concept. Teachers may also feel the need to assess students on their understanding of the literature studied. Often these assessments are administered by requiring students to answer questions about their memory of facts from the literature: whether Ponyboy was a Greaser or a Soc, whether S. E. Hinton was a man or a woman, whether Dan'l Webster was a frog or a toad.

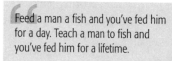 Feed a man a fish and you've fed him for a day. Teach a man to fish and you've fed him for a lifetime.

—Saying

Such assessments, although easy to grade and presumably objective, are questionable because they require the repetition of superficial knowledge and do not enable students to construct any new meaning during the process of assessment. I would advocate instead some kind of extended writing, which is more likely to encourage complex thinking through which students can synthesize and extend their knowledge. To write an extended essay on the year's worth of literature centered on the theme of negotiating thresholds, students might do the following:

> During the year you have read about a great many characters negotiating a variety of thresholds, some successfully, some not. For your final exam, your task is to write an essay in which you select three literary protagonists from our year's reading and explain how effectively each one negotiated a significant threshold in the literature. Each protagonist should come from a different unit of study. To do this, you will need to:
>
> - Describe the threshold being negotiated (e.g., a conflict between two social groups, a conflict between two sets of goals, a change between two stages of maturity, etc.)
> - Describe the conflicts involved and why the situation is problematic for the protagonist
> - Describe how the threshold is negotiated
> - Evaluate whether the threshold was well negotiated or not
>
> From your description of these three protagonists' experiences, draw a conclusion about how to negotiate a threshold. Make sure to refer to all three protagonists and contrast their negotiations.

Evaluating this kind of final exam will take you much longer than it takes to grade an objective test. You can't take these essays and run them through a scanner, then compute the grade by adding up the number of correct answers. Rather, you have to read them carefully and apply some kind of evaluative criteria, likely involving a complex set of factors: the detail of the reviews of the protagonists' experiences, the faithfulness to some kind of language standard, the insight of the synthesis at the end, and so on.

Although a rubric can reduce the chance of impressionistic (and therefore inconsistent) grading, you are being subjective in your evaluation, a problem that causes many teachers to resort to the factual assessments that support authoritarian schooling.

In many schools teachers are urged to use objective evaluations. Furthermore, when administrators decide that teachers' final grades are due within a day of the last exam period, they strongly discourage teachers from using extended writing on final exams.

However, extended writing gives the students the opportunity to develop their writing skills, synthesize personal and textual knowledge, and construct new knowledge through their reflection on the year's experiences and engagements with literature. In my view, providing them with this opportunity more than makes up for whatever additional time you must spend grading them and whatever consequences come from risking subjectivity in your evaluation.

Assessment Developed by Students

Another way to approach a final assessment is to dedicate class time toward the end of the course to having students generate tasks and questions through which their engagement with the course can be evaluated. This kind of assessment fits well with a teaching approach in which students help to plan the curriculum, with any approach that falls within a constructivist perspective, and with the overarching concept of self-determination. Essentially, it relies on students to reveal what they have learned through their identification of authentic tasks and projects that demonstrate how they have constructed the purpose of the class. Students could either generate a menu of tasks, projects, or questions, or negotiate a classwide project. They could then be called on to develop a scoring rubric through which their work would be evaluated and possibly participate in the evaluation themselves.

Taking this approach requires a key role for the teacher, that of insuring that students generate tasks that meet both their own sense of authenticity and the school's notion of rigorous assessment. Students need to know that if they design a frivolous assessment, you have a responsibility to the community to replace it with something more fitting. Teachers might need to identify a set of guidelines for student-designed assessments. You might specify, for instance, that the culminating text must

- account for material from each individual unit of study from the course
- synthesize knowledge across the various units
- meet the expectations of some literate community
- reveal a construction of new knowledge
- communicate effectively with the specified audience

You might identify other requirements, depending on the particular experiences you and your students have had within the course. If, for instance, your overarching concept is designed to address a community-wide problem, such as environmental contamination, students might submit their final exams to the city mayor or to another official. Doing so would both provide them with an opportunity for social action and give them an audience for their exams beyond the teacher.

Designing this assessment could follow any one of a number of processes. Students could start by generating possible tasks in small groups, and then explain them to the whole class, with the teacher orchestrating the discussion. Once each group has presented its ideas, the class as a whole could negotiate some kind of agreement as to which one would serve as the most fruitful opportunity for a final assessment. Another possibility would be for the class to generate a menu of exam possibilities from which individual students or collaborative groups could choose.

Identify Culminating Texts

In Chapter 2, you began thinking about a whole course curriculum and particular units within it. For this curriculum, identify a set of culminating texts that students might produce in conjunction with the year's overarching themes. Present them in the manner described above

- In language addressing the students, write a description of the text that students will ultimately produce.
- Explain its relationship to the course emphasis.
- In bulleted items, present the specific requirements for successfully producing the text.

Taking this approach is a departure from the other assessments reviewed in this chapter in that the specific mode of assessment is developed at the end, rather than the beginning, of the course. It does meet the spirit of the general approach, however, in that it is responsive to the content and process of the instruction that leads to it. What distinguishes this approach is that the students determine what is significant about the class and identify assessment vehicles through which they can synthesize their understanding and create new knowledge.

CULMINATING TEXTS FOR TEACHERS

Throughout this chapter I have referred to the ways in which teachers can produce texts during the year as ways to construct meaning from their teaching. A teacher's text production can also demonstrate to students that the teacher is a learner in the class. I'll next review some possible ways in which you can compose a text that contributes to your own learning and can show others how you have changed through your teaching.

Work That Parallels Student Work

One way to reflect on your teaching is to produce the same culminating assignment that your students are producing. This approach works best on open-ended projects, such as keeping a portfolio, producing a multimedia text that synthesizes your experiences and understandings, or maintaining a journal or log in which you do a naturalistic study of your own teaching.

Portfolio

If you were to keep a process portfolio, your exhibits could include student work that taught you something about your teaching, feedback on unit evaluations, excerpts from a log you've kept on your teaching, or other artifacts through which you learned how to be a better teacher. As with student portfolios,

> A reflective pedagogy represents—and requires—dependable strategies and introspective dimensions. Like the conscious and unconscious rhythms of the body, there is a corporeal and visceral texture to teaching. There are lineaments that are profoundly familiar, if inexplicable. Teaching is sustained and stabilized by the recognized images that repeated reflection offers—the predictable academic sequences and settings of communication and exchange.
>
> —Patricia C. Phillips

the purpose would be to reflect on what you've learned, rather than to showcase your best work. Students would undoubtedly be interested in knowing what you learned from teaching them and how you will teach differently as a result of their experiences in your class.

Multimedia Project

You could produce a creative or multimedia project that represents what you've experienced and learned through your teaching. A good example of this comes from Cindy Cotner, a teacher in central Oklahoma. A few years ago Cindy was an administrator with the Oklahoma Writing Project and also a school consultant for the Oklahoma Endowment for the Humanities. She ran terrific workshops for students in which she helped them use art across the curriculum. She was also enrolled in a graduate program at the University of Oklahoma, where I was teaching. For one of my courses, Cindy created a collage that synthesized her understanding of what it means to be a teacher. A reproduced version of her collage was published in the *English Journal,* the leading practitioner journal in the field (see *English Journal,* 1996, 85 (5), p. 62). Producing some kind of creative work that represents your teaching experiences might fascinate your students and help them view artistic composing as more legitimate in school.

Teaching Log

If your students are keeping journals or reading logs, you could also maintain a teaching log in which you reflect on your teaching. Through a teaching log you can identify problems with your teaching and think about how to make appropriate changes. You can think about how a unit is working and whether it works better for some students than others. You can think about classroom dynamics, school politics, curriculum debates, media views of education, or other issues that affect how you think about your work. A number of excellent books have been published that feature teachers reflecting on their own practice. This reflection often begins with the kinds of observations teachers make in their teaching logs.

Ethnographic Experiments

In Chapter 2 I referred to Luis Moll's idea of conducting inquiries into what he calls the *cultural resources* of students by getting to know students and their families outside school. His work in the Tucson area is designed to bridge the cultural gap between middle-class teachers and the working class Mexican American students they teach. These students often do poorly in school, yet engage in sophisticated cognitive lives at home and in the community. Moll's idea is for teachers to get a better understanding of students' competencies outside school and adjust instruction so that the students can build on these strengths and resources in their classroom work.

This work entails getting out into the community and observing students and their families at work. You might not feel comfortable inviting yourself into the homes of your students, and that's understandable. There are, however, arenas in which you may feel more at ease, such as community centers, public parks, after-school programs, the YMCA, or other centers of public activity. You might coach a youth sports team, get involved in scouting, or otherwise participate in community life so as to better understand the strengths of students that aren't so apparent in school. The main consequence of this action would be to rethink your teaching so as to build on these strengths in students' formal academic evaluation.

Moll also believes that communities will develop greater respect and trust for teachers if teachers develop these sorts of relationships. Students will be more likely to trust that a teacher's decisions are in their interests and less likely to resist both the system and individual teachers.

Moll has found that community studies of this sort work best when they are conducted by teams of teachers. Working in a team allows for the sharing of ideas and impressions, collaboration in the development of new teaching approaches, and support for one another's efforts. Conducting ethnographic experiments is obviously a lot of work and would place great demands on your time. They have the potential, however, to help you teach in ways that recognize and take advantage of the strengths your students have that are typically overlooked in schools.

Frame Experiments

In *Teaching Writing as Reflective Practice (1995)*, George Hillocks argues that teachers can learn a great deal about their teaching by conducting frame experiments; that is, by adopting a disposition about teaching that involves continual inquiry into the consequences of teaching methods. These might involve comparative studies, such as teaching two classes differently and contrasting student work produced in response to the two approaches. They might involve experimenting with new methods—using more drama, using small groups in different ways, trying writing workshops—and taking careful notes on the changes that result in the classroom.

Studies of Classroom Relationships

In *Inside City Schools: Investigating Literacy in Multicultural Classrooms, (1999)* Sarah Freedman and colleagues report on a project in which a group of teachers studied the ways in which relationships played out in the classrooms in response to changes they made in their teaching. Unlike Hillocks, who was interested in how teaching affects student schoolwork, the teachers working with Freedman were concerned with how to set up strong classroom communities. In a typical study, a teacher in an urban, multiracial school would assign literature that focused on racial conflict and observe how relationships among students changed. For teachers interested in the relational aspects of schooling, this approach can reveal the kinds of feelings that often simmer beneath the surface of classroom order.

Electronic Conversations

Another activity you can engage in is to subscribe to a professional·*listserve*. A listserve is a computer-mediated discussion conducted through email. Anyone anywhere on earth with a computer can subscribe for free. Usually listserve discussions are organized around topics from very broad to very specific. NCTE-talk, for instance, is simply about teaching English and can cover any issue raised by its subscribers. Teachers Applying Whole Language (TAWL) is more specific; still more focused is Gay, Lesbian, Bisexual Teachers of Speakers of Other Languages (GLESOL).

Books on Teacher Research

Allen, J., Cary, M., & Delgado, L. (1995). *Exploring blue highways.* New York: Teachers College Press.

Anderson, G., Herr, K., & Nihlem, A. (1994). *Studying your own school: An educator's guide to qualitative practitioner research.* Thousand Oaks, CA: Corwin Press.

Atwell, N. (1998). *In the middle: New understandings about writing, reading, and learning* (2nd ed.). Portsmouth, NH: Heinemann.

Cochran-Smith, M., & Lytle, S. (Eds.) (1993). *Inside/outside: Teacher research and knowledge.* New York: Teachers College Press.

Freedman, S. W., Simons, E. R., Kalnin, J. S., Casareno, A., & The M-CLASS teams. (1999). *Inside city schools: Investigating literacy in multicultural classrooms.* New York: Teachers College Press.

Gallas, K. (1994). *The languages of learning: How children talk, write, dance, draw, and sing their understanding of the world.* New York: Teachers College Press.

Gallas, K. (1995). *Talking their way into science: Hearing children's questions and theories, responding with curricula.* New York: Teachers College Press.

Gallas, K. (1997). *Sometimes I can be anything: Power, gender, and identity in a primary classroom.* New York: Teachers College Press.

Goswami, D., & Stillman, P. (Eds.). (1987). *Reclaiming the classroom: Teacher research as an agency for change.* Portsmouth, NH: Heinemann.

Krogness, M. M. (1995). *Just teach me, Mrs. K: Talking, reading, and writing with resistant adolescent learners.* Portsmouth, NH: Heinemann.

Mohr, M., & MacLean, M. (1987). *Working together: A guide for teacher-researchers.* Urbana, IL: National Council of Teachers of English.

Noden, H. R. (1999). *Image grammar: Using grammatical structures to teach writing.* Portsmouth, NH: Heinemann.

Pappas, C., & Zecker, Z. L. (1998). *Teacher inquiries in literacy teaching-learning: Learning to collaborate in elementary urban classrooms.* Mahwah, NJ: Erlbaum.

Ray, R. (1993). *The practice of theory: Teacher research in composition.* Urbana, IL: National Council of Teachers of English.

Rief, L. (1992). *Seeking diversity: Language arts and adolescents.* Portsmouth, NH: Heinemann.

Wells, G., Bernard, L., Gianotti, M. A., Keating, C., Konjevic, C., Kowal, M., Maher, A., Mayer, C., Moscoe, T., Orzechowska, E., Smieja, A., & Swartz, L. (1994). *Changing schools from within: Creating communities of inquiry.* Toronto: OISE Press; Portsmouth, NH: Heinemann.

Whitin, P. (1996). *Sketching stories, stretching minds.* Portsmouth, NH: Heinemann.

Wilhelm, J. D. (1997). *You gotta BE the book.* New York: Teachers College Press; Urbana, IL: National Council of Teachers of English.

Rationale

Return to the rationale you wrote earlier. Reread it and see how well it fits your unit as you are developing it. If need be, reconsider your rationale by adjusting its focus, adding or revising major points, adding or revising the evidence you provide, adding to or revising your rebuttals, and revoicing your rhetoric and points to suit potential readerships.

A listserve can provide a broad-based conversation that's unavailable in any single school. It can help you see how teaching conditions are in other schools, how teachers approach problems from other perspectives, and how you can form professional networks to help you grow as an educator. You could prepare a listserve portfolio in which you print out contributions that you found provocative and reflect on how they've helped you rethink your teaching. Students would be interested to know that you view yourself as part of a larger community of inquiry and that your experiences with them are central to your identity as a person.

A large index of email discussion groups is available at http://www.ncte.org/rte/links5.html#E-mail Discussion Groups. The National Council of Teachers of English (http://www.ncte.org) also hosts its own array of listserves concerned with the teaching of English.

FINAL THOUGHTS

This chapter has focused on

- how to think about instructional goals for the whole year (or other time limit for a course)
- how to develop those goals within the umbrella provided by a set of overarching concepts
- how to identify a related set of units that contribute to the conversation centered on those concepts
- how to assess students on the projects in which they synthesize their knowledge for the whole course
- how to construct meaning from your own teaching through a range of inquiries that generally are known as *teacher research, practitioner research, action research,* or *reflective practice.*

In the next chapter, I look at how to develop individual units within the context of these whole-course goals.

CHAPTER 5

Setting and Assessing Unit Goals

This chapter moves from course-level planning to unit-level planning, with a focus on identifying the major assessments: Knowing how students will be assessed should help you make decisions about how to plan the particular lessons of the unit. I review both conventional and alternative assessments. Conventional assessments are ones you are probably already familiar with from your own schooling: analytic essays, extended definitions, research reports, and so on. Alternative assessments are derived from the kinds of knowledge reviewed in Chapter 3: exploratory, narrative, connected, multimedia/multigenre ways of knowing, and unconventional and/or creative modes of expression. On the whole, I recommend a balanced approach that involves both conventional and alternative assessments.

PRELIMINARIES

In this chapter we will set goals for individual units that contribute to the course-long conversation about negotiating thresholds. Once again, we will "plan backwards" in thinking about assessment, that is, I will think first about what kinds of culminating texts students could ultimately produce from engagement with the unit material. These texts will then serve as goals when planning the path of instruction, a topic we will take up in Chapters 6 through 8. These are also the texts you will assess to give students grades for the class.

Constructing Units, Constructing Texts

Throughout this book, I have used metaphors of *construction* to help illustrate processes of teaching and learning. I would like to extend that metaphor now to give you a concrete idea of how to think about planning unit goals and the instruction that leads to them. I encourage you to think of your classroom as a *construction zone,* to borrow an analogy suggested by Dennis Newman, Peg Griffin, and Michael Cole (1989). To work within this zone, you should begin with some kind of plan.

If you were building a house, you would undoubtedly begin by envisioning what the house would look like when it was finished. You might even draw or build a small model of that final product to help you see your ultimate goal during the process of construction. You would also prepare a blueprint, a detailed set of plans to help you build the house according to a set of specifications.

The model and blueprint provide you with a goal and a plan for realizing it, but also allow for flexibility, depending on circumstances that may arise. If your plans call for a skylight, yet you learn during construction that softwood trees drop debris on the house, you might abandon the skylight idea. If you are building the foundation and unearth a subterranean spring, you will probably move the house to a different location on the lot or change the blueprint to allow the water to flow through the house. If your work crew comes up with an idea for routing the plumbing more efficiently, you might change some of the infrastructure design. If your goals change, you will adjust the blueprint and model accordingly. You might, for instance, meet and marry a gourmet cook and decide to change your standard kitchen design to a deluxe design.

In other words, beginning with a sense of your outcome and a design for realizing it does not lock you into a rigid plan. Rather, it provides you with a goal and a pathway that you can adjust in response to changing conditions. Following your plan regardless of intervening events can cause your house to slide into a sinkhole. However, if you try to build a house without any idea of what it's supposed to look like, you might end up with a stairway that leads nowhere.

The task in this chapter is to envision what students will be working toward as a consequence of their engagement with the unit texts and activities. These goals will come in the form of culminating texts that you will assess. The construction metaphor applies simultaneously to two things: one is your design of the unit itself; the other is the texts that students will build within the unit. Both are goal-directed acts that require the use of tools and materials.

Both teachers and students also produce texts whose ultimate form will be assessed. In other words, just as a home owner or building inspector eventually evaluates the quality of a new home, you will ultimately be responsible for saying how well your students construct these culminating texts. In turn, your students will form judgments about the way in which you have designed your text: the instructional unit.

> I've come to realize that a defining characteristic of good teaching is to push on the existing order of things.
>
> —Mike Rose, *Possible Lives*

Conceptualizing Your Unit Focus

All the planning you do in a unit will occur in terms of the unit focus. Once again, you are caught within a tension described previously: Whose unit of study is this, and who gets to decide what it is about? Conventionally, a teacher is the primary decision maker in the classroom. In this tradition, the teacher would pick the unit topic, decide what's important for students to learn about it, and then fashion goals and assessments, lessons, activities, and so on so that students could make progress toward grasping the unit concepts. Taking this approach, the teacher needs to think through the concept under study and plan carefully so that students can explore the key issues in a detailed and connected way.

For instance, in a unit on discrimination, you might think through what it means to discriminate, perhaps starting with examples from your own experiences or from the media. When a parent prohibits a seven-year-old from watching a PG-13 movie, is this discrimination against the child? When a teacher tends not to call on a student who earnestly makes embarrassing statements, is this discrimination against the student? When a person who is conned out of money says he or she has been "gypped," is this discrimination against Gypsies? Your consideration of a broad series of examples could help you identify what you think is important to understand about discrimination and plan instruction appropriately.

Some, however, feel that when a teacher takes such a strong role in planning, students' engagement with the unit becomes limited to whatever the teacher finds most important. In our example, this focus might preclude students from considering other aspects of discrimination that could enrich their work during the unit. Another approach, then, might be for the teacher to take a less assertive role in identifying the unit concepts and to let them emerge through the students' participation in the unit.

I have described different degrees of control a teacher might exert in planning the course of study. I believe that the principles of planning in this book will allow you to take either approach, or one in between. Regardless of the approach you take, you will benefit from thinking through the concept as clearly as possible before, during, and after your design of the unit. As I've said before, planning is a recursive process that involves continual reconsideration with each new act and decision.

Setting Goals

In Chapter 3, I reviewed a range of ways in which students might know something. As you might imagine, it would be very difficult to provide opportunities for assessing all kinds of knowing in each and every unit. Rather, you should try to provide diverse assessments over the course of the whole year. For any individual unit of instruction, you should provide a more limited set of major assessments. In other words, for each unit of instruction, you should identify a small set of culminating texts for students to produce. If you choose them wisely, students will have plenty of work on their hands, and not just busy work, but significant construction of new and important knowledge.

In Chapters 6 through 8, I will show how your daily activities and discussions should also include opportunities for multiple ways of knowing. As a teacher, you will be responsible for grading both major assessments and the smaller assignments that lead up to them. To return to the construction metaphor, you will evaluate not only the finished house, but also some (but not all) stages of production. In this chapter, although, I focus on the major graded texts that students produce during a unit. I will concentrate on planning these culminating texts that students will work toward, which often occupy the latter portion of the unit. For now, we are thinking about what the house as a whole will ultimately look like.

Reflective Writing Prompt

To what extent do you agree with the construction metaphor as a way to think about teaching and learning? What is the basis of your beliefs? Can you think of a different metaphor that would describe your beliefs better? If so, try to extend this metaphor as far as you can.

Conventions and Alternatives

Buildings, like academic knowledge, tend to be constructed through the use of conventional tools. To drive a nail, most carpenters will use a hammer. To divide a board in two, most use a saw. School, too, has its conventional tools. Students are likely to write with a pen, pencil, or keyboard, and to write on paper. And in school they typically use these tools to take notes and write correct answers on exams or to write analytically.

But in constructing buildings and doing school, you don't always follow the conventions. To get from the ground floor to the second floor of a house, most people would build a straight staircase, or perhaps one with a single, right-angle turn near the bottom. But you could also build a spiral staircase, put in an elevator, install a firefighter's pole, plant exterior vines for climbing in and out of windows, or leave a pogo stick by the front door. Although most people wouldn't choose these options, the fact that straight staircases are conventional does not mean that there aren't other ways of getting to the second floor and back.

School functions similarly. There are certain established ways of doing things that often make alternatives hard to see. These well-established ways are deeply ingrained in our ways of conceiving of school, because school was that way when we were kids and has been that way for generations. Under such conditions, it's hard to imagine alternatives. If things were different, it just wouldn't be school. What's so difficult to see under these circumstances is that these ways of schooling were developed in response to a different set of circumstances than exist today and might not fit today's conditions so well.

James Wertsch (1991) illustrates this kind of problem by describing the history of the typewriter keyboard, known as the QWERTY keyboard because of the position of the first keys on the top row. Most people assume that the layout of keys is designed to make typing easier. If you have grown up using computer keyboards rather than typewriters, you probably couldn't imagine any other reason for arranging keys.

Actually, the opposite is true: The QWERTY layout is designed to *slow down* a fast typist. When typewriters were first invented, they were not electrified. The imprint of a letter on the page came about when a typist struck a key, which was attached to a wire with a corresponding letter on the other end. This letter was propelled forward to strike a thin ribbon containing ink, which in turn struck the paper and put the letter on it. If a typist went too fast, the wires would get all tangled up. So, to slow fast typists down, the keyboard was arranged to make typing somewhat clumsy and therefore slower and less likely to jam up the typewriter.

In spite of many advances in technology, the QWERTY keyboard has endured, even though most word processing programs have options that enable you to switch to a more efficient arrangement. We just can't imagine it any other way, and we even assume that the structure is designed to make things work better.

Conventions of schooling can act in similar ways: There are ways of doing things that are part of school, and if we do them differently it just doesn't seem like school any more. If we envision alternatives, they seem to lack legitimacy because they're different from what we know and are comfortable with. We assume that the ways of

Vignette

The following is one of those bits of trivia that people forward around the Internet. I've never been able to figure out if it's true or not, but if it isn't, it ought to be.

The U. S. standard railroad gauge (distance between rails) is 4 feet, 8.5 inches. That's a rather odd number. So, why is that gauge used? It's used because that's the way they built them in England and the first U. S. railroads were built by English expatriates.

So, why did the English build them like that? Because the first rail lines in Europe were designed and built by the same people who built the prerailroad tramways, and that's the gauge they used.

Why did they use the same gauge then? Because the people who designed and built the tramways used the same jigs and tools that they used for building wagons, which used that same wheel spacing.

Okay, so why did the wagons use that odd wheel spacing? Well, when they tried to use any other spacing, the wagons were prone to breaking down on some of the old long-distance roads, because that's the spacing of the old wheel ruts.

So, who built these old, rutted roads? The first long-distance roads in Europe were built by imperial Rome for the benefit of its legions. The roads have been used ever since.

And the ruts? The initial ruts, which everyone had to match for fear of destroying the wagons, were first made by Roman war chariots. Since the chariots were all made to certain specifications for, or by, imperial Rome, they were all alike in the matter of wheel spacing. The U.S. standard railroad gauge of 4 feet, 8.5 inches derives from the original specification for an Imperial Army war chariot. But, one nagging question remains: Why did the design of the Roman war chariots incorporate that specific wheelbase?

Answer: Because the chariots were designed to be just wide enough to accommodate the back ends of two warhorses. So, the next time you are handed some oddball specification and you assume that some horse's ass was responsible for coming up with it, you may be exactly right.

schooling are the best and most efficient ways to educate students, because we've never known anything different.

In this chapter I am going to ask you to think about school as it might be, rather than as it is. In this book I am not trying to prepare you to function comfortably within schools as they exist, but I am asking you to rethink what schooling is and how you can make it more authentic, dynamic, purposeful, and fulfilling for both students and teachers. Doing so requires you to think of alternatives to what is conventional.

I will use the ways of knowing outlined in Chapter 3 to help think of culminating texts that students might produce for different units identified in Chapter 4 for the sophomore year curriculum. If you were a house builder, would you build the same house for all people, regardless of the size of their families, their living priorities, the weather conditions that affect the house, and other factors?

Probably not. An unmarried computer programmer on the Florida coast and a married Amish couple with five children and four dogs in northern Pennsylvania would require different abodes. Similarly, different students have different needs that can be

Vignette

I've always found it odd that much school assessment relies on students' ability to memorize information, but schools provide very little instruction in how to remember things. The field of cognitive psychology, which focuses on memory, has identified a number of tricks that people can use to remember things better. One is to "chunk" information; that is, to think of things in clusters that have some kind of relationship. Another is to associate something with a memorable image.

An example: My daughter, Alysha, was recently studying for her final exams for eighth grade. For her science exam, she had to remember a vast amount of information from the semester's study. She was having trouble remembering that Jupiter's moon Io has a volcanic surface, so we tried to think of a way to help her learn this fact. Our solution: We sang, to the tune of the Seven Dwarves' song "Hi-ho, hi-ho, it's off to work we go," "Io, Io, it has a volcano." She sang this song incessantly the rest of the evening. The item, incidentally, did not end up being on the test. But I'll bet that she remembers it much longer than all the questions that were.

met through studying English in your class. Your challenge is to plan assessment so that it allows students of different makeups and backgrounds to have the same opportunities for success, for living well.

> Education is not filling a pail but the lighting of a fire.
> —William Butler Yeats

Although I distinguish between conventional and alternative assessments, both follow the constructivist principles outlined in the first few chapters of this book. I am not providing information on how to develop objective tests that ask students to repeat information, distinguish Dan'l Webster from Daniel Webster, or otherwise memorize and repeat things that they will soon forget. Rather, all the assessments that follow engage students in the synthesis of previously learned knowledge and the construction of new knowledge. Even though they are nearly ubiquitous in schools, the common means of assessment— true/false questions, multiple-choice questions, matching problems, fill-in-the-blank statements, and short-answer questions— play no role in the kind of instruction I outline in this book. If I were to hire you to build my house, I'd watch you work and look at how well some of your completed houses withstood wear and tear, rather than ask you if it's true or false that clapboard siding insulates better than vinyl, especially when the answer might be, "It depends."

Field Observation

In the school you are visiting, how would you describe the assessments on a continuum from conventional to alternative? What does this approach to assessment tell you about the assumptions held in the school about teaching and learning? What are the consequences of this approach in terms of deeming students capable or incapable? How equitable is the school's approach to assessment; that is, to what extent does it provide avenues for success for the whole range of students enrolled in the school?

In producing their culminating texts, students will inevitably demonstrate their knowledge of characters' names, literary events, and so on. They will do so, however, in service of thinking in complex ways, rather than in the low-level cognitive task of memorization. In advocating a constructivist approach, I am not saying that factual knowledge is unimportant. I am saying, rather, that students will forget the facts if they are not put to good use.

UNIT GOALS AS UNIT ASSESSMENTS

I will discuss assessment in two sections. First, I will identify what I think of as conventional kinds of assessments. These fit well with the typical structure of school, focusing on detached analysis of texts with an emphasis on maintaining a distant stance from the topic. Second, I will identify a range of alternative assessments that provide opportunities for learning through exploratory, narrative, connected, multimedia/multigenre, unconventional, and creative modes and forms.

In making this distinction I am not saying that an analytic paper is never creative, exploratory, or the like. I hope, indeed, that conventional schooling provides avenues for dynamic engagement with texts and other people, even though many studies of classrooms say that it does not. The distinction between conventional and alternative assessments is based on the findings of recent research in human development, cultural psychology, rhetoric, intelligence, semiotics, gender, and other fields. This research has provided legitimacy, if not widespread acceptance, for considering a broader range of texts and learning processes than English classes customarily provide.

In describing these assessments, I will focus primarily on the final form they will take. In the chapters that follow, I will shift attention to the teaching and learning processes that lead to the production of these forms. Traditionally, teaching has focused on the proper look of a final product, without teaching students procedures for producing them. Here, I will consider the product students are working toward, and in later chapters I will describe how to teach students how to construct these final texts.

Even though I am beginning by describing the ultimate form, it's important to understand that *these forms are the culminating texts that follow from engaging in social action.* In other words, I will present the criteria for writing a good argument (the final form you will assess), but the argument will come from learning how to engage in the social action of argumentation. Similarly, I will describe a narrative, but the narrative you will grade follows from students' learning to think about and represent their experiences through the process of narration.

When you think about unit goals, you need to keep *both the final form and the social action that produces it* in mind. If you focus on form only, you run the risk of overlooking the social purposes these forms serve. It's important to know textual features for particular kinds of writing (or other text)—to know the distinct traits that go into an argument, a response log, a book review, and so on. It's equally important to know that these traits are more than just parts to produce. They enable writers to meet particular social goals. *It's vital, then, to stress the social purposes of any texts you evaluate, particularly the ways in which they enable writers to communicate with specific groups of readers.*

Each assessment that follows includes a set of elements. First, students are presented with the general task (to write a personal narrative, to write a literary analysis, etc.). Beneath the statement of the general task is a set of bulleted items. These items will serve five primary purposes:

1. To provide students with a clear set of parameters for producing their texts
2. To provide students with an understanding of how their work will be evaluated

3. To provide teachers with a set of goals to guide their teaching
4. To identify for teachers what they need to teach students to do
5. To provide teachers with criteria to guide their assessment.

The assignments do more than simply tell students what to do. They also outline responsibilities for both you and your students.

Discussion Topic

How have the process, product, and purpose of learning been handled in schools you've observed? What reasons do teachers give for the kinds of attention they give to each? How do you evaluate their approach to process, product, and purpose?

Conventional Assessments

In this section I look at ways to identify assessments that fit within the overriding values of school, yet can be produced in ways that students find meaningful and that enable them to engage in significant social action. Thinking analytically is a key skill not only for school success, but for participating in many of society's activities and professions. It certainly ought to be central to any language arts program offered in school, although it should *not* be the only kind of thinking and writing evaluated in school. All the assessments I describe in this section involve some kind of analytic or argumentative writing. Writing of this sort is widely assigned in school and used on high-stakes assessments that involve writing.

Analytic or argumentative writing also ought to be the occasion for new learning. In many classes I have observed, analytic writing is produced through what's known as the five-paragraph or three-point theme, which includes a one-paragraph introduction, a three-paragraph body, and a one-paragraph conclusion that reiterates the introduction. The three points covered in the essay's body frequently consist of ideas from the teacher's lecture notes, rather than new insights by the student writer. As many observers of classrooms have said, instruction in five-paragraph themes, while perhaps teaching some lessons about paragraphing and thesis and support, too often focuses on the production of a form rather than on the generation of ideas. I encourage you to make *engagement with content* the primary consideration in writing instruction, with attention to form coming later. To borrow an architectural phrase, form should follow function. Yet function should have a form in mind.

Table 5.1 provides examples of different types of conventional assessments found at the Virtual Library of Conceptual Units at http://www.coe.uga.edu/~smago/VirtualLibrary/index.html. In the left column under "Unit" are listed the authors of the units in the Virtual Library; note that most units are coauthored. The type of assessment is indicated by an x in the appropriate column.

Extended Definition

One conventional form students can learn to produce is the extended definition. Extended definitions serve as the basis for most laws and governing rules, as well as for any kind of scientific classification. Consider, for instance, proposing a law to

TABLE 5.1 Virtual Library: Examples of Conventional Assessments

Unit	Literary Analysis Essay	Comparison/ Contrast Essay	Five-Paragraph Theme	Persuasive Essay	Research
	Goal				
Askari					
Barrett Endres Stinchcomb					
Begnaud Evans	X				
Behr Reece Watkins					
Bryan Skorupski		X			X
Camp Davis Harris			X		
Cockrill Hall Long				X	
Deroshia					X
Hedden Orr Shroyer					
Hollingshead Wood					
Johnson	X				
Loggins Taggart Thomas					
Rachmuth Shuler					
Siegmund Stroud Hasty	X	X			
Swann Williams					

control sexual harassment in the workplace. In order to enforce such a law, you would need to define what it means to harass someone, what it means for that harassment to be of a sexual nature, and what it means to do this in a workplace. You would need to define these terms clearly enough that a group of independent observers (e.g., a jury) could say with some certainty whether a particular action was or was not an act of sexual harassment in the workplace. A carefully worded, specific, and well-illustrated definition is particularly important in potentially ambiguous cases.

Thematic literature units can provide opportunities to work at developing extended definitions. Often they center on topics such as progress, loyalty, success, courage, and other aspects of culture and character that require definition in order to be understood in literature. In the sophomore curriculum, the unit on discrimination would be a good place to include instruction in writing extended definitions. Writing an extended definition of discrimination could help students think through what it means to act in discriminatory ways.

Some literature might present blatant cases of discrimination, such as the legally-instituted racism described by Richard Wright in his autobiography *Black Boy*. Other cases are less clear. Through the process of defining and illustrating discrimination, students can help clarify for themselves how to evaluate social interactions in which they engage personally and that they observe through news media.

A unit on discrimination could feature sustained attention to the question of how discrimination is defined and illustrated, with classroom activities including personal writing, discussions of literature, and efforts to consider the two in terms of one another. You would need to provide formal instruction in how to define abstract concepts; A good instructional sequence is described by Larry Johannessen, Elizabeth Kahn, and Carolyn Walter in *Designing and Sequencing Prewriting Activities*. You could provide the following prompt for a culminating text in which students define and illustrate what it means to discriminate:

> Throughout the unit we have considered the effects of discrimination, on both the person who discriminates and the person discriminated against. We have looked at questions of discrimination in a variety of situations, using examples from current events, from your personal experiences, and from literature. In some cases, there has been disagreement on what counts as discrimination. Your task is to write an essay in which you provide an extended definition of discrimination. To do so, provide the following:
>
> - A general introduction in which you provide an overview for your definition.
> - A set of *criteria* or rules that state clearly what discrimination is and is not.
> - For each criterion, an *example* from literature, current events, or your personal experiences that illustrates the rule at work. At least half your examples must come from the literature studied in class.
> - For each criterion, a *counterexample* from literature, current events, or your personal experiences that appears to meet the conditions of the rule yet lacks some essential ingredient. At least half your counterexamples must come from the literature studied in class.

- For each example and counterexample, a *warrant* that clearly explains why the rule is or is not being met.
- For your whole argument, a *counterargument* expressing the viewpoint of someone who might disagree with you.
- For the counterargument, a *rebuttal* in which you defend your position.
- Conventional grammar, spelling, punctuation, and usage throughout your essay
- Evidence of having written at least one rough draft that has been submitted for peer evaluation

I should reiterate that these bulleted items serve a variety of purposes. The most obvious purpose is to inform students what they are responsible for and what you will grade. They also specify a set of responsibilities for you as a teacher. If you are going to grade something, then you need to teach students how to do it.

Literary Analysis

Literary analysis is, for many English teachers, the bread-and-butter of writing instruction. In most cases, however, students are evaluated on their ability to write an analysis of a literary work already studied in class. Under such circumstances, students inevitably rely on the teacher's interpretation to form the substance of their own analysis. They are evaluated, then, on their skill at reproducing the teacher's analysis to the teacher's satisfaction.

This approach does not serve them well as a tool for analyzing new literature. Indeed, it suggests a teaching approach in which the teacher's role is to provide a good interpretation for students to replicate on the assessment. Consider, however, what would happen if students were evaluated on their ability to analyze a work of literature that they had never seen before. Not only would this approach evaluate their independent analytic abilities, it would suggest to the teacher that the purpose of instruction is to teach analytic skills rather than to provide a preferred interpretation, no matter how insightful.

Let's say, then, that in the sophomore unit on coming-of-age literature, the teacher helps students see a common pattern in such stories. Coming-of-age stories typically begin with some illustration of a protagonist's immature behavior at the outset, a critical experience that results in a major realization, and a transformation to more mature behavior by the end. Class activities could focus on seeing how protagonists negotiate the threshold of this critical experience and thinking about what kinds of transformations they undergo. As part of this literary analysis, students could engage in reflection on personal transformations that have followed from critical experiences, thus recognizing this pattern in their own lives.

Teachers could then evaluate students' ability to recognize and interpret this pattern with an essay based on a choice of literary works, none of which has been covered in class. The students' task would be to identify and analyze the transformation in the independently read story possibly through a culminating text produced in response to this prompt:

From the literary choices provided, read one work of literature and write an essay in which you analyze the protagonist's coming-of-age experience. In your essay, make sure that you:

- Provide a general thesis for the paper, explaining the protagonist's primary transformation during the course of the story.
- Describe the protagonist's immature behavior at the beginning of the story, including specific examples from the text.
- Describe clearly the key event that causes the character to change. In doing so, explain why this event, rather than others in the story, causes the protagonist to come of age.
- Describe the significant changes taking place in the protagonist following the coming of age experience, including specific examples from the text.
- Draw a conclusion about how people change as a result of significant events and how these changes can be considered as a coming of age.
- Follow rules of conventional grammar, spelling, punctuation, and usage throughout your essay
- Give evidence of having written at least one rough draft that has been submitted for peer evaluation

Argumentation

Argumentation is another staple of school writing, a common form of writing in many professions, and the way in which most conflicting points of view come into contact. In order to prove a point, you need to argue it; that is,

- have a thesis (e.g., a belief that conflicts between peer groups in school must be resolved)
- support it with a set of claims (e.g., antagonism has increased, tension is .. greater in hallways, there is less unity at school functions, etc.)
- back each claim with evidence (e.g., fights have grown more frequent, students self-segregate in the cafeteria, some students have posted hateful websites, etc.)
- anticipate a counterargument (e.g., the problem is not so great because there have been few outbreaks of violence thus far)
- and rebut the counterargument (e.g., the problem must be addressed before a crisis takes place, rather than after it happens)

Even if you never become a lawyer or serve on a political talk-show panel, knowing careful argumentation can help you see clearly on issues you care about yet over which there is disagreement.

Many different parts of the English curriculum can serve as opportunities for instruction in argumentation. Students can argue for interpretations of literature or for ways to view literary movements. For the sophomore curriculum, the unit on conflict with authority could provide the occasion for students to argue for a particular interpretation of a character's actions. Once again, they would do so using a literary work that is new to them, rather than one that the class has already discussed. And once again, your role as teacher would be to teach interpretive and argumentative strategies, rather than to provide good interpretations. The students could write their arguments in response to the following prompt:

> From the literary choices provided, read one work of literature and write an argument in which you analyze the protagonist's conflict with an authority figure. In your argument, evaluate the protagonist's approach to resolving the conflict. In producing your argument, make sure that you do the following:
>
> - Provide a governing *thesis* in which you explain the conflict and provide a general evaluation of the protagonist's actions
> - Support this thesis with a set of *claims*—the reasons that support your interpretation
> - Back each claim with *evidence* from the story
> - Anticipate and explain a *counterargument,* which is a disagreement with your interpretation
> - Rebut the *counterargument* with additional reasons in support of your argument
> - Follow rules of conventional grammar, spelling, punctuation, and usage throughout your essay
> - Give evidence of having written at least one rough draft that has been submitted for peer evaluation

Research Report

Another conventional kind of assessment found in school is the research report. Such reports are produced in many disciplines and professions, and often are required in school curricula. A good report on a significant topic can make an important contribution to people's knowledge about issues that matter to them. These reports are focused on facts, but use these facts in the service of constructing knowledge about a topic.

In English classes, students could write research reports on issues related to the unit concept they are studying. The Shakespeare unit from the sophomore curriculum, for instance, could involve students in doing library research on the historical context of *Julius Caesar.* This research could serve a variety of purposes: evaluating the historical accuracy of the play, learning more about characters of interest, informing an understanding of the play's plot, and so on.

For the discrimination unit, students could conduct research on the Civil Rights movement, the women's suffrage movement, or any variety of discrimination battles waged in local, U.S., or world history. By sharing these reports with their classmates, students could provide a good context for discussing questions of discrimination that arise in the literature.

Research reports in schools tend to follow a particular written formula, established before other media became available to students. When resources allow, teachers ought to take advantage of opportunities many students now have to use computers, videos, and related technologies to produce their research reports. The form of the report might vary if students have the capability to produce a documentary film instead of a written report, for instance.

A research report might be written in response to the following prompt:

We have been studying questions of discrimination in the literature we have read and in your personal knowledge of the world. For your culminating project, produce a research report on some historical instance of discrimination. The topic may be of international significance (e.g., apartheid in South Africa), important in U.S. history (e.g., reverse discrimination lawsuits in college admissions), or of local/community interest (e.g., a skateboarding restriction on community sidewalks). Your report should meet the following requirements:

- It may be in any form of your choice: writing, film, interview recordings, computer graphics, and so on, or in any combination of these forms.
- The report should be guided by some perspective you take on the issue.
- If written, your report should include a minimum of 1,000 words (roughly four typed pages).
- If produced in some other medium or combination of media, your report should comprise at least a 10-minute presentation.
- Your presentation should follow some clear organizational pattern that follows from your report's thesis.
- The information you provide must come from a minimum of five sources.
  - These sources can be *secondary*—sources such as books or encyclopedias that someone else has written and from which you take information.
  - These sources can be *primary*—sources that you personally investigate, such as interviews you conduct, observations you make, documents you study, and so on.

Alternative Assessments

In this section I will present other kinds of culminating texts that can form the basis of assessment. While less traditionally assessed in schools, they are every bit as legitimate in terms of how people think, act, communicate, and represent meaning throughout society. In addition, I will review ways of evaluating the kinds of exploratory thinking and writing that students do in the process of producing culminating texts.

Table 5.2 provides examples of different types of alternative assessments found at the Virtual Library of Conceptual Units at http://www.coe.uga.edu/~smago/ VirtualLibrary/index.html. In the left column under "Unit" are listed the authors of the units in the Virtual Library; note that most units are coauthored. The type of alternative assessment is indicated by an x in the appropriate column.

Exploratory Thinking and Writing

In Chapter 3 I reviewed Douglas Barnes's views of exploratory and final draft uses of speech. Much of what you evaluate in school will be final drafts. One problem with schooling in general is that it focuses on these final products without providing opportunities for students to engage in—and be rewarded for—the informal, tentative,

TABLE 5.2 Virtual Library: Types of Alternative Assessments

Unit	Goal							
	Portfolio	Journal	Question Asking	Creative Writing	Multimedia Project	Performance/ Presentation	Curriculum Design	Personal Essay
Askari	X	X		X	X	X		X
Barrett Endres Stinchcomb	X			X	X	X		
Begnaud Evans	X	X	X					
Behr Reece Watkins	X	X		X				
Bryan Skorupski			X	X	X	X		
Camp Davis Harris		X			X	X		
Cockrill Hall Long	X	X				X		
Deroshia		X		X			X	
Hedden Orr Shroyer		X		X				
Hollingshead Wood		X		X		X		
Johnson								X
Loggins Taggart Thomas		X	X					X
Rachmuth Shuler				X		X		X
Siegmund Stroud Hasty		X						
Swann Williams	X	X		X	X	X		

experimental processes that lead to them. Here I will look at four kinds of exploratory work you can evaluate: portfolios, journals, rough drafts, and student-generated questions about literature.

Portfolios.   In Chapter 4, I identified the *process portfolio* as a way of evaluating students according to what they have learned about their learning, often through their reflection on exploratory texts they have produced on their way to more formal products. You could also use portfolios in individual units. I will review two such ways next.

1. *Course-long portfolio preparation.* In Chapter 4, I proposed that a process portfolio could serve as one of the final evaluations for a whole course of study. If you make this choice, you need to attend to portfolio preparation during each unit, having students identify exploratory work done for the unit that has generated significant new learning. The work they select would be included in the portfolios prepared for the course as a whole. You would not evaluate the exhibits until you are evaluating the whole portfolio; that is, you would not grade the exhibits students turn in during the individual units.

You could, however, periodically devote class time to having students discuss which of their exploratory efforts have been significant learning experiences and work through a process of reflection with them on how to prepare a reflective statement for an individual exhibit. In this way, you would be preparing students for their course-long portfolio throughout the year or semester, giving exploratory work attention and value in everyday instruction.

2. *Portfolios for individual units.* Following the ideas of the course-long process portfolio described in Chapter 4, you could have students keep shorter portfolios for individual units of study, or perhaps for each marking period. These would require more frequent selections of exhibits gathered from a more limited pool of items. You could outline their responsibilities for a unit portfolio as follows:

> Throughout the unit you have had a lot of experiences with literature and other art forms. In response to these texts, you have produced a variety of pieces of writing, art, and other forms of expression. Presumably, you have learned something about yourself, the literature, how to write, how to read, and other things.
>
> Prepare a portfolio in which you present things you've produced that have resulted in your most valuable learning. We will call these things *exhibits.* The exhibits you present do not need to be your best work. Often we learn the most from our rough drafts, our frustrated efforts, and other experiences that do not yield our best products. *You will not be graded on the quality of the exhibits that you include.* Rather, you will be graded on how carefully you reflect on what you learned from producing them.
>
> Your portfolio should include:
>
> - A title page with name and date.
> - A minimum of four items that serve as your exhibits. You must include a minimum of one exhibit for each week of the unit. Your portfolio may include additional exhibits if you wish, including things from outside this class.
> - A written statement that identifies and discusses significant learning based on each exhibit, consisting of a minimum of 200 words.

- A longer *synthesis paper,* in which you discuss how these exhibits as a whole reveal what you've learned both about yourself and about the material we have studied, consisting of a minimum of 750 words (roughly three typed pages).

Journals. Students can also keep journals in which they think through their engagement with the unit topics, with exploratory writing serving as the medium for their thinking. Writing used this way can serve as a tool for discovering new ideas.

Journals come in a variety of forms. I will next review a series of journal types, describing them briefly and then including a possible way to present them to students as goals.

1. *Personal journal.* A personal journal is an open-ended opportunity for students to write whatever they think or feel in response to the unit's content and processes, however they might be experiencing them. Ideally, the journal will involve a strong component of reflection, of thinking through ideas and emotions, of developing a personal response to the unit. It should not simply summarize readings or discussions. You can make reflection one of the requirements of the assignment and include attention to reflection in your assessment.

In Chapter 15, I discuss why journals will not be appropriate in all settings. They are, however, useful tools for many teachers and students for thinking through their ideas about a topic. One solution is to make them optional, so that students who benefit from them will have the opportunity to do so, but students whose families discourage introspection in school will not be caught in a conflict. You could present the journal as follows:

Keep a journal in which you think through ideas and feelings that you have in response to the material we study, the class discussions and activities that we engage in, and any other engagement you have with the unit topic. The following issues will be factors in the way I grade your journal:

- Your journal does not need to follow the conventions of textbook English. Rather, the purpose is to think about the class without worrying about the form your thoughts take.
- Do not simply summarize the literature we read in the class. Although you need to refer to these texts, the primary purpose of your journal is to think about your response to these texts, rather than to provide summaries of what they say. In other words, your journal should focus on how you have engaged with the literature.
- You are welcome, though not required, to reflect on personal issues that occur to you in relation to your consideration of the literature.
- Your journal should include a minimum of 500 words of writing (roughly two typed pages) per week. For each entry, put the date of the writing at the beginning.
- Keep in mind that *I am required to share any thoughts or suggestions of violence, suicide, substance abuse, family abuse, or other harmful behavior with the school counselors.*

- If there are any pages in your journal that you do not want me to read, please mark them with an X at the top.

These last two items raise one of the trickiest questions about journals—how to treat issues of confidentiality. You want students to write honestly in their journals, yet they know you will read them. You also may be obligated to report information about destructive behavior to parents, school authorities, or both. Students need to know how you are going to read their journals and what you will do with certain kinds of information. Often, students use assignments like this as a way of asking for help when they don't know of any other way.

2. *Reading log.* A more structured kind of journal, with a more specific purpose, is the reading log. Here students use journal pages with vertical lines down the middle, writing down significant passages from literature on the left side and writing their comments, responses, questions, and interpretations on the right. The purpose of these journals is to encourage students to attend carefully to the language of the literature and to read reflectively, pausing to think about particular passages before moving along. Some students do find this process cumbersome and the interruptions to their reading more a distraction than a source of discovery. A reading log could follow from a prompt like this:

Keep a reading log in response to the literature we are studying during this unit. To keep your log:

- Divide each page with a vertical line down the center.
- On the left side of each page, record significant passages from the literature you read.
- On the right side, across from each passage, do any or all of the following:
  1. Ask *questions* that would help you understand the passage better
  2. Give your personal *response* to the passage
  3. Give your personal *evaluation* of the passage
  4. Think through a possible *interpretation* of the passage
- Write a minimum of three entries for each work of literature studied.
- Remember that your journal does not need to follow the conventions of textbook English. Rather, the purpose is to think about the literature without worrying about the form your thoughts take.
- Keep in mind that *I am required to share any thoughts or suggestions of violence, suicide, substance abuse, family abuse, or other harmful behavior with the school counselors.*

3. *Dialogue Journal.* A dialogue journal is a journal shared by two or more people, in which they carry on a discussion about a shared topic. The discussion

---

Reflective Writing Prompt

Many educators believe that *getting to know their students* is essential to teaching effectively and that all good teaching starts with efforts to get students to reveal important things about themselves. Journals, memoirs, and other introspective writing are often used not just for the purpose of having students reflect on their experiences, but also for the purpose of enabling teachers to learn more about their students' lives.

Some people find such reflection invasive. Some parents, for instance, protest strongly when teachers require introspective writing, saying that a student's personal life is of no importance in learning an academic discipline and is none of a teacher's business. Some students are very private and don't wish to produce writing on personal topics that others will read about.

Think about this tension and how you would resolve it. What is the benefit of introspective writing to the student? To the teacher? Should introspective writing be required of all students to the same degree? At what point do introspective writing assignments become invasive? Should teachers who require introspective writing of students share their own introspective writing with their students, and, if so, how personal ought this writing to be?

is conducted through written exchanges, and the topic is the unit they are studying. Traditionally, a dialogue journal has been handwritten, with students physically handing over the journal to their partner(s) when they have finished their conversational turn. These partners could conceivably include anyone who's interested in participating, including the teacher, parents, and students who are not enrolled in the class.

Dialogue journals can also be kept through electronic mail, without the unwieldy problem of carrying the journal around and handing it to one another at the completion of a turn. Electronic dialogue journals can also include any number of participants. In either case, the idea is to provide a forum for discussion beyond what the classroom offers.

A dialogue journal might be prompted as follows:

> With at least one other person, maintain a dialogue journal in which you discuss the issues raised in class. You may keep your dialogue journal in a regular writing notebook, or you may provide printouts of a discussion you maintain over email. In keeping your dialogue journal, remember:
>
> - Your journal does not need to follow the conventions of textbook English. Rather, the purpose is to think about the class without worrying about the form your thoughts take.
> - Do not simply summarize the literature we read in the class. Your discussion should include questions, analysis, reflection, and evaluation. It should be evident that you are learning something new through your dialogue.
> - Make sure that you include attention to each text studied in the unit.
> - You are welcome, though not required, to reflect on personal issues that occur to you in relation to your consideration of the literature.
> - All participants in your dialogue journal should make roughly equal contributions.
> - Keep in mind that *I am required to share any thoughts or suggestions of violence, suicide, substance abuse, family abuse, or other harmful behavior with the school counselors.*

Rough Drafts.   Another way to evaluate exploratory thinking is to have students turn in rough drafts of their work. You can do this in several ways. For each piece of extended writing they do, students could be required to produce one or two rough drafts. For each of these drafts, small groups of students could evaluate one another's work and provide recommendations for improvement. (See Appendix C for one way to structure these response groups.)

An alternative is for students to turn their rough drafts in to you for feedback. You could also have students seek a reader from outside class, which could be a parent or other significant adult. Keep in mind that in school, teachers are almost exclusively the evaluators of students' work. Having students write for other audiences can help them learn about the notion of audience, which many rhetoricians stress is essential to effective writing and communication.

When students turn in final drafts, have them staple all outlines, notes, drafts, and feedback to the formal version that you
will evaluate. In this way, you can track their progress and ensure
that they are working at extended composition with their writing.
Evaluating rough drafts should merely consist of making sure that
they have been done. If the goal is to allow preliminary work to
be exploratory, then putting a grade on its quality is questionable.

> Education is what you learn in books,
> and nobody knows you know it but
> your teacher.
>
> —Virginia Cary Hudson

Asking Questions.   Students rarely pose questions in school. Observers of classrooms
have made some rather astonishing discoveries about how frequently students initiate
inquiries of their own. In one study, students asked, on average, one question each
month. It's hard to imagine establishing a school culture based on principles of inquiry
and constructivism when students so rarely pose the questions that guide their learning.

Simply telling students to ask questions is often frustrating because they have
been conditioned to view school as a place where every question has a correct answer. In school when you ask students to ask questions, they often come up with
questions that sound a lot like the ones at the end of their textbook chapters: Which
character did what? What was the name of the character who did such-and-such? The
mirror they provide for schooling is not one I find attractive to look into.

One way you can evaluate students, then, is to teach them to ask questions. I
see this as an issue of exploratory talk because they will need to talk about the texts
in order to generate their questions, and the questions they pose ought to inquire
into the open-ended territory that exploratory talk helps them investigate. For now,
I will simply give an example of how to present this challenge to students. In Chapter 8, I will give a better idea of how to prepare students for doing it.

I will create this assignment for the study of *The Outsiders* in a unit on gangs,
cliques, and peer-group pressure, but it can easily be adapted to any unit. The assignment is somewhat unique in that, rather than evaluating students on their construction of meaning *after* reading, it places the job of literary discussion entirely in
their hands. After many years of leading class discussions myself—relying on my
own clever questions to guide our analysis—I shifted this responsibility to students.
I would lead some discussions, but primarily for the purpose of helping students develop procedures for leading their own. The following prompt assumes that I will
teach a sequence similar to that described in Chapter 8 and that the students will understand what the terms refer to.

> To discuss S. E. Hinton's *The Outsiders,* the class will organize into six small
> groups, with each group responsible for leading a discussion of two chapters of
> the novel. Each group will use one full class period to discuss its chapters. To
> lead your discussion, you may adopt any format: regular English class, nonvio-
> lent talk-show format, town meeting, courtroom, or other mode of your choice.
> Your discussion should involve all of the following:
>
> - Each group member should take a roughly equal part in leading the
>   discussion
> - You should make an effort to include each other class member in your
>   discussion

Vignette

When I taught, I experimented with a lot of different ways to give quizzes. While I don't like quizzing students on assigned reading, I found it was often necessary, particularly when they had to read a book required by the curriculum but that they disliked.

One idea I tried was, instead of asking questions and having students provide answers to show that they'd read the assigned chapters, asking them to pose five questions that indicated that they'd read the material. My reasoning was that we could then use their questions as the basis for our discussion. This was a great idea in theory, and I was very proud of it, until I began to see the kinds of questions the students asked.

Almost all the questions requested an obvious, factual answer. I was distressed about this until I began to think of how poorly I'd prepared them for the task. I had assumed that they knew how to pose questions. Throughout their schooling, however, they'd experienced questions exactly of the sort they were producing for me. To them, a question posed in school was a question about a fact. Why would they ask different kinds of questions for me, especially when I was going to grade them on those questions? The experience caused me to jettison the idea, even though I'd been so pleased with myself for thinking it up. I realized that if I wanted students to ask open-ended, authentic questions, I needed to teach them how to do it and make it clear that such questions were legitimate and highly valued in my classroom.

- The questions you pose should not ask for factual information from the story, unless those facts help explore open-ended questions (questions without a single correct answer)
- The questions you pose should include at least one in each of the following categories:
  - Inferences about characters or events within the text
  - Generalizations from the text to society at large
  - The effects of literary form or technique
  - The purpose of a particular event in terms of the text's meaning
  - Evaluations of the literature
  - Emotions students experienced in response to the story
  - Personal connections to the story
- During the discussion, you should also work at getting students to elaborate on their initial comments

Book Clubs and Literature Circles. A less formal way of getting students to talk in exploratory ways is to have them discuss literature through book clubs or literature circles, which I introduced in Chapter 2. The teacher plays a less directive role in these settings than in the student-led whole-class discussions I have just described. In book clubs and literature circles, students either determine their own approach to discussion or are assigned open-ended roles that enable them to come up with questions and procedures of their own. Any of these three methods is worth trying, possibly in combination so that students have opportunities for self-directed discussions with different degrees of direction and freedom.

Narrative Knowing

Recall Jerome Bruner's contention that narrative knowing, while typically overlooked in schools, has just as crucial a role in human history as paradigmatic knowing. Yet schools, and English teachers, tend to overlook this type of knowing when it comes to assessment. I next identify ways in which you can evaluate students' prospects for knowing their worlds through a narrative construction.

Personal Narrative.   Much literature is presented around a story that portrays something about the human condition. Often readers relate to literature by recounting a personal story that parallels the issues depicted in it. One thing students can do, then, as a way of engaging with the unit themes, is write, act, or otherwise produce a personal narrative in which they relate a significant event from their own lives. For the hypothetical sophomore curriculum I am developing, these events would involve negotiating a threshold, with particular attention to one of the unit concepts.

Let's say, for instance, that the students are studying the unit on conflict with authority. One kind of writing they could do would be to relate a narrative about a conflict with authority that they have experienced. Their task might be the following:

> Write about a personal experience in which you had a conflict with someone in authority. The authority figure might have been an adult (a parent, teacher, coach, etc.) or a peer in an authority position (a team captain, student government leader, etc.). Through your narrative, you should convey the following:
>
> - Your relationship with the person with whom you came in conflict
> - The nature of your conflict
> - How both you and the other person viewed the conflict
> - If you resolved it, how; if you didn't, explain what happened
> - What you learned through the experience
>
> You do not need to explain these things in this order, and you don't need to announce or label any of them (that is, you don't need to have a paragraph beginning, "My relationship with so-and-so was . . ."). Rather, you should, at some point in your narrative, relate them in some way.

Retelling Literary Narratives.   Another kind of narrative would adopt the perspective of a literary character to relate an incident from literature. Literature is always told through some narrator's perspective. As some (Booth, 1974; M. W. Smith, 1991) have argued, that perspective is characterized by human limitations; that is, the narrator has limitations that enable him or her to tell only part of the story and to tell it in ways that are biased or unreliable.

Having students retell stories from the perspectives of other characters is one way to help them understand a narrative perspective, how it affects how a story is told, and how it helps to distinguish a narrator from an author. You could prompt such a narrative as follows:

> Take an extended passage from one of the works of literature we have read during this unit and retell it from the perspective of any character other than the original narrator. Your narrative should:
>
> - Include the same basic actions, events, and characters of the original narration, unless your narrator was somehow obscured from seeing or knowing about some

- Be told in a voice that is recognizable as that of your designated narrator; that is, it should include this character's personality, dialect, diction, opinions, and other traits
- Reflect your narrator's perspective on what happened

Connected Knowing

In Chapter 3, I reviewed ways in which schools do not provide many opportunities for relational or connected learning. I would like to suggest a few ways in which you can plan assessments that take connected knowing into account.

Collaborative Learning.   One way you can be responsive to connected knowers is to provide opportunities for collaboration on graded work. For instance, you can allow students to conduct their research reports (see earlier discussion) or creative and multimedia projects (discussed later) in teams. As I will review in later chapters, you can also plan to include collaborative learning in the activities that lead to the production of culminating texts.

Affective Response.   Attention to students' emotional responses to literature is also minimized in schools. Through the use of journals, student-generated discussions, narratives, and other kinds of assessment, you can increase the opportunities for students' affective responses to literature to be included in your evaluations of their schoolwork.

Exploratory Learning Opportunities.   Connected knowing is often associated with tentative, exploratory learning. I have reviewed a number of possible ways to allow for exploratory expression in assessed schoolwork: journals, student-generated discussions, process-oriented writing instruction, and so on.

Multimedia or Multigenre Productions

Gardner's work on multiple intelligences suggests that students ought to have opportunities to generate knowledge through texts and processes that move beyond the conventional academic emphasis on analytic writing. Much of this section on alternative assessment has provided ideas on how to extend students' opportunities for response and interpretation beyond detached analysis. I would also argue that students ought to be able to work in media other than writing. Some of the most remarkable work I have seen from high school students has come through multimedia productions, including art, music, dance, live or videotaped performance, and various combinations of these modes and others.

I should add that some rather intriguing multimedia productions do not necessarily reveal deep engagement with the literature. In one class I observed, for instance, a student baked a cake and decorated it in the fashion of a story's setting, and the class then ate it. It was not clear what they learned from this process, other than that the cake looked very tasty. It's possible that, rather than letting some works of art stand on their own, you would ask that students either write or verbally present an explanation of their work's significance in order to help you evaluate it.

Later in this book (Chapters 11 and 12) I will present transcripts from discussions that took place among students during and following their production of multimedia interpretations of literature. These transcripts present compelling evidence that multimedia productions can provide a powerful vehicle for high-level engagement with literature. They can also serve a very important function in students' interpretive processes, helping them generate images of literature that can then form the basis for a response or an interpretation. This strategy can be particularly useful for students who resist reading literature, especially if they have difficulty knowing how to produce images of what they read (see Wilhelm, 1997).

In Chapter 12 I will review one kind of assignment, called a *body biography,* that can serve as an image-generating tool. For now, I will simply provide one very open-ended assignment that you can adapt to a variety of units. I will specify a unit from the sophomore curriculum, but as you'll see, you can easily modify it for any unit of study.

You have read a complex work of literature in Shakespeare's *Julius Caesar.* To show what you have learned through your engagement with this play, create an interpretive text in any form of your choice: collage, painting, poetry, music, drama, sculpture, performance art, or other textual form. You are also welcome to combine forms to produce your text. Furthermore, you may use different forms within a form—that is, you can include a gravestone with epitaph, a haiku, a song, an encyclopedia entry, a movie review, and so on, all within a single interpretive text. Your text should include the following:

- It should in some way depict your understanding of the play. This understanding might be about any of the following:
  - The play's characters and their actions and relationships
  - How the play has helped you learn something about yourself and your world
  - Roman history
  - Shakespeare as a playwright
  - Another topic of your choice
- It should make some kind of reference to the play, even if it focuses on you and your current world
- You may produce your text individually or in a group of any size up to five
- You will have two class periods in which to work on your text; you must do all additional work outside class
- You must prepare a 3 to 5 minute presentation of your text to the class in which you explain its significance and what it reflects about your understanding of the play.

Unconventional (for School, Anyhow) Genres

Another type of assessment is to have students produce writing (perhaps in combination with other media) in genres that are not ordinarily produced by students for school assessments. The following list of possibilities is hardly exhaustive and is intended primarily to prime the pump of your imagination. When making assignments, you will need to identify the traits that should be involved in such texts, specify what they are, and be responsible for teaching students how to produce them.

Book or Film Review. Movie reviews are available through a variety of media. Countless examples of the genre can be found in newspapers, on television, and on the Internet. Students could study the genre and its elements and produce reviews of texts they read in class. This kind of assessment might be particularly useful if you choose a book-club arrangement for a unit or if you will have the opportunity to publish the reviews for other students to share.

Guide Book. Another kind of text students could produce would be a guide book. For a unit on peer groups, for instance, students could produce a guide book for incoming students. The book could review the various social groups among the student body and could include pictures, descriptions, interviews, and other methods of characterizing the different groups within the school. I would caution students that they should try to present each group in a fair and respectful manner, as students are often tempted to portray groups they don't belong to in unflattering ways.

Letter to the Editor. Students could write letters to the editor of a publication in which they express their opinions on some topic of importance to them. This task might follow from instruction in expository or persuasive writing, but students will see that letters to the editor often lack the formality of the kinds of analytic writing they learn to do in school. If you've read many letters to the editor, you'll know that they also often lack any semblance to thoughtful logic. By having students read one another's letters and responding to them, you may help students avoid producing the kinds of rants often published in newspapers.

Children's Book. Students could produce a children's book geared to the unit's theme. For the unit on *Julius Caesar,* for instance, students could retell a scene from the play, presenting it in the style of children's books they have studied. The assignment could conceivably bridge two different units, with students producing their book in the form of a parody.

Other. My intention here is to help you think about alternative kinds of texts that students could produce, rather than to provide you with an all-inclusive list. The possibilities are virtually limitless. I'm counting on you to think of others. One of my former students, for instance, had her students design the covers for hypothetical compact discs, with album themes related to the literary themes they were studying. I was delighted to hear of her idea, for it meant that she was taking the principles from her preservice education and using them to generate new ideas about teaching. I'm hoping that this book will serve the same purpose for you, rather than simply provide you with a limited set of assignments to give.

Creative Writing

Students can also generate creative work of their own in a variety of forms. In using the term *creative writing* I am referring to works of poetry, fiction, drama, and other fictive modes. I also assume, however, that any other kind of writing students do can include creative elements.

Here I will review two kinds of creative writing that students can do, writing that corresponds to the unit concepts and writing that follows the conventions of particular genres.

Writing Related to the Unit Concept.   Students can produce a poem, play, story, or other piece that concerns the unit concept. You could ask them, for instance, to produce some kind of literary work that includes a conflict with authority. You could either have students produce a particular form (poem, story, etc.) or have the assignment be open-ended, allowing students to choose their own medium or combination of genres.

Evaluating creative writing is difficult for many teachers, who find it too subjective to assess. As a result, many teachers don't assign it. But eliminating creative work from the curriculum because it's hard to grade can limit the ways in which students learn through their engagement with literature and other texts. Rather than disallowing open-ended thinking and writing, teachers should think of open-minded ways of assessing it. The following assignment is one way for you to specify assessment criteria without compromising the open-ended ways in which students may proceed:

> During the unit we have read a variety of literary works concerned with the theme of conflict with authority. Now it is your turn to write one. Using a medium or combination of media of your choice, produce a literary work that includes a conflict with an authority figure. In doing so, keep in mind the following:
>
> - You may use any literary form, or combination of literary forms, you choose
> - You may supplement your writing with other media: graphics, sound, movement, and so on
> - Your text should in some way involve a conflict with an authority figure
> - While you needn't resolve the conflict (and many conflicts go unresolved), you do need to show in some way the aftermath of the conflict and its consequences

Genres.   Students can also produce literature in a particular genre. If the sophomore curriculum were to include a unit on parody, for instance, they could both study parodies and produce them. An assignment that George Hillocks thought up long ago still works quite well. The idea is for students to study a writer with a distinctive style, such as Edgar Allan Poe or the narrative voice of Holden Caulfield. After characterizing that style, the students parody it with a kind of text that provides a humorous contrast, such as a children's story or nursery rhyme. Following a careful reading of Poe's style and characterization of his tendencies—dark images, macabre themes, recurring terms, and so on—for example, students could retell Humpty Dumpty, Jack and Jill, or another children's story using Poe's style. The prompt for students might appear as follows:

> Take a Mother Goose rhyme or another children's story and retell it in the style of Edgar Allan Poe. In your parody:
>
> - Remain faithful to the main elements of the children's rhyme or story
> - Tell the story in a voice that uses elements of Edgar Allan Poe's narrative style, including:

Unit Design

Identify Possible Goals

Identify a set of possible goals for the unit you are designing. Keep in mind that you should avoid the temptation of including too many major assessments in a single unit. You should instead focus on a few tasks that students can do well and that you can teach them how to do within the time limits of the unit.

For now, identify a small set of goals. Include both conventional and alternative forms of assessment. You needn't write out complete assignments at this point. In Chapter 6, you will narrow down your list and provide details for the assignments you intend to include in your unit.

- Common themes
- Typical sentence structures
- Recurring words
- Method of narration (e.g., first person)
- Narrative perspective

Exaggerate these elements so that they are clearly recognizable and humorous

ASSESSING CULMINATING PROJECTS

Grading student work can be a perplexing task. How do you know that all work that receives a B has similar qualities that can be distinguished from all work that receives an A or a C? How you make this distinction is especially important when a student or parent questions your grading decisions. How can you answer their challenge in ways that are defensible? One way is to develop a *rubric* to guide your decisions. A rubric is a scale that specifies how to differentiate between one level of performance and another. In its simplest form, a rubric for a 100-question multiple-choice test might simply be:

90–100 items correct:	A
80–89 items correct:	B
70–79 items correct:	C
60–69 items correct:	D
59 or fewer items correct:	F

Yet life in a constructivist classroom is not so clear-cut. When grading essays, portfolios, narratives, multimedia projects, drama, and so on, you need to specify how you will distinguish between an A and a B, a B and a C, and so on.

Earlier I said that one thing you need to have as a teacher—one thing you owe your students and your community—is *high expectations* for what your students will learn and produce. Teaching from a constructivist perspective is one way to have high expectations, because you are asking your students to engage with the course in a much more complex way than is available through memorization and recitation. You are asking them to be responsible for determining the rules by which they will evaluate literature, the understanding that they personally take from the material and activities, and the meaning that they construct from the literature. That's asking a lot. But your students will, for the most part, appreciate the fact that you respect them enough to commit yourself to this kind of teaching and learning. And if you demonstrate to them that you perceive yourself as a learner too, you'll reinforce the notion that learning is a lifelong process.

But doing all this is more work. It's much easier to borrow someone else's objective test and answer sheet than to read a pile of essays and evaluate them in fair and respectful ways. You might guess by now that I think that what's best for students is not always easiest for teachers. Next I'll suggest ways to think about how to make distinctions between one grade and another. I'll use the portfolio as an example of how to develop a scoring rubric for an open-ended assignment such as the ones described earlier.

The following is a series of questions you might ask in thinking about assessment:

- What might students learn from doing this, and how do I know that they've learned it?
- What conventions do students need to follow in order to produce an acceptable form of this genre? These could include issues ranging from the need for a particular form of English (e.g., textbook English) to the need for criteria in an extended definition.
- What level of detail is required to treat the topic sufficiently?
- What degree of cohesion should a student achieve?
- To what degree has the student met each point in the assignment?

The portfolio assignment includes some clear, unambiguous requirements (e.g., a minimum number of exhibits, an explanation of each, and a synthesis paper). Some students believe that simply producing the minimum requirements should earn them a high grade. In evaluating portfolios, you need to decide exactly what a student should earn for each level of performance you find in response to the assignment.

The portfolio assignment also includes some requirements that are more open to interpretation. In particular, the essay in which students explain how they learned about their own learning process is open-ended. You need to address how you will treat these issues when assigning grades to portfolios.

Assuming that your school follows the traditional A through F grading system, the following is one possible rubric for assessing the portfolio project described in the previous section:

A grade of A will be awarded to portfolios that

- are turned in on time
- include the minimum components
- meet minimum expectations for each component (e.g., minimum number of words)

- clearly explain how each exhibit served as the source of significant learning about the self, the materials, and/or the learning process
- clearly explain in the synthesis paper how the individual exhibits contribute to an overall set of related learning experiences explained in terms of a related set of points

A grade of B will be awarded to portfolios that

- are turned in on time
- include the minimum components
- meet minimum expectations for each component (e.g., minimum number of words)
- clearly explain how each exhibit served as the source of significant learning about the self, the materials, and/or the learning process
- do not clearly explain in the synthesis paper how the individual exhibits contribute to an overall set of related learning experiences explained in terms of a related set of points

A grade of C will be awarded to portfolios that:

- are turned in on time
- include the minimum components
- meet minimum expectations for each component (e.g., minimum number of words)
- do not clearly explain how each exhibit served as the source of significant learning about the self, the materials, and/or the learning process
- do not clearly explain in the synthesis paper how the individual exhibits contribute to an overall set of related learning experiences explained in terms of a related set of points

A grade of D will be awarded to portfolios that

- are turned in on time
- include the minimum components
- do not meet minimum expectations for the components (e.g., the synthesis paper does not provide a synthesis; the commentaries are less than a page long or do not indicate reflection on learning)
- do not clearly explain how each exhibit served as the source of significant learning about the self, the materials, and/or the learning process
- do not clearly explain in the synthesis paper how the individual exhibits contribute to an overall set of related learning experiences explained in terms of a related set of points

A grade of F will be awarded to portfolios that:

- are turned in after the specified due date
- are turned in on time yet do not include the minimum components (cover page, eight exhibits, eight commentaries, synthesis paper)

Prepare Rubric

For one of the culminating texts you identified previously, prepare a scoring rubric. This rubric should clearly distinguish among the kinds of performances acceptable for each of the five possible grades (A, B, C, D, F).

- do not meet minimum expectations for the components (e.g., the synthesis paper does not provide a synthesis; the commentaries are less than a page long or do not indicate reflection on learning)
- do not clearly explain how each exhibit served as the source of significant learning about the self, the materials, and/or the learning process
- do not clearly explain in the synthesis paper how the individual exhibits contribute to an overall set of related learning experiences explained in terms of a related set of points

While it will not solve all problems, a rubric of this sort will help you evaluate the portfolios in a fairly consistent manner. Using rubrics is particularly helpful at the beginning of your career, when you are learning how to assess for the first time. You will find them especially useful when you experience fatigue from grading; that is, when you've been grading for a while, your attention begins to slip, and you need a reference point for making distinctions among performances. You will also find rubrics useful if your grading decisions are challenged by a student, parent, or administrator. If your rubric makes clear distinctions and you can demonstrate how your grading is informed by these distinctions, you will have fewer headaches to contend with.

Before departing this section on rubrics, I should stress that they can be difficult to develop without having read a number of student papers to see the range of traits they include. If you are reading this book in conjunction with a practicum, you would benefit from asking your mentor teacher if you may grade papers, or at least read them, as part of your experience. Doing so will help you think about what makes for good writing in particular situations and how to assess writing in ways that are related to what the teacher has taught about it.

FINAL THOUGHTS

This chapter has focused on the setting of unit goals. The purpose of these goals is to articulate the evaluative destination students are headed for, which in turn helps a teacher identify instructional responsibilities. While focusing on the final forms of the texts I have tried to stress that these texts should serve as the culmination of some kind of meaningful engagement of students with the literature, the class, and their worlds. This engagement and the social action it involves are fundamental to the educational process. The culminating texts provide the teacher with a concrete product to assess that represents the students' engagement.

One important point to remember is that *the planning process is recursive.* In other words, you don't necessarily set unit goals at the beginning never to revisit them. Rather, most of what you do in instructional planning is *provisional.* You think about goals and assessments in terms of the unit concepts, sketch them out as I've done in this chapter, work on lessons and activities that help students work toward those goals, and then go back and reconsider the assessments in terms of what's realistic. Sometimes your original theories and assumptions don't work so well once you put them in motion.

Recently, for instance, I saw a fascinating British Broadcasting Company series called *Walking with Dinosaurs* on the Discovery Channel. Based on their discoveries of bones, eggs, and other remnants of dinosaur society, scientists had developed theories of what dinosaurs looked like, what their posture was, how they moved, what they ate, how they lived, and so on. For *Walking with Dinosaurs,* however, they needed to work with computer animators to reconstruct what the dinosaurs looked like as they interacted with their prehistoric world. When they began putting the creatures in motion on animation screens, they realized that some of their theories needed revision. Program producer Jaspar James described the process as follows:

> It used to be thought that the hugely long necks of sauropods were for reaching for the tops of trees, like giraffes. As you'll notice though, our Diplodocus do quite the opposite. Their long necks reach out and sweep around in an arc to eat vegetation at ground level. We have paleontologist Kent Stevens to thank for this re-evaluation of their feeding habits. Kent did on a computer what could never have been done with the real skeletons. He made careful measurements of all the vertebrae that make up a *Diplodocus'* neck and then made a computer model which allowed him to study how the neck as a whole could move. Because of the way that the bones fit together, Kent found that it would have been impossible for the animal to ever get its head much higher than the horizontal. It simply did not have a swan-like bendy neck. But its head could, without any problem, reach down to ground level—in fact it could reach a fair way beneath it! The animal, then, could get to a large sweep of vegetation, without even moving its huge body. This kind of study hadn't been done before with the real bones because their size and weight makes it impossible to play around with them in this way. (http://www.bbc.co.uk/dinosaurs/tv_series/production2.shtml)

My point is not to instruct you about dinosaurs, but to show you how you need to adapt your plans as you make new discoveries—first, when planning, and second, when putting your ideal unit in motion with students. How they move, what they feed on, how their brains work, how they affect their environment, and so on will surely cause you to rethink your plans. As you work through your unit, you should continually reconsider the goals and assessments you developed early on.

Books about Assessing Student Learning

Airasian, P. W. (1996). *Assessment in the classroom.* New York: McGraw-Hill.

Allison, L., Bryant, L., & Hourigan, M. (Eds.). (1997). *Grading and the post-process classroom.* Portsmouth, NH: Heinemann.

Anson, C. M. (Ed.). (1989). *Writing and response: Theory, practice, and research.* Urbana, IL: National Council of Teachers of English.

Ause, C., Brunjes, H. E. B., & Spear, K. I. (1993). *Peer response groups in action: Writing together in secondary schools.* Portsmouth, NH: Heinemann.

Bizanno, P. (1993). *Responding to student poems: Applications of critical theory.* Urbana, IL: National Council of Teachers of English.

Darling-Hammond, L., Ancess, J., & Falk, B. (1995). *Authentic assessment in action: Studies of schools and students at work.* New York: Teachers College Press.

DeFabio, R. Y. (1994). *Outcomes in process: Setting standards for language use.* Portsmouth, NH: Heinemann.

Flynn, T., & King, M. (Eds.). (1993). *Dynamics of the writing conference: Social and cognitive interaction.* Urbana, IL: National Council of Teachers of English.

Freedman, S. W. (1987). *Response to student writing* (NCTE Research Report No. 23). Urbana, IL: National Council of Teachers of English.

Fulwiler, T. (Ed.). (1987). *The journal book.* Portsmouth, NH: Heinemann.

Harp, B. (Ed.). (1994). *Assessment and evaluation in student-centered programs* (2nd ed.). Norwood, MA: Christopher-Gordon.

Harris, M. (1986). *Teaching one-to-one: The writing conference.* Urbana, IL: National Council of Teachers of English.

Hewitt, G. (1995). *A portfolio primer: Teaching, collecting, and assessing student writing.* Portsmouth, NH: Heinemann.

Johnston, P. H. (1992). *Constructive evaluation of literate activity.* New York: Longman.

Johnston, P. H. (1997). *Knowing literacy: Constructive literacy assessment.* York, ME: Stenhouse.

Shaughnessy, M. P. (1977). *Errors and expectations: A guide for the teacher of basic writing.* New York: Oxford University Press.

Spandel, V., & Stiggins, R. J. (1990). *Creating writers: Linking assessment and writing instruction.* New York: Longman.

Spear, K. I. (1987). *Sharing writing: Peer response groups in English classes.* Portsmouth, NH: Heinemann.

Stiggins, R. J., & Conklin, N. F. (1992). *In teachers' hands: Investigating the practices of classroom assessment.* Albany, NY: SUNY Press.

Stipek, D. J. (1993). *Motivation to learn.* Boston: Allyn & Bacon.

Strickland, K., & Strickland, J. (1998). *Reflections on assessment: Its purposes, methods and effects on learning.* Portsmouth, NH: Heinemann.

Valencia, S., Hiebert, E. H., & Afflerbach, P. P. (Eds.). (1994). *Authentic reading assessment: Practices and possibilities.* Newark, DE: International Reading Association.

Welch, N. (1997). *Getting restless: Rethinking revision in writing instruction.* Portsmouth, NH: Heinemann.

White, E., Lutz, W., & Kamusikiri, S. (Eds.). (1996). *Assessment of writing: Politics, policies, practices.* New York: Modern Language Association of America.

Yancey, K. B., & Huot, B. (1997). *Assessing writing across the curriculum: Diverse approaches and practices.* Norwood, NJ: Ablex.

Zak, F., & Weaver, C. C. (Eds.). (1998). *The theory and practice of grading writing: Problems and possibilities.* Albany, NY: SUNY Press.

Refining the Unit Focus

This chapter moves from the general discussion of goals and assessment in Chapter 5 to a more specific discussion of a unit on coming of age for the hypothetical sophomore curriculum described in Chapter 4. Here, I walk through how I might identify a unit topic within the sophomore curriculum, how I might go about selecting materials, and how I might identify a small set of goals for the unit. I make an effort to think aloud during my planning process to illustrate how you might make decisions during unit design.

In Chapter 5 I identified a variety of conventional and alternative assessments that could serve as goals for a unit of instruction. As you can imagine, you would never try to do all these assessments in a single unit. Rather, for any one unit, you should select a few that would provide students the opportunity to be assessed through a range of ways of knowing. In this chapter, I will take one unit of instruction and identify a set of goals that students could work toward. I will identify the unit goals as many teachers do, on the basis of my own judgment about what students will learn. You could adapt these decision-making principles to identify goals in collaboration with either colleagues or students.

WHOLE-COURSE CONSIDERATIONS

I will approach this task within the context of the sophomore curriculum discussed in the previous two chapters. Remember that for any course, you should have a limited set of overarching concepts. Trying to do too much will likely result in confusion.

I reviewed a number of possible types of overarching concepts in Chapter 4. Here, I will get more specific. I will identify a small set of concepts, with no more than one from any single type, for the sophomore curriculum. I will then provide a brief rationale for each.

- *Negotiating thresholds (theme):* I have previously described the appropriateness of this theme for the sophomore year course. In brief, sophomores tend to adopt a group orientation and can benefit from considering ways of negotiating the contact they have with other groups.

These groups include social groups within their peer culture, groups formed by different age and grade levels within their school, and the general distinction between the adolescent and adult worlds that they are transversing.

- *Self-determination (stance):* I want my students to develop the stance that they are capable of learning on their own and that my role is to teach them how to learn. If we succeed, they will find the course useful after they leave it, and they will not view me as a mere fact dispenser whose utility ends the day of the last exam. Facts, of course, will be central to the knowledge they learn in my class. But the facts will not be an end in themselves. Rather, they will serve as tools for students to use as they construct knowledge. Students will learn how to find facts on their own, how to distinguish a fact from a fraud, how to use facts to construct new paradigmatic and narrative knowledge. In other words, they will learn how facts function. Doing so will be part of our overall effort to help them understand and realize their potential for learning independently and knowing what they need to know.
- *Dramatic images (strategy):* My experiences as a teacher have taught me the importance of having students generate images that help them visualize literature. Louise Rosenblatt (1978) has described this ability as generating an *evocation* of a literary work, which provides the basis for literary response. Students can render their understanding of literature through a variety of means, including art, drama, dance, and other artistic and theatrical forms. As I will illustrate in Chapters 11 and 12, this strategy not only provides students with a way to represent their understanding, but can also contribute to the understandings they reach.

In Chapter 4, I identified a series of culminating texts that students could produce for final exams in relation to these over-arching concepts. In this chapter, I will narrow my scope to a single unit within this whole course and identify goals for that unit. Beginning with Chapter 7, I will then begin to plan instruction that will help students achieve these goals.

> Finals, the very name of which implies that nothing of importance can happen after it.
>
> —David Lodge

CONCEPTUAL UNIT ON COMING OF AGE

I will illustrate unit design through a unit on coming-of-age literature, one of the units I previously identified for the sophomore curriculum. I will plan this unit as the first unit of the school year. This unit provides an appropriate beginning because the literature fits well with the kinds of transitions that students make in moving from ninth grade to tenth. Often the summer has placed them in situations that have enabled significant transformations of the sort explored in coming-of-age literature. This unit will allow students to reflect on these experiences in ways much richer than those afforded by the "what I did last summer" essays that occasionally start the new academic year.

Materials

I will assume that my choices for materials will be constrained by the curriculum and the literature anthology. For the purposes of demonstration, I'll select a set of texts that were in the anthologies I used when I taught high school English and that tend to be reprinted in new ones. For the unit's major work, I'll select a canonical young-adult novel, *A Separate Peace*. My purposes in making these relatively safe and conventional choices is that they are typical of the kinds of materials that will be available to you in most public schools.

The materials are:

Poems

Robert Frost: "The Road Not Taken"
Langston Hughes: "Mother to Son"

Short Stories

Richard Wright: "The Man Who Was Almost a Man"
Alice Munroe: "Red Dress"
Nicolai Chukovski: "The Bridge"
Irwin Shaw: "Peter Two"
Alice Walker: "Everyday Use"

Novel

John Knowles: *A Separate Peace*

Unit Goals

For the major unit goals, I want to select assessments that evaluate a range of ways of knowing. I also want to establish certain principles and routines that I can use to help give the year a comfortable sense of rhythm and continuity. In addition to these considerations, I will describe assessment of two types:

- *In-process texts and activities:* activities students do as part of their learning *during* the unit. These texts and activities are designed to be exploratory, with attention given primarily to what students learn. The final look of their product is of less concern.
- *Culminating texts and activities:* activities students do toward the *end* of the unit. These texts and activities should be more concerned with expectations for form, although they should also serve as opportunities for new learning.

In-process texts and activities ought to contribute to students' ability to produce satisfying culminating texts and activities.

There are dozens of worthwhile goals you could set for any unit of instruction. To help focus the students' attention on a set of goals they can realize in rich and productive ways, you should identify a small set of goals to serve as the major assessments for the unit. These goals should be consistent with the overarching concepts for the course as a whole. When you plan other units within the curriculum, you should vary the goals and assessments to account for the multiple ways of knowing outlined in Chapter 3.

> Those students get the highest grades who take their responsibilities of educating me the most seriously.
>
> —Theodore Roethke

For the coming-of-age unit, I want to provide for a range of ways of knowing that fit within the three overarching concepts I've identified. In other words, I want students to begin to understand how to negotiate thresholds, to develop a stance that they will determine much about their own learning, and to learn procedures for generating images to represent literary relationships and actions. From the menu of goals I described in Chapter 5, a number suit these purposes well. I will next describe one possible set of goals that would fit within my conception of the curriculum as a whole and within the role of this particular unit within that curriculum. The goals are numbered for convenience rather than to suggest an order of importance.

In-Process Texts and Activities

Self-determination is among the year's overarching concepts. I hope that during the course of the year, students will develop the stance that they are in control of their learning. I want them to believe that they know what they want to learn and how to learn it.

But hoping isn't enough. I need to make sure that I teach them ways of learning that contribute to that kind of confidence and authority. Teaching for self-determination requires that I help students learn procedures for setting goals and posing questions that they would like to answer. I therefore want to start the year by identifying texts and activities through which students can learn some procedures for asking questions. If they have had a typical education, they are probably inexperienced at posing their own questions about their schoolwork; they have spent most of their school life answering questions asked by teachers.

Field Observation

In a school you're visiting, note the frequency with which students ask questions and note the type of questions they ask. What do the amount and kinds of questions they ask tell you about their understanding of how school works?

Because of their inexperience at asking questions, I want to give students opportunities that have two features:

- They may take risks and make mistakes without being punished by a bad grade
- They have the opportunity to work collaboratively and receive feedback while learning, as part of an instructional scaffold

Two of the goals I identified in Chapter 5 can potentially provide these opportunities: keeping a response log and leading student-generated discussions. I will next describe what these goals might look like. In describing them, I'll review the teaching responsibilities you set for yourself when identifying the responsibilities you set for students.

Goal 1: Response Log.   I am indebted to Cindy O'Donnell-Allen, whose senior English class I observed for a year, for this approach to using response logs. I describe her class in greater detail in Chapter 12. While Cindy didn't invent response logs—they've been around for quite some time—she developed a way of teaching students how to use them that I felt was very effective. I'll flesh out this approach in Chapter 8.

Briefly, Cindy valued the overarching concept of self-determination and felt that one way to help students achieve it was to use response logs as a tool for learning different ways of thinking about literature. She did not want them to rely on her for their interpretations, which she felt would do them little good once they left her class. Rather, she wanted them to develop both a stance that they were competent and insightful readers and a set of strategies for pursuing their insights and questions. Based on her years of teaching, however, she felt that her students had been conditioned to answer questions rather than ask them. They therefore needed to be taught different kinds of questions to ask. They also needed to be taught the specific format of the response log, which was used rarely in her school district.

Next I'll provide one way to specify the task of keeping a response log. As reviewed in Chapter 5, the assignment includes a general description of the task and a set of specific components. For each component listed, the teacher would need to (a) provide appropriate instruction and (b) determine a fair and appropriate assessment.

> Keep a reading log in response to the literature we are studying during this unit. To keep your log:
>
> - Divide each page with a vertical line down the center.
> - On the left side of each page, record significant passages from the literature you read.
> - On the right side, across from each passage, do any or all of the following:
>   1. Ask *open-ended questions* that would help you understand the passage better
>   2. Give your personal *response* to the passage (i.e., any thoughts you have in connection with it)
>   3. Give your personal *evaluation* of the passage
>   4. Think through a possible *interpretation* of the passage
> - Have at least one question of each type for each work of literature studied.
> - Remember that your journal does not need to follow the conventions of textbook English. Rather, the purpose is to think about the literature without worrying about the form your thoughts take.
> - Turn your response log in every two weeks. I will read your log and respond to your comments. If you make an entry that you do not want me to read, place an X at the top of the page.
> - Keep in mind that *I am required to share any thoughts or suggestions of violence, suicide, substance abuse, family abuse, or other harmful behavior with the school counselors.*

If you set this as a goal for students, you also assume an important set of teaching responsibilities. Many observers of schools have noted that teachers are very good at giving assignments, but not always so good at teaching students how to do the things they assess. For the reading-log goal, you need to teach students knowledge in two areas:

- The genre of the reading log, including not just the format, but the social practices that produce it. These would include taking an inquiring stance,

using writing for exploratory purposes, understanding the importance of taking risks, and realizing that some schoolwork will not be penalized for being incorrect.
- Procedures for posing the four types of entry described: questions, personal response, personal evaluation, and interpretation.

Goal 2: Student-Generated Discussions. A related kind of assignment would be to teach students how to generate their own questions for whole-class discussions of literature. Again, taking this approach would depart radically from students' customary experiences in school, where they come to class with the expectation that the teacher will carry the interpretive load for them.

A further departure of this assignment is that students will learn how to ask open-ended questions rather than those with correct answers. As with the response-log assignment, you will have to teach students how to do this, given their likely lack of experience with inquiry in school and likely belief that in school, only correct answers matter.

I am adapting the following assignment from my own teaching in Illinois high schools. My purpose was to give students authority in their approach to reading and responding to literature. I found that if I did my job well, the students often asked questions that resulted in compelling discussions conducted entirely by students. The following is the task I would set for them, adapted to the coming-of-age unit. I will elaborate in Chapter 8 on how I taught my students how to lead these discussions. For the purposes of convenience, I will use *A Separate Peace* by John Knowles for this assignment. As you'll see, you can easily substitute other books for students to read and discuss.

> To discuss John Knowles's *A Separate Peace,* the class will organize into six small groups, with each group being responsible for leading a discussion of two chapters of the novel. Each group will use one full class period to discuss its chapters. To lead the class, you may adopt any format you wish: regular English class, nonviolent talk-show format, courtroom scene, town meeting, or other mode of your choice. Your discussion should involve all of the following:
>
> - Each group member should take a roughly equal part in leading the discussion
> - You should make an effort to include each other class member in your discussion
> - The questions you pose should not ask for factual information from the story, unless those facts help explore open-ended questions (those without a single correct answer)
> - The questions you pose should include at least one in each of the following categories:
>   - Inferences about characters or events within the text
>   - Generalizations from the text to society at large
>   - The effects of literary form or technique

Reflective Writing Prompt

In your own education, did your teachers teach you how to do the things they were assessing you on? What were their assumptions about their role as teachers? In their approach, what responsibilities did you have as a student? What was the overall effect of this approach on your learning? What have you learned from your own schooling that you can apply to your approach to teaching?

- Purpose of a particular event in terms of the text's meaning
- Evaluations of the literature
- Emotions students had in response to the story
- Personal connections to the story
- During the discussion, you should also work at getting students to elaborate on their initial comments

Once again, when you give this assignment, you also assign yourself a set of teaching responsibilities. You need to make sure that students know how to work in groups, which may be an unfamiliar format for them. I describe how to do this in Chapter 9. Primarily, you need to teach them how to ask questions of the type you are requiring. They probably are inexperienced in answering open-ended questions, much less asking them. Your teaching responsibilities, then, will be centered on teaching students how to distinguish the question types, ask appropriate questions within them, and discuss them in exploratory ways. I would encourage you to adopt an inquiry stance toward the issues, so that when students disagree they *argue to learn* rather than *argue to win*. They might also view discussion as co-*constructed,* or *dialogic;* that is, they work together to use exploratory talk to construct new ideas. Discussion needn't be based on disagreement, but rather can work toward agreement through the participation of many.

Note that the assignment also includes options on how to create different formats for leading the discussions. Some students feel comfortable leading discussions as teachers. In fact, they often enjoy the opportunity to imitate certain distinctive teachers they've had over the years—this may include imitating you. Other students prefer to adapt a game-show or talk-show format or to put characters on trial and call class members up to testify. I've always found that students get more out of their discussions when they choose their own format. What you need to stress is that you will be evaluating them according to the criteria specified in the assignment and that if they can have a little fun while meeting them, that's great.

You should also stress that some formats might detract from their ability to satisfy the assignment's requirement and you might specify which program formats could detract from the exploration of ideas. I would discourage violent or profane talk-show formats.

One final point: I am proposing the response log and student-generated discussions as goals for early in the year. You can then either have students repeat them for future units or build on them with different assignments. For instance, if you see that students are learning how to generate insightful questions, you might use a book club or literature circle approach for a unit later in the year. In this approach, after reading a common set of texts relative to a unit concept, students would break into small groups to discuss a major work (e.g., a novel) of their choice. This process would enable students to draw on their knowledge of how to pose questions to lead their own discussions of their book club literature. It would provide a good extension of the skills learned in the response log and student-led discussions and contribute to their self-determination as learners.

My approach here does depart from that suggested by the originators of the book club and literature circle approaches. They tend to rely more on students' spontaneous ability to generate questions, rather than having the teacher teach question

Vignette

A note on homework: The amount of homework you can assign will vary, depending on the rules of the school you teach in. In some schools, you can assign as much homework as you please. In fact, children are increasingly suffering from back injuries that doctors and chiropractors attribute to the heavy backpacks they carry around for school.

In other schools, the amount of homework you assign will be controlled by the administration. I spent some time in a middle school a few years ago in which the principal decreed that teachers could assign homework only one night a week. He specified further that math teachers could assign homework on Mondays, English teachers on Tuesdays, history teachers on Wednesday, science on Thursdays, and nobody over the weekend.

But that's not all. The school football team played its games on Tuesday afternoons. To help boost attendance, he declared that if a student could produce a ticket stub as proof of going to the game, the student was excused from homework that night. And so during the football season, English teachers couldn't assign homework.

And the school was nominated for a Blue Ribbon School of Excellence award that year.

---

types prior to setting up the clubs and circles. In their own writing about these approaches, they describe excellent results without the instruction on question posing that I describe. You might want to experiment with different sequences to see which way works best for you.

Discussion Topic

Many educational reformers recommend that schools would educate students better if they were to require more homework. Do you believe that by assigning more homework, you will be a better English teacher?

Culminating Texts and Activities

The in-process assessments are designed to teach students strategies for learning both stance and procedures for personal inquiry. They focus on the process of inquiry more than on the precision of the final product. For culminating texts and activities, your focus includes attention to the final form of the effort and how it meets particular conventions. This attention to form does not eliminate attention to process, but rather stresses the idea that certain kinds of texts have particular features that readers expect to find. These formal features serve as codes to help readers invoke the appropriate reading conventions. The more faithfully a writer works within these conventions, the more likely readers will be in tune with the writer's intentions.

A simple example: A reading log does not call for correct answers or conventional English because the emphasis is on using writing as a tool for thinking, rather than on producing an impeccable product. A reader who invokes the wrong

> "Needless to say, my students are constantly challenging me to redefine old insights, to crack open my treasured chestnuts of truth, to learn what I don't know, and to confront my own process of writing in order to help them. This last is perhaps the most educational aspect of my teaching."
>
> —Julia Alvarez

conventions might consider students bad writers when they are in fact using the logs as intended. It behooves a writer to know which conventions to call on in producing a particular kind of writing. Culminating texts should be responsive to the need for appropriate conventional form.

For the sophomore curriculum, we want to work within the whole course's overarching concepts. In addition to the stance of *self-determination,* we want to make sure that the unit addresses the theme of *negotiating thresholds* and the strategy of *dramatic images.* A number of the culminating texts identified in Chapter 5 can contribute to these emphases. Students could write a personal narrative related to the unit theme, or they could write a literary analysis, which would provide opportunities for both narrative and paradigmatic knowing during the unit. Finally, they could produce an artistic text through which they could demonstrate their understanding of the unit themes and represent their knowledge through a dramatic image.

I will next give some possible ways of providing assignments to help students reach these goals.

Goal 3: Personal Narrative Related to the Unit Theme.
Students in their sophomore year are at an age when transforming experiences are likely to occur, moving them to new stages of maturity. One way to draw on these life events is to have students write personal narratives about significant experiences that have resulted in a sense that they have entered a new age characterized by greater worldly wisdom and accomplishment. In Chapter 5, I described one possible assessment of this type for a unit on conflict with authority. You could easily adapt this assessment to the unit on coming of age.

As you will see in Chapter 7, it's possible to link this culminating text to an introductory activity for the unit as a whole. That is, students could begin the unit by writing about a personal experience that triggered a transformation from immaturity to maturity. I have used these narratives in ways consistent with the overarching concept of generating dramatic images: Students take their narratives, share them in small groups, select or develop a single narrative from the various possibilities, produce a script, and perform their sketch before the class. Through this activity students can see a variety of coming-of-age narratives prior to reading. This repeated engagement with the script can help them develop schematic knowledge of how such stories tend to unfold, thus aiding their ability to write literary analyses (see goal 4).

Students can then, during the unit, return to their own narratives and develop them into more polished pieces of writing. To help them understand the expectations for this text, you could give the following instructions:

Write about a personal experience you've had in which you had a coming-of-age experience. Through your narrative, you should convey the following:

- The immature behavior that you exhibited prior to the experience
- A transforming experience through which you gained significant new knowledge and maturity
- The mature behavior that you exhibited following the experience

- A reflection on why this experience, rather than others, had the power to cause such a significant change in your wisdom and maturity
- An understanding of appropriate language conventions for narrative writing

You are not required to explain these events in this particular order, although you may do so if you wish. The purpose of the narrative is to enable you to think about what counts as a significant experience for you and what effects those experiences have on your development toward adulthood.

As with other unit goals, this assignment identifies both student responsibilities and teacher responsibilities. Students need to understand how to produce a narrative and what, in particular, a coming-of-age narrative includes. The activity described above can be useful in teaching this knowledge. I will elaborate on this instruction in the chapters that follow.

Goal 4: Literary Analysis.   As noted, the production of personal narratives and the study of narratives produced by others can help students recognize the script typically followed in coming-of-age literature. This knowledge in turn can help them analyze a story for an explication of the coming-of-age script. As I have argued previously, it's most useful for students to analyze a story they have not studied in class for this task. If they analyze a story you have already discussed, you can't be sure whether they're simply parroting the class's interpretation or not. To demonstrate what they have really learned about coming-of-age literature, they should have the opportunity to read a story and analyze it on their own. The task you present them might look as follows:

From the literary choices provided, read one work of literature and write an essay in which you analyze the protagonist's coming-of-age experience. In your essay, make sure that you:

- Provide a general thesis for the paper, explaining the protagonist's primary transformation during the course of the story.
- Describe the protagonist's immature behavior at the beginning of the story, including specific examples from the text.
- Describe clearly the key event that causes the character to change. In doing so, explain why this event, rather than others in the story, causes the protagonist to come of age.
- Describe the significant changes taking place in the protagonist following the coming-of-age experience, including specific examples from the text.
- Draw a conclusion about how people change as a result of significant events.
- Follow rules of textbook grammar, spelling, punctuation, and usage throughout your essay.
- Give evidence of having written at least one rough draft that has been submitted for peer evaluation.

Note that the last requirement suggests that students will have the opportunity to work on this essay over time, producing several drafts. It's possible that you would

Unit Design

Refining Your Focus

You have thus far identified overarching concepts and goals for the course. You have also identified possible materials and goals for a single unit of study.

At this time, you will refine your unit plan to identify the goals that will suggest an appropriate instructional design. To refine your unit, do the following:

- Reconsider the materials you originally selected, reducing your list to a set that you can reasonably teach within the time limits of your unit.
- Identify a small set of *culminating texts* that students can produce. Producing these texts should allow your students to meet the unit goals. For these culminating texts:
  - Make sure that you are using both conventional and unconventional forms of assessment.
  - Make sure that the goals are consistent with the overarching concepts of the whole course.
  - For each text, identify a set of bulleted criteria that will help you outline your teaching responsibilities, help your students understand their responsibilities, and help you develop an assessment rubric.
- Identify a small set of in-process texts that students can produce. Producing these texts should allow your students to meet the unit goals. For these in-process texts:
  - Make sure they help students work toward the unit goals and culminating texts.
  - For each text, identify a set of bulleted criteria that will help you outline your teaching responsibilities, help your students understand their responsibilities, and help you develop an assessment rubric.

When you are done, exchange your work with other students and critique one another's plans. Use this feedback for further refinement of your unit design.

---

restrict them to in-class writing to ensure that they are providing an interpretation on their own.

Goal 5: Multimedia Project.   Finally, students can produce a multimedia project of their choice. I tended to provide an opportunity like this for every unit we studied. At times I would make them optional for extra credit; at times I would require them. For many students, the greatest learning took place through these projects. Undoubtedly, the greatest fun came in producing them. Often, my most unmotivated and least successful students would spend extraordinary amounts of time in preparation, particularly when their efforts resulted in a performance.

Some groups of students would spend entire weekends writing, practicing, performing, and filming their interpretations. They would insist on showing their videotapes to the class, who typically received them with laughter, respect, and appreciation. I'm confident that videotaped performances from the 1980s are still prized possessions of many of my former students.

Rationale

Return to the rationale you wrote earlier. Reread it and see how well it fits your unit as you are developing it. If need be, reconsider your rationale by adjusting its focus, adding or revising major points, adding or revising the evidence you provide, adding to or revising your rebuttals, and revoicing your rhetoric and points to suit potential readers.

The assignment should be open-ended, as should your criteria for evaluating them. Because students may choose to work in a medium in which they are not trained or talented (e.g., they might not have experience in the theater), you should base your evaluation on what they learned from the process of producing the project. This might entail having students provide an explanation of what their artistic interpretation means and what they learned from doing it. The following is one way to phrase your instructions to students:

> You have read a number of literary works that concern the theme of coming of age. To show what you have learned through your engagement with this literature, create an interpretive text in any form of your choice: collages, paintings, poetry, music, drama, sculpture, performance art, or other textual form. You are also welcome to combine forms to produce your text. Your text should include the following:
>
> - It should in some way depict your understanding of coming-of-age experiences
> - It should make some kind of reference to at least one work of literature studied during the unit
> - You may produce your text individually or in a group of any size up to five.
> - You will have two class periods in which to work on your text; you must do all additional work outside class.
> - You must prepare a 3 to 5 minute presentation of your text in which you explain to the class its significance and what it reflects about your understanding of coming of age experiences and/or literature.

FINAL THOUGHTS

In this chapter I have given an idea of how you might develop a manageable set of goals for a single unit. These goals fall within the overarching concepts that guide the whole course. They provide opportunities across a broad range of the ways of knowing identified in Chapter 3. In the next chapter, I go to the beginning of the unit to describe ways of designing introductory activities that help students develop the kinds of schematic knowledge they'll need to work successfully toward these goals.

7 Introductory Activities: Gateway to the Unit Concepts

In this chapter I talk about what I think is a key part of any unit: the introductory activity. Such activities help students develop an appropriate "cognitive map" for the concepts that are key to the unit. I describe four kinds of introductory activities: writing about personal experiences, opinionnaire/survey, scenarios/case studies, and writing about related problems. I illustrate each with a possible introduction for different units in the hypothetical sophomore curriculum. I also encourage you to think of other ways to introduce a unit's concepts.

By now you have identified your unit goals in the form of a set of assessments. Through these assessments, your students will both

- demonstrate learning that you can assess, and
- learn new things for themselves through their process of producing their texts.

Both you and your students now know what you are building toward. It's possible that things will happen along the way to cause these plans to change somewhat, but for the most part you have a set of goals to guide your planning of the unit.

How, then, to begin? I will continue with the construction metaphor by returning to the idea of providing an instructional scaffold, which I introduced in Chapter 2. In construction, scaffolds help support those parts of a building that are in the process of being built. They are gradually removed as the building becomes more solid and self-supporting. Teaching can provide the same support for learners.

I should stress one weakness of the scaffolding metaphor before continuing. Both scaffolds and buildings are inert. Both instruction and learners are dynamic. Different buildings will be supported by a scaffold in more or less the same ways. Different learners, however, will understand, use, and reconstruct an instructional scaffold in different ways. It's very important when using the scaffolding metaphor to understand this key distinction.

The general idea of the metaphor is that a scaffold can provide support during the earliest stages of learning. As learners demonstrate that they have grasped the concepts stressed in the instruction, the teacher's support is gradually removed. The active, dynamic quality of learning, however, will likely produce differences in

- the particular goals that each student has in relation to the goals the teacher has
- the ways in which different students understand and use the unit concepts

- the particular tools that different students use in order to reach their goals
- the ways in which different students use those tools
- the pace at which different learners grasp the concepts
- the degree to which teachers change their own thinking during the process of teaching

You should not assume, then, that by providing a scaffold everything will be hunky-dory. Rather, you should be attentive to the dynamics at work with you and your students, the materials, and the tasks to make sure that your students are indeed getting support and that you are all building the same building; or, if they are building a different building, understand what might be gained by changing your plans.

In this chapter I will describe how to use a particular kind of scaffold called an introductory activity. An introductory activity is designed to help students develop the kind of schematic knowledge they need to understand the unit's key concepts and problems. It thus provides them with a blueprint for the knowledge they will construct during the unit.

In designing your unit, you should ask, What knowledge will students need in order to work successfully toward the unit goals? This question raises the problem of deciding who gets to decide which knowledge is important. In most educational settings in the United States, adults exclusively make this decision. Often, these adults are far removed from the classroom: textbook writers, politicians who mandate standardized testing, curriculum directors from the district office, and so on. Within the classroom, teachers typically make whatever decisions are available after these external mandates are met.

In this book, I have suggested ways for students to have at least some say in what they think is important to learn. In considering what knowledge students will need during the unit, you should try to seek a balance between what you know from your perspective as a professional educator and what students can tell you through their engagement with the course during the year. As noted in other parts of this book, you can collaborate with students on curriculum planning in some cases as a way of understanding their goals and purposes for studying English.

I will review here some possible ways for you to introduce students to concepts that will likely be central to the literature they study. As you will see, all provide some opportunity for reconstruction by students. All of the types of introductory activities I describe are designed to have students wrestle with problems similar to those faced by characters in literature. The activities either directly or indirectly ask students to draw on their own experiences in similar kinds of situations to think about either the structure of experience (e.g., the script for a coming-of-age experience) or the substance (e.g., evaluating characters' decisions in problematic situations). By thinking through these questions prior to reading, students will be able to use the blueprint for experience, and the script for action based on this blueprint, to help them understand the characters' actions in the texts they read.

The assumption behind this approach is that students typically have some kind of experiences that they can draw on to assist them with new learning. Unfortunately, students often view their personal knowledge as irrelevant to understanding schoolwork and flounder in areas where they could flourish. The introductory activities I'll describe in this chapter are designed to help students recognize and use their knowledge to help them make connections with the literature they read and provide them with material for the texts they produce.

It's important to know that many texts require knowledge that students are not likely to have. There are times when students simply need factual information of some kind to help them understand something in their reading. During my earliest years of teaching, I assigned students Robert Frost's "The Silken Tent," a poem about a large Arabian tent that, as the sun rose higher in the sky, relied on its central mast for support rather than the guys that had supported it early in the day. From my days as a Boy Scout, I knew that guys were the ropes that supported the tent externally, going from pegs in the ground to loops at the top of the tent wall.

A group of girls, however—evidently with no camping experience—interpreted the guys as "boys" and thought that they were a metaphor for the ways in which a girl relies on boyfriends during adolescence and on herself as she matures. Why they were hanging from a tent was not so clear. In any case, their interpretation was based on their personal construction of the terms of the poem. Not a bad interpretation, though probably not what Frost had in mind. This anecdote illustrates the problem that often key knowledge in literature lies outside students' experiences and requires some more explicit teaching approach. While in general I don't feel that lecturing accomplishes what teachers think it does, I do see occasions when it's useful for students to be provided with relevant facts as aids to their reading. As I've noted previously, there are those who would disagree with me on this point. I'd suggest thinking and talking about both sides of this issue as you go through your career.

In this chapter, I will describe a set of activities designed to help students draw on knowledge they already have as a way of preparing them for problems they will come across in the unit's literature. I will describe four kinds of activities: personal experience writing, opinionnaire/survey, scenarios/case study, and writing about related problems. I will link each of the four types of activities to one of the units in the sophomore curriculum. I would suggest varying the kinds of introductory activities you use, given that you don't want your teaching to become too predictable. In this chapter I'll show how you might provide consistent kinds of introductory activities without getting into an instructional rut. I also offer these four types of introductions as possibilities, rather than as the only ways in which you could introduce a unit. I hope that you think about the metaphor of the cognitive map and generate your own approaches to designing such activities.

One thing to keep in mind is that the learning process should be recursive. By that I mean that these introductory activities are designed to enable students to draw on their prior personal knowledge to help them understand issues that come up in literature. In turn, the students' engagement with the literature should help them come to a better understanding of their personal knowledge and experiences. You can help students make these connections in your instructional design by having them return to the introductory activity after their engagement with the literature. For instance, when students write about relevant personal experiences prior to reading, they can return to these narratives later in the unit and develop them into more formal pieces of writing. This process

Reflective Writing Prompt

Think back on your own learning as a student. To what extent were you encouraged to draw on your personal life as a way of understanding schoolwork? What do you feel the consequences were for your learning? What does the extent to which you were encouraged to think about your personal life tell you about your teachers' assumptions about the purpose of schooling?

helps students use their prior knowledge to inform their understanding of the literature, and the literature to enrich their understanding of their personal experiences.

Table 7.1 provides examples of different types of introductory activities found at the Virtual Library of Conceptual Units at http://www.coe.uga.edu/~smago/VirtualLibrary/index.html. In the left column under "Unit" are listed the authors of

TABLE 7.1   Virtual Library: Types of Introductory Activities

Unit	Introductory Activity				
	Personal Experience	Opinionnaire/ Survey	Scenarios/ Case Studies/ Current Events	Writing Related to Unit Concept	Original Approaches
Askari				X	
Barrett Endres Stinchcomb			X		
Begnaud Evans			X		
Behr Reece Watkins					X
Bryan Skorupski	X			X	
Camp Davis Harris	X				
Cockrill Hall Long					X
Deroshia			X		
Hedden Orr Shroyer				X	
Hollingshead Wood	X				
Johnson					X
Loggins Taggart Thomas	X		X		
Rachmuth Shuler	X			X	
Siegmund Stroud Hasty	X				
Swann Williams		X			

the units in the Virtual Library; note that most units are coauthored. The type of introductory activity is indicated by an x in the appropriate column.

WRITING ABOUT PERSONAL EXPERIENCES

Students can write informally—perhaps in journals or reading logs—about experiences they've had that are similar to those of the characters they will study. The act of writing can promote reflection about important experiences that will help students relate to the problems confronted by the characters in the literature. In having students produce appropriate personal-experience writing, you need to think about the key concepts and problems in the literature and design a writing prompt that will help students think about personal experiences that may contribute to their understanding of these concepts and problems.

For my hypothetical sophomore curriculum, half the units are thematic. The key literary theme should provide you with the topic for your prompt. Other kinds of units can also allow for personal experience writing as an introduction, particularly if the units involve a theme. The unit on *Julius Caesar,* for instance, includes a set of related themes that are likely to be familiar to students: betrayal, ambition, and so on. These topics can provide the basis for personal writing that will help prepare students for the actions of the literary characters.

For the sophomore curriculum I've designed, it would make a great deal of sense to begin the year by having students write about a personal experience in which they came of age. This introductory activity would meet a number of curricular ends:

- It would make students' first writing of the year in the narrative genre, which many argue is more familiar and accessible, and more developmentally appropriate for younger students, than is the paradigmatic mode. Students' initial writing, then, would be something they would have an opportunity to feel successful about.
- It would introduce students to the key problems and concepts of the unit.
- It would give them explicit knowledge of the script of coming-of-age literature.
- It could serve as the basis of a classroom drama.
- It could provide the first draft for the unit goal of writing a personal narrative.

An alternative activity involving personal experience writing would be to have students interview a significant person in their lives, perhaps a parent, and then prepare a narrative of that other person's experience. You do need to be careful about requirements to involve parents, however. When I discussed this idea with a group of teachers a few years ago, one of them said that if a teacher gave her this assignment, she'd take a zero rather than do it, due to years of abuse she'd experienced at home. One thing I've learned from years of teaching is that you can't always assume that students come from stable homes or that they've grown up the way you have. It's a good idea to build in options rather than requiring parental input, perhaps allowing students to substitute a significant adult for a parent if they wish.

The prompt for the students' personal experience writing should ask them to describe the situation in ways that prepare them for their subsequent reading and writing. Keeping in mind the unit goal identified in Chapter 6, you might come up with the following prompt. The prompt should be specific enough to get students to think about the full range of problems involved, yet not so detailed as to override the spontaneity of their writing.

> Write about a personal experience you've had that was a coming-of-age experience, that is, one that caused you to grow up in some way. Make sure to explain:
>
> - The immature behavior that you exhibited prior to the experience
> - A transforming experience through which you gained significant new knowledge and maturity
> - The mature behavior that you exhibited following the experience
>
> You are not required to explain these events in this particular order, although you may if you wish. Keep in mind that other students will read about the experience you write about.

This last statement is necessary any time you ask students to share their writing. You should never require students to share what they've written if you haven't advised them of this step ahead of time. Students should always have the option of not sharing if they feel uncomfortable reporting their experiences to others.

Note that this prompt is less detailed than the prompt for the culminating text that they produce for their unit goal. The idea is to get them writing somewhat freely about the experience, for them to use writing as a tool for thinking about how experiences can contribute to maturity. Note, too, that the prompt includes a brief, accessible definition of "coming-of-age experience" to help set the stage for the rest of the unit.

It's important to have some kind of follow-up to an introductory activity of this type so that students can compare their responses to those of other students and have the opportunity to benefit from one another's reflections. Here are some possible ways to follow up personal writing:

- Have students get in small groups, read one another's narratives, and characterize the kinds of experiences that result in significant change. Then, have each group report to the whole class, with the teacher orchestrating its contributions into a discussion on significant experiences and the kinds of changes they can promote.
- Have students get in small groups, read one another's narratives, then choose one or several to use as the basis for a short play to be performed before the class. Following performances of these plays, the class could discuss the kinds of scripts developed by each group for coming-of-age stories. These scripts could serve as the basis for analyses of stories during discussions and ultimately for an analytic essay that students would write on an unfamiliar story based on the coming-of-age theme.
- Have students get in small groups and describe the characteristics of a good coming-of-age narrative. Have each group report to the whole class, with the teacher orchestrating a discussion on the traits of good narratives of this type. Have students revise their narratives based on the qualities identified during this discussion, creating a second draft of the narrative they will produce as a culminating text.

Field Observation

In the school you are visiting, what kinds of background knowledge do the teachers include in their instruction when introducing new ideas? Through what kinds of classroom processes do teachers orchestrate students' accessing or acquiring this knowledge (e.g., lecture, activity, discussion, etc.)? What does their approach to background knowledge suggest about teachers' assumptions about teaching and learning?

OPINIONNAIRE/SURVEY

An opinionnaire or survey is a set of controversial statements designed to get students thinking about issues they will later encounter in the literature. At times the statements might come directly from the literature itself. For instance, I once developed an opinionnaire for an American literature unit on protest literature that included one statement that was paraphrased from one of the texts the class was going to read, Thoreau's "Civil Disobedience": "The best government is the one that governs the least." If the literature provides no such provocative statements, you will need to develop them yourself based on the issues that students will eventually think through while reading.

For the sophomore unit on discrimination, you could use an opinionnaire as a way to get students to think about issues prior to reading. One possible set of statements is as follows:

Each of the following statements expresses an opinion. Rate each statement from 1 (strongly disagree) to 5 (strongly agree).

1. Any set of beliefs is okay, as long as you believe in them sincerely.
2. I tend to go along with whatever my friends are for, even if I disagree with them.
3. People should always try to understand and tolerate other people, no matter how different they are.
4. If you move to a new country, you should adapt to the culture as quickly as possible so that you fit in.
5. I try not to notice people's physical characteristics. That way, I treat everyone the same.
6. I would never date anyone from outside my religion.
7. I never judge people on the basis of their appearance.
8. If you know where people live, you can tell a lot about them.
9. It's harmless to tell jokes about people in which they appear stupid because of their race, hair color, nationality, and so on.
10. Laws are designed to make society fair for all of its citizens.

The key to writing an effective opinionnaire is to use statements that will invite disagreement among students. This disagreement should lead to discussions of issues central to the problems that will arise in the literature. All the statements in this example are designed to help students think through what they already know about discrimination and to refine their ideas in light of contrasting opinions expressed by classmates.

One thing to be careful about is writing items that in some communities might be viewed as invasive. For instance, item 6 in this opinionnaire could conceivably draw protests from some parents because they might view the ensuing discussion as an attack on their belief system.

You can use opinionnaires in a variety of ways:

- Pass them out and go over the items in order, having a discussion of each.
- Have students complete the opinionnaire individually, then discuss their responses in small groups, and finish with a whole-class discussion.

The advantage of the second approach is that it enables all students to partici-pate in the discussion. In a whole-class discussion on a topic that invites strong opin-ions, some less assertive students will have few opportunities to speak. By adding the small-group stage, you will allow for greater participation, particularly among students who feel inhibited by the whole-class setting or who benefit from engaging in exploratory talk.

SCENARIOS/CASE STUDIES

Scenarios and case studies describe problematic examples of people who find them-selves in thorny situations that parallel the circumstances of the literary characters. Scenarios tend to be briefer and intended for small-group discussions followed by a whole-class comparison of the small-group decisions. Case studies tend to be more detailed and complex and used for more extensive study, such as when small groups lead the whole class in an analysis of a single case. Appendix B includes an exam-ple of a case study that is designed according to a court-case analysis.

The basic structure and design process of the two are similar, however. Once again, you should write the scenarios or case stud-ies at the intersection of what the literature provides and what the students have experienced. In the sophomore year unit on conflict with authority, you could design an introductory activity based on a set of scenarios requiring students to evaluate how such problems are negotiated. The following activity could serve this purpose:

> Campus agitators are rarely, if ever, students or faculty from the scientific disciplines; they tend to come out of the social sciences, which are relatively inexact in their researches, and the humanities, which are and should be preoccupied with unanswerable questions.
>
> —Samuel B. Gould

Each of the following scenarios involves an individual coming in conflict with an authority figure. In a small group of four stu-dents, read each one carefully. Then, as a group, rank the char-acters according to how much you admire them, putting 1 by the scenario in which you admire the character's behavior the most, 2 by the scenario in which you admire the character the second most, and so on. You must rank all five of the scenarios—no ties.

1. Justin Time was on his high school football team. He didn't start, but was a reserve linebacker who often played when the team went into special defenses. After a tough loss, the coach mistakenly thought he heard Justin laugh at something as the team was walking back to the locker room. Enraged that a player was not taking defeat seriously enough, the coach ordered Justin to crawl across the parking lot on his elbows in front of the whole team and a few hundred spectators, yelling at him at the top of his lungs the entire time. Justin thought that a good team player always did what the coach said, so although he initially denied that he had been the one who'd laughed, he ended up following his coach's orders without arguing.
2. Sybil Rights was a bright young woman, although her grades didn't always reflect it because she didn't always do what her teachers wanted her to do. One time her history teacher gave the class an assignment in which they were to outline the entire chapter from the textbook that dealt with the U.S. government's decision to drop the atomic bomb on Japan.

Although every other student in the class did the assignment, Sybil refused, saying that it was just busy work and that she would not do assignments that she thought were a waste of her time. She decided that she could spend her time better by actually learning something about this incident, so she wrote an essay on the morality of the bombing that she intended to enter in the school's annual essay competition. She ended up getting a zero on the assignment, which lowered her grade for the marking period from a B to a C.

3. Mo Skeeto was a young U.S. soldier stationed in France in World War II. His troop was one of many battling the enemy in a hilly region of Europe. The enemy was well positioned at the top of a hill, and the Americans couldn't seem to gain any ground in spite of their superior numbers. Finally, an order came down from the commanding officer that Mo's troop should charge the hill. It occurred to him that his troop was being sacrificed to create a diversion so that other troops could make a sneak attack from behind while the enemy was fighting Mo's troop off. Mo thought that this was a stupid plan that was doomed to failure and that his life was going to be sacrificed needlessly. Yet he followed his orders, charged the hill, was killed along with everyone else in his troop. Sure enough, the master plan failed. After Mo's troop was wiped out, the sneak attack from behind was successfully rebuffed and the enemy still held the hill.

4. Robin DeBanks had a job working at the local hardware store after school. Usually she did whatever was necessary, such as unpacking boxes, working the cash register, or putting price tags on merchandise. She almost always had something to keep her busy. One day, however, a heavy rainfall kept business down. At one point there were no customers in the store and she had taken care of all the little jobs, so she was standing around doing nothing. Her boss hated to pay her for nothing and so told her to scrub the linoleum floor of the store with an abrasive cleaner, a job that Robin reckoned hadn't been done in years. She thought that this task was utterly ridiculous and a waste of her time, but she didn't want to risk losing her job, so she got a bucket, a brush, and some cleanser and went to work.

5. Frazier Nerves stayed out too late with his girlfriend one night, and his parents reacted by grounding him, confining him to his room every night for a month. He thought that this punishment was excessively harsh, but knew that arguing would only make matters worse. Still, he had a great desire to see his girlfriend; not only was he madly in love with her, but he also knew of other boys who found her attractive and he thought that if they were not to date for a month he might lose her to someone else. Desperate to maintain his relationship with his girlfriend but fearful of parental repercussions, Frazier started sneaking out through his window every night after his parents had gone to bed for a late-evening rendezvous with her. He made it through the month without getting caught and with his relationship still intact.

An alternative to writing the scenarios yourself is to take a set of stories from the news. A typical year provides an abundance of current events related to many thematic units of literature. For a unit on conflict with authority, you might find stories about athletes coming in conflict with their coaches, workers coming in conflict with their bosses, students coming in conflict with teachers and administrators, and so on. The main thing to keep in mind is that these stories should illustrate a variety of kinds of conflicts and resolutions (or nonresolutions) so that students think about the problem in complex ways.

Regardless of how you identify the scenarios or cases, you could have students rank the characters' actions from most admirable to least admirable. They could do this individually, then discuss their rankings in small groups, and then compare their responses in an all-class discussion. The discussions should encourage students to examine closely their attitudes toward authority figures and consider carefully the kinds of dilemmas the literary characters will face.

> "My educational experiences from early childhood through adolescence were highly regimented and disciplined. They fit the "domesticating" rather than the "liberating" mode of learning and teaching insightfully distinguished by Paulo Freire. Literacy was taught for the sake of knowledge that focused primarily on a prescribed abstract understanding of the world that did not always accord with reality. . . . Education was an act of transferring textbook knowledge . . . from teachers, who commanded absolute authority, to students, whose minds were regarded as empty vessels to be filled. Learners were expected to be passively compliant, denied or restricted in self-expression, voice, and creativity. Schools provided formal, rigid classroom settings that seemed to me to imprison students' young minds.
>
> —Esther Ngan-Ling Chow"

WRITING ABOUT RELATED PROBLEMS

Tom McCann, chair of the English department at West Chicago (Illinois) High School, has spent a great deal of time thinking of ways to teach students how to write arguments. One of his ideas works well as an introductory activity. The format for the activity is based on advice columns such as Dear Abby. The idea is to think of situations that come up in literature, and then present students with a letter to an advice columnist that describes a similar kind of situation. Their job is then to write to the person offering a solution to the problem.

In the sophomore curriculum, the unit on gangs, cliques, and peer pressure would be well suited to an introductory activity of this type. Let's say that the class will read S. E. Hinton's *The Outsiders* as the unit's major work of literature. You could prepare a letter to the Answerline columnist that anticipates the dilemmas raised in the novel, and have students write a letter back arguing in favor of a particular solution. The prompt for their writing could look like this:

Pretend that you are a famous newspaper columnist who gives advice to people who write letters to you. Often their problems concern crucial moments in their lives that they need advice about. What kind of advice would you give to the following person? Make sure that when you write your response you are supportive of the person's problems and give a thoughtful answer. Make sure, too, that whatever your advice, you give several reasons why the person should follow it. Also make sure that you explain why your recommended course of action is better than others that the person might follow.

Dear Answerline,
   I have a problem that I need your advice about. I have to go to you because I can't tell my parents. They'd just yell at me and ground me if they thought I was in any kind of trouble. Please help me figure out what to do.

The problem actually starts with my best friend. We're both part of a group that always hangs around together. We always stick together, right or wrong. If one of us gets in a fight, the rest are there to help out. If one of us is in trouble, the others are always there. Every time I've ever had a problem, my friends were there to make things right. I could never let any of them down, especially my best friend, Chris, who's always been there for me.

But now I'm worried that things have gone too far. There's another group in our school that we've always had trouble with. They think they're better than we are and always put us down. Usually we just yell things back at them, or sometimes get in a fight, and it's over till the next time. But last week they burned Chris's car. Now everybody wants revenge. And Chris has got a gun and wants to use it.

I don't know what to do. If I say I think it's gone too far, they'll call me chicken. If I say I don't want to go along with them, they'll think I'm disloyal. If I call the police, my best friends might get arrested. If I warn the other group, my friends may get hurt. If I lose my friends, I won't have anybody left.

What should I do?

Sincerely,

Fearful in Fredericksburg

The students' job is to write to Fearful, offering a solution to the problem. After all the students are done, you could follow the same sequence outlined in the other introductory activities: Have students compare their answers in small groups, then have a whole-class discussion in search of a solution.

This introduction, like the personal experience narrative introducing the coming-of-age unit, could additionally serve to prepare students for more formal writing later in the unit. In a unit using this kind of introduction, you could have a goal of producing an argument about problem resolution in an independently read work of literature. The Answerline letter could both introduce students to the literature and introduce them to argumentative writing. Subsequent instruction could focus on making, supporting, and warranting claims and rebutting alternative solutions.

Discussion Topic

In your experience as a student, what kinds of background information have teachers provided you with prior to reading? How did they provide it for you (e.g., lecture, activity)? How did the background information affect your reading? Why?

FINAL THOUGHTS

This chapter has focused on writing introductory activities that prepare students for issues that come up in literature. My focus has been on drawing on prior knowledge that students can connect with new knowledge. As noted previously, some kinds of reading might require an introduction that helps acquaint students with unfamiliar realms of knowledge. I imagine that if you teach literature from diverse cultures and nations, you

Unit Design

Design Introductory Activity

Using the procedures outlined in this chapter, design an introductory activity for the unit you are planning. When you are done, exchange your introductory activity with another student or group of students for feedback on its appropriateness for your unit focus.

will need to help students understand different issues, relationships, literary styles, and other aspects of the texts that may be quite different from what they know through exposure to Western literary traditions. The questions you should ask are, What does one need to know in order to read this text with the appropriate expectations? How can I help students access the knowledge that will prepare them for this reading? You should also be aware that many people in the field, both practicing teachers and theorists, would prefer that readers go ahead with their readings without such preparation. They argue that students' initial constructions are part of their process of meaning making and should not be tainted by the teacher's sense of what's important to know.

It's worth noting that in order to be successful with this approach to teaching, you might need to consider another kind of prior knowledge—prior knowledge about how to "do school." As I've noted elsewhere, students are going to be enculturated to authoritative, transmission-oriented approaches to schooling. In the constructivist classroom, they will be expected to act quite differently, by relating their personal knowledge and experiences to their school learning, by asking questions instead of answering them, by constructing knowledge instead of receiving it. In an important sense, then, you will likely have to spend some time helping students relearn how to be students. In other words, they will need prior knowledge about how to "do school" properly in your class. The unit introductory activity can be an important step in helping them learn a different way of being a student.

Books Concerning Introductory Activities

Johannessen, L. R. (1992). *Illumination rounds: Teaching the literature of the Vietnam War.* Urbana, IL: National Council of Teachers of English.

Kahn, E. A., Walter, C. C., & Johannsessen, L. R. (1984). *Writing about literature.* Urbana, IL: National Council of Teachers of English.

Smagorinsky, P., McCann, T., & Kern, S. (1987). *Explorations: Introductory activities for literature and composition, grades 7–12.* Urbana, IL: National Council of Teachers of English.

Smith, M. W. (1991). *Understanding unreliable narrators: Reading between the lines in the literature classroom.* Urbana, IL: National Council of Teachers of English.

8 The Construction Zone: Building Toward Unit Goals

This chapter illustrates unit design with the development of a complete unit of instruction on the topic of coming of age for the hypothetical sophomore curriculum. I develop the extended metaphor of construction as a way to think about both unit design and student learning. I make an effort to discuss unit design as a *situated practice;* that is, the decisions you make are dependent on the situation you teach within. The unit I design here begins with a set of goals and keeps those goals in mind as a way to keep the instruction focused and purposeful. Classes are planned with anticipated amounts of time for each segment of instruction. As you'll see, planning—even when so carefully designed—is still messy, and must include the flexibility to change. Indeed, as I think my way through the unit I reconsider and revise some of the plans I made at the beginning. My purpose is to try to be realistic about how planning is important for coherent instruction but should always be responsive to new circumstances.

THINKING OF YOUR CLASS AS A CONSTRUCTION ZONE

In this chapter I will describe how to plan classes so that students can work productively toward the unit goals. I continue using the construction metaphor I have used throughout the book, characterizing the classroom as a *construction zone.* In this construction zone, teachers help students build and reflect on texts they find useful and important.

If the unit goals are thoughtfully set so that they help students engage with the unit concepts, they should enable students to work toward the production of texts that are meaningful in two ways:

- The *process* of planning and constructing texts will enable students to synthesize prior knowledge and build new knowledge. Both the teacher and other students are available to co-construct or provide help during this process. This process of composition is usually exploratory, with new ideas discovered as the work of construction unfolds.
- The *product* of the text itself will be a text that they can reflect on for continued learning. The text will also serve to communicate students' understandings to others and enable them to reflect on the unit problems in

new ways. My reference to the product does not describe only the finished text. It also refers to the text at any point during the composing process, when its builder(s) can step back, consider its form, and either revise or build on it. And I should stress that a text is never really finished, even though it may achieve an assessable form for school purposes. If the text matters to the student, then it will undergo continual revision, if not tangibly, then psychologically, as the student continues to think through the ideas that generated the text.

Students will build these texts through the use of *tools*. These tools can include language (primarily speaking and writing) and their particular uses (e.g., exploratory talk, analytic essays, reading logs, and so on). In the workshop of our classroom, we also allow for a broader *tool kit* for text construction. This kit might include music, movement in dance and drama, various tools for producing art, computers and their capabilities, and other instruments that students might find useful in producing texts.

Classroom members' use of these tools will come within an environment overseen by you, the teacher. In your leadership role you will help students learn how to use tools effectively, draw on necessary resources, act as productive crew members, and understand the nature and purpose of the texts they are constructing. At times you might be a facilitator, at times you might provide clear and explicit information, at times you might turn over leadership responsibilities to students. At times you might work along with students, constructing texts according to the same guidelines they are following. You might also produce texts from research that you are conducting on the relationship between your teaching and their learning, or on their lives outside the classroom, so that you better understand how to build on their knowledge and strengths.

You will use your good judgment about which role is most appropriate for which circumstances and needs. You will make these judgments with an awareness of the overall context in which you are teaching, including your department, your school, your community, and your state. You should be a good citizen of all these social groups, keeping in mind that one responsibility of citizenship is to work for change when systems don't serve their constituents well.

MY APPROACH IN THIS CHAPTER

This chapter is written as though I am thinking aloud while planning a unit. I will reveal my thinking as an instructional planner, using the principles I've outlined in this book. One thing that you will see is that I will make an initial set of plans that I will adjust as the unit goes on. As a teacher, you will always have an ideal unit in mind that you must accommodate to the situations in which you teach.

At times, your instruction must be modified because of the external structure of schooling, such as the approach of a deadline (e.g., the end of a grading period) or the resources provided by your school (e.g., the presence or absence of Internet access). At other times, an administrative decision might require you to adjust your

Books about Tools for Learning

Cole, M. (1996). *Cultural psychology: A once and future discipline.* Cambridge, MA: Harvard University Press.

Lave, J. (1988). *Cognition in practice.* New York: Cambridge University Press.

Lee, C. D., & Smagorinsky, P. (Eds.). (2000). *Vygotskian perspectives on literacy research: Constructing meaning through collaborative inquiry.* New York: Cambridge University Press.

Moll, L. C. (Ed.). (1990). *Vygotsky and education: Instructional implications and applications of sociohistorical psychology.* New York: Cambridge University Press.

Newman, D., Griffin, P., & Cole, M. (1989). *The construction zone: Working for cognitive change in school.* New York: Cambridge University Press.

Tharp, R. G., & Gallimore, R. (1988). *Rousing minds to life: Teaching, learning, and schooling in social context.* New York: Cambridge University Press.

Tulviste, P. (1991). *The cultural-historical development of verbal thinking* (M. J. Hall, Trans.). Commack, NY: Nova Science Publishers.

Vygotsky, L. S. (1978). *Mind in society: The development of higher psychological processes* (M. Cole, V. John-Steiner, S. Scribner, & E. Souberman, Eds.). Cambridge, MA: Harvard University Press.

Vygotsky, L. S. (1987). Thinking and speech. In R. Rieber & A. Carton (Eds.) and N. Minick (Trans.). *The collected works of Lev Vygotsky* (Vol. 1, pp. 39–285). New York: Plenum.

Wells, G. (Ed.). (1994). *Changing schools from within: Creating communities of inquiry.* Toronto: OISE Press; Portsmouth, NH: Heinemann.

Wells, G. (in press). *Thinking with Vygotsky.* New York: Cambridge University Press.

Wertsch, J. V. (1985). *Vygotsky and the social formation of mind.* Cambridge, MA: Harvard University Press.

Wertsch, J. V. (1991). *Voices of the mind: A sociocultural approach to mediated action.* Cambridge, MA: Harvard University Press.

planning (e.g., you might be told to stop what you're doing and prepare your students for a standardized test).

Other things can intervene from without and require you to change your plans: There might be a fire alarm, or a pep rally, or a snow day, or a school tragedy, or a field trip. You also might adjust to situations that take place within your class, such as some instruction's taking longer than you'd anticipated or human relations issues that need immediate attention. Your use of a plan, therefore, is always provisional.

I will begin with an instructional plan that, due to various constraints, I will modify as I go along. I do this to simulate *some,* though hardly all, of the conditions that you will face in a school. Things rarely go exactly as planned in school and part of my job is to adjust to new circumstances. For starters, however, I will try to plan as carefully as possible. I'd rather be too prepared than underprepared for the complicated business of teaching. Just as I'd never try to build a house without a blueprint, I wouldn't try to teach without a plan.

I will also show what daily plans look like. I will describe them specifically, right down to an anticipated amount of time I will spend on each activity. Some readers might find such microlevel planning to be a bit too heavily scripted. The purpose, however, is not to write a script, but to try to anticipate how classes will go from day to day. One frustration often felt by early-career teachers, particularly in student teaching, is that they have a good sense of educational theory but little idea of how to implement it on a daily basis. I'll try to show how the instructional principles I've outlined look in daily classes, in sequences of classes known as *lessons,* and in the larger units of instruction in which they occur.

One word on lessons before we continue: It's important to design good individual lessons that are related to the unit goals. It's also important for the lessons to be interrelated and to build cogently toward the unit goals. If we think in terms of our construction metaphor: Let's say you are making a shirt, and you design and construct excellent individual components: a sleeve, a collar, another sleeve, front and back pieces, and so on. While they might be fine pieces individually, if they are not coordinated to suit a particular reason for wearing a shirt—to stay warm in winter, to match a pair of shoes, to evoke a feeling or mood—then the shirt might both lack overall coherence and serve its purpose poorly. Lessons within a unit, too, must both stand individually to meet a unit's goals and work together coherently to serve the unit as a whole.

Field Observation

In the school you are visiting, what are the expectations for teachers in terms of instructional planning? Are they expected to have plans? If so, how detailed are the plans expected to be? How closely are the teachers expected to follow the plans? Are they expected to write their own plans, or to follow the plans provided by their commercial textbooks or district curriculum? Are their plans reviewed formally (e.g., by an administrator)? What are the consequences of the teachers' approaches to planning for student learning? Can you distinguish one lesson from another and see how they fit within overall unit goals?

PRELIMINARIES

Teaching Language

As a teacher, I also have many responsibilities to my students. One is to teach aspects of language use. Typically, language use is addressed through what's called *grammar.* Grammar is usually taught through grammar books that emphasize the identification of the parts of sentences, with the goal of having students learn a "standard" version of English. There are several problems with this approach:

> Teachers are expected to reach unattainable goals with inadequate tools. The miracle is that at times they accomplish this impossible task.
>
> —Haim G. Ginott

- Research for nearly a hundred years has repeatedly shown, almost without exception, that *teaching grammar apart from usage does not significantly change the way people speak or write.* Some have even argued that teaching grammar is *detrimental* to students' development as writers because (1) it takes time away from productive writing instruction and (2) it reduces the whole, great, dynamic field of literature, writing, and language to its most minute elements, assessing students on these elements at the expense of attention to the glory and wonder of *belles lettres.*
- Research in sociolinguistics has questioned the privileged role of textbook English. Sociolinguists have argued that different circumstances call for different syntax, vocabulary, intonation, and other aspects of *communication.* Effective language instruction, according to sociolinguists, emphasizes how to use language for communication, not how to restrict language use to a single variety. Among these varieties is textbook English, but one thing that savvy communicators know is that this variety of English is inappropriate in some

settings (e.g., a country-and-western or blues song). There are many different standards for using language, each dependent on the situation in which it is used. Textbook English is but one of these standard forms.

- One consequence of emphasizing textbook English and downgrading the use of other varieties is that *people who speak other varieties at home are made to feel defective and outcast in school.* Effective language instruction should emphasize the situational nature of language use. It should respect the varieties students use in some contexts and help teach them the *codes,* or rules, of others. In this way they will recognize the qualities of their home speech while learning varieties of the language that can serve them well in other situations. From this perspective, it is important for students to learn the conventions of textbook English, for it is the preferred version of the language in many circumstances. These conventions should not, I contend, be taught as isolated grammar lessons, but instead should be embedded in instruction geared toward situational communication.

- Politically, referring to one version of English as "standard" and others as "nonstandard," "dialect," or "vernacular" establishes one version as the norm and other versions as deviant or defective. By implication, *speakers* of other versions are deviant or defective. Sociolinguists have stressed the need to view all language use as situational and all judgments about language use as political. In this view, considering varieties and their speakers to be nonstandard is bigoted.

I'll confess that in my early years of teaching at the university level, I was quite effective at persuading my students that teaching grammar in isolation is counterproductive. I was so effective that some of my students bombed in job interviews because they launched into wondrous diatribes against the teaching of formal grammar—not, unfortunately, what the principal conducting the interview wanted to hear. I have since become more aware of the need to balance teachers' understanding of the limits of grammar instruction with their savvy in negotiating the political environments of schools. I may well persuade you that grammar instruction, conducted apart from language usage, will have negligible or possibly detrimental effects on your students' speaking and writing. Just don't mention this during a job interview.

You then have yourself a dilemma. If you accept the belief that discrete grammar instruction has historically failed and that all judgments about language variation are political, and if you are expected to teach grammar in your job in ways that boost test scores, you will be caught between a rock and a hard place. Welcome to the world of public school teaching.

I recommend that you address language instruction through brief, daily attention to language issues at the start of each class. These relatively short (5–10 minutes) lessons have gone by a variety of names: minilesson, Daily Oral Language, and others, although they don't always describe the same thing. Some Daily Oral Language programs are prepackaged, for instance, and are done in the same way in diverse classes across the nation. I've sat in schools with "open classroom" architecture—no walls—and observed teachers all down the line teaching the exact same lesson at the exact same time and on the exact same part of their classroom chalkboards, each a mirror image of the other.

Other approaches are entirely situational, with teachers using this time to address language issues that arise in their students' writing and speaking. As you can guess, I prefer this approach. I imagine that the rationale for the uniform approach is that all students in the school are getting the exact same instruction, an approach that is justified by its democratic intentions. The rationale for the situational approach is that all students might not need the same instruction and so teachers should adjust their instruction to local circumstances.

I'll leave the choice of which way to go to you. Let's assume that you decide to do language instruction this way instead of through week-long drills. In keeping with my construction metaphor, I'll refer to these sessions as occasions for *tool sharpening*. Language, as I've maintained throughout this book, is an essential tool in discovering, representing, and communicating knowledge. To use it well, you need to maintain it and know how to use it under different conditions. Being able to label the teeth and handle of a saw is all well and good, but won't prevent you from cutting off your hand while using it. Our emphasis in the daily tool-sharpening session will be to give attention to ways in which language is appropriately put to use, with particular efforts to relate the knowledge from these sessions to the texts the students are producing during the unit.

There will be plenty of attention to the King's English. There's little advantage, for instance, in using homonyms incorrectly, in using apostrophes to form ordinary plurals, in writing run-on sentences. And so the tool-sharpening sessions will attend to issues of usage that, if not learned, could potentially limit students' potential for school success, job placement, earning potential, and other possible sources of happiness. They will also give attention to the ways in which using a different set of language codes can serve social and communicative ends well.

You might identify a set of categories to which you will devote your tool-sharpening sessions. For instance, you might want to rotate across a set of topics that would include the following:

- Status markers (i.e., grammar or usage that stigmatizes people as being uneducated), including subject-verb disagreement, pronoun-referent mismatch, and so on (see Noguchi, 1991)
- Usage
- Standardized-test-question format
- Sentence combining (i.e., combining clauses and phrases to create sentences of greater syntactic complexity)
- Language variation (i.e., knowing when particular varieties of English are appropriate)
- Punctuation
- Parallel structure
- Roots, prefixes, and suffixes
- Context clues for vocabulary meaning
- Politics of grammar (e.g., consequences of the use of masculine pronouns for general reference)
- History of language (e.g., word etymology, British and American English, etc.)

This list is not exhaustive; you could undoubtedly add other categories. In this chapter, I will illustrate possible tool-sharpening emphases for these different categories.

Books on Grammar Use and Language Instruction

Baron, D. (1994). *Guide to home language repair.* Urbana, IL: National Council of Teachers of English.

Farr, M., & Daniels, H. (1986). *Language diversity and writing instruction.* Urbana, IL: ERIC Clearinghouse on Reading and Communication Skills.

Hillocks, G. (1986). *Research on written composition: New directions for teaching.* Urbana, IL: ERIC Clearinghouse on Reading and Communications Skills and National Conference on Research in English.

Hunter, S., & Wallace, R. (Eds.). *The place of grammar in writing instruction: Past, present, future.* Portsmouth, NH: Heinemann.

Hymes, D. (1974). *Foundations in sociolinguistics: An ethnographic approach.* Philadelphia: University of Pennsylvania Press.

Noden, H. R. (1999). *Image grammar: Using grammatical structures to teach writing.* Portsmouth, NH: Heinemann.

Noguchi, R. R. (1991). *Grammar and the teaching of writing: Limits and possibilities.* Urbana, IL: National Council of Teachers of English.

Shaughnessy, M. P. (1977). *Errors and expectations: A guide for the teacher of basic writing.* New York: Oxford University Press.

Strong, W. (1986). *Creative approaches to sentence combining.* Urbana, IL: National Council of Teachers of English.

Weaver, C. (1996). *Teaching grammar in context.* Portsmouth, NH: Heinemann.

Reflective Writing Prompt

Think back to your own education. How was the grammar or language instruction handled? What do you see as the purpose of the grammar/language instruction you received? How would you evaluate the effectiveness of the approach used to teach it? What were the effects of this instruction on the whole range of students in your classes? What were the assumptions behind the grammar/language instruction you received?

Many of the particular lessons are aimed at addressing areas that persistently affect language usage (e.g., using homonyms properly, knowing roots and suffixes, matching pronouns to antecedents), and that sophomores might need help with.

Keep in mind that although I am suggesting possibilities for tool-sharpening sessions, *in my actual teaching I would probably adjust them in response to situations that arose during the unit.* You'll see, for instance, that later in the unit the tool sharpening is designed to address issues of language use that arise in student writing. I hope that your own use of these sessions will be based on topics that you identify from your own classroom situations as possibly beneficial. So remember that, although the plans that follow might imply that I'm using the tool-sharpening sessions in prescriptive ways, if I were to teach this unit I would likely make many adjustments, depending on what I thought my students needed.

Getting Started: Outlining the Unit

In identifying the unit *goals*, I have identified my basic teaching *responsibilities*. I will need to teach students how to pose questions for two kinds of inquiry: (1) the individual act of keeping a reading log, and (2) the group activity of leading a class discussion. I will need to teach them how to produce a narrative about a coming-of-age experience, including the story script behind such narratives. I will need to teach them how to recognize this story script in stories written by others so that they can

Vignette

I taught full-time in three school districts, each with a different kind of schedule. The first school divided the year into four quarters, with students changing classes and teachers every nine weeks. The second school used a semester system. For the most part, students stayed in the same class for the whole year, with grades due each nine weeks. The third school used semesters, but divided each into three six-week marking periods.

Each system required a different approach to organization. The first school made it difficult to establish long-term goals, teach across the year with continuity, or take a patient approach to student development, because teachers were not likely to teach any one student in all four quarters. The second approach allowed for greater continuity, and the nine-week marking periods encouraged process-oriented teaching. The third approach discouraged a process-oriented approach because there was an imperative to record grades for the six-week report cards.

Time parameters provide important constraints on your teaching; you need to know what they are and teach within them.

analyze how others make sense of the maturation process. I will provide daily attention to issues involved in language use and communication. And I will provide students with an open-ended opportunity to construct the unit's meaning through a multimedia project of their own choice.

This is my initial, ideal sense of how I envision the unit. Because, however, I teach within constraints, I will ultimately modify these goals in response to several factors. One is the limitation imposed by the length of the marking period. Another is the need for extensive instruction on procedures early in the year, which will require me to spend time teaching some things that will in turn force sacrifices in others. A third problem I will face is the students' fatigue with the topic. As the unit goes on, I will need to monitor the extent to which continued engagement with the topic will be productive. And so I need to be aware of not only the forces that constrain my teaching from outside the classroom, but also the dynamics that take place within it, when making decisions about how to adjust my initial conception and planning of the unit.

My teaching of the unit should also keep whole-course goals in mind. For the whole semester, students will be keeping a portfolio. I need to include regular attention to what might go into these portfolios: what the purpose is, what might make a good exhibit, how to reflect on an exhibit's contribution to their learning. Because many students will never have kept a portfolio before, I will need to devote some explicit instructional time to how to select and reflect on an exhibit.

These are the responsibilities, then, that I have to my students. I can also assume some learning responsibilities of my own. As a teacher, you can produce some portion of these texts along with your students. They might be interested, for instance, in knowing of some of your own coming-of-age experiences through a narrative or multimedia text you produce. You might keep your own portfolio about what you learned about teaching from your experiences during the year.

In addition, you should always *teach reflectively*, as I reviewed at the end of Chapter 4. In other words, through your evaluation of students, you should always be evaluating your teaching. If students are not learning, how could you change the environment or the structure or content of the lessons? Do some groups of students perform better in your class than others, and if so, why? Are you less patient with some students than with others, and can you identify a reason for and consequences of your response to them? How do students treat one another in your class, and are there changes you can make to promote better human relations?

In turn, the students have the responsibility for taking advantage of the opportunity you have provided. If your instruction is designed in thoughtful ways, they ought to use these tools and activities to grow to the greatest extent possible in their quest toward the unit goals. Through production of these texts, the class can become a construction zone where there is an ethic of productivity within a respectful environment. As I'll illustrate in Part II, Chapter 12, you'll rarely be 100 percent successful in achieving such a classroom. You can set up your class, however, to encourage most students toward that end.

> As far as I'm concerned, "whom" is a word that was invented to make everyone sound like a butler.
>
> —Calvin Trillin

CONTEXTS OF TEACHING

As I've maintained throughout this book, you do not teach in a vacuum. Rather, you teach within a set of confines or constraints. These can be useful in that they provide a set of guidelines for appropriate decision making. They can also, of course, be limiting by restricting your choices. Whether you like them or not, however, they exist and provide the context for your teaching. It's important, then, to understand where you teach, whom you teach, and those with whom you teach.

The School and Community Context

Your teaching should be responsive to your students and their needs. I don't claim that you can simply take the unit I outline in this chapter and teach it anywhere. In writing this book for a broad audience, I face the problem that a unit well-suited for one context might be less useful in another. I will therefore provide a context for the unit based on schools where I've taught as well as schools I've observed. The school profile is typical of many schools across the United States. The unit is very similar to units I've taught in schools like these.

My hypothetical school is a comprehensive public senior high school of 2,000 students. It lies in the metropolitan area of an urban center and includes students from across the economic spectrum. It has a three-track system, with the tracks labeled honors, regular, and basic; for the upper grades there are more specialized tracks, such as advanced placement and vocational. The sophomore curriculum I'm designing will be for students in the regular track.

The racial makeup of the student body is 50 percent European American, 20 percent African American, 10 percent Asian American, 10 percent Hispanic American, 5 percent Native American, and 5 percent mixed race. Slightly fewer than half the students live in homes with both their biological parents. Eighty percent of the senior class will have a part-time job at some point during the senior year. Sixty percent of each freshman class will graduate on time (i.e., within four years); 15 percent will move to another district, 10 percent will drop out, 1 percent will be expelled for disciplinary reasons, and 14 percent will graduate after completing additional course work. In a typical graduating class, 40 percent of seniors go to four-year colleges, and half of those eventually receive degrees; 20 percent go to two-year colleges; 20 percent go to trade schools; and 20 percent enter the workforce.

The town is characterized by the lack of consensus often found in diverse communities. In a typical year, the town newspaper will report frequently on

- disputes about property taxes that fund education, with many citizens writing letters to the editor questioning whether the schools provide enough quality to merit tax increases
- concern about school discipline, with many citizens believing that declining behavioral standards are affecting the overall quality of education
- disagreements about the role of religion in school, with some believing that Christian morality should be explicitly taught and some opposing any mention of Christianity (e.g., "Christmas holiday")
- different notions of educational standards held by various community members
- conflicting views on how the town's cultural diversity should be reflected in the curriculum
- questions about whether and how to diversify the faculty and administration to reflect the community's racial makeup
- the belief by minority parents that their children are singled out by school disciplinarians for punishment
- the belief by white parents that minority students get special treatment
- concerns about safety, teen pregnancy, and drug or alcohol abuse among the community's teenagers, fueled by a belief that there has been a decline in students' character that should be addressed through the school curriculum
- beliefs that students' character is the province of the home, and should not be tampered with by teachers and their values
- other areas of disagreement among the school's diverse constituents

Time Considerations

I will plan the unit on *coming of age* for a school that has 50-minute class periods, a common length of time for school organization. The school year is divided into two semesters, each of which is partitioned in half in what are called quarters. A quarter lasts roughly nine weeks. Grades are due at the end of each quarter, with final grades due at the end of semesters. At the halfway point of each quarter, the euphemistically named progress reports (a.k.a. "failure notices") must be sent home for any student who is in danger of receiving a grade of D or lower for the grading period or for any student whose grades reveal a decline in performance.

These grading periods help define the limits of the units. If you decide to teach eight units for the year, you should plan on roughly four to five weeks per unit, keeping in mind that you always lose days to pep rallies, school assemblies, field trips, snow days, and so on. You also end up devoting class periods to either standardized test preparation or the actual testing.

> This was really the great discovery of why I would want to teach: I could go on learning! I didn't have to be the one who knows. How dreary! What Frost said about writing poetry ("No surprise for the writer, no surprise for the reader") also holds true for teaching. Unless a teacher is making discoveries in the classroom, rediscovering the text with the "beginner's mind" that Zen masters talk about, the class lacks the magical sense of possibility and discovery.
>
> —Julia Alvarez

As I've noted previously, the best-laid plans are inevitably thwarted, and you need to constantly revise your plans to suit new conditions. But, regardless of what happens, you will need to provide closure to your unit of instruction as the grading period comes to an end so that the students' report card grades reflect their performance on the unit's culminating texts. The main consequence of this deadline is that your instructional planning is never ideal, but designed and modified to function within the parameters of your school's schedule.

Back to School

The beginning of the school year has some fairly predictable rituals. The week before school starts, there are typically meetings that help teachers get into their autumn routines. There are often preliminary meetings for new faculty members, where they may be given a greeting by the district and school administrators, a tour of the school, a guide to school policies, information about the chain of command to go through to solve problems, a doughnut and some coffee, and so on. The whole faculty will often then meet for a period of time (all or part of a day). Here the principal gives an optimistic talk designed to put everyone in a positive frame of mind. Then it's on to a coffee break, where teachers swap greetings and stories of their summer's activities. This is likely followed by departmental meetings, where the chair offers a greeting, more encouraging words, and an agenda for the year.

There might be further breakout groups, with perhaps teachers of a particular preparation or team (a cross-disciplinary group of teachers who share the same set of students) meeting to discuss their curriculum and instruction for the year. Finally, teachers might be given time to go to their classrooms for individual preparations for the school year: hanging posters, filling in the gradebook, organizing seats, making sure class sets of books are on the shelves, and doing whatever other housekeeping is necessary before students enter class on the first day of school. Teachers and students often view the return to school in the same bittersweet way: They are sad to see summer and its pace come to an end, but glad to be back in school with their friends.

SETTING UP SHOP: GETTING STARTED WITH STUDENTS

Mostly, the first day of school is a time of getting reacquainted, of getting back into the routine of school. Students will come to class ready to see old friends and socialize. When students think of returning to school, they don't think, "What will I learn about writing and literature this year?" They think, "Who's in my class, and who's my teacher (mean, nice, hard, strict, easy, etc.)?"—usually in that order. These concerns are foremost on their minds when they come into class on the first day.

Much of what happens throughout the first day of school is clerical. Teachers take attendance, find that so-and-so has moved to another state and should be scratched from the roster, tolerate the students who drift in late claiming they couldn't find the room, and so on. They then might pass out the class textbook and record which student received which book. Often, teachers then take time to lay out a set of rules students must abide by in the class. Teachers typically try to be positive to start the year, although some begin by spelling out the series of disciplinary consequences that follow from any violations of the class rules. This whole set of housekeeping activities might take the first 30 minutes or so. Teachers might use the remaining time by beginning a lesson (groans), assigning homework (bigger groans), or otherwise delving into the academics of school.

This time could also be used to take an *inventory* of students' interests and performance levels. Throughout the first few weeks of school, you should look for opportunities for students to tell you about themselves. You can do this in a number of ways:

1. *Personal experience writing:* If you do not plan to solicit personal experience writing as part of the unit itself, you might ask students to provide you with a piece of writing in which they tell of some significant event from their recent past—not the classic "what I did last summer" exercise, but an assignment that encourages students to write about something that will help you get to know them and their interests better. Through this writing you can learn about the students and what they find significant and also get a sense of their development as writers. Both pieces of information should inform how you teach. In the coming-of-age unit, personal experience writing is already built into the unit design.

2. *Owner's manual:* You could also learn about your students by having them provide you with an owner's manual for themselves. You might need to review what these should include:
   - A description of the product and its intended use
   - Instructions on how to assemble it (optional)
   - A diagram of what it looks like in action
   - Instructions on how to operate and maintain it
   - How to know when it's not working properly
   - What steps to take to fix it

   Students usually have fun writing about themselves in this way, and you can learn about their personalities, interests, and writing from these manuals.

3. *Parent/guardian introduction:* Another way to learn about students is by having a parent, guardian, or other significant adult in the students' lives provide a letter of introduction. You might contrive a situation: The student is new to a setting, and this person is writing the letter that will provide entrée. As I noted previously, you should always be careful about requiring parental involvement, as some students may come from troubled homes.

4. *Survey:* You could prepare a survey in which you ask students to tell you things about themselves. One set of questions might be:

   Please answer each question as honestly as possible. Your answers will help me get to know you as a person and also help me to know how to teach this class well.

   1. What kind of reading did you do over the summer? Please tell:
      - the *type* of reading (newspaper, magazine, novel, etc.)
      - the *amount* you read (five pages a day, two pages a week, none, etc.)
      - the *names* of things you read (*Rolling Stone* magazine, *Flowers in the Attic*, etc.)

2. Who is your favorite author? What have you read by this author? Why do you consider this author your favorite?
3. What kinds of things do you particularly dislike to read? Why do you find them so awful?
4. What's your favorite thing about school?
5. What's your least favorite thing about school?
6. What kind of writing did you do over the summer? Please tell:
   * the *type* of writing (letters to friends, email, a novel, etc.)
   * the *amount* you wrote (five pages a day, two pages a week, none, etc.)
7. What purposes do you use writing for outside school?
8. If you could change one thing about the writing you do in school, what would it be?
9. If you could change one thing about the reading you do in school, what would it be?
10. What would you most like to learn about in this class?
11. If you could give me one piece of advice about how to teach this class, what would it be?
12. If you could change the way school is run, what changes would you make?
13. What are your favorite things to do outside school?
14. Do you think your favorite things from outside school should be part of what you do for grades in school? Please explain.
15. Do your grades in school accurately reflect how smart you are? Please explain.

From a survey of this type, you can get a sense of what students' experiences with literature and writing are, what their attitudes toward school are, and how you might look for opportunities to build on their interests for more effective teaching and learning.

5. *Response to literature:* Finally, you could do a kind of diagnostic inventory to see how students make sense of their reading. You could have them read a short work of literature and write a response in which they explain how they make sense of it. Their responses could be in the form of a short essay, an imaginative piece they produce, or answers to a series of questions you ask about the work.

From whatever combination of inventories you use, you should get a sense of where the students stand academically and where their interests lie. This knowledge can help you choose appropriate texts to read and develop a suitable set of expectations.

My hypothetical classes will include a diverse set of students, representative of the racial composition and economic range of the school as a whole. Their writing reveals a wide span of fluency, from students with a strong voice and facility with language to those who find writing painfully difficult. Some students read widely on their own, others rarely read at all. Some have computers in their homes, others lack even typewriters. My instruction, then, needs to account for a wide range of students so that all can benefit in some way.

STARTING THE UNIT

In Chapter 7 I described a set of possible ways to introduce a unit. I briefly described an appropriate introductory activity for the coming-of-age unit. Here I will show how you might plan this activity in greater detail. My thinking is, as usual, constrained by time limitations. I have roughly five weeks in which to teach the unit. I am dedicating an extra week to this unit because the beginning of the year often involves lost time to administrivia (passing out books, etc.) and usually requires greater attention to procedures and routines than will be needed subsequently. That leaves me with about four weeks in which to run a writing workshop before the marking period ends. These time parameters are not hard-and-fast time limits, but rather approximations of how much time I'll budget for each. As the unit unfolds and I make adjustments to situations that arise, I'll similarly rethink the time frame for each unit.

Every class period will include a couple of minutes at the beginning to take attendance and take care of housekeeping duties (reading announcements, passing back papers, etc.), followed by about 10 minutes of tool sharpening. That leaves just under 40 minutes of time for the unit, although we might need a few minutes at the end of the period to straighten out the room if we've moved the desks for a small-group activity or performances. Leaving the room orderly for the next class is particularly important if, as an early-career teacher, you have to teach in a number of different classrooms and are always on someone else's turf.

The first day of class has already been devoted to housekeeping and one of the inventories I identified earlier. For convenience's sake, I'll say that the first day of school is on a Monday, although it doesn't always work out that way. And so I'll begin my planning on Tuesday of the first week of school, with the understanding that in many school systems the second day of school might fall on a Friday, with the weekend making it difficult to start the year with academic continuity. Of course, I'll hope that nobody pulls a fire alarm, or that a bird or bee doesn't fly in my classroom window, or that a maintenance crew doesn't come to fix the radiator in the middle of class, or that the grounds crew doesn't mow the grass outside my window so that we can't hear one another talk over the noise . . . but if these things do happen (and at some point during the year they will), we'll forge ahead nonetheless.

On Tuesday, I'll want to move into the introductory activity right after doing our tool sharpening. We'll start with the writing prompt for the personal narratives about a coming-of-age experience. I'll then need to spend a few minutes teaching students how to work in small groups, because it's likely that they are inexperienced with collaborative learning in school. I'll want them to compare their narratives in small groups and follow this small-group activity with a whole-class discussion of what goes into such narratives.

In some units, I'd follow the whole-class discussion by having students get back in groups and produce plays based on one or more of the narratives. In the coming-of-age unit I'm designing here, however, I've already committed too much time to teaching question posing later in the unit. So, though I think that producing plays would be a good activity for this unit, I'll have to jettison the dramatic interpretations and look for opportunities in other units to include theatrics. It's possible, too, that students will dramatize the classes in which they lead their discussions, so there will conceivably be opportunities during this unit to have students work within the course's overarching concept of generating dramatic images.

Following is one way to lay out a daily plan for this sequence. One caution: Any time you give students either a writing prompt or a small-group task, you need to *provide them with a hard copy of the instructions.* You can write the instructions on the board, display them on an overhead, or distribute photocopies or mimeographed sheets. They will not remember the instructions if you simply say them aloud. They will need to have a written version of the task to use as a reference point.

Discussion Topic

In one school I taught in, the district superintendent told the faculty that all teachers should have lesson plans written so that they could tell you on September 1 exactly what they would be doing on March 1. What do you think was the rationale behind this request? Do you agree or disagree with this reasoning? Why?

Day 2 (Tuesday)

3 minutes: Attendance, housekeeping.
5 m.: Tool sharpening: Usage *(they're, their, there).*
15 m.: Provide hard copy of the following prompt and have students write.

> Write about a personal experience you've had in which you had a *coming-of-age* experience, that is, one that caused you to grow up in some way. Make sure to explain:
>
> - The immature behavior that you exhibited prior to the experience
> - A transforming experience through which you gained significant new knowledge and maturity
> - The mature behavior that you exhibited following the experience
>
> You are not required to explain these events in this particular order, although you may if you wish. Keep in mind that other students will read about the experience you write about.

15 m.: Have students get in groups of four or fewer. Because this is the first time for small-group work in this class, model how to form and work in a group first (see Chapter 9). Then provide hard copy of the following instructions and go over them together:

> Each student in your group should read your experience aloud. Then, as a group, identify the following, based on the experiences written about in your group:
>
> - The traits that characterize immature behavior
> - The reasons that the transforming experiences enable people to change
> - The traits that characterize mature behavior
>
> (optional) Have students proofread to see if they've used *there, their,* and *they're* properly.

As students work, circulate to answer questions and help them focus on the task.

9 m.: Begin a whole-class discussion of the small-group conclusions. Record bulleted versions of the points made by each group. This discussion will need to be continued on the following day.

3 m.: Return seats to original positions; prepare to depart.

A few things before moving along to day 3:

As you can imagine, it's hard to say exactly how long any one segment will last. The purpose of the plan is to *anticipate* how the class will go, rather than to have the plan dictate a schedule. Your decision regarding the end of one episode and the beginning of the next will follow from your judgment about students' progress. If you teach the same preparation several times in one day, it's possible that some classes will move further along in the sequence than others in the same time period. The plan provides you with a flexible scheme for your classes.

A note on transitions: It's a good idea to make the transitions between episodes fairly crisp. Some educators strongly advocate instruction that uses time efficiently, with both classrooms and lessons designed to avoid unproductive uses of time. While I think that teaching should provide opportunities to stretch out and explore topics and ideas in depth, I agree that avoiding time *wasting* is a good idea. Transitions are one area where you can emphasize such efficiency.

Related to this issue is the time at the end of class. Students are often inclined to stand up and gather near the classroom door as the bell approaches. When I taught, I had a simple rule that nobody could leave the class unless everyone was seated. Although it took me a few days to establish this rule at the beginning of the year, once students learned it, they required little reinforcement. Having a simple rule like this enables you to restore the room's order on days when the class activities promote a little chaos.

Okay, on to day 3. We'll need to continue the discussion about the content of narratives. We then begin instruction on how to keep a reading log. I borrow the instructional sequence on reading logs—what educators call a lesson—from the high school teaching of Cindy O'Donnell-Allen, who began her senior English class this way. She had originally simply assigned the reading logs, but discovered that students were so heavily conditioned to answering questions in school that they had difficulty posing them. She thus scaffolded their reading-log responses by going through a kind of sequence that I strongly recommend in this book. The sequence involves the following stages:

1. The teacher introduces a skill, strategy, or procedure to the whole class. This introduction includes
   - a clear explanation of the nature of the task (e.g., what a reading log is and why they're keeping it)
   - explicit information about the expectations for what the students will do (e.g., use the log to pose particular kinds of questions and try to answer them)
   - modeling of how to do this, using accessible materials so that the students can clearly follow the explanation
2. Students are then asked to work collaboratively on a similar kind of problem, using accessible materials so that they can succeed in their initial learning (e.g., they would be provided with an accessible work of literature and, as a

group, pose a set of questions about it). The collaboration can take place in groups of two to four students.

3. Students get feedback on these initial efforts. This feedback can come from peers (e.g., groups exchange and critique one another's efforts) or from the teacher. If the teacher provides the response, he or she would need to collect and respond to the work by the next class session.

4. Students get these critiques back. If the class is ready to move forward, they can then begin with a reading-log entry that they keep individually, which in turn gets some kind of feedback from peer or teacher. If the initial log entries do not come close to expectations, the small-group stage might be repeated.

To summarize: The sequence Cindy used went from *teacher modeling* in a *whole-group* setting, to *small-group practice* with immediate *feedback,* to *individual application* of the procedure. This sequence is a good example of one kind of instructional scaffold. If applied rigidly, a teacher might move along before students are ready. And so one characteristic of flexibly scaffolding students' learning is that the teacher should be attentive and sensitive to how they are performing and adjust the teaching according to what they need. A second characteristic of a flexible scaffold is that the teacher should not simply expect students to do things as modeled, but encourage them to generate new ideas about how to do the task. The purpose, then, is not to get students to mimic the teacher faithfully, but to use the teacher's modeling as a way to learn a new way of thinking about something.

This is also a good time to reiterate one of the long-standing questions about the scaffolding metaphor, that being Searle's question, "Who's building whose building?" The question is fundamentally concerned with the issue of whether the teacher's way is the one and only right way to do things. The answer is, of course not. There are many different ways in which a text can be built and read, each with different purposes and effects.

In the response-log sequence of instruction, it's clear that the teacher is imposing a value on students; that is, the teacher is specifying a stance toward literature and procedures for taking that stance. Some critics would accuse me of being hegemonic here by imposing my view of literature on students. They would say that I'm requiring students to be reflective readers, even if that's not their inclination or preference. And I would have to say that they're right, that's what I'm doing.

I would justify my imposition in terms of what I think is deficient in most school instruction. Students are rarely given opportunities to ask questions, give personal evaluations, make personal connections, or respond in personal ways to the literature they read in school. When I saw Cindy go through this sequence of teaching students *how* to engage in response, I was impressed with her understanding that students would have difficulty inventing their own procedures for asking questions. She assumed that they would benefit from being taught some ways of generating open-ended questions to provide themselves with richer reading experiences. It's true that she decided whose building would get built. But I'm convinced that, for too many students, the lot might still be vacant if she hadn't.

There are occasions, then, when I think it's beneficial for you to impose an agenda on students and teach them how to do a particular thing in a particular way. Primarily, I think it's important to do so when there's a good way to do something that they would be unlikely to think up on their own.

Unit Design

Examine Lessons in Model Units

In the Virtual Library of Conceptual Units at http://www.coe.vga.edu/~smago/Virtual Library.html, choose a unit and look at the author's design of lessons. What is the purpose of the lessons? What kinds of scaffolding do the lessons entail? How are the lessons related to the unit's goals and assessments? To what extent do the lessons involve constructive activity by the students? How do the individual lessons contribute to the students' overall growth and learning in terms of the unit concept? How would you assess the sequencing and relationship of the individual lessons relative to one another? Who's building whose building?

Following these principles, your scheduling for the next few days might look like this:

Day 3 (Wednesday)

3 minutes: Attendance, housekeeping.

5 m.: Tool sharpening: Roots, prefixes, and suffixes: Review of words including the prefixes *co* and *com* (with): *company, comfort, companion, community, collaborate, coalition, coexist,* and so on.

20 m.: Complete discussion from day 2. Each group should offer its views on immature and mature behavior and the kinds of incidents that can trigger the transformation from one to the other. Your role is to record their contributions, using either the board or an overhead projector. While recording, look for opportunities to have students engage in discussion with one another, particularly when groups come up with conflicting points of view or information or when their ideas can productively build on one another's. Students should also be keeping their own notes to help them learn the kind of script they will analyze in one of the unit's culminating projects.

5 m.: Provide closure to the discussion by having students summarize the class's views on coming-of-age experiences and making sure that students understand that they will need this information to succeed on subsequent assignments.

15 m.: Begin the reading-log instruction. This might break down as follows:

> **3 m.:** Explain briefly what a reading log is and what it looks like.
>
> **2 m.:** Pass out a brief, accessible work of literature (e.g., Frost's "The Road Not Taken").
>
> **2 m.:** Pass out the assignment sheet for keeping a reading log, which is:

Keep a reading log in response to the literature we are studying during this unit. To keep your log:

- Divide each page with a vertical line down the center
- On the left side of each page, record significant passages from the literature you read

- On the right side, across from each passage, do any or all of the following:
  1. Ask *open-ended questions* that would help you understand the passage better
  2. Give your personal *response* to the passage (i.e., any thoughts you have in connection with it)
  3. Give your personal *evaluation* of the passage
  4. Think through a possible *interpretation* of the passage
- Have at least one question of each type for each work of literature studied
- Remember that your journal does not need to follow the conventions of textbook English. Rather, the purpose is to think about the literature without worrying about the form your thoughts take.
- Turn your response log in every two weeks. I will read your log and respond to your comments. If you make an entry that you do not want me to read, place an X at the top of the page.
- Keep in mind that *I am required to share any thoughts or suggestions of violence, suicide, substance abuse, family abuse, or other harmful behavior with the school counselors.*

8 m.: Review the assignment, with a promise to spend time in class the next day learning how to do it.

2 m.: Preparation for departure.

Day 4 (Thursday)

3 m.: Attendance, housekeeping.

10 m.: Tool sharpening: Standardized testing format: word-analogy problems (e.g., *robin: bird* as *poodle:* _____ (a) animal (b) dog (c) collie (d) noodle).

15 m.: Model how to maintain the log by thinking aloud as you read "The Road Not Taken." To illustrate your entries, make them on an overhead projector as you think aloud. Make sure to include at least one entry of each of the four types identified in the assignment: *open-ended questions* that would help students understand the passage better, personal *response* to the passage, personal *evaluation* of the passage, and a possible *interpretation* of the passage. Encourage students to ask questions about the process and about each type of entry.

3 m.: Students then choose collaborators to work with while you pass out a new work of literature (e.g., Langston Hughes's "Mother to Son").

16 m.: Groups of students read the poem and work on producing responses of each type, using the split-page notebook format you modeled earlier. As students work, circulate among the groups to answer questions and help students maintain their focus.

3 m.: Students restore their desks to the original positions and prepare to depart.

Day 5 (Friday)

3 m.: Attendance, housekeeping.

Plan Week 1

Plan the first week of instruction for your unit. It needn't be for the first week of school. Your first week's plan should include the following:

- Some kind of inventory for assessing students' knowledge and needs
- Evidence that the instruction is clearly tied to your unit goals
- Instruction in procedures for how to reach the unit goals
- Establishment of classroom routines
- Daily plans, including the amount of time anticipated for each episode

10 m.: Tool sharpening: Punctuation: apostrophes (with emphasis on apostrophe placement with singular and plural possessives and on not using apostrophes to form plural nouns).

10 m.: Each group exchanges its response-log entries with those of another group for the purpose of providing a critique. Their task is to evaluate whether each group has made an appropriate entry for each of the four types.

15 m.: Whole-class discussion to follow up the small-group critiques. Your role is to ask different groups to volunteer their entries for each type. The class then sees a range of possible ways to provide each type of entry.

12 m.: Assign the first story of the unit, Alice Munro's "Red Dress." Make the link between the story script of their personal narratives on coming of age and the structure of the series of stories they are about to read.

Homework: Have students complete the reading of the story and turn in a response-log entry on Monday. Include a caution that any out-of-class reading is likely to be followed by a content quiz to ensure that they've read it.

The first week of school is now over. You've accomplished a lot. You have learned a lot about the students from reading their inventories and their personal experience narratives, and from listening to students discuss their conceptions of immature and mature behavior. You have established some important routines: the daily tool-sharpening sessions and the movement from whole class to small group to individual performance. You have taught students how to use the tool of writing in what's likely a new way, for the purpose of thinking through their response to literature and posing questions about it. You have introduced the coming-of-age literature and helped students see the script it tends to follow, all prior to their reading the literature. And because you had planned the week in advance, you didn't stay up each night till the wee hours trying to figure out what to do on the next day.

WEEK 2

In the second week of school, you can begin to focus on analyzing the coming-of-age script in a series of short stories. Students will have additional opportunities to construct their own questions about the stories in their reading logs. Once again, you will scaffold the students' learning by starting with a teacher-led, whole-class discussion of the story script. Once you are confident that students can read this script without your guidance, they apply their knowledge in small-group analyses of stories. Finally, you will evaluate them on their ability to recognize this script individually. In addition, you will begin to prepare them for the semester's goal of keeping a portfolio.

The first day of the second week will require some extra work to help get students back into the mind-set of school and the issues of the unit. It's a long way from Friday to Monday in the mind of a student. While some are so gung ho about school that they can't wait for classes to start again after Friday's final bell, many turn their attention immediately and entirely to other things that interest them: their friends, their extracurricular activities, their socializing, their jobs, their families, their communities of faith, and much more. Especially this early in the year, you'll need to help them get their minds back on the unit. It's possible that they're not accustomed to having continuity of the sort that you're encouraging, and that they're not expecting last week's classes to affect what they learn this week. You'll need, then, to establish the importance of continuity in your class.

You'll also need to do a couple of things on Monday that may be unpleasant. You'll need to do something to make sure that the students read the story you assigned on Friday. Typically, teachers give quizzes in which they ask a set of questions about key events from the story. If students remember the story but forget exactly who did what, then they can fail the quiz. In addition to requiring the recall of arbitrary knowledge, this kind of quiz reinforces the idea that literature study consists of the recollection of isolated factoids.

In my years of teaching, I found that if I didn't provide some sort of quiz, then a number of students simply wouldn't do the reading. I had originally believed that if I made my classes interesting, then students would do the work. I had been persuaded that if I needed to rely on extrinsic motivators such as quizzes, there was something wrong with my teaching. I therefore made reading assignments with the belief that if the literature and classes were worthwhile, my students would do the reading.

My faith in the widespread intrinsic motivation of my students turned out, however, to be overly optimistic. I found that without some kind of incentive, a significant number of students would ignore the reading. I'd then come to class with the expectation of having a discussion and realize that very few students were participating, while the others spent the class avoiding eye contact with me. I resigned myself to the idea that, in the real world of my classes, I did not have the ideal students that people talked about in books about education. I needed to come up with some way to motivate my students to come to class prepared, aside from how interesting I thought my classes would be.

After trying several different ways of quizzing students on the reading assignments, I finally settled on what I call a *summary quiz*. These are quite simple. Students were asked to write a brief summary of the story, making sure to include key details from the beginning, middle, and end of the story or chapters.

These quizzes served the purpose of rewarding students for doing the reading, without punishing them for confusing the details. They also served the purpose of having students recall the story prior to our discussing it, thus in a sense clearing some of the cobwebs early in the class—cognitive psychologists would say the quiz would bring the story into short-term memory. Finally, they gave students an opportunity to write, rather than simply to give one-word answers to questions. I found, then, that summary quizzes did the basic work of encouraging students to do the unit's reading, while also serving beneficial purposes in terms of students' learning. They took a little longer for me to grade, but I've found that making school convenient for the teacher does not always make school enriching for students.

A second new area to cover in the second week of school is the introduction of the semester's portfolio assignment and instruction in how to select appropriate exhibits. The portfolio instruction would be a briefer form of lesson than the reading-log instruction. From this point on, you will need to provide regular attention to the portfolios so that students are working on them throughout the semester. Because of time constraints facing the unit as a whole, you will sacrifice some of the tool-sharpening sessions to help students understand their portfolio responsibilities.

Earlier, I provided a possible *rubric* to use in your final evaluation of the portfolios. As the semester goes on and you give continuing attention to their portfolio production, you may begin to introduce the rubric as a way to help students understand how they'll be evaluated. Doing so at this early point in the year, however, would be overwhelming and likely counterproductive.

One of the methods used in the portfolio instruction is a *freewrite*. Technically, a freewrite is an open-ended approach to writing in which students simply begin writing about whatever occurs to them and continue, ideally without pausing, for a given period of time. The idea is to focus on the act of writing itself without worrying about spelling, grammar, or other aspects of form. Freewriting is a good example of an exploratory use of writing, used for the purpose of generating and exploring ideas.

The freewrite below is what's sometimes called a *focused freewrite;* that is, one in which the topic is specified. Here, the freewrite retains its essential quality of encouraging students to use writing as a tool for thinking through a question without worrying about the quality of the product. The emphasis is then on the ideas generated, even if they might come out roughly phrased or punctuated. There's plenty of time to polish them up later in revising and editing opportunities.

Day 6 (Monday)

3 m.: Attendance, housekeeping.

30 m.: Introduction to portfolio assignment (in place of tool sharpening). This segment will include a number of different stages:

> **8 m.:** Have students do a *freewrite* in response to the following prompt: What did you learn in this class during the first week of school? What did you learn it from?
>
> **5 m.:** Follow-up to freewrite: Have some students volunteer to share what they've written. On the board, distinguish between two aspects of their portfolios: the stimulus for learning (which will become the *exhibit*), and the account of learning (which will become the *reflective writing*).

2 m.: Pass out the portfolio assignment, which is:

Throughout the semester you have had a lot of experiences with literature and other art forms. In response to these texts, you have produced a variety of pieces of writing, art, and other forms of expression. Presumably you have learned something about yourself, the literature, how to write, how to read, and other things.

Your culminating project for the semester is to prepare a *portfolio* in which you present things you've produced that have resulted in your most valuable learning. We will call these things *exhibits.* The exhibits you present do not need to be your best work. Often we learn the most from our rough drafts, our frustrated efforts, and other experiences that do not yield our best products. *You will not be graded on the quality of the exhibits that you include.* Rather, you will be graded on how carefully you reflect on what you learned from producing them.

Your portfolio should include:

- Title page with name and date
- A minimum of eight items that serve as your exhibits. You must include a minimum of two exhibits for each of the four units we studied. Your portfolio may include additional exhibits if you wish, including things from outside this class.
- Reflective writing that identifies and discusses significant learning based on each exhibit, consisting of a minimum of 200 words for each exhibit.
- A longer *synthesis paper* in which you discuss how these exhibits as a whole reveal what you've learned this year about both yourself and the material we have studied, consisting of a minimum of 1,000 words (roughly four typed pages).

15 m.: Read through the assignment. Focus on explaining what an *exhibit* is and give illustrations from the examples provided by students from their freewriting. Stress that the accompanying *reflective writing,* and not the quality of the exhibit, will be the basis for the portfolio grade. Link the portfolio assignment and the reading log to the overarching concept of seeking self-determination as learners. Explain that students will do two units in each of the semester's two marking periods and that they'll need at least two exhibits from each unit. Ask for questions about the assignment and their responsibilities.

8 m.: Introduce the idea of a summary quiz. Have students write and turn in a summary quiz for "Red Dress."
6 m.: Have students get in small groups to compare their reading-log entries for "Red Dress." From their entries, each group should prepare one question to pose to the class on the following day.
3 m.: Return desks to original locations; exeunt.

Here I introduce another routine: Students will use their reading-log entries as ways to initiate class discussions. One managerial note: In these first few weeks of school, you will need to monitor small-group work carefully. Many students will be inexperienced in participating in small groups. You will need to make sure that students are seated in discrete groups and understand their task. You will also need to make judgments about groups that are unproductive. In Chapter 9, I discuss ways of managing students' work in small groups.

On day 7, we will discuss the story in two ways. First of all, students will have an opportunity to pose their own questions, using their reading-log entries as the basis. Because I want students to have opportunities to provide one another with feedback on their reading-log entries as part of the scaffolding process, I'll have them get in small groups to hear one another's questions and responses to the text. After critiquing one another's questions, each group can then formulate a single question to pose to the class. I'm assuming a class size of about 25 students (though I'm painfully aware that in some schools the number is higher—sometimes much higher).

You'll typically, then, have six to seven small groups operating at once during any small-group activity. In the plan that follows, I'll make a conservative estimate that each group's question will yield a discussion of 2 to 5 minutes. This estimate could be off by quite a bit, however. Planning time for discussion is an inexact science, since you never know where an open-ended discussion will go. You should be prepared, then, to readjust your planning any time a discussion is involved. One advantage of preparing a whole unit in advance is that if a discussion falls far short of its anticipated time, you can simply move to the next part of the plan, rather than being left with a large stretch of unplanned dead time at the end of a class period. These dead periods often occur in the classes of early-career teachers. Sometimes they occur when an administrator is conducting an evaluation. You can avoid the problem with careful planning.

Day 7 (Tuesday)

3 m.: Attendance, housekeeping.

10 m.: Tool sharpening: Language variation: Have students identify a set of appropriate and inappropriate circumstances for saying the following:

> "I ain't got nothing to do."
>
> "I am devoid of activities with which to engage myself."

Follow with these questions: On what occasions do we use the rules for proper speech that we learn in school? On what occasions do we use other rules? What determines the rules for propriety that we follow?

20 m.: A representative from each of the previous day's small groups poses the group's question to the class. These questions form the basis for the class's initial discussion of the story. Your role is to moderate this discussion, with an emphasis on prompting students to elaborate their responses.

15 m.: Guide a discussion in which students look at the story in terms of its coming-of-age script. The questions that structure this discussion follow the questions students will respond to in satisfying the unit goal: What immature behavior does the protagonist show at the beginning of the story? What significant event causes change? What mature behavior does the protagonist show at the end? Why does this event, above all others, cause this change?

2 m.: Homework assignment: Have students read Richard Wright's "The Man Who Was Almost a Man." Prepare for exeunt.

On day 8, I'll want to reinforce the procedures we used to respond to "Red Dress." We'll go through a very similar process in discussing it as a way to reinforce the method of analysis before beginning to turn over the interpretive responsibilities to the students.

Day 8 (Wednesday)

3 m.: Attendance, housekeeping.

7 m.: Tool sharpening: Status markers: pronoun use in prepositional phrases (e.g., "between you and me" instead of "between you and I").

10 m.: Summary quiz on "The Man Who Was Almost a Man"

10 m.: Have students get in small groups to compare their reading-log entries for "The Man Who Was Almost a Man." From their entries, each group should prepare one question to pose to the class.

20 m.: A representative from each group poses the group's question to the class. These questions form the basis for the class's initial discussion of the story. The teacher's role is to moderate this discussion, with an emphasis on prompting students to elaborate on their responses.

Day 9 (Thursday)

3 m.: Attendance, housekeeping.

10 m.: Tool sharpening: History of language: Neologisms from the entertainment industry (*prequel, docudrama, shockudrama, mockudrama, infotainment, edutainment, infomercial, advertorial,* etc.)

15 m.: Guide a discussion in which students look at the story in terms of its coming-of-age script. The questions that lead this discussion follow the questions students will respond to in satisfying the unit goal: What immature behavior does the protagonist show at the beginning of the story? What significant event causes change? What mature behavior does the protagonist show at the end? Why does this event, above all others, cause this change?

10 m.: Pass out copies of *A Separate Peace* and tell students that within a few weeks they will begin discussing it in student-led discussions. They will need to read ahead in order to succeed in leading their discussions.

12 m.: Homework: Have students read Nicolai Chukovski's "The Bridge." Students may begin reading in the remaining time in the period.

Day 9 illustrates one thing that will happen during any unit: You will have a segment of time remaining in a class. Students will often plead for you to grant them "free time" and tell you that all their other teachers do this (although you'll have trouble corroborating this claim with testimony from these other teachers). In fact, students will tell you that they deserve a "free day" every so often, again saying that other teachers allow them all the time. Yet, if you look around the school, you tend to find every class being conducted as normal. My advice is to take these claims with a grain of salt and go ahead with your instructional plans.

In any case, there will be days when you conclude something with 10 to 20 minutes remaining. Rather than letting students talk for the remainder of the period, you

Vignette

I know of one teacher who deliberately leaves "free time" at the end of every class. During this time, she talks informally with students about their lives outside class. The purpose of this is twofold. First of all, she learns more about the students and what their lives are about—their circumstances, their interests, their responsibilities, their activities, their friends, and so on. Establishing this relationship helps her understand her students' strengths and needs better, and also helps develop a connection that makes classroom relations better.

Second of all, it helps to promote students' beliefs that the teacher cares about them individually and as a group. Presumably, if students know that their teacher cares about them, they will be more likely to buy into the teacher's decisions about pedagogy, classroom management, and so on.

can either take care of housekeeping chores (e.g., passing out books) or allow them to begin their homework. I can imagine few circumstances that would justify using class for "free time," given how precious your instructional time is.

The plan for day 10 will rest on the assumption that students are ready to begin the second phase of the scaffolding process by doing the analysis of the coming-of-age script in small groups, without your explicit guidance. If I were teaching real groups of students, I might not begin this transition at this point. I would, rather, make an informal assessment of students' grasp of the story script based on the way the class discussions go. I might make this transition after only one story, or I might decide that the class needs at least one more whole-class experience with the analysis before moving to the small-group stage. For the purposes of planning, however, I will assume that two stories will suffice for the teacher-led stage, and that two more in small groups will prepare them for their individual analyses.

One question you might ask yourself is, Does it matter what order I go in with the stories? Is there an optimal sequence for reading and discussing them in learning the unit concepts? I would say that there are probably different consequences for different sequences. "The Man Who Was Almost a Man" concerns an African American boy, his father, and a gun; "Red Dress" concerns a white Canadian girl, her mother, a dress, and a dance. Each would cover different ground and raise different issues, and reversing the order of the texts would no doubt cause a slightly different reading of each. Whether one sequence is more optimal than another is open to question.

Each story discussion will still begin with students generating whole-class discussion questions in small groups, based on their reading-log responses. This procedure accomplishes several ends:

- It gives students a concrete goal for the use of their reading logs.
- It allows discussions to explore aspects of the story that might not come up in the analysis of the story script.
- It provides students with continual feedback on the kinds of entries they are making in their reading logs.

Day 10 (Friday)

3 m.: Attendance, housekeeping.

5 m.: Tool sharpening: Usage: Distinguish proper usage of *between* and *among, less* and *fewer.*

10 m.: Summary quiz on "The Bridge."

7 m.: Have students get in small groups to compare their reading-log entries for "The Bridge." From their entries, each group should prepare one question to pose to the class.

20 m.: A representative from each group poses the group's question to the class. These questions form the basis for the class's initial discussion of the story. Your role is to moderate this discussion, with an emphasis on prompting students to elaborate on their responses.

5 m.: Collect reading logs for the first teacher evaluation.

As you can see, day 10 did not get all the way to the small-group analysis of the story script, focusing instead on the students' questions about the story. Monday's class will be dedicated to their first small-group analysis of a story apart from your direct guidance.

You have also given yourself an assignment for the weekend: to evaluate their response logs. It's important to turn these back to students fairly quickly so that they can continue to use the logs and can use your feedback for future entries. Grading papers over the weekend is probably not your idea of an ideal getaway, but it's something you'll end up doing if you want your students to learn how to write.

Your willingness to dedicate time to reading student writing will earn their gratitude and likely distinguish you from most in the teaching profession. Extensive writing is much more likely to take place in the English class than anywhere else in the school curriculum, and extensive writing takes time to grade. Let's say you devote one minute to each student each week. That's an absurdly small amount of time, but if you have 150 students, then that's two and a half hours of time outside the classroom that you invest in their writing. Spend ten minutes on each student and that's fifteen hours. Your school will probably give you planning time (which often ends up being grading time, or form-filling-out time), but not fifteen hours a week. And so you will undoubtedly end up spending time at home with a stack of student papers at your side. Your students will recognize this dedication and appreciate you for it.

Week 3 will involve the students in their small-group analyses of two stories, and then in their individual analyses.

One thing you'll notice is that so far, classes have not been interrupted by any pep rallies, holidays, field trips planned by other teachers, assemblies, and other intrusions into your teaching. There's no construction crew tearing up the sidewalk outside your window. There's no maintenance team brewing a vat of tar with noxious odors wafting through your classroom, all in preparation for reroofing the area right above your classroom. There's no school marching band practicing all day long on the other side of the thin wall of your classroom. There have been no 100-degree days that leave you and your students limp with

> My basic conclusion is contained in the aphorism "Less is more." I believe that the qualities of mind that should be the goal of high school need time to grow and that they develop best when engaging a few, important ideas, deeply. Information is plentiful, cheap; learning how to use it is often stressful and absolutely requires a form of personal coaching of each student by a teacher that is neither possible in many schools today nor recognized as an important process.
>
> —Theodore Sizer, *Horace's Compromise*

Plan Week 2

Plan the second week of instruction for your unit. Your plan should include the following:

- Continuity from week 1's instruction
- Evidence that the instruction is clearly tied to your unit and course-long goals
- Instruction in procedures for how to reach the unit goals
- Classroom routines
- Daily plans, including the amount of time anticipated for each episode

heat exhaustion, too weather-beaten to move alertly through the instruction. My plan is somewhat unrealistic in that it does not include any of these impediments or others. In a real teaching situation, I would likely have modified my plans to fit with the scheduling problems, administrative decisions initiated elsewhere in the school, and other acts of improvidence. For now, I'll concentrate on making the plans, because without a plan, there won't be anything to modify.

WEEK 3

Day 11 (Monday)

3 m.: Attendance, housekeeping.

10 m.: Return reading logs, go over both strengths (e.g., share exemplary entries) and common types of problems (do *not* use individual students' writing as negative examples). Reiterate expectations for the logs in light of the first two weeks' performance.

35 m.: Have students get in small groups and analyze the story script for "The Bridge." Provide them with hard copy of the following assignment:

> For "The Bridge," write an essay in which you analyze the protagonist's coming-of-age experience. In your essay, make sure that you:
>
> - Provide a general thesis for the paper, explaining the protagonist's primary transformation during the course of the story.
> - Describe the protagonist's immature behavior at the beginning of the story, including specific examples from the text.
> - Describe clearly the key event that causes the character to change. In doing so, explain why this event, rather than others in the story, causes the protagonist to come of age.
> - Describe the significant changes taking place in the protagonist following the coming-of-age experience, including specific examples from the text.
> - Draw a conclusion about how people change as a result of significant events.

2 m.: Return seats to original positions; prepare to depart.

It's quite possible that 35 minutes won't be enough time for the students to do this assignment well. You should monitor the groups carefully to see if they're working diligently at the task, and if they are and do not finish, allow them a finite amount of time at the beginning of the next class to complete the assignment. Because the students are required to produce an essay rather than a set of short answers to these questions, I'll assume that they need extra time and so will let them continue the following day.

You can either require one paper from each group or require each student to write a paper based on the group's discussion. If each student writes, you will have a lot of grading on your hands. Students will, however, benefit from the experience. You will make many decisions in your career that reflect this balance: The more you expect and require of your students, the more work you are giving to yourself.

Day 12 (Tuesday)

3 m.: Attendance, housekeeping.
10 m.: Tool sharpening: Sentence combining: making compound sentences using *and, but, so, or,* or a semicolon.
37 m.: Students finish their small-group task. When they finish, they can begin reading Irwin Shaw's "Peter Two."

At this point we are about halfway through the unit and still have some major work ahead of us. I will therefore vary the routine for tomorrow's class by moving straight from the summary quiz to the students' analysis of "Peter Two" for the story script. This will be their final preparation for their individual analysis of a new story. You could either give them a choice of stories to read from their anthology or simply assign one for their individual analysis.

The advantage of having choice is that they might grasp some stories better than others and so produce a better essay. Realistically, however, they are not likely to read five or six stories in order to choose one. A pragmatic solution is simply to assign one, such as Alice Walker's "Everyday Use," or to give them a smaller set of stories to choose from. From your point of view, it's good to have them writing on different stories so that there's greater variety in your own reading experience when you grade their papers.

Day 13 (Wednesday)

3 m.: Attendance, housekeeping.
10 m.: Tool sharpening: Roots, prefixes, suffixes: words that include *dom* (home) (e.g., *domestic, domicile, domain,* etc.)
10 m.: Summary quiz on "Peter Two"
27 m.: Begin analysis of "Peter Two" in small groups, following the same guidelines used with "The Bridge."

Day 14 (Thursday)

3 m.: Attendance, housekeeping.
10 m.: Tool sharpening: History of language: words derived from names of Greek and Roman gods (mercurial, Olympian, saturnine, etc.)

5 m.: Remind students that they should be saving possible texts for portfolio exhibits; ask for suggestions for possible exhibits from the last week's work.
30 m.: Complete analysis of "Peter Two," turn in.
2 m.: Return seats to original locations; prepare to depart.

Day 15 (Friday)

3 m.: Attendance, housekeeping.
5 m.: Tool sharpening: Usage: Homonyms (*hear/here; hair/hare; higher/hire; heir/air*)
10 m.: Make the assignment for their individual assessment. The assignment is similar to the one given for their small-group analysis:

> From the literary choices provided, read one work of literature and write an essay in which you analyze the protagonist's coming-of-age experience. In your essay, make sure that you:
>
> - Provide a general thesis for the paper, explaining the protagonist's primary transformation during the course of the story.
> - Describe the protagonist's immature behavior at the beginning of the story, including specific examples from the text.
> - Describe clearly the key event that causes the character to change. In doing so, explain why this event, rather than others in the story, causes the protagonist to come of age.
> - Describe the significant changes taking place in the protagonist following the coming-of-age experience, including specific examples from the text.
> - Draw a conclusion about how people change as a result of significant events.
> - Follow rules of textbook grammar, spelling, punctuation, and usage throughout your essay.
> - Give evidence of having written at least one rough draft that has been submitted for peer evaluation.

32 m.: Students begin reading the story. They should bring in a draft of their essay by the following Tuesday.

The requirement to provide evidence of at least one draft with peer evaluation helps you set the schedule for next week. You'll need to provide time in class for peer evaluation and to teach the students how to critique one another's work. Including this step in the sequence can provide benefits in several ways:

- Students will benefit from the peer feedback and produce better essays.
- The process of responding to several other papers will give students experience in reading analyses of the type they're writing and possibly make them more astute critics of their own writing.
- Students will learn another routine that you will use in your class, the use of peer-response groups to provide feedback on drafts of their writing. By regularly participating in these groups, they are being encouraged to view writing as a process that requires several iterations before being considered complete.

Plan Week 3

Plan the third week of instruction for your unit. Your plan should include the following:

- Continuity from week 2's instruction
- Evidence that the instruction is clearly tied to your unit and course-long goals
- Instruction in procedures for how to reach the unit goals
- Feedback from both students and teacher on initial drafts of work that uses criteria similar to those that will be used in formal assessments
- Continued establishment and development of classroom routines
- Daily plans, including the amount of time anticipated for each episode

The requirement to bring the drafts in on Tuesday creates a somewhat disembodied day on Monday. You don't want to begin a new sequence of classes that would immediately be interrupted by Tuesday's peer-feedback session. And you don't want to waste the day. You can, however, use Monday productively by devoting more concentrated attention to their semester's portfolio assignment. You have spent part of one period introducing this assignment to them, but you have an opportunity with Monday's class to return to this assignment and help the students both identify an appropriate exhibit and work on producing an accompanying reflective essay.

After the peer-response feedback to the analytic essays, you have two unit goals left to work toward: the student-led discussions on their outside novel, and their personal narratives on coming-of-age experiences. If you provide careful instruction on how to do these successfully, you will likely run over the initial time budget of five weeks and infringe further on the writing workshop. You will always have to make decisions about what to do in these cases. For this opening unit, I think it's important to work toward both these goals, and so will plan to include them at the expense of a few days off the writing workshop.

My reasoning is that the first unit of the year will always require more instructional time than other units, because I am teaching students how to do things that I will expect of them later in the year. In subsequent units, for instance, I will want to have students lead discussions of the outside novels. I will not, however, need to teach the students how to pose the questions, because I will do that in the coming-of-age unit.

Similarly, if I have students keep response logs, I can simply make the assignment rather than spending a few days teaching them how to keep one. The year's first unit includes more explicit teaching of routines and procedures than other units, and therefore inevitably takes longer to teach. While I hate to scale back the workshop that follows, its greatest strength—its open-ended quality—makes it flexible in adjusting to other needs.

Of course, others would undoubtedly disagree with me, saying that the workshop, and not the unit, should take priority. There are legitimate arguments in support of that decision. My point here is not to dispute them, but rather to say that when you teach, you inevitably make decisions that constrain your other choices. The most important thing is to make principled, defensible choices, even if they are subject to disagreement by respected colleagues.

WEEK 4
Day 16 (Monday)

3 m.: Attendance, housekeeping.

15 m.: Tool sharpening: Politics of grammar: Have students freewrite about the differences and similarities between the grammar taught in textbooks and the grammar used in their homes, and the usefulness of each. Follow-up discussion: Why is one form of language "official" and others not? Who decides which form of language is best? What are the consequences of using different versions of English in different circumstances? (Note that this topic could potentially run well over 15 minutes!)

5 m.: Tell students that they will devote the day to selecting good portfolio exhibits. Remind them that a good exhibit is not necessarily a good product, but a source of important learning. It could be an individually produced exhibit or something produced in a group.

10 m.: Have students freewrite about the most important things they've learned during the class so far. Remind them that their learning could be about themselves, about their learning processes, about particular stories, about how to read literature in satisfying ways, about how to write well, or about anything else that they consider significant learning. Have them link the learning to some artifact that they could use as an exhibit.

12 m.: Have students volunteer to share their learning experiences. Your role is to classify the experience, write a brief statement about what the student learned, and catalog the relevant exhibit.

5 m.: Demonstrate what an exhibit would look like in a portfolio. Include the artifact, followed by a page or so of reflection on how it contributed to significant learning. Distinguish between a *summary* of how it was produced and a *reflection* on how it contributed to learning. Students' freewrites could serve as the basis of their reflections for particular exhibits. Remind students that for each unit of study during the semester, they will need a minimum of two exhibits. Remind them that they will need to bring rough drafts of their essays to class on Tuesday, with zeros assigned to students who do not bring them.

On day 17 you'll need to teach students how to respond to one another's papers. There are different approaches you can take to doing this. The most open-ended approach is to have each student read his or her paper aloud to the group and have students provide feedback afterwards. I have found that, particularly early in the year, students benefit from having a particular set of feedback responsibilities. In my experience, they don't spontaneously know how to provide feedback, since for many of them it's a new experience.

My approach was to organize students into groups of four (obviously, some groups might be of different sizes, depending on that day's attendance). I would provide a hard copy of a set of three proofreading responsibilities, all derived from the assignment they were following. For the coming-of-age analytic papers, these responsibilities might be as follows:

1. Read the whole paper carefully. For your feedback, focus your attention on the writer's *clear description of the three major parts of the story:* the immature behavior at the beginning, the significant experience that caused change, and the mature behavior at the end. In the margins of the paper, make comments about how clearly the writer has described these three parts of the story. Then, at the end of the paper, write a brief summary of your recommendations for how to improve the paper in this regard.

2. Read the whole paper carefully. For your feedback, focus your attention on the writer's *introduction to the paper and conclusion about transforming experiences.* In the margins of the paper, make comments about how effectively the writer has introduced the paper and how well the conclusion follows from the analysis. Then, at the end of the paper, write a brief summary of your recommendations for how to improve the paper in this regard.

3. Read the whole paper carefully. For your feedback, focus your attention on the writer's use of *paragraph divisions, grammar, usage, and punctuation.* Wherever appropriate, provide suggestions on how to improve the presentation of the essay. Then, at the end of the paper, write a brief summary of your recommendations for how to improve the paper in this regard.

Each student would read the paper of each other student in the group. The system worked as follows:

1. For round 1, each student would pass his or her paper to the left. Students would then critique this paper according to the first responsibility identified (analysis of the three main parts of the story).

2. When students were finished with this round, they would again pass papers to the left for round 2, so that they were reading a new paper, taking on the second responsibility (critiquing the introduction and conclusion).

3. When finished, they would again pass papers to the left for round 3 (copyediting).

4. Following round 3, the papers would be passed to the left, so that they would be returned to their authors. Each author, then, would have three separate sets of feedback, each with a different focus. This feedback, along with the first draft, would get handed in along with the final copy of the paper.

This approach to critiquing, while somewhat methodical, worked quite well for my students, particularly after they'd done it a few times and understood the procedure and purpose of the activity. Like other new procedures, this one will require more careful instruction and monitoring the first time students do it.

You may find the explicit instruction in day 17 to be spelled out with overstated simplicity. I've found, however, that without such clear explanation, a number of students will not understand how the procedure works. Taking a few minutes to walk through your procedures will save you time later and make your class more comprehensible to your students.

You could also take this opportunity to distribute and discuss the rubric you will use to grade the students' essays and have them use the rubric in their peer-group evaluations of one another's first drafts. Keep in mind that a rubric's greatest strength is also its greatest weakness. Its strength is that it provides you with a clear way of discriminating between an A and a B, a B and a C, and so on. And, unless you teach in a very innovative school, you'll have to make those distinctions every time you assign and grade student work.

Having a rubric, especially at the beginning of your career, will help you make criterion-based decisions about which grade to assign a piece of student work. Inevitably, someone will question your grading decisions. If you can demonstrate that your grading is consistent and principled rather than idiosyncratic, you'll have a much easier time defending your evaluations. Meetings such as parent conferences then become much more manageable and less stressful.

On the other hand, a rubric can result in fairly rigid approaches to assessment. To return to the construction metaphor, it establishes a strict building code that students' constructions must meet in order to pass inspection. In terms of the question, Who's building whose building?, the answer is necessarily, The students are building buildings designed according to the teacher's code. It's important, then, to have a rubric that enables students to build within the code, yet not have every building look exactly alike regardless of their living needs.

It's important to think of the effects of using any particular evaluative tool on student work. A building code designed for one kind of building in one part of the country might not work well for buildings designed elsewhere for other purposes. An inspection code written for a restaurant in Milwaukee would not take into account the structural needs of a skyscraper in San Francisco, where the possibility of an earthquake necessitates the use of particularly strong materials in configurations designed to resist the effects of tremors. The inspection code dictates much about how a building will be constructed.

Similarly, a grading rubric provides both constraints and opportunities for how students will construct their texts in school. Just as a building code in San Francisco ensures that buildings will be strong enough to withstand an earthquake, a good rubric may require students to do things that they wouldn't do by choice, yet that are good things for them to know how to do.

Is there only one code available for evaluating the soundness of a student text? No, there are many available, each encouraging the production of a different kind of text. The question then becomes, What kind of text are students being encouraged to produce? Does the evaluative instrument—the rubric—limit students more than it enables them? Does the rubric take into account the possibility that a student's idea for a functional text might be judged as insufficient according to the rubric? Does the rubric deny students the opportunity to construct an innovative text by specifying the terms of production?

One final point: The question of which standards to use when evaluating writing raises an important issue about the nature of writing. Is a piece of writing good or bad without respect to who's reading it? I will urge you to think about the idea proposed by Martin Nystrand that the quality of writing is a function of the relationship between writers and readers. In this view, good writing is writing that is in tune with its readers. A highly technical research report might be a splendid piece of work to other researchers, yet might be obscure gobbledygook to the person on the street.

The text itself is not good or bad; rather, different readers are more or less in tune with the writing conventions used by the writer.

The use of rubrics typically imposes a single set of conventions and expectations on student writing. Most frequently rubrics represent the conventions preferred by the text's sole reader, the teacher. As a teacher, then, you should consider ways to provide both varied readerships for your students' writing, and varied or flexible ways in which to evaluate their work.

These are perplexing questions faced in any school assessment (or, for that matter, in any assessment anywhere). I would justify the instructional approach outlined here by saying that yes, the goal of instruction is to produce a particular kind of text in a particular kind of way. I think it's worthwhile to do because the goal is to teach students *generative* ways of reading, that is, procedures for how to do something. Throughout the year, I'll teach them procedures for reading in other ways as well. My intention, then, is to teach them a repertoire of procedures for using literacy tools; to teach them that they have a tool kit available that they can use in a variety of ways. Each tool provides both constraints and opportunities, and it's important to understand both when using them.

Finally, evaluation, like death and taxes, is one of the inevitabilities of life in school. You can't teach in most schools without giving a grade. And you need to grade in ways that students (and often their parents) find consistent, equitable, and defensible. A rubric is a way to specify the code you're using to evaluate student work.

If you're uncomfortable writing the code by which you assign students their grades, you could look for alternatives, such as dedicating class time to having students produce the rubrics. While helping with the question of who's building whose building, it would raise a different set of questions, such as, Do students' expectations for a soundly constructed text meet expectations by which these texts will be judged elsewhere? Is the process of arriving at these judgments an experience so worthwhile that it outweighs the importance of meeting adult standards for text production? These are serious and difficult questions that you must weigh in any reconsideration of how to identify the standards by which student work is formally evaluated.

For this book, I will assume that, for much student work, you will be the one doing the primary evaluation. One persistent criticism of school writing is that it's done exclusively for the teacher, resulting in writing that is stale and meaningless to students. You can address this problem by having students write for readerships outside the classroom (see, for instance, Appendix C of this book). For analytic work of the type being assessed here, it's likely that you, as one long enculturated to the domain of English, will have a good understanding of which standards analytic writing should meet and can write a fair and defensible rubric for evaluating the students' texts.

Here is a possible rubric for essays analyzing coming-of-age literature:

To receive an A on this paper a student must do the following:

1. Provide a general thesis for the paper that explains the protagonist's primary transformation during the course of the story. The explanation should involve an *inference* about the character's transformation.

2. Describe the protagonist's immature behavior at the beginning of the story, including specific examples from the text.
3. Describe clearly the key event that causes the character to change. This description should be aided by a clear explanation of why this event, rather than others in the story, causes the protagonist to come of age. This explanation should involve an *inference* about the power of this event for the protagonist.
4. Describe the significant changes taking place in the protagonist following the coming-of-age experience, including specific examples from the text.
5. Draw a conclusion about how people change as a result of significant events, making a link between the transformation of the protagonist and transformations made by people from the student's knowledge outside literature.
6. Follow rules of textbook grammar, spelling, punctuation, and usage throughout.
7. Give evidence of having written at least one rough draft that has been submitted for peer evaluation.

To receive a B on this paper a student must do the following:

1. Provide a general thesis that explains the protagonist's primary transformation during the course of the story. The explanation should involve an *inference* about the character's transformation, although the inference might not be explained in great detail.
2. Describe the protagonist's immature behavior at the beginning of the story, including at least one specific example from the text. The examples might lack the detail found in papers receiving As, however.
3. Describe the key event that causes the character to change. This description should be aided by an explanation of why this event, rather than others in the story, causes the protagonist to come of age. This explanation may involve an *inference* about the power of this event for the protagonist, although the inference may not be explained as clearly as those found in papers receiving As.
4. Describe the significant changes taking place in the protagonist following the coming-of-age experience, including at least one example from the text.
5. Draw a conclusion about how people change as a result of significant events, making a link between the transformation of the protagonist and transformations made by people from the student's knowledge outside literature. This connection, however, might be stated without great elaboration.
6. Follow rules of textbook grammar, spelling, punctuation, and usage throughout, with some variation from textbook form.
7. Give evidence of having written at least one rough draft that has been submitted for peer evaluation.

To receive a C on this paper a student must do the following:

1. Provide a general thesis for the paper that explains the protagonist's primary transformation during the course of the story. The explanation does not provide a well-explained *inference* about the character's transformation.
2. Describe the protagonist's immature behavior at the beginning of the story, including at least one example from the text.
3. Describe clearly the key event that causes the character to change. This description should be aided by an explanation of why this event, rather than others in the story, causes the protagonist to come of age. This explanation does not provide a well-explained *inference* about the power of this event for the protagonist.
4. Describe the significant changes taking place in the protagonist following the coming-of-age experience, including at least one example from the text.
5. Draw a conclusion about how people change as a result of significant events, making a link between the transformation of the protagonist and transformations made by people from the student's knowledge outside literature. This link might be made only tenuously, however.
6. Follow rules of textbook grammar, spelling, punctuation, and usage throughout, with some exceptions.
7. Give evidence of having written at least one rough draft that has been submitted for peer evaluation.

To receive a D on this paper a student must do the following:

1. Provide a general thesis for the paper that explains the protagonist's primary transformation during the course of the story. The thesis might be sketchy, however, and lacks an inference about the character's transformation.
2. Describe the protagonist's immature behavior at the beginning of the story, illustrated by a briefly worded example.
3. Describe the key event that causes the character to change, without an explanation of why this event had significant powers of transformation for the protagonist.
4. Describe the significant changes taking place in the protagonist following the coming-of-age experience, without the provision of a well-described example.
5. Not draw a conclusion about how people change as a result of significant events or make a clear link between the transformation of the protagonist and transformations made by people from the student's knowledge outside literature.
6. Include frequent infelicities in grammar, spelling, punctuation, and usage throughout.
7. Give evidence of having written at least one rough draft that has been submitted for peer evaluation, yet not necessarily evidence of having followed the recommendations provided by peers.

To receive an F on this paper a student must do the following:

1. Give evidence that the student did not read the story, with evidence indicated by the absence of information about initial immaturity, a transforming event, or ultimate mature behavior.

As I've said, there are other ways to organize and conduct peer-response groups. I describe a different way in Appendix C, showing how response groups can be set up so that students play the role of different kinds of audiences when responding to other students' writing.

I should also reiterate that generating a rubric out of thin air can be difficult. As you gain experience in reading student writing, you will have a firmer basis on which to understand what to expect from students in your school, what the prevailing standards are, and how to distinguish one level of performance (and thus one grade) from another. At this point in your career, I recommend reading as much student writing as possible and discussing grading criteria with experienced teachers to help you think about how to develop rubrics.

Day 17 (Tuesday)

3 m.: Attendance, housekeeping.
10 m.: Tool sharpening: Standardized-test-question format: Multiple-choice vocabulary items.
3 m.: Have students organize into groups of four (some groups may have an odd number).
5 m.: Distribute hard copies of the proofreading responsibilities and review them.
5 m.: Using one group to illustrate, model how group members rotate their papers. Have them begin by holding their own papers. Have them pass them to the left. When this is accomplished, say that they should do critique 1 from the handout for this paper. Have them pass the papers to the left again, saying that for this round they do critique 2. Have them pass the papers to the left again, saying that for this round they do critique 3. Have them pass the papers to the left again, back to their authors.
22 m.: Have students follow these procedures for critiquing one another's papers. Circulate among the groups to help them with the procedures and answer other questions.
2 m.: Return desks to original positions; prepare to depart. Tell students that final copies are due on Thursday. They may be typed or handwritten.

You've now reached a major break in the unit. Students are in the process of completing their first formal writing of the year. You have three major goals remaining from your original plan: student-led discussions of the novel, personal narratives on coming-of-age experiences, and an open-ended multimedia text in which they synthesize their understanding of the unit. You have two questions: Is there time to do all of these? And, assuming the answer is yes, Which order is best to follow? Here you will likely make a judgment based on how you see your students progressing.

It's possible that you would decide to make the multimedia text an optional assignment done for extra credit, which would reduce the amount of class time you'd devote to it. For this unit, because time is growing short, that's what I'll do.

If you decide to do the other two, you'd need to make other judgments. Have the students had sufficient time to read their outside novel to lead discussions on it? Are they fatigued right now from writing their analytic essays, thus making it a poor time to go straight into another major piece of writing? Moving in either direction would have its advantages and disadvantages.

For this unit, I'll decide to do the novel first and the personal experience narratives second as a way to provide a break between the pressures of producing two extended pieces of writing. I might, however, need to provide students with some class time to catch up on their reading of the novel, since they have been both reading short stories and writing analytic papers outside class for the past few weeks.

Day 18 (Wednesday)

3 m.: Attendance, housekeeping.

10 m.: Explain the multimedia project option (in place of tool sharpening); give a due date of two weeks.

37 m.: Students are given class time to work on their revisions or to read *A Separate Peace*. Remind them that they should be maintaining their reading logs for the novel. Also remind them that their essays are due the following day. You serve as a resource for students who have questions about their essays or about the novel.

Day 19 (Thursday)

3 m.: Attendance, housekeeping (collect papers).

7 m.: Tool sharpening: History of language: words derived from names (*guillotine, leotard, sandwich, gerrymander,* etc.)

40 m.: Students are given class time to read *A Separate Peace*. Remind them that they should be maintaining their reading logs for the novel.

In assigning essays to several classes' worth of students, you have also assigned yourself a tremendous amount of work in grading them. One way to manage this responsibility is to plan days such as this one during which students are productively engaged in a worthwhile task and you have time to begin your grading. I think it's important to return student work as soon as possible. Scheduling days like this can help you provide a quick turnaround so that students get feedback while their efforts are still fresh in their minds. In this case, it also allows them to move forward with their reading, which might have been set back by the other work they've been doing outside class.

For Friday's class, you'll begin teaching them how to pose the kinds of questions that they'll be using in their presentations. Meanwhile, they'll be able to continue reading the novel outside class and over the weekend. You, too, will have homework over the weekend, since you'll have the goal of returning their essays to them on Monday.

Ordinarily you'd collect response logs today, but will do so next week because (1) you've got your hands full grading essays, and (2) you'll want students to use them as they complete their reading of *A Separate Peace*. The response logs will take the place of the summary quizzes as your evidence that students have done the reading, unless the student-led groups decide to include a quiz as part of their class.

Vignette

This might be a good time to address the tendency of people to say, "A good teacher always . . ." *In general,* I'd say that good teachers get students' papers back as quickly as possible. Unfortunately, there are times—and sometimes years—when your life outside school makes it hard for you to live up to the ideal of the "good teacher" who "always" does this or that. There are some pretty good teachers who get divorced and have to care for three children by themselves, who suffer the death of a loved one, who must work a second job to make ends meet, or who endure other hardships. These circumstances make it hard to chaperone school dances, return papers the next day, arrive early and stay late to meet with students, and so on. My hope is that you're the best teacher that your circumstances allow you to be, and that you'll be sympathetic when someone else's personal life requires his or her teaching to take second priority on occasion. Some very good teachers have had some very bad years and have needed the support of their colleagues to get through them.

Day 20 (Friday)

3 m.: Attendance, housekeeping.
10 m.: Tool sharpening: Syntax: Dangling participles (e.g., "Crashing against the rocks, the seagulls flew just above the waves.")
10 m.: Pass out and review responsibilities for student-led discussions:

To discuss John Knowles's *A Separate Peace,* the class will organize into six small groups, with each group being responsible for leading a discussion of two chapters of the novel. Each group will be responsible for one full class period to discuss its chapters. To lead your class, you may adopt any format you wish: regular English class, irregular English class, nonviolent talk-show format, courtroom scene, town meeting, or other mode of your choice. Your discussion should involve all of the following:

- Each group member should take a roughly equal part in leading the discussion
- You should make an effort to include every other class member in your discussion
- The questions you pose should not ask for factual information from the story, unless those facts serve to help explore open-ended questions (i.e., those without a single correct answer)
- The questions you pose should include at least one in each of the following categories:
  - Inferences about characters or events within the text
  - Generalizations from the text to society at large
  - The effects of literary form or technique
  - The purpose of a particular event in terms of the text's meaning
  - Evaluations of the literature
  - Emotions students had in response to the story

Plan Week 4

Plan the fourth week of instruction for your unit. Your plan should include the following:

- Continuity from week 3's instruction
- Evidence that the instruction is clearly tied to your unit and course-long goals
- Instruction in procedures for how to reach the unit goals
- Clear attention to assessment criteria
- Continued establishment and development of classroom routines
- Daily plans, including the amount of time anticipated for each episode

- Personal connections to the story
- During the discussion, you should work at getting students to elaborate on their initial comments.
- Your discussion should occupy the whole class period.

5 m.: Explain that they'll need to organize into six groups of roughly even size (ideally, four, though the number will depend on the number of students enrolled). Have students pick their groups and organize into them.

2 m.: Explain that you will give them practice in generating the seven types of questions they should ask, using a story from the ones they have studied to this point (e.g., "The Bridge"). The procedure will be for you to define each type of question and give an example and for each group then to come up with a similar type of example from the same story.

10 m.: Define what an *inference* is (an educated guess about something that's not literally stated). Provide an illustration of an inferential question about "The Bridge" (e.g., "What is the protagonist's attitude toward leaving home?") and explain clearly why it requires an inference. Have each group generate an inferential question about the story and invite groups to share theirs with the class. Clarify how each question generated by students meets the expectations for this question type.

8 m.: Define a *generalization to larger society* (what the story is saying about life in general). Provide an illustration of an inferential question about "The Bridge" (e.g., "What is the author saying about the necessity of making a break with the family in order to grow up?") and explain clearly why it requires a generalization. Have each group generate a generalization question about the story and invite groups to share theirs with the class. Clarify how each question generated by students meets the expectations for this question type.

2 m.: Return seats to original positions; prepare for departure.

Monday's class will then be devoted to two things: returning the analytic essays and reviewing strengths and weaknesses, and continuing with the questioning instruction. Because you'll be going over the papers, you will bypass the tool sharpening for the day.

Vignette

I remember something that happened to me when I was in the eighth grade. I'd taken a history test and not done too well. The teacher reviewed the tests in our class, and illustrated some idiotic responses to the exam questions by reading answers from some students in his other class, whose names he provided along with their answers. The answers were indeed dumb, and along with everyone else I chuckled, thinking, what knuckleheads these kids are. Later that day, I learned from some friends that he'd done the same thing in his other class, using my answers among others as objects of ridicule. I still remember how humiliated I felt to be publicly named as a bad student.

WEEK 5

Day 21 (Monday)

3 m.: Attendance, housekeeping.

15 m.: Return the analytic essays. Explain how you used the rubric to determine grades. Review common strengths and weaknesses of the papers, being careful not to single out any individual student's difficulties for public discussion. Tell students that if they wish to submit a revision of their papers, they may submit it on Friday.

10 m.: Define what *literary form and technique* are (i.e., techniques such as irony, figurative language, etc.). Provide an illustration of a question about technique for "The Bridge" (e.g., "What does the girl on the bicycle symbolize in the story?") and explain clearly why the question requires an understanding of technique or form. Have each group generate a question about the story's form or technique and invite groups to share theirs with the class. Clarify how each question generated by students meets the expectations for this question type.

10 m.: Define what a *significant event* is (an event that causes substantive changes in the lives of the characters). Provide an illustration of a question about significant events for "The Bridge" (e.g., "Why is the story called 'The Bridge'?") and explain clearly why this question is centered on the significance of an event. Have each group generate a question about the story's significant events and invite groups to share theirs with the class. Clarify how each question generated by students meets the expectations for this question type.

10 m.: Define an *evaluation* (a judgment about the quality of the literary work or parts thereof). Provide an illustration of an evaluative question about "The Bridge" (e.g., "Did you think that the characters were realistic? Why or why not?") and explain clearly why it requires an evaluation. Have each group generate an evaluative question about the story and invite groups to share theirs with the class. Clarify how each question generated by students meets the expectations for this question type.

2 m.: Return seats to original positions; prepare to depart.

Day 22 (Tuesday)

3 m.: Attendance, housekeeping.

10 m.: Tool sharpening: Address recurring problems from students' essays.

10 m.: Define what an *emotional response* to a story is (how the story made them feel). Provide an illustration of an emotional question about "The Bridge" (e.g., "What emotions did you experience when the bicycle went off the bridge?") and explain clearly why it involves an emotional response. Have each group generate a different emotional question about the story and invite groups to share theirs with the class. Clarify how each question generated by students meets the expectations for this question type.

10 m.: Define what a *personal connection* to a story is (a connection between the reader's personal experiences and those of literary characters). Provide an illustration of a question requiring a *personal connection* for "The Bridge" (e.g., "What would you have done if you'd been in the protagonist's situation at the end of the story?") and explain clearly why it requires a personal connection. Have each group generate a personal connection question about the story and invite groups to share theirs with the class. Clarify how each question generated by students meets the expectations for this question type.

15 m.: Have different groups take responsibility for different sections of the book. You could do this through voluntary assignment or through a lottery of some sort. It's possible that students who did not want to read the whole book would lobby heavily for early chapters. A lottery system would take the pressure off you about which groups lead which discussions and add incentive for all students to complete the book.

Once the discussion-leading responsibilities are distributed, remind students that the format of the discussion is up to them. Successfully led student discussions have come in all manner of formats. Encourage students to have fun with the assignment, though not at the expense of their discussion-leading responsibilities. They should plan to lead their discussion for a full class period, however, and so should make sure that their planning, while including a minimum set of questions from the type prescribed, also poses other questions for students to discuss. They might look to their reading logs to see what other kinds of questions they could pose for their discussions.

You might distribute your grading rubric prior to the small-group preparations. The following is one way to differentiate the grades for student performances:

Rubric for grading student-led discussions

A discussion receiving an A will be characterized by the following:

1. Each group member takes a roughly equal part in leading the discussion.
2. The discussion will include at least 75 percent of the other students in the class.
3. The questions posed will only ask for factual information when those facts serve to help explore open-ended questions (i.e., those without a single correct answer).
4. The questions include at least one from each of the following categories:
   - Inferences about characters or events within the text

- Generalizations from the text to society at large
- The effects of literary form or technique
- The purpose of a particular event in terms of the text's meaning
- Evaluations of the literature
- Emotions students had in response to the story
- Personal connections to the story.
5. The discussion occupies the entire class period.

A discussion receiving a B will be characterized by the following:

1. Each group member takes a roughly equal part in leading the discussion, although some students speak noticeably more than others.
2. The discussion will include at least 50 percent of the other students in the class.
3. The questions posed will only ask for factual information when those facts serve to help explore open-ended questions (i.e., those without a single correct answer).
4. The questions include at least one from most of the following categories:
   - Inferences about characters or events within the text
   - Generalizations from the text to society at large
   - The effects of literary form or technique
   - The purpose of a particular event in terms of the text's meaning
   - Evaluations of the literature
   - Emotions students had in response to the story
   - Personal connections to the story
5. The discussion occupies the entire class period.

A discussion receiving a C will be characterized by the following:

1. Some group members speak substantially more than others.
2. The discussion will include less than half the other students in the class.
3. The questions posed will occasionally ask for factual information that does not serve to help explore open-ended questions (i.e., those without a single correct answer).
4. The questions include at least one from at least four of the following categories:
   - Inferences about characters or events within the text
   - Generalizations from the text to society at large
   - The effects of literary form or technique
   - The purpose of a particular event in terms of the text's meaning
   - Evaluations of the literature
   - Emotions students had in response to the story
   - Personal connections to the story
5. The discussion occupies most of the class period.

A discussion receiving a D will be characterized by the following:

1. Some group member do most of the talking.

Plan Week 5 (if necessary)

Plan the fifth week of instruction for your unit. Your plan should include the following:

- Continuity from week 4's instruction
- Evidence that the instruction is clearly tied to your unit and course-long goals
- Instruction in procedures for how to reach the unit goals
- Clear attention to assessment criteria
- Continued establishment and development of classroom routines
- Daily plans, including the amount of time anticipated for each episode

2. The discussion includes no more than 25 percent of the other students in the class.
3. The questions frequently request factual information.
4. The questions include less than half of the following categories:
   - Inferences about characters or events within the text
   - Generalizations from the text to society at large
   - The effects of literary form or technique
   - The purpose of a particular event in terms of the text's meaning
   - Evaluations of the literature
   - Emotions students had in response to the story
   - Personal connections to the story
5. The discussion ends well before the class period ends

A discussion receiving an F will be characterized by the following:

1. The discussion leaders give little evidence of having read the book.
2. The discussion leaders give little evidence of having prepared questions of any kind.
3. The discussion ends well before the class period ends.

Students may use whatever time remains to begin working on their preparations.

2 m.: Return desks to original positions; prepare for departure.

Day 23 (Wednesday)

3 m.: Attendance, housekeeping.
47 m.: Students work in small groups preparing their questions and formats.

Day 24 (Thursday)

3 m.: Attendance, housekeeping.

47 m.: Students work in small groups preparing their questions and formats.

Day 25 (Friday)

3 m.: Attendance, housekeeping (collect revised essays, final reading logs for the unit).

47 m.: Student group leads discussion of Chapters 1 and 2.

WEEK 6

Day 26 (Monday)

3 m.: Attendance, housekeeping.

47 m.: Student group leads discussion of Chapters 3 and 4.

Day 27 (Tuesday)

3 m.: Attendance, housekeeping.

47 m.: Student group leads discussion of Chapters 5 and 6.

Day 28 (Wednesday)

3 m.: Attendance, housekeeping (collect multimedia projects).

47 m.: Student group leads discussion of Chapters 7 and 8.

Day 29 (Thursday)

3 m.: Attendance, housekeeping.

47 m.: Student group leads discussion of Chapters 9 and 10.

Day 30 (Friday)

3 m.: Attendance, housekeeping.

47 m.: Student group leads discussion of Chapters 11 and 12.

We've now reached the end of the sixth week. It's time to reassess the length of the unit. In spite of our original plans to include a formal personal narrative on a coming-of-age experience, we should probably bring the unit to a close and dedicate the remaining three weeks of the marking period to the writing workshop. One compromise would be to suggest this personal narrative as a possible topic during the workshop. Because one feature of such workshops, however, is student determination of topic and form, you should keep it optional. It's entirely possible that at this point, the students will be starting to burn out on the topic of coming of age anyhow and will be glad to have the opportunity to think about something completely different.

Note that you haven't given an exam on the outside novel; rather, the evaluation has been on student-led discussions. You may want to include some kind of assessment of students' engagement with the novel. You could, for instance, require a portfolio exhibit that clearly indicates a reading of the whole novel. It's also possible that you would accept student response logs as evidence that they have read and engaged with the novel.

One final thing to do, perhaps on Monday of the following week, is to give the students an opportunity to evaluate the unit. Throughout this book I've advocated the idea that you should always be assessing both your students and your own teaching. If the students have performed consistently well on their writing and discussion leading, it's likely that your instruction was effective. If they didn't, then you need to think back on how you taught the class and consider ways that you could teach differently for the learning you seek. If it worked better for some groups of students than for others, you might need to give some thought to the question of why this happened.

Another way to evaluate your teaching is to ask the students how they experienced the unit. These evaluations can range from the relatively simple to the rather complex. Here is one opinionnaire that invites students to give you feedback on their impressions of the unit.

> Please answer each question that follows. You do not need to put your name on this evaluation. Your comments will strongly influence my efforts to revise the unit for the next group of students, so I'd appreciate your complete honesty in responding. Keep in mind that I'm much more likely to act on thoughtful answers than on those that are glib or sarcastic.
>
> 1. We read the following literature during the unit. Please write your honest opinion of each work of literature, and recommend whether or not I should use it next year.
>   Poems
>   "The Road Not Taken"
>   "Mother to Son"
>   Short Stories
>   "The Man Who Was Almost a Man"
>   "Red Dress"
>   "The Bridge"
>   "Peter Two"
>   "Everyday Use"
>   Novel
>   *A Separate Peace*
> 2. What did you learn from keeping your reading log? Did you feel that you were adequately taught how to keep one? Please explain. Do you think that keeping a reading log would be a good idea for units that we do later this year? Why or why not?

3. What did you learn from writing your analytic essay? Did you feel that you were adequately taught how to write it? Please explain. How would you recommend that I do this next year?
4. What did you learn from leading your discussion? Did you feel that you were adequately taught how to conduct it? Please explain. How would you recommend that I do this next year?
5. What would you recommend that I do the same if I teach this unit again to other students?
6. What would you recommend that I do differently?
7. What suggestions can you make for the way in which we learn about language, literature, and writing for the rest of this year?

With this evaluation, students can let you know what they found positive and negative about the unit. I found their feedback particularly useful the first time I taught a unit, because the first time you teach something you're likely to make the most errors in judgment. Your students can be good informants about the strengths and weaknesses of your unit design, the materials you selected, the adequacy of your instruction, and so on.

FINAL THOUGHTS

I have taken you through this unit as I might plan it for a group of hypothetical students. One thing I have illustrated is the way you make modifications in your plans depending on the circumstances. My original plans for the unit were a little ambitious for the first unit of the year, it turns out, and I had to jettison two of the original five goals for the unit. If I were to teach this unit later in the year, I might have time to include these two, because I wouldn't need to spend a week or so of instructional time teaching students how to keep reading logs and lead discussions. If I teach these procedures now, I can simply assign them later on and expect that students will know how to do them.

Because I think that the narrative and multimedia project fit well with the overarching course concepts, I might make efforts to include them as goals in subsequent units. Students could write about personal experiences with discrimination, peer pressure, or another unit focus, and could produce a multimedia project for virtually any unit. Abandoning them here, then, does not suggest that they are unimportant, nor does it delete them from the year's activities. It simply shifts the possibilities that I have for how to design the rest of the year's units.

As I look ahead, I have laid the groundwork for a number of learning opportunities that students have in the units to follow. Students have now had six weeks of enculturation to the ideas that

> **Field Observation**
> How compatible is this approach to teaching with the teaching you observe in a school you're visiting? What advantages and disadvantages do you see to teaching in the ways you're observing in a school? How do they compare with the advantages and disadvantages that follow from the approach outlined here?

- they can use both writing and talking for exploratory purposes
- they are responsible for generating the questions that initiate the class's literary discussions

Rationale

Return to the rationale you wrote earlier. Reread it and see how well it fits your unit as you are developing it. If need be, reconsider your rationale by adjusting its focus, adding or revising major points, adding or revising the evidence you provide, adding to or revising your rebuttals, and revoicing your rhetoric and points to suit potential readers.

- their writing will be treated as a process involving several drafts
- their writing will be viewed as a social act that will have readers other than the teacher—in this case, other students, but as the year progresses, readers outside the classroom
- part of their job in the class is to reflect on how they learn

Subsequent units should build on these attitudes so that students view the class as a construction zone in which their role is to be active builders.

Before ending this chapter on unit design, I would like to emphasize that I have demonstrated *one* possible way to design a unit on coming of age. You could do it quite differently, particularly if you taught this unit to other students, with other texts available, with a different emphasis, or at a later point in the year. My intention has been to show how a unit of instruction fits in with an overall curricular context, is responsive to a variety of constraints, and is designed to meet its own stated goals. I'm hoping that you can now move from this demonstration to the planning of units that suit you, your students, and your curriculum well.

> To teach is to learn twice.
>
> —Joseph Joubert

PART 2

LIFE IN CLASSROOMS

In Part I of this book, I outlined a way to think about how to plan instruction. In Part II, I talk about life in classrooms. Chapter 9 is designed to be mostly practical, talking about how to arrange your classroom physically and how to manage the social life that follows from particular physical organizations. Chapters 10 through 12 are devoted to descriptions of classrooms that have used the principles behind the instructional approach outlined in Part I. Through these chapters I show how students and teachers talk during particular kinds of discussions and how different instructional contexts and tasks encourage different ways of talking about literature.

The classrooms I describe here are real, having served as the sites for research I've conducted on how students make meaning in English classes. All discussion transcripts reported were tape-recorded, transcribed, and analyzed in order to draw conclusions about how people talk about literature, especially when the discussions are set up in particular ways. For this book, I'll focus on the transcripts alone and not dwell on the technical aspects of conducting research. At the end of each chapter I'll provide references to more detailed articles for those who want to learn more about the processes that went into the collecting, processing, reducing, analyzing, and interpreting of the data.

I recorded the discussions described in Chapter 10 during my last year of teaching at Oak Park and River Forest High School in Illinois. The analysis of the transcripts was later conducted with Pam Fly, at the time a doctoral student at the University of Oklahoma, where I taught from 1990 to 1998. The chapter describes how students talk in relation to their teachers. I contrast two types of teachers, those who take authoritative approaches and those who try to get students to talk during discussions. I then look at how the students talked to one another when they moved from the teacher-led discussions to small-group discussions, finding remarkable differences in the discussions of students of these different types of teachers. The discussions reported here should correspond very well to the instruction described in Chapter 8, since the students are discussing some of the same short stories that are included in that unit and are discussing them in the context of a coming-of-age sequence.

Chapter 11 looks at student work from a public alternative school. Because all the students were recovering substance abusers, and because I agreed to keep their identities confidential, I need to be discreet about some details of the school and students. My hope is that all have recovered from their addictions and have gone on to lead productive lives. I therefore need to protect their identities as carefully as possible when publicly discussing their schoolwork. In this chapter, I look at the ways in which the students interpret a short story through any medium of their choice. Most chose artistic or dramatic vehicles for their interpretations. Through a set of interviews they provided while watching a tape of their interpretive process, they describe in fascinating detail the kinds of learning that can take place through artistic composing.

Chapter 11 also describes classrooms outside the English department where I saw highly engaged students producing texts that they found useful and important. The texts, for the most part, were not written. Rather, they were clothing produced in a home economics sewing class, horse-ranch plans for an agriculture class, and house designs in both a home economics and an architectural design class. I describe these classes to help illustrate my belief that the emphasis in school should be on encouraging students to compose meaningful texts, with the medium of the text (writing, drawing, etc.) fitting the needs of the occasion.

Chapter 12 looks at students from the public high school class of Cindy O'Donnell-Allen, whose classroom has been featured elsewhere in this book. Cindy allowed me to study her class on two occasions, once to study a small set of student writers and a second time for a more extensive study of her students' broader composing activity. In Chapter 12 I describe her students' productions of *body biographies,* a kind of creative multimedia composition that she adapted for the purposes of literary interpretation. By studying the transcripts of the discussions they engaged in while working, we were able to document both the cognitive and the social processes that students go through while producing artistic interpretations of literature.

Chapters 10 through 12 are designed to show you the kinds of learning that can potentially take place through the process of exploratory talk and multimedia composing. They also show some students who use open-ended learning opportunities in unproductive ways. On the whole, these chapters show the potential for students' constructive action, as well as some potential problems that might ensue, when teachers establish the kind of constructivist learning environment outlined in Part I of this book.

> " If we want to bring about change in students, we need to restructure schools—not individual teachers or individual students. It seems that a great deal of effort is always expended on creating structures to transport into schools, rather than on considering what changes need to be made in elements that mediate school activity to bring about a desired change. We need to flip the idea of stages of cognitive development, age-bound grade levels, etc., over. Students should move through different activities that provide multiple paths to learning and development. The content of activity is what is important.
>
> —William E. Blanton "

Setting Up Your Classroom

T his chapter gives attention to how to set up the physical arrangement of your class-room. I begin with the consequences of different ways of arranging the seats and discuss ways to involve students in designing the classroom. I offer some advice on lead-ing discussions and then give extended attention to how to set up small groups so that students get the most out of them. I close with some ideas on classroom management, in particular the need to make your class interesting and engaging so as to keep stu-dents involved.

Classrooms have a fairly standard arrangement that has been remarkably durable over time and across disciplinary boundaries. When you envision a classroom, you probably see the following:

> In my mind's eye I keep seeing rows. Rows of desks, running horizontal across a room, light yellow wooden tops, pale beige metal legs, a shallow depression for pencils at the far edge, and chairs of the same material, separate from the desks, movable. The windows—tall and running the length of the classroom—are on the left. Light streams through. . . . The scenes are all mixed together—grade school with graduate school—but always the windows along one side of the room, and always the desks in rows.
>
> —Jane Tompkins

- The desks are in rows, facing the front of the room.
- The teacher is positioned at the front of the room, often standing, at times behind a lectern.
- There is a chalkboard behind the teacher where key information can be recorded for later testing purposes and where homework assignments are listed.
- The walls of the room have some sort of bookshelves where reference books and perhaps class sets are stored.

There are, of course, variations. Science classes, for instance, are often conducted in labs, with sinks and other apparatus avail-able for various experiments. In class after class, school after school, however, you tend to find something resembling the arrangement I have described.

Many critics have pointed out that this arrangement both fol-lows from, and in turn contributes to, traditional values and processes of schools. The teacher, standing at the front, is the fo-cal point of the class. The students, seated and facing the teacher, are thus compelled to view the teacher as the center of classroom life. This arrangement is not benign, but helps to shape the classroom dynamics. Think of the ways in which classrooms typically function. The teacher does most of the talking, and the students' role is to listen to the teacher, record knowledge that might be assessed, and then return that knowledge to the teacher on a test.

The classroom organization actually discourages students from talking to each other and funnels all student remarks to the teacher. This pattern reinforces other aspects of classroom life, such as the tendency for student work to be written for, and evaluated by, the teacher alone. When students are seated in rows facing the teacher, they tend to make any contributions during discussions to the teacher rather than to other students. When this pattern exists, it's hard to call the exchange a discussion.

Rather, what you tend to get is a teacher serving as the primary speaker, with students occasionally filling in information when the teacher provides an opening. This information is offered to the teacher for approval, rather than to other students for their consideration and response. Even on occasions when students respond to one another's contributions, their remarks are spoken toward the front of the room where the teacher volleys them back out to other students.

Observe some classrooms and see how often you find exceptions. I found that when I tried to have discussions, it was very difficult to get the students to speak to each other, because they had been so heavily conditioned to speak to the teacher. In this chapter I will talk about the environment of the classroom and how you can set it up to change the ways in which both teachers and students talk to each other.

Reflective Writing Prompt

Think back on your own schooling. Was there much variation in the seating arrangements of the classrooms you were in? How did different arrangements suggest appropriate ways of interacting? How did different arrangements suggest different conceptions of knowledge? How did different arrangements suggest different conceptions of authority?

SEATING ARRANGEMENT

One way to change the discussion patterns in your classroom is to change the seating arrangement. I strongly recommend that you not set up the seats in rows facing the front. Unless the seats are bolted to the floor—and in older schools, they actually were—you can move them into any configuration that your imagination and the available space allow. I have taught under circumstances where there were simply too many students in too small a space to get very imaginative about how to set up the seats. Whenever possible, however, I tried to set them up so that students were looking at one another as much as they were looking at me.

You could, for instance, set the seats up in a circle, with you simply occupying one of the seats rather than being the class's focal point. If you have a class of over twenty or so students, this can create problems because the circle gets so large that it's hard to hear what people across the room are saying. An alternative is to set the class up in a U-shape, with you roaming the middle while orchestrating discussions. Often your space limitations create problems of distance, which can be solved by using two U's, one within the other. This arrangement will have some students looking at the backs of other students' heads, but will at least make it possible for students to face many of their classmates and thus encourage discussions rather than teacher-mediated dialogues.

Other arrangements can break up the teacher-centered organizations of classrooms. I've seen teachers use tables rather than desks, so that the class is organized in small groups. Some teachers would never do this because students could more easily copy one another's work. However, the assumption behind using tables is that it's a good thing to collaborate and see one another's work, since it's likely that different students will construct different responses. The concern about copying comes mainly from teachers who require correct answers that can be copied for undeserved credit.

Other teachers set up class so that there are two sets of short rows that face each other, with a lane down the center that the teacher can occupy. The effect of these alternative ways of setting up seats is that students are encouraged to talk directly to one another, rather than to view the teacher as the conduit for all contributions. Furthermore, the arrangement positions students as contributors rather than receivers of knowledge. That's what we're trying to accomplish through the principles of teaching and learning that are behind this book.

> My early years in school were quite miserable. I had a stammer and I wrote with my left hand. So I was made to sit in the back of the room and could move up only as my stammer improved and I switched to my right hand.
>
> —Maurice Sendak

Of course, some teachers don't *want* their students to talk, which is perhaps why they set up the classrooms to focus attention on their own utterance and discourage students from talking to one another. And you'll find that by encouraging talk, you'll get some students who talk about things that are not germane to the academic focus of the class. That is one consequence of having an open-ended, constructivist, student-centered class: Some students take liberties with the freedoms you provide.

This nonacademic use of opportunities has discouraged many teachers from teaching in open-ended ways. My view is that constructivist classrooms simply make nonacademic uses of time more overt. As I reviewed in Chapter 1, the fact that a student is sitting quietly is no guarantee that the student is listening or learning. Many of history's most elaborate daydreams have come during school lectures and discussions.

LEARNING STUDENTS' NAMES

However you set up your room, you should make an effort to learn your students' names as quickly as possible. One way to do this is to tell them that they may sit wherever they wish, but that they need to sit in the same place every day to make it easier for you to learn their names. You can then prepare a seating chart, which will enable you to do three things:

- Take attendance quickly and easily.
- Call students by name during discussions, even on the first day of class.
  Calling them by name will help them feel noticed and important.
- Learn their names more quickly.

The seating chart, then, is designed to help you do the housekeeping chore of taking attendance quickly so that you can spend more class time with their education and to help you get to know your students more quickly. Used in this way, it is a means of enablement rather than control.

Alternatively, you could write each student's name on an index card and replicate their seating choices on your desk. This provides students with greater flexibility in where they sit while still providing you with a reference for remembering each student's name. It's a tad more cumbersome than seating charts, but somewhat less restrictive.

STUDENT-DESIGNED ENVIRONMENTS

So far I have talked about the ways in which you might set up the classroom. As an alternative, you could dedicate time at the beginning of the year to having students design their own learning environment. The idea for doing this comes from my observations of Cindy O'Donnell-Allen's class. She did not invent the idea of having a student-designed environment; however, she did it very well, and her methods are worth sharing.

The year I observed her teach, her class started out in the school library because her classroom was being remodeled. When they finally moved into their classroom (an epic tale in and of itself), Cindy spent a few class sessions in which the students worked in small groups to generate ideas about how they wanted the class organized and outfitted. Each small group in each class generated a wish list of things they would want for the classroom decor.

In each class she then had a class discussion in which each group offered its ideas, which she catalogued on the board. Some of the ideas were a bit far-fetched, but many were feasible. The class decided which they wanted and could get hold of, either by collecting money or finding as hand-me-downs. From the contributions of all her classes, she made a master list of room decorations and accoutrements and then put the students in charge of rounding them up.

The students pooled their resources to turn their ideas into reality. They pitched in money to buy a new faux-oriental rug, a used couch, a used chair, and an end table. Students donated such items as plants, posters, candles, an aquarium, and a microwave oven frequently used to make popcorn, heat soup, and prepare other comestibles during class. The classroom was located in the business department, and the students voted to retain the large business desks rather than take the conventional desks they were scheduled to receive. Their interior design activities counted toward their grades, primarily in terms of participation points.

The arrangement of these items varied, depending on the needs of the occasion. The desks were usually in a U-shape but were frequently moved for small-group work, class theatrics (Cindy began her career as a speech and drama teacher), and other activities that required a fluid setting. Cindy used the classroom walls to display student work, including the writing and art that students produced as part of their study of literature, participation in writing workshops, and other classwork.

Thus, rather than making executive decisions about the ways in which to organize the room physically, you can consult students and have them help decide how it should look. I find it unlikely that they would conclude that the best possible arrangement would be to sit in rows facing the teacher at the front of the room.

> I could never say that I have no idea of the way students respond to my pedagogy; they give me constant feedback. When I teach, I encourage them to critique, evaluate, make suggestions and interventions as we go along. Evaluations at the end of a course rarely help us improve the learning experiences we share together. When students see themselves as mutually responsible for the development of a learning community, they offer constructive input.
>
> —bell hooks

Field Observation

In a school you are visiting, take note of the classroom arrangement. Who decided on this arrangement? What kinds of interactions does it encourage, and what kinds does it discourage? What assumptions about knowledge are suggested by the classroom arrangement? What assumptions about authority are suggested by the arrangement? What alternatives for classroom arrangement are possible in this setting? What consequences might follow from alternative approaches to arranging the classroom?

DISCUSSION-LEADING TECHNIQUES

Changing the physical arrangement of the classroom can provide new channels for classroom interaction, but doesn't guarantee them. If you are teaching seventh graders, they are likely to have had six years of conditioning to reinforce the idea that the teacher is the only person in the room who may be spoken to, either formally or informally. If you teach twelfth graders, the conditioning is even more powerful. Breaking students out of this expectation often requires more than changing the organization of the furniture, no matter how critical a first step that might be.

I used a couple of techniques with high school students to get them to talk directly to one another. I've found that I need to do the same thing with college students, who have had even more conditioning to traditional patterns of interaction. One is to explicitly tell students to talk to each other and not to me. In discussion settings, students will, even when responding to other students' remarks, usually face the teacher. I would break in and say, "Face Roberta, not me," or "Don't respond to Roberta by talking to me; look at her when you respond to her comment." It's amazing how difficult it is for students to do this, but if you make explicit remarks like this often enough, you can help to change the patterns.

A second technique I've used is to remove myself from students' sight lines when a discussion is going well. I do this by standing in the doorway, sometimes slightly in the hallway, so that students can't use me as their intermediary during discussions. They have to look at one another, since there is no teacher standing at the front for their approval. Their contributions can then take on more the character of exploratory talk—sometimes contentious, sometimes co-constructed, but in general less likely to be offered for my approval and more likely to be what I consider an authentic discussion.

Vignette

A few years ago I made about ten observations of a first-grade student teacher in a public school. She observed that her students, even at this tender age, had been heavily conditioned to a particular way of doing school. In particular, they were accustomed to doing things at a brisk pace and in an orderly manner. She, in contrast, wanted to take more time with projects, to move at a more thoughtful pace. When asked if the students had trouble with the crisp schedule they were expected to follow, she said, "No, no, see, they're really good at that. . . . unpacing them and unstructuring them is what's hard."

She pointed out that for many students, first grade was actually their third year in the school system because they had attended both kindergarten and "transition," a year of school between kindergarten and first grade. In other words, even as first graders the students had already spent *half their lives* being conditioned to a particular way of doing school, one that already made it difficult to change their patterns. If that's the degree of socialization they have had in first grade, you can imagine how hard you'll need to work at changing their expectations for schooling by the time they reach middle or high school.

Books About Classroom Discussions

Barnes, D. R. (1992). *From communication to curriculum* (2nd ed.). Portsmouth, NH: Heinemann.

Barnes, D. R., Britton, J. & Torbe, M. (1990). *Language, the learner, and the school* (4th ed.). Portsmouth, NH: Heinemann.

Bellack, A., Kleibard, H., Hyman, R., & Smith, F. (1966). *The language of the classroom.* New York: Teachers College Press.

Cazden, C. B. (1988). *Classroom discourse: The language of teaching and learning.* Portsmouth, NH: Heinemann.

Cazden, C. B., John, V. P., & Hymes, D. (Eds.). (1972). *Functions of language in the classroom.* New York: Teachers College Press.

Marshall, J. D., Smagorinsky, P., & Smith, M. W. (1995). *The language of interpretation: Patterns of discourse in discussions of literature* (NCTE Research Report No. 27). Urbana, IL: National Council of Teachers of English.

Mehan, H. (1979). *Learning lessons.* Cambridge, MA: Harvard University Press.

Nystrand, M. (1997). *Opening dialogue: Understanding the dynamics of language and learning in the English classroom.* New York: Teachers College Press.

SMALL GROUPS

Another way to change the patterns of classroom discussions is to have students work in small groups. As you've seen from Part I of this book, I think that small-group work should be part and parcel of most instructional sequences. It doesn't work simply by telling students to get in groups, however. It takes a bit of preparation in order for small groups to work effectively. Keep in mind that for many students, working in small groups will be a new and unusual experience. You need to put considerable thought into getting them set up, teaching students how to work in them, and making the group goal clear and explicit.

> I complain about the physical space of my classroom. The ceiling is low, the chairs small and childish. Dusty chalkboards line the walls. An ancient wooden podium is forcibly chained to the Formica table. It depresses my spirit. I rearrange the chairs, the table, breaking the static rows into dynamic circles, but the whitewashed cement-block walls still weigh me down. I think I need a better stage, better props, to be a better teacher.
>
> —Christa L. Walck

Setting Up

I've seen several different ways of forming small groups. I'll review them next, then make a case for using one rather than others. I should say right away that my own preference is not the preference of all. You might experiment with different approaches to setting up groups in order to find what works best for your students.

Random Organization

A random organization groups kids on the basis of some arbitrary characteristic, such as

- their place in the attendance book (e.g., a teacher goes down the attendance roster and assigns kids numbers, with students getting together with students assigned the same number)

- where they're sitting (e.g., the teacher says something like, "Everyone in this row is in group 1, everyone in this row is in group 2 . . .")

The primary virtue of organizing groups in this way is that it gets the job done quickly. However, groups formed in this way can end up with odd collections of people. Some might dislike each other personally, others might have incompatible work styles, you might consolidate all of the most or least engaged students in one group, and so on. In general, I'd avoid forming groups randomly, unless their dynamics are not important for the project.

Stratification

In this approach, a teacher tries to distribute the students evenly across the various groups. The criteria for distribution might include any combination of the following:

- The teacher's perception of their ability
- Gender
- Race
- Social class

This approach has the advantage of bringing students in touch with students they might not get to know otherwise. It can also be defended in that it can make sure that each group has at least one capable student who can take on a teaching role to help others with their learning.

There is also a downside to this approach. If you distribute students according to your perception of their ability, you may be defining ability in narrow ways that overlook strengths students may have in solving problems or negotiating group processes. If you focus on ability (or at least your perception of it) alone, you might end up grouping together students who work poorly together. I have often seen groups formed this way, where one student simply did the task without involving the others out of fear that the others would compromise his or her grade through their contributions.

If you sort students according to some apparent trait, such as race, you may be contributing to those students' feelings that they are singled out unfairly. I have seen classes, for instance, where the racial composition was roughly six African American students and twenty European American students. When using small groups, the teacher sorted the African American students across the groups. My sense from watching their expressions was that the students felt that their race was being used as a way to prevent them from working together, even though the teacher's stated goal was to help integrate the class.

One thing to keep in mind is that your students will be involved in many subcommunities, only some of which will be evident on the surface. It's easy to look at a trait such as race and decide that it's bad for all students of a single race to work together consistently. But it's often more complicated than that. When I taught, I found that students who came to the high school from the same neighborhoods and feeder schools tended to group together. I also found that students who shared an activity (e.g., football players) tended to group together. These groupings often crossed racial lines. Singling out students for race, then, overlooks other ways in which they might form communities with other students.

Student Choice

A third way of organizing groups is to let students choose their own partners. After trying other methods, I found that this way worked best for me, although, like the other approaches, it had its downside. In my experience, giving students choice about their co-workers made them much more convivial about doing schoolwork. They looked forward to the opportunity to construct something with people they wanted to be with and with whom they worked productively.

Although the groups were undoubtedly homogenous in many ways, they tended to be stratified in terms of the range of achievement they brought to the group. That is, I found that the best students in class rarely chose one another as work partners. Rather, their friendships provided them with emotional support of the type that is very enabling when working collaboratively. When students chose their own groups, then, they did so because they understood how they complemented one another in ways that were far beyond my grasp.

One great benefit of this approach was that, because they were working with friends, students usually had a stake in the success of the other people in their group. They would therefore not only try to produce a good product for their group, but they would also take an interest in how well the other people were learning the concepts for their subsequent individual performance. I found that the other two approaches to group formation rarely created situations in which students cared about the success of the other group members and took efforts to make sure that they were learning. I found that this frequently happened, however, when students chose their own partners.

This approach, like others, produced groups that were unproductive. Typically, this occurred when students' social goals overrode their academic focus and their attention wandered. Over the years, I found that if I had five groups of students working within a class, three or four would work with little need for my intervention. That left me with a relatively minor management problem.

My main approach to such groups was to stand near them while they were working. Often a teacher's proximity will affect a group's attention to the task. The group work was often graded, so the group grade was also an incentive for working productively on the task. If neither of these approaches worked, then I needed to intervene and tell them that they could no longer work together. I gave them the choice of how to disband. If other groups would take them, then they could join; if not, then their choice was to work with whomever they could find as partners other than the people whose company they had forfeited.

The emphasis on choice, then, had its limitations. On the whole, I found that this method resulted in the most consistently satisfactory performance of my students, both from their standpoint and from mine.

> "Time remains a constructive metaphor for teaching and learning. Sequences, recursive patterns, new encounters, and repeated habits form the cartography of time, travel, and exchange in territories of teaching. If unceasing, time is negotiable, offering opportunities and obstacles, shared encounters and privileged moments. . . . Who does control the time of learning? In what ways? And what are the consequences?
>
> —Patricia C. Phillips"

Setting Up and Operating Groups

Once you've decided on a method for determining group makeup, you still have some work to do to make sure that the groups function smoothly. I will review two aspects of group management: physical arrangement and task definition.

Vignette

A friend told me about a colleague who was very skilled in what some have called the "presentational" or "frontal" teaching style—that is, he primarily stood before his students and talked, giving wise and informed lectures about the topic of study. My friend tried to get him to experiment with using small groups as a way to let the students do some of the talking, and lo and behold, one day his colleague gave it a try.

His colleague entered the staff room later in the day, saying that he'd never use small groups again. The students, he said, had no idea how to talk to one another and mostly sat there frustrated. My friend asked him what their task had been, and the colleague said that they'd been asked to discuss the furniture imagery of *Wuthering Heights.* My friend was unable to persuade him that the problem was not with small groups, but with the lack of preparation they'd had for the task. The colleague went back to his customary method of teaching, convinced that small groups "don't work."

Physical Arrangement

Steve Kern, with whom I did a number of presentations and workshops in the 1980s, used to tell a story about his initial experiences in using small groups. He'd done his student teaching under the mentorship of Larry Johannessen, an experienced teacher who spent a great deal of time thinking about small-group formation and process. When Steve took over Larry's class in midyear, the students were so well enculturated to small-group work that he simply had to say, "Get in small groups," and in moments they'd be organized and ready to go.

Then, when he began his first teaching job the following year, he assumed that all students everywhere would respond in the same way. When he told students to get into groups in the first week of school, however, he had a mess on his hands. Students were splayed about the room haphazardly, to the point where he couldn't tell who was in which group. Some groups sat in a line rather than in a closed group. In general, the students had no idea of what it meant to form a group. Steve found that part of his job at the beginning of the year, then, was to teach them how to form a group and work together.

Doing so might seem a little silly and overly simplistic at first, but if you do it well early in the year then your students will be like Larry's students thereafter and need minimal prompting to get going. Here are some things you might do when you put students into groups the first time:

- Tell them that if you look at the class and can't clearly distinguish one group from another, then the groups are not properly formed.
- Take one group and model the way students should sit: facing inward so that they form a closed circle, able to see the face of each other group member, desks making contact so that they can hear one another talk.
- Have other students get in their groups, providing you with clear lanes throughout the room so that you can easily circulate while they work.
- Praise groups that are well formed and explain the virtues of their formation clearly to the class.

Only when students have formed groups this way should you go on to the next step, which is giving them their task.

Group Task

It should be absolutely clear to students what their task is in the group. As I said in Chapter 8, *you should always provide a hard copy of any instructions you give for group work.* The assignment that you know so clearly in your own head is quite fleeting to students; no sooner are the words out of your mouth than they are swept away by the faintest classroom breeze. And so you need to pass out a copy of the task to each group, write it on the board, or display it on an overhead. Otherwise, you'll spend much of the class going around from group to group, explaining the assignment to them again. I've seen groups wait for a half hour before the teacher finally got to them to tell them what they should have been provided with at the beginning of the class.

The task itself should be open-ended. There's not much point in putting students in groups to answer factual questions. Working in groups works best when students have the opportunity to exchange ideas, disagree, and construct something new. Group tasks can thus either involve the *synthesis* of conflicting ideas or the *co-construction* of new knowledge through discussion.

Group Size

People disagree on the optimal size for small groups. I prefer not to give an exact number for how large a group ought to be, although I think that once past a certain size, groups are too large to function well. It all depends on the task, however. For instance, if your goal is to simulate a jury (see the activity in Appendix B), you might want to have a group of twelve.

For most small-group activities, I prefer to set a limit of four, allowing five when you have an odd number of students in the class. Note that I have set a maximum size rather than a precise size. Because of my belief in allowing students choice in group composition, I think it's a good idea to allow them some choice in how large their groups should be.

Part of that choice should be the choice to work alone. You should be careful to see whether a person is working alone by choice or being ostracized by other groups. If a student is being deliberately outcast, then you might look for ways to get someone to invite that person as a partner.

Teacher Role during Group Work

Once groups are formed, given their task, and hard at work, your role as a teacher is to circulate about the room. As you move around, you should listen to the conversations taking place. If students are getting away from the task, you can remind them of their responsibilities. If they are in an interesting discussion about the task, you can eavesdrop. If they have questions, you should try to answer them. In general, then, your job is to be present to help them accomplish the group goals.

One practical suggestion I'd give is to always circulate so that you always have vision of the whole class. Typically, this means that you circulate on the perimeter

Books on Small Group Process

Abercrombie, M. L. J., & Terry, P. M. (1978). *Talking to learn: Improving teaching and learning in small groups.* Guildford, NY: Society for Research into Higher Education.

Adams, D. M., & Hamm, M. (1996). *Cooperative learning: Critical thinking and collaboration across the curriculum.* Springfield, IL: C. C. Thomas.

Barnes, D. R., & Todd, F. (1995). *Communication and learning revisited: Making meaning through talk.* Portsmouth, NH: Heinemann.

Bean, J. C. (1996). *Engaging ideas: The professor's guide to integrating writing, critical thinking, and active learning in the classroom.* San Francisco: Jossey-Bass.

Marshall, J. D., Smagorinsky, P., & Smith, M. W. (1995). *The language of interpretation: Patterns of discourse in discussions of literature* (NCTE Research Report No. 27). Urbana, IL: National Council of Teachers of English.

Nystrand, M., Gamoran, A., & Heck, M. J. (1992). *Using small groups for response to and thinking about literature.* Washington, DC: U. S. Department of Education, Office of Educational Research and Improvement, Educational Resources Information Center.

Peterson, P., Wilkinson, L., & Hallinan, M. (Eds.) (1984). *The social context of instruction: Group organization and group processes.* New York: Academic Press.

Thelen, H. A. (1954). *Dynamics of groups at work.* Chicago: University of Chicago Press.

of the classroom with your back to the wall and your eyes looking inward. Of course, you don't do this walking awkwardly sideways like a merry-go-round horse doing a penguin imitation, but rather at a more natural gait. If you stop and talk to a group, always position yourself so that you can see the other groups. I've seen teachers who stop and visit with a group, positioning themselves so that they're facing the corner and losing their vision of the class. With their back turned, they encourage off-task behavior on the part of some students, and the occasional hurling of debris around the room. Maintaining vision of the class should become second nature for teachers monitoring small-group work.

Another approach is to rotate among the groups. Sitting in on different groups as they work allows you to mix in with the students and participate with them in their discussion. You need to be careful that you don't act too much the teacher here and take over as the Great Authority. If you are able to check your teacher persona at the door and fit in with the kids, then this approach may work well for you.

CLASSROOM MANAGEMENT

The term *classroom management* for many conjures the notion of discipline, better known as punishment. I will try to persuade you that the best classroom management plan is *not* concerned with punishment, but instead is focused on engaging students with interesting and worthwhile things to do. Students who are busy working on projects that interest them are less likely to be disruptive than are students who are bored or unchallenged. I will call my approach to management the *flow* approach, using the ideas of Mihalyi Csikszentmihalyi that I described previously.

To review briefly: Csikszentmihalyi has found that people are happy who are engaged in activity that involves roughly equal degrees of skill and challenge. When immersed in such an activity, they lose all sense of time. He gives the example of a rock climber who takes hours to scale a rock wall and thinks that it has taken minutes. We have all had such experiences. They are frequently reported by athletes who lose track of time because they are so heavily immersed in the activity of playing the game.

The sad news is that I have not often seen flow experiences in the core academic classes I have observed in school. These classes, including English, often rely on lectures and the memorization of facts, rather than on the kinds of constructive flow activities I've seen elsewhere in the curriculum. In contrast with the flow activities that take place during deep engagement with a sport, in school kids are more typically given a list of the rules of the game, which they must memorize and be tested on. Their memory of the rules, rather than their playing of the game, is often the basis for instruction and assessment.

In my view, then, the best classroom-management technique you can use is to make your classroom a place where flow experiences become more likely. You will still have some students whose behavior is at odds with your goals; I'm making no guarantees here. But I'd rather rely on interesting, challenging, engaging work than on punitive measures to keep my students on task. In most cases, you'll need some incentives, particularly grades, to help students stay focused. You'll also need rules that lay out consequences of disruptive behavior. But these external guidelines, I think, should be secondary means of control and incentive. The emphasis should be on the academic work rather than on the behavior, so that classroom management is tied to effective teaching rather than existing as a separate set of techniques.

Of course, you're teaching English, not playing a ball game, and there's no doubt that it's harder to create flow experiences for most kids in English than in their favorite sport or other activity. One of my most memorable experiences as an educator came when I observed a driver's education class that included some of my own students from a "basic"—that is, low track—class. I'd had difficulty all year getting these boys to get involved with the reading, writing, and language instruction that were the core of our curriculum. Watching them in the driver's ed class, however, was quite a revelation.

The driver's education class was conducted in the simulation room, which was a large room with twenty-five or so simulated car cabs complete with dashboard, steering wheel, brakes, and other accessories for driving. The students would sit in the simulated cabs. In front of them, on a large screen taking up the front of the classroom, they viewed a film that provided a view of the road through a car's windshield. I felt myself in an odd time warp as I viewed the same grainy driver's education films that I had seen as a high school student in the sixties as the cinematic car, fins and all, negotiated contrived traffic situations. The students felt as though they were actually driving their simulated cars. They would turn on their signals when the film slowed for them to make a turn, hit the brakes when a car pulled out in front of them, and otherwise "drive" their cars in response to the conditions presented by the film.

Books on Flow Experiences

Csikszentmihalyi, M. (1975). *Beyond boredom and anxiety.* San Francisco: Jossey-Bass.

Csikszentmihalyi, M. (1990). *Flow: The psychology of optimal experience.* New York: Harper & Row.

Csikszentmihalyi, M., & Csikszentmihalyi, I. S. (Eds.). (1988). *Optimal experience: Psychological studies of flow in consciousness.* New York: Cambridge University Press.

Csikszentmihalyi, M., & Larson, R. (1984). *Being adolescent: Conflict and growth in the teenage years.* New York: Basic Books.

Csikszentmihalyi, M., Rathunde, K., & Whalen, S. (1993). *Talented teenagers: The roots of success and failure.* New York: Cambridge University Press.

At one point, the film was speeding smoothly along at about sixty miles per hour when suddenly a car swerved onto the screen in the path of the "drivers," seeming to come from out of nowhere. At that point, I was watching one of my basic English students, who was so engrossed in his driving that he spun his steering wheel violently and then actually fell out of his seat from the momentum of the turn. Fortunately, he was wearing his seat belt or he might have flown out of his cab entirely and crashed into the student in the next lane. Many other students in the class had the same reaction, and there was much embarrassed laughter among the students over the incident. My own thought immediately was, How could I make that happen in my class? How could I make the activities so real to students that they would actually fall out of their chairs from involvement?

Although I can't claim that I did this consistently, I did teach classes where students seemed surprised and bothered to hear the bell ring at the end of the period. They were, in all likelihood, the best classes I ever taught. I could tell because students would continue the discussion topic as they left the class for the passing period. When I was able to achieve this state—when students were so engrossed in activity or discussion that they lost track of time—I never had behavioral problems. This won't happen for you every day, and it won't happen with all groups of students. But I do feel that it's an ideal that you should strive for, one that makes behavioral management a function of engaged learning, rather than engaged learning a consequence of behavioral management.

Unit Design

In the unit you are designing, have you taken the classroom arrangement into account? If not, how could you set up your classroom to encourage the kinds of learning your unit is designed to promote?

In your unit, have you set aside time to teach students how to participate in small-group activities? To what extent do your plans take into account the issues raised in this chapter?

FINAL THOUGHTS

In this chapter I have reviewed some practical ways to think about setting up your class and conducting it. In the remaining chapters in Part II, I will give examples from real class discussions of how classes conducted according to these principles might unfold.

Discussion Topic

How is it possible to teach so that students have flow experiences in an English class?

CHAPTER 10
How Ways of Talking Affect Ways of Learning

This chapter includes some excerpts from real classroom discussions that involved the short stories included in the coming-of-age unit designed in Chapter 8. I contrast two approaches that teachers took to discussion leading. In one, the teachers assumed most of the interpretive responsibilities themselves. When the students tried to talk about thematically related short stories in small groups, they had a great deal of trouble coming up with interpretations of their own. In the other, the teachers used four techniques for getting students to participate in the discussions: prompting students to generate a context for their interpretation, prompting students to elaborate on their responses, building on student contributions to generate questions, and making the process of analysis explicit. The students of these teachers talked much more extensively when discussing stories in small groups. I conclude that students learn how to talk about literature when teachers use their teaching role to prompt students to think about literature during discussions, rather than to provide students with an authoritative or preferred interpretation.

How do you teach such things? Knowing that frontal learning has its limits, and using the Socratic method, I asked questions and reacted to their responses. I was careful to be encouraging in my answers, agreeing first with what I could support, and only afterwards rebutting with a counterargument or a fact. But the students rebelled: how could I put them on the spot that way? How dare I ask questions to which I already knew the answers?

—Tikva Simone Frymer

In previous chapters I talked about common patterns of interaction that take place in classrooms and the consequences of these patterns for how students learn. To review: The most common physical arrangement for classrooms is for teachers to stand at the front of the class, with students facing forward in rows. This arrangement makes the teacher the focus of attention for students. The teacher spends much of the period talking and explaining. As often happens during lectures, this talk consists of "official" information—either facts about the subject or opinions that are rendered so authoritatively that they stand as facts. The role of students is to listen to what the teacher says, speak when called upon, respond to what the teacher asks, and direct any and all remarks to the teacher. The content of the discussion will then become the basis for an examination, possibly written by someone other than the teacher (the author of the anthology's teacher's manual, a departmental or district committee, a colleague, etc.).

In this chapter I will describe what happens in actual classrooms where these patterns do and don't occur. By and large, they do occur. In his studies of classroom discussions of literature, James Marshall found that English teachers experience tensions that give them competing goals. On the one hand, they want discussions to be spontaneous, free-flowing, improvisational, exploratory—to be, in the words of one, a "jam session." On the other hand, they have a conventional interpretation of literature in mind that they want students to arrive at, thus requiring them to shape the students' contributions toward a particular end. Marshall found that classroom discussions of literature were characterized by the following:

- Teachers dominated the talk, often talking up to 80 percent of the time. Teachers' remarks tended to be information, questions, or responses to students. Student remarks almost always supplied information in response to teachers' questions about the text. The teachers' emphasis on the literature was academic rather than personal. By this I mean that they focused on the text as an object of study independent of students' personal associations or emotions in response to it.
- Typically, each student contribution was brief and followed by a teacher response. Students rarely talked directly to one another. Students rarely posed their own questions; their contributions were mainly answers to teachers' questions. They rarely volunteered their own interpretation; they mainly supplied responses that assisted the teacher's interpretation. If viewed solely on their own, the students' remarks made little sense. They only made sense when understood in the context of the larger interpretation and monologue provided by the teacher.

> Our job is not to make up anybody's mind, but to open minds and to make the agony of the decision-making so intense you can escape only by thinking.
>
> —Fred Friendly

The overall effect of these patterns was that teachers would provide an interpretation of a text, with students serving primarily to slot information in occasionally. Students' contributions were usually folded into their teacher's preconceived interpretation, which itself was often derived from the official interpretation of authoritative literary critics. The discussions stayed on track because teachers used their responses to students' remarks to weave together their preferred interpretation. The teachers ultimately controlled the direction, pace, content, and organization of discussions. This control made it unlikely for discussions to resemble a jam session.

These patterns were almost inevitable in spite of teachers' stated goals to make themselves "disappear" from discussions and let students take control of the interpretation. Teachers stated that they wanted to recede into the background and let students take over. By doing so, they would help students develop independent interpretive skills. Yet the conflicting goal of learning conventional interpretations rarely allowed for these free-flowing, student-run discussions to occur.

Field Observation

Get permission from a student to follow him or her around to several classes throughout the school; that is, to shadow the student as he or she goes through the routines of school. During a typical school day, what kinds of activities do students engage in? What is their primary role as students as they go across the curriculum? What frame of mind might they be in when they arrive for your class? How should your knowledge of their frame of mind affect your decisions about how to teach them in an English class?

A CONTRAST OF TWO APPROACHES TO DISCUSSION

Without the opportunity to practice interpretive skills in discussions, students are not likely to learn them for independent use. In this chapter, I will look at what students learn from talking about literature in different ways. I draw on discussions of four teachers. Two of them taught in ways similar to the one characterized by Marshall. The other two prompted students to construct and elaborate on their construction of the text's meaning.

To answer the question of what students learned from these approaches, I studied students' discussions in small groups following the teacher-led discussions. My assumption was that if students learned procedures for interpreting literature during teacher-led discussions, then they would use that knowledge when interpreting literature in small-group discussions that followed. That's the assumption behind instructional scaffolding as I've outlined it in this book. I'll next describe how the different discussions unfolded, with the goal of understanding the consequences of different approaches to leading discussions.

The four teachers were Mr. Harris, Mr. Stone, Ms. Sanders, and Mr. Azarov (all pseudonyms, as are all student names). Harris and Sanders tended to speak much more frequently than their students, and did so with the intention of providing their preferred interpretation. Stone and Azarov made more balanced contributions and did so primarily for the purpose of involving students in the interpretive process. When their students moved to small groups to discuss stories, the students of Harris and Sanders tended to have very brief discussions, doing little beyond the minimum. In their small-group discussions, the students of Stone and Azarov delved into the stories in depth.

The students were all high school sophomores studying coming-of-age literature. Mr. Azarov taught honors students; the other three taught regular track classes. The stories they discussed were from the class literature anthology and were read as part of the teachers' coverage of the sophomore curriculum. The stories discussed in these classes were among the stories outlined in Chapter 8 of this book: "The Bridge" and "Peter Two."

The main question I tried to answer was: If teacher-led and small group discussions are set up and managed in more or less the same ways, how will different teaching approaches influence the ability of students to talk on their own? What I found confirmed what I suspected; that teaching in the manner described by Marshall provided students with few skills of their own for interpreting literature. Mr. Harris and Ms. Sanders were the primary speakers in their discussions, both occupying the floor and providing the bulk of the interpretation. When their students moved to small groups to discuss a story based on the same theme and script, they had few interpretive tools to prompt and sustain their discussion.

Mr. Stone and Mr. Azarov took a different role, limiting their talk to the following:

- Prompting students to generate a context for their interpretation
- Prompting students to elaborate on their responses
- Building on student contributions to generate questions
- Making the process of analysis explicit

Reflective Writing Prompt

Think back to literary discussions you've been involved in throughout your education. For the most part, whose interpretation counted? To what degree did discussions resemble jam sessions? How were students treated when they offered interpretations or responses that were different from those of the teacher? What were the consequences of these processes on the ways you learned to think about literature?

When their students moved to small groups, their discussions were detailed and elaborate. The students showed evidence that they had learned ways of talking about literature during the teacher-led discussions.

I next give examples from the different discussions that illustrate these differences.

> *I asked a question. I can't remember now what it was. It doesn't matter. The point was that out of the foxhole of my terror, I grabbed a question and lobbed it out there at the massed troops–the enemy. My students. I will never forget the wave of astonishment, of blessed relief, that followed. Half a dozen hands went up, a little explosion of volunteers. I couldn't believe it. They're doing it! They're being students! They think I'm a teacher!*
>
> –Patricia Hampl

Prompting Students to Generate a Context for Their Interpretation

Mr. Harris was an experienced teacher who had taught the sophomore curriculum for many years. His familiarity with the literature was evident in his discussions, in which he served as the primary speaker. He tended to share lengthy personal experiences that illustrated the plight of the literary characters. In doing so, he modeled the kind of personal response to literature often encouraged by transactional literary theorists such as Louise Rosenblatt. Often these personal connections were riveting and relevant to the literary dilemma.

In doing this, however, Mr. Harris did not appear to help students learn how to generate relevant personal examples themselves. In the following discussion, for instance, he posed questions about the behavior of the protagonist from "The Bridge." A student provided a brief factual response. Mr. Harris then took this response and generated a hypothetical situation that helped illuminate the character's situation.

Mr. Harris:	Rachel, what happens after he jumps into the water?
Rachel:	He saves the girl.
Mr. Harris:	Is it an easy saving?
Rachel:	No, because the current pulls them under.
Mr. Harris:	That is described in great detail. Why do you suppose the author describes the saving in such great detail?
Student:	[inaudible]
Mr. Harris:	It has to be arduous for anything to be important. It has to be difficult. For example, if it were easy to play the guitar, we would all be Eric Clapton. But all of us probably have sat down with either our guitar or somebody else's guitar. The first thing you find out is that it sort of hurts and it is hard to keep the frets down. So you get one chord and you struggle for a while, like row, row your boat. You got to change it, and it is difficult. Now, if it is a matter of just hopping off a two foot bridge into three feet of water and saying, "Don't be silly. You're all right, honey," that is not going to be something that changes him very much. But in the act of saving itself, one particular thing happens between the two people. Can you remember what that is?

Presumably, the reference to rock legend Eric Clapton will build on students' interests and help them see the connection between their own worlds and those of the characters in the story. The problem is that Mr. Harris produced this context without engaging students at all in the process. Because they had no involvement in generating this connection, they did not learn how to do it for themselves. Here, for instance, is a complete episode in the small-group discussion of Mr. Harris's students. They are responding to questions about the story script for "Peter Two":

Ellen:	[Reads from assignment sheet] "What characteristics does the protagonist have at the beginning of the story that you would call immature? Give examples and explain why they are immature."
Betty:	I don't know.
Judy:	Wait, I forgot the story. Let me get my book right here.
Ellen:	I think that at the beginning of the story, he thinks that to be mature, he's going to be six feet tall, he's going to have arms of steel, and he thinks he's going to be in control.
Judy:	He watches TV too much.
Ellen:	And he thinks he's rebelling by eating grape seeds just because his mother is not there.
Ginny:	Good answer.
Ellen:	Somebody else talk. (pause) Does anyone else have any more reasons why he is immature?
Betty:	Nope.

This discussion was typical in the discussions that took place among Mr. Harris's and Ms. Sanders's students. In this small group, the students produced an acceptable answer and then moved on to the next question. Although Mr. Harris had provided them with an interesting personal connection to the story, the students appeared to have learned no procedures for making personal connections of their own. Simply modeling a response, then, appears to be insufficient in teaching students how to respond on their own.

> In most English classes the short story has become a kind of literary specimen to be dissected. Every time a story of mine appears in a Freshman anthology, I have a vision of it, with its little organs laid open, like a frog in a bottle.
>
> —Flannery O'Connor

Mr. Stone's approach was different. He used questioning techniques that prompted the students to generate their own context for their interpretation. As should be evident from the following transcripts, his students were then able to produce a relevant context in their small-group discussions. In the following excerpt from one whole-class discussion, he pushed a student to provide a context for interpreting the character of Peter in "Peter Two":

Patsy:	He thought it was so mature to, well, he was eating grapes and staying up late with, he was eating grapes and grape seeds and staying up late and watching TV without his mother's approval.
Mr. Stone:	Okay, eating grapes and seeds and a couple of other examples. He was staying up late.
Patsy:	Yeah.
Mr. Stone:	And he was also—
Patsy:	Watching TV.

Mr. Stone:	And watching TV when told not to. And these fall into the category of what?
Patsy:	Huh?
Mr. Stone:	These all have something in common.
Patsy:	Well, disobeying.
Mr. Stone:	Okay. He was disobeying his mother. All right. Now what can you do with this? In other words, what are you trying to tell us by bringing up these points?
Patsy:	That he thought he was mature by disobeying his mother. He thought it made him a more mature person and older by doing things he wasn't supposed to do.
Mr. Stone:	Thought he was mature through these acts. Okay, and what does Patsy think? Do you agree with it?
Patsy:	What? No.
Mr. Stone:	Why not?
Patsy:	He was just showing how immature he is by doing that.
Mr. Stone:	And what criterion of a definition of maturity are you using to make this judgment? Why is this, you are saying that this is, in fact, immature even though he thought he was mature. That is what you are saying, right?
Patsy:	Yes.
Mr. Stone:	Why? You are saying he is immature because of something and that because is your definition. And what is it about your definition that allows you to make this judgment?

Mr. Stone's technique here is to take a student's contribution and ask her questions about it. The questions are designed to get her to place the story in a broader context—what it means to be mature. The goals for the unit as a whole were different from those outlined in Chapter 8 of this book. The goal for Mr. Stone's students was to produce an extended definition of maturity, which they generated through their analysis of a series of coming-of-age stories. Attention to this goal, and the context it provided, was then central to these discussions.

The task of producing the definition, however, was the responsibility of the students. Mr. Stone used whole-class discussions to help students generate this context. His method was to urge students to pursue their ideas through questions and prompts, rather than by providing examples of relevant contexts. Although the excerpt I've shown involves only one student, that student is moved to generate a context in some detail.

When Mr. Stone's students moved to their small-group analysis of "The Bridge," they were then able to generate contexts of their own for interpreting the character's maturation. Here is the way one small group discussed the story. The students were using the same set of questions that Mr. Harris's students used in their small group, asking about the character's transformation from immature to mature:

Veronica:	The protagonist was very insecure.
Kay:	Why is he insecure?

Hope:	Why is he insecure? Because he stayed home all the time and didn't want to go on this trip.
Kay:	So that was immature?
Tammy:	That was insecure.
Hope:	Insecure, which is immature.
Tammy:	Yeah.
Kay:	Why is immaturity insecurity?
Tammy:	[reads from assignment sheet] ". . . that you would call immature?"
Kay:	Why is insecure immature? By staying home, is that immature?
Tammy:	No, he had no friends.
Kay:	No friends is insecure?
Hope:	No, he's insecure and insecurity is immaturity.
Kay:	The second question asks, "Explain why . . ."
Tammy:	You have to know yourself and he doesn't; therefore he's insecure.
Hope:	Insecure means no self-knowledge.
Tammy:	Yeah.
Kay:	Okay, he had no self-knowledge. Now, why is that immature?
Tammy:	Because he was too protected.
Hope:	It's immature because—
Kay:	He was protected.
Hope:	Yeah. He was seventeen, he was afraid to go out. Well, actually—
Kay:	He was old enough to know—
Hope:	Right.
Kay:	He spent his life at home.
Hope:	He was never really out.
Veronica:	Maybe he was a hermit. I don't know why. He just like stayed at home with his family. I feel sorry for him.
Hope:	He's one of those people you don't want to know. How is no self-knowledge immature?
Tammy:	Let me explain this one. You see, like, no self-knowledge, that leads to—I don't know.
Kay:	He has no idea what the outside world is.
Tammy:	You have to know yourself, and by knowing yourself, you know your limits.
Hope:	Yeah.

This discussion shows that the students have picked up on how to push themselves toward a more detailed context for thinking about the story. They appear to have adopted Mr. Stone's method of posing questions that seek an elaboration. He never told them during the discussion that he was teaching them a strategy, yet they seem to have picked it up through routine participation in his method.

Discussion Topic

These are some questions my colleague Mark Faust asks preservice teachers about literature discussions:

What are literature discussions discussions of? Or, What do we talk about when we talk about literature?

What are literature discussions for?

What counts as an appropriate topic for a literature discussion that takes place in school?

What should teachers do to start literature discussions?

What should teachers do during literature discussions?

What should students know in order to participate in literature discussions?

How do teachers know what students know, and how should this knowledge affect a teacher's role in literature discussions?

Does a teacher's role depend on what students know?

Does a teacher's role depend on what kinds of things students say?

Is there any obligation for the class to stay on topic? If so, how do you know when you're off topic? Whose topic is it that you're off?

Prompting Students to Elaborate on Their Responses

A second effective discussion-leading technique teachers used was to prompt their students to develop partial or initial responses. Mr. Azarov, for instance, had a method of repeating student statements in the form of a question in order to prompt them to elaborate:

Jane:	. . . it seems like she is just this mother figure. He is kind of scared of her.
Mr. Azarov:	He is kind of scared of his grandmother?
Jane:	Yeah. Like she is kind of turning against him.
Mr. Azarov:	She is turning against him?

Methods like this one appeared quite effective in getting students to develop their own self-prompts for elaborating when they discussed stories in small groups. Mr. Azarov's students engaged in longer, more detailed analysis of the literature in their small groups than did students of teachers who elaborated on student responses themselves. Both Azarov and Stone had a unique way of providing such prompts; no particular method seemed more effective than another. The key issue was that they developed some way of getting students to pursue their ideas, rather than providing the elaboration themselves. Both teachers' methods prevented their discussions from following the customary "IRE" pattern in which

- the teacher *initiates* a topic
- a student *responds* briefly
- the teacher then *evaluates* and elaborates on the student's response, often at length

> In a typical history classroom where the teacher was lecturing about Genghis Khan's invasion of China and conquest of Beijing in 1215, only 2 out of 27 students were thinking about China when they were signaled. One of the 2 was remembering the meal he had when he last ate out with his family at a Chinese restaurant, and the other was wondering why Chinese men wore their hair in a ponytail. None mentioned Genghis Khan or Beijing or 1215.
>
> —Mihaly: Csikszentmihalyi, Kevin Rathunde, Samuel Whalen, *Talented Teenagers*

Building on Student Contributions to Generate Questions

Another effective discussion-leading technique was for teachers to ask questions based on student contributions. This is known as *uptake*. Asking uptake questions is very different from coming to class prepared with a list of discussion questions that you ask regardless of the situation. The following sequence illustrates how a teacher took a student's comment about the protagonist in "The Bridge" and used it as the basis for a follow-up question:

Larry:	You don't have a male figure if you are a man, and you don't have a reference because you see things a little differently because men and women have different—
Mr. Azarov:	Yeah, he has just got a grandmother and an aunt in the house, and he has just lost his mother. It doesn't seem like he ever had a father around. So you are saying you wouldn't call it immaturity? You would call it—
Fred:	Innocence.
Larry:	No. I think it is more what is going on in the house.
Mr. Azarov:	Just a reflection of the life, the way he has been growing up?
Esther:	I don't think there is anything really wrong with him, like, hiding in the bushes, because when what they talk about this, this aunt had like four kids and stuff, and maybe he didn't have his own room to go to or something, and he would like to be by himself. And just like [another student] said, no one knows that he's there till he's picked or his grandma makes a comment or something and she doesn't know he is there. But he can still feel like everything is that's going on so he doesn't miss something.

Here, Mr. Azarov is going with the flow of the discussion. Rather than setting the direction of the discussion by asking predetermined questions, he is basing his questions on student interpretations. His questions, then, are designed to get students to elaborate on or defend their ideas. And as you can see, Esther is the one who extends the observation about the character.

You'll recall that the teachers described by Marshall felt a tension between wanting to go with the flow and wanting to lead students down an interpretive path. Inevitably, they led their discussions toward a conventional interpretation. The teachers I studied who provided a conventional interpretation ended up teaching few procedures for students to adopt in their own interpretations. Those who went with the flow by using methods such as uptake were more likely to have

- large-group discussions in which students, rather than the teacher, provided the elaborations
- small-group discussions in which students engaged in extended inquiry into the story's meaning

MAKING THE PROCESS OF ANALYSIS EXPLICIT

A final effective discussion-leading strategy was for the teacher to make the process of analysis explicit. Teachers did this by calling attention to procedures for interpreting literature, as in the following sequence:

Mr. Stone:	Okay, now what does that tell you about him? For some reason we are bringing these up and saying they are evidence that he is mature, isn't that what you are saying? That he is mature. We are saying that all of these things help us to classify this behavior as immature behavior, but I don't see any reason to make that classification based on the definition that we have up there [on the chalkboard] so far. What do we need to do? Does anyone disagree with the judgment that all of this is immature? Is there anyone contesting that? What's missing now? Something is missing. We don't have anything to make the judgment by, so we need to decide what part of the definition allows us to make that judgment. Is your hand up, Gary?
Gary:	You could say for a definition that bragging about stuff is being immature, or boasting about it would be a sign of immaturity.
Mr. Stone:	Bragging or boasting says Gary. Well, note that that would be a definition of immature. What does a mature person do?
Gary:	They don't need to brag.
Mr. Stone:	A sign of maturity is not bragging.
Gary:	They already know who they are.
Mr. Stone:	Oh, now you just said something different. Because they what?
Gary:	They already know who they are.
Mr. Stone:	So it sounds as though you are saying the criterion should be self-knowledge. The reason for that, Gary, as you pointed out so astutely, is that the mature person has self-knowledge. Any response to that?

In posing such questions as "What do we need to do?" and "What's missing now?" Mr. Stone pointed out to students that in order to pursue their consideration of the story, they needed to make a procedural move: "We need to decide what part of the definition allows us to make that judgment."

This brief exchange also illustrates Mr. Stone's use of uptake, such as his summary of Gary's remarks and following question, "Any response to that?" There is also an instance when he paraphrases Gary's statement, "A sign of maturity is not bragging," as a way to get Gary to elaborate his comment.

As should be clear by now, the combination of these techniques added up to an approach designed to *teach students how to talk, and thus think, about literature.* The way of talking was exploratory rather than authoritative, inquiry-based rather than geared toward official interpretations. And as the small-group

Field Observation

Do one of the following:

1. Observe the class of another teacher.

    Make observational notes of the following:

    Comparison of teacher talk versus student talk (length of time, number of contributions, length of contributions)

    The kinds of questions teachers ask (uptake, predetermined, open-ended, informational, etc.)

    The direction of the discussion (toward a preconceived interpretation, free-flowing, etc.)

    The purpose of teacher contributions (to get students to elaborate, to lead to a particular interpretation, etc.)

    Draw inferences about what students are learning from taking part in the discussion and about what they will be able to do on their own as a result of their participation.

2. Audiotape or videotape your own teaching, and play back the tape. Make observational notes of the following:

    Comparison of your talk versus student talk (length of time, number of contributions, length of contributions)

    The kinds of questions you ask (uptake, predetermined, open-ended, informational, etc.)

    The direction of the discussion (toward a preconceived interpretation, free-flowing, etc.)

    The purpose of your contributions (to get students to elaborate, to lead to a particular interpretation, etc.)

    Draw inferences about what students are learning from taking part in the discussion and about what they will be able to do on their own as a result of their participation.

discussions revealed, this approach was far more effective in promoting student talk than was the authoritative approach used by the other teachers observed.

Discussion Topic

What is the purpose of a discussion about literature? Do college English classes and secondary school English classes share the same purposes, and should they be conducted with the same processes? Why or why not?

FINAL THOUGHTS

The classes I've described illustrate an important facet of good instructional scaffolding. In previous chapters, I described a sequence of going from teacher-led discussions to small-group discussions to individual performance. The classes I've described here show that simply going through this sequence does not necessarily accomplish anything. Rather, they show that *teaching only scaffolds when it engages the students in some kind of joint activity that teaches them procedures for how to learn.*

All the teachers I studied were attempting to provide a scaffold of support for student learning. Effective instructional scaffolding, however, involves a dynamic interaction between students and teacher and not simply the modeling of a learning process or the presentation of information. Teachers whose students engaged in fruitful small-group activities *cultivated student expertise*, rather than issuing expert opinions.

These classes also show how small groups are not a panacea. Rather, they are an extension of the continuum of discussions enacted during the school year. How they function depends on the prevailing language of the classroom. Because they are an extension of prior classes, it's unlikely that they'll work effectively in classes where the teacher dominates classroom talk for the most part. Teachers who have struggled with small groups might benefit from examining their own discussion-leading styles in order to make their classes more flexible and interactive. Teachers who have had success with small groups might be more cautious in recommending them to others. Teachers need to attend to the total environment they create in their classrooms and to look at particular instructional methods and classroom episodes as they relate to learning and instruction as a whole.

Discussion Plans

Unit Design

Look at the literature discussions you have planned for your unit. How carefully scripted are they? What kinds of contributions will students make to the discussions you've planned? To what extent is it likely that they will promote a joint activity that teaches students interpretive strategies?

Details on This Research

Marshall, J. D., Smagorinsky, P., & Smith, M. W. (1995). *The language of interpretation: Patterns of discourse in discussions of literature* (NCTE Research Report No. 27). Urbana, IL: National Council of Teachers of English.

Smagorinsky, P., & Fly, P. K. (1993). The social environment of the classroom: A Vygotskian perspective on small group process. *Communication Education, 42,* 159–171.

Smagorinsky, P., & Fly, P. K. (1994). A new perspective on why small groups do and don't work. *English Journal, 83*(3), 54–58.

CHAPTER 11 Multimedia Composing with a Big Tool Kit

This chapter again provides illustrations from real classrooms. The emphasis here is on classes in which students are given opportunities for multimedia/multigenre composing. I first look at some classes across the curriculum where such composing is commonplace, including agriculture classes where students design horse ranches, home economics classes where students make clothing and do interior design, and architectural design classes where students design houses. I argue that these classes provide opportunities for the kinds of collaborative, extended composing processes often valued by writing teachers. I then look at an English class where students interpreted a short story through drama, dance, music, and drawing. The interpretations they came up with through these media were quite sophisticated and compelling. I conclude that students ought to get more opportunities for these kinds of interpretations, given their potential for enabling sophisticated thinking and interpretation.

Throughout this book I have tried to persuade you that *people learn from making, and reflecting on, things that they find useful and important.* These things are *texts,* and the process of constructing them is called *composing.* To most English teachers, a composition is a piece of writing, usually some kind of formal essay. I will try to show you that writing, while the most highly valued form of composition in school, is just one of many ways in which students can produce useful and meaningful texts.

In previous chapters, I talked about the need to view writing as one essential tool in a *tool kit* that students draw on to produce their schoolwork. In this chapter, I will describe composing that I've observed both across the curriculum and in an English class. The students that I describe here give strong evidence that there should be a more legitimate role in school for what I've called *multimedia composing*, that is, composing that is done from a big tool kit containing a variety of means of production.

BACKGROUND

My interest in multimedia composing comes from my own experiences as a teacher. After I'd been teaching for a few years, the high school in which I taught instituted a speech program. Every sophomore in the school would devote one semester to an untracked course that involved the students in public speaking, oral interpretation, improvisation, role-playing, and other activities involving oral communication. At that time I taught juniors and wanted to be able to follow up the speech program with students in their subsequent learning. With release time provided by my supervision of a student teacher, I was able to observe a number of speech classes, discuss their purpose with the teachers, find out what the students were learning, and build on the speech-program activities with my juniors.

My incorporation of the speech activities into the junior curriculum profoundly affected my approach to teaching. My classes had always been activity oriented, but my exposure to the dynamic activities in the speech classes opened up new possibilities to me. The juniors who'd taken speech had learned a great array of skills that served them well in interpreting literature. They had learned, for instance, the art of oral interpretation and would, without much prompting, bring in all manner of musical accompaniment, elaborate sets, costumes, and even special effects to enhance their performances. I still have a powerful memory of one group of boys—not among my strongest students—performing a nocturnal scene from Nathaniel Hawthorne's "Young Goodman Brown." To do so, they came attired in dark robes and brought props that suggested the supernatural. They then not only fogged the room with a cauldron of dry ice, but added pyrotechnics by darkening the room and striking a lighter beneath the jet from an aerosol can, providing a memorable (if perilous) rendition of the literary moment.

In the following years, in addition to the core of writing I required, I increasingly encouraged students to represent their understanding of literature through unconventional types of compositions. I did so even after changing jobs and teaching in a school that did not have the preparatory speech program. My rationale for emphasizing multiple forms of compositions was that the students were, almost without exception, highly engaged in the projects they would undertake, often far more so than they were when being evaluated through writing.

In particular, students who were low achievers were often among the most enthusiastic and productive workers on these projects. Students who were loath to turn in simple homework assignments would spend all weekend producing elaborate video productions dramatizing their interpretations of literary relationships. Above all, the students, besides being engaged, were clearly demonstrating an understanding of literature in ways not accessible through their writing. Not only were they active and involved, they were learning in the process.

A RATIONALE FOR AN EXPANDED TOOL KIT

I have since had the opportunity to observe classrooms across the school curriculum to see how students make meaning in different subject areas. What I learned surprised me quite a bit. After observing both core academic courses—English, math, science, and history—and courses elsewhere in the school, I found that often the most interesting learning comes in the classes that stand relatively low in academic status. And some of the most tedious classes I observed were the ones students needed to take in order to go to college.

My judgment is based on the degree to which I could see students engaged in learning that was

- process-oriented
- constructive
- meaningful
- extended
- connected
- social
- useful

Many teachers of writing say that good writing instruction should promote these virtues. What I found was that they were more likely to occur in classes where students were composing a nonwritten text. The question I was forced to ask myself was, If we justify writing instruction because it promotes the construction and communication of meaning, and if other kinds of texts have the same potential yet achieve it more often, then why do we value writing above all other forms of textuality? As a teacher of writing, I was intrigued. And as a teacher of English who had found value in multimedia composing, I was doubly intrigued.

> **Reflective Writing Prompt**
>
> In your experiences as a student, how has your most useful and meaningful learning taken place? What kinds of classes have you found the least interesting, challenging, and transforming? Based on this reflection, how can you conduct your English class so as to make it interesting, challenging, and transforming for your students?

Based on my observations, I came to the unpopular conclusion that promoting *writing across the curriculum* is misguided. Rather, the emphasis should be on *composing across the curriculum,* through whatever medium is appropriate. Much writing across the curriculum is dull and uninspired—students doing word problems instead of formulas in math, writing an explanation of a scientific phenomenon when a diagram would communicate it better, and the like. Focusing exclusively on the tool of writing, rather than on the act of composing, both overestimates the value of writing and underestimates the value of other tools.

My purpose is *not* to argue that writing is trivial. My purpose is both to argue that English teachers should shift their emphasis to processes of composition and to consider the potential that other tools have for enabling students to compose useful and meaningful texts. As English teachers, you'll always have an obligation to teach writing. I'm trying to show that writing does not have the *exclusive* potential for enabling the construction of meaning, but should be considered the primary tool in students' tool kits for making things that they find useful and important.

COMPOSING ACROSS THE CURRICULUM

A few years ago I had the opportunity to spend time visiting about 20 percent of the classes in a large high school. I tried to visit at least one class in each subject area offered in the school. My original purpose was to study writing across the curriculum. I was initially disappointed to find that there was actually very little writing across the curriculum. As an English teacher, I had always assumed that students needed to write across the curriculum in order to develop the kinds of powerful thinking that writing can enable.

What I saw was different from what I expected. This kind of surprise, incidentally, is one of the reasons I find research so valuable: So frequently, it helps me learn a different reality than I anticipated.

What I saw surprised me in a few different ways. First, when students did write, their writing tended to be very brief: notes from a teacher's lecture, short answers on tests, and not much else. The writing, then, did not involve students in any extended process of composition or produce anything I'd call a useful text. It served primarily as the medium to record facts, either to prepare for a test or on the test itself.

Second, I was surprised to find that, across the curriculum, students were engaged in all manner of composition, featuring all the virtues I described previously. Students would willingly compose texts that they found useful and meaningful. They would spend considerable time on them; in some courses, the entire semester's work was devoted to the production of a single text. To compose them, students would need to synthesize their knowledge from a range of academic disciplines. They would need to learn the particular conventions of the field of study they were working within and produce a text that included those conventions.

The text needed to be something that they wanted to produce and would ultimately find useful. They would discuss their texts and composing processes with the teacher and other students and redo parts that required improvement. In short, these students were composing texts in all the ways that writing theorists say are important and that justify the idea of writing across the curriculum.

However, almost without exception, these students were producing texts through a medium other than writing. They were sewing, drawing, acting, painting, and, in general, reaching deep into their tool kits for the means of composing. In this chapter, I will describe some of those classes and the kinds of texts that the students produced. First I'll describe a sewing class. I've referred to this class earlier in this book. The home economics department in general was not regarded as a beehive of intellectual activity by most people in the school. One home ec teacher I interviewed said that other teachers in the building referred to home economics courses as basket weaving. This supposedly derogatory term showed a lack of understanding of two things: the seriousness with which home economics students treated their composing, and the difficulty of weaving baskets (a point made to me by a Native American student I taught in Oklahoma).

Even the home ec teachers, I think, underestimated the degree of intelligence it took to produce good work in their classes. When I asked one teacher what students needed in order to succeed, she said, "Common sense." After watching her students in action, I would have to disagree. I'd say that they needed a range of abilities that required intelligence and other qualities, particularly patience. Calling these "common sense" greatly underestimated the cognitive sophistication of the students.

In the coed sewing class I observed, every student in the class was on task for virtually the entire period. For their course projects, the students could construct any product that required sewing. Most made clothing that they would wear, and therefore were greatly concerned about getting the final product right. They were using what Howard Gardner would call spatial intelligence as they measured their own bodies and then cut sections of material that would fit their personal forms properly. In addition, they needed to make decisions about the colors and patterns that suited their own complexions, hair color, and body shape, as well as the mood they hoped to convey through their appearance.

As teenagers, they were very sensitive about the way they looked, and therefore were deeply concerned about the choices they made and the craft behind their work. When they would make a section of clothing, try it on, and find it didn't fit properly, they would immediately undo their work and try it until they got it right. Their process of production was highly social, with students asking one another's opinions, helping each other with problems, and providing feedback and support for one another's efforts. The teacher played a similar role, providing hands-on help for students who were having difficulties with their work. When students would finish a garment, they would display it with pride to their classmates, who would admire it and praise their work.

I can't imagine that these students could produce a more meaningful text than an article of clothing that they would wear to school. Their involvement with these projects was most evident when, with a few minutes remaining in the class, the teacher told the students that they would need to begin cleaning up so they could leave at the bell. Students were surprised to find that the period was almost over, and their faces tightened with frustration because they would have to abandon their projects in midstitch. Earlier in this book I referred to the idea of *flow* learning experiences, which take place when someone is so wrapped up in an activity that he or she loses track of time. In my observations across the school curriculum, I found flow activities primarily in classes like the sewing class. In these classes, students were so engrossed with their work that the class period seemed to go by in minutes and they had to snap out of their state of involvement in order to get back on the school schedule.

When I observed these same students in their other classes, I rarely saw the same level of interest, involvement, commitment, or energy. A student who would readily tear out a stitch and redo it would complain when asked to revise an essay for an English class. A student who was concerned with the most minute details of stitchwork would wonder why history papers should be written with impeccable citations. Of course, there were some students who valued both their sewing and their writing. Doug, a senior whose writing I studied in detail that year, produced three teddy bears and a pair of boxer shorts for the sewing class and a wide range of compositions for his two English classes (creative writing and senior English). He took great care with all the texts he produced for these classes.

Most of the other students I observed, however, took their sewing much more seriously than they took their writing. In other words, students who would compose meaningful texts in their home ec classes with great concern for precision and appearance could not see the point of composing written academic texts with similar attention to the requirements of propriety of form. In spite of these students' remarkable personal investment in their productions, in the eyes of the school the home ec classes were marginal, not central to the core of academic knowledge, physically located on the margins of the school building, and generally regarded as appropriate primarily for non-college-bound students.

My observations in this high school took me to other parts of the building typically believed to be nonacademic. Among the most fascinating parts of the school was the agriculture department, located on the edge of the school facility in a distant, detached building it shared with the athletic department's weight-training room.

One class I observed focused on equine management and production and required students to design a functional, profitable horse ranch. To do so, students needed to understand the living and breeding needs of a specific breed of horse and design an appropriate environment for it. They needed to know the proper size of the stalls for their breed, the design of the breeding area, the layout of the paddocks, the size of the exercise area, and other aspects of spatial layout. They also needed to understand the climate of the area they were building the ranch in. This knowledge would affect decisions about roof pitch (e.g., the angle best for snow or rain runoff), building height (e.g., the proper height in a tornado belt), landscape (e.g., where to place facilities to avoid flooding during heavy rainfall), and so on. To complete their ranch successfully, students needed to know how to

- design the interior road system for maximum efficiency in manure disposal and other daily maintenance
- calculate the mix of the feeds to provide proper nutrition for the specific breed and functions of their horses
- design the barn so that the office where business would be conducted would not be affected by veterinary lab odors or other distractions
- design living quarters for farmhands that allowed comfort at minimal cost
- otherwise synthesize a tremendous amount of working knowledge of horses, meteorology, mathematics, human cultures, nutrition, breeding, veterinary science, cultural difference, and other aspects of horse-ranch management in their production of a drawing of the layout of their ranches

As in the sewing class, the students produced these drawings in a dynamic, purposeful environment. Students composed several drafts of their ranches, which they would show to their teacher and other students throughout their process of production. They relied on one another's expertise to assist them in their compositions. They frequently revised their ideas as they worked toward a final conception of their ranch. Like the students in the sewing class, they took this work very seriously. And, like the students in the sewing class, they were not taken very seriously by the other students, faculty, and administrators in the school.

Similar processes took place in the extended composition of texts in the architectural design and interior design classes I observed. The two classes overlapped: The teachers of the courses were in close contact, the classes frequently had cross-enrollments, and the students were able to coordinate their work for the two classes. In other words, they could build a model house for the architectural design course and furnish its rooms for the interior design course. Both classes, like the equine management class, were informal and involved almost continual talk among students as they worked on their projects. Students were encouraged to get feedback at every stage of production from both teachers and peers and to go out into the field for help from parents, construction engineers, and interior decorators.

In the architectural design class, the students' primary goal was to prepare the floor plans for and construct a model of a 1,200- to 1,800-square-foot home. The home had to include a minimum of one full bath, a kitchen, two bedrooms, and a two-car garage. Students were required to design the home down to the smallest detail, including the placement of light switches, and to take into account the cost-effectiveness of the materials they chose for their construction. Most students had external audiences for their products, such as judges in competitions they were encouraged to enter.

To build their homes, the students had to incorporate knowledge of math, physics, engineering, geometry, and other disciplines. They had to take into account the environment in which the home would be built, considering such factors as whether the soil and water table allowed for a basement, whether the summer temperatures warranted air-conditioning, and so on. Above all, the homes had to be *functional;* students were to determine who would live in the house and how the layout would meet the inhabitants' needs. Typically, the hypothetical residents were the students themselves, causing them to give great thought to their own living needs and the relationship of those needs to the materials and layout of the home.

Students had to consider the placement and shape of closets, the routing of ducts and electrical wiring, and all other aspects of house design. The text they composed—the house design—was meaningful because they had to create an area that would support the ways in which they wanted to conduct their lives. In the process, they had to consider whether they wanted to have a family, read books in a quiet study, entertain large groups of people, cook elaborate meals, engage in indoor recreation, or engage in other pursuits that would influence the design of the home.

Construction of the model houses took place through the course of the semester. As a result, students were in a continual state of drafting, with each plan graded throughout the course. Students had steady access to one another, the teacher, and all of resources of the classroom, and in addition were encouraged to study existing homes and construction sites. Students were thus involved in a lengthy process of composition that produced a text that helped define them as people.

The interior design class shared a similar concern with, as the teacher said, "being able to move things around in space." Students had to take into consideration line design, color, proportion, a sense of rhythm and balance in a room, and other factors that make a room attractive and functional. Students were responsible for designing a "dream home" that fit a defined lifestyle, which they identified through an early written consideration of their career plans, their marriage and family plans, and their hobbies and interests. They then designed the interior of their home around those thoughts and feelings. Their ultimate composition was a floor plan decorated with sample swatches.

> "Who dares to teach must never cease to learn.
>
> —John Cotton Dana

The homes, according to the teacher, needed "to be comfortable, to be useful, to be a good place to be." In order to make the home a "good place to be," students needed to think about the relationship between their own needs and the structure of the environment in which they would live. To establish this relationship, students needed to learn about functional spatial design, and thus engaged in such preliminary projects as redesigning a faulty kitchen. Through such instruction students learned the effects of different layouts and how to match different effects with different needs.

In all tasks, students could work collaboratively, though each student had to turn in an individual project. Like the architectural design students, the interior design students frequently worked outside class to increase their expertise, going to home furnishing stores to examine and bring to class samples of tile, wallpaper, and other materials. Like the architecture and equine-management classes, the course involved a lengthy process of learning and composition, with the semester's work synthesized in the design of a single, functional product. According to the teacher, "It's not a class where you say, well, turn it in at the end of the hour. It's an ongoing project. It's started from the first day of class; it's not a project you can finish next week or next month. It can just keep on building. I don't know that there's really an end to it."

My purpose with these descriptions is to help give you an idea of how students compose elsewhere in the school, particularly in areas where you might think there's little going on academically. Although they typically have less stature in the hierarchy of the school, such courses have much that core academic classes can learn from. In the next section, I'll talk about multimedia composing that I've observed in the English curriculum, where I had an opportunity to spend more time with the students to learn about how they learned.

Field Observation

In a school you're visiting, observe a teacher, or a set of teachers, from a discipline other than English. In your observations, try to identify the following:

- What the teacher considers "knowledge"
- How the teacher teaches that knowledge
- How the students are asked to show what they know
- What they learn through the process of showing it
- How the teacher grades their products
- The degree to which students are in the flow of learning

If possible, interview the teacher, using questions based on your observations, with the goal of understanding the teacher's view of knowledge and how students best develop and reveal it.

MULTIMEDIA COMPOSING IN ENGLISH

As I've said at many points in this book, English classes can be the sites of multimedia composing, although they are more likely to require students to write. I have had the opportunity to observe and talk with students who interpreted literature with art, dance, music, and drama. Through these interpretations they learned new things about the stories they read and about themselves. I'll next describe one such class I observed, the story the students read, and the way I studied their composing processes. The school was an alternative school for students who were recovering from substance abuse. I chose this school because, as an alternative school, it was more likely to value alternative approaches to teaching and learning. I also had a good working relationship with the teacher, who was well-versed in the work of Howard Gardner, came from an artistic family himself, and frequently used the arts in conjunction with the English curriculum. I can't reveal the names of anyone from the school, including the teacher, because I agreed to keep everyone's identity confidential as a condition of being allowed to work with the students.

In order to study their composing processes, we filmed students as they read a story, chose collaborators (or decided to work alone), discussed possible tools for interpretation, discussed the story's meaning, and worked out an interpretive text such as a dance, a painting, a song, or other type of composition. They could choose the materials for their interpretation from an abundant set of supplies provided by the teacher, including pens and paper for writing.

The story they responded to was William Carlos Williams's "The Use of Force." (See http://www.bnl.com/shorts/stories/force.html for an online version of this story.) In this story a doctor narrates an account of a house call he makes during a diphtheria epidemic. The doctor must extract a throat culture from a young girl who has displayed symptoms of the illness. The girl battles him savagely and hysterically to prevent him from examining her throat, and her parents try to help the doctor by holding her down and shaming her into complying. During the course of the struggle the doctor develops contempt for the parents and passion toward the girl. Against his rational judgment, the doctor becomes lost in "a blind fury" to attack and subdue her. In "a final unreasoning assault," he overpowers the girl and discovers her "secret" of "tonsils covered with membrane." The story ends with a final act of fury in which the girl attacks the doctor "while tears of defeat blinded her eyes."

After filming students as they produced their interpretations, we played back the video for several groups and asked them to recall and discuss what they had been thinking about during their reading and response. Through this procedure we learned much about how these students developed their interpretive texts. The students we interviewed included

- one boy who drew a picture representing the relationship between the two central characters in the story
- two girls who choreographed a dance representing this same relationship
- four boys who worked on a sophisticated keyboard synthesizer to create a soundtrack that represented the changing moods and rhythms of the story
- a group of three boys and one girl who scripted and dramatized the story

Through the interviews, the students revealed that they had engaged in a variety of processes that teachers value in writing. The students

- drew on a wealth of personal experiences to inform their reading of the story and to compose their texts
- empathized with the characters by relating parallel experiences
- imbued their texts with personal meaning
- represented their understanding symbolically
- drew on previously read texts both to inform their reading and to create their own texts
- drew on historical knowledge to interpret the story and create their own texts
- produced compositions that were sensitive to the mood and tempo of the story
- generated alternative endings to the story that focused on characters' emotional states rather than on the story's literal action
- viewed their work on this text as part of a larger composing process
- recognized the ambiguity of the story, their own texts, and human experience
- strove to communicate their understanding of the story to others

Additionally, the process of creating these interpretive texts served a dual purpose: The students' thoughts both *shaped and were shaped by* the texts they composed. In other words, two simultaneous processes took place. On the one hand, as you would expect, students' thoughts about the story served as the material from which they developed their interpretations. On the other hand—and more significantly—*the process of composing their texts changed the way they thought about the story.* I'll next illustrate how these processes occurred.

All students reported drawing on personal experiences to compose their texts. Martha, who participated in the choreographed interpretation, played the role of the girl in the story. She said in her interview that she empathized strongly with the girl. She said that she, too, hated to have people look inside her and get to know her. She said that she hated going to the dentist and have him open her mouth to look inside. Just like the girl in the story, she often fought the dentist's efforts to look within her. I found her own description of these feelings quite moving. I will therefore quote them at some length.

Martha: It's tough for me. When I was hiding from [Jane in the dance] she was the doctor and I was the daughter, the little girl, and it was just like me. I hate people trying to find out who I am so I was basically hiding the way I always hide but I was hiding to be somebody else. I felt like I was hiding in the little girl, but it was me that was hiding, because I do that all the time. I hide from everybody.

Q: Did you feel for the character then?

Martha: Oh, yeah, I felt for the character. When I was dancing I was thinking about what I would do. I hated what the doctor did to her. I wanted to kill him.

Later in the interview Martha returned to her feelings about her character.

Martha: My feelings for the kid started when I was reading the story because there have been many times when I have had some problems. I'm like, I'm okay, get away. In a way I kind of knew how this girl was feeling whenever the doctor was trying to get into her mouth. I am like that with dentists. I hate dentists. I won't let them get into my mouth. I'm afraid they're going to pull out my teeth. It scares me. I try to keep my mouth shut, too. I put myself in her position through the whole story knowing she was scared and very insecure because she knows she is going to die. She knows through the whole story she's going to die. She doesn't want her parents to know about it.

Q: Is it just dentists? Earlier you were talking about how you don't like people in general getting inside you. So was it just a dentist or was it—

Martha: Well, for people to know me, I don't like for anyone to know me, it is really scary for people to know me. Who I am or anything like doctors, and stuff like that. I don't like them to look inside my mouth. With her I feel like she doesn't want the doctor to know she is dying because I am pretty sure because she could feel her tonsils. She knows she is dying. She knew it, she knew it was there and she knew she was going to die and she didn't want her mom to know. She didn't want her parents to know.

Martha's portrayal of the girl through her role in the dance, then, was informed by tremendous fears similar to those experienced by her character. The experience of playing out those fears through her participation in the dance allowed her to make a strong personal connection with the main character in the story.

Martha and her collaborator, Jane, created spatial relationships to show the emotional relationships between characters. Jane reported that they showed the antagonistic relationship between the doctor and girl through their positioning relative to one another: "When the doctor is trying to get her around to his way of thinking, we figuratively did it by going around in circles opposite each other."

Jane and Martha also created spatial relationships to show the characters' emotional states during the story. In order to do so, they needed to reconstruct the story line. In Williams's text the story ends with the girl attacking the doctor in a blind fury following his forcible extraction of the throat culture. Jane and Martha decided to focus on the doctor's feelings, rather than to follow the story line strictly. According to Jane:

> We did another dance at the very end and we were practicing on it and, like, she's sheltered, like the little girl is hidden. She won't let anybody find out what her secret is and that's what she's doing. She is hiding and the doctor is trying to follow in her footsteps to try to figure out what is going on. And at the very end when it says that she did have [diphtheria], in the dance we made her die. She just fell and the doctor picked her up and carried her. Because, like, we were going to have the doctor die with her because it was like the third patient he had died and he was dying inside, but [our teacher] didn't really like that. And after we started thinking, you know, how he gets underneath the skin real hard, it is like we started thinking about it too and he doesn't really die. He tries to help her and stuff. We went further than the story went.

Here Jane and Martha attempted to represent the figurative death of the character by physically having her die. After their teacher's intervention, they tried another approach, as described by Jane.

> That is when they finally figured it out. It is, like, at the very end they walked together. It's like they walk two steps and when you do a little pause, the doctor shelters her and just looks at her because he's died with her. His whole life has just gone down the drain because it's another kid; he feels it's all his fault this time. And that is how I really felt when I was doing the dance.

In their interpretation, they focused on the characters' emotions rather than on the literal story line provided by Williams. Their focus on the doctor's emotions required them to rewrite the ending. In some schools, their decision would be treated as a wrong interpretation because it departed from the literal story line. In a constructivist classroom, however, the girls had the opportunity to focus on the part of the story that held the most meaning for them and to reconstruct it for interpretive purposes.

A final point on this interpretation: In Chapter 3, I discussed the possibilities of engaging in a narrative way of knowing. Narrative knowledge involves verisimilitude, the likeness of truth, the creation of characters and events that represent emotional and social truths without replicating them. Well-formed narratives are distinguished by their believability even while they contain falsehoods. The reconstructed ending of Jane and Martha's interpretation carries powerful emotional resonance, even if it departs from the original story's literal conclusion. I would argue that the dramatic medium of dance allows for this interpretation in ways not typically provided in school.

A group of four boys approached their interpretation quite differently. They used a sophisticated keyboard instrument to compose a soundtrack that depicted the changing moods and rhythms of the story. None of the four students was a trained musician. The keyboard instrument, however, provided such a great range of sounds and dubbing capabilities that even a person with limited knowledge could program it for a soundtrack. The boys reported that their musical accompaniment was intended to represent the story line.

Cory:	They had this funky, like, Star Trek sound going on and I said, "This has nothing to do with the little girl not wanting to show her parents how she had the disease that could kill her," and they were, like, "r-r-r-r-r," and they had this funky sound on, and I was, like, you know, at first, you know, you need to have like a fight going, and then at the end where she was so enraged over— so enraged from defeat, that kind of mellowed out some because it, it would show the feelings and the end of defeat that the little girl was going through.
Q:	So did you say that the loud part showed the rage?
Cory:	Yeah, and her struggling, you know, how, having a kind of an intense sound because of her struggling, not wanting to open her mouth, not wanting to let that, that doctor do a throat culture.
Q:	Uh huh. And then the mellow sound was her—
Jake:	Defeat.

Rather than altering the story line to represent a particular emotional truth, these students tried to enhance the story line through a musical accompaniment. Providing this match required them to discuss in depth what they thought the story meant so that they could find the appropriate sounds to tell the story musically.

The compositions, then, revealed the students' thinking about the story. Simultaneously, *the process of composing the texts changed their thinking about the story.* Jane, one of the dancers, reported that her feelings about the doctor changed through her portrayal of him.

I finally figured out what it is like to be in the position of the doctor. That is why I didn't hate the doctor so much because I knew how he felt. . . . [I learned about] how the doctor felt. I knew his feelings, but knowing it and feeling it is totally different things. [I learned] about myself, that I can feel their feelings. I see how they feel.

A similar process was reported by other students I interviewed. A boy named Dexter drew a picture of the relationship between the doctor and the girl (see Fig-

FIGURE 11.1

ure 11.1). He said that the meaning of the drawing changed as his picture developed. For instance, Dexter's depiction of the doctor was quite threatening. Yet he revealed that when he started his drawing he was not certain what the threatening figure would stand for.

Dexter: I wasn't really sure if it was him going to be the doctor or not until the end of the story, I mean, until the end of the drawing, because I was thinking, well, it could be this person that she, that she has imaged in her mind and uh—or this could be an analogy of diphtheria, but then I said it doesn't matter. It's just a doctor. It was going through her mind, [inaudible] but I liked to read. The first time I'd read the doctor; the second, the analogy. It's just through that one story.

Q: So you mean, even after you drew the face and everything, it wasn't the doctor yet?

Dexter: Uh huh. I mean, it could have been a lot of things. It depends on your viewpoint of the picture, but what I was thinking is—it was the doctor and then it was an analogy of the whole attitude of the story, and then it was the, her parents' attitude, or the parents, especially her parents.

Dexter's understanding of the identity of the dominant figure in the drawing changed as he continued to draw the picture and think about the story. Some of these meanings (such as the mother or the disease) occurred to him *as he was drawing* and thinking about how to interpret the characters. These meanings are not evident from looking at the drawing, where the figure looks like a man, most likely the doctor. Not only did the picture represent Dexter's view of the characters, but the process of drawing the picture enabled him to develop new ideas about the story.

The dramatic production by the group of four also involved processes that developed their thoughts about the story. When discussing the dress Suzie would wear in her role as the girl, the students considered how it fit with the way in which they viewed the tone of the production.

Bart:	I don't know. That dress, it would make it look like she was a little—it just wouldn't look right just to fit the whole atmosphere of the play.
Wes:	I didn't think it would either, because she said it was real pretty, and I didn't think that would get—
Donnie:	See, the reason we thought about this is because in the story it says a little, fully dressed girl.
Suzie:	Not if you see the dress, then you would understand. It is like, it is real baggy, and it has flowers on it and stuff.
Wes:	I thought it would have one of them, like, penitentiary or work dresses, or like a sweater or cardigan.
Q:	You would think that would be a good dress to wear?
Wes:	That is what I pictured in my mind, something drab, not something fancy.

Their discussion about how to represent the relationships in the story helped them think clearly about the characters. Similarly, they discussed how the film *The Exorcist* might influence their depiction of the girl's transformation from withdrawn to enraged. During this discussion, Wes realized that he viewed the girl as "possessed," which enabled him to envision her in a particular way and interpret the story appropriately. Bart, too, developed his thinking about the story by thinking about it in terms of previous classes. He said that during the production of the play, "I was thinking about the extended definition of what abuse is, because they were talking about if you are a child abuser. Is it really abuse if someone cuts their hand and you give them a shot? That is hurting them, but it is to help them out later. I was thinking about that. How ambiguous abuse can be. What abuse means."

Through his participation in the play, Bart continued his previous deliberation on the definition of abuse. His efforts to represent the doctor's treatment of the girl forced him to reconsider other academic material from the curriculum and integrate it into his view of the story and his beliefs about abuse, a prominent topic among students in this substance abuse treatment center.

Discussion Topic

To what extent is multimedia composing appropriate in an English class? How would you justify multimedia composing if it were opposed by students, parents, colleagues, or administrators?

FINAL THOUGHTS

In this chapter I have tried to show two things. One is that, across the curriculum, it's more important to think in terms of *composing* than to assume that writing is the best and only vehicle for helping students think about subject matter. The illustrations I've given make a strong case that English teachers can learn a great deal from observing teachers from other disciplines and trying to understand what it means to construct meaning outside the realm of English.

Multimedia Composing

Look back through the unit you are designing. To what extent are your students involved in meaningful composing? How can you revise your unit so as to encourage the kinds of learning described in this chapter?

The second thing I've tried to show is that in an English class, there is potential for great learning through media other than writing. The students I've described here produced meaningful texts through a variety of media. From what I could tell, all of their composing activity got them in the flow of learning. I believe strongly that what they accomplished through their compositions was much more worthwhile than listening to a lecture on the story and passing a test on it. Instead, using the constructivist principles of the teacher's instruction, they composed texts that both represented their understanding of the story and, in the process, enabled them to understand both the story and themselves better.

Detailed Reports of These Studies

Smagorinsky, P. (1995). Constructing meaning in the disciplines: Reconceptualizing writing across the curriculum as composing across the curriculum. *American Journal of Education, 103,* 160–184.

Smagorinsky, P. (1995). Multiple intelligences in the English class: An overview. *English Journal, 84*(8), 19–26.

Smagorinsky, P. (1996). Multiple intelligences, multiple means of composing: An alternative way of thinking about learning. *NASSP Bulletin, 80*(583), 11–17.

Smagorinsky, P. (1997). Artistic composing as representational process. *Journal of Applied Developmental Psychology, 18,* 87–105.

Smagorinsky, P. (1997). Personal growth in social context: A high school senior's search for meaning in and through writing. *Written Communication, 14,* 63–105.

Smagorinsky, P. (1999). The world is a stage: Dramatic enactment as response to literature. In B. J. Wagner (Ed.), *Building moral communities through drama* (pp. 19–38). Stamford, CT: Ablex.

Smagorinsky, P. (2002). If meaning is constructed, what's it made of?: Toward a cultural theory of reading. *Review of Educational Research.*

Smagorinsky, P., & Coppock, J. (1994). Cultural tools and the classroom context: An exploration of an alternative response to literature. *Written Communication, 11,* 283–310.

Smagorinsky, P., & Coppock, J. (1994, Fall). Exploring an evocation of the literary work: Processes and possibilities of an artistic response to literature. *Reader,* 62–74.

Smagorinsky, P., & Coppock, J. (1994). Exploring artistic response to literature. In C. K. Kinzer & D. J. Leu (Eds.), *Multidimensional aspects of literacy research, theory, and practice* (pp. 335–341). *Forty-Third Yearbook of the National Reading Conference.* Chicago: National Reading Conference.

Smagorinsky, P., & Coppock, J. (1995). The reader, the text, the context: An exploration of a choreographed response to literature. *Journal of Reading Behavior, 27,* 271–298.

Smagorinsky, P., & Coppock, J. (1995). Reading through the lines: An exploration of drama as a response to literature. *Reading and Writing Quarterly, 11,* 369–391.

CHAPTER

12 Building Body Biographies

This chapter offers a glimpse at more multimedia and multigenre composing, this time in a different teacher's class in a more mainstream school. The students produced interpretations of *Hamlet* through a *body biography,* a life-sized human outline that students would fill with significant images and language from the play. I describe the classroom, the *Hamlet* unit, and the assignment. I then present a set of discussions that took place as students composed their body biographies. The discussions reveal that, as with the students described in Chapter 11, the students in this class exhibited sophisticated thinking about a difficult work of literature as they produced their artistic interpretations. The discussions also revealed that the interactions in different groups were quite different in terms of the human relationships established, with some groups working cooperatively and others involving conflict and abusive treatment. I conclude with a general endorsement of collaborative work of this type, with the understanding that it does not guarantee full cooperation among all students.

In Chapter 11, I described multimedia composing (a) across the curriculum in a mainstream high school and (b) in the English curriculum of an alternative school. Throughout this book, I have tried to impress on you that the environment in which you teach will place limitations on the ways in which you teach. The alternative school provided a setting where teachers had far more freedom in how to teach than you'll find in most mainstream schools. The alternative school revealed that it's possible for students to compose meaningful multimedia texts as a way to interpret literature and for their composition of those texts to help them arrive at new meaning about both themselves and the literature. Once I'd found that this was possible I wanted to know whether teachers in mainstream schools, surrounded by mandates and authoritative teaching traditions, could include such activities in their English classes.

REFLECTING ON MY OWN TEACHING

Of course, I knew it was possible, because I'd done it myself, both in a school where the speech program supported alternative ways of teaching and in one where many of my colleagues taught in the manner of Mr. Harris, whom I profiled in Chapter 10. In both schools, I was blessed with bright and knowledgeable colleagues who, almost without exception, were highly regarded by their students. The different environments, however, supported and encouraged different ways of teaching.

I was fortunate that in both places, I was able to teach in ways that suited my notion of effective instruction. In the second of these two schools, however, my teaching went more against the grain of the teaching practices that my students were accustomed to. When students complained about my teaching—and no matter where or how you teach, you'll get complaints—it was often because students felt they were getting something different from what their friends were getting in other classes. They were worried about falling behind, even if they weren't quite sure where the race was headed or why they were running it. My feeling was that you can't fall behind if you're not headed in the same direction.

From these experiences, I knew that the environment of teaching affects how well your teaching practices will be understood and appreciated. This environment is provided by administrators who set policies and preside over teaching evaluations, by colleagues who set the norms for how English gets taught, and by students who tend to feel that whatever's normal is probably right. All of these come within the larger contexts of community values, district and state policies, high-stakes assessment movements, the political climate, and other factors.

The alternative school had provided an environment that supported alternative ways of teaching and learning. The therapeutic mission of the school promoted academic instruction that involved reflection and personal realization, since a successful student was one who kicked the habit. My question was, in a different kind of school, one with traditional values and practices, could a teacher include multimedia composing in ways that were taken seriously?

Again, I knew from my own career experiences that it was possible. I'd taught in ways that produced highly insightful interpretative texts. I'd drawn this conclusion from my informal observations of my students at work and from the quality of the products they'd produced. What I had never had, however, was the chance to study and understand the *processes* students went through to produce these compositions. Describing these processes, it seemed, was necessary in order to persuade other people that students are doing far more than "just drawing" when interpreting literature through an artistic medium.

MULTIMEDIA COMPOSING IN A MAINSTREAM SCHOOL

My opportunity finally came during the year I observed the classroom of Cindy O'Donnell-Allen, who taught in a mainstream high school in Oklahoma. Cindy's school was similar to the more traditional school I had taught in: college prep curriculum, highly regarded faculty, diverse student body, and generally traditional approaches to curriculum and instruction. After beginning her career in another part of the state, Cindy had taken this job several years before. From the beginning, she had taught in ways that were different from those of the majority of her colleagues. Her mother's work as a kindergarten teacher had opened her eyes to the possibilities of using a cross-disciplinary teaching approach that involved students heavily in activity. Her first teaching assignment as a speech and drama teacher had also influenced her belief in the importance of having students take active roles in the classroom.

She also had a number of means of support, which turned out to be important to her in her efforts to teach against the grain. Several of her colleagues tried to pressure her into teaching more conventionally. She was able to resist these efforts in part because of her determination to teach in ways she found effective and in part because she had external support for using them. The midlevel administrator in her school who oversaw the English department was a great admirer of her work. This admiration led to support for Cindy's teaching, which enabled her to persist even when her risks want awry or when other members of her faculty expressed their disapproval of her methods.

Cindy also found support from outside the school. She maintained her membership in the National Council of Teachers of English and the Oklahoma Council of Teachers of English, both of which supported the kinds of unconventional teaching she practiced. She attended a summer institute of the local affiliate of the National Writing Project, an organization that advocates process-oriented teaching. She maintained her affiliation with the Writing Project throughout her teaching career, including a term of service on the advisory board. Ultimately, she founded a teacher-research group within the Writing Project. This group met every month to discuss and support one another's classroom research projects. In addition, she became active in the organization responsible for the Advanced Placement exam, frequently making presentations at their conferences about how to teach AP courses in constructivist ways.

Through these memberships, she came in contact with teachers from other schools with whom she could share ideas, find kindred spirits, and discuss ways to persist in the face of resistance. She also found people who could recommend good books about teaching and with whom she could discuss the books' merits and applications. This reading proved to be very influential in the teaching practices she adopted for her classroom.

She also continued her education, enrolling in a master's degree program that further supported her efforts to teach in learner-centered, process-oriented, multimedia, growth-oriented ways. Through this program, she came in contact with texts, students, and faculty whose influences helped her modify and develop her ideas about teaching. Earning a master's degree also increased her authority within her school and gave her further license to teach according to her principles. Finally, it helped tie her in with a local community of like-minded teachers, an important network for any teachers who find their ideas about teaching unique in their own schools.

Through the university Cindy got an email account, which enabled her to stay in contact with people she met in her professional activities and to subscribe to professional listserves (i.e., electronic discussions on a particular topic). Her ability to connect electronically with teachers around the world gave her a broadened sense of community and an understanding that even if her methods were unusual in her school, they were part of a vibrant teaching tradition that was ardently practiced worldwide.

My point with this extensive description is to let you know that, in many schools, the prevailing environment will support authoritative, text-centered, and form-oriented

Books Involving Progressive Education

Applebee, A. (1974). *Tradition and reform in the teaching of English: A history.* Urbana, IL: National Council of Teachers of English.

Dewey, J. (1916). *Democracy and education: An introduction to the philosophy of education.* New York: The Free Press.

Dewey, J. (1928). *Progressive education and the science of education.* Washington, DC: Progressive Education Association.

Graham, P. A. (1967). *Progressive education from Arcady to academe: A history of the Progressive Education Association, 1919–1955.* New York: Teachers College Press.

Jackson, P. W. (1998). *John Dewey and the lessons of art.* New Haven, CT: Yale University Press.

Jervis, C., & Montag, C. (1991). *Progressive education for the 1990s: Transforming practice.* New York: Teachers College Press.

Pflaum, S. W., & Pignatelli, F. (1993). *Celebrating diverse voices: Progressive education and equity.* Newbury Park, CA: Corwin.

Winick, M. P. (1978). *The progressive education movement: An annotated bibliography.* New York: Garland.

teaching. In order for you to adopt the principles I advocate in this book, it's possible that you will need to teach against the grain. Doing so requires confidence and persistence, and is greatly helped by finding support. While being in the minority, you are rarely alone in your own building, and it's important to find colleagues with whom you can provide a rationale and base of support for your teaching approach.

In order to persist over time, you'll find it useful to affiliate yourself with broader teaching communities where you can continue to discuss the merits of teaching in unconventional ways and come in contact with books, speakers, colleagues, and other resources that help you extend your knowledge. By finding these communities and networks of like-minded colleagues, you will find that your approach is part of a long-standing tradition of teaching often called *progressive*.

THE CLASSROOM

I next turn to a more particular description of Cindy's class. I've already made reference to it in previous chapters, and here will try to give some idea of the flavor of her arrangement of the classroom and her methods of teaching. I will then describe a particular episode that took place in February when her students composed multimedia interpretations of Shakespeare's *Hamlet* through an artistic medium called a body biography. This description will focus on the composing processes the students went through to produce these interpretations, which we studied by analyzing transcripts of the discussions they engaged in while working.

> The secret to education is respecting the pupil.
>
> —Ralph Waldo Emerson

Earlier, I described the way in which Cindy set up the classroom environment by having her students brainstorm ideas for the room's decor and then putting them in charge of putting their plan into effect. Within this student-constructed environment, she strove to allow all students opportunities for making personal connections and thinking open-endedly about problems through classroom activities. She also stressed conventional academic literacies, with the understanding that part of students' success comes through their knowledge of how to "do school." Her class included

- a reader-response pedagogy (i.e., one that provides for individual readers to make personal constructions of meaning for literature)
- process-oriented classes designed to promote personal reflection and growth among students
- activity-based and student-centered methods of developing literacy skills
- reliance on students' life experiences to inform their understanding of literature and to provide the basis for their writing topics
- frequent use of small groups, exploratory discussion, response logs, and nontraditional assessment
- attention to conventions of language use, particularly writing and the genres of academic discourse
- attention to unconventional genres and their potential for promoting learning

Reflective Writing Prompt

How was Shakespeare handled when you studied it in high school? What were the teacher's goals in teaching his plays? What role did the teacher and students play in classroom interactions? What did you learn from studying Shakespeare?

I have given examples of how these values looked in practice elsewhere in this book. I will next describe a particular unit that she taught to begin the second semester of the students' senior year. It would qualify as a conceptual unit as outlined in previous chapters, as it focused on the work of a single author, Shakespeare. As is typical of the senior British literature curriculum, the Shakespeare unit was required within the department, with *Hamlet* the text of choice. I will describe the general outline of the unit and then focus on the ways in which students talked while working in small groups on their body biography compositions.

THE *HAMLET* UNIT

Cindy's role during their reading of *Hamlet* was, in some ways, similar to the role she had taken in previous conceptual units. The class involved a great deal of student activity and performance. Cindy tried to link the language and themes of the play to what students already knew, although without requiring disclosure of experiences related to the play's more sensitive themes (e.g., incest).

However, the challenges of reading such a difficult work of literature caused her to be far more directive in her teaching than she ordinarily was. She had deliberately chosen accessible literature during the first semester. Her reasoning was that if they started with more readable literature, students would more easily make personal connections and then apply methods of personal response independently. The choice of more accessible literature to start with, then, was part of her effort to scaffold their learning.

Shakespeare, however, presented greater challenges because of the complexity and unfamiliarity of the language in the play. She included more direct instruction on certain aspects of the play. This instruction included explicit lessons on interpreting Shakespearean language, borrowing from Robinson's *Unlocking Shakespeare's Language* (1989). Robinson's lessons are designed to help students understand the vocabulary, syntactic structures, and other arcane aspects of Shakespearean language.

For their reading of *Hamlet,* Cindy drew heavily on her background as a drama teacher. She stressed performance-based activities and teaching strategies to help students interpret the text independently. The room was set up so that students could get up and take part in performances. Their desks were set up in a two-tiered U-shape with the class sofa, originally placed at an angle in a back corner of the room, moved to the center of the inner U. This arrangement left a large space in the front and center of the room that functioned as a stage. During the reading of the play, students gathered comfortably in this open area on the couch, seats, and carpet. At the front of the class was a record player and TV that she used for audio and videotape versions of the play.

Cindy began the unit by having students participate in a summary choral reading she had written that included lines from the play bridged with modern-day language. They referred to this activity later in the unit when they created their own study guides for each act of the play. These study guides required students to

- create titles for each scene
- write a summary of the scene
- list and describe each character's function in the scene
- select and respond to what they saw as the most significant conflict and quotation from the scene

Students later used these study guides to help them complete class projects and to study for quizzes and the blue-book essay exam Cindy gave at the end of the unit.

Students performed their reading of the play. A revolving cast of students would stand in the open space at the front of the classroom while reading their lines, with the intention of giving some idea of relationships and action of the play. Cindy alternated such readings with both the Zeffirelli film version of *Hamlet* and an audio performance that she played on a portable, battered record player from an earlier epoch. When she broke out the record player for the first time, I wrote the following in my observation notes:

> This looks like a stereo from when I was in elementary school, circa maybe 1960, with a needle like a nail, a turntable like a potter's wheel in one of those vomit-brown fold-up carrying cases where the top half becomes the speakers. On goes the record, crackling as the needle hits the vinyl, popping along in accompaniment to the dialogue of the play. . . . After a few lines Cindy stopped the turntable with a pause knob, asked some questions, then started it up again, record grinding back into motion, carving another divot into the vinyl.

Well, so much for the technological revolution. At any rate, through Cindy's use of audio, video, and student readings, the class was exposed to different interpretations of the characters as they proceeded through the acts and became acquainted with the ancient technology of the phonograph record.

Periodically, Cindy would conduct an interview with students, who would play various roles from the play. The purpose was to have them explain their characters and their understanding of their relationships. The students also performed group *freeze frames* in which they chose an event from the play, decided why it was the most important one they had read, worked out a modern interpretation of it, titled it, and then performed it for the class. After other students tried to guess which event they were performing, the group's defense of its choice served as a springboard for additional class discussion of the entire scene. Through this activity the students were able to

- discuss the play in their own language
- interpret it through depictions that represented their own worlds
- translate Shakespeare's language so that they could express their own experiences and concerns through Shakespearean themes and characters

THE BODY BIOGRAPHY ASSIGNMENT

At the conclusion of the play, Cindy organized the class into five groups, with each group responsible for interpreting a different character through a *body biography*. She had adapted this activity from an idea she'd come across in her professional reading, in an article in the *English Journal* published by the National Council of Teachers of English (see Underwood, 1987). For this activity, each group was provided a large sheet of butcher paper on which to trace the outline of one of the students. Within this outline they drew pictures, wrote words, and included key lines from the play that they believed represented significant aspects of the character's personality, experiences, actions, and relationships. The assignment she gave them was as follows:

Body Biography

For your chosen character, your group will be creating a *body biography*—a visual and written portrait illustrating several aspects of the character's life within the play.

You have many possibilities for filling up your giant sheet of paper. I have listed several, but please feel free to come up with your own creations. As always, the choices you make should be based on the text, for you will be verbally explaining (and thus, in a sense, defending) them at a showing of your work. Above all, your choices should be creative, analytical, and accurate.

After completing this portrait, you will participate in a showing in which you will present your masterpiece to the class. This showing should accomplish these objectives. It should:

- review significant events, choices, and changes involving your character
- communicate to us the full essence of your character by emphasizing the traits that make her/him who s/he is
- promote discussion of your character (esp. regarding gender issues in the play)

Body Biography Requirements

Although I expect your biography to contain additional dimensions, your portrait *must* contain:

- a review of significant happenings in the play
- visual symbols
- an original text
- your character's three most important lines from the play

Body Biography Suggestions

1. *Placement*—Carefully choose the placement of your text and artwork. For example, the area where your character's heart would be might be appropriate for illustrating the important relationships within his or her life.
2. *Spine*—Actors often discuss a character's spine. This is her/his objective within the play. What is the most important goal for your character? What drives her/his thoughts and actions? This is her/his spine. How can you illustrate it?
3. *Virtues and Vices*—What are your character's most admirable qualities? Her/his worst? How can you make us visualize them?
4. *Color*—Colors are often symbolic. What color(s) do you most associate with your character? Why? How can you effectively work these colors into your presentation?
5. *Symbols*—What objects can you associate with your character that illustrate her/his essence? Are there objects mentioned within the play itself that you could use? If not, choose objects that especially seem to correspond with the character.
6. *Formula Poems*—These are fast, but effective, recipes for producing a text because they are designed to reveal a lot about a character. (See the additional handouts I gave you for directions and examples.)
7. *Mirror, Mirror. . . .*—Consider both how your character appears to others on the surface and what you know about the character's inner self. Do these images clash or correspond? What does this tell you about the character?
8. *Changes*—How has your character changed within the play? Trace these changes within your text and/or artwork.

Students were initially given one day of class time to prepare their body biographies. Since the school used a block schedule, these periods lasted 84 minutes. Cindy also told students that they were welcome to use her room before or after school and during any periods when she wasn't teaching to work on their projects. This extra time included a 30-minute period right before lunch called Overtime, when teachers made themselves available to any student who wished to drop in for extra help.

Cindy adjusted the schedule when she decided that the majority of students were working diligently on the assignment yet not making enough progress to finish by her original deadline. Toward the end of the period, then, she made an adjustment and decided to give them an extra period to conclude their work.

I next describe the processes that took place as they composed their body biographies.

WHAT STUDENTS LEARNED THROUGH THEIR COMPOSING OF BODY BIOGRAPHIES

In Chapter 11, I described learning that took place when students interpreted "The Use of Force" through artistic media of their choice. I relied on students' memories of what they had been thinking while composing, stimulated by a videotape that they watched of themselves in the process of composition. In Cindy's class, we took a different approach. We placed a tape recorder with each group to record the discussions they engaged in while working. To do so, we had to spread the groups out: One worked in the hallway, one worked in a vacant class next door, and the other three were dispersed throughout the room so that the recordings would not be obscured by conversations from other groups. We were successful in recording four of the five groups so that we could understand how they talked as they collaborated on their body biographies.

We next had the tapes transcribed and spent several months reading them carefully in order to try to understand what students had learned during their group compositions. We found that all four of the groups we studied were able to come up with a good interpretation of their character and represent it in their body biographies. We also found that two of the groups functioned quite harmoniously and two did not. I will next use selected examples from the group discussions to explain both their interpretations and their social relationships. Each discussion was quite long, taking up at least one block period, so I'll only offer excerpts to illustrate the processes we found.

Composing Processes for Body Biographies

One group of four girls (one of whom was mostly absent) interpreted the character of Ophelia in their body biography (see Figure 12.1). One way that the group understood Ophelia was by thinking about her as if she were a modern teenager. They did this in spite of the fact that, when making the assignment, Cindy had decided not to require personal connections to the characters. She would ordinarily encourage such responses, but did not want to require students to talk publicly about their personal experiences with the controversial themes of incest, murder, betrayal and so on that run throughout the play. In this case, her respect for her students' sense for privacy and propriety outweighed her beliefs about response to literature.

In the following excerpt, the girls discuss Ophelia's relationship with her father and how they might depict it. In their consideration of this relationship, they talk about Ophelia as if she were a friend:

Carly:	What else did she do? She had, oh, she talked to Hamlet. Oh, and she had followed her dad, she obeyed her dad.
Sherri:	Right.
Ann:	That's right, I forgot about that.
Sherri:	Draw it in kind of a little circle. She wasn't scared of Hamlet, was she?
Carly:	No—

FIGURE 12.1   Ophelia

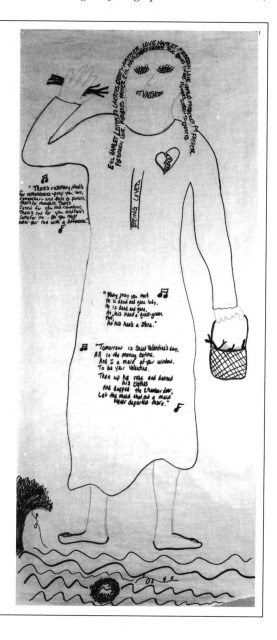

Hair:
EVIL HAMLET LISTEN TO LAERTES OBEY FATHER.
LOVE HAMLET.
FORBIDDEN LOVE. HAMLET MURDERED MY FATHER.
FORBIDDEN LOVE. MURDERED FATHER. EVIL
HAMLET. OBEY FATHER.
TRUE, BONES, TWIGS, FLOWERS, LISTEN TO
LAERTES

Eyes:
HAMLET FATHER

Mouth:
ST. VALENTINE

Heart:
HAMLET

Spine:
BEING LOVED

"There's rosemary, that's for remembrance—pray you love,
remember—and there is pansies, that's for thoughts.
There's fennel for you and columbines. There's rue for you,
and here's some for me. Oh you must wear your rue with a
difference."

"Nay, pray you mark
He is dead and gone lady,
He is dead and gone,
At his head a grass-green turn.
And his heels a stone."

"Tomorrow is Saint Valentine's day.
All in the morning betime.
And I a maid at your window.
To be your Valentine.
Then up he rose and donned his clothes
And dupped the chamber door.
Let the maid that out a maid.
Never departed more."

Ann:	But she was hurt by him.
Carly:	She was really hurt by him, though.
Ann:	If we had an old study guide—
Carly:	Oh, my gosh, if we could just even go through the book. She did so much more that we're not even thinking of, let's see—
Sherri:	What about that part where Hamlet says, "You're not who you think you are"? Remember that time—

Ann:	When he tells her to go to the nunnery?
Carly:	Oh yeah, was that—? She must have a real low self-esteem. We should probably put that down there.
Sherri:	A low self-esteem?
Ann:	Well, I mean, how could you have a high one with all those people around you telling you what to do and—
Carly:	Yeah, really.
Ann:	Telling you to go to the nunnery.
Carly:	Do we ever hear her and, like, Laertes talking, like maybe we should put something like Laertes in there.
Ann:	Yeah, Laertes told her not to date Hamlet.
Sherri:	Oh, that's right.
Carly:	What else?

This excerpt shows how they thought about Ophelia in terms of their own understanding of how girls act in society. Both their comments about Ophelia's self-esteem (a relatively modern concern) and their teen language (e.g., the order "not to date Hamlet") suggest that they viewed Ophelia in light of their modern experiences as teenage girls. By making this connection with the character, they constructed an interpretation of the ways in which Ophelia established relationships with other characters in the play.

This brief excerpt shows how their personal connection, and their effort to depict Ophelia's relationships in the play, led them to discuss the character in ways that showed some insight into her psyche. One common kind of criticism that you can anticipate when doing things like body biographies is that some people—including students, colleagues, and parents—will think you're watering down the curriculum by having students "just draw pictures" instead of doing cognitive work. This brief excerpt shows that there's more going on than drawing pictures—the students need to discuss the character in order for the picture to make sense.

In this next section I'll show other examples of the kind of symbolic and inferential thinking that students do when just drawing pictures. The research base that I draw these examples from should, I think, provide a rationale that can effectively refute the idea that this kind of work is in any way lightweight or unchallenging cognitively. In my view, the real concern for any parent, student, or teacher should be that schoolwork can reduce a complex text like *Hamlet* to something trivial. I assume that some might view drawing pictures as trivial. I hope that I'll show here that such is not the case. I think that I could much more easily show that a factual exam that requires the relatively low-level cognitive process of memorization would be a far more trivial way to engage with the play.

We consistently found that the students in all groups engaged in symbolic thinking while composing their body-biography interpretations. I'll next give examples from a couple of different groups of the kinds of symbolic and inferential thinking involved in producing the texts.

The group that interpreted Gertrude included five students: Rita, Jack, Dirk, Bob, and James. As you will see later, this group was highly problematic in terms of its social relationships. In spite of the interpersonal dynamics, they produced a compelling interpretive text (see Figure 12.2) for their body biography.

FIGURE 12.2   Gertrude

"What have I done that thou dar'st wag thy tongue. In noise so rude against me."

"Sweets to the sweet! Farewell! I hoped thou shouldst have been my Hamlet's wife. I thought thy bride-bed to have decked, sweet maid, and have not strewed thy grave!"

"I doubt it is no other than the main. His fathers death and our o'hasty marriage"

"and for your part Ophelia, I do wish that your good beauties be the happy cause of Hamlet's wildness."

"Mother, you have my father much offended."

"Oh, speak to me no more. These words like daggers enter in my ears. No more, sweet Hamlet."

On arm:
I am so confused
I am a couch because I want everyone to be comfortable
I wish everything would work out.
I hope Hamlet is okay.
I dream of Hamlet and Ophelia together.

On head:
HAMLET
CLAUDIUS
OPHELIA

On necklace: Claudius

On loin: LUST

In split heart: Hamlet Claudius

In whole heart: OPHELIA

The group spent a great deal of time discussing what they felt was a central event in the play, the accidental poisoning of Gertrude by Claudius. They drew a goblet falling from her hand to represent this incident on the literal level. From there, they began to discuss how the poisoning led to a series of events, passions, and relationships. As they discussed how to depict the falling goblet, Rita said, "I think we need to put something about how she really did like Ophelia, but I don't know how."

From there the group decided to consider Gertrude's loyalties in the play, particularly those toward three key characters: Claudius, Hamlet, and Ophelia. They discussed her divided loyalties between Claudius (her second husband and the brother of her first husband, King Hamlet) and Hamlet (her son who disapproved of her second marriage and suspected Claudius of murdering King Hamlet). They represented these loyalties in two ways, both in her *heart* and in her *head.*

The group decided to draw two hearts, one split between Claudius and Hamlet and one devoted to Ophelia. Dirk explained to Bob what the divided hearts symbolized:

Bob:	Working on her heart?
Dirk:	We're going to show, like, Claudius and Ophelia, and the broken hearts is going to be where she was disgracing, finding out that Claudius was trying to poison her.
Bob:	So, which one is gonna be her—
Dirk:	That one, yeah.
James:	What about King Hamlet?
Dirk:	[inaudible] Hamlet decided to have [Ophelia] as a [inaudible] and to marry her and then at the end [Gertrude] finds out that Ophelia dies and she is heartbroken about this. And [Gertrude] is heartbroken about Claudius, trying to find out, she finds out that Claudius was trying to kill her. That's what we're going to do.

Dirk's account of the play was not entirely accurate in that Claudius intends to poison Hamlet's drink, not Gertrude's. Gertrude is the one, however, who drinks from the poisoned goblet. Claudius watches without intervening so he won't implicate himself in the poisoning. The effect of Claudius's killing Gertrude, however, is the same. In their presentation of the body biography to the class the following week, Rita explained that in the divided heart, "One is Hamlet, Claudius, and she is split between them. Then she has a big heart for Ophelia because I really think she liked her."

The discussion of the character's head followed. This discussion paralleled the one about the heart. Early on Rita had decided to draw the head as a skull. Later they decided to divide it into three sections and devote each to a character central to Gertrude's feelings. As Rita noted, each of these characters was someone Gertrude felt "torn" about.

Bob:	Do we divide her head in the middle?
Rita:	Yeah, you know why?
Bob:	Because she loves Claudius, she loves Hamlet Senior.
Rita:	We should crack it. You know, like when cartoon characters, like, are skiing and they, like, hit something—
Bob:	Oh yeah, and it, like, separates.
Rita:	—and their whole body is, like, cracked, and they go, like— Because she's got all these different parts, or—

The body biography composition, then, was not simply a drawing. It evolved through what we thought was a very sophisticated discussion of a very difficult work of literature. What's notable is that this discussion took place entirely without the benefit of adult guidance. While Cindy had provided direction during the reading of the play, the group's discussion, interpretation, and composition came about independently. As should be evident from the discussion, the students' talk was exploratory and constructive, often building on one another's contributions to create a collaborative idea. This kind of talk is quite different from the interpretive opportunities that students get in the authoritative discussions reviewed in Chapter 10.

Students in the group that interpreted Ophelia (see Figure 12.1) built on their personal connection to the character to interpret her symbolically in their text. The assignment called for the students to use both art and writing to interpret the character. The girls in this group came up with the original idea of combining art and writing when they decided to draw Ophelia's hair in the form of phrases:

Carly:	What are we going to put for her to obey her dad?
Ann:	I don't know, we need some kind of symbol.
Carly:	Maybe in her hair.
Ann:	We could put something, and then have, like, "Listen to dad"—
Carly:	See, we could put on her hair, instead of actually drawing hair, we could write "Dad" in, like, the curves, do you know what I am saying?
Ann:	Yeah, I think so.
Sherri:	Okay, but we can't draw it in back of her, she's, like—
Ann:	We could put, like, "Listens to dad, obeys dad, dad died," et cetera.
Carly:	Yeah, Dad slash Hamlet.
Ann:	We could like list all of the things that made her go crazy in her hair.
Carly:	Okay, yeah! That's awesome! Good idea, okay.
Ann:	Okay, but I don't think I'm going to turn that into a coffin.
Carly:	Okay, that's good because that would be—I'm sorry if I put my butt in your face—I'll draw it in her hair.
Ann:	And her hair has to be brown, too, that's what color her hair was.
Carly:	Okay, can I, with chunks of black, like one letter being black or something. Okay, I'm going to, is it okay if I write a song in here?
Sherri:	Uh huh.
Carly:	Okay, where is her first song? What does she say first? She says something really interesting first. Where's the, no, okay, maybe not. Should I just put all of her songs because they're not very long and they all say something interesting? Or should I put that—?

This example illustrates a process I described in Chapter 11 that I think is a key aspect of composing a meaningful text. That is, not only does the text represent their thinking, but the process of composing the text enables the students to reflect on their ideas in such a way that they generate new meaning. The process works in this way:

1. The group works out a way of functioning socially (which, as I'll show next, does not always happen the way you'd hope).
2. Group members generate images of the play that they picture in their heads and then try to describe to the other students.
3. Other students then respond to these proposed images and compare them to their own images of the same character, scene, or relationship. This response usually requires students to clarify both their image and their reasons for believing it is fitting and to discuss which images best suit the play as they understand it.
4. Individual group members then explain to one another the image that they think should go into the body biography. In doing so, the group needs to discuss why they think particular images are apt. This discussion typically involves a return to the text they're interpreting so that students can defend particular interpretations.
5. When they reach agreement through discussion, they draw the image into the body biography.
6. Once included on the body biography, each word and image then becomes part of a text that they can use as a source of further reflection, discussion, and interpretation.

We saw this process in each group composition. Another example comes from the body biography of Laertes produced by June, Lisa, Troy, Venus, and Courtney (see Figure 12.3). Here they discuss how to depict Laertes' relationship with Hamlet, whose death he causes. In the discussion, the students generate images of the character in their effort to come up with the text of their body biography:

Courtney:	Should I draw him stabbed?
June:	That looks good.
Courtney:	Like a little quotation. He looks like—write, "I will kill you."
June:	Right, write revenge.
Courtney:	Hamlet jumps in the grave and starts choking Laertes? So, which one is which?
June:	Well, whoever chokes Laertes.
Troy:	This is a long, long poem.
Cindy:	[The period is almost over.] You need to make arrangements to finish up in my class. You can use my room all you want or you can take your thing with you; it is completely up to you. You can use my room almost anytime.
June:	Oh, what should I write here?
Courtney:	I don't know.
June:	And right here I will put—uh, blood.
Courtney:	Write, "You murderer" or something.

To this point, the discussion primarily served to move them toward agreement on what had literally happened in the play and how to symbolize the characters' feel-

FIGURE 12.3 Laertes

Thought balloons from head:
OH POLONIUS! WOE IS ME! OH OPHELIA!
SHE FELL FROM A TREE!
HAMLET MUST DIE!

"It is here, Hamlet, Hamlet, thou art slain; no
medicine in the world can do thou good. In thee
there is no half an hour's life, . . . The King, the
King's to blame." p. 171

Death comes to his dad
Now Laertes is mad
He's back to seek revenge
That will make the killer cringe
His sis fell from a tree
And now she is free
From the circle of madness
And Infinite sadness
Laertes challenges Hamlet, Lord
Puts poison on his sword
He cuts Hamlet when he's down
Everyone now surrounds
To see who will perish
For the kingdom they cherish
He was stabbed, while distraught
By his own sick plot
But before he dies
Says to Hamlet—I apologize
He blames the mess on the king
In his hand death rings
The king receives what he deserves
It's the ghost that Hamlet serves
Now all royalty is dead
So Fortinbras is the new head.

"I will do't, and for that purpose I'll annoint my
sword. . . . I'll teach my point with this contagion,
that, if I gall him slightly, It may be death.

"Let come what comes, only I'll be revenged
most thoroughly for my father."

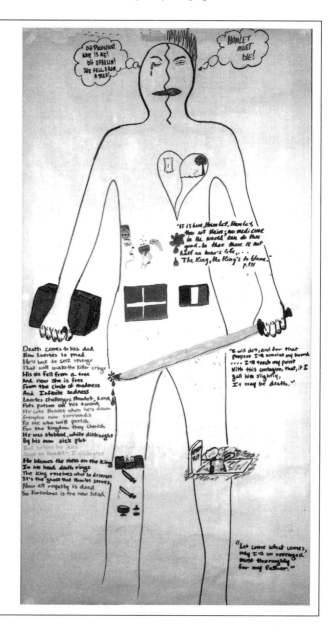

ings toward one another. This effort prompted June to return to *Hamlet* to pose an
important question about the character's motivation. As Cindy walked past their
group on her rounds, she heard:

June: But why did Hamlet come to Laertes?
Cindy: They were fighting.
June: I don't know why.
Courtney: Yeah, but why did he start? Because Laertes was in the grave and
           then he went and jumped after him? What did Laertes say?

Cindy:	And Hamlet tells him to "Hold off thy hands." So Laertes is apparently the one that does it first. He warns him, he says, "Get away from me. There is something in me that you don't want to mess with."
June:	So this is Laertes here?
Courtney:	Right.
Lisa:	I don't know, write "murderer" or something. Okay, what about, just say that, like—
June:	Okay, have you got some quotations? I think we write the quotations on here, right?
Lisa:	Yeah.
Venus:	And then, I don't know, there are two more [quotes to write down in the assignment].
June:	Is this where they were fighting in the grave?
Venus:	No, it is when he tells them, it is when they are fighting and he tells them that the king knows.
June:	Okay, okay, look then, we should write this by his wound. Okay, then we should do it right here where he stabbed him and kills him. So maybe we should do, like, by the stab, you know.

I should point out that the students in this group were not exceptional students. Their grades fell in the B–C range. At one point June was in danger of failing the semester and had to do extra work to bring her grade up. Yet here she shows herself to be a thoughtful reader of a complex play, generating questions to help her understand this key relationship. The reason she posed these questions was that her group needed to use the body biography to represent the character and to know the character she needed to pose questions that would help her group explore his relationships.

The discussion transcripts illustrated a number of similar instances that thoroughly rebut the idea that these are just drawings. Rather, they are interpretive texts that are produced through extensive discussion and reflection on the meaning of the play, conducted almost entirely without the intervention of an expert adult.

Establishing Working Relationships

So far I have described the potential of collaborative body biographies for promoting discussions that depend on high-level inferences about the literary characters. In analyzing the discussion transcripts, we also learned that the groups collaborated with different degrees of social cohesiveness. Of the four groups we analyzed, we found that the Laertes and Ophelia groups performed up to Cindy's highest hopes for both the cognitive complexity of their work and the social dynamics through which they worked.

Field Observation

Observe a class in which students are engaged in literary discussion. If possible, observe small-group as well as whole-class discussions. Make note of the following:

- What is the purpose of the discussion? Who is in control of the topic and direction?
- What kinds of contributions do the students make to the discussion?
- If students are not contributing, what are they doing instead?
- What would you estimate is the degree of participation among students generally?
- What conclusions can you draw about your observation of this discussion?

The Gertrude and Claudius groups, however, while completing the task, did so in ways that we found distressing. Certain students in these groups were, at times, cruel to one another and quite willing to let others do the work for them. The Gertrude group produced a remarkable body biography nonetheless, primarily because Rita spent considerable time outside class working on it. The dynamics of the Claudius group, however, showed up in the careless attitude that one group member took toward the task and the body biography's appearance.

I will next review examples of both the constructive dynamics of the Ophelia group and what we considered to be the destructive dynamics of the Gertrude and Claudius groups. I will conclude by thinking about both the benefits and risks of conducting class in ways that are open-ended and allow students both personal and intellectual freedom.

Ophelia Group

The four girls in the Ophelia group worked with remarkable cohesiveness. Indeed, they could serve as the poster girls for constructivist classrooms. Their discussion was characterized consistently by the following kinds of statements:

Affirmation: These statements affirmed the worth of another group member's contribution. They were more than simple statements of agreement. Instead, they praised another girl's contribution and, by implication, the girl herself.

Inclusion: These statements invited other students to participate in the project. Most often they were offered to more quiet, less assertive students in order to give them roles and opportunities to contribute.

Courtesy: These statements conveyed consideration toward another student, often in the form of a routine civility.

I could offer an abundance of illustrations from this group's interactions as evidence of the great potential of small groups for promoting student learning and social skills. I will highlight one example to show the group's supportive way of working together. The following exchange took place shortly after they began working. Ann had lain down to be traced and worried that her fingers appeared to be fat because the outline had inflated their appearance. Throughout the transcripts of all groups, we often found girls expressing a concern about looking fat, even from the petite Rita in the Gertrude group. We found that their interactions were consistent with other reports that express alarm about girls' self-esteem. Here is how their conversation unfolded:

Ann:	Oh, not bad—okay, we could go over it with, like, the marker and make it look a little thinner.
Sherri:	Your fingers are not that fat, so don't worry.
Carly:	It is like, oh, finger exercises. Okay, let's—was she wearing a dress? That might be easier, oh, she was wearing the dress, then we'll just put on a dress.
Ann:	Yeah, because they went, like, tight here and then they just, like, all the way down.

Carly:	Do you want to do that?
Sherri:	Yeah, weren't you saying you were just going to do bare feet?
Carly:	Yeah, we'll do bare feet, okay.
Ann:	You wanna trace your sketch?
Carly:	Okay, is it okay if I go ahead and, like, do the dress?
Ann:	Yeah.
Carly:	You sure?
Ann:	Yeah.
Carly:	Any of you guys want to do it?
Sherri:	No, it doesn't matter.
Ann:	I wouldn't know where to begin.

This excerpt illustrates patterns that recurred often during their collaboration. Ann's self-deprecating remark about the size of her fingers was immediately met with an affirmation from Sherri and Carly's humorous effort to dissolve her anxiety. The girls then began to discuss how to represent their character on the body biography. First, however, they discussed the roles each would take in the interpretation. Carly tried to include the others in the production, only taking a role for herself after offering it to the others. Her effort at inclusion was met with Ann's self-deprecating remark about her ability to provide a good drawing. They then began a discussion of how to depict the character's literal appearance, based on how she'd appeared in the play and film. The group went on to support one another in the production of a thoughtful interpretive text.

On the whole, the relationships established by this group fit well with Cindy's ideal notion of how students would perform. The students

- chose a character to interpret
- engaged in exploratory discussion
- discussed and clarified possible images to include in their body biography
- used these discussions to come to a more sophisticated understanding of the play
- reflected on the images of their text for further understanding
- treated one another with respect, support, and appreciation

We see this group as illustrating the potential students have to negotiate the open-ended structure Cindy provided. In particular, this group illustrates the kinds of productive and cohesive social relationships that students can establish in this context. In this all-girl group, these relationships appeared to support girls during moments when they expressed negative self-esteem.

> I attempt to organize a more student-centered classroom. While I have personally advocated an emphasis upon group work, collaborative learning, and hands-on experiences . . . as better for women, I now worry about the impact of the group dynamics on men of color and women. Too many faculty . . . remain unaware of the research from women's and ethnic studies demonstrating how racism and sexism from the broader culture become replicated in classroom and group dynamics.
>
> —Sue V. Rosser

Gertrude and Claudius Groups

I next describe the dynamics that took place within two other groups. When we studied the discussion transcripts, we were very disturbed by some of the interactions that took place. Before I present and discuss them, I'd like to ward off one possible interpretation of what follows.

The students who did not use the body biography activity as Cindy envisioned they might were, in general, disaffected and disengaged from school. Their grades were poor for the most part, but not because the students lacked intelligence. For reasons that we could not discern—and in some cases, that their parents found baffling—they did the least amount of work possible and consistently undermined other students' efforts to take the work seriously. We were particularly bothered by this because Cindy intended that her educational design would help to motivate students who were turned off to school.

In many cases, her goals were indeed realized. Most of the students whose interactions I report here were not honor-roll students. They were typical high school kids in the spring semester of their senior year. For the most part, they were far more interested in the prom, in graduating, in next year's plans, and in their social lives than they were in schoolwork. As these discussion transcripts indicate, however, they discussed *Hamlet* in relatively sophisticated ways while producing their body biographies.

However, there were also cases where the liberties that students were granted were simply abused, as were the feelings of other students. It's important to note that these students were equally disengaged during other parts of the class and, according to both school records and parental reports, school in general. We see, then, the small-group activity simply making their lack of involvement more overt than you'd see in a class where students are expected to sit quietly and listen.

The two groups I'll next review, in contrast to the Ophelia group, often engaged in exchanges characterized by the following socially destructive traits:

Discourtesy: These statements showed a lack of consideration for another student and often were insulting or demeaning.

Resistance to discourtesy: These statements occurred when, following a discourteous statement, a student would respond with a further discourtesy.

Apathy: These statements explicitly conveyed a lack of engagement with or motivation for schoolwork.

In the Gertrude group, Jack provided the axis for the group's social relations. Jack was tall, forceful, and talkative, often overpowering other students in the group socially. He had a way of delivering abusive statements with a chuckle. He directed most of his derogatory comments to Rita, the only girl in the group, and Dirk, the only African American.

Rita was task oriented and grade conscious and was the impetus for most academic work within the group. She frequently made self-deprecating remarks both during this assignment and at other points during the year. She was particularly worried about being fat and unattractive, in spite of standing 5 feet 2 inches, weighing 105 pounds, and being described as pretty in unsolicited comments made by various people throughout the year.

Rather than being met with affirmations following her self-critical remarks, she instead made herself vulnerable to the taunting of Jack. The group's relations were established early in their discussion. Rita served as the figure for their body biography, and after a girl from a neighboring group had finished tracing her outline, the following exchange took place:

Rita: Don't smell my breath whatever you do.

Jack: You already ate one bag [of chips] a minute ago. Rita, you're a pig. That's why we had to size down your thighs. We had to do a little constructive surgery.

Rita: My crotch is not that low.

Jack: No, that is a pretty low crotch. Do you want me to fix that for you?

Dirk: Well, what are we supposed to do—draw you buck naked or something?

Jack: No, Dirk, please.

Dirk: I'm pretty sure—

Jack: Don't go there, man.

Dirk: We'll just draw some lines like she had clothes on and that is why her crotch is so low.

Jack: All right, tell me how high, Rita, like up in there?

Rita: That's good, I don't care what it looks like.

Jack: It's a good thing.

Dirk: We'll draw the chi-chi's now.

James: Man, that is, that is weird.

Rita: No boobs. [Laughter] I don't have any, and no, you're not going to draw any.

Dirk: She lookin'—

Jack: Yeah, she looks—we can reconstruct, but we can't reconstruct that much.

This early exchange illustrates processes that took place frequently during their discussion. Rita served as the subject of various insults, primarily from Jack. These abusive remarks toward Rita, we found, discouraged collaboration and cohesion in working on the project. Ultimately, Jack spent much of the period talking off-task while Rita and others worked on the interpretation, only to have Jack insult their work, typically with a chortle.

In addition to feeding on Rita's insecurities about her appearance, Jack's comments toward Dirk were at times blatantly racist. In the following segment Dirk made a reference to a black marker he was using for his contribution to the body biography, and Jack insulted him repeatedly:

Jack: What's up, Bucky?

Dirk: I had black.

Jack: What's so great about black? Black stinks.

Dirk: You got a point? Huh? I smell good. What're you talking about?

Jack: You smell so good—if you took a bath.

Dirk: I was going to mention that I found some markers in the drawer.

Jack:	Hey, what are you doing, son?
Dirk:	Same thing you're doing, son.
Jack:	Well, now what are you doing? You're just messing everything up.
Dirk:	Come on now.
Jack:	Just take your black marker and get away from me, man. You hear me, boy?

This segment needs little explanation, other than to say that it illustrates the destructive relationships that Jack initiated within the group. Because Rita ended up working on the body biography outside class, their finished product was quite remarkable. When we listened to the tape of their discussion, however, we were discouraged to learn that the process of construction had included such exchanges.

A second problem that affected both this group and the Claudius group was the varying degrees of commitment of the different students. Both groups included students who performed poorly in school, primarily because they consistently did not complete assignments. In the Gertrude group, two of the five students did not pass the class and one passed with the lowest possible grade, though each was given plenty of opportunities, encouragement, and incentives to perform.

These degrees of commitment resulted in widely varying efforts to contribute to the group effort. One key episode in the small-group discussion came early when the students were discussing the time frame Cindy had provided to complete the body biographies. In considering how they would need time outside class, the group interacted as follows:

Rita:	You guys, we're not coming in for Overtime—I'll do some of this over the weekend.
Jack:	Rita's, like—sacrifice. We're not coming in. You're right, I ain't coming in.
Rita:	She should have given us, like, two periods to do this in.
James:	Shoot, I can't do this, I gotta work.

When Rita declared that she would work on the body biography at home, the other group members lost all urgency in contributing equally to the project. From this point on, the transcript became characterized by Rita's efforts to initiate an interpretation. Meanwhile, Jack led a series of unrelated discussions about the film *Forrest Gump,* an upcoming car wash sponsored by the cheerleaders, the impending state basketball tournament, the merits of different brands of shoes, their preferences in snack foods, and other topics that students might discuss outside the classroom.

The image we developed was of a work crew consisting of one or two people getting the job done while the rest stand around, leaning on their shovels and shooting the breeze. When I was a college student I had summer jobs where this sort of thing happened, and I always resented the way in which we all got equal credit for the work I did. The parallels between those experiences and the dynamics we saw in this group were striking.

The Claudius group also had problematic dynamics. This group included two students who were hostile to Cindy throughout the semester and in general hostile toward school and other students. When in groups, they tended to undermine other students' efforts to work productively on the task. The next excerpt shows how Jerry tended to work against the group goals, demonstrating an apathy that showed up in his group's body biography. The group was discussing how they might draw a crown on Claudius's head as part of their depiction of his character (see Figure 12.4):

Jay:	The crown can be something that stands, he stands for.
Cale:	Somebody draw the crown.
Jay:	For incest.
Cale:	Draw the crown, what?
Jay:	Well—
Jerry:	What are we supposed to do now? Don't be disappointed if this doesn't look so good.
Cale:	I don't understand. [inaudible] Jerry! Jerry, why did you do that?
Jerry:	Because it doesn't matter what it looks like as long as we get our representation. He told me to draw the crown, and I said, "Okay, but don't get mad at me if I draw it badly." And everybody goes—[makes a grumbling noise]
Cale:	That looks like trash, Jerry. Jerry, that is one rotten crown, dude.
Jerry:	Do you like it? Incest!
Cale:	Actually, incest could be adultery.
Jerry:	Oh, who cares.

In looking at the body biography, we had to agree with Cale that Jerry had drawn one rotten crown, dude. Jerry's remarks, like Jack's in the Gertrude group, need little explanation. He appeared eager to impress on others his apathy and to inscribe it in the group's body biography. In doing so he undermined the kinds of relationships that can lead to the productive sorts of discussions we saw in other groups.

In this case, Jerry interpreted Cindy's assignment as a license to produce a sloppy interpretation. Cindy had told the students that they would get graded on the ideas they were representing, rather than on the quality of their artwork. Her thinking was that she didn't want to reward good artists and punish the artistically challenged, since the goal of the activity was literary analysis and not art. Jerry's view that "it doesn't matter what it looks like" was typical of his indifferent attitude toward school and the other students in his group. The other students did not appreciate the trashy appearance of his drawing or his general conduct during the group activity.

FINAL THOUGHTS

In studying the group transcripts, then, Cindy and I came to the understanding that simply working in groups does not produce miracles. Rather, students need to believe that the process of the group work is worthwhile to them. We decided that there needs to be some degree of *goal congruency* between teacher and students if the students are to work faithfully without direct guidance or supervision. In planning

FIGURE 12.4   Claudius

In crown:
Incest Murder Power $
Deceit

"That cannot be since I am still possessed of these effects for which I did the murder, My crown, mine own ambition, and my queen. May one be pardoned and retain th' offense?"

I am deceitful and selfish.
I wonder if Hamlet knows I killed his father.
I hear the voices of those I've met in the past.
I see them writhing in pain.
I want power beyond my wildest dreams.
I am deceitful and selfish.
I pretend that I am guiltless.
I feel remorse.
I touch the lives of many men who often end up dead.
I worry that one day they will seek the ultimate revenge.
I cry at the loss of my crown and my queen.
I am deceitful and selfish.
I understand that my actions hurt others.
I say death to all those who oppose me.
I dream of better times.
I try asking for forgiveness.
I hope it will be given.
I am deceitful and selfish.

" 'Tis unmanly greif. It shows a will most incorrect to heaven. A heart unfortified, a mind impatient. An understanding simple and unschooled."

"Shy Now. You Speak—Like A Good Child And A True Gentleman. That I Am Guiltless of Your Father's DEATH!"

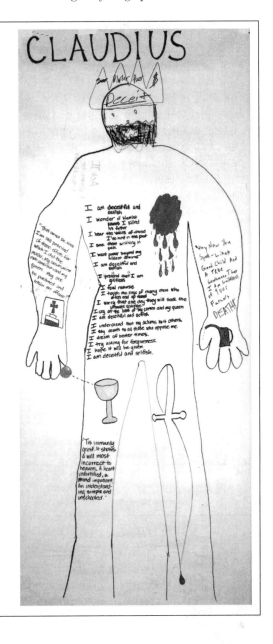

the body biography task, Cindy had found a task that she believed would fit with her overall goals for a dynamic, meaning-centered classroom. And for many students, it surely was. We see these exceptions as demonstrations of the challenges that teachers face, rather than as reasons not to conduct open-ended classrooms. Teaching authoritatively might make the problems less visible, but would not make them go away.

Vignette

The April 1994 issue of the NCTE journal *College English* included an article that caused quite a ruckus among writing teachers. In "Fault Lines in the Contact Zone," Richard E. Miller reported on an incident that took place in a California community college in which a student wrote a paper for an open-ended class assignment. The assignment, taken from a widely used college composition textbook, asked students to write a report on some incident of group behavior. Miller described the paper as follows:

> One [student] responded with an essay detailing a drunken trip he and some friends made to "San Fagcisco" to study "the lowest class . . . the queers and the bums." The essay recounts how the students stopped a man on Polk Street, informed him that they were doing a survey and needed to know if he was "a fag." From here, the narrative follows the students into a dark alleyway where they discover, as they relieve themselves drunkenly against the wall, that they have been urinating on a homeless person. In a frenzy, the students begin to kick the homeless person, stopping after "30 seconds of non-stop blows to the body," at which point the writer says he "thought the guy was dead." Terrified, the students make a run for their car and eventually escape the city. (p. 392)

The assignment never specified that the students needed to write about something that the teacher would like. And as it turned out, the student knew that the teacher, who was gay, would find it offensive. The student himself came from Kuwait and held a culturally learned contempt for homosexuals.

The assignment in the book assumed that students are good people and would write about legal, morally acceptable behavior. Because there were no cautions against writing hatefully about an offensive action, the student produced an essay well within the acceptable boundaries of the assignment.

If a student turned a paper like this in to you, how would you evaluate it, and would you take any action beyond the evaluation?

Unit Design

Engagement

Look back over the unit you've designed. To what degree have you encouraged students to become engaged with the class? To what degree might students use open-ended learning opportunities in unproductive ways? How might you address these issues in your unit design?

Rationale

Return to the rationale you wrote earlier. Reread it and see how well it fits your unit as you are developing it. If need be, reconsider your rationale by adjusting its focus, adding or revising major points, adding or revising the evidence you provide, adding to or revising your rebuttals, and revoicing your rhetoric and points to suit potential readers.

Discussion Topic

How should a teacher work with unmotivated students? Is it a teacher's responsibility to motivate a student? What are the various causes of disengagement from school? How might they be addressed?

Field Observation

Observe a classroom, looking for students who are disengaged or disaffected. Report and reflect on the following:

- In what ways do they show their lack of interest in school?
- How do they respond to the class structure?
- How do they affect the engagement of other students in the class?
- What might be the source of their disengagement or disaffection?
- Is there a way to change the environment or type of activity to help increase their engagement?
- If not, how might the teacher conduct the class so as to modify the effects of their disengagement?

Detailed Descriptions of These Studies

O'Donnell-Allen, C., & Smagorinsky, P. (1999). Revising Ophelia: Rethinking questions of gender and power in school. *English Journal, 88*(3), 35–42.

Smagorinsky, P. (2002). If meaning is constructed, what's it made of?: Toward a cultured theory of reading. *Review of Educational Research*.

Smagorinsky, P., & O'Donnell-Allen, C. (1998). The depth and dynamics of context: Tracing the sources and channels of engagement and disengagement in students' response to literature. *Journal of Literacy Research, 30,* 515–559.

Smagorinsky, P., & O'Donnell-Allen, C. (1998). Reading as mediated and mediating action: Composing meaning for literature through multimedia interpretive texts. *Reading Research Quarterly, 33,* 198–226.

Smagorinsky, P., & O'Donnell-Allen, C. (2000). Idiocultural diversity in small groups: The role of the relational framework in collaborative learning. In C. D. Lee & P. Smagorinsky (Eds.), *Vygotskian perspectives on literacy research: Constructing meaning through collaborative inquiry* (pp. 165–190). New York: Cambridge University Press.

The Original Body Biography Assignment

Underwood, W. (1987). The body biography: A framework for student writing. *English Journal, 76,* 44–48.

PART 3

RETHINKING THE CURRICULUM

In Part III I ask you to rethink your assumptions about three aspects of teaching English: the multicultural curriculum, character education, and educational standards. As many have noted, it's impossible to teach without a bias of some sort, without values, without an agenda. All your actions are value laden in some way. Even seemingly innocuous decisions, such as how to organize the furniture in your room, have implications for how learning takes place. Other decisions you make will also affect what and how students will learn in your class.

In Chapter 13, I discuss questions that you need to consider in planning a curriculum. Mostly these stem from efforts to broaden the literary canon. The canon consists of those texts thought to be essential reading: the works of Shakespeare, *The Adventures of Huckleberry Finn, The Scarlet Letter,* and "the usual prisoners" that you could undoubtedly name based on your experiences of being a student. In the last decade or two, there has been an effort to be more inclusive; that is, to replace some of these canonical works with literature by more diverse authors: minorities, women, international writers, writers of diverse gender orientation, and so on. In this chapter I discuss the ways in which modern concerns about the literature curriculum raise a new set of questions.

In Chapter 14 I address the movement toward *character education.* Modern youth are perceived to be morally deficient and in need of an educational intervention to improve their character and thus make schools safer and healthier places for learning. In this chapter I critique the most common notions of character and character education and provide an alternative way of thinking about both. I then proceed to discuss how this reconception of character education might look in thematic units of instruction.

In Chapter 15 I review two kinds of national standards movements, one for students and one for teachers. Educators are increasingly called on to be accountable, that is, to demonstrate their effectiveness. Standards movements have arisen because of a widespread belief that schools are failing children. In this chapter I question this assumption, while at the same time arguing that schools can serve students better. I then look at the assumptions behind the International Reading Association/National Council of Teachers of English standards project, which identifies what all students should know following their experience in an English curriculum.

I next turn to the National Board for Professional Teaching Standards' effort to create a national certification for master teachers. Throughout these analyses, I try to get you to consider the questions, What does it mean to be a knowledgeable student? and What does it mean to be a master teacher? In the end, I argue that the profession will be best served if teachers use these projects as a springboard for developing their own standards for teaching and learning.

On the whole, these chapters continue with the general intention of this book: to ask you to question the assumptions behind beliefs about teaching and learning and to understand as clearly as possible why you teach as you do.

13 Rethinking the Curriculum from a Multicultural Perspective

I n this chapter I think about how the current emphasis on multiculturalism has created new dilemmas for teachers. Expanding the canon has helped to present a more pluralistic worldview in the curriculum and has allowed a broader range of students to find their experiences represented in school. These changes, like any other drastic changes, have also raised new questions for teachers. I explore in depth three types of challenges facing teachers as the curriculum expands to include a new range of authors: how to teach ironic texts about social issues, how to approach a curriculum that is designed to change students' attitudes, and how to teach texts selected to represent a particular group of people.

If you read the newspapers and follow current events, you're no doubt painfully aware that schools are often singled out for being the cause of much societal failure. While sometimes viewed as a recent phenomenon, the tendency to attack schools when something goes wrong outside them has been around for some time—at least as long as I've been alive. Right around the time I was starting school, the Soviet Union launched *Sputnik,* the first space satellite. The United States responded with increased emphasis on science and mathematics education, which I experienced to little avail. The assumption was that U.S. schools were deficient in these areas; how else to explain our laggardly performance in the space race?

Preparing students for rocket science is but one of many missions identified for U.S. schools. Participation in virtually any aspect of adult life is often believed to originate in K–12 education. The presence of so many (often conflicting) missions is, I think, one of the main reasons schools make such easy targets for their critics. When schools are believed to have an infinite number of purposes and missions, they inevitably fail to meet somebody's (or everybody's) expectations. And as the diverse groups that make up our nation increasingly stress their uniqueness and the importance of their needs—particularly insofar as schools ought to meet them—the goals of schooling become even more difficult to agree on.

"Celebrate diversity" has become a slogan in many schools. Yet diversity has proven to be very difficult to celebrate for most communities. Rather, it has challenged people to be their open-minded best, something that a lot of people have trouble being. Being open-minded, after all, requires people to respect and accommodate the goals and values of others, even though doing so may affect their own prospects for fulfillment.

Indeed, the celebration of diversity, like the occasional Mardi Gras, has ended up being somewhat of a riot. The anti-affirmative action backlash of the 1990s has revealed a resentment by some groups of whites toward minorities in their competition for admissions and scholarships, jobs and promotions, and other benefits. Further backlash is evident in the current wave of criticism of multiculturalism in school curricula. Critics (usually white, but not always) bemoan what they view as a decline in standards and quality that follows from the inclusion of a heretofore unrecognized voice or heritage. These tensions are distressing for those who, with the best of intentions, want to promote harmony and common understanding by using the curriculum as a tool for learning about different cultures. Instead of finding a new celebration of diversity, however, they often see their efforts to enlighten students about one another's cultures lead to aggravated competition and stress among various groups.

Educators are then left with a paradox. Schools have always had a mission to promote equality, democracy, and citizenship. They have managed this mission unevenly over the years. Many immigrants from early in the twentieth century, for instance, dropped out of school because they couldn't speak English. My uncles, born in Belarus (formerly Belorussia), immigrated to the United States with my grandmother in 1916. With no English to begin with, they dropped out of school in early adolescence and became painters, relieving the school of the problem of how to educate them with their limited English proficiency. And until the latter part of the century, the goal of immigrants was to assimilate, rather than to retain an ethnic identity. Diversity was less of an issue for schools then. In spite of their diverse backgrounds, the goal was to make people more or less the same. The slogan for the times might aptly have been "Celibate diversity."

At the outset of the twenty-first century, pluralism has taken on a different meaning to many. First, immigrant groups are simply more visible, consisting largely of people of color, in contrast to the waves of white Europeans who immigrated in the first half of the twentieth century. Second, the emphasis has shifted from assimilation to maintaining an ethnic and cultural identity. While the U.S. population is not necessarily more diverse than it was in previous eras, diversity is both more evident and viewed differently.

This new vision has made teaching much more complicated than it was a few generations ago. At that time, it seemed right and natural for schools to use the curriculum as a tool for assimilation. In the literature curriculum, this meant reading literature by the standard-bearers of American society: writers who were white and male, and mostly of British or American origins. The societal shift toward ethnic rather than national identity has shown up in disagreements over what students should study in school. Rather than endorsing a literary canon of works by white males, citizens of various backgrounds want to see their own heritages reflected in the curriculum.

In other words, they want to read books by authors who are like them, who represent the world from their point of view. From this perspective, the curriculum of assimilation establishes the white middle class as society's norm and views all others in terms of its deficits relative to this norm. Diversifying the curriculum would help to establish the legitimacy of other perspectives as well, instead of having them viewed as inferior alternatives to middle-class culture.

The paradox, then, is that schools have a mission to promote a sense of community and citizenship, yet must pursue it in a climate of cultural competition for a voice in the process of schooling. Few communities have been successful in managing the tensions of this paradox smoothly. The solutions, such as diversifying the curriculum, have rarely succeeded in satisfying all stakeholders in the school system. Educators are then left with a perplexing question: If they are to celebrate cultural and ethnic diversity, can they simultaneously promote a civic identity?

In particular, how do teachers accomplish this through the English curriculum? English classes seem particularly fertile grounds for these tensions to come out in the open. Students must read books. Which ones? The selection of any text feeds into the tensions outlined so far. If teachers choose one book, that means they're not choosing others. If teachers exclude a book from the curriculum, are they engaging in censorship? On what grounds, then, do teachers base their decisions on what to teach? Considering these questions might entail a reflection on these issues:

1. In a society composed of countless cultural groups with distinct histories and identities, how can teachers include the voices and experiences of all or most of society's various cultures? In striving for multicultural inclusion, which of the myriad groups should teachers single out for students to be exposed to? Should the selection be driven by race, religion, ethnicity, continent of origin, region within the United States, political values, or some other factor? If teachers choose according to one of these criteria, on what basis do they then choose the voices from within each group?

2. Should the potential offensiveness of a work be a consideration in the selection process? Is the profane and racially inflammatory language of James Baldwin's *Blues for Mister Charlie* a sufficient reason not to use it in the classroom? Are the persistent use of the word *nigger* and the overwhelmingly bigoted views of the characters in *Huckleberry Finn* good reason for students not to read it?

3. Should the particular moral, social, or political values imparted through a text be a consideration in the selection process? For example, should the antibusiness values of Charles Dickens's *Hard Times* work against its selection? And should the context of instruction determine the volatility of the values? For instance, does the pro-environment ideology of Dr. Seuss's *The Lorax* make it an unacceptable book in an area dependent on the timber industry, but acceptable in the grain belt? Does the anti-Christian theology of *The Autobiography of Malcolm X* exclude it from the curriculum in the Bible Belt, but make it acceptable in more pluralistic areas? Should teachers seek to teach texts in a value neutral way in the classroom and thus focus on literary merit rather than ideology, or is doing so simply a different ideology? Should the question of values be of greater or lesser importance than the literary merit of the works, or is it even possible to disentangle the two? For that matter, is it possible to define "literary merit" so that there is consensus among all of a community's stakeholders and participants?

4. Should the potential community response to particular topics enter into teachers' consideration of what to include in the curriculum? How does the prostitution of *Sister Carrie* affect teachers' thinking as curriculum builders?

Should the communist sympathies of Richard Wright in *Native Son* discourage its inclusion in the curriculum in a conservative community? How do teachers justify the inclusion of *Romeo and Juliet* when teen suicide is a crisis?

5. Should teachers seek to achieve a balance of positive and negative images in the depiction of various cultural groups? If teachers have their students read Ralph Ellison's *Invisible Man,* for instance, should they attempt to balance the oppression with an uplifting story of African American accomplishment, such as Colin Powell's *My American Journey: An Autobiography?*

6. Should teachers choose texts that are often misunderstood due to the author's use of sophisticated literary techniques, such as ironic distance between the author's views and those of the speaker, as found in Swift's "A Modest Proposal"? In particular, should teachers exclude texts such as Faulkner's *Light in August,* where the speaker expresses racist views?

7. Should the author's personal life matter? Should teachers exclude Ezra Pound because he was a fascist and anti-Semitic? Or Shakespeare because of the negative portrayal of Jews in *The Merchant of Venice?* Should Coleridge be eschewed because he smoked opium? Should students read Lillian Hellman, even though she was unfaithful to her husband and smoked and drank heavily? Should Martin Luther King, Jr.'s plagiarism and extramarital affairs make him persona non grata in the English class? Should Patrick Henry's ownership of slaves lead him to be eliminated as a voice of liberty?

8. Can a member of one cultural group authentically write about the experiences of another? Can white authors authentically depict Native American characters? Can a Cheyenne-Arapaho male authentically depict life from the perspective of a Winnebago woman? Can a middle-class African American write an authentic story about life "in the hood"? When writers do depict characters from other cultures, how do teachers evaluate them for inclusion in the curriculum?

9. At what point do the selection principles become censorship, given that any effort at inclusion inevitably results in the exclusion of something, and any kind of exclusion is based on some kind of discrimination?

10. If teachers involve students in curriculum planning or allow them to read books entirely of their own choice, can these issues be sidestepped?

11. Can teachers solve any or all of these problems by providing an appropriate instructional context for the literature used in their classroom? In other words, can teachers teach any problematic text in such a way that it can be a potentially valuable experience for any student? Or are some texts prohibitively problematic, particularly in certain communities? We might assume that the profanity, sex, drugs, and violence in John Updike's *Rabbit Redux* would invite parental protest in many communities. But might books such as *Little Women* also cause a commotion in communities with a great sensitivity to women's issues?

These questions are not meant to be comprehensive, but simply to reveal the conundrum facing anyone who wishes to diversify the curriculum. In many cases, the issues are sidestepped by relying on a combination of

- commercial anthologies, which must pass through the scrutiny of various stakeholders to get approval at the state level and so are largely inoffensive (and therefore, many find, insipid)

- canonical literature, which will generally withstand scrutiny though is not foolproof

Yet resorting to these old reliable texts means that the curriculum will undergo little change. Whether that's good or bad depends on what's in the curriculum, the ways in which it serves students, and whose perspective provides the judgment of what's good or bad.

I will next review some of the issues in multicultural education that have vexed me the most as a teacher. I'll not attempt to settle the questions, for they are quite contentious and open to different interpretations. They are they kinds of issues you're likely to encounter in your teaching at some point. I offer them here as illustrations of the complexities of teaching English in the twenty-first century.

THE ADVENTURES OF TEACHING *HUCKLEBERRY FINN*

The Adventures of Huckleberry Finn is one of the most celebrated, widely read, and frequently protested books in the history of American letters. You've probably been assigned this novel at least once in your schooling, probably more. Those who believe that *Huckleberry Finn* is a work of great literary merit have interpreted the text through a recognition of Twain's use of dramatic irony. The irony comes through the distinction he has created between his own views and those of the speaker, Huck. That was the way I was taught to read the novel, and the explanation has always made sense to me. If you don't accept this distinction, you would probably have a hard time justifying the novel's use in school.

Understanding this distinction is important because Huck's views are frankly racist. Let us look at Huck's narration in a passage from Chapter 31, "You Can't Pray a Lie":

Once I said to myself it would be a thousand times better for Jim to be a slave at home where his family was as long as he'd got to be a slave, and so I'd better write a letter to Tom Sawyer and tell him to tell Miss Watson where he was. But I soon give up that notion for two things: she'd be mad and disgusted at his rascality and ungratefulness for leaving her, and so she'd sell him straight down the river again; and if she didn't everybody naturally despises an ungrateful nigger, and they'd make Jim feel it all the time, and so he'd feel ornery and disgraced. And then think of me! It would get all around that Huck Finn helped a nigger to get his freedom; and if I was ever to see anybody from that town again I'd be ready to get down and lick his boots for shame. That's just the way: a person does a low-down thing, and then he don't want to take no consequences of it. Thinks as long as he can hide, it ain't no disgrace. That was my fix exactly. The more I studied about this the more my conscience went to grinding me, and the more wicked and low-down and ornery I got to feeling. And at last, when it hit me all of a sudden that here was the plain hand of Providence slapping me in the face and letting me know my wickedness was being watched all the time from up there in heaven, whilst I was stealing a poor old woman's nigger that hadn't ever done me no harm, and now was showing me there's One that's always on the lookout, and ain't a-going to allow no such miserable doings to go only just so fur and no further, I most dropped in my tracks I was so scared. Well, I tried the best I could to kinder soften it up somehow for myself by saying I was brung up wicked, and so I warn't so much to blame, but something inside of me kept saying, "There was the Sunday school, you could 'a' gone to it; and if you'd 'a' done it they'd 'a' learnt you there that people that acts as I'd been acting about the nigger goes to everlasting fire.

As a high school teacher I assigned *Huckleberry Finn* to my American literature students for many years. Yet the responses of my African American students made me increasingly uneasy about the role of the book in the education of my students. In the paragraph just cited, the word *nigger* appears four times, and it recurs routinely throughout the book. The white characters repeatedly assert and assume that blacks are property for them to use as they please and that God supports their subjugation.

A detached reader can make the argument that Twain is showing us that these beliefs are wrong; that the white characters who have bone-deep beliefs about the subhumanity of blacks have themselves been drawn by Twain to exhibit hypocrisy, avarice, and other negative traits. In contrast, Jim is noble, honest, and deeply sympathetic.

These are the conventional readings of the novel, the ones we learned in school and the ones we in turn teach to our students. Yet as I've reviewed in previous chapters, reading is a constructive process. Teachers can give their preferred interpretations, and students can pass tests on them, but this does not stop readers from seeing something else in the literature. At least two types of alternative readings make *Huckleberry Finn* a problematic book to teach in school.

The first comes from those students who feel degraded by the language of the text—most frequently African American students, though others may be similarly offended. Just as students I've described in previous chapters have initiated responses to literature with their emotional resonance with the language of the text, students may find the racist perspective and language of Huck's narration not merely offensive, but extremely painful. I've spoken with many educators who pooh-pooh this response, saying that the students shouldn't be so sensitive. Rather, they say, *Huckleberry Finn* is a great work of art and therefore students' trivial feelings should be dismissed. Only an unsophisticated reader, they say, could fail to see the ironic distance between Twain's own views on bigotry and those expressed by the speaker, Huck.

From this perspective, emotional readings are inferior to analytic readings. Students should rise above their emotional response and become more detached. Doing so will enable them to regard *Huckleberry Finn* as a masterpiece and appreciate its commentary on society. This perspective represents the way in which literature is traditionally taught in schools: Analysis is preeminent, the teacher's interpretation is more authoritative than the students' response, and the locus of power resides with the teacher and his or her affiliation with the community of professional literary critics.

My own experiences in teaching *Huck Finn* to multiracial classes, however, have suggested to me that "understanding" the novel is only one of many responses people may legitimately have to it. Many black students I have taught have acknowledged the differences in beliefs between author and speaker and have recognized the novel's literary merit. Yet they still have been deeply hurt by the attitudes expressed

Vignette

I was observing a high school class not long ago in which the text under discussion was Steinbeck's *Of Mice and Men*. The class was about two-thirds white, one-third black. Some students had complained about the language of the book, including the profanity and the use of, as one girl called it, "the N word." The teacher opened a discussion of the book's language and why they considered it offensive. The class was divided on the question of the book's offensiveness. One white boy persistently said that the students were seniors and should be mature enough to handle the language and should get over it if they were offended. Several black students and one white girl said that they found "the N word" offensive and didn't like the book.

The teacher said that she understood why they might not like the language, but that the book was a classic and was worth reading. The students shouldn't allow the presence of one word to ruin their appreciation for the rest of the book. The book, if anything, showed the ignorance of the characters who used the N word. After continuing with this line of reasoning, she moved along to the next lesson.

The teacher's response sounded to me very familiar, because it echoed almost verbatim my own explanations to students about why they shouldn't find *Huck Finn* offensive when I first taught it to mixed-race classes. After class, she and I talked about the question over lunch with a small group of her colleagues in the school's English department, and all said that they did pretty much the same thing: When kids complain about offensive language, they explain that students ought not be offended because the characters are only revealing their ignorance. The teachers in the faculty lounge all agreed that after they explained the situation, their students all understood and stopped complaining.

I've always been outnumbered when I've taken the position that the use of dramatic irony makes it difficult for students to appreciate the literary merit of texts that include abusive language. Perhaps I'm also losing the argument with you. Rather than persuading you that I'm right, I'll simply ask you to listen to your students and not assume that when they stop talking after your explanations, the reason is that they've been persuaded by your logic.

by Huck and requested that we please not read any more stories that use the word *nigger*. If *Huckleberry Finn* is truly a great book, then students should have great experiences with it. I don't think this is possible unless we treat the book emotionally as well as intellectually.

A second type of alternative reading comes when readers take what Michael W. Smith has called a submissive stance in response to a text. When this happens, readers accept the authority of the narrator without question. Many readers do not respond to *Huckleberry Finn* as ironic, but accept the surface meaning instead. Teachers try to remedy this kind of reading by explaining the dramatic irony. I can't say, however, that these explanations always work.

Here, then, is my dilemma with regard to *Huckleberry Finn* and other books that potentially degrade readers. Traditional school approaches to reading literature invest authority in the teacher's explanations, based on the teacher's training in the perspective of professional critics. The values of a relatively small number of readers set the terms for the reading practices of the far more populous reading public. These ordinary readers within the general reading public, however—including students—do not affiliate themselves with critics, but read for other purposes and with other criteria. Respecting their responses means investing the students with the right to decide what matters about literature.

As a teacher, which approach will you take? How will you respond to students who feel offended by a writer's characterization of their cultural identity? Will you avoid teaching texts that are potentially offensive to your students? What will be the basis for your decisions?

USING MULTICULTURAL EDUCATION TO BROADEN STUDENTS' MINDS

One of the reasons I have always valued education is that it has brought me in contact with ideas that I never would have otherwise considered. Through my education I have read *The Communist Manifesto, The Analects of Confucius, The Koran,* and countless other texts that have challenged the ways in which I had grown up to think about the world. Like many who take up education as a profession, I have often assumed that we all not only benefit from exposure to a variety of ideas, but *want* to see the world from as many perspectives as possible in order to get the clearest sense of our own personal beliefs.

You needn't be a sociologist, however, to know that not everyone seeks a broader view of the world. Yet teachers often feel that they have a duty to provide enlightenment for their students whether they want it or not. We feel this need especially strongly when we see hatred and discrimination played out in school. A racial slur scrawled on the lavatory wall, boys calling girls "bitches" and other degrading names, students saying that something they don't like is "gay"—these and other incidents are disturbingly common in our schools. As members of the school community, we feel the need *to do something* to change students' attitudes and make them more respectful and tolerant. And because books have always been our medium of passing along great ideas, we often attempt to address issues of bigotry and discrimination through changes in curriculum.

In doing so we have found out a few things. One is that not everyone wants to be exposed to new ideas; many people are quite content with the ones they have. Indeed, people are often fiercely loyal to the ideas they have grown up with and would feel that they were betraying their homes and communities if they were to change. As a result they often adamantly resist what they feel are attempts to indoctrinate them into new ways of thinking and end up becoming more entrenched in their beliefs than ever.

This resistance has led to a second realization, that books don't have the same transforming effect on many people that they have on people who end up being English teachers for a living. As I've argued throughout this book, much research in reading stresses the constructive nature of the reading process, with the text providing a blueprint from which readers construct meaning based on their personal histories, their cultural backgrounds, and the orientations they've learned toward reading.

Student readers do not all approach reading in the open-minded way that most college-educated English teachers do. Students, I've found, construct meanings that may differ from what we think they might learn from texts we assign with a didactic intent. As a consequence, our efforts to address what we perceive as attitude problems through curricular change often backfire when the students resist the ideas altogether, reconstruct them to justify their preconceived beliefs, or reject them through the frameworks that guide their reading.

We can find many examples of the ways in which this process works. One infamous example took place at the University of Texas at Austin in the early 1990s. Many people in the English department were disturbed by the increasing outbreaks of hostility over civil rights issues in the Austin community. The coordinators of the freshman composition program decided that one way to get students to be more sensitive to one another was to involve them in the analysis of Supreme Court cases that concerned civil rights issues.

The course covered the same type of writing instruction that students would ordinarily get in a freshman composition course, with a special emphasis on learning how to construct and critique legal arguments. The course also gave great attention to the process of writing arguments, with students producing several drafts of each assignment, working together in writing groups, doing collaborative research in the library, participating in peer critiques, and otherwise sharing their developing essays with other students and the teacher. Judged on the basis of its method of teaching writing, the course was exemplary in its pedagogy for teaching students to critique and write arguments with expertise.

The idea of using court cases as the basis of study was also inspired. Almost everyone loves a good court case. The courtroom drama is a staple of television and film and has served as the basis of classroom simulation games (see, for instance, Appendix B of this book). The trouble with the course came through its selection of which court cases to study. The cases all concerned civil rights issues of some sort, including racial prejudice, gay/lesbian rights, and women's issues. Some members of the faculty opposed the content of the course because they felt that the intent was to indoctrinate students into politically correct viewpoints. They took their case to the local newspapers, who were very happy to report to the public the controversy in the radical English department.

The uproar got national press attention and was even the subject of a panel at a national conference in which members of the English department aired their differences in public. The issue was equally inflammatory among students, who defended both sides of the case with passion, yet little persuasion. In the end a number of prominent faculty members left the university, and the curriculum was modified to mollify those who remained.

The University of Texas case is but one of many I could have cited. Many schools have attempted a similar sort of enlightenment plan using literature or courses in multiculturalism to help change attitudes, only to run into resistance. Teachers are stuck in the middle of a problem that seems to have no clear solution: We are too idealistic to sit back and allow bigotry to go on unchecked, yet when we attempt to address it through academic measures we seem to exacerbate the problem. Perhaps we are too impatient; perhaps the initial hostility is something we must go through in order to achieve long-term change. And perhaps we are wrong in thinking that it is our duty to change people's deeply ingrained beliefs about society, in spite of how destructive we find them. After all, from their perspective, *we* are the ones who are being destructive.

The questions I would pose to you are: Is it your responsibility as a teacher to teach such demeanors as tolerance and open-mindedness? To what extent should you be concerned with the teaching of values? If you teach values, should you teach particular values, or simply engage students in the consideration of moral dilemmas from which they derive their own values? What happens when students are taught values at home that you find offensive? How do you work effectively with your colleagues in discussing these issues, particularly when you disagree?

> I believe that in my teaching I am passing on a torch that too many people believe is dying with my generation: the torch that is set aflame by the burning love of literature. My students love the books they read as I loved them; they see in them a promise, a possibility, a richness of life they can find nowhere else.
>
> —Mary Gordon

TEXTS SELECTED TO REPRESENT A PARTICULAR GROUP OF PEOPLE

A third type of text that presents problems for teachers concerned with issues of diversity is one that is chosen to represent a particular group of people. Many curricula are now being rewritten to reflect concern for global consciousness, racial and ethnic diversity, gender issues, and other sensibilities that extend the curriculum beyond the traditional canon. One problem with diversifying reading lists is that the world is indeed a diverse place. While we have relatively few genders to complicate the selection of materials, we have many, many countries, most of which are composed of members of widely varying cultures, religions, ethnicities, and social classes, all of which may have had different characteristics at different points in history.

Representing the world's diverse people is not possible, given this broad range. We need, then, to think about how to go about stocking our new culturally diverse curriculum. Our first task would be to whittle down the possibilities. But which countries should our anthologies represent? In choosing writers to represent Africa, should we choose authors from Madagascar, Ivory Coast, Egypt, South Africa, or someplace else? And after we have made these decisions, we are faced with the problem of diversity within nations. Typically in anthologies we now see writers identified as representing one country or another, even such extraordinarily diverse nations as India, Russia, China, Brazil, and others. Should our Brazilian representative be from the indigenous rain-forest peoples? The descendant of a German expatriate? A surfer dude from Rio de Janeiro?

Even if we restrict our choices to authors from the United States, we face the same problems. Which writers represent which groups of people? Should we attempt to represent all racial and ethnic groups who inhabit the United States? Which voices represent Latinos, who originate from such distinct nations as Cuba, Mexico, Puerto Rico, Panama, Venezuela, and many others? The group known as Native Americans is considerably more diverse, with somewhere in the neighborhood of 400 different tribes. These various tribes originate from different parts of the continent, speak different languages, have developed different cultures, and were often at war with one another for centuries. Which tribes should speak for such a diverse race of people?

We also have the question of how these groups should be represented, particularly when they are represented through a limited set of texts. We can see this problem through the example of Richard Wright's commonly taught autobiography *Black Boy*. Without question, this book has great historical and literary significance and should be read by all Americans who seek an understanding of American society. Wright is one of the century's most important writers, and his story teaches us much about the oppressive racism in Mississippi in the early part of the century. Read, for instance, the following passage:

> One afternoon I was wheeling my barrow toward the pond when something sharp sank into my thigh. I whirled; the dog crouched a few feet away, snarling. I had been bitten. I drove the dog away and opened my trousers; teeth marks showed deep and red.
>
> I did not mind the stinging hurt, but I was afraid of an infection. When I went to the office to report that the boss's dog had bitten me, I was met by a tall blonde white girl.
>
> "What do you want?" she asked.
>
> "I want to see the boss, ma'am."
>
> "For what?"
>
> "His dog bit me, ma'am, and I'm afraid I might get an infection."
>
> "Where did he bite you?"
>
> "On my leg," I lied, shying from telling her where the bite was.
>
> "Let's see," she said.
>
> "No ma'am. Can't I see the boss?"
>
> "He isn't here now," she said, and went back to her typing.
>
> I returned to work, stopping occasionally to examine the teeth marks; they were swelling. Later in the afternoon a tall white man wearing a cool white suit, a Panama hat, and white shoes came toward me.
>
> "Is this the nigger?" he asked a black boy as he pointed at me.
>
> "Yes, sir," the black boy answered.
>
> "Come here, nigger," he called me.
>
> I went to him.
>
> "They tell me my dog bit you," he said.
>
> "Yes, sir."
>
> I pulled down my trousers and he looked.
>
> "Humnnn," he grunted, then laughed. "A dog bite can't hurt a nigger."
>
> "It's swelling and it hurts," I said.
>
> "If it bothers you, let me know," he said. "But I never saw a dog yet that could really hurt a nigger."
>
> He turned and walked away and the black boys gathered to watch his tall form disappear down the aisles of wet bricks.

Wright experienced this humiliation in 1924. Widely publicized hate crimes occurring seventy-five years later suggest that such experiences still take place. And there's no doubt that it's important for texts like Wright's to be part of our students' education.

Unfortunately, however, *Black Boy* and books from its era are frequently the only texts used to represent the African American experience in U.S. schools. Studies of U.S. curricula have found that Wright, Maya Angelou, Lorraine Hansberry, and Zora Neale Hurston are the African American authors most often included in curricula. All four writers focus on experiences from the Jim Crow era, before the Civil Rights movement began in the 1950s. It appears, then, that "the black experience" in the United States, at least as presented in schools, is one of poverty and hopeless oppression. Surely this image, while still describing the lives of too many, should not be the sole depiction of modern African American life. Indeed, such texts, framed in the segregationist times of the past, do little to shed light on the complexity and problems of what it means to live in a modern racist society.

I wish to emphasize again that these texts are exceptional works of literature and are essential reading for concerned citizens. But when they are among the few texts selected to depict the lives of African American citizens, they offer a very narrow, negative, and potentially destructive view of the experiences of black Americans. As the new century dawns, we unquestionably have far too many minority group citizens whose lives are adversely affected by discrimination. But we also have a strong, growing black middle class and prominent, successful African American leaders in all sectors of society. Should American schoolchildren be exposed to a view of African Americans that focuses almost exclusively on vitriolic, dead-end encounters with whites? Are black and white people encouraged to develop a sense of kinship with one another through exclusive exposure to such texts?

A related problem in these texts is the lumping together of "white people" as a monolithic, generally evil group. In *Black Boy,* Wright repeatedly makes statements such as "White people looked upon Negroes as a variety of children." To Wright, the white people of his community were undoubtedly quite homogeneous and could be regarded as a single culture. But many white people have very little in common with one another. An Israeli American, Hasidic Jewish delivery-truck driver from New York City, an Italian American, Catholic ACLU lawyer from Tampa, an Orthodox Greek American hairstylist from Chicago, a Norwegian American chimney sweep from rural Minnesota, a Lithuanian American, Buddhist racehorse trainer from Louisville, and a mixed-nationality atheist real-estate developer from the suburbs of Sacramento are all white people, but do they represent "white America" any more than young Richard Wright represents "black America"?

My questions for you are: If you have a goal of diversifying the curriculum to represent varied cultural groups, on what basis do you make your selections? How do you teach your selections without essentializing the cultural groups—that is, without reducing a diverse set of people to a small set of traits? What is getting represented through your selection of texts? How can you help your students to understand the complexities of multicultural education through your inclusion of multicultural texts?

Field Observation

For a class you're observing, look through the anthology used for the class. If you look at the beginning of the book, you'll find the book's editors, writers, and compilers. Does the group represent a broad spectrum of U.S. society? Is it important for the book to be produced by people from diverse backgrounds? Why or why not?

Now look through the book. To what extent does the anthology try to represent different cultural groups? What images does it consistently present of various groups?

Look at the kinds of assignments required of students. To what extent do they ask the students to engage with the kinds of issues raised in this chapter or with other issues that you find important?

Observe the teacher's use of the book. To what extent does the teacher follow the anthology's teaching script? In what ways do the students engage with the text, the class, and the teacher? To what extent does this engagement affect (a) the classroom or school community, and (b) the students' identity with their home cultures?

Diversity Issues

Look back through the unit you're designing. How have you treated issues of diversity? Are issues of culture represented in ways that are superficial and stereotypical? Are there ways you could revise your unit so that your attention to diversity is responsive to issues raised in this chapter?

FINAL THOUGHTS

If I could answer the questions I've raised, I could retire on my robust consulting fees. Like most, I'm better at posing these questions than coming up with definite answers. The tensions I've described will not go away; you will inevitably deal with them in your own teaching. At the center of these tensions is the pressure to acknowledge and respect diversity and the pressure to promote kinship and citizenship among all members of the school community. That sense of kinship needn't be, and most likely won't be, idyllic. Diverse people often disagree about what is best for the group as a whole. Seeking consensus often silences those on the margins of power. Finding kinship and community among diverse constituents, then, is often much more difficult than multicultural slogans would lead you to believe.

Discussion Topic

How should teachers address cultural differences in their teaching? Consider both the design of the curriculum and the process of classroom instruction.

Books About the Literature Curriculum and/or Censorship

Applebee, A. N. (1993). *Literature in the secondary school: Studies of curriculum and instruction in the United States* (NCTE Research Report No. 25). Urbana, IL: National Council of Teachers of English.

Beach, R. W., & Marshall, J. D. (1997). *Teaching literature in the secondary school.* Harcourt Brace Jovanovich.

Miller, S., & McCaskill, B. (1993). *Multicultural literature and literacies: Making space for difference.* Albany, NY: SUNY Press.

Moffett, J. (1988). *Storm in the mountains: A case study of censorship, conflict, and consciousness.* Carbondale, IL: Southern Illinois University Press.

Nussbaum, M. C. (1997). *Cultivating humanity: A classical defense of reform in liberal education.* Cambridge, MA: Harvard University Press.

Power, B., Wilhelm, J., & Chandler, K. (1997). *Reading Stephen King: Issues of censorship, student choice, and popular literature.* Urbana, IL: National Council of Teachers of English.

Rabinowitz, P., & Smith, M. W. (1997). *Authorizing readers: Resistance and respect in the teaching of literature.* New York: Teachers College Press.

Reichman, H. (1993). *Censorship and selection: Issues and answers for schools.* Chicago, IL: American Library Association.

Tax, M., & Agosin, M. (1995). *The power of the word: Culture, censorship, and voice.* New York: Women's Organization for Rights Literature and Development.

Rethinking Character Education

This chapter considers the question of character education, an old idea that has received renewed attention at the turn of the century because of concerns about teen sex, drug use, and violence. In this chapter I review how character is conceived, disputing some widely held beliefs about what character is and where it's located. I then link questions of character education to issues raised throughout this book, in particular my preference to approach it in constructivist rather than authoritative ways. I finally discuss how character education can be included in thematic units of instruction, illustrating the point with ideas on two thematic units, one on success and the other on peer groups, cliques, and gangs.

> Whatever success we have as teachers is measurable really only by what our students continue to take with them through their lives. And that is something we will never know.
>
> —Gayle Pemberton

These are tough times to be a kid. David Berliner and Bruce Biddle report the following facts about modern youth:

- In the 1990s, high school prostitution rose by over 260 percent
- Minors commit just under 50 percent of all criminal acts
- Over 50 percent of all murders are committed by unemployed teenagers
- Ten percent of middle schools employ security guards at their graduations
- Bullying, suicide, delinquency, violence, and dropping out of school are all increasing and regarded as critical problems

And that's just in Japan. In the United States there is evidence of similar problems among the nation's youth. As the twenty-first century begins, surveys of teens reveal that cheating, lying, stealing, alcohol use, and violence are commonplace occurrences. And, like the U.S. workplace, schools have lately become the sites of highly publicized violence.

As has often been the case throughout the history of U.S. schools, people have looked to the curriculum for a solution to a problem in society. One educational response to these alarming trends is what is known as *character education*. Many now believe that educating students with attention to character development can instill values that contribute to safe, stable, and secure schools and communities. These efforts reveal an interest in helping students learn not just the 3 Rs but also what some call the fourth and fifth Rs: right and wrong. Presumably, if schools provide character development, students will behave in more morally responsible ways.

Reflective Writing Prompt

Should schools be concerned with developing students' character? If so, what do you think student character is, and how do you think schools can provide character education? If not, why not?

WHAT DO WE TALK ABOUT WHEN WE TALK ABOUT CHARACTER?

If we're going to talk about character education, then it's a good idea to figure out what we mean by character. In this section, I'll talk about two things: what character is, and where it's located. In both cases, I'll first review the way character is most typically conceived in character curricula, and then I'll offer a different approach to thinking about it.

What Character Is

As I write this chapter, over thirty states have received federal funding to support character education. In addition, a number of private organizations are devoted to the issue of character development in youth. Often, character-education initiatives involve collaborations among schools, private organizations, businesses, communities of faith, and other organizations interested in the cultivation of a wholesome youth.

With my colleague Joel Taxel I have read a number of character-education curricula, as well as the information provided by several private organizations devoted to character education. These programs, while different in many ways, share a set of general beliefs about what character is and where it's located.

In the majority of programs we've looked at, character is represented as a set of traits. A typical list would be respect, responsibility, trustworthiness, caring, justice, and citizenship. I've come across far more extensive lists, however. In one state, the character curriculum includes twenty-seven traits identified by state politicians. Some are straight from the Boy Scout creed (trustworthy, loyal, helpful, etc.); some are dispositions (cheerful); some appear designed to make life easier for adults (punctual, school pride); and one is tied to belief systems (respect for the creator).

A character-education program is usually implemented to dissuade students from engaging in sex, drugs, and violence. One document presents this rationale succinctly: "Character education has proven to be a positive force in reducing disruptive behavior, alcohol and drug abuse, and teen pregnancy." Actually, it's hard to find any proof for the effectiveness of any character-education program. By and large the programs are implemented on faith more than on demonstrated improvements in any student's character.

This faith is based on a belief that character is not relative. Instead, it emerges from what the CHARACTER COUNTS! Coalition calls "objective criteria of virtue" that young people may adopt as ground rules for life. This organization, like others, argues that character is something that transcends race, creed, politics, gender, and wealth. One's circumstances, then, are not a factor in one's character. Rules of

Field Observation

Is safety or student conduct an issue in the school you are visiting? Try to find the following:

- Teachers' perceptions of changes in school safety and student behavior over the years and the reasons for those changes
- Facts about changes in school safety and student behavior
- Measures taken to improve school safety and student behavior, either through security or the curriculum
- If those measures exist, what the assumptions are behind them
- If those measures exist, what their effects are

conduct do not vary according to circumstances, and different cultures cannot conceive of character in different ways.

The main point I wish to make is that character is typically conceived as consisting of a set of traits that adults identify or, if they are believed to be objective criteria of virtue, that preexist in human nature. These traits are not open to question and in many conceptions of character education can be transmitted to students by adults. I know of schools that try to transmit them over the school's public address system, with a "character trait of the week" broadcast along with the daily announcements.

Where Character Is Located

I will next consider the question of where character is located. This might seem to be an odd question. It's possible that you, like most character educators, assume that character resides in the individual. It is something that a person either has or doesn't have. In this view, problems in schools arise from individual students who lack character. The character-education program, then, is designed to add character to those deficient individuals.

Consider, for instance, the following premise behind the character-education program in California:

The word "character" is derived from the Greek word "to mark" or "to engrave," and is associated with the writings of philosophers such as Plato and Aristotle. People with good character habitually display good behavior, and such habits are embedded, or marked, on a person. While there may be no specific consensus on a list of desirable character traits, there is considerable agreement on desirable moral values that underlie these traits.

Throughout history thoughtful philosophers and educators have been concerned about the cultivation of character traits and virtues such as honesty, courage, perseverance, loyalty, caring, civic virtue, justice, respect and responsibility, and trustworthiness. The consensus is that these traits (and others like them) are not innate and thus must be acquired through teaching and practice in the home and in the schools. Traits, or virtues, must be transmitted to be internalized. Children learning these lessons, however, should not behave solely based on a set of principles or rules, but rather they must learn to behave with understanding. It is an important function for educators, therefore, to help form children into adults who behave well, who demonstrate good "external conduct," and who understand why that sort of behavior is important.

This statement assumes that it is the job of (presumably virtuous) adults to transmit character to students, in the process shaping them into well-behaved citizens. This approach would appear to assume that a problem such as school violence is a problem with the character of the individual students who act violently. The solution, then, is to transmit better character traits to them. The assumptions behind the California approach are typical of character curricula.

In my view, the focus on the individual is misguided. I think character is something that's part of the *environment* in which human relationships are established

Vignette

Recent Efforts to Improve School Discipline

When I was a high school student in the 1960s, there was a national movement to grant students greater freedom. Ever since then, there have been efforts to promote greater discipline. I guess we can't have it both ways. Among the recent measures taken to improve school discipline are the following:

- Instituting school courtesy policies that require students to address teachers respectfully (e.g., as "ma'am" or "sir") or face detention
- Requiring a school uniform, or toughening dress codes
- Granting principals the authority to take action against students for unacceptable off-campus behavior that has a direct link to school safety (e.g., sending an email threat to another student from an off-campus computer)

What effects do you feel that these initiatives will have on student behavior?

and developed. Rather than viewing character on a person-by-person basis, this approach would view character as a *community* issue. Typical character-education programs ask, What's wrong with these individual kids who have sex, do drugs, and act violently, and how can we instill in them better character traits to prevent these behaviors? Taking a community-based perspective would shift the question dramatically, asking instead, What is taking place in the environment that is promoting such destructive actions?

Some of the character-education programs currently in operation take such a community-focused approach, viewing character education as a shared responsibility among parents, teachers, administrators, and community members. Adults in the community are expected to take responsibility for acting in ways that model a set of virtues for students to emulate. This approach to character education tries to create an environment conducive to good citizenship. The assumption is that when human relationships (rather than individual people) become the focus, attention shifts to creating an environment in which people will be less inclined to act in destructive ways.

HOW STUDENTS LEARN

In Part 1 of this book, I reviewed theories of learning that provide the basis for the teaching approach I endorse. You will recall that typically in schools, knowledge is viewed as a commodity or thing that can be transmitted intact from text or teacher to students. I outlined an alternative conception of teaching and learning, one that views knowledge as constructed rather than objective and transmittable.

Constructivist approaches to teaching and learning are less likely to assume that you can improve students' character by announcing character traits to them and showing them good models of people with character. Instead, they assume that students will construct their own codes of behavior no matter what you say to them. An educator's role, then, is to guide and assist this process of construction through attention to the environment, materials, and activities that students manipulate, interpret, and reconfigure.

I will next outline two approaches to character education. The first one, which I call a *didactic* approach, is the one I most typically see in character-education curricula. It is based on a transmission, authoritative view of teaching and learning. The second approach rarely appears in character-education programs, and indeed is often reviled by character educators and directors of private organizations dedicated to character development. I call this a *reflective* approach. As you might guess, this approach is well aligned with constructivist assumptions about how people learn.

Didactic Approach

One state's character-education program defines character education as "the process by which positive personality traits are developed, encouraged and reinforced through example, study (history and biography of the great and good) and practice (emulation of what has been observed and learned)." The adults determine what is good and present it to the students as something to gravitate toward. The students' role is to mimic the exemplary.

The curriculum, then, includes exemplars of people who depict good character. Their ethical behavior can serve as the model for youth to follow, likely in accordance with the sort of objective criteria for virtue discussed previously. I call this approach *didactic* because it is designed to impart a moral code of conduct. Students then are expected to follow and eventually adopt the rules of behavior that make up this code.

As I noted before, didactic approaches rely on a transmission pedagogy. I have critiqued this approach throughout this book and might try your patience if I were to do it again. And so I will next turn to the approach that I prefer, a *reflective* pedagogy for character education.

Reflective Approach

In a reflective approach, students consider problematic situations and the kinds of moral judgments required to negotiate them. Ultimately, their task is to develop and live by standards of moral conduct that they develop through reflecting on what's right and wrong, particularly when situations are complex. Key to this approach is the assumption that life is too complicated to be reduced to a fixed set of rules. The curriculum, then, focuses on complex issues that students reflect on to determine for themselves what moral action requires.

While the particular activities and assessments of reflective approaches might vary, what they share is a focus on a constructivist approach to developing a code of ethics. In most cases I would imagine that students would settle on the same codes of behavior impressed on them through didactic approaches. In a reflective approach, however, the process of instruction would emphasize the students' engagement with the issues and the resolutions they come up with for considering moral dilemmas.

The assumption here is that they will more likely abide by rules that they develop themselves than by rules that others try to instill in them. Furthermore, a reflective approach is more responsive to complex moral situations. A complex situation requires a consideration of character that is not available through the emulation of the great and good. The great and good must often be selectively portrayed in order to appear exemplary. When I was a boy, Thomas Jefferson was offered as an ex-

Vignette

Persecution of Jews has occurred throughout Western history. My Jewish grandparents lived during a particularly ugly period of genocide. They were born in the 1880s in what's now called Belarus. Right around the time of their birth, Czar Alexander II was assassinated. Although the assassin was not a Jew, false rumors incited mobs to attack Jews in over 200 cities. These attacks became known as "pogroms," meaning "devastation" or "riot." These were mob attacks, either approved or condoned by the authorities, against a religious or racial minority. Although the government did not organize pogroms, its anti-Semitic policy between 1881 and 1917 made them possible. Official persecution of Jews led to a belief that pogroms were legitimate, and those involved in them were neither discouraged nor punished.

My grandparents fled their homeland in the early 1900s to escape the ethnic cleansing carried out through pogroms. If they had accepted an inflexible set of character traits in which honesty was the only policy, they would undoubtedly have been murdered during the anti-Semitic genocide of the time. In resisting and escaping from government-supported death squads, they exhibited the courage that often appears on lists of desirable character traits. Yet they were also unpatriotic toward their government, disloyal to government officials and policies, and, I imagine, downright uncheerful much of the time. I suspect that they told a lie or two and perhaps used forged credentials to make their escape. To me they are heroic people, yet they might not measure up to the traits typically emphasized in didactic approaches to character development.

emplar of the worthy life. The storybook version of Jefferson overlooked the fact that he owned slaves and fathered children by one without acknowledging them as his own—a deadbeat dad. Jefferson, like the rest of us, was a person of contradictions and flaws. Only through selective portrayal does he become an exemplar.

I make this point because I believe that character and life are more complex than typical character-education programs make them out to be. We need, then, a definition of character that has some flexibility and takes the context of moral action into account. Let me illustrate with an example that is often found in school history books, of the slave escape route known as the Underground Railroad. The Underground Railroad is customarily presented as a great illustration of courage, both of the slaves and of the abolitionists who assisted them.

From the standpoint of typical character-education programs, however, the Underground Railroad is highly problematic. In escaping, the slaves were breaking the laws of the South, thus being bad citizens. They were also not living up to their responsibilities as slaves or showing their masters respect. They were highly untrustworthy because they would lie to protect one another. And some, such as Nat Turner, initiated bloody rebellions against their captors, which most white southerners found unjust.

I find it absurd to think that the travelers and guardians of the Underground Railroad lacked character. They were admirable and courageous because they were resisting an unjust system. A didactic approach appears to provide little accommodation for the kind of relativistic thinking required to reach this conclusion, however. I find that rigid rules are far more limiting than enabling in helping students examine complex situations, either those presented in school or those they experience in their lives.

If a student must drive someone to the hospital in an emergency, it's likely he or she will break traffic laws in doing so quickly. If a student is asked by a drug dealer to let a friend know that cocaine is available, the student might lie to protect the friend from destructive behavior. While perhaps extreme, these examples illustrate the kinds of complex situations that students face quite often. A didactic approach is much better at addressing straightforward situations, but provides few tools for thinking about the kinds of problematic situations that complicate the idea of moral action.

TEACHING CHARACTER THROUGH THEMATIC UNITS

I will next illustrate ways to include character education in the literature curriculum. Teaching through conceptual units, particularly those organized around a theme, has great potential for presenting character issues in a reflective, community-based way. I will review two very different ways to do this. First I'll describe a unit on success that I used with high school juniors. Then I'll outline some possibilities for teaching a unit on gangs, cliques, and peer-group pressure for the sophomore curriculum outlined in Part I.

A Unit on Success

It should not surprise you to learn that when I taught American literature to juniors, I tried to organize the literature into recurring themes: the literature of protest, the American dream, success, self-reliance, progress, justice, and so on. Although I did not consciously develop a character curriculum, I was always interested in having students think about the themes in terms of their own developing sense of morality and code of conduct.

The unit on success centered on a topic of great interest to my students. The notion of success is also a focus of much American literature. Students' notions of success were often tied up in money, glamour, and the material benefits they afford. It seemed like a good idea to explore how basing a conception of success solely on fame and fortune overlooks both the negative consequences of such gloried lives and the possibilities for success to come through other types of achievement.

Over the years I used a variety of texts that provided a balance in perspective. I tried to avoid selecting texts in which business values are consistently cast in a negative light—not so easy given the way in which big business is often depicted as the breeding ground for greed and avarice. I always felt that the unit was more effective if I avoided oversimplification in both exemplars of success and caricatures of evil. (See Appendix A for possible texts to include in this unit.)

Unit Goal

Given my goal of having students determine for themselves what it means to be a success, I set as a major objective the writing of an extended definition of the term *success*. Extended definitions of this sort require students to generate a set of criteria that state the principles behind the concept and then to illustrate each criterion with examples that meet them and contrasting examples that appear to meet them yet lack some fundamental element (see, for instance, the courtroom activity described in Appendix B). In order to write their definitions effectively, students needed to consider a range of examples of success. Many of these were provided by the literature. In addition, examples could come from students' own knowledge of and experience in the world, as well as from their independent reading and knowledge of popular culture, including song, film, and television.

Introductory Activity

Students' own beliefs about success provided the starting point for our discussions about the topic. One way to help students draw on their own knowledge would be to write a set of scenarios or find items in the news that illustrate problematic instances of success. These might include a person who becomes famous by committing a crime, a person who sacrifices career interests to be a homemaker, a person who gets elected school president through a dirty campaign, a person who makes a fortune but has no friends, a person who sets modest goals and reaches them, and so on. Students would then make judgments about the characters in the scenarios, perhaps ranking them according to their relative degrees of success. In doing so the students would be considering the concept on their own terms to prepare them for thinking about the issues that arise in their reading.

The ultimate goal of this discussion would be to form the basis of an extended definition of success that students would refine and illustrate as the unit progressed. I usually moved students into small groups for the generation of criteria so that each student would have an opportunity to participate in this part of the process. Students could then collaborate on generating the criteria and also have the chance to revise them as their own conceptions of success developed through the course of the unit.

An initial discussion of this sort can help students consider issues of character in ways that are highly meaningful to them. If, for instance, they feel that a wealthy, famous, professional athlete is not a success because he is conceited, self-centered, arrogant, and involved in multiple paternity suits, then they have identified issues of character that they feel are important. The point is not to coerce students into believing that money is a source of corruption, but to have them think carefully about whether money in and of itself is a mark of success.

Among the examples students consider should be people with wealth and fame and also humility, grace, compassion, and generosity. These might include those who use their time, money, and influence to establish foundations that support community projects, raise scholarship money, fund medical research, support civic and humanitarian initiatives, and so on. The question that always emerges from these considerations is, Of all these attributes, which are the ones that allow a person to be considered a success? By delineating what counts as good character and contrasting it with what only appears to be good character, students are coming closer to developing an ethical code they can live by.

Ranking Activity

The reading and discussion of the unit texts should help students refine the criteria they develop through this introductory activity. Other activities during the unit could help students come to an understanding of what they value in others and themselves. One activity I used was a ranking activity for thinking about the characters in *Death of a Salesman*. In small groups, students ranked the characters according to two scales: first, from most materialistic to least materialistic, and second, from most respected to least respected.

Although the rankings varied somewhat, they were also remarkably consistent and followed a pattern that students found both surprising and unsettling. The characters that they consistently found the most materialistic (Ben, Hap, Willie) were the characters that they respected the least, and the characters that they found the least materialistic (Linda, Bernard, Biff) were the ones they respected the most. This realization only came about in the whole-class discussion in which each group shared its rankings and all rankings were assembled on the chalkboard.

Students' recognition of this conflict often resulted in a reexamination of their own values, since most students initially were not troubled by their own materialism. After this activity, however, they had to reevaluate their values because they realized that in being materialistic, they were acting in ways they themselves did not respect.

Benefits of Reflection

I should add that this clarification did not cause students to completely abandon any sense of materialism. In fact, students helped me see possible benefits of desiring some degree of wealth. A number of students argued that having the goal of wealth helped them to develop other virtues through which they would achieve it: a work ethic, self-discipline, responsibility, and so on. Just as they were beginning to develop a more sophisticated understanding of what success entails, so was I.

In each case, I should stress, the realizations came about through reflection on why we believed as we did, reflections that often resulted in changes in those beliefs. I am skeptical that such changes would have occurred if I had instead taken a didactic approach and told students that they needed to be more disciplined and responsible, or if the principal had announced over the loudspeaker that the character trait of the week was discipline. By coming to that understanding themselves through their own consideration of what they valued, students adopted the beliefs with a certain passion and commitment to live better lives.

Unit on Peer Groups, Cliques, and Gangs

The study of peer groups can also be a good opportunity to explore questions of character. If we consider the overarching theme for the sophomore curriculum in Part I—negotiating thresholds—we see that these thresholds often require difficult moral choices. The study of peer groups can help students come to terms with a variety of issues that they face and that are central to the literature they study (see Appendix A for possible texts):

- Peer groups can provide the rules of conduct that adolescents follow. Therefore, understanding how they operate is important to understanding what kinds of rules the groups promote.

- Peer groups typically position themselves in opposition to other groups. These include other peer groups, adults, and the larger civic community. If a peer group encourages or requires behavior that is dangerous to themselves or others, students benefit from thinking about the consequences of belonging to them.

- As part of this opposition, peer groups often view other groups as threatening in some way. They therefore act in antagonistic ways toward them. Here I refer not only to rival groups that are on somewhat even footing, but also to groups on unequal footing, when one has some kind advantage in cultural capital. In school, for instance, there's usually a group generally thought by faculty to be "good" (e.g., jocks, student council members, etc.) and groups thought to be "bad" (known variously as burnouts, freaks, greasers, and other derogatory names). The jocks usually have greater capital within the school than the burnouts, and the two groups are inevitably at odds with one another.

- Related to the issue of opposition, some peer groups adopt values that condone predatory actions. A number of such cases have made the national news, including the ritual rape of girls and the routine taunting of social groups with little power in the school.

In planning a curriculum to address these thresholds, I would use a reflective, community-based approach. Typically, when a member of an outcast social group acts out in school, the behavior is treated as a problem of the individual student who lacks character. I would argue instead that these conflicts need to be addressed as a question of human relationships. Character education ought to address the whole environment in which socially unacceptable behavior takes place, rather than focusing solely on those who act out.

Some recent instances of school violence have involved students who have been treated as outcasts by other students. *Under no circumstances do I condone the kinds of violent responses they have chosen or excuse them from having personal responsibility for their actions.* I think, however, that attributing the violence solely to their bad character, without giving more thought to how the adults and other students in the school might treat one another differently, will do little to address the root causes of the problem and prevent it from happening again.

> ## Field Observation
>
> In a school you're visiting, make note of the different peer groups you can identify. Describe the following:
>
> - The characteristics of the students in each group
> - The reasons they appear to belong together
> - The ways in which they negotiate differences with other groups
> - The ways in which teachers treat members of different groups
> - The kind of influence that group members appear to have in the overall functioning of the school

Character Traits That Are Relational

Before getting too far into my description of this unit, I would like to introduce a new character trait, one that I haven't seen in any of the lists of traits of existing character-education programs. That trait is *empathy*. I think that there are a couple of reasons that empathy and similar traits don't make the list of essential traits.

First, empathy is viewed as an emotional skill rather than as a character trait. Referring to the perspectives outlined in Chapter 3, I'd say that the traits you typically see in character curricula reflect a masculine, or authoritarian conception of the world, rather than a feminine, or connected view. Interestingly, most of the character-education programs I've looked at have been the work of men. I am not surprised, then, to see that aside from the recurrence of "caring" on lists of essential traits, good character is not viewed as having an affective dimension.

Even the view of care found in the documents of character-education programs has a patronizing, rather than a relational, view of caring. The CHARACTER COUNTS! web page, for instance, defines caring as follows:

> Be kind • Be compassionate and show you care • Express gratitude • Forgive others • Help people in need

The Character Education Partnership, in outlining its fourth principle that the school must be a caring community, states:

> The school itself must embody good character. It must progress toward becoming a microcosm of the civil, caring, and just society we seek to create as a nation. The school can do this by becoming a moral community that helps students form caring attachments to adults and to each other. These caring relationships will foster both the desire to learn and the desire to be a good person. *All children and adolescents have a need to belong, and they are more likely to internalize the values and expectations of groups that meet this need.* The daily life of classrooms, as well as all other parts of the school environment (e.g., the corridors, cafeteria, playground, and school bus), must be imbued with core values such as concern and respect for others, responsibility, kindness, and fairness. (emphasis added)

The vision offered here again seems to fall short of defining care in terms of empathy. Rather, what I see is the assumption that all children will wish to belong to the core social group of the community, and that mainstreamers can make this core group more inviting by treating all with kindness. This vision does not take into consideration the possibility that members of other social groups may wish to be understood and accepted on their own terms. For mainstreamers to accept socially marginal people on their own terms, they would need to take an empathic stance toward them.

The second reason empathy is overlooked is that considering empathy as a character trait requires one to take a community-based perspective rather than an individualistic one. By and large, exercising empathy means trying to view the world through someone else's experiences and emotions. The whole thrust of taking an empathic approach is on understanding others rather than on developing individual virtues. Character then becomes defined in terms of one's relationships with others, particularly with those who are different.

The emphasis of character education then shifts from building strong individuals to building strong communities. If a student becomes violent in school, at least part of the solution needs to be an effort to understand why that person acted out and to consider how the school climate might have contributed to those actions. Again, *taking this approach does not accept or approve of the antagonistic behavior.* It does, however, consider how the behavior of others—including adults—might be a factor in creating feelings of ill will.

I would like to introduce a second term that should be central in this process, *compathy,* an obscure etymological cousin of both empathy and sympathy. Empathy refers to the projection of oneself into the personality of another in order to achieve better understanding. Sympathy describes a sameness or affinity of feelings between two or more people. Compathy refers to *feeling with* another person. It requires not simply projecting and understanding, but making an effort to *live through* that person's emotions, to resonate with that person's experiences and responses.

Acting with compathy is extremely difficult. I suspect that it's not in many dictionaries because it's so hard to do that it's barely even a word. It strikes me as a very important thing to try to do, however. Many people who are violent, disruptive, or resistant in school are in some way alienated from what they perceive to be the school's mainstream social life. It seems, then, that the first step in reducing their feelings of separation and opposition is to try to understand and share their perspective and feelings.

From what I can tell, hoping that they want to become more like you does not reduce their feelings of estrangement. In fact, a didactic approach seems to encourage what's called the *pathetic fallacy*. This occurs when you project your own personality into that of others and attribute *your* emotions to *them*. Taking an empathic or compathic approach, in contrast, requires one to make this projection with the goal of understanding and experiencing another person's sense of the world.

The unit I'm proposing on peer pressure, then, will be one based on the idea that students can learn to understand the perspectives and emotional responses of people from other groups. Rather than laying out a whole unit of instruction, I will describe some activities that could be included in a thematic study of gangs, cliques, and peer-group pressure, particularly in a school where there is concern about conflict between members of opposing social groups. I will describe an introductory activity for the unit, some recurring kinds of considerations, and some culminating texts that students could produce.

Introductory Activity

To introduce a unit on peer pressure that would promote empathy among groups, a teacher could look to current events to identify a well-known incident involving a conflict between peer groups in a school. Once the class agreed on an incident to work with, the students could divide into small groups, with each group taking a role from among the participants in the conflict under consideration. The following are possible roles:

- The student(s) from one of the social groups
- The student(s) from the other social group
- Members of the school security or disciplinary force
- The school principal
- A teacher (real or hypothetical) who could have been present during the outbreak
- Member(s) of other social group(s) determined by the class

Each group would then be responsible for creating a narrative of the incident from the perspective of its character. The medium for presenting the narrative could be the choice of the members of the group. They could write a story using their character as narrator, write and possibly perform a play depicting the events through the eyes of their character, create a computer-based animation of the events, or develop some other form for their presentation to the class.

Student groups would then present their narratives, giving the class an opportunity to see the same event played out from different points of view. Following the presentation the whole class could consider a series of questions:

- Is there an objective way to view the incident?
- How is each participant's actions and perspective justified?
- How is each participant's actions a function of a social-group identity?
- How do the social groups position themselves relative to other social groups?
- In what ways do the different social groups both understand and misunderstand one another?
- What efforts have they made to empathize with one another?
- What might be gained and lost from extending such empathy?
- To what extent is there compathy among the different groups, and what are the consequences of this degree of compathy?

I would like to take a moment to reiterate a few of the underlying assumptions about this approach. First, it is reflective rather than didactic. The students are not being presented with exemplars to imitate, but rather are being asked to think about what it is like to be another person, exemplary or not. Second, the emphasis is not on instilling missing traits in deficient characters, but on working toward a consideration of the value of a particular way of being. Third, the emphasis is not on changing particular, deficient students, but on creating a climate in which issues of character are fundamental to relationships among people.

This introductory activity should set the stage for the concepts to be emphasized during the unit. I will next describe a few ways in which they could be reexamined during the course of the unit.

Personal Experience Writing

Students could, at various points, write about experiences they have had with peer-group pressure or group conflict. They could be asked to consider these experiences from various angles. One would be to take the perspective of people within their group who are trying to get them to behave in particular ways. These ways needn't be negative. Although peer groups often provide pressure to act against perceived antagonistic groups, they can also promote prosocial behavior.

Students could also take the point of view of people against whom they align themselves: parents, teachers, antagonistic peer groups, and so on. This kind of writing could be informal, with students using some kind of journal to explore how other people in their worlds exist in relationship to them. It could also end up being formal, with students producing Faulkneresque accounts featuring multiple narrations of the same event, following the pattern of the unit's introductory activity.

Writing in Response to Literature

Students could also work at taking different perspectives in their study of literature. Through both role-playing and writing, students could try to see the world through the eyes of different characters. *The Outsiders* features two groups, the Socs and the Greasers. These are enduring categories in public schools in the United States. *The Outsiders* is narrated by Ponyboy, one of the Greasers. Students could retell different sections of the story from the perspective of another character from either of the two groups. The texts the students produce would serve to help them see situations from the perspectives of others. At the same time, they could meet more conventional goals of English classes:

- Learning strategies for reading literature (e.g., understanding narrative perspective)
- Understanding and adapting language use (e.g., knowing the worldviews, dialects, and vocabularies of particular characters)
- Writing in a conventional genre (e.g., narratives)

Discussion Topic

Do you think that it's the role of schools to promote character development? If so, how should they do it? If not, who is responsible for moral education?

FINAL THOUGHTS

Mandated changes in curriculum often require teachers to set aside additional time to do something that they would not ordinarily do, and the result is yet more fragmentation in the curriculum and less time for students to learn from their engagement with literature. While undoubtedly the character-education movement could have that effect, I also think that it can be incorporated into the instruction that is already taking place in ways that make literary engagement more enriching and meaningful to students.

The approach I have described fits well with constructivist approaches to teaching, in which students' knowledge comes through their own activity and is implicated in their development of concepts. I have argued that this approach will contribute more to students' character development than didactic approaches, which fit with authoritative approaches to schooling, in which students are expected to master material provided by teachers and texts. I believe that mastery, as conceived here, is only apparent; that is, students can memorize lists of virtues and pass tests on them, but will not necessarily adopt them. I am much more confident that a reflective, community-based approach to character education is much more likely to help students develop virtues that they believe in their bones and then live by.

Books About Moral and Character Education

Amundson, K. J. (1991). *Teaching values and ethics: Problems and solutions.* Arlington, VA: American Association of School Administrators.

Benninga, J. (1991). *Moral, character and civic education in the elementary school.* New York: Teachers College Press.

Damon, W. (1988). *The moral child.* Cambridge, MA: Harvard University Press.

Durkheim, E. (1961). *Moral education: A study in theory and application of the sociology of education.* New York: The Free Press.

Gauld, J. (1993). *Character first: The Hyde School differences.* San Francisco: ICS Press.

Huffman, H. A. (1994). *Developing a character education program.* Alexandria, VA: Association for Supervision and Curriculum Development.

Kilpatrick, W. (1992). *Why Johnny can't tell right from wrong.* New York: Simon & Schuster.

Kurtines, W., & Gewirtz, J. L. (Eds.). (1991). *Handbook of moral behavior and development.* Hillsdale, NJ: Erlbaum.

Lickona, T. (1991). *Educating for character: How our schools can teach respect and responsibility.* New York: Bantam.

Noddings, N. (1992). *The challenge to care in schools: An alternative approach to education.* New York: Teachers College Press.

Nucci, L. (1986). *Moral development and character education: A dialogue.* Berkeley, CA: McCutchan.

Purpel, D. (1988). *The moral and spiritual crisis in education: A curriculum for justice and compassion.* Granby, MA: Bergin & Garvey.

Ryan, K., & Lickona, T. (1992). *Character development in schools and beyond.* Washington, DC: Council for Research in Values and Philosophy.

Sichel, B. (1988). *Moral education: Character, community and ideals.* Philadelphia: Temple University Press.

Vincent, P. F. (1994). *Developing character in students.* Chapel Hill, NC: New View Publications.

Wynne, E., & Ryan, K. (1993). *Reclaiming our schools: A handbook for teaching character, academics and discipline.* Columbus, OH: Charles Merrill.

Unit Design

Return to the unit that you planned in Part I. Does the existing unit design provide opportunities to include attention to issues of character?

CHAPTER 15 Rethinking Standards for Teaching English

This chapter looks at national standards projects for the teaching of English language arts. I first review a set of different definitions for standards and the implications of using any one of them rather than the others. I then consider two standards projects, one for student performance and one to evaluate teachers. I next argue that teachers ought to develop their own standards rather than relying on those developed by others. To help generate discussion about what one's standards might be, I review questions teachers could consider to think about standards. Ultimately, I believe that a grassroots effort to think about standards would greatly invigorate teaching and help teachers come to a clearer understanding of why they teach the way they do. I believe that principled practice would be a likely outcome of a profession-wide discussion of educational standards.

Reflective Writing Prompt

If you were to grade the national public school system, what grade would you give it? What would be the basis for your assessment?

If you were to grade the middle or high school you attended, what grade would you give it? What would be the basis for your assessment?

Schools have always been among our most cherished institutions. They have been given the charge of teaching children what they need to know to be the next generation of productive citizens, however that might be defined. As I noted in Chapter 13, however, the pluralistic makeup of our nation has made it hard to agree on the purpose of education. And as society grows more complex and cultural groups seek a stronger identity, the educational mission increasingly becomes a source of disagreement.

To some, school is a place for the transmission of Western culture and preparation for success in college and career. To others, it's a place for people of privileged backgrounds to critique their advantages and adopt more democratic values. School is also viewed as a place where people learn the life skills that some parents don't have time to teach. Some believe that the purpose of public education is to make sure that each cultural group is included and accounted for in the curriculum. These are just a few of the countless beliefs about the mission of public education and how it should be carried out.

It's little wonder, then, that schools, given the task of accomplishing so much, are so often found to accomplish so little. Beliefs about the effectiveness of schools are paradoxical. When polled about schools, people tend to say two things:

- The school in their own community is doing a fine job (usually graded an A or B)
- Schools in general are doing a bad job (usually graded C–F)

It's easy to speculate on the reasons for this difference. One explanation is that schools on the whole are actually doing a pretty good job, as argued by David Berliner and Bruce Biddle (1995) in *The Manufactured Crisis: Myths, Fraud, and the Attack on America's Public Schools*. These authors maintain that evidence often cited to demonstrate the decline of education—including standardized test scores, the quality of the teaching force, and so on—can be interpreted to show *improvements* in the quality of education. Their argument that U.S. schools are increasingly effective is bolstered by the confidence expressed by most people in their own local system, which is the one they have the greatest knowledge and understanding of.

The belief that schools are a mess, however, is widespread and axiomatic among many people. Berliner and Biddle argue that it's to some people's advantage to hold and proclaim the belief that schools are in bad shape. Doing so, they say, supports other social agendas and shifts blame for societal problems to the convenient scapegoat of school. Because pretty much everyone goes to school, pretty much anything that happens afterwards can be blamed on education. With school missions always expanding and with schools taking on increasing responsibilities, it becomes progressively more difficult to do all things well.

It also becomes easier to identify a single goal of schooling (e.g., educating students about Western history) and use it as the sole measure of a school's effectiveness, regardless of how well the school is meeting its other missions. And with information (as well as misinformation and disinformation) increasingly accessible, it's easy to find things wrong with society for which schools can be held accountable, no matter how slim the association between the two.

To give but one example: Most schools now aim to ensure the learning of all children, and will be sued if they don't. In taking on this mission, they make a commitment to caring for and educating children who are autistic, learning disabled, teen parents, physically disabled, nonnative speakers of English, emotionally traumatized, physically and emotionally abused, and possessed of other special social, cognitive, emotional, or physical needs. Providing an equitable and appropriate education for these students requires the dedication of great funds, often in terms of extremely low teacher-to-student ratios and special facilities. While external funds are available to support such efforts, they also require funding from the district's tax base and finite school budget. Creating low teacher-to-student ratios in one part of the building often results in higher ratios in other classrooms.

Or, let's say that a health crisis comes up. In the 1980s, AIDS became an epidemic that very quickly was addressed through the school curriculum. Devoting additional time to AIDS education means devoting less time to the gerund, the periodic table of elements, or whatever else it displaces. Toward the end of the twentieth century, schools also began instituting programs to address problems with teen substance abuse, and such ideas as Red Ribbon Week were born. Red Ribbon Week activities include health education across the curriculum, school assemblies, and other interventions designed to dissuade students from drinking or using drugs. While they're learning about drugs, they're learning less about Nathaniel Hawthorne, isosceles triangles, the Civil War, and other traditional school subjects.

In addition to time, these programs require funds. Committing funds to any one area means taking them from someplace else. And so the debate team's travel budget might get cut, the science teachers might tape newspapers over the windows when showing films rather than having new curtains, the art and music programs might be discontinued, the swimming team might be eliminated, and so on.

As you can imagine, each of these decisions will anger some percentage of the population, who will feel that the school isn't doing a very good job. And this feeling will be exacerbated when the truism about the decline of education is repeated by every politician running for office, every talk-show host in search of higher ratings, every editorial writer, every college professor whose incoming students fall short in some area, and others who express views about education through public forums.

The fairly relentless criticism of schools has resulted in calls for schools to be more accountable. People want to know how their tax dollars are being spent and what they're getting for their money. They want some way to grade the schools on the job they're doing and recourse when the marks are low. Evaluating schools, like evaluating students, requires an understanding of what's being evaluated and an instrument for performing the evaluation. Making schools accountable, then, requires

- a statement on the purpose of schooling
- a statement on what it means to be well schooled in terms of that purpose
- a means through which to evaluate schools according to these beliefs

Educational historians have found that complaints about education are as old as the public school system itself. The end of the twentieth century, however, brought about one significant change: actual efforts to develop and implement ways of making schools accountable. Among these have been efforts to develop *standards* to guide schooling.

These standards movements have been very controversial, for a variety of reasons:

- Many educators believe that both teaching and learning are too complex to be assessable by a single instrument
- Effective teaching methods in one context (e.g., an AP English class) might be ineffective in another (e.g., an English class with large numbers of nonnative speakers and mainstreamed special-education students)
- Students enter school with such great variation in readiness and resources that it's difficult to set expectations for learning that will suit them all.
- Teachers have historically resisted efforts to compare teaching performances and reward excellent teachers, preferring instead a wage scale based entirely on seniority.

> One looks back with appreciation to the brilliant teachers, but with gratitude to those who touched our human feelings.
>
> —Carl Jung

Yet the political climate has made it inevitable that educators must come up with some kind of standards if they are to have credibility with their various stakeholders.

Vignette

In the early 1960s, my father was active in our school district's Parent-Teacher Association (PTA) in northern Virginia. I had three sisters and a brother, and so my parents became acquainted with a good number of teachers in the district as we went through school. After seeing considerable variation in the quality of teachers we got in school, my father felt that it was unfair for the great teachers to be paid the same as the poor ones. He had a saying: A good teacher is always underpaid, a bad teacher is always overpaid. To help address what he felt was an inequity in reward for different levels of performance, he proposed a merit pay system to the PTA and school district.

This plan met with tremendous opposition from the teachers, who argued that it's impossible to come up with a plan that distinguishes exceptional teachers from the rest. Ultimately, the plan was rejected, primarily due to the teachers' resistance to being comparatively evaluated.

This incident has been played out in many communities across the country, both in the 1960s and since. The greatest opposition to evaluations of teaching comes from teachers themselves, and indeed teachers have been among the most vocal critics of the standards projects I'll discuss in this chapter. I've always found it to be ironic that teachers grade students routinely, and accept this as central to their work, yet strongly resist efforts to have their own teaching performances graded.

WHAT DO WE TALK ABOUT WHEN WE TALK ABOUT STANDARDS?

A fundamental question that teachers should discuss when developing standards is: What do we mean when we refer to standards? One of the problems in the national debate over standards is that different people in the same conversation often have different definitions in mind. I'll next review three definitions that people use when discussing standards.

Meaning 1: Making Things the Same for All Students

This notion of standards is evident in the idea of a centralized core curriculum. If students in every school study the same content at the same time, presumably, Americans will have a common knowledge base and better sense of nationhood. This meaning of standards is also at work in the idea of "standard English," which presumes that there is a single, official set of rules for grammar and usage that should govern speech in all situations. We additionally see this notion of standards behind standardized tests; that is, tests taken by all students nationwide (or worldwide) at a particular point in schooling. The test makers claim, and many people believe, that these tests provide a reliable and valid way of comparing the effectiveness of all schools whose students take the tests.

Meaning 2: Minimum Level of Performance

President Clinton called for a national goal of all third graders' being able to read. He never clearly explained what he meant by this, but I see this as a good example of a standard specifying a minimum level of performance. We also see this notion of standards at work in many state-mandated curriculum documents that identify grade-level performance levels that all students must achieve. These competencies are described at the low end—the lowest acceptable level of performance for promotion to the next grade.

Meaning 3: Typology of Experiences

This meaning of standards is the one found in the National Council of Teachers of English/International Reading Association (NCTE/IRA) standards I'll describe later. It refers to a range of areas in which students have experience. The level of performance, however, is never described, nor are all students expected to meet the standards in the same way. Take, for instance, NCTE/IRA standard # 2: "Students read a wide range of literature from many periods in many genres to build an understanding of the many dimensions (e.g., philosophical, ethical, aesthetic) of human experience." This standard does not specify how much literature, how wide a range, which periods or genres, which literary works, or what degree of understanding a student should reach. It also does not state that each student should read the same literature or come to the same understanding. Rather, it describes a competency—reading broadly to understand life broadly. The phrasing is deliberately vague to allow individual teachers to apply it to the needs of their particular students.

STANDARDS FOR WHOM?

The standards movement has affected most school subject areas, and has had two prongs. One effort has been to identify standards for what an educated *student* ought to know in a particular discipline. The other has been to identify what a skilled *teacher* can do. Developing standards for these two groups has been undertaken by different organizations, all with different approaches. Each standards project has suffered from internal disagreements and squabbling, inevitable criticism from people outside the project, charges of invalidation from critics, and the general discord that you would expect from projects of this scope and political delicacy.

My goal in this chapter is to outline the standards efforts as they have been conceived. Because I think it's impossible to develop a national set of standards for either teachers or students that everyone will like, I'll avoid playing the critic here, and instead urge you to read the standards documents yourself and the views of their antagonists. Ultimately, I think that the standards ought to serve as points of departure for a reflective teacher, rather than guidelines to follow. My emphasis, then, will be on asking you to read them carefully, think about the values behind them, and think about what they do and don't provide you as a prospective teacher of English.

Standards for Students

The Standards for English Language Arts was a joint undertaking by the National Council of Teachers of English (NCTE) and the International Reading Association (IRA). Their object was to come up with a set of standards that would govern all learning in the discipline, grades K–12. The organizations decided to approach this task by developing a single set of standards for all grades.

This approach was quite different from that developed by other national organizations. The national standards for math and science, for instance, identify competencies that students need at particular grade levels. Here is one of the standards written by the National Council of Teachers of Mathematics:

In grades K–4, the study of mathematics should emphasize problem solving so that students can—

- use problem-solving approaches to investigate and understand mathematical content;
- formulate problems from everyday and mathematical situations;
- develop and apply strategies to solve a wide variety of problems;
- verify and interpret results with respect to the original problem;
- acquire confidence in using mathematics meaningfully.

The standard is written so that it applies to students within a particular range of schooling and so can include a greater degree of specificity than is possible with the NCTE/IRA standards. While less specific than many critics would prefer, the mathematics standard also suggests a minimum level of performance in that students must verify and interpret results, rather than simply engage in problem solving.

The NCTE/IRA standards needed to be written very broadly so that they would apply to all students, no matter how old, no matter where in school, no matter what their native language, no matter what their circumstances. Writing standards for all students requires a certain vagueness, and indeed the documents provided by the NCTE argue that their lack of specificity is their greatest strength. Because they don't prescribe how to teach, when to teach, what to teach, and so on, they may be interpreted by savvy teachers to suit the needs of particular students in particular communities.

The standards' vagueness, however, has also been a source of criticism, because the standards don't do what critics want. Critics of education want other definitions of standards to apply. First, they want to see standards that set a baseline level of performance so that "social promotions"—promotions from one grade to the next without evidence of achievement or progress—are not possible. These critics argue that a school diploma ought to certify that a graduate has a certain, measurable degree of knowledge. The NCTE/IRA standards deliberately avoid saying what this level of knowledge is.

Second, critics want greater uniformity across schools so that a high school graduate in one part of the country knows roughly the same things as a high school graduate in another. Critics often point to the way a valedictorian of one high school is not comparable to the valedictorian of another, as evidenced by standardized tests scores, college success, and other measures. At the other end of the spectrum, they point to infamous cases of students graduating from high school without being able

FIGURE 15.1   The NCTE/IRA List of Standards for the English Language Arts

The vision guiding these standards is that all students must have the opportunities and re-sources to develop the language skills they need to pursue life's goals and to participate fully as informed, productive members of society. These standards assume that literacy growth begins before children enter school as they experience and experiment with literacy activi-ties—reading and writing, and associating spoken words with their graphic representations. Recognizing this fact, these standards encourage the development of curriculum and in-struction that make productive use of the emerging literacy abilities that children bring to school. Furthermore, the standards provide ample room for the innovation and creativity es-sential to teaching and learning. They are not prescriptions for particular curriculum or in-struction.

Although we present these standards as a list, we want to emphasize that they are not distinct and separable; they are, in fact, interrelated and should be considered as a whole.

1. Students read a wide range of print and nonprint texts to build an understanding of texts, of themselves, and of the cultures of the United States and the world; to acquire new information; to respond to the needs and demands of society and the workplace; and for personal fulfillment. Among these texts are fiction and nonfiction, classic and contemporary works.
2. Students read a wide range of literature from many periods in many genres to build an understanding of the many dimensions (e.g., philosophical, ethical, aesthetic) of human experience.
3. Students apply a wide range of strategies to comprehend, interpret, evaluate, and appreciate texts. They draw on their prior experience, their interactions with other readers and writers, their knowledge of word meaning and of other texts, their word identification strategies, and their understanding of textual features (e.g., sound-letter correspondence, sentence structure, context, graphics).

to read. Such instances inflame the calls for accountability to restore the meaning of a school diploma.

The dispute over standards, then, is in part a dispute over definitions. It also rep-resents an ancient struggle between those who find diversity energizing and those who find it disruptive. The standards as written allow for great diversity because they spec-ify so little. Critics argue, however, that because they specify so little, it's possible that students will come out of schools with neither uniform nor baseline knowledge.

Figure 15.1 lists the standards developed by the NCTE and the IRA for what stu-dents should know through their engagement in English language arts.

Discussion Topic

Find out if your state has developed its own standards project or state curriculum. Contrast it with the NCTE/IRA standards. How are they similar? How are they dif-ferent? What assumptions does your state make about what's important about being a literate citizen and about how studying English in school can help bring that liter-acy about? What definitions of standards does the state curriculum or standards proj-ect rely on?

4. Students adjust their use of spoken, written, and visual language (e.g., conventions, style, vocabulary) to communicate effectively with a variety of audiences and for different purposes.
5. Students employ a wide range of strategies as they write and use different writing process elements appropriately to communicate with different audiences for a variety of purposes.
6. Students apply knowledge of language structure, language conventions (e.g., spelling and punctuation), media techniques, figurative language, and genre to create, critique, and discuss print and nonprint texts.
7. Students conduct research on issues and interests by generating ideas and questions, and by posing problems. They gather, evaluate, and synthesize data from a variety of sources (e.g., print and nonprint texts, artifacts, people) to communicate their discoveries in ways that suit their purpose and audience.
8. Students use a variety of technological and information resources (e.g., libraries, databases, computer networks, video) to gather and synthesize information and to create and communicate knowledge.
9. Students develop an understanding of and respect for diversity in language use, patterns, and dialects across cultures, ethnic groups, geographic regions, and social roles.
10. Students whose first language is not English make use of their first language to develop competency in the English language arts and to develop understanding of content across the curriculum.
11. Students participate as knowledgeable, reflective, creative, and critical members of a variety of literacy communities.
12. Students use spoken, written, and visual language to accomplish their own purposes (e.g., for learning, enjoyment, persuasion, and the exchange of information).

Standards for Teachers

The NCTE/IRA standards for students have resulted in disagreements both within the teaching profession and between the professional organizations and their public critics. A standards project developed at roughly the same time has created very great controversy, primarily within the profession. This standards project was the work of the National Board for Professional Teaching Standards (NBPTS). This group hoped to describe what good teaching is and then to develop an assessment vehicle for rewarding teachers who meet the standards.

This standards project is distinct not only in its focus (teachers rather than students) but in the definition it uses. Like the NCTE/IRA standards for students, the NBPTS standards identify categories of performance. And like the NCTE/IRA standards, they avoid specifying a uniform content that teachers need to know.

In contrast, however, the very purpose of the NBPTS standards is to identify baseline measures of performance; that is, the NBPTS uses the definition of standards that specifies a minimum level of teaching competence. And it does so at the *high* end of the spectrum. In other words, the NBPTS's goal is not to outline the lowest acceptable level at which a teacher can perform. Rather, it is trying to identify *excellence* and outline the minimum performance at which one can be labeled a superior

Standards Books Published by the NCTE

Crafton, L. K. (1996). *Standards in practice, grades K–2*. Urbana, IL: National Council of Teachers of English.

Elementary Section Steering Committee of NCTE. (1997). *The literate life: Exploring language arts standards with a cycle of learning*. Urbana, IL: National Council of Teachers of English.

Hydrick, J. (1996). *Parent's guide to literacy for the 21st century*. Urbana, IL: National Council of Teachers of English.

Myers, M. (1996). *Changing our minds: Negotiating English and literacy*. Urbana, IL: National Council of Teachers of English.

Myers, M., & Spalding, E. (Eds.). (1997). *Assessing student performance*. Urbana, IL: National Council of Teachers of English.

National Council of Teachers of English. (1995). *Teaching literature in high school: The novel*. Urbana, IL: Author.

National Council of Teachers of English. (1995). *Teaching the writing process in high school*. Urbana, IL: Author.

National Council of Teachers of English. (1996). *Guidelines for preparation of teachers of English language arts*. Urbana, IL: Author.

National Council of Teachers of English. (1996). *Motivating writing in middle school*. Urbana, IL: Author.

National Council of Teachers of English. (1996). *Teaching literature in middle school: Fiction*. Urbana, IL: Author.

National Council of Teachers of English. (1996). *Teaching reading and literature: Grades 4–6*. Urbana, IL: Author.

National Council of Teachers of English. (1997). *Teaching reading and literature in early elementary grades*. Urbana, IL: Author.

National Council of Teachers of English and International Reading Association. (1996). *Standards for the English language arts*. Urbana, IL and Newark, DE: Authors.

NCTE/IRA Joint Task Force on Assessment. (1994). *Standards for the assessment of reading and writing*. Urbana, IL, and Newark, DE: National Council of Teachers of English and International Reading Association.

Sierra-Petty, M. (1996). *Standards in practice, grades 3–5*. Urbana, IL: National Council of Teachers of English.

Smagorinsky, P. (1996). *Standards in practice, grades 9–12*. Urbana, IL: National Council of Teachers of English.

Wilhelm, J. D. (1996). *Standards in practice, grades 6–8*. Urbana, IL: National Council of Teachers of English.

teacher. The reward the NBPTS offers is a national teaching certificate that singles a teacher out as being among the nation's finest practitioners.

This project has been met with resistance on two levels. The first is that the NBPTS describes excellent teaching of a particular type, making it so that excellent teachers of other types are not deemed meritorious. The second is a disagreement with the way in which candidates are scored, even among those who agree with the NBPTS's vision of excellent teaching. The terms of this debate are outlined in a special theme issue of the NCTE journal *Voices from the Middle*, published in 1995, which is well worth reading as a primer for understanding disputes in the field.

I will next present the standards for teaching English Language Arts at two levels, early adolescence (generally for middle-school teachers) and adolescence and young adulthood (generally for high school teachers). The standards were independently developed by two different groups of subject-area experts. In the listings that follow, the levels of performance are not specified. The NBPTS is continually developing and refining scoring rubrics that distinguish levels of performance according to each of these competencies.

NBPTS Standards for Early Adolescence (Ages 11–15)/ English Language Arts

Preparing the Way for Productive Student Learning

I. Knowledge of Students

Accomplished EA/ELA teachers systematically acquire a sense of their students as individual language learners.

II. Curricular Choices

Accomplished EA/ELA teachers set attainable and worthwhile learning goals for students and develop meaningful learning opportunities while extending to students an increasing measure of control over how those goals are pursued.

III. Engagement

Accomplished EA/ELA teachers elicit a concerted effort in language learning from each of their students.

IV. Learning Environment

Accomplished EA/ELA teachers create a caring, inclusive and challenging environment in which students actively learn.

V. Instructional Resources

Accomplished EA/ELA teachers select, adapt and create curricular resources that support active student exploration of literature and language processes.

Advancing Student Learning in the Classroom

VI. Reading

Accomplished EA/ELA teachers engage their students in reading and responding to literature, and in interpreting and thinking deeply about literature and other texts.

VII. Writing

Accomplished EA/ELA teachers immerse their students in the art of writing.

VIII. Discourse

Accomplished EA/ELA teachers foster thoughtful classroom discourse that provides opportunities for students to listen and speak in many ways and for many purposes.

IX. Language Study

Accomplished EA/ELA teachers strengthen student sensitivity to and proficiency in the appropriate uses of language.

X. Integrated Instruction

Accomplished EA/ELA teachers integrate reading, writing, speaking and listening opportunities in the creation and interpretation of meaningful texts.

XI. Assessment

Accomplished EA/ELA teachers use a range of formal and informal assessment methods to monitor student progress, encourage student self-assessment, plan instruction and report to various audiences.

Supporting Student Learning through Long-Range Initiatives

XII. Self-Reflection

Accomplished EA/ELA teachers constantly analyze and strengthen the effectiveness and quality of their teaching.

XIII. Professional Community

Accomplished EA/ELA teachers contribute to the improvement of instructional programs, advancement of knowledge, and practice of colleagues.

XIV. Family Outreach

Accomplished EA/ELA teachers work with families to serve the best interests of their children.

NBPTS Standards for Adolescence and Young Adulthood (Ages 14–18+)/English Language Arts

Preparing the Way for Productive Student Learning

I. Knowledge of Students

Accomplished AYA/ELA teachers systematically acquire a sense of their students as individual language learners.

II. Knowledge of English Language Arts

Accomplished AYA/ELA teachers know their field and draw upon this knowledge to set attainable and worthwhile learning goals for students.

III. Engagement

Accomplished AYA/ELA teachers actively involve each of their students in language learning.

IV. Fairness

Accomplished AYA/ELA teachers demonstrate through their practices toward all students their commitment to the principles of equity, strength through diversity, and fairness.

V. Learning Environment

Accomplished AYA/ELA teachers create an inclusive, caring and challenging classroom environment in which students actively learn.

VI. Instructional Resources

Accomplished AYA/ELA teachers select, adapt and create curricular resources that support active student exploration of language processes and of a wide range of literature.

Advancing Student Learning in the Classroom

VII. Integrated Instruction

Accomplished AYA/ELA teachers frequently integrate reading, writing, speaking and listening opportunities in English studies and across the other disciplines.

VIII. Reading

Accomplished AYA/ELA teachers engage their students in reading and responding to literature, as well as interpreting and thinking deeply about literature and other sources.

IX. Writing

Accomplished AYA/ELA teachers immerse their students in the art of writing for a variety of purposes.

X. Discourse

Accomplished AYA/ELA teachers foster thoughtful classroom discourse that provides opportunities for students to listen and speak in many ways and for many purposes.

XI. Language Study

Accomplished AYA/ELA teachers strengthen student sensitivity to and proficiency in the appropriate uses of language.

XII. Assessment

Accomplished AYA/ELA teachers use a range of formal and informal assessment methods to monitor student progress, encourage student self-assessment, plan instruction and report to various audiences.

XIII. Self-Reflection

Accomplished AYA/ELA teachers constantly analyze and strengthen the effectiveness and quality of their teaching.

XIV. Professional Community

Accomplished AYA/ELA teachers contribute to the improvement of instructional programs, advancement of knowledge, and practice of colleagues in the field.

XV. Family Outreach

Accomplished AYA/ELA teachers work with families to serve the best interests of their children.

Readings on the NBPTS Standards for English Teachers

Barbieri, M., & Rief, L. (Eds.). (1995). National certification [Special theme issue]. *Voices from the Middle, 2*(4).

Christenbury, L. (Ed.). (1994). *English Journal, 83* (7). The debate begun in this issue was continued in the following issues: September 1995; March 1996; April 1996; January 2000.

As you can see, the two sets of standards are fairly similar. In the sections that follow, I will refer to these standards as I explore other questions. For now, I simply ask you to read through these descriptions, and possibly to go to the NBPTS website (www.nbpts.org) where the standards are fleshed out. You can also get more information on how the board assesses teachers to identify their proficiency relative to these standards.

Keep in mind that my purpose here is for you to think about these standards, rather than to adopt them. The sections that follow are intended to give you additional ways of thinking about them.

Field Observation

1. In the school you are visiting, what are the expectations for students? What assumptions underlie these expectations? How are these expectations communicated to students? How does the school respond to students who do and don't meet these expectations?

2. In the same school, what are the expectations for teachers? What assumptions about good teaching underlie these expectations? How are excellent teachers rewarded? Is there any effort to address problems with the teaching of those who are not believed to be excellent?

3. If you were to use the appropriate set of NBPTS standards to evaluate a teacher you are observing, how would the teacher rate? Is the evaluation fair? Do the standards overlook any of the teacher's strengths?

DEVELOPING STANDARDS: ISSUES TO CONSIDER

You have so far seen the outlines of two standards projects, both designed to improve the teaching and learning of the discipline called English or language arts. I would ultimately argue that these standards, rather than settling the questions, should serve as the basis for new conversations about what it means to have standards for teaching and learning in our field. From a constructivist point of view, the question then becomes; Which standards will you adopt and revise for your own purposes? On what basis do you use these standards to guide your teaching?

I will next explore issues that I think should be behind the consideration of educational standards. As you might guess, these forays are designed to raise, rather than answer, questions.

What Is English?

When developing standards for English language arts, teachers need to define their discipline. In some ways this task is easy, for the subject of English has historically included the teaching and learning of literature, writing, and language. As society becomes more complex and interdependent, however, drawing the boundaries of a discipline becomes more difficult. Indeed, interdisciplinary learning becomes more important. "Writing," for instance, describes a broad set of practices. Does it include writing business letters? Keyboarding skills? Handwriting? Songwriting? Writing across the curriculum and thus in other disciplines? Deciding what's included helps to decide what the standards ought to address.

Beyond the question of how to define a traditional strand of the curriculum such as writing, teachers need to think about what else is involved in a modern conception of English language arts. The study of film and television? Of opera and popular music? Uses of the Internet? Art and dance? Most teachers recognize the difficulty of circumscribing the field of English language arts. Doing so, however, is critical in deciding what kinds of standards should apply.

> My commitment to engaged pedagogy is an expression of political activism. Given that our educational institutions are so deeply invested in a banking system, teachers are more rewarded when we do not teach against the grain. . . . Ideally, education should be a place where the need for diverse teaching methods and styles would be valued, encouraged, seen as essential to learning. Occasionally students feel concerned when a class departs from the banking system. I remind them that they can have a lifetime of classes that reflect conventional norms.
>
> —bell hooks

Whose Standards?

The standards of both the NCTE/IRA and the NBPTS are based on values that are consistent with those that underlie this book. I would say that they rest on principles promoting teaching and learning that are

- student centered rather than centered on teachers' knowledge
- activity oriented rather than inactive
- constructivist rather than transmitted and received
- interaction based and collaborative rather than individual
- multidirectional rather than unidirectional
- open-ended rather than predetermined
- exploratory and inquiry based rather than authoritative
- built on the transaction between texts and students' personal lives rather than being solely text based

As such, the standards are not values neutral, but have a liberal perspective. My use of the term *liberal* is only partly political. I mean that the standards assume that *education is an experience that changes people* (both students and teachers) rather than an institution designed to preserve and perpetuate historical values. Teachers and students are therefore inquirers and explorers who share (and question) authority. Knowledge is thus constructed and protean, and learning is a growth process requiring reflection and inquiry. The values with which we grow up are thus not necessarily the best values for all, or even for ourselves, but they are continually evolving through exposure to and contrast with diverse sets of beliefs.

These liberal values are not shared by all members of the general public or all members of the teaching profession. To give one example: I was teaching a graduate course in the teaching of writing and one of the texts we read touted the benefits of

> It is important that students bring a certain ragamuffin, barefoot irreverence to their studies; they are not here to worship what is known, but to question it.
>
> —Jacob Bronowski

introspective writing, such as journals and personal experience narratives. One of the teachers in the class taught at a rural, Bible Belt middle school and said that she could never use any of the activities recommended in the book in her school district. She then showed us a letter that a religious organization had distributed to parents in her community, urging them to sign it and send it to their board of education. The letter appears here in its entirety:

> I am the parent of_____who attends_____School. Under U. S. legislation and court decisions, parents have the primary responsibility for their children's education, and pupils have certain rights which the schools may not deny. Parents have the right to assure that their children's beliefs and moral values are not undermined by the schools. Pupils have the right to have and to hold their values and moral standards without direct or indirect manipulation by the schools through curricula, textbooks, audio-visual materials, or supplementary assignments.
>
> Accordingly, I hereby request that my child be involved in NO school activities or materials listed below unless I have first reviewed all the relevant materials and have given my written consent for their use:
>
> - Psychological and psychiatric examinations, tests, or surveys that are designed to elicit information about attitudes, habits, traits, opinions, beliefs, or feelings of an individual or group;
> - Psychological and psychiatric treatment that is designed to affect behavioral, emotional, or attitudinal characteristics of an individual or group;
> - Values clarification, use of moral dilemmas, discussion of religious or moral standards, role-playing or open-ended discussions of situations involving moral issues, and survival games including life/death decision exercises; death education, including abortion, euthanasia, suicide, use of violence, and discussions of death and dying;
> - Curricula pertaining to alcohol and drugs;
> - Instruction in nuclear war, nuclear policy, and nuclear classroom games;
> - Anti-nationalistic, one-world government or globalism curricula;
> - Discussion and testing on inter-personal relationships; discussions of attitudes toward parents and parenting;
> - Education in human sexuality, including premarital sex; extra-marital sex, contraception, abortion, homosexuality, group sex and marriages; prostitution, incest, masturbation, bestiality, divorce, population control, and roles of males and females; sex behavior and attitudes of student and family;
> - Pornography and any materials containing profanity and/or sexual explicitness;
> - Guided fantasy techniques; hypnotic techniques; imagery and suggestology;
> - Organic evolution, including the idea that man has developed from previous or lower types of living things;
> - Discussions of witchcraft, occultism, the supernatural, and Eastern mysticism;
> - Political affiliations and beliefs of student and family; personal religious beliefs and practices;
> - Mental and psychological problems and self-incriminating behavior potentially embarrassing to the student or family;
> - Critical appraisals of other individuals with whom the child has family relationships;

- Legally recognized privilege and analogous relationships, such as those of lawyers, physicians, and ministers;
- Income, including the student's role in family activities and finances;
- Non-academic personality tests; questionnaires on personal and family life and attitudes;
- Autobiography assignments; log books, diaries, and personal journals;
- Contrived incidents for self-revelation; sensitivity training, group encounter sessions, talk-ins, magic circle techniques, self-evaluation and auto-criticism, strategies designed for self-disclosure (e.g., zig-zag);
- Sociograms; sociodrama; psychodrama; blindfold walks; isolation techniques.

The purpose of this letter is to preserve my child's rights under the Protection of Pupil Rights Amendment (the Hatch Amendment) to the General Education Provisions act, and under its regulations as published in the Federal Register of Sept. 6, 1984, which became effective Nov. 12, 1984. These regulations provide a procedure for filing complaints first at the local level, and then with the U. S. Department of Education. If a voluntary remedy fails, federal funds can be withdrawn from those in violation of the laws. I respectfully ask you to send me a substantive response to this letter attaching a copy of your policy statement on procedures for parental permission requirements, to notify all my child's teachers, and to keep a copy of this letter in my child's permanent file. Thank you for your cooperation.

Sincerely,_____

Copy to: School Principal
Child's Teachers

Anyone submitting this letter to a school system would seek the prohibition of the sorts of activities typically associated with the pedagogy called for in both standards projects. My approach to character education (outlined in Chapter 14), for instance, would be unacceptable according to this document. So would any introductory activities that engaged students in reflection on their beliefs, or any use of reading logs, or any efforts to build literary understanding on personal knowledge or experience. I imagine that you'd have to greatly modify the principles of practice I use in this book to be considered a good teacher in such places.

My point is not to criticize either the standards or those communities that reject them. My point is simply to clarify that the standards are driven by a liberal ideology that is not shared by all. I think it would be healthy to have additional standards projects to help balance our perspective on the issue of standards and schooling. I would like to see what English language arts standards would look like if developed by

- parents from various conservative or orthodox religious groups
- urban minority parents (or subgroups therein)
- rural parents
- a gay/lesbian task force
- students
- dropouts
- K–12 English language arts teachers who are not members of the IRA or the NCTE

- teachers at exclusive private schools
- English language arts teachers in each school district in the United States

I think that the national dialogue about standards would be much better informed if we heard from these groups and others. My question to you as a prospective teacher is, When you think about an ideology for teaching, what is it and what kinds of standards emerge from it?

Discussion Topic

To what extent is teaching ideological? If an ideology is behind a teaching approach, what are the consequences for students who hold a different set of beliefs? What standards for both teachers and students emerge from different ideologies?

Goals for Schooling and Students and Notions of the Ideal Adult

All teachers, as I have said throughout this book, teach with goals in mind. I also think that they teach with a sense of what someone is like following an education. The Greeks used the word *telos* to describe our sense of an optimal outcome or ideal destination. I think that in order for teachers to discuss standards, they need to uncover for themselves what kind of citizen they are hoping to encourage through their instruction.

A number of educational writers have proposed that education should cultivate particular traits. I next present a list of some I have come across in my recent reading. Many of these traits suggest different goals and practices for education. Schools, say these writers, should be devoted to producing students, and ultimately adults, who are

- caring (Noddings, 1992)
- subversive (Postman & Weingartner, 1987)
- thoughtful (Brown, 1993)
- culturally literate (Hirsch, 1987)
- civic minded (Stotsky, 1991)
- imaginative (Bogdan, 1992)
- democratic (Dewey, 1966)
- joyous (Newman, 1996)
- virtuous (Bennett, 1993)
- politically liberated (Freire, 1970)
- personally liberated (Montessori, 1964)
- self-motivated (Csikszentmihalyi & Larson, 1984)
- scientific (Piaget, 1952)
- skeptical (Foucault, 1972)
- reflective (Schon, 1991)
- free (Greene, 1988)
- domestic (Martin, 1995)
- inquiring (Dewey, 1960)
- compassionate (Jesus Christ, n.d.)

Books That Present Conceptions of the Ideal Adult

Bennett, W. J. (Ed.). (1993). *The book of virtues: A treasury of great moral stories.* New York: Simon & Schuster.

Bogdan, D. (1992). *Re-educating the imagination: Toward a poetics, politics, and pedagogy of literary engagement.* Portsmouth, NH: Heinemann.

Brown, R. G. (1993). *Schools of thought: How the politics of literacy shape thinking in the classroom.* San Francisco: Jossey-Bass.

Csikszentmihalyi, M., & Larson, R. (1984). *Being adolescent: Conflict and growth in the teenage years.* New York: Basic Books.

Dewey, J. (1960). *The quest for certainty.* New York: Putnam.

Dewey, J. (1966). *Democracy and education: An introduction to the philosophy of education.* New York: The Free Press.

Foucault, M. (1972). *The archaeology of knowledge and the discourse on language.* New York: Pantheon.

Freire, P. (1970). The adult literacy process as cultural action for freedom. *Harvard Educational Review, 40,* 205–212.

Greene, M. (1988). *The dialectic of freedom.* New York: Teachers College Press.

Hirsch, E. D. (1987). *Cultural literacy: What every American should know.* Boston: Houghton Mifflin.

Jesus Christ (n. d.). Cited in *The Holy Bible.*

Martin, J. (1995). *The schoolhome.* Cambridge, MA: Harvard University Press.

Montessori, M. (1964). *The Montessori method* (A. E. George, Trans.). Cambridge, MA: Robert Bentley.

Newman, F. (1996). *Performance of a lifetime: A practical-philosophical guide to the joyous life.* New York: Castillo International.

Noddings, N. (1993). *The challenge to care in schools: An alternative approach to education.* New York: Teachers College Press.

Piaget, J. (1952). *The origins of intelligence in children.* New York: Norton.

Postman, N., & Weingartner, C. (1987). *Teaching as a subversive activity.* New York: Dell.

Schon, D. A. (Ed.). (1991). *The reflective turn: Case studies in and on educational practice.* New York: Teachers College Press.

Stotsky, S. (Ed.). (1991). *Making connections between civic education and language.* New York: Teachers College Press.

This list is not intended to be comprehensive. My point is that teachers are future oriented. They see their work as having consequences for how students turn out. They also believe that there are better and worse ways to turn out. These beliefs have implications for the kinds of teaching they do and the kinds of expectations they have for students. Any effort to develop standards for students needs to acknowledge what these assumptions are and account for them.

Metaphors for Schooling

Another way to help think about standards is to consider metaphors for the process of schooling. A number of metaphors are commonly used to describe schools and their functions. I'll review a few, with examples of their implications for teaching and learning.

School as Factory

When school is viewed as a factory, teachers are seen as workers and students as products. Both become forms of capital. Schooling conducted in this way seeks a uniform set of procedures and products and the most efficient way of production. Schools must be accountable in measurable ways (test scores, cost/production ratios, etc.). Preserving the chain of command is important, suggesting a hierarchy running from administrators at the top to students on the bottom.

School as Health Care

In this view of schooling, students are viewed as diseased, and it is the teacher's job to cure them. Diagnosing deficiencies and providing corrective instruction is a central teaching practice. Students are largely viewed in terms of their deficits, and teachers' success comes through their rate of curing.

School as Prison

This metaphor has been quite durable among students for many generations. Adults, too, can see school as a place designed to punish offenders. Writing teachers have often lamented the ways in which disciplinarians use writing in punitive ways (e.g., writing "I will not . . ." a hundred times). Schools in which teachers are required, on the first day of school, to explain classroom management plans that center on escalating forms of punishment seem to reinforce students' idea that school is a prison.

School as War

It's common to hear teaching described as conducted "on the front lines" or "in the trenches." Sadly, this characterization often comes from teachers themselves. This bellicose notion of teaching presents students and teachers (and teachers and administrators, teachers and parents, etc.) as being in a perpetual state of opposition and combat. Students are thus seen as a group that needs to be conquered or subdued because of the threat they pose to teachers' security and authority.

School as Athletics

This metaphor is similar to the school as war viewpoint, though the combat is not quite so deadly and the competition is with other students rather than with the teacher. Teachers put students through drills on fundamentals as preparation for high-stakes, winner-take-all competitions (i.e., exams). The metaphors to describe the teacher are not consistent. On the one hand, educators often describe the teacher as a benevolent coach who gives personal advice, nurtures students along, and is warm and friendly. I played competitive sports for many years and don't remember meeting a coach quite like this. Most yelled a lot, seemed to dislike their players (especially the ones who weren't very good), and were much more concerned with their own coaching records than with their players' development as human beings. Yet this image persists among educational writers, most of whom I must conclude probably never played competitive, organized sports.

Vignette

Back when I was substitute teaching in central New Jersey in the mid-1970s, I worked in a junior high school that had what they called "The Opportunity Room." The Op, as students called it, was where they were sent when they misbehaved. I visited The Op on a few occasions to see how the school's discipline problems were handled. For the most part they were punished with writing. At least one student was always covering the chalkboard with repeated writing of "I will not throw the garbage can at the teacher" or whatever else the student might have done.

Imagine, then, the English teacher who tries to persuade this student that writing is the key to success, a significant form of self-discovery, a tool for learning, a means to a better future. I'm not excusing the disruptive behavior. I'm saying that you can't punish students by making them do work that, elsewhere in the building, you're trying to convince them will lead to greater success and happiness.

Teacher as Gardener

Teaching is also seen as a form of cultivation. Teachers provide a fertile ground for growth, plant their seeds with care, know the proper type and amount of stimulation for each type of plant, and otherwise raise a crop of healthy, hearty, prosperous students through tender loving care. On the downside of this metaphor, teachers weed out the bad students or separate the grain from the chaff. In general, though, healthy growth through care and nourishment are the primary goals of schooling as gardening.

Teaching as Construction

I've already described this metaphor in detail throughout this book (in case you've forgotten).

Summary

Each of these metaphors has different implications for how to teach and what kind of student comes out in the end. The list is probably not comprehensive. My point is that teachers who consider the issue of educational standards ought to examine their metaphors for schooling to help identify their assumptions about what they expect students to do and how they mean to help them do it.

> **Reflective Writing Prompt**
> What metaphor would you use to describe your beliefs about teaching, learning, and schooling? Try to extend your metaphor as far as possible.

USING STANDARDS TO DEVELOP STANDARDS

To close this book, I will ask you to begin a conversation that you will likely be engaged in throughout your teaching career. That conversation will address several questions: What is an educational standard? Why do I hold this belief? What standards will be behind my own teaching? How will my teaching reflect standards for both myself and my students?

I have been teaching for almost twenty-five years now and still labor over these questions. Rather than considering them a burden, I find the ongoing effort to answer them energizing, challenging, inspiring, and enlightening. I have had involvement with both the NCTE/IRA and NBPTS projects, and while they've been immensely frustrating at times, the discussions surrounding their development have forced me to think about my work as a teacher much more clearly. I hope that as I leave you with these questions, you will find that your own career is a quest to think carefully about what you do and why you do it. In essence, engaging with these questions will inevitably lead to the development of principled practice, which is where I began this book and where I hope you begin yours.

> Leont'ev says, "Thus the movement of an animal along a fence is subordinate to the 'geometry,' becomes assimilated by it, and carries it within itself." And, having learned how fences (the Alaska pipeline, 10-lane interstate highways, the expansion of residential areas) transform animals' paths of migration, how they hasten alongside the fence until they die of lack of water, I can suddenly picture the importance of what he's saying: that the actual physical (and social) geometry in which our activity engages becomes part of the psychological engine of the activity. One can imagine the various "fences" that clutter the landscape of, for example, education. The students and teachers trotting alongside those fences, trusting that at some point the fence will end and they will be able to cross over and get back on the path before they die of thirst—and some of them who assimilate the fence and begin to say, "The fence IS the path."
>
> —Helena Worthen

Discussion Topic

With a small group of students or teachers, consider each NCTE/IRA standard and answer the following questions:

- To what degree should these standards include attention to baseline levels of performance and uniform content for all students (i.e., the two definitions of standards eschewed by the IRA and the NCTE)?
- Do you agree with each of the twelve standards as a central focus of English instruction?
- What standards are missing that you would add?
- How do your standards fit with the overriding values of the citizens and faculty of the communities in which you have taught or observed?
- How do you put these standards into practice?
- What notion of the ideal adult, and what metaphors about schooling, are suggested by your revised standards?
- How will you assess students' meeting of these standards?

Unit Design

Unit Design

1. Look back through the unit you have designed. Which standards are at work in your expectations for students? These standards might come from the NCTE/IRA project, but more fruitfully would come from your own consideration and discussion of appropriate standards. How useful do you find these standards in thinking about student learning?

2. How would your unit design be evaluated from the standpoint of either set of NBPTS standards (i.e., middle or high school)? What aspects of your teaching are these standards sensitive to? Are there any teaching strengths that might be overlooked by these standards? How useful do you find these standards in helping you to evaluate your own teaching?

3. In what ways might your understanding of multicultural literature, character education, or educational standards cause you to reconsider and revise the rationale you provide for your unit?

Afterword: Theory in Practice

In this book I have raised questions about some truisms that dominate and limit public discussions about education. One is that schools are doing a terrible job. While I think that schools can do much better, I agree with Berliner and Biddle's view that there's little evidence to support the widely held and wildly circulated assumption that schools are in a state of decline and disarray.

I've also questioned the notion that schools are hotbeds of political correctness. Quite the contrary. Study after study has shown that schools are actually quite conservative places, driven primarily by authoritative approaches to teaching that have dominated Western schools since the time of the ancient Greek academies. It's quite true that many highly quotable radicals advocate more reformist pedagogies, but I doubt if you'll see many of them at work (either the radicals or the pedagogies) in actual schools.

I would like to take on another truism, now that you've presumably read this book. That truism is: Teachers aren't interested in theory. Arthur Applebee (1993) quotes one teacher who, when asked about contemporary literary theory, said that theories are "far removed from those of us who work the front lines!" (p. 122). The remark is quite revealing about what I think is the real nature of the problem. I would say that the problem is not that teachers reject theory. I suspect that this teacher could not effectively work "in the trenches" or "on the front line" without some theory of what she's doing (see Chapter 15 for the "school as war" metaphor for teaching). Regardless of how you perceive classroom work (war, gardening, incarceration, etc.), you have a set of beliefs about what you're working toward, how you should get there, which materials best enable a good trip, and so on. Indeed, the teacher quoted by Applebee conveys many of her beliefs about teaching simply by declaring that she's on the front line.

What I think that this teacher, and many others, reject is the way theory is presented. Typically, theorists present their ideas through an array of specialized, polysyllabic terms (ventriloquation, deconstruction, interinanimation, etc.) that require them to explicate extensive sets of formal rules and abstractions. I've done this in a lot of my own writing. Teachers' interests are more pragmatic, and so wading through the technical language and abstract concepts of the theoretical specialist can be daunting and unproductive. As a result, many teachers say that theory is impractical and irrelevant. What I think they're really saying is that *theorists* are impractical and irrelevant, at least to their needs. My goal is to criticize neither theorists for doing their work, nor teachers for doing theirs. Rather, I simply aim to explain what I think is a crucial problem in sorting out what is and isn't useful for a classroom teacher.

In this book I have tried to present a theoretically grounded approach to teaching. I have tried to do this without getting the project bogged down in the task of the theoretician, which is to focus primarily on an elaboration of concepts through technical language. I've done my share of that in other things I've written for readers with other interests.

My approach, rather, has been to present *theory as an extended metaphor,* much as the teacher does in locating herself on the battlefield of instruction. The essence of the theory I've proposed is that people learn by making, and reflecting on, things that they find useful and important. They do so through a process of composition in which they develop goals, locate appropriate tools and materials, develop plans, and construct a text. Throughout this process of composition they revise their goals and plans to meet arising circumstances, use new tools and materials as needed, reflect on the emerging text, and reconsider how and why they're making it.

This process enables learners to construct new meaning as they work, both through emerging ideas and those that come through reflecting on the text during production. The learners I refer to include both those we call teachers and those we call students, although I think that their roles can get merged in dynamic classrooms. While the texts constructed by learners may reach a point of temporary completion, they are part of an ongoing effort to construct meaning, and so may serve as points of reflection for the development of new compositions. Texts, then, are occasions for learning both through the process of composition and reflection on the product, both on its provisional form during composition and on its equally provisional form when completed for school assessment.

All of this composing takes place in some kind of social context. The context of construction has a lot to do with the kinds of compositions and composition processes that are valued and encouraged. The context includes things outside the classroom: a state-mandated curriculum, a set of district policies, the role of parents in policymaking, the pressures exerted by colleagues, and so on. Often, these social forces encourage authoritarian approaches to schooling and the production of texts with particular features (e.g., textbook English, five paragraphs, etc.).

The context also includes the way in which you set up your classroom. If you place the seats in rows facing you at the front, you discourage the use of speech as a tool for exchanging and constructing ideas among students. If you allow for multimedia composing, then you open up students' tool kits for constructing meaningful texts. An act or text is rarely meaningful in and of itself. Rather, it takes on meaning through the validating effect of the environment. If a teacher only values five-paragraph themes and a student submits a statue to interpret a novel, then the statue will have no significance or worth in this context, regardless of what the student has learned or how the statue might be appreciated in another context.

Books on Vygotskian Activity Theory

Chaiklin, S., & Lave, J. (Eds.). (1996). *Understanding practice: Perspectives on activity and context.* New York: Cambridge University Press.

Cole, M. (1996). *Cultural psychology: A once and future discipline.* Cambridge, MA: Harvard University Press.

Cole, M., Engestrom, Y., & Vasquez, O. (Eds.). (1997). *Mind, culture, and activity: Seminal papers from the Laboratory of Comparative Human Cognition.* New York: Cambridge University Press.

Engestrom, Y., Miettinen, R., & Punamaki, R-L. (Eds.). (1999). *Perspectives on activity theory.* New York: Cambridge University Press.

Lave, J. (1988). *Cognition in practice.* New York: Cambridge University Press.

Lee, C. D., & Smagorinsky, P. (Eds.). (2000). *Vygotskian perspectives on literacy research: Constructing meaning through collaborative inquiry.* New York: Cambridge University Press.

Moll, L. C. (Ed.). (1990). *Vygotsky and education: Instructional implications and applications of sociohistorical psychology.* New York: Cambridge University Press.

Newman, D., Griffin, P., & Cole, M. (1989). *The construction zone: Working for cognitive change in school.* New York: Cambridge University Press.

Rogoff, B. (1990). *Apprenticeship in thinking: Cognitive development in social context.* New York: Oxford University Press.

Rogoff, B., & Lave, J. (Eds.). (1984). *Everyday cognition: Its development in social context.* Cambridge, MA: Harvard University Press.

Rogoff, B., & Wertsch, J. V. (Eds.). (1984). *Children's learning in the "zone of proximal development."* San Francisco: Jossey-Bass.

Tharp, R. G., & Gallimore, R. (1988). *Rousing minds to life: Teaching, learning, and schooling in social context.* New York: Cambridge University Press.

Tobach, E., Falmagne, R. J., Parlee, M. B., Martin, L. M. W., & Kapelman, A. S. (Eds.). (1997). *Mind and social practice: Selected writings of Sylvia Scribner.* New York: Cambridge University Press.

Tulviste, P. (1991). *The cultural-historical development of verbal thinking* (M. J. Hall, Trans.). Commack, NY: Nova Science Publishers.

One other thing is important in order for the metaphor of construction to be useful as a theory of teaching: You need to get fulfillment from doing work. I mean this in several ways. First of all, I mean that what I've outlined in this book will require a lot of work from you. You can't go on cruise control and let the teacher's manual or curriculum do all of the thinking and teaching for you. Rather, you need to view instructional design as stimulating, intellectually challenging, important work that can potentially put you in the flow. You need to get satisfaction out of putting a lot of effort into something with the understanding that it will probably result in a provisional product that you'll need to revise. You need to enjoy the challenge of aligning goals and practices, of devising activities that students will find engrossing and enlightening, of channeling your creativity into the production of the text that serves as your unit of instruction.

You also need to be prepared to do work in response to what your students produce. Grading papers takes a lot of time. But it's unlikely that students will learn to

Books on Vygotskian Activity Theory

van der Veer, R., & Valsiner, J. (1991). *Understanding Vygotsky: A quest for synthesis.* Cambridge, MA: Blackwell.

Vygotsky, L. S. (1978). *Mind in society: The development of higher psychological processes* (M. Cole, V. John-Steiner, S. Scribner, & E. Souberman, Eds.). Cambridge, MA: Harvard University Press.

Vygotsky, L. S. (1987). *The collected works of Lev Vygotsky: Vol. 1. Problems of general psychology* (R. Rieber & A. Carton, Eds.; N. Minick, Trans.). New York: Plenum.

Vygotsky, L. S. (1993). *The collected works of L. S. Vygotsky: Vol. 2. The fundamentals of defectology (abnormal psychology and learning disabilities)* (R. Rieber & A. Carton, Eds.; J. Knox & G. Stevens, Trans.). New York: Plenum.

Vygotsky, L. S. (1997). *The collected works of Lev Vygotsky: Vol. 3. Problems of the theory and history of psychology* (R. Rieber & J. Wollock, Eds.; R. van der Veer, Trans.). New York: Plenum.

Vygotsky, L. S. (1997). *The collected works of Lev Vygotsky: Vol. 4. The history of the development of higher mental functions* (R. Rieber, Ed.; M. J. Hall, Trans.). New York: Plenum.

Wells, G. (Ed.). (1994). *Changing schools from within: Creating communities of inquiry.* Toronto: OISE Press; Portsmouth, NH: Heinemann.

Wells, G. (in press). *Thinking with Vygotsky.* New York: Cambridge University Press.

Wells, G., & Chang-Wells, G. L. (1992). *Constructing knowledge together: Classrooms as centers of inquiry and literacy.* Portsmouth, NH: Heinemann.

Wertsch, J. V. (1985). *Vygotsky and the social formation of mind.* Cambridge, MA: Harvard University Press.

Wertsch, J. V. (1991). *Voices of the mind: A sociocultural approach to mediated action.* Cambridge, MA: Harvard University Press.

Wertsch, J. V. (1996). *Mind as action.* New York: Oxford University Press.

Wertsch, J. V., del Rio, P., & Alvarez, A. (1995). *Sociocultural studies of mind.* New York: Cambridge University Press.

write unless they're writing, and it's unlikely that they'll grow as writers without your earnest, engaged response to their papers. There will be times when grading a volume of student writing (or other composing) will be a grind. But the overall satisfaction that you get from participating in their growth should overcome whatever time commitment is involved in evaluating their work.

You also need to be prepared to do work alongside your students. Sometimes this means doing a project of the same type they are doing: writing with them during a writing workshop, keeping a portfolio about your teaching as they keep one about their learning. Sometimes it means doing a project to understand better how they are learning: doing a frame experiment to understand the effects of your instruction, charting the development of relationships that follow from a change in your teaching. Sometimes it means conducting an ethnographic experiment in order to learn more about your students' lives outside school so that you can teach them in ways that build on their strengths. Becoming an actively reflective practitioner will require an inquiring stance and the time that it takes to enact it. But doing so can make your work as a teacher much more stimulating than it would be if you were simply to pass out the handouts that accompany your commercial literature anthology and grade them with an electronic scanner.

Your students also need to have some kind of work ethic. I think that students do, but that much school instruction dulls it, at least with regard to schoolwork. I found that when I involved my students in constructive, productive activity, they would work pretty hard and feel pretty good about what they produced. Of course, this doesn't happen with everything you do. Some things you teach in the English curriculum are not going to light a fire under every student. But you can make an effort to teach so that it happens as often as possible.

My notion of work is not of the nose-to-the-grindstone variety, although there are times when that's what you need to do. Rather, it refers to the labor of love, the transforming potential of authentic, constructive, productive activity. I think that, whatever else a standards document might measure, all great teachers love what they do and do it with passion. If they stay up till 2 A.M., it's not because they don't know what to do the next day, it's because they're so involved with their work that they lose track of time. When you teach with this kind of engagement and passion, you won't need a standards document to tell you that you're an exceptional teacher. Your students will know, and will show their appreciation and respect in ways that you just can't get through a national teaching certificate.

This extended metaphor I've outlined embodies a theory that goes under more than one name. I use the terms *activity theory* or *cultural-historical activity theory*, based primarily on the work of Lev Vygotsky. I'll not belabor the technical aspects of the theory now, but if you continue with your formal education and are interested in understanding the basis for the teaching approach I've laid out in this book, you might look for courses in which Vygotsky's work is featured. If you wish to take on the ambitious task of reading this challenging work on your own, you might look into the texts listed on pp. 342–343.

Reading them might be a stretch and a challenge. But think about what you ask your students to do: to read texts that are at the limits of what they grasp, to grow into new ways of thinking, knowing, and doing. Should you expect anything less of yourself?

REFERENCES

Abercrombie, M. L. J., & Terry, P. M. (1978). *Talking to learn: Improving teaching and learning in small groups*. Guildford, NY: Society for Research into Higher Education.

Ada, A. F., Harris, V. J., & Hopkins, L. B. (1993). *A chorus of cultures: Developing literacy through multicultural poetry*. Carmel, CA: Hampton-Brown.

Adams, D. M., & Hamm, M. (1996). *Cooperative learning: Critical thinking and collaboration across the curriculum*. Springield, IL: C. C. Thomas.

Adler, M. J. (1999). *The great ideas: A lexicon of Western thought*. New York: Scribner.

Airasian, P. W. (1996). *Assessment in the classroom*. New York: McGraw-Hill.

Allen, J., Cary, M., & Delgado, L. (1995). *Exploring blue highways*. New York: Teachers College Press.

Allison, L., Bryant, L., & Hourigan, M. (Eds.). (1997). *Grading and the post-process classroom*. Portsmouth, NH: Heinemann.

American Association of University Women. (1995). *The AAUW Report: How schools shortchange girls*. New York: Marlowe.

Amundson, K. J. (1991). *Teaching values and ethics: Problems and solutions*. Arlington, VA: American Association of School Administrators.

Anderson, G., Herr, K., & Nihlem, A. (1994). *Studying your own school: An educator's guide to qualitative practitioner research*. Thousand Oaks, CA: Corwin Press.

Anson, C. M. (Ed.). (1989). *Writing and response: Theory, practice, and research*. Urbana, IL: National Council of Teachers of English.

Apple, M. W. (1982). *Education and power*. Boston: Routledge & Kegan Paul.

Applebee, A. (1974). *Tradition and reform in the teaching of English: A history*. Urbana, IL: National Council of Teachers of English.

Applebee, A. N. (1981). *Writing in the secondary school*. Urbana, IL: National Council of Teachers of English.

Applebee, A. N. (1986). Musings . . . principled practice. *Research in the Teaching of English, 20*, 5–7.

Applebee, A. N. (1993). *Literature in the secondary school: Studies of curriculum and instruction in the United States* (NCTE Research Report No. 25). Urbana, IL: National Council of Teachers of English.

Applebee, A. N. (1996). *Curriculum as conversation: Transforming traditions of teaching and learning*. Chicago: University of Chicago Press.

Arbib, M. A., Conklin, E. J., & Hill, J. A. C. (1987). *From schema theory to language.* New York: Oxford University Press.

Atwell, N. (Ed.). (1989). *Workshop 1 by and for teachers: Writing and literature.* Portsmouth, NH: Heinemann.

Atwell, N. (1998). *In the middle: New understandings about writing, reading, and learning* (2nd ed.). Portsmouth, NH: Heinemann.

Ause, C., Brunjes, H. E. B., & Spear, K. I. (1993). *Peer response groups in action: Writing together in secondary schools.* Portsmouth, NH: Heinemann.

Banks, J. A. (1998). *An introduction to multicultural education* (2nd ed.). Boston: Allyn and Bacon.

Barbieri, M. (1994). *Workshop 6: The teacher as writer.* Portsmouth, NH: Heinemann.

Barbieri, M., & Rief, L. (Eds.). (1995). National certification [Special theme issue]. *Voices from the Middle, 2*(4).

Barnes, D. R. (1992). *From communication to curriculum* (2nd ed.). Portsmouth, NH: Heinemann.

Barnes, D. R., Britton, J., & Torbe, M. (1990). *Language, the learner, and the school* (4th ed.). Portsmouth, NH: Heinemann.

Barnes, D. R., & Todd, F. (1995). *Communication and learning revisited: Making meaning through talk.* Portsmouth, NH: Heinemann.

Baron, D. (1994). *Guide to home language repair.* Urbana, IL: National Council of Teachers of English.

Beach, R. W. (1993). *A teacher's introduction to reader-response theories.* Urbana, IL: National Council of Teachers of English.

Beach, R. W., & Marshall, J. D. (1991). *Teaching literature in the secondary school.* Harcourt Brace Jovanovich.

Bean, J. C. (1996). *Engaging ideas: The professor's guide to integrating writing, critical thinking, and active learning in the classroom.* San Francisco: Jossey-Bass.

Belanoff, P., & Dickson, M. (Eds.). (1991). *Portfolios: Process and product.* Portsmouth, NH: Heinemann.

Belenky, M. F., Clinchy, B. M., Goldberger, N. R., & Tarule, J. M. (1986). *Women's ways of knowing: The development of self, voice, and mind.* New York: Basic Books.

Bellack, A., Kleibard, H., Hyman, R., & Smith, F. (1966). *The language of the classroom.* New York: Teachers College Press.

Bennett, W. J. (Ed.). (1993). *The book of virtues: A treasury of great moral stories.* New York: Simon & Schuster.

Benninga, J. (1991). *Moral, character and civic education in the elementary school.* New York: Teachers College Press.

Berliner, D. C., & Biddle, B. J. (1995). *The manufactured crisis: Myths, fraud, and the attack on America's public schools.* New York: Longman.

Bizanno, P. (1993). *Responding to student poems: Applications of critical theory.* Urbana, IL: National Council of Teachers of English.

Black, L., Daiker, D., Sommers, J., & Stygall, G. (Eds.). (1994). *New directions in portfolio assessment: Reflective practice, critical theory, and large-scale scoring.* Portsmouth, NH: Heinemann.

Bloom, A. (1987). *The closing of the American mind.* Touchstone.

Bloom, B. (Ed.). (1956). *Taxonomy of educational objectives: Cognitive and affective domains.* New York: David McKay.

Bogdan, D. (1992). *Re-educating the imagination: Toward a poetics, politics, and pedagogy of literary engagement.* Portsmouth, NH: Heinemann.

Bomer, R. (1995). *Time for meaning: Crafting literate lives in middle and high school.* Portsmouth, NH: Heinemann.

Booth, W. (1974). *A rhetoric of irony.* Chicago: University of Chicago Press.

Bransford, J. D. (1979). *Human cognition: Learning, understanding and remembering.* Belmont, CA: Wadsworth.

Britton, J., Burgess, T., Martin, N., McLeod, A., & Rosen, H. (1975). *The development of writing abilities (11-18).* London: Macmillan Education Ltd. for the Schools Council.

Brown, R. G. (1993). *Schools of thought: How the politics of literacy shape thinking in the classroom.* San Francisco: Jossey-Bass.

Bruner, J. (1983). *Child's talk: Learning to use language.* New York: Norton.

Bruner, J. (1986). *Actual minds, possible worlds.* Cambridge, MA: Harvard University Press.

Bruner, J. (1996). *The culture of education.* Cambridge, MA: Harvard University Press.

Calfee R., & Perfumo, P. (1996). *Writing portfolios in the classroom.* Hillsdale, NJ: Erlbaum.

Calkins, L. M. (1994). *The art of teaching writing.* Portsmouth, NH: Heinemann.

Capossela, T. L. (1993). *The critical writing workshop: Designing writing assignments to foster critical thinking.* Portsmouth, NH: Heinemann.

Cazden, C. B. (1988). *Classroom discourse: The language of teaching and learning.* Portsmouth, NH: Heinemann.

Cazden, C. B. (1992). *Whole language plus: Essays on literacy in the United States and New Zealand.* New York: Teachers College Press.

Cazden, C. B., John, V. P., & Hymes, D. (Eds.). (1972). *Functions of language in the classroom.* New York: Teachers College Press.

Chaiklin, S., & Lave, J. (Eds.). (1996). *Understanding practice: Perspectives on activity and context.* New York: Cambridge University Press.

Charlton, J. (Ed.). (1994). *A little learning is a dangerous thing: A treasury of wise and witty observations for students, teachers, and other survivors of higher education.* New York: St. Martin's Press.

Christenbury, L. (Ed.). (1994). *English Journal, 83*(7).

Christenbury, L. (Ed.). (1995). Multiple intelligences. Special theme issue of *English Journal, 84*(8).

Clifford, J. (Ed.). (1991). *The experience of reading: Louise Rosenblatt and reader-response theory.* Portsmouth, NH: Heinemann.

Coates, J. (1993). *Women, men and language* (2nd ed.). New York: Longman.

Cochran-Smith, M., & Lytle, S. (Eds.). (1993). *Inside/outside: Teacher research and knowledge.* New York: Teachers College Press.

Cohen, E. (1994). *Designing groupwork: Strategies for the heterogeneous classroom.* New York: Teachers College Press.

Cole, M. (1996). *Cultural psychology: A once and future discipline.* Cambridge, MA: Harvard University Press.

Cole, M., Engestrom, Y., & Vasquez, O. (Eds.). (1997). *Mind, culture, and activity: Seminal papers from the Laboratory of Comparative Human Cognition.* New York: Cambridge University Press.

Crafton, L. K. (1996). *Standards in practice, grades K-2.* Urbana, IL: National Council of Teachers of English.

Csikszentmihalyi, M. (1975). *Beyond boredom and anxiety.* San Francisco: Jossey-Bass.

Csikszentmihalyi, M. (1990). *Flow: The psychology of optimal experience.* New York: Harper & Row.

Csikszentmihalyi, M., & Csikszentmihalyi, I. S. (Eds.). (1988). *Optimal experience: Psychological studies of flow in consciousness.* New York: Cambridge University Press.

Csikszentmihalyi, M., & Larson, R. (1984). *Being adolescent: Conflict and growth in the teenage years.* New York: Basic Books.

Csikszentmihalyi, M., Rathunde, K., & Whalen, S. (1993). *Talented teenagers: The roots of success and failure.* New York: Cambridge University Press.

Damon, W. (1988). *The moral child.* Cambridge, MA: Harvard University Press.

Daniels, H. (1994). *Literature circles: Voice and choice in the student-centered classroom.* York, ME: Stenhouse.

Darling-Hammond, L., Ancess, J., & Falk, B. (1995). *Authentic assessment in action: Studies of schools and students at work.* New York: Teachers College Press.

DeFabio, R. Y. (1994). *Outcomes in process: Setting standards for language use.* Portsmouth, NH: Heinemann.

Delpit, L. (1995). *Other people's children: Cultural conflict in the classroom.* New York: The New Press.

Dewey, J. (1916). *Democracy and education: An introduction to the philosophy of education.* New York: The Free Press.

Dewey, J. (1928). *Progressive education and the science of education.* Washington, D. C.: Progressive Education Association.

Dewey, J. (1934). *Art as experience.* New York: Berkeley Publishing Group.

Dewey, J. (1960). *The quest for certainty.* New York: Putnam.

Dewey, J. (1964). *John Dewey on education: Selected writings* (R. Archambault, Ed.). Chicago: University of Chicago Press.

Dewey, J. (1966). *Democracy and education: An introduction to the philosophy of education.* New York: The Free Press.

Durkheim, E. (1961). *Moral education: A study in theory and application of the sociology of education.* New York: The Free Press.

Eckert, P. (1989). *Jocks and burnouts: Social categories and identity in the high school.* New York: Teachers College Press.

Eisner, E. (Ed.). (1985). *Learning and teaching the ways of knowing.* Eighty-fourth Yearbook of the National Society for the Study of Education, Part II. Chicago: University of Chicago Press.

Elementary Section Steering Committee of NCTE. (1997). *The literate life: Exploring language arts standards with a cycle of learning.* Urbana, IL: National Council of Teachers of English.

Ellis, J. M. (1997). *Literature lost: Social agendas and the corruption of the humanities*. New Haven, CT: Yale University Press.

Engestrom, Y., Miettinen, R., & Punamaki, R-L. (Eds.). (1999). *Perspectives on activity theory*. New York: Cambridge University Press.

Erikson, E. (1950). *Childhood and society*. New York: Norton.

Erikson, E. (1980). *Identity and the life cycle*. New York: Norton.

Farr, M., & Daniels, H. (1986). *Language diversity and writing instruction*. Urbana, IL: ERIC Clearinghouse on Reading and Communication Skills.

Finders, M. J. (1997). *Just girls: Hidden literacies and life in junior high*. New York: Teachers College Press; Urbana, IL: National Council of Teachers of English.

Fly, P. K. (1991, April). *Teaching the literary character analysis in AP English*. Paper presented at the annual convention of the Oklahoma Council of Teachers of English, Oklahoma City.

Flynn, T., & King, M. (Eds.). (1993). *Dynamics of the writing conference: Social and cognitive interaction*. Urbana, IL: National Council of Teachers of English.

Foucault, M. (1972). *The archaeology of knowledge and the discourse on language*. New York: Pantheon.

Freedman, S. W. (1987). *Response to student writing* (NCTE Research Report No. 23). Urbana, IL: National Council of Teachers of English.

Freedman, S. W., Simons, E. R., Kalnin, J. S., Casareno, A., & The M-CLASS teams. (1999). *Inside city schools: Investigating literacy in multicultural classrooms*. New York: Teachers College Press.

Freeman, P. R., & Schmidt, J. Z. (Eds.). (2000). *Wise women: Reflections of teachers at midlife*. New York: Routledge.

Freire, P. (1970). The adult literacy process as cultural action for freedom. *Harvard Educational Review, 40,* 205–212.

Freire, P. (1995). *Pedagogy of the oppressed*. New York: Continuum.

Fulwiler, T. (Ed.). (1987). *The journal book*. Portsmouth, NH: Heinemann.

Gallas, K. (1994). *The languages of learning: How children talk, write, dance, draw, and sing their understanding of the world*. New York: Teachers College Press.

Gallas, K. (1995). *Talking their way into science: Hearing children's questions and theories, responding with curricula*. New York: Teachers College Press.

Gallas, K. (1997). *Sometimes I can be anything: Power, gender, and identity in a primary classroom*. New York: Teachers College Press.

Gardner, H. (1983). *Frames of mind: The theory of multiple intelligences*. New York: Basic Books.

Gardner, H. (1993). *Multiple intelligences: The theory into practice*. New York: Basic Books.

Gardner, H. (1999). *The disciplined mind: What all students should understand*. New York: Simon and Schuster.

Gardner, H. (1999). *Intelligence reframed: Multiple intelligences for the 21st century*. New York: Basic Books.

Gauld, J. (1993). *Character first: The Hyde School differences*. San Francisco: ICS Press.

Gee, J. (1990). *Social linguistics and literacies: Ideology in discourses*. New York: Falmer.

Gilligan, C. (1982). *In a different voice: Psychological theory and women's development.* Cambridge, MA: Harvard University Press.

Giroux, H. (Ed.). (1997). *Counternarratives: Cultural studies and critical pedagogies in postmodern spaces.* New York: Routledge.

Goldberg, M. R. (1997). *Arts and learning: An integrated approach to teaching and learning in multicultural and multilingual settings.* New York: Longman.

Goswami, D., & Stillman, P. (Eds.). (1987). *Reclaiming the classroom: Teacher research as an agency for change.* Portsmouth, NH: Heinemann.

Graham, P. A. (1967). *Progressive education from Arcady to academe: A history of the Progressive Education Association, 1919-1955.* New York: Teachers College Press.

Grant, C. (Ed.). (1997). *Dictionary of multicultural education.* Phoenix, AZ: Oryx Press.

Graves, D., & Sunstein, B. (1992). *Portfolio portraits.* Portsmouth, NH: Heinemann.

Greene, M. (1988). *The dialectic of freedom.* New York: Teachers College Press.

Harp, B. (Ed.). (1994). *Assessment and evaluation in student-centered programs* (2nd ed.). Norwood, MA: Christopher-Gordon.

Harris, M. (1986). *Teaching one-to-one: The writing conference.* Urbana, IL: National Council of Teachers of English.

Harris, V. J. (Ed.). (1993). *Teaching multicultural literature in grades K–8.* Norwood, MA: Christopher-Gordon.

Hayes, J. R. (1992). A psychological perspective applied to literacy studies. In R. Beach, J. L. Green, M. L. Kamil, & T. Shanahan (Eds.), *Multidisciplinary perspectives on literacy research* (pp. 125–140). Urbana, IL: National Conference on Research in English and National Council of Teachers of English.

Heath, S. B. (1983). *Ways with words.* New York: Cambridge University Press.

Hewitt, G. (1995). *A portfolio primer: Teaching, collecting, and assessing student writing.* Portsmouth, NH: Heinemann.

Hill, B. C., Johnson, N. J., & Noe, K. (1995). *Literature circles and response.* Norwood, MA: Christopher-Gordon.

Hillocks, G. (1972). *Observing and writing.* Urbana, IL: National Council of Teachers of English.

Hillocks, G. (1986). *Research on written composition: New directions for teaching.* Urbana, IL: ERIC Clearinghouse on Reading and Communications Skills and National Conference on Research in English.

Hillocks, G. (1995). *Teaching writing as reflective practice.* New York: Teachers College Press.

Hillocks, G., McCabe, B., & McCampbell, J. (1971). *The dynamics of English instruction, grades 7–12.* New York: Random House.

Hirsch, E. D. (1987). *Cultural literacy: What every American should know.* Boston: Houghton Mifflin.

Hollins, E. R. (1996). *Culture in school learning: Revealing the deep meaning.* Mahwah, NJ: Erlbaum.

Honor Teacher Awards. (2000, May 14). *The Atlanta Journal-Constitution,* Section Q.

hooks, b. (1994). *Teaching to transgress: Education as the practice of freedom.* New York: Routledge.

Huebner, D. (1985). Spirituality and knowing. In E. Eisner (Ed.), *Learning and teaching the ways of knowing* (pp. 159–173). Chicago: National Society for the Study of Education.

Huffman, H. A. (1994). *Developing a character education program.* Alexandria, VA: Association for Supervision and Curriculum Development.

Hunter, S., & Wallace, R. (Eds.). *The place of grammar in writing instruction: Past, present, future.* Portsmouth, NH: Heinemann.

Hydrick, J. (1996). *Parent's guide to literacy for the 21st century.* Urbana, IL: National Council of Teachers of English.

Hymes, D. (1974). *Foundations in sociolinguistics: An ethnographic approach.* Philadelphia: University of Pennsylvania Press.

Hynds, S. (1997). *On the brink: Negotiating literature and life with adolescents.* New York: Teachers College Press.

Jackson, P. W. (1998). *John Dewey and the lessons of art.* New Haven, CT: Yale University Press.

Jacobsohn, R. W. (1998). *The reading group handbook: Everything you need to know to start your own book club.* New York: Hyperion.

Jervis, C., & Montag, C. (1991). *Progressive education for the 1990s: Transforming practice.* New York: Teachers College Press.

Johannessen, L. R. (1992). *Illumination rounds: Teaching the literature of the Vietnam War.* Urbana, IL: National Council of Teachers of English.

Johannessen, L., Kahn, E., & Walter, C. C. (1982). *Designing and sequencing prewriting activities.* Urbana, IL: ERIC and National Council of Teachers of English.

Johnston, P. H. (1992). *Constructive evaluation of literate activity.* New York: Longman.

Johnston, P. H. (1997). *Knowing literacy: Constructive literacy assessment.* York, ME: Stenhouse.

Josselson, R. (1996). *Revising herself.* New York: Oxford University Press.

Kagan, J., & Coles, R. (Eds.). (1971). *12 to 16: Early adolescence.* New York: Norton.

Kahn, E. A., Walter, C. C., & Johannsessen, L. R. (1984). *Writing about literature.* Urbana, IL: National Council of Teachers of English.

Keene, E. O., & Zimmermann, S. (1997). *Mosaic of thought: Teaching comprehension in a reader's workshop.* Portsmouth, NH: Heinemann.

Kilpatrick, W. (1992). *Why Johnny can't tell right from wrong.* New York: Simon & Schuster.

Kintsch, W. (1977). *Memory and cognition* (2nd ed.). New York: Wiley.

Kitao, S. (1989). *Reading, schema theory, and second language learners.* Tokyo: Eichosha Shinsha.

Kohlberg, L. (1981). *The philosophy of moral development.* San Francisco: Harper & Row.

Krogness, M. M. (1995). *Just teach me, Mrs. K: Talking, reading, and writing with resistant adolescent learners.* Portsmouth, NH: Heinemann.

Kurtines, W., & Gewirtz, J. L. (Eds.). (1991). *Handbook of moral behavior and development.* Hillsdale, NJ: Erlbaum.

Ladson-Billings, G. (1997). *The dreamkeepers: Successful teachers of African-American children.* San Francisco: Jossey-Bass.

Lakoff, R. (1975). *Language and woman's place*. New York: Harper and Row.

Langer, J. A., & Applebee, A. N. (1987). *How writing shapes thinking: A study of teaching and learning* (NCTE Research Report No. 22). Urbana, IL: National Council of Teachers of English.

Lave, J. (1988). *Cognition in practice*. New York: Cambridge University Press.

Lazear, D. G., & Ray, H. (1999). *Eight ways of knowing: Teaching for multiple intelligences*. Arlington Heights, IL: Skylight Training.

Lee, C. D. (1993). *Signifying as a scaffold for literary interpretation: The pedagogical implications of an African American discourse genre* (NCTE Research Report No. 26). Urbana, IL: National Council of Teachers of English.

Lee, C. D., & Smagorinsky, P. (Eds.). (2000). *Vygotskian perspectives on literacy research: Constructing meaning through collaborative inquiry*. New York: Cambridge University Press.

Lensmire, T. J. (1994). *When children write: Critical re-visions of the writing workshop*. New York: Teachers College Press.

Lensmire, T. J. (2000). *Powerful writing, responsible teaching*. New York: Teachers College Press.

Lickona, T. (1991). *Educating for character: How our schools can teach respect and responsibility*. New York: Bantam.

Llewelyn, S., & Osborne, K. (1990). *Women's lives*. New York: Routledge.

Lloyd-Jones, R., & Lunsford, A. A. (1989). *The English Coalition Conference: Democracy through language*. New York and Urbana, IL: Modern Language Association and National Council of Teachers of English.

Loveless, T. (1999). *The tracking wars: State reform meets school policy*. Washington, DC: Brookings Institution Press.

Lucas, S. (1999). *Tracking inequality: Stratification and mobility in American high schools*. New York: Teachers College Press.

Luke, A. (1988). *Literacy, textbooks and ideology*. New York: Falmer.

Maher, F., & Tetreault, M. (1994). *The feminist classroom*. New York: Basic Books.

Mahiri, J. (1998). *Shooting for excellence: African American and youth culture in new century schools*. New York: Teachers College Press.

Mandler, J. M. (1984). *Stories, scripts, and scenes: Aspects of schema theory*. Hillsdale, NJ: Erlbaum.

Marshall, J. D., Smagorinsky, P., & Smith, M. W. (1995). *The language of interpretation: Patterns of discourse in discussions of literature* (NCTE Research Report No. 27). Urbana, IL: National Council of Teachers of English.

Martin, J. (1995). *The schoolhome*. Cambridge, MA: Harvard University Press.

McCormick, T. M. (1994). *Creating the nonsexist classroom: A multicultural approach*. New York: Teachers College Press.

McLaren, P. (1997). *Life in schools: An introduction to critical pedagogy in the foundations of education*. Addison-Wesley.

McMahon, S. I., Raphael, T. E., & Goatley, V. J. (Eds.) (1997). *The book club connection: Literacy learning and classroom talk*. New York: Teachers College Press.

Mehan, H. (1979). *Learning lessons*. Cambridge, MA: Harvard University Press.

Mehan, H., Villanueva, I., Hubbard, L., & Lintz, A. (1996). *Constructing school success: The consequences of untracking low-achieving students*. New York: Cambridge University Press.

Miller, J. B. (1986). *Toward a new psychology of women* (2nd ed.). Boston: Beacon Press.

Miller, R. E. (1994). Fault lines in the contact zone. *College English, 56,* 389–408.

Miller, S., & McCaskill, B. (1993). *Multicultural literature and literacies: Making space for difference.* Albany, NY: SUNY Press.

Mills, S. (1995). *Feministic stylistics.* New York: Routledge.

Moffett, J. (1988). *Storm in the mountains: A case study of censorship, conflict, and consciousness.* Carbondale, IL: Southern Illinois University Press.

Moffett, J., & Wagner, B. J. (1992). *Student-centered language arts, K–12* (4th ed.). Portsmouth, NH: Heinemann.

Mohr, M., & MacLean, M. (1987). *Working together: A guide for teacher-researchers.* Urbana, IL: National Council of Teachers of English.

Moll, L. C. (Ed.). (1990). *Vygotsky and education: Instructional implications and applications of sociohistorical psychology.* New York: Cambridge University Press.

Montessori, M. (1964). *The Montessori method* (A. E. George, Trans.). Cambridge, MA: Robert Bentley.

Moore, D., & Davenport, S. (1988). *The new improved sorting machine.* Madison, WI: National Center on Effective Secondary Schools.

Myers, M. (1996). *Changing our minds: Negotiating English and literacy.* Urbana, IL: National Council of Teachers of English.

Myers, M., & Spalding, E. (Eds.). (1997). *Assessing student performance.* Urbana, IL: National Council of Teachers of English.

National Council of Teachers of English. (1995). *Teaching literature in high school: The novel.* Urbana, IL: Author.

National Council of Teachers of English. (1995). *Teaching the writing process in high school.* Urbana, IL: Author.

National Council of Teachers of English. (1996). *Guidelines for preparation of teachers of English language arts.* Urbana, IL: Author.

National Council of Teachers of English. (1996). *Motivating writing in middle school.* Urbana, IL: Author.

National Council of Teachers of English. (1996). *Teaching literature in middle school: Fiction.* Urbana, IL: Author.

National Council of Teachers of English. (1996). *Teaching reading and literature: Grades 4–6.* Urbana, IL: Author.

National Council of Teachers of English. (1997). *Teaching reading and literature in early elementary grades.* Urbana, IL: Author.

National Council of Teachers of English and International Reading Association. (1996). *Standards for the English language arts.* Urbana, IL and Newark, DE: Authors.

NCTE/IRA Joint Task Force on Assessment. (1994). *Standards for the assessment of reading and writing.* Urbana, IL, and Newark, DE: National Council of Teachers of English and International Reading Association.

Nelms, B. F. (Ed.). (1988). *Literature in the classroom.* Urbana, IL: National Council of Teachers of English.

Newman, D., Griffin, P., & Cole, M. (1989). *The construction zone: Working for cognitive change in school.* New York: Cambridge University Press.

Newman, F. (1996). *Performance of a lifetime: A practical-philosophical guide to the joyous life.* New York: Castillo International.

Ng, S., & Bradac, J. (1993). *Power in language: Verbal communication and social influence*. Newbury Park, CA: Sage.

Noddings, N. (1992). *The challenge to care in schools: An alternative approach to education*. New York: Teachers College Press.

Noden, H. R. (1999). *Image grammar: Using grammatical structures to teach writing*. Portsmouth, NH: Heinemann.

Noguchi, R. R. (1991). *Grammar and the teaching of writing: Limits and possibilities*. Urbana, IL: National Council of Teachers of English.

Nucci, L. (1986). *Moral development and character education: A dialogue*. Berkeley, CA: McCutchan.

Nussbaum, M. C. (1997). *Cultivating humanity: A classical defense of reform in liberal education*. Cambridge, MA: Harvard University Press.

Nystrand, M. (1986). *The structure of written composition: Studies in reciprocity between writers and readers*. Orlando, FL: Academic Press.

Nystrand, M. (1997). *Opening dialogue: Understanding the dynamics of language and learning in the English classroom*. New York: Teachers College Press.

Nystrand, M., Gamoran, A., & Heck, M. J. (1992). *Using small groups for response to and thinking about literature*. Washington, D.C.: U. S. Department of Education, Office of Educational Research and Improvement, Educational Resources Information Center.

O'Donnell-Allen, C., & Smagorinsky, P. (1999). Revising Ophelia: Rethinking questions of gender and power in school. *English Journal, 88*(3), 35–42.

Oakes, J. (1985). *Keeping track: How schools structure inequality*. New Haven, CT: Yale University Press.

Oakes, J., Quartz, K. H., Ryan, S., & Lipton, M. (2000). *Becoming good American schools: The struggle for civic virtue in school reform*. San Francisco: Jossey-Bass.

Orenstein, P. (1994). *SchoolGirls*. New York: Doubleday.

Pappas, C., & Zecker, Z. L. (1998). *Teacher inquiries in literacy teaching-learning: Learning to collaborate in elementary urban classrooms*. Mahwah, NJ: Erlbaum.

Peterson, P., Wilkinson, L., & Hallinan, M. (Eds.). (1984). *The social context of instruction: Group organization and group processes*. New York: Academic Press.

Pflaum, S. W., & Pignatelli, F. (1993). *Celebrating diverse voices: Progressive education and equity*. Newbury Park, CA: Corwin.

Piaget, J. (1952). *The origins of intelligence in children*. New York: Norton.

Piaget, J. (1995). *The essential Piaget* (H. E. Gruber & J. J. Voneche, Eds.). Northvale, NJ: Jason Aronson.

Pipher, M. (1994). *Reviving Ophelia: Saving the selves of adolescent girls*. New York: Putnam's.

Postman, N., & Weingartner, C. (1987). *Teaching as a subversive activity*. New York: Dell.

Power, B., Wilhelm, J., & Chandler, K. (1997). *Reading Stephen King: Issues of censorship, student choice, and popular literature*. Urbana, IL: National Council of Teachers of English.

Probst, R. E. (1988). *Response and analysis: Teaching literature in junior and senior high school*. Portsmouth, NH: Heinemann.

Purpel, D. (1988). *The moral and spiritual crisis in education: A curriculum for justice and compassion.* Granby, MA: Bergin & Garvey.

Purves, A., Rogers, T., & Soter, A. (1995). *How porcupines make love III: Readers, texts, cultures in the response-based literature classroom.* New York: Longman.

Rabinowitz, P., & Smith, M. W. (1997). *Authorizing readers: Resistance and respect in the teaching of literature.* New York: Teachers College Press.

Ravitch, D. (1991). *The American reader: Words that moved a nation.* New York: HarperCollins.

Ray, R. (1993). *The practice of theory: Teacher research in composition.* Urbana, IL: National Council of Teachers of English.

Reichman, H. (1993). *Censorship and selection: Issues and answers for schools.* Chicago, IL: American Library Association.

Rief, L. (1992). *Seeking diversity: Language arts and adolescents.* Portsmouth, NH: Heinemann.

Robinson, R. (1989). *Unlocking Shakespeare's language: Help for the teacher and student.* Urbana, IL: National Council of Teachers of English.

Rogoff, B. (1990). *Apprenticeship in thinking: Cognitive development in social context.* New York: Oxford University Press.

Rogoff, B., & Lave, J. (Eds.). (1984). *Everyday cognition: Its development in social context.* Cambridge, MA: Harvard University Press.

Rogoff, B., & Wertsch, J. V. (Eds.). (1984). *Children's learning in the "zone of proximal development."* San Francisco: Jossey-Bass.

Romano, T. (1995). *Writing with passion: Life stories, multiple genres.* Portsmouth, NH: Heinemann.

Rose, M. (1989). *Lives on the boundary: The struggles and achievements of America's underprepared.* New York: Penguin.

Rose, M. (1995). *Possible lives: The promise of public education in America.* Boston: Houghton Mifflin.

Rosenbaum, J. (1976). *Making inequality: The hidden curricula of high school tracking.* New York: John Wiley & Sons.

Rosenberg, S. (1988, Fall). Getting into Kenyon. *Kenyon College Alumni Bulletin, 8–9.*

Rosenblatt, L. M. (1978). *The reader, the text, the poem: The transactional theory of literary response.* Carbondale, IL: Southern Illinois University Press.

Rosenblatt, L. M. (1996). *Literature as exploration* (5th ed.). New York: Modern Language Association.

Ryan, K., & Lickona, T. (1992). *Character development in schools and beyond.* Washington, DC: Council for Research in Values and Philosophy.

Sadker, M., & Sadker, D. (1994). *Failing at fairness: How America's schools cheat girls.* New York: Scribner's.

Schön, D. A. (Ed.). (1991). *The reflective turn: Case studies in and on educational practice.* New York: Teachers College Press.

Schurr, S. L. (1995). *Prescriptions for success in heterogeneous classrooms.* Columbus, OH: National Middle School Association.

Searle, D. (1984). Scaffolding: Who's building whose building? *Language Arts, 61,* 480–483.

Shaughnessy, M. P. (1977). *Errors and expectations: A guide for the teacher of basic writing.* New York: Oxford University Press.

Shor, I. (1996). *When students have power: Negotiating authority in a critical pedagogy*. Chicago: University of Chicago Press.

Sichel, B. (1988). *Moral education: Character, community and ideals*. Philadelphia: Temple University Press.

Sierra-Petty, M. (1996). *Standards in practice, grades 3–5*. Urbana, IL: National Council of Teachers of English.

Sigel, I. E., & Brody, G. H. (Eds.) (1990). *Methods of family research: Biographies of research projects (Vol. 1): Normal families*. Hillsdale, NJ: Erlbaum.

Sizer, T. R. (1992). *Horace's compromise: The dilemma of the American high school*. Boston: Houghton Mifflin.

Smagorinsky, P. (1991). *Expressions: Multiple intelligences in the English class*. Urbana, IL: National Council of Teachers of English.

Smagorinsky, P. (1995). Constructing meaning in the disciplines: Reconceptualizing writing across the curriculum as composing across the curriculum. *American Journal of Education, 103*, 160–184.

Smagorinsky, P. (1995). Multiple intelligences in the English class: An overview. *English Journal, 84* (8), 19–26.

Smagorinsky, P. (1996). Multiple intelligences, multiple means of composing: An alternative way of thinking about learning. *NASSP Bulletin, 80*(583), 11–17.

Smagorinsky, P. (1996). *Standards in practice, grades 9–12*. Urbana, IL: National Council of Teachers of English.

Smagorinsky, P. (1997). Artistic composing as representational process. *Journal of Applied Developmental Psychology, 18*, 87–105.

Smagorinsky, P. (1997). Personal growth in social context: A high school senior's search for meaning in and through writing. *Written Communication, 14*, 63–105.

Smagorinsky, P. (1999). The world is a stage: Dramatic enactment as response to literature. In B. J. Wagner (Ed.), *Building moral communities through drama* (pp. 19–38). Stamford, CT: Ablex.

Smagorinsky, P. (2002). If meaning is constructed, what's it made of?: Toward a cultural theory of reading. *Review of Educational Research*.

Smagorinsky, P., & Coppock, J. (1994). Cultural tools and the classroom context: An exploration of an alternative response to literature. *Written Communication, 11*, 283–310.

Smagorinsky, P., & Coppock, J. (1994, Fall). Exploring an evocation of the literary work: Processes and possibilities of an artistic response to literature. *Reader, 62–74.*

Smagorinsky, P., & Coppock, J. (1994). Exploring artistic response to literature. In C. K. Kinzer & D. J. Leu (Eds.), *Multidimensional aspects of literacy research, theory, and practice* (pp. 335–341). *Forty-Third Yearbook of the National Reading Conference*. Chicago: National Reading Conference.

Smagorinsky, P., & Coppock, J. (1995). The reader, the text, the context: An exploration of a choreographed response to literature. *Journal of Reading Behavior, 27*, 271–298.

Smagorinsky, P., & Coppock, J. (1995). Reading through the lines: An exploration of drama as a response to literature. *Reading & Writing Quarterly, 11*, 369–391.

Smagorinsky, P., & Fly, P. K. (1993). The social environment of the classroom: A Vygotskian perspective on small group process. *Communication Education, 42*, 159–171.

Smagorinsky, P., & Fly, P. K. (1994). A new perspective on why small groups do and don't work. *English Journal, 83*(3), 54–58.

Smagorinsky, P., McCann, T., & Kern, S. (1987). *Explorations: Introductory activities for literature and composition, grades 7–12.* Urbana, IL: National Council of Teachers of English.

Smagorinsky, P., & O'Donnell-Allen, C. (1998). The depth and dynamics of context: Tracing the sources and channels of engagement and disengagement in students' response to literature. *Journal of Literacy Research, 30,* 515–559.

Smagorinsky, P., & O'Donnell-Allen, C. (1998). Reading as mediated and mediating action: Composing meaning for literature through multimedia interpretive texts. *Reading Research Quarterly, 33,* 198–226.

Smagorinsky, P., & O'Donnell-Allen, C. (2000). Idiocultural diversity in small groups: The role of the relational framework in collaborative learning. In C. D. Lee & P. Smagorinsky (Eds.), *Vygotskian perspectives on literacy research: Constructing meaning through collaborative inquiry* (pp. 165–190). New York: Cambridge University Press.

Smith, M. W. (1991). *Understanding unreliable narrators: Reading between the lines in the literature classroom.* Urbana, IL: National Council of Teachers of English.

Smith, P. M. (1985). *Language, the sexes and society.* New York: Basil Blackwell.

Smitherman, G. (1977). *Talkin and testifyin: The language of black America.* Boston: Houghton Mifflin; Reprint, Detroit: Wayne University Press, 1986.

Sommers, C. H. (2000). The war against boys. *The Atlantic Monthly, 285*(5), 59–74).

Spandel, V., & Stiggins, R. J. (1990). *Creating writers: Linking assessment and writing instruction.* New York: Longman.

Spear, K. I. (1987). *Sharing writing: Peer response groups in English classes.* Portsmouth, NH: Heinemann.

Spring, J. (1976). *The sorting machine: National educational policy since 1945.* New York: David McKay.

Stiggins, R. J., & Conklin, N. F. (1992). *In teachers' hands: Investigating the practices of classroom assessment.* Albany, NY: SUNY Press.

Stipek, D. J. (1993). *Motivation to learn.* Boston: Allyn & Bacon.

Stotsky, S. (Ed.). (1991). *Making connections between civic education and language.* New York: Teachers College Press.

Stotsky, S. (1999). *Losing our language: How multicultural classroom instruction is undermining our children's ability to read, write, and reason.* New York: The Free Press.

St. Pierre, E., & Pillow, W. (Eds.). (2000). *Working the ruins: Feminist poststructural theory and methods in education.* New York: Routledge.

Strickland, K., & Strickland, J. (1998). *Reflections on assessment: Its purposes, methods and effects on learning.* Portsmouth, NH: Heinemann.

Strong, W. (1986). *Creative approaches to sentence combining.* Urbana, IL: National Council of Teachers of English.

Tannen, D. (1989). *Talking voices.* New York: Cambridge University Press.

Tax, M., & Agosin, M. (1995). *The power of the word: Culture, censorship, and voice.* New York: Women's Organization for Rights Literature & Development.

Taylor, J. M., Gilligan, C., & Sullivan, A. M. (1995). *Between voice and silence: Women and girls, race and relationship.* Cambridge, MA: Harvard University Press.

Tchudi, S. (1991). *Planning and assessing the curriculum in English language arts.* Alexandria, Va: Association for Supervision and Curriculum Development.

Tharp, R. G., & Gallimore, R. (1988). *Rousing minds to life: Teaching, learning, and schooling in social context.* New York: Cambridge University Press.

Thelen, H. A. (1954). *Dynamics of groups at work.* Chicago: University of Chicago Press.

Thorne, B., Kramarae, C., & Henley, N. (1983). *Language, gender, and society.* Rowley, MA: Newbury House.

Tiedt, P. L., & Tiedt, I. M. (1999). *Multicultural teaching: A handbook of activities, information, and resources* (5th ed.). Boston: Allyn & Bacon.

Tierney, R., Carter, M., & Desai, L. (1991). *Portfolio assessment in the reading-writing classroom.* Norwood, MA: Christopher-Gordon.

Tierney, R., & Pearson, P. D. (1986). *Schema theory and implications for teaching reading: A conversation.* Champaign, IL: University of Illinois at Urbana-Champaign.

Tobach, E., Falmagne, R. J., Parlee, M. B., Martin, L. M. W., & Kapelman, A. S. (Eds.). (1997). *Mind and social practice: Selected writings of Sylvia Scribner.* New York: Cambridge University Press.

Todd, A. D., & Fisher, S. (Eds.). (1988). *Gender and discourse: The power of talk.* Norwood, NJ: Ablex.

Tulviste, P. (1991). *The cultural-historical development of verbal thinking* (M. J. Hall, Trans.). Commack, NY: Nova Science Publishers.

Tyler, R. (1949). *Basic principles of curriculum and instruction.* Chicago: University of Chicago Press.

Underwood, W. (1987). The body biography: A framework for student writing. *English Journal, 76,* 44–48.

Valencia, S., Hiebert, E. H., & Afflerbach, P. P. (Eds.). (1994). *Authentic reading assessment: Practices and possibilities.* Newark, DE: International Reading Association.

Van der Veer, R., & Valsiner, J. (1991). *Understanding Vygotsky: A quest for synthesis.* Cambridge, MA: Blackwell.

Vincent, P. F. (1994). *Developing character in students.* Chapel Hill, NC: New View Publications.

Vine, H., & Faust, M. (1993). *Situating readers: Students making meaning of literature.* Urbana, IL: National Council of Teachers of English.

Vygotsky, L. S. (1978). *Mind in society: The development of higher psychological processes* (M. Cole, V. John-Steiner, S. Scribner, & E. Souberman, Eds.). Cambridge, MA: Harvard University Press.

Vygotsky, L. S. (1987). *The collected works of Lev Vygotsky: Vol. 1. Problems of general psychology* (R. Rieber & A. Carton, Eds; N. Minick, Trans.). New York: Plenum.

Vygotsky, L. S. (1993). *The collected works of L. S. Vygotsky: Vol. 2. The fundamentals of defectology (abnormal psychology and learning disabilities)* (R. Rieber & A. Carton, Eds.; J. Knox & G. Stevens, Trans.). New York: Plenum.

Vygotsky, L. S. (1997). *The collected works of Lev Vygotsky: Vol 3. Problems of the theory and history of psychology* (R. Rieber & J. Wollock, Eds.; R. Van der Veer, Trans.). New York: Plenum.

Vygotsky, L. S. (1997). *The collected works of Lev Vygotsky: Vol. 4. The history of the development of higher mental functions* (R. Rieber, Ed.; M. J. Hall, Trans.). New York: Plenum.

Wagner, B. J. (Ed.). (1999). *Building moral communities through educational drama.* Stamford, CT: Ablex.

Walkerdine, V. (1990). *Schoolgirl fictions.* New York: Verso.

Weaver, C. (1996). *Teaching grammar in context.* Portsmouth, NH: Heinemann.

Webster, Y. O. (1997). *Against the multicultural agenda.* Westport, CT: Praeger.

Welch, N. (1997). *Getting restless: Rethinking revision in writing instruction.* Portsmouth, NH: Heinemann.

Wells, G. (Ed.) (1994). *Changing schools from within: Creating communities of inquiry.* Toronto: OISE Press; Portsmouth, NH: Heinemann.

Wells, G. (in press). *Thinking with Vygotsky.* New York: Cambridge University Press.

Wells, G., Bernard, L., Gianotti, M. A., Keating, C., Konjevic, C., Kowal, M., Maher, A., Mayer, C., Moscoe, T., Orzechowska, E., Smieja, A., & Swartz, L. (1994). *Changing schools from within: Creating communities of inquiry.* Toronto: OISE Press; Portsmouth, NH: Heinemann.

Wells, G., & Chang-Wells, G. L. (1992). *Constructing knowledge together: Classrooms as centers of inquiry and literacy.* Portsmouth, NH: Heinemann.

Welner, K. G., & Oakes, J. (2000). *Navigating the politics of detracking.* Arlington Heights, IL: Skylight Publications.

Wertsch, J. V. (1985). *Vygotsky and the social formation of mind.* Cambridge, MA: Harvard University Press.

Wertsch, J. V. (1991). *Voices of the mind: A sociocultural approach to mediated action.* Cambridge, MA: Harvard University Press.

Wertsch, J. V. (1996). *Mind as action.* New York: Oxford University Press.

Wertsch, J. V., del Rio, P., & Alvarez, A. (1995). *Sociocultural studies of mind.* New York: Cambridge University Press.

Wheelock, A. (1992). *Crossing the tracks: How "untracking" can save America's schools.* New York: Free Press.

White, E., Lutz, W., & Kamusikiri, S. (Eds.). (1996). *Assessment of writing: Politics, policies, practices.* New York: Modern Language Association of America.

Whitin, P. (1996). *Sketching stories, stretching minds.* Portsmouth, NH: Heinemann.

Wilhelm, J. D. (1996). *Standards in practice, grades 6–8.* Urbana, IL: National Council of Teachers of English.

Wilhelm, J. D. (1997). *You gotta BE the book.* New York: Teachers College Press; Urbana, IL: National Council of Teachers of English.

Wilhelm, J. D., & Edmiston, B. (1998). *Imagining to learn: Inquiry, ethics, and integration through drama.* Portsmouth, NH: Heinemann.

Winick, M. P. (1978). *The progressive education movement: An annotated bibliography.* New York: Garland.

Wynne, E., & Ryan, K. (1993). *Reclaiming our schools: A handbook for teaching character, academics and discipline.* Columbus, OH: Charles Merrill.

Yancey, K. B. (Ed.). (1992). *Portfolios in the writing classroom: An introduction.* Urbana, IL: National Council of Teachers of English.

Yancey, K. B., & Huot, B. (1997). *Assessing writing across the curriculum: Diverse approaches and practices.* Norwood, NJ: Ablex.

Yancey, K. B., & Weiser, I. (Eds.). (1997). *Situating portfolios: Four perspectives.* Urbana, IL: National Council of Teachers of English.

Zak, F., & Weaver, C. C. (Eds.). (1998). *The theory and practice of grading writing: Problems and possibilities.* Albany, NY: SUNY Press.

APPENDIX A

Texts for Thematic Units

This appendix provides outlines for units of instruction built around literary themes and genres. For each unit I provide a set of possible texts and a possible conceptual focus. Keep in mind that my intention here is to suggest possibilities rather than to prescribe a curriculum; there are many other units that you could develop, and different texts and focuses for each of the units that I outline. The lists of texts are intended to be responsive to a range of readers in terms of age, reading ability, interests, and so on, so that the unit themes can be adapted to readers of different grade levels, from different communities, and so on. The lists comprise both canonical works and less familiar texts, including literature, film, and popular music. There are far more texts listed than you would ever teach in any single unit; rather, the idea is to provide an idea of what is possible for teaching a particular theme. I would always hope that any teachers using these lists would use their own knowledge and imagination to make the instruction work for their own students and circumstances.

One way to preview literature is to consult one of the many hypertext libraries available on the Internet. I provide links to hypertext libraries at http://www.coe.uga.edu/~smago/Links/Links2LWL.htm#OnlineTexts.

THE AMERICAN DREAM

Poetry

Hughes, Langston: "I, Too, Sing America"

Sandburg, Carl: "Cool Tombs"

Sassoon, Siegfried: "The Case for the Miners"

Teasdale, Sara: "Barter"

Whitman, Walt: "I Hear America Singing"; "Song of Myself"; "Song of the Open Road"

Williams, William Carlos: "Pastoral"

Short Stories

Gordon, Roxy: "Pilgrims"

Owens, Louis: "Soul-Catcher"

Tallmountain, Mary Randle: "Tender Street"

Novels

Amis, Martin: *Money*

Bellow, Saul: *The Adventures of Augie March*

Burns, Olive Ann: *Cold Sassy Tree*

Cooper, James Fenimore: *The Deerslayer*

Dreiser, Theodore: *Sister Carrie; An American Tragedy*

Ellison, Ralph: *Invisible Man; Juneteenth*

Erdrich, Louise: *The Beet Queen; The Bingo Palace; Love Medicine*

Fitzgerald, F. Scott: *The Great Gatsby*

Kesey, Ken: *Sometimes a Great Notion*

Lewis, Sinclair: *Babbitt*

Mailer, Norman: *An American Dream*

Miller, Sue: *Family Pictures*

Mitchell, Margaret: *Gone with the Wind*

Momaday, N. Scott: *House Made of Dawn*

Morrison, Toni: *Beloved*

Proulx, E. Annie: *The Shipping News*

Redding, J. Saunders: *Stranger and Alone*

Rolvaag, O. E.: *Pure Gold*

Twain, Mark: *The Gilded Age; The Adventures of Huckleberry Finn*

Tyler, Anne: *Saint Maybe*

Updike, John: *Rabbit Run*

Wharton, Edith: *Ethan Frome*

Wright, Richard: *Native Son*

Nonfiction

American Slave Narratives: An Online Anthology
       <http://xroads.virginia.edu/~Hyper/wpa/wpahome.html>

Declaration of Independence

Faulkner, William: Nobel Prize acceptance speech

The Federalist Papers

Kennedy, John Fitzgerald: Inaugural address

King, Martin Luther: Christmas sermon on peace

The Lincoln-Douglas debates

Malcolm X: *Message to the Grass Roots*

Mayflower Compact

Moon, William Least Heat: *Blue Highways*
Rawick, George P. (Ed.): *The American Slave: A Composite Autobiography*
Steinbeck, John: *Travels with Charley*
Thoreau, Henry David: *Walden*
Whitman, Walt: *Democratic Vistas*

Drama

Albee, Edward: *The American Dream*
Miller, Arthur: *Death of a Salesman*
Serling, Rod: *Requiem for a Heavyweight*

Autobiographies

Brown, Claude: *Manchild in the Promised Land*
Cofer, Judith Oritz: *Silent Dancing*
Dillard, Annie: *An American Childhood*
Franklin, Benjamin: *Autobiography*
Hellman, Lillian: *An Unfinished Woman*
Kingston, Maxine Hong: *The Woman Warrior*
Powell, Colin: *My American Journey: An Autobiography*

Films

Citizen Kane
The Godfather trilogy
It's a Wonderful Life
Meet John Doe
Mr. Deeds Goes to Town
Mr. Smith Goes to Washington

Key Concepts and Problems

What is the American dream? What is American about it? To what extent is it relative to time and place? To what extent is it stable and enduring? How can the dream turn into a nightmare? How can it be an illusion? With what does the American dream come in conflict?

ANIMALS AS SYMBOLS
Fables/Fairy Tales/Folktales

Aesop: "The Fox, the Crow, and the Cheese"; "The Dog in the Manger"
Baring-Gould, W. S. (Ed.): *The Annotated Mother Goose*
Beauty and the Beast
Fernandez, Cayento: "The Bee and the Owl"; "The Monkey and the Pig"
Gay, John: "The Turkey and the Ant"; "The Wild Boar and the Ram"
Grimm, Jacob and Wilhelm: "The Golden Bird"; "The Golden Goose"; "The Wolf and the Fox"

Krylof, Ivan: "The Cuckoo and the Eagle"; "The Wolf and the Mouse"; "The Cat and the Nightingale"

Perrin, J. B.: "The Cat and the Bat"; "The Two Goats"

Phaedrus: "The Fox and the Dragon"; "The Ant and the Fly"

Tales of China: "The Mule and the Lion"; "The Lion and the Mosquitoes"

Tales of India: "The Stupid Monkeys"; "How the Rabbit Fooled the Elephant"

Tales of the Winnebago: "The Hare"

The Bible

The golden calf (Exodus 32, 33:1–6)

The lost sheep (Luke 15:3–7)

Poetry

Blake, William: "The Tiger"

Chalfi, Raquel: "Porcupine Fish"

Dickey, James: "The Bee"

Dickinson, Emily: " 'Hope' is the thing with feathers"; "A Narrow Fellow in the Grass"

Lawrence, D. H.: "Snake"

Moore, Marianne: "The Monkeys"

Rilke, Rainer Maria: "The Panther"

Roethke, Theodore: "Snake"

Schwartz, Delmore: "The Heavy Bear"

Tennyson, Alfred, Lord: "The Eagle"

Whitman, Walt: "A Noiseless Patient Spider"

Short Stories

du Maurier, Daphne: "The Blue Lenses"

Novels

Adams, Richard: *Watership Down*

Orwell, George: *Animal Farm*

Key Concepts and Problems

What do the characters represent? How can you tell? In what ways are the characters like people? What is the author saying about people, through the use of animals as symbols?

CHANGING TIMES

Poetry

Masters, Edgar Lee: *Spoon River Anthology*

Short Stories

Anderson, Sherwood: "Winesburg, Ohio"
Faulkner, William: "Go Down, Moses"
Irving, Washington: "Rip Van Winkle"

Novels

Achebe, Chinua: *Things Fall Apart*
Aluko, T. M.: *One Man, One Wife*
Faulkner, William: *The Hamlet; The Town; The Mansion; The Rievers*
Kesey, Ken: *Sometimes a Great Notion*
Lampedusa, Giuseppe di: *The Leopard*
Mahfouz, Naguib: *Midaq Alley*
Marquez, Gabriel Garcia: *One Hundred Years of Solitude*
Mitchell, Margaret: *Gone with the Wind*
Paton, Alan: *Cry, the Beloved Country*
Tarkington, Booth: *The Magnificent Ambersons*
Wharton, Edith: *Age of Innocence*
Wolfe, Thomas: *You Can't Go Home Again*

Autobiographies

Eastman, Charles Alexander: *From the Deep Woods to Civilization*
Mandela, Nelson: *Long Walk to Freedom*

Drama

Hellman, Lillian: *The Little Foxes*
Wilder, Thornton: *Our Town*
Williams, Tennessee: *The Glass Menagerie; A Streetcar Named Desire*

Films

The Last Picture Show
The Misfits

Songs

Haggard, Merle: "Are the Good Times Really Over for Good?"
Springsteen, Bruce: "Glory Days"

Key Concepts and Problems

How has society changed over time? What are the old values and conditions? What are the new values and conditions? What has caused these changes? How do the characters adapt to the changes? What is the author saying about human nature through the action in the story?

CHARACTER AS SYMBOL

Mythology

Daedalus and Icarus

Prometheus

Sisyphus

The Bible

The members and the body (1 Corinthians 12:12–30)

The prodigal son (Luke 15:11–32)

The rich man and lazarus (Luke 16:19–31)

The sower (Matthew 13:1–9, 18–23)

Poetry

Blake, William: "The Chimney Sweep"

Eliot, T. S.: "The Hollow Man"

Overstreet, Bonaro W.: "John Doe, Jr."

Robinson, Edwin Arlington: "Miniver Cheevy"

Thomas, Dylan: "The Hand That Signed the Paper"

Wordsworth, William: "The Solitary Reaper"

Short Stories

Cather, Willa: "The Sentimentality of William Tavener"

Cheever, John: "The Swimmer"

Collier, John: "The Chaser"

Connell, Evan, Jr.: "The Condor and the Guests"

Hawthorne, Nathaniel: "Young Goodman Brown"

Lawrence, D. H.: "The Rocking Horse Winner"

Poe, Edgar Allan: "The Masque of the Red Death"

Novels

Barth, John: *A Prayer for Owen Meany*

Hawthorne, Nathaniel: *The Scarlet Letter*

Melville, Herman: *Billy Budd*

Drama

Miller, Arthur: *The Crucible*

Films

Platoon

Tron

Key Concepts and Problems

Define symbol, allegory, and parable. What clues tell the reader that the characters are acting as symbols? What do the characters and elements of the story symbolize? How do they work together consistently to form a pattern that readers can interpret and draw conclusions from? What is the author trying to say through the symbols used in the story?

CHARACTERIZING AN AUTHOR'S STYLE

Prose Writers

Faulkner, William: "Barn Burning"; stories from *Go Down, Moses;* "Mule in the Yard"; "Old Man"; "Red Leaves"; "A Rose for Emily"; "Spotted Horses"; "That Evening Sun"; "Wash"; selections from *The Portable Faulkner*

Hemingway, Ernest: Stories from *In Our Time;* "Old Man at the Bridge"; "The Short Happy Life of Francis Macomber"; "The Snows of Kilimanjaro"

Twain, Mark: "The Celebrated Jumping Frog of Calaveras County"; *A Connecticut Yankee in King Arthur's Court; Life on the Mississippi;* "The Man That Corrupted Hadleyburg"; "The Mysterious Stranger"; *Pudd'nhead Wilson*

Poets

Dickinson, Emily: "Dear March—Come in"; " 'Hope' is the thing with feathers"; "The Grass so little has to do"; "What mystery pervades a well!"; "A Thought went up my mind today"

Frost, Robert: "Stopping by Woods on a Snowy Evening"; "The Road Not Taken"; "Neither Out Far Nor In Deep"; "Desert Places"; "The Secret Sits"

Key Concepts and Problems

What distinguishes the author in terms of (a) themes, (b) views of society, (c) views of human nature, (d) sentence structure, (e) language, and (f) literary techniques? How are these manifested in the writer's literature? How does knowledge of these features help us understand unfamiliar works by this writer?

COMEDY

Novels

Austen, Jane: *Pride and Prejudice*

Bellow, Saul: *Henderson the Rain King; Herzog*

Burgess, Anthony: *Enderby*

Fielding, Henry: *Tom Jones*

Smith, Lee: *Family Linen; Oral History*

Toole, John Kennedy: *A Confederacy of Dunces*

Wodehouse, P. G.: *The Inimitable Jeeves*

Drama

Barrie, J. M.: *The Admirable Crichton*

Chase, Mary: *Harvey*

Coward, Noel: *Weatherwise*

Gay, John: *The Beggar's Opera*

Goldsmith, Oliver: *She Stoops to Conquer*

Jonson, Ben: *Volpone*

Molière: *Tartuffe*

Shakespeare, William: *A Midsummer Night's Dream; Much Ado about Nothing; As You Like It*

Sheridan, Richard Brinsley: *The Rivals; The School for Scandal*

Wilde, Oscar: *The Importance of Being Earnest*

Key Concepts and Problems

What literary techniques (irony and so forth) does the playwright use to achieve a comic effect? What purpose does the comedy have? Why is comedy an effective means of making a serious point? Do you laugh at yourself as you see humor in the drama? Why or why not? What are the characteristics of comic characters? What are typical characteristics of comic plots?

COMING OF AGE

Poetry

Cofer, Judith Ortiz: "Crossings"

Short Stories

Anderson, Sherwood: "I'm a Fool"

Chukovski, Nicolai: "The Bridge"

Hurst, James: "The Scarlet Ibis"

Lessing, Doris: "Through the Tunnel"; "A Sunrise on the Veld"

McCullers, Carson: "Like That"

Munro, Alice: "Red Dress"

Updike, John: "A & P"

Walker, Alice: "Everyday Use"

Wright, Richard: "The Man Who Was Almost a Man"

Novels

Alcott, Louisa May: *Little Women*

Arguedas, Jose Maria: *Deep Rivers*

Baldwin, James: *Go Tell It on the Mountain*

Bennett, Kay: *Kaibah*

Conway, Jill Ker: *Road from Coorain*

Dorris, Michael: *Guests*

Grass, Günter: *The Tin Drum*

Guest, Judith: *Ordinary People*

Kincaid, Jamaica: *At the Bottom of the River*

Kingsolver, Barbara: *Bean Trees*

Knowles, John: *A Separate Peace*

Laye, Camara: *The Dark Child*

Le Guin, Ursula: *Very Far Away from Anywhere Else*

McCullers, Carson: *The Heart Is a Lonely Hunter*

Milosz, Czeslaw: *The Issa Valley*

Parks, Gordon: *The Learning Tree*

Paterson, Katherine: *Jacob Have I Loved*

Rolvaag, O. E.: *The Third Life of Per Smevik*

Twain, Mark: *Tom Sawyer*

Autobiographies

Beauvoir, Simone de: *Memoirs of a Dutiful Daughter*

Dillard, Annie: *An American Childhood*

Mitchell, Emerson Blackhorse: *Miracle Hill: The Story of a Navajo Boy*

Singer, Isaac Bashevis: *A Day of Pleasure: Stories of a Boy Growing Up in Warsaw*

Films

Stand by Me

Key Concepts and Problems

What is the definition of maturity? What examples of immature behavior do the protagonists exhibit before their coming-of-age experiences? What examples of mature behavior do they exhibit after their coming-of-age experiences? What is the key incident that causes the protagonist to change? What particular characteristics does this incident have that affect the protagonist so profoundly? What are the similarities among the experiences of the characters in the various stories? How truly do these experiences reflect those of real people? In what ways does the reader have empathy for the protagonist? How does this empathy affect the reader's comprehension?

CONFLICT WITH AUTHORITY

The Bible

The golden calf (Exodus 32, 33:1–6)

Poetry

Alexie, Sherman: "The Lone Ranger and Tonto Fistfight in Heaven"

Short Stories

Baldwin, James: "The Man Child"
Cather, Willa: "The Sentimentality of William Tavener"
Deal, Bordon: "Antaeus"
du Maurier, Daphne: "The Old Man"
Lavin, Mary: "The Story of the Widow's Son"
Ortiz, Simon J.: "Woman Singing"
Vonnegut, Kurt, Jr.: "Harrison Bergeron"
Wright, Richard: "The Man Who Was Almost a Man"

Novels

Alcott, Louisa May: *Little Women*
Golding, William: *Lord of the Flies*
Mathews, John Joseph: *Sundown*
McNickle, D'Arcy: *The Surrounded*
Orwell, George: *Animal Farm*
Potok, Chaim: *The Chosen*
Steinbeck, John: *The Red Pony*

Drama

Chayefsky, Paddy: *The Mother*
Shakespeare, William: *Romeo and Juliet*

Key Concepts and Problems

Who is the authority figure? What characteristics does this figure have? From what sources does the authority derive his or her power? What are the characteristics of the protagonist? What causes them to clash? What is the outcome of the clash? How is the clash resolved? What does the protagonist learn through the clash?

CONNOTATION AND IMAGERY
Poetry
Connotation

Davis, Frank Marshall: "Four Glimpses of Night"
Hughes, Ted: "Wind"
Jarrell, Randall: "Bats"
Owen, Wilfred: "Arms and the Boy"
Robinson, Edwin Arlington: "Richard Cory"
Shapiro, Karl: "The Fly"; "Auto Wreck"
Smith, Stevie: "Zoo"
Wilbur, Richard: "Still Citizen Sparrow"; "Firetruck"

POETRY

Imagery

Browning, Robert: "Meeting at Night"

Grenelle, Lisa: "It Was Cold in the House"

Hayden, Robert: "Those Winter Sundays"

Housman, A. E.: "On Moonlit Heath and Lonesome Bank"

Keats, John: "To Autumn"

Rich, Adrienne: "Living in Sin"

Sarton, May: "A Parrot"

Sassoon, Siegfried: "The Rear Guard"

Shelley, Percy Bysshe: "Lines: When the Lamp Is Shattered"

Thwaites, Michael: "The Gull"

Key Concepts and Problems

Connotation

Which words in the poem are especially vivid? Why do they have exceptional impact? Are the connotative words consistent? That is, do they work together to convey a sense of harshness, a sense of gentleness, or another particular feeling? How can readers use their imaginations to picture more about the poem and its subject from these connotative words? How do the connotative words help the poet convey meaning?

Imagery

Which words in the poem convey an image? Are the images consistent, working together to portray a particular mood or feeling? How can readers use their imaginations to picture more about the poem and its subjects from these images? How do the images help the poet convey meaning?

COPING WITH LOSS

Prayers

Last rites

Mourner's Kaddish

Poetry

Browning, Robert: "My Last Duchess"

Burns, Robert: "Auld Lang Syne"

Dickinson, Emily: "Because I could not stop for Death"; "I heard a Fly buzz-when I died"

Frost, Robert: "Out, Out"; "After Apple-Picking"; "Fire and Ice"

Gray, Thomas: "Elegy Written in a Country Churchyard"

Hopkins, Gerard Manley: "Spring and Fall to a Young Child"

Housman, A. E.: "To an Athlete Dying Young"

Keats, John: "Ode to a Nightingale"; "La Belle Dame Sans Merci"

Poe, Edgar Allan: "The Raven"; "Annabel Lee"
Stevens, Wallace: "Domination of Black"
Tennyson, Alfred, Lord: "In Memoriam"
Thomas, Dylan: "Do Not Go Gentle into That Good Night"
Whitman, Walt: "When Lilacs Last in the Dooryard Bloomed"

Short Stories

Borges, Jorge Luis: "The Circular Ruins"
Brooke, Rupert: "The Dead"
Chekhov, Anton: "Enemies"
Faulkner, William: "A Rose for Emily"
Galsworthy, John: "The Apple Tree"
Harjo, Joy: "The Woman Who Fell from the Sky"
Hemingway, Ernest: "Hills Like White Elephants"
Joyce, James: "The Dead"; "A Painful Case"
Kafka, Franz: "The Judgment"
Marquez, Gabriel Garcia: "Tuesday Siesta"
Porter, Katherine Anne: "The Grave"
Shenendoah, Joanne: "Dance of the North"
Steinbeck, John: "Flight"
Tolstoy, Leo: "The Death of Ivan Ilych"

Novels

Agee, Philip: *A Death in the Family*
Devoto, Pat Cunningham: *My Last Days as Roy Rogers*
Guest, Judith: *Ordinary People*

Nonfiction

Baldwin, James: *Notes of a Native Son*

Drama

Arrabal, Fernando: *Picnic on the Battlefield*
Miller, Arthur: *A View from the Bridge*

Songs

Bugguss, Suzy: "Letting Go"
Clapton, Eric: "Tears in Heaven"
McEntire, Reba: "The Greatest Man I Never Knew"
Wolf, Kate: "Medicine Wheel"

Key Concepts and Problems

What is lost? What do the characters lose through the loss? What do they gain? How do the characters cope with grief? How does their coping affect them? How do they change? How are the grievers treated by others? How does this treatment affect them? What is the author saying about the human ability to cope with great loss?

COURAGE
Mythology

Hercules

Poetry

Kipling, Rudyard: "Gunga Din"

Short Stories

Agee, James: "A Mother's Tale"
Buck, Pearl: "Guerilla Mother"
Connell, Richard: "The Most Dangerous Game"
Freeman, Mary E. Wilkins: "The Revolt of Mother"
Hemingway, Ernest: "A Day's Wait"
London, Jack: "To Build a Fire"
Poe, Edgar Allan: "The Cask of Amontillado"
Vasconcelos, Jose: "The Boar Hunt"

Novels

Carter, Forrest: *The Vengeance Trail of Josey Wales*
Cather, Willa: *Death Comes to the Archbishop*
Crane, Stephen: *The Red Badge of Courage*
Ellison, Ralph: *Invisible Man*
Hemingway, Ernest: *The Old Man and the Sea*
Markandaya, Kamala: *Nectar in a Sieve*
Trumbo, Dalton: *Johnny Got His Gun*
Welty, Eudora: *The Robber Bridegroom*

Autobiographies

Angelou, Maya: *I Know Why the Caged Bird Sings*
Giovanni, Nikki: *Gemeni*
Yevtushenko, Yevgeny: *A Precocious Autobiography*

Drama

Buck, Pearl: *The Rock*

Fletcher, Lucille: *Sorry, Wrong Number*

Nonfiction

Wiesel, Elie: *Night*

Films

The Lost Weekend

The Man Who Shot Liberty Valance

Key Concepts and Problems

What is the definition of courage? What key incident tests the protagonist's courage? How does the character respond to this challenge? Is the character's action courageous? Why or why not? What values in conflict bring about situations calling for courage? Would a courageous action in one situation necessarily be regarded as courageous in the context of another? Why or why not?

CULTURAL CONFLICT

Poetry

Chrystos: "Not Vanishing"

Hardy, Thomas: "The Man He Killed"

Owen, Wilfred: "Anthem for Doomed Youth"; "Strange Meeting"

Short Stories

Achebe, Chinua: "A Man of the People"

Buck, Pearl: "The Frill"

Isherwood, Christopher: "The Berlin Stories"

Kipling, Rudyard: "The Man Who Would Be King"

Nicol, Abiosch: "The Devil at Yolahun Bridge"

Peters, Lenri: "Parachute"

Popkes, Opal Lee: "Zuma Chowt's Cave"

Rubadiri, David: "Stanley Meets Mutesa"

Tapahonso, Luci: "The Snakeman"

Warrior, Emma Lee: "Compatriots"

Novels

Alexie, Sherman: *Reservation Blues; Indian Killer*

Beti, Mongo: *Mission to Kala*

Conrad, Joseph: *Heart of Darkness*

da Cunha, Euclides: *Rebellion in the Backlands*

Ekwensi, Cyprian: *People of the City*

Forster, E. M.: *A Passage to India*

Gaup, Ailou: *In Search of the Drum*

Gordimer, Nadine: *Livingstone's Companions*

Greene, Graham: *The Human Factor*

James, Henry: *The American*

Lawrence, D. H.: *The Plumed Serpent*

Munonye, John: *The Only Son*

Orwell, George: *Burmese Days*

Power, Susan: *The Grass Dancer*

Qoyawayma, Polingaysi: *No Turning Back*

Scott, Paul: *The Jewel in the Crown; The Day of the Scorpion; The Towers of Silence; A Division of the Spoils*

Tan, Amy: *The Joy Luck Club*

Thiongo, Ngugi wa: *The River Between*

Nonfiction (Essays)

Cheng, Nien: "Life and Death in Shanghai"

Orwell, George: "Shooting an Elephant"

Autobiographies

Fire Lame Deer, Archie: *Gift of Power: The Life and Teachings of a Lakota Medicine Man*

Rogers, John: *Red World and White*

Song

Johnny Clegg & Savuka: *Third World Child*

Key Concepts and Problems

In what ways are the cultures different? Is one culture more powerful than the other? If so, in what ways? In the author's view, is one culture superior to the other? If so, in what ways? Do you agree with the author's judgment? What is the outcome of the clash? Is the outcome "fair"? Why or why not? How do characters change as a result of their experience with another culture?

THE DETECTIVE

Short Stories

Doyle, Sir Arthur Conan: Sherlock Holmes stories

Gilbert, Michael: "The Oyster Catcher"

Hocky, Mary: "Stranger on the Night Train"

Mayor, Ralph H., Jr.: "The Buried Treasure of Oak Island"

Novels

Chandler, Raymond: *The Big Sleep*

Christie, Agatha: *Murder on the Orient Express; The Murder of Roger Ackroyd*

Francis, Dick: *Banker*

Hoeg, Peter: *Smilla's Sense of Snow*

James, P. D.: *Death of an Expert Witness; Shroud for a Nightingale*

Murray, Stephen: *A Cool Killing*

Paretsky, Sara: *Killing Orders; Deadlock; Indemnity Only*

Peters, Elizabeth: *The Deeds of the Disturber*

Sayers, Dorothy L.: *Murder Must Advertise*

Scoppetone, Sandra: *Playing Murder*

Tey, Josephine: *Brat Farrar*

Wilzien, Valere: *Murder at the PTA Luncheon*

Key Concepts and Problems

What qualities does the detective have that help in solving crimes? What are typical patterns and properties of detective stories? What sorts of obstacles does the detective encounter? How does he or she overcome them? What qualities allow the detective to triumph over adversaries?

DISCRIMINATION

Poetry

Angelou, Maya: "On the Pulse of Morning"

Short Stories

Abrahams, Peter: "Tell Freedom"

Hutchinson, Alfred: "Road to Ghana"

Johnson, Dorothy M.: "A Man Called Horse"

Le Guma, Alex: "Where Are You Walking Around, Man?"

Luthuli, Albert: "The Dignity of Man"

Muro, Amado: "Cecilia Rosa"

Soyinka, Wole: "Telephone Conversation"

Thomas, Piri: "Puerto Rican Paradise"

Walker, Alice: "Everyday Use"

Novels

Alexie, Sherman: *Reservation Blues; Indian Killer*

Ekhart, Alan: *A Sorrow in Our Hearts*

Gaines, Ernest: *A Lesson before Dying*

Greene, Bette: *The Drowning of Stephan Jones*

Griterson, David: *Snow Falling on Cedars*

Hinton, S. E.: *The Outsiders*

Hurston, Nora Zeal: *Their Eyes Were Watching God*

Lee, Harper: *To Kill a Mockingbird*

Markandaya, Kamala: *Nectar in a Sieve*
Morrison, Toni: *Beloved*
Walker, Alice: *The Color Purple*
Walker, Margaret: *Jubilee*
Weisel, Elie: *Night*
Wright, Richard: *Native Son*

Nonfiction (Essays)

Baldwin, James: "The Discovery of What It Means to Be an American"
Hughes, Langston: "Fooling Our White Folks"
King, Martin Luther, Jr.: "Letter from a Birmingham Jail"
Longauex y Vasquez, Enriqueta: "The Mexican-American Woman"
Redding, Saunders: "American Negro Literature"

Nonfiction (Books)

Debo, Angie: *And Still the Waters Run*
Greene, Melissa Fay: *Praying for Sheetrock*
Terkel, Studs: *Division Street: America*
Weatherford, Jack: *Native Roots; Indian Givers*

Autobiographies

Angelou, Maya: *I Know Why the Caged Bird Sings*
Frank, Anne: *Diary of a Young Girl*
Wright, Richard: *Black Boy*

Drama

Hansberry, Lorraine: *A Raisin in the Sun*
Shakespeare, William: *Othello*
Shaw, George Bernard: *Pygmalion*
Wilson, August: *Ma Rainey's Black Bottom*

Films

Clearcut
Dance Me Outside
Do the Right Thing
Guess Who's Coming to Dinner?
In the Heat of the Night
The Long Walk Home
Once Were Warriors
Shindler's List

Smoke Signals
A Soldier's Story
Swing Kids

Documentary Films

Eyes on the Prize
Martin Luther King, Jr.: From Memphis to Montgomery

Song

Belafonte, Harry: "Kwela" (Listen to the Man)

Key Concepts and Problems

Why is the character being discriminated against? In what ways is the character different from the group that's discriminating? Does the character want to be accepted? Why or why not? What forms of discrimination is the character subject to? How is the character affected by discrimination? How is the conflict resolved? What in the environment leads to discrimination? What makes discrimination more likely in one environment than in another?

THE EPIC HERO
The Bible

David (Samuel 16–18; Kings 1–2)
Joseph (Genesis 37–50)
Moses (Exodus 1–19)
Ruth (Ruth)

Epic Poetry

Beowulf
The Epic of Gilgamesh
Homer: *The Odyssey*
The Song of Roland

Novels

Barth, John: *The Sot-Weed Factor*
Bellow, Saul: *Herzog*
Clarke, Arthur C.: *2001: A Space Odyssey*
Ellison, Ralph: *Invisible Man*
Gardner, John: *Grendel*
Hemingway, Ernest: *The Old Man and the Sea; For Whom the Bell Tolls*
Norris, Frank: *The Octopus*

Steinbeck, John: *The Grapes of Wrath*
Sykes, Gerald: *The Center of the Stage*

Key Concepts and Problems

What are the characteristics of an epic? What are the characteristics of the epic hero? What are the characteristics of the epic hero's quest? How are the elements of the hero and the quest similar and different from story to story? Why are such characters heroic? Do we have such heroes in society today? Why or why not?

THE FAMILY

Poetry

Bode, Carl: "The Bad Children"
Brooks, Gwendolyn: "The Children of the Poor"
Carver, Raymond: "Photograph of My Father in His Twenty-Second Year"
Dickey, James: "The Bee"
Hayden, Robert: "Those Winter Sundays"
Roethke, Theodore: "My Papa's Waltz"
Plath, Sylvia: "Daddy"; "The Disquieting Muses"

Short Stories

Bambara, Toni Cade: "Raymond's Run"
Boles, Paul Darcy: "The Night Watch"
Chekhov, Anton: "Enemies"
Freeman, Mary E. Wilkins: "The Revolt of Mother"
Gray, Nicholas Stuart: "The Star Beast"
Hesse, Hermann: "A Man by the Name of Ziegler"
Jackson, Charles: "A Night Visitor"
Kelley, William Melvin: "Brother Carlyle"
Morrison, Toni: "Recitatif"
Steinbeck, John: "Flight"
Stuart, Jesse: "Love"
Williams, William Carlos: "The Use of Force"

Novels

Allende, Isabel: *House of the Spirits*
Bell, Betty Louise: *Faces in the Moon*
Blue, Rose: *Goodbye, Forever Tree*
Burns, Olive Ann: *Cold Sassy Tree*
Cross, Gillian: *On the Edge*

Faulkner, William: *As I Lay Dying*
Dorris, Michael: *Morning Girl*
Irwin, Hadley: *What about Grandma?*
Lamott, Anne: *Rosie; Crooked Little Heart*
Maloney, Ray: *The Impact Zone*
Mazer, Norma Fox: *Three Sisters*
Smiley, Jane: *A Thousand Acres*
Stowe, Harriet Beecher: *Uncle Tom's Cabin*
Tan, Amy: *The Joy Luck Club*

Autobiographies

Allende, Isabel: *Paula*
Angelou, Maya: *Singin' and Swingin' and Gettin' Merry Like Christmas; Gather Together in My Name*
May, Lee: *In My Father's Garden*
McBride, James: *The Color of Water: A Black Man's Tribute to His White Mother*
McCourt, Frank: *Angela's Ashes*
Schlissel, Lillian (Ed.): *Women's Diaries of the Westward Journey*

Nonfiction

Griffin, Garah Jasmine (Ed.): *Beloved Sisters and Loving Friends*

Drama

Shepard, Sam: *Paris, Texas*

Films

A River Runs through It

Key Concepts and Problems

What is the definition of a family? What do family members share? What types of conflicts occur within families? How are they resolved? What goals do families have? How do family needs affect the behavior of the characters in the story? What outside influences affect the family? Are these influences good or bad? Why?

THE FOLK HERO
Folktales/Legends

Irving, Washington: "The Legend of Sleepy Hollow"
Tales about such legendary figures as Crispus Attucks, Barney Beal, Bowleg Bill, Pecos Bill, Paul Bunyan and Babe, Annie Christmas, Mike Fink, John Henry, Jack the Giant Killer, Casey Jones, Joe Magarac, and Betty Zane

Key Concepts and Problems

What are the characteristics of the folk hero? What are the characteristics of the folk hero's quest? What types of obstacles does the folk hero encounter? What qualities enable the folk hero to triumph? What forces in a culture produce folk literature?

FRIENDS AND ENEMIES

Short Stories

Fante, John: "The Odyssey of a Wop"
Galsworthy, John: "The Apple Tree"
Maugham, Somerset: "The Letter"
Oliver, Diane: "Neighbors"

Novels

Auel, Jean: *The Clan of the Cave Bear*
Bradbury, Ray: *Fahrenheit 451*
Bridgers, Sue Ellen: *Home before Dark*
Cary, Joyce: *The Horse's Mouth*
Cervantes, Miguel de: *Don Quixote*
Dumas, Alexandre: *The Three Musketeers*
Forster, E. M.: *A Passage to India*
Greene, Bette: *Summer of My German Soldier; Morning Is a Long Time Coming*
Greene, Graham: *Brighton Rock*
Guy, Rosa: *The Friends*
Hesse, Hermann: *Demian; Narcissus and Goldmund; Siddhartha*
Hunt, Irene: *Across Five Aprils*
Kazantzakis, Nikos: *Zorba the Greek*
Kerr, M. E.: *I'll Love You When You're More Like Me*
Knowles, John: *A Separate Peace*
Lawrence, D. H.: *Women in Love*
Le Guin, Ursula: *Very Far Away from Anywhere Else*
Mahy, Margaret: *Catalogue of the Universe*
Myers, Walter Dean: *Hoops*
Oates, Joyce Carol: *Solstice*
Paterson, Katherine: *Jacob Have I Loved; The Bridge to Terabithia*
Puig, Manuel: *The Kiss of the Spider Woman*
Steinbeck, John: *Of Mice and Men*
Strasser, Todd: *Friends Till the End*
Zalben, Jane Breskin: *Here's Looking at You, Kid*

Drama

Serling, Rod: *In the Presence of Mine Enemies*

Films

Ma Vie en Rose (My Life in Pink)
Twilight of the Gods

Key Concepts and Problems

What draws friends together? What causes people to be enemies? How do the characters try to settle their differences? How are the conflicts resolved? What is the author trying to say about the nature of friendship? What is the author trying to say about the nature of conflict?

FRONTIER LITERATURE

Novels

Allen, Hervey: *The Forest and the Fort*

Brown, Dee: *Wave High the Banner*

Cather, Willa: *Obscure Destinies; My Antonia*

Cooper, James Fenimore: *The Last of the Mohicans; The Pioneers*

Fletcher, Inglis: *Roanoke Hundred*

Forbes, Esther: *Paradise*

Garland, Hamlin: *Moccasin Ranch*

Giles, Janice Holt: *Land beyond the Mountains*

Mason, F. Van Wyck: *The Young Titan*

MacLachlan, Patricia: *Sarah Plain and Tall; Skylark*

Richter, Conrad: *Free Man; Light in the Forest*

Rolvaag, O. E.: *Giants in the Earth*

Swanson, Neil: *The Silent Drum*

Vaughan, Carter: *The Invincibles*

Welty, Eudora: *The Robber Bridegroom*

Widdemer, Margaret: *The Golden Wildcat*

Key Concepts and Problems

What is the goal of the settlers? What is their attitude toward (a) nature, (b) Native Americans, and (c) the law? How do they try to achieve their goal? Who or what are their allies in achieving their goal? What are their obstacles? How do the properties of a frontier help determine the form of a frontier story? What are typical characteristics of heroes in frontier stories? How does the perspective of the narrator invite particular responses and sympathies of readers? What are the consequences of these responses and sympathies for developing a perspective on Western expansion and native people?

GANGS, CLIQUES, AND PEER-GROUP PRESSURE

Short Stories

Andreyev, Leonid: "Nippie"

Cozzens, James Gould: "The Animals' Fair"

Hwang, S. T.: "The Donkey Cart"

Langdon, John: "The Blue Serge Suit"

Stafford, Jean: "Bad Characters"

Taylor, Elizabeth: "Nice and Birds and Boy"

Vaca, Nicolas C.: "The Purchase"

West, Jessamyn: "Live Life Deeply"

Novels

Hinton, S. E.: *Rumble Fish; The Outsiders*

Morrison, Toni: *The Bluest Eye*

Peterson, P. J.: *Corky and the Brothers Cool*

Drama

Rose, Reginald: *Dino*

Shakespeare, William: *Romeo and Juliet*

Films

The Breakfast Club

Pretty in Pink

Sixteen Candles

West Side Story

Key Concepts and Problems

What are the values of the group applying pressure? Why have group members adopted these values? Why do they try to impose them? In what ways is the protagonist different from the group? How does the protagonist respond to the pressure? How does the protagonist change during the story? What are differences among gang, clique, and peer group? Why do kids join? Why do such groups form?

GENDER ROLES

Fairy Tales

"Cinderella"

"Hansel and Gretel"

Poetry

Chester, Laura: "Eyes of the Garden"

Collins, Judy: "Albatross"

Short Stories

Faessler, Shirley: "A Basket of Apples"

Freeman, Mary E. Wilkins: "The Revolt of Mother"

Hemingway, Ernest: "The Short Happy Life of Francis Macomber"

Huang, Veronica: "Backstage"

Hurston, Zora Neale: "Sweat"

Rau, Santha Rama: "Who Cares?"

Thurber, James: "The Secret Life of Walter Mitty"

Toer, Pramoedya Ananta: "Inem"

Walker, Alice: "Everyday Use"

Novels

Arnow, Harriette: *The Dollmaker*

Chopin, Kate: *The Awakening*

Hurston, Zora Neale: *Their Eyes Were Watching God*

Langton, Jane: *Her Majesty; The Boyhood of Grace Jones*

Lindbergh, Anne Morrow: *Gift from the Sea*

Walker, Alice: *The Color Purple*

Drama

Shaw, George Bernard: *How He Lied to Her Husband*

Films

9 to 5

Tootsie

Victor/Victoria

Key Concepts and Problems

How are the roles of males and females presented in the literature? What is the point of view of the narrator toward these roles? What is the point of view of the author toward these roles? How do these roles reflect the values of the culture and era of the story's setting? To what extent are these roles consistent with attitudes toward gender roles in your community?

INFLUENCES ON PERSONALITY

Novels

Burns, Olive Ann: *Cold Sassy Tree*

Childress, Alice: *A Hero Ain't Nothin' but a Sandwich; Rainbow Jordan*

Greene, Hannah: *I Never Promised You a Rose Garden*

Lipsyte, Robert: *One Fat Summer*

Myers, Walter Dean: *It Ain't All for Nothin'*

Peck, Robert Newton: *Justice Lion*
Sleator, William: *House of Stairs*
Stewart, Mary: *The Crystal Cave*
Torchia, Joseph: *Kryptonite Kid*
Twain, Mark: *The Adventures of Huckleberry Finn*

Key Concepts and Problems

What influences do the characters face? Consider such factors as family, religion, friends, media, laws and rules, temperament, intellect, talent, and values. Which of these influences are good? Which are bad? Which influences are the greatest? How does the character respond to the influences? What does the character discover at the end? How does this realization affect the character?

IRONY

Note: The approach to studying irony is adapted from the work of Wayne Booth and Michael W. Smith (see in particular Smith, 1991).

Clue 1: Straightforward Warning in Author's Own Voice

Barry, Dave: "God Needs the Money"

Breathed, Berke: *Bloom County* cartoons

cummings, e. e.: "the Cambridge ladies who live in furnished souls"

Larson, Gary: *The Far Side* cartoons

Nemerov, Howard: "Santa Claus"

Royko, Mike: "Silence Is the Best Sport"

Simon, Paul: "The Dangling Conversation"

Twain, Mark: "My Watch"

Clue 2: Known Error Proclaimed

Baker, Russell: "Addals of Medicid"

Barry, Dave: "What Is and Ain't Grammatical"; "Great Baby! Delicious!"

Benchley, Robert: "Whoa!"; "French for Americans"

Buchwald, Art: "Fresh Air Will Kill You"

Perelman, S. J.: "Waiting for Santa"

Clue 3: Conflict of Facts within the Work

Capek, Karel: "The Last Judgment"

cummings, e. e.: "i sing of Olaf, glad and big"

Daudet, Alphonse: "The Death of the Dauphin"

Gardner, Mona: "The Dinner Party"

Hardy, Thomas: "The Man He Killed"; *Satires of Circumstance*

Henry, O.: "The Ransom of Red Chief"
Kerr, Orpheus C.: "The Latest Improvements in Artillery"
Lowell, Amy: "Fireworks"
Madgett, Naomi Long: "The Mother Saki"; "The Interlopers"
Shelley, Percy Bysshe: "Ozymandias"
Smith, Stevie: "Zoo"

Clue 4: Conflict of Style

Hubbard, Kim: *A Letter from the Front*
Lehrer, Tom: "Fight Fiercely, Harvard"
Locke, David Ross: "Nasby Shows Why He Should Not Be Drafted"
Marquis, Don: "warty biggins, the toad"
Mull, Martin: "Straight Talk about the Blues/Ukelele Blues"
Parker, Dorothy: "From the Diary of a New York Lady"
Twain, Mark: "Unspoken War Prayer"

Clue 5: Clash of Beliefs

Barry, Dave: "God Needs the Money"
Buchwald, Art: "Is Your City Worth Saving?"
Clough, Arthur Hugh: "The Latest Decalogue"
Franklin, Ben: "The Sale of the Hessians"
Newman, Randy: "Short People"; "Let's Drop the Big One"
Olson, Elder: "Plot Improbable, Character Unsympathetic"
Paxton, Tom: "What Did You Learn in School Today?"
Royko, Mike: "A Great Fish, the Bullhead"
Springsteen, Bruce: "Nebraska"
Swift, Jonathan: "A Modest Proposal"

Overall Review of Irony

Blume, Judy: *Tales of a Fourth Grade Nothing*
Heller, Joseph: *Catch-22*
Kubrick, Stanley: *Dr. Strangelove*
Rice, Anne: *Interview with the Vampire*
Shepherd, Jean: *In God We Trust, All Others Pay Cash*
Swift, Jonathan: *Gulliver's Travels*
Twain, Mark: *The Adventures of Huckleberry Finn*
Vonnegut, Kurt, Jr.: *Slaughterhouse Five*
Wells, H. G.: *The War of the Worlds*
Wibberley, Leonard: *The Mouse That Roared*
Zindel, Paul: *The Effect of Gamma Rays on Man-in-the-Moon Marigolds*

Key Concepts and Problems

There are five clues for recognizing irony (identified by Wayne Booth, and listed above). Does this work include one or more of these clues? If so, when we reject the surface meaning of the piece, what is the author really saying?

THE JOURNEY
The Bible

Exodus

Epic Poetry

Homer: *The Iliad; The Odyssey*

Short Stories

Glancy, Diane: "The Orchard"

Hawthorne, Nathaniel: "Young Goodman Brown"

Renville, D.: "Siobhan La Rue in Color"

Novels

Adams, Richard: *Watership Down*

Hemingway, Ernest: *The Old Man and the Sea*

Melville, Herman: *Moby-Dick*

Momaday, N. Scott: *The Way to Rainy Mountain*

Steinbeck, John: *The Grapes of Wrath*

Tolkien, J. R. R.: *The Hobbit*

Twain, Mark: *The Adventures of Huckleberry Finn*

Nonfiction

Iyer, Pico: *Video Night in Kathmandu: And Other Reports from the Not-So-Far East*

Moon, William Least Heat: *Blue Highways*

Autobiographies

Guthrie, Woody: *Bound for Glory*

Schlissel, Lillian (Ed.): *Women's Diaries of the Westward Journey*

Films

El Norte

Thelma and Louise

Song

Mitchell, Joni: "Woodstock"

Key Concepts and Problems

What is the character's quest? What is the vehicle for the journey? What does the character value in getting there, that is, what does the character view as sacred, dispensable, profane? What help does the character receive along the way? How does he or she view this help? What physical and character traits enable the journey to continue? What changes does the character experience along the way? What destinations does the character reach? Ultimately, what is the meaning of the journey?

JUSTICE
Poetry

Anzaldua, Gloria: "How to Tame a Wild Tongue"

Davis, Frank Marshall: "Giles Johnson, Ph.D."

La Farge, Peter: "As Long As the Grass Shall Grow"

Miriktani, Janice: "Breaking Silence"

Mitsui, James: "Destination: Tule Lake Relocation Center, May 20, 1942"

Okita, Dwight: "In Response to Executive Order 9006"

Okubo, Mine: "Holding Center, Tanforan Race Track Spring 1942"

Walker, Margaret: "For My People"

Novels

Bambara, Toni Cade: *The Salt Eaters*

Carlisle, Henry, and Carlisle, Olga Andreyev: *The Idealists*

Dostoyevsky, Fyodor: *Crime and Punishment*

Faulkner, William: *Light in August*

Le Guin, Ursula: *The Dispossessed*

Melville, Herman: *Billy Budd*

Steiner, George: *The Portage to San Cristobal of A.H.*

Taylor, Mildred: *Roll of Thunder, Hear My Cry*

Toomer, Jean: *Cane*

Uchida, Yoshiko: *The Invisible Friend*

Wells-Barnett, Ida B.: *Crusade for Justice*

Wouk, Herman: *The Caine Mutiny*

Wright, Richard: *Native Son*

Autobiographies

Black Elk, with John G. Neihardt: *Black Elk Speaks*

Mandela, Nelson: *Long Walk to Freedom*

Moody, Anne: *Coming of Age in Mississippi*

Standing Bear, Luther: *My People, the Sioux*

Nonfiction

Ehrenreich, Barbara and English, Deidre: *The Sexual Politics of Sickness*

King, Martin Luther, Jr.: "Letter from a Birmingham Jail"

Thoreau, Henry David: "Civil Disobedience"

Drama

Peckinpah, Sam: *Noon Wine*

Rose, Reginald: *Twelve Angry Men*

Shakespeare, William: *The Merchant of Venice*

Song

Johnny Clegg & Savuka: "Bombs Away"

Key Concepts and Problems

What is the definition of justice? Where do the characters in the story get their concept of justice? Is the behavior of the characters in the story just? Why or why not? What are the difficulties involved in achieving justice? In what ways can punishment be justly related to crime? What is the relationship between justice and mercy? What is the source of one's concept of justice?

THE LEADER

Short Stories

Deal, Bordon: "Antaeus"

Guthrie, A. B., Jr.: "Old Mother Hubbard"

Novels

Bonham, Frank: *Durango Street*

Cormier, Robert: *The Chocolate War; After the First Death; The Bumblebee Flies Anyway*

Forman, James: *A Ceremony of Innocence*

French, Michael: *The Throwing Season*

Golding, William: *Lord of the Flies*

Hinton, S. E.: *The Outsiders; That Was Then, This Is Now; Rumble Fish*

L'Engle, Madeleine: *A Ring of Endless Light*

O'Brien, Robert: *Z for Zachariah*

Schaefer, Jack: *Shane*

Stevenson, Robert Louis: *Treasure Island*

Twain, Mark: *Tom Sawyer*

Zindel, Paul: *Harry and Hortense at Hormone High*

Films

Dave

Hoosiers

Key Concepts and Problems

What are the qualities of a leader? Why do others follow such a person? What type of leadership does the leader offer? What is the leader's purpose? How is this character regarded by the others in the story? How does the leader change during the story?

LOSS OF INNOCENCE
Mythology
Pandora's box
Phaethon
Deirdre and the sons of Usna

The Bible
The Creation and the Fall (Genesis 1–3)

Poetry
Cullen, Countee: "Youth Sings a Song of Rosebuds"
Millay, Edna St. Vincent: "Childhood Is the Kingdom Where Nobody Dies"
Roethke, Theodore: "Dinky"
Stafford, William: "In the Old Days"; "Time"
Thomas, Dylan: "Fern Hill"

Short Stories
Hawthorne, Nathaniel: "Egotism, Or the Bosom Serpent"
Joyce, James: "Araby"
Shaw, Irwin: "Peter Two"
Updike, John: "You'll Never Know, Dear, How Much I Love You"
Warren, R. P.: "Blackberry Winter"

Novels
Baldwin, James: *Go Tell It on the Mountain*
Carter, Forrest: *The Education of Little Tree*
Gipson, Fred: *Old Yeller*
Hawthorne, Nathaniel: *The Marble Faun*
Hunter, Kristin: *God Bless the Child*
Knowles, John: *A Separate Peace*
Rawlings, Marjorie: *The Yearling*
Salinger, J. D.: *The Catcher in the Rye*
Smith, Betty: *A Tree Grows in Brooklyn*
Soyinka, Wole: *Ake: The Years of Childhood*
Steinbeck, John: *The Red Pony*

Song
Johnny Clegg & Savuka: "The Promise"

Key Concepts and Problems

What is innocence? In what ways is the character originally innocent? What causes the "fall"? How is the character affected by the fall? Is the character better off, or worse? Why? What has the character learned from this experience?

LOVE
Poetry

Burns, Robert: "A Red, Red Rose"

Donne, John: "The Ecstasy"

Graves, Robert: "Symptoms of Love"

Herrick, Robert: "Delight in Disorder"

Lowell, Amy: "The Taxi"

Roethke, Theodore: "Elegy for Jane"

Shakespeare, William: "Sonnets 18, 29"

Shapiro, Karl: "How Do I Love You?"

Yeats, William Butler: "The Lover Tells of the Rose in His Heart"

Short Stories

Hughes, Langston: "A Good Job Done"

Kerckhoff, Joan: "Talk to Me, Talk to Me"

O'Connor, Flannery: "Everything That Rises Must Converge"

Novels

Austen, Jane: *Pride and Prejudice*

Brontë, Charlotte: *Jane Eyre*

Brontë, Emily: *Wuthering Heights*

du Maurier, Daphne: *Rebecca*

Faulkner, William: *Light in August*

Hemingway, Ernest: *A Farewell to Arms*

Joyce, James: *Ulysses*

Kundera, Milan: *The Unbearable Lightness of Being*

Marquez, Gabriel Garcia: *Love in the Time of Cholera*

McCullers, Carson: *The Heart Is a Lonely Hunter*

Percy, Walker: *The Second Coming; The Moviegoer*

Rhys, Jean: *Wide Sargasso Sea*

Walker, Alice: *The Color Purple*

Woolf, Virginia: *Orlando*

Drama

Chayefsky, Paddy: *Marty*

Shakespeare, William: *A Midsummer Night's Dream; Romeo and Juliet*

Films

Out of Africa

Key Concepts and Problems

What is the definition of romantic love? What enables the lovers to become intimate with each other? How do the characters in the story illustrate the definition of romantic love? How do they fall short of the definition? Is there such thing as weak love, or can love only be strong? How does a love relationship affect an individual? How do individuals in love affect each other? How does romantic love develop?

LOYALTY

The Bible

Abraham and Isaac (Genesis 22:1–19)

Cain and Abel (Genesis 4:1–16)

The golden calf (Exodus 32, 33:1–6)

Joseph and his brothers (Genesis 37:1–36)

Poetry

Brooks, Gwendolyn: "The Preacher: Ruminates behind the Sermon"

Masters, Edgar Lee: "The Village Atheist"

Muir, Edwin: "Moses"

Nemerov, Howard: "Santa Claus"

Prettyman, Quandra: "When Mahalia Sings"

Shapiro, Karl: "151st Psalm"

Spender, Stephen: "What I Expected"

Yeats, William Butler: "The Second Coming"

Short Stories

Babel, Isaac: "Awakening"

Baldwin, James: "My Childhood"

Chavez, Fray Angelico: "Hunchback Madonna"

Frame, Janet: "The Reservoir"

Haycox, Ernest: "A Question of Blood"

Hughes, Langston: "Salvation"

Mendoza, Durango: "Summer Water and Shirley"

O'Flaherty, Liam: "The Fairy Goose"

Silko, Leslie Marmon: "The Man to Send Rain Clouds"

Swados, Harvey: "Claudine's Book"

Novels

Gipson, Fred: *Old Yeller*

Potok, Chaim: *The Chosen; The Promise*

Nonfiction

Chief Joseph of the Nez Perce: Speech of surrender

Gettysbury Address

King, Martin Luther, Jr.: "Letter from a Birmingham Jail"

Pledge of Allegiance

Red Jacket: *An Indian Speaks*

Thoreau, Henry David: "Civil Disobedience"

Drama

Chayefsky, Paddy: *Holiday Song*

Films

The Bridge on the River Kwai

On the Waterfront

Key Concepts and Problems

What is loyalty? What are the different kinds of loyalty? What causes someone to feel loyal? What forces can compete with one's loyalty? How does one choose between being loyal or disloyal? How does one judge someone who has acted disloyally?

THE MYTHIC HERO

Mythology

Bellerophon

Jason

Orpheus

Perseus

Theseus

Nonfiction

Information about such heroes, past and present, as Neil Armstrong, Cesar Chavez, Joan of Arc, Benito Juarez, John F. Kennedy, Martin Luther King, Jr., Teddy Roosevelt, Nelson Mandela, Babe Ruth, Tecumsah, Mother Teresa, and the like.

Key Concepts and Problems

What are the characteristics of the mythic hero? What are the characteristics of the mythic hero's quest? What becomes exaggerated about a mythic hero? What gets overlooked?

NEW KID ON THE BLOCK
Novels

Blume, Judy: *Tiger Eyes*

Carter, Alden: *Growing Season*

Cleaver, Vera: *Where the Lilies Bloom*

Guy, Rosa: *New Guys around the Block*

Kerr, M. E.: *Him She Loves?*

Myers, Walter Dean: *The Outside Shot*

Key Concepts and Problems

What is different about the newcomer? How is this character received by the others? How does the character respond to this reception? How does the character adapt to the new environment? How does the character change during the story? Is this positive or negative? Why?

OPTIMISM/PESSIMISM
Mythology

Sisyphus

Poetry

Arnold, Matthew: "Dover Beach"

Blake, William: "The Marriage of Heaven and Hell"

Brontë, Emily: "Ah! Why, Because the Dazzling Sun"

Coleridge, Samuel Taylor: "Frost at Midnight"; "The Rime of the Ancient Mariner"

Eliot, T. S.: "The Wasteland"; "The Hollow Men"

Hardy, Thomas: "The Man He Killed"

Pope, Alexander: "An Essay on Man"

Shelley, Percy Bysshe: "Ode to the West Wind"

Tennyson, Alfred, Lord: "Ulysses"

Wordsworth, William: "The World Is Too Much with Us"; "Tintern Abbey"; "It Is a Beauteous Evening"

Yeats, William Butler: "Sailing to Byzantium"

Novels

Camus, Albert: *The Stranger*

Conrad, Joseph: *Lord Jim*

Dostoyevsky, Fyodor: *Crime and Punishment; Notes from the Underground*

Gascar, Pierre: *The Season of the Dead*

Mann, Thomas: *The Magic Mountain*

Voltaire: *Candide*

Drama

Beckett, Samuel: *Waiting for Godot*

O'Neill, Eugene: *The Hairy Ape*

Simpson, N. F.: *One Way Pendulum*

Sartre, Jean-Paul: *No Exit*

Shakespeare, William: *Macbeth; Hamlet*

Key Concepts and Problems

Is the piece optimistic, pessimistic, or neutral in outlook? What clues tell you what the outlook is? Do you agree with the author's vision? Why or who not? What evidence do you see in the real world that either supports or refutes the author's vision? What facts and conditions contribute to one's evaluation of experience? To what extent do such attitudes come from the way the world is? To what extent do they come from a person's temperament?

THE OUTCAST

Poetry

Hughes, Langston: "Brass Spittoons"

Robinson, Edwin Arlington: "Mr. Flood's Party"

Rosenberg, Isaac: "The Jew"

Sassoon, Siegfried: "Does It Matter?"

Thomas, Dylan: "The Hunchback in the Park"

Short Stories

Capote, Truman: "Jug of Silver"

Gallico, Paul: "The Snow Goose"

Gorky, Maxim: "Her Lover"

Harte, Bret: "The Outcasts of Poker Flat"

Laurence, Margaret: "The Half Husky"

Matheson, Richard: "Born of Man and Woman"

Munro, Alice: "Red Dress"; "Day of the Butterfly"

Parker, Dorothy: "Clothe the Naked"

Peretz, I. L.: "The Outcast"

Rovere, Richard: "Wallace"

Singer, Isaac Bashevis: "Gimpel the Fool"

Novels

Dickens, Charles: *Great Expectations; David Copperfield*

Field, Rachel: *Hepatica Hawns*

Petry, Ann: *The Street*

Smith, Betty: *A Tree Grows in Brooklyn*

Steinbeck, John: *Of Mice and Men*

Autobiographies
Wright, Richard: *Black Boy*

Drama
Brecht, Bertolt: *Galileo*
Rose, Reginald: *Thunder on Sycamore Street*
Williams, Tennessee: *The Glass Menagerie*

Films
Pretty in Pink
Valley Girl

Key Concepts and Problems
In what ways is the outcast different from society? Why does society reject this character? To what extent does the character reject himself or herself? How does the character feel about rejection? How does the character try to resolve this rejection?

PARODY
Prose
Columns by distinctive writers such as Andy Rooney, Molly Ivins, Dave Barry
Several short stories by a writer with a distinctive style, such as Edgar Allan Poe
Several examples from a distinctive genre, such as lab reports, fairy tales, recipes, sports writing

Key Concepts and Problems
What are the distinctive features of a writer's style? Consider (a) themes, (b) sentence structure, (c) commonly used words or word types, (d) point of view, (e) types of details, and (f) types of literary techniques. What are the distinctive features of a given genre in terms of structure? *Assignment:* Write a distinctive genre piece (such as a recipe, lab report, fairy tale, or sports writing) in the style of the writer studied.

PERSUASION
Poetry
Hopkins, Gerard Manley: "Pied Beauty"
Marvell, Andrew: "To His Coy Mistress"
Shakespeare, William: "Sonnets"
Yeats, William Butler: "The Second Coming"

Short Stories
Babel, Isaac: "Gedali"; "The Story of My Dovecote"
Gogol, Nikolay: "The Overcoat"

Hemingway, Ernest: "The Short Happy Life of Francis Macomber"
Joyce, James: "The Dead"
Lawrence, D. H.: "The Prussian Officer"
Roth, Philip: "The Conversion of the Jews"
Tolstoy, Leo: "Where Love Is, God Is"
Updike, John: "Pigeon Feathers"

Novels

Camus, Albert: *The Stranger*
James, Henry: *Daisy Miller; What Maisie Knew*
Joyce, James: *A Portrait of the Artist as a Young Man*
Swift, Jonathan: *Gulliver's Travels*

Nonfiction (Essay)

Swift, Jonathan: "A Modest Proposal"

Key Concepts and Problems

What philosophical ideas and attitudes toward life does the author seem to hold? What does the author seem to value most dearly? How does the author present his or her personal values, attitudes, and philosophical ideas in the work? What does the writer do to persuade the reader to agree with these ideas and attitudes? Is the writer rhetorically persuasive? Why or why not? What is the range of rhetorical techniques— overt and covert—that a writer may use to persuade a reader that his or her personal values, attitudes, or philosophical ideas are right or worthy of serious consideration?

THE PICARESQUE HERO
Epic Poetry

Byron, George Gordon, Lord: *Don Juan*

Novels

Bellow, Saul: *Henderson the Rain King; The Adventures of Augie March*
Berger, Thomas: *Little Big Man*
Cary, Joyce: *The Horse's Mouth*
Cervantes, Miguel de: *Don Quixote*
Defoe, Daniel: *Moll Flanders*
Faulkner, William: *The Rievers*
Fielding, Henry: *Tom Jones; Joseph Andrews*
Goldman, William: *The Princess Bride*
Lesage, Alain René: *The Adventures of Gil Blas Santillana*
Mann, Thomas: *Felix Krull*
Smollett, Tobias: *Roderick Random*

Swift, Jonathan: *Gulliver's Travels*
Twain, Mark: *The Adventures of Huckleberry Finn*
Voltaire: *Candide*

Key Concepts and Problems

What are the characteristics of the picaresque hero? How does the protagonist fit this description? What does the hero learn from travel adventures? How is the hero affected by the lack of a stable family? What is the author trying to say about society, based on the adventures of the hero? What is the relationship between the characteristics of the hero and the form of the story?

POINT OF VIEW

Short Stories

Greenburg, Dan: "Catch Her in the Oatmeal"
Helprin, Mark: "Letters from the *Samantha*"
James, Henry: "A Bundle of Letters"
Malamud, Bernard: "The Prison"
Parker, Dorothy: "But the One on the Right"
Petrakis, Harry Mark: "The Journal of a Wife Beater"
Poe, Edgar Allan: "The Fall of the House of Usher"
Updike, John: "A & P"

Novels

Dorris, Michael: *A Yellow Raft in Blue Water*
Erdrich, Louise: *The Beet Queen*
Faulkner, William: *As I Lay Dying*
Gardner, John: *Grendel*
Oz, Amos: *Black Box*
Twain, Mark: *The Adventures of Huckleberry Finn*

Key Concepts and Problems

How old is the narrator? How does this affect his or her reliability? How smart is the narrator? How does this affect his or her reliability? What is the narrator's socioeconomic status? How does this affect his or her reliability? What are the narrator's values and beliefs? How do they affect his or her reliability? What is the narrator's purpose in telling the story? How is the narrator's knowledge about the other characters limited? Is there testimony or action that conflicts with the narrator's version of events and people? If there is more than one narrator, which one is most reliable? Why? Is there significant distance (emotional, intellectual, psychological, moral) between the reader and the narrator? Explain. How does the reliability of the narrator affect the reader's understanding of a story? How does the narrator's involvement influence the impact of the story?

PROGRESS
Short Stories
Faulkner, William: "The Bear"; "Delta Autumn"

Novels
Bellow, Saul: *Henderson the Rain King*

Berger, Thomas: *Little Big Man*

Crichton, Michael: *Jurassic Park*

Kesey, Ken: *Sometimes a Great Notion*

Kosinski, Jerzy: *Being There*

Le Guin, Ursula: *The Word for World Is Forest*

Momaday, N. Scott: *The Way to Rainy Mountain*

Sinclair, Upton: *The Jungle*

Vonnegut, Kurt, Jr.: *Slaughterhouse Five*

Wells, H. G.: *The Time Machine*

Wolf, Adolf: *Legends Told by the Old People*

Nonfiction
Mailer, Norman: *Of a Fire on the Moon*

Thoreau, Henry David: *Walden*

Films
The Gods Must Be Crazy

Song
Johnny Clegg & Savuka: "Inevitable Consequence of Progress"

Key Concepts and Problems
What is the definition of progress? Consider progress in terms of (a) technology, (b) the human spirit, (c) the expansion of "civilization," and (d) the evolution of the human intellect. Do the behavior and events of the story represent progress? Why or why not? What is the author's attitude toward progress? Do you agree?

PROPAGANDA
Novels
DeVries, Peter: *Witch's Milk*

Lessing, Doris: *Documents Relating to the Sentimental Agents in the Volyen Empire*

Orwell, George: *1984; Animal Farm*

Nonfiction
Gold, Philip: *Advertising, Politics, and the American Culture*

Hawthorn, Jeremy (Ed.): *Propaganda, Persuasion, and Polemic*

Jowett, Garth S., and Victoria O'Donnell: *Propaganda and Persuasion*

Orwell, George: *Writers and Leviathan*

Rank, Hugh: *Analyzing Persuasion: 10 Teaching Aids*

Films

The Manchurian Candidate

Triumph of the Will

Key Concepts and Problems

What are the characteristics of propaganda? How can we recognize it? What distinguishes propaganda from other forms of persuasion?

PROTEST LITERATURE

Poetry

Dunbar, Paul Laurence: "Sympathy"

Hughes, Langston: "Dream Deferred"; "Ballad of the Landlord"

Jeffers, Lance: "On Listening to the Spirituals"

McKay, Claude: "The White House"

Randall, Dudley: "The Idiot"

Short Stories

Freeman, Joseph: "From Bohemia to Russia"

London, Jack: "A Night with the Philomaths"

Mailer, Norman: "The Patron Saint of MacDougal Alley"

Novels

Bellamy, Charles: *The Breton Mills*

Kesey, Ken: *One Flew over the Cuckoo's Nest*

Orwell, George: *Animal Farm*

Sinclair, Upton: *The Jungle*

Ward, Elizabeth Stuart Phelps: *The Silent Partner*

Nonfiction

Anthony, Susan B.: "Woman Wants Bread, Not the Ballot!"

Catt, Carrie Chapman: "The World Movement for Woman Suffrage, 1904 to 1911: Is Woman Suffrage Progressing?"

Cleaver, Eldridge: *Soul on Ice*

Declaration of Independence

Dunbar, Roxanne: "Female Liberation as the Basis for Social Revolution"

Henry, Patrick: Speech to the Virginia Convention

Hentoff, Nat: "The War on Dissent"
King, Martin Luther, Jr.: "Letter from a Birmingham Jail"
Paine, Thomas: *The Crisis*
Thoreau, Henry David: "Civil Disobedience"

Autobiographies

Malcolm X, with Alex Haley: *The Autobiography of Malcolm X*

Films

Cool Hand Luke
Do the Right Thing
Matewan
Norma Rae

Documentary Films

Eyes on the Prize
Martin Luther King, Jr.: From Memphis to Montgomery

Key Concepts and Problems

What conditions have prompted the protest? What steps does the writer suggest we take in making a protest? Is there a common series of steps that the writer suggests taking in protesting? Does the writer suggest the point at which we should abandon the protest, that is, is a radical alternative, such as violence, appropriate in the situation in question? Is the protest justified? Why or why not? What are the differences between fictional and nonfictional protests? What are the typical forms of protest literature?

THE PURITAN ETHIC

Elementary Texts

McGuffy's Reader
The New England Primer

Poetry

Bradstreet, Anne: "To My Dear and Loving Husband"
Taylor, Edward: "Meditation Six"

Short Stories

Hawthorne, Nathaniel: "The Minister's Black Veil"; "Young Goodman Brown"
Twain, Mark: "The Man That Corrupted Hadleyburg"; "The Mysterious
    Stranger"

Novels

Hawthorne, Nathaniel: *The Scarlet Letter*

Nonfiction

Edwards, Jonathan: *Sinners in the Hands of an Angry God*
Mather, Cotton: *Essays to Do Good*

Drama

Miller, Arthur: *The Crucible*

Key Concepts and Problems

What are the central beliefs of the Puritans? What are the characteristics of the Puritan ethic? What historical factors contributed to the development of these principles? How was life for the Puritans different from life today? How was it similar to life today? Why did Puritanism die in America? To what extent does the Puritan ethic survive in the United States today?

REALISM/NATURALISM
Poetry

Masters, Edgar Lee: *Spoon River Anthology*
Robinson, Edwin Arlington: "Cliff Klingenhagen"; "Miniver Cheevy"

Short Stories

Anderson, Sherwood: selections from *Winesburg, Ohio*
Garland, Handin: selections from *Main Travelled Roads*
Jewett, Sarah Orne: selections from *The Country of the Pointed Firs*

Novels

Cather, Willa: *The Professor's House*
Crane, Stephen: *The Red Badge of Courage; Maggie*
Dreiser, Theodore: *Sister Carrie; An American Tragedy*
Glasgow, Ellen: *Barren Ground*
Howells, William Dean: *A Modern Instance*
James, Henry: *Daisy Miller*
Lewis, Sinclair: *Main Street*
Norris, Frank: *McTeague*
Sinclair, Upton: *The Jungle*
Wharton, Edith: *Ethan Frome*
Wright, Richard: *Native Son*

Key Concepts and Problems

What are the characteristics of realism and naturalism? What historical influences shaped these forms? How are they different from other literary forms? How does the literature exemplify these forms? How is naturalism an extreme extension of realism? What unique types of observations do the forms of realism and naturalism allow the authors to make?

THE PSYCHOLOGY OF BRITISH LITERARY CHARACTERS: CHAUCER TO THE MODERNS

Poetry and Prose (Listed Chronologically)

Sir Gawain and the Green Knight

Chaucer, Geoffrey: *The Canterbury Tales*

Malory, Sir Thomas: *Le Morte d'Arthur*

Spenser, Edmund: *The Faerie Queene*

Shakespeare, William: *Hamlet*

Milton, John: *Paradise Lost*

Austen, Jane: *Pride and Prejudice*

Byron, George Gordon, Lord: *Don Juan*

Shelley, Mary: *Frankenstein*

Brontë, Emily: *Wuthering Heights*

Dickens, Charles: *David Copperfield*

Hardy, Thomas: *Jude, the Obscure*

Shaw, George Bernard: *Arms and the Man*

Eliot, T. S.: "The Love Song of J. Alfred Prufrock"

Conrad, Joseph: *Heart of Darkness*

Woolf, Virginia: *To the Lighthouse*

Key Concepts and Problems

How is the psychology of the characters influenced by the attitudes of the times in which they were written? How does the psychology of these characters change over time? What is responsible for these changes? What is the same about the characters over time? What conclusions can we draw about human nature, based on our study of these characters?

RESPONSIBILITY

Novels

Cather, Willa: *My Antonia*

Kerr, M. E.: *Gentlehands*

Milkowicz, Gloria: *The Day the Senior Class Got Married*

Newton, Suzanne: *I Will Call It Georgie's Blues*
Southerland, Ellease: *Let the Lion Eat Straw*
Stone, Bruce: *Half Nelson, Full Nelson*
Sweeney, Joyce: *Center Line*
Zindel, Paul: *The Pigman*

Drama

Rose, Reginald: *Thunder on Sycamore Street*

Key Concepts and Problems

What value systems are the characters being influenced by? How strenuously are the value systems being imposed? From where do the characters derive their sense of responsibility? What forces are testing this sense? How do the characters respond to these forces? How is the conflict resolved? What is the author trying to say about value systems and responsibility in particular? Distinguish among duty, obligation, expectation, responsibility, and promise.

RITES OF PASSAGE

Mythology

Irish: The prince of the Lonesome Isle; The lade of Tubber Tintye
Navajo: Twin warriors
Greek: Actaeon; Phaethon and Phoebus; Psyche and Cupid
Sumerian: *Inanna's descent to the Netherworld*

The Bible

Story of Job (Job 1–42)

Poetry

Gunn, Thom: "Black Jackets"
Parker, Dorothy: "Indian Summer"
Thomas, Dylan: "Poem in October"

Short Stories

Clinton, Michelle T.: "Humiliation of the Boy"
Cohoe, Grey: "The Promised Visit"
Fox, Robert: "A Fable"
Meckel, Christo: "The Lion"
Silko, Leslie Marmon: "Tony's Story"
Steinbeck, John: "Flight"
Wallace, Karen: "Mary"

Novels

Dickens, Charles: *Oliver Twist*

Elfman, Blossom: *First Love Lives Forever*

Gibbons, Kaye: *Ellen Foster*

Momaday, N. Scott: *House Made of Dawn; The Ancient Child*

Panshin, Alexi: *Rite of Passage*

Stine, Robert L.: *Twisted*

Welch, James: *Winter in the Blood*

Nonfiction

Sheehy, Gail: *Passages*

Key Concepts and Problems

What is initiation/rite of passage? What actually changes as the result of an initiation or rite of passage? What is the character initiated into? What state is the character leaving? Could the character have made the same transformation without the rite of passage? Why or why not? How does the character change during the story?

ROMANCE
Fairy Tales

"Cinderella"

"Snow White"

Mythology

Persephone

Perseus

Romulus and Remus

The Bible

Jesus (Matthew, Mark, Luke, John)

Moses (Exodus 1–19)

Poetry

Keats, John: "La Belle Dame Sans Merci"

Tennyson, Alfred, Lord: "The Lotus Eaters"

Short Stories

Colette: "The Secret Woman"

Collier, John: "The Chaser"

Hemingway, Ernest: "Hills Like White Elephants"

Poe, Edgar Allan: "William Wilson"

Novels

Brontë, Charlotte: *Jane Eyre*

Brontë, Emily: *Wuthering Heights*

Burroughs, Edgar Rice: *Tarzan*

Cain, James M.: *The Postman Always Rings Twice*

Cervantes, Miguel de: *Don Quixote*

Cheever, John: *Oh, What a Paradise It Seems*

Crutcher, Chris: *Running Loose*

Davis, Terry: *Vision Quest*

du Maurier, Daphne: *Rebecca*

Estey, Dale: *A Lost Tale*

Golding, William: *The Princess Bride*

Holland, Isabelle: *Summer of My First Love*

Kerr, M. E.: *Gentlehands; Him She Loves?; I Stay Near You*

Lee, Mildred: *The People Therein*

Le Guin, Ursula: *Very Far Away from Anywhere Else*

Lipsyte, Robert: *Jack and Jill*

Lyle, Katie: *Dark but Full of Diamonds*

Malory, Sir Thomas: *Le Morte d'Arthur*

Marshall, Katherine: *Christie*

Mazer, Harry: *I Love You, Stupid!*

McCullough, Colleen: *The Thorn Birds*

Mitchell, Margaret: *Gone with the Wind*

Myers, Walter Dean: *Motown and Didi*

Tolkien, J. R. R.: *Lord of the Rings*

Vonnegut, Kurt, Jr.: *Slaughterhouse Five*

Drama

Goethe, Johann Wolfgang von: *Faust*

Shakespeare, William: *A Midsummer Night's Dream; Romeo and Juliet; The Tempest*

West, Jessamyn: *The Massacre at Fall Creek*

Wilkinson, Brenda: *Ludell and Willie*

Zindel, Paul: *The Pigman*

Films

Fatal Attraction

Play Misty for Me

Key Concepts and Problems

How does the world of innocence come into play in each selection? What kind of quest does the hero pursue in each story? How are they similar and how are they different? How do magic, mystery, and miracles function in these selections? What roles do vision and revelation play in these selections? What sorts of fulfillment do the characters seek? What are the typical elements and patterns of romance? What problems tend to frustrate romantic possibilities in ironic romances? Why does irony so often enter into romantic stories?

SATIRE
Fables
Aesop: *Fables*
di Prima, Diane (Ed.): *Various Fables from Various Places*
Thurber, James: *Fables for our Time*

Cartoons
Breathed, Berke: *Bloom County*
Martin, Joe: *Mr. Boffo*

Political Cartoons
Trudeau, Garry: *Doonesbury*

Poetry
Cleghorn, Sarah: "The Golf Links Lie So Near the Mill"
Clough, Arthur Hugh: "The Latest Decalogue"
cummings, e. e.: "i sing of Olaf, glad and big"
Donne, John: "Song"
Hardy, Thomas: "Satires of Circumstance"
Masters, Edgar Lee: selections from *Spoon River Anthology*
Robinson, Edwin Arlington: "Miniver Cheevy"
Sassoon, Siegfried: "Base Details"
Shelley, Percy Bysshe: "Ozymandias"
Smith, Stevie: "Zoo"

Short Stories
Boll, Heinrich: "Action Will Be Taken"
Daudet, Alphonse: "The Death of the Dauphin"
King, Thomas: "A Seat in the Garden"
Machado, Anibal Monteiro: "The Piano"
Maupassant, Guy de: "The Necklace"
Saki: "The Interlopers"

Novels
Austen, Jane: *Pride and Prejudice*
Dickens, Charles: *Hard Times*
Heller, Joseph: *Catch-22*
Mahfouz, Naguib: *Smalltalk on the Nile*

Orwell, George: *Animal Farm*
Smiley, Jane: *Moo*
Swift, Jonathan: *Gulliver's Travels*
Twain, Mark: *The Adventures of Huckleberry Finn; Pudd'nhead Wilson*
Wibberly, Leonard: *The Mouse That Roared*

Drama

Patrick, John: *Teahouse of the August Moon*
Shaw, George Bernard: *Arms and the Man*
Wilde, Oscar: *The Importance of Being Earnest*

Films

Being There
Dr. Strangelove
The Front Page
His Girl Friday
Hollywood Shuffle
Network
The Player
Wag the Dog

Key Concepts and Problems

What is the definition of satire? What is the specific target of ridicule within the work? How does the satirist use character and event to ridicule the target? How does the ridicule of the target within the work apply to the real world? What are the satiric devices used in the selections and how are they used?

SCIENCE FICTION

Short Stories

Selections from *The Science Fiction Hall of Fame*

Novels

Adams, Douglas: *The Hitchhiker's Guide* series
Asimov, Isaac: *I, Robot; The Foundation* series
Blish, James: *Star Trek Logs*
Brooks, Terry: *Sword of Shannara* series
Clarke, Arthur C.: *Childhood's End; 2001: A Space Odyssey*
Delaney, Samuel: *Nova; The Einstein Intersection*
Harrison, Harry: *Stainless Steel Rat* series
Heinlein, Robert: *Stranger in a Strange Land*
Herbert, Frank: *Dune* series

Le Guin, Ursula: *Wizard of Earthsea* trilogy

Lem, Stanislaw: *Solaris*

McCaffrey, Anne: *Dragonriders of Pern* series

Wells, H. G.: *The War of the Worlds; The Time Machine*

Zelazny, Roger: *Amber* series

Films

Invasion of the Body-Snatchers

Star Wars

2001: A Space Odyssey

Key Concepts and Problems

What are the conditions of the world the author has created? How is this world different from our own? How is it the same? What is the protagonist's quest? What obstacles does the protagonist face? How does he or she overcome them? How does the character change during the story? How is the author using the futuristic setting to make observations about today's people? How do the special conditions of the story relate to its form?

SELF-RELIANCE

Poetry

Auden, W. H.: "The Unknown Citizen"

Dickey, James: "The Bee"

Dickinson, Emily: "The Soul selects her own Society"; "There is a solitude of space"

Frost, Robert: "Into My Own"; "The Silken Tent"; "The Road Not Taken"; "Desert Places"

Moore, Marianne: "The Mind Is an Enchanting Thing"

Nemerov, Howard: "Life Cycle and the Common Man"

Reid, Alistair: "Curiosity"; "Propinquity"

Swenson, May: "The Pure Suit of Happiness"

Taggard, Genevieve: "The Enamel Girl"

Whitman, Walt: "Song of Myself"; "A Noiseless Patient Spider"

Wordsworth, William: "I Wandered Lonely As a Cloud"

Short Stories

Melville, Herman: "Bartleby the Scrivener"; "The Piazza"

Novels

Baldwin, James: *Nobody Knows My Name*

Gibbons, Kaye: *Ellen Foster*

Melville, Herman: *Moby-Dick*

Twain, Mark: *The Adventures of Huckleberry Finn*

Nonfiction (Essays)

Emerson, Ralph Waldo: "Self-Reliance"

Thoreau, Henry David: "Civil Disobedience"

Films

Cool Hand Luke

The Lost Weekend

On the Waterfront

Key Concepts and Problems

What is self-reliance? To what extent should an individual interact with and be influenced by society? What distinguishes self-reliance, anarchy, alienation, and self-centeredness? What are the advantages and disadvantages of self-reliance? Do you agree with the author's viewpoint? Compare the basis of authority of the self to the basis of authority of society. How does a self-reliant attitude influence one's behavior in relationships?

A SENSE OF PLACE

Poetry

Crane, Stephen: "A Man Said to the Universe"

Eliot, T. S.: "The Love Song of J. Alfred Prufrock"

Lanier, Sidney: "Song of the Chattahoochee"

Walker, Alice: "Everyday Use"

Whitman, Walt: "I Hear America Singing"

Short Stories

Hemingway, Ernest: "A Soldier's Home"

Hinojosa-Smith, Rolando: "This Writer's Sense of Place"

Hogan, Linda: "Amen"

Smith, Patricia Clark: "Flute Song"

Novels

Cisneros, Sandra: *The House on Mango Street*

Farrell, James: *Studs Lonigan* trilogy

Faulkner, William: *The Hamlet; The Town; The Mansion*

Hurston, Zora Neale: *Their Eyes Were Watching God*

McNickle, D'Arcy: *Wind from an Enemy Sky*

Mitchell, Margaret: *Gone with the Wind*

Momaday, N. Scott: *The Way to Rainy Mountain*

Autobiographies

Blackmarr, Amy: *House of Steps: Adventures of a Southerner in Kansas*

May, Lee: *In My Father's Garden*

Nonfiction

Algren, Nelson: *Chicago: City on the Make*

Irving, Washington: *A Tour on the Prairie*

Kotlowitz, Alex: *There Are No Children Here: The Story of Two Boys Growing Up in the Other America*

Mitchell, Joseph: *Up in the Old Hotel*

Royko, Mike: *One More Time: The Best of Mike Royko*

Terkel, Studs: *Chicago*

Songs

"America the Beautiful"

Jackson, Alan: "Home"

Keb Mo: "More Than One Way Home"

Little Feat: "Atlanta"

Pizzarelli, John: "I Like Jersey Best"

Rogers and Hammerstein: "Oklahoma!"

The Smashing Pumpkins: "Bullet with Butterfly Wings"

Taylor, James: "Copperline"; "Carolina in my Mind"

Weatherly, James: "Midnight Train to Georgia"

Films

Boyz in the Hood

The Horse Whisperer

Key Concepts and Problems

In what ways does the author use images (including all five senses) to character-ize the place? What emotions is the author trying to evoke through the senses? What attitudes is the author trying to create toward the place? How successful is the author in evoking emotions and attitudes for people who know the place and for people who don't? What is the overall effect of the work in creating a sense of place?

SOCIAL RESPONSIBILITY

Poetry

Coleridge, Samuel Taylor: "Work without Hope"

cummings, e. e.: "i sing of Olaf, glad and big"

Durem, Ray: "Award"

Hughes, Langston: "I, Too, Sing America"

Overstreet, Bonero W.: "John Doe, Jr."

Patchen, Kenneth: "Nice Day for a Lynching"

Short Stories

Bennett, Hal: "Dotson Gerber Resurrected"
Camus, Albert: "The Adulterous Woman"
Cheever, John: "The Swimmer"
Crane, Stephen: "The Open Boat"
Hawthorne, Nathaniel: "My Kinsman, Major Molineux"
Oates, Joyce Carol: "Saul Bird Says: Relate! Communicate! Liberate!"
Wright, Richard: "The Man Who Saw the Flood"

Novels

Faulkner, William: *Intruder in the Dust*
Hawthorne, Nathaniel: *The Scarlet Letter*
Heller, Joseph: *Catch-22*
Orwell, George: *1984*
Parks, Gordon: *A Choice of Weapons*
Porter, Katherine Anne: *Ship of Fools*
Sinclair, Upton: *The Jungle*
Stein, Gertrude: *Three Lives*
West, Rebecca: *The Thinking Reed*

Nonfiction

Emerson, Ralph Waldo: *The American Scholar*
Thoreau, Henry David: *Walden*

Drama

Arrabal, Fernando: *Picnic on the Battlefield*
Miller, Arthur: *A View from the Bridge*
Shaw, George Bernard: *Major Barbara*

Song

Johnny Clegg & Savuka: "One (Hu)man, One Vote"

Key Concepts and Problems

What is the individual's relationship to society? What types of obligations (moral, legal, etc.) does a citizen have to society? How do we fulfill these obligations? What happens if we do not? What must we sacrifice for the greater good? How do we lose from this sacrifice? How do we gain?

SUCCESS

Poetry

Auden, W. H.: "The Unknown Citizen"
Conoski, Victor: "Money"

Dickinson, Emily: "Success is Counted Sweetest"

Frost, Robert: "The Road Not Taken"

Robinson, Edwin Arlington: "Richard Cory"

Shagoury, Charles: "Schizophrenia on Madison Avenue"

Shelley, Percy Bysshe: "Ozymandias"

Short Stories

Cather, Willa: "The Sculptor's Funeral"

Hemingway, Ernest: "The Short Happy Life of Francis Macomber"

Thurber, James: "The Secret Life of Walter Mitty"

Novels

Alger, Horatio: *Struggling Upward, or, Luke Larkin's Luck*

Anaya, Rudolfo: *Bless Me, Ultima*

Dickens, Charles: *Great Expectations*

Fitzgerald, F. Scott: *The Great Gatsby*

Liu, Aimee E.: *Face (Face)*

Marshall, James V.: *Walkabout*

Petry, Ann Lane: *The Street*

Wells, H. G.: *The Island of Dr. Moreau; The Time Machine*

Wilde, Oscar: *The Picture of Dorian Gray*

Wolfe, Tom: *Bonfire of the Vanities*

Nonfiction (Essays)

Emerson, Ralph Waldo: "The Conduct of Life"

Drama

Hansberry, Lorraine: *A Raisin in the Sun*

Miller, Arthur: *Death of a Salesman*

Serling, Rod: *Requiem for a Heavyweight*

Shakespeare, William: *Macbeth*

Wilson, August: *The Piano Lesson*

Films

Clockers

Forrest Gump

Good Will Hunting

His Girl Friday

Hollywood Shuffle

It's a Wonderful Life

La Bamba

Mr. Smith Goes to Washington

Primary Colors

You Can't Take It with You

Songs

Brooks, Garth: "Against the Grain"

Burton, Michael: "Night Rider's Lament"

Madonna: "Material Girl"

Sinatra, Frank: "My Way"

Key Concepts and Problems

What values of a society help to determine what counts as success? Can success according to one criterion affect success according to another? If success is defined according to the acquisition of power and money, what are possible consequences for both the successful person and others? Do different social and cultural groups define success in different ways? How can individuals develop systems of beliefs and codes of conduct that enable them to consider themselves a success?

TECHNOLOGY, NATURE, AND SOCIETY

Poetry

Blake, William: "London"; "The Chimney Sweep"

Hobson, Geary: "Buffalo Poem #1"

Wordsworth, William: "The World Is Too Much with Us"

Short Stories

Bruchac, Joseph: "Bears"

London, Jack: "To Build a Fire"

Szilard, Leo: "Voice of the Dolphins"

Updike, John: "The Music School"

Novels

Dickens, Charles: *David Copperfield; Oliver Twist*

Ing, Dean: *Systemic Shock*

Norris, Frank: *The Octopus*

Orwell, George: *1984*

Sinclair, Upton: *The Jungle*

Smith, Martin Cruz: *Stallion Gate*

Steinbeck, John: *The Grapes of Wrath*

Nonfiction

Burke, James: *Connections*

Emerson, Ralph Waldo: *Nature*

Mailer, Norman: *Of a Fire on the Moon*

Thoreau, Henry David: *Walden*

Wolfe, Tom: *The Kandy-Kolored Tangerine-Flake Streamline Baby*

Films

Continental Divide
Dr. Strangelove
The Stepford Wives
2001: A Space Odyssey
Robocop

Key Concepts and Problems

Does human nature change depending on whether the environment is dominated more by nature than by machine? How do machines affect the ways in which people live? How does the natural world affect the ways in which people live? When nature comes into conflict with technology, which one triumphs? Why? Is technological change positive, negative, or neutral? Why?

THE TRAGIC HERO

Epic Poetry

Homer: *The Iliad*

Novels

Conrad, Joseph: *Lord Jim*
Hardy, Thomas: *Tess of the D'Urbervilles*
Mann, Thomas: *Doctor Faustus*
Updike, John: *Rabbit Run*
Wharton, Edith: *Ethan Frome*

Drama

Aeschylus: *Prometheus; Persae; Oresteia; Agamemnon*
Chekhov, Anton: *The Cherry Orchard*
Euripides: *Medea; Heracles*
Ibsen, Henrik: *Hedda Gabler; The Wild Duck*
O'Neill, Eugene: *The Emperor Jones*
Shakespeare, William: *Hamlet; King Lear; Macbeth; Othello*
Shaw, George Bernard: *St. Joan*
Sophocles: *The Oedipus Cycle; Prometheus Bound; Antigone*

Key Concepts and Problems

What are the characteristics of the tragic hero? How is the character affected by fate? Does the tragic hero have free will? What is characteristic of tragic plot structure? How do you feel about what happens to the tragic hero? What statement about life is the author making through the tragic hero?

THE TRICKSTER

Folktales/Fables/Children's Stories

Aesop: "The Fox, the Crow, and the Cheese"
Grimm, Jacob and Wilhelm: "Little Red Riding Hood"

Harris, Joel Chandler: Br'er Rabbit stories
La Fontaine: Reynard the Fox stories
Dr. Seuss: *The Cat in the Hat; The Cat in the Hat Comes Back*

The Bible

The Fall (Genesis 3)

Epic Poetry

Homer: *The Odyssey*
Milton, John: *Paradise Lost*

Short Stories

Alexie, Sherman: "Somebody Kept Saying Powwow"
Benet, Stephen Vincent: "The Devil and Daniel Webster"
Brant, Beth: "Coyote Learns a New Trick"
Conley, Robert J.: "Wili Woyi"
Dorris, Michael: "Groom Service"
Earling, Debra: "Jules Bart"; "Giving Too Much—August 1946"
Henry, O.: "The Ransom of Red Chief"
Salisbury, Ralph: "Aniwaya, Anikawa, and the Killer Teen-Agers"
Twain, Mark: "The Man That Corrupted Hadleyburg"; "The Celebrated
    Jumping Frog of Calaveras County"

Novels

Bulgakov, Mikhail: *The Master and Margarita*
Cary, Joyce: *The Horse's Mouth*
Dickens, Charles: *Oliver Twist*
Kesey, Ken: *One Flew over the Cuckoo's Nest*
O'Brien, Flann: *At Swim-Two-Birds*
Twain, Mark: *Tom Sawyer*

Drama

Jonson, Ben: *Volpone*
Moliere: *Tartuffe*

Key Concepts and Problems

What are the characteristics of the trickster? What are the trickster's motives? How does the trickster affect the other characters? Would you classify the trickster as good or bad? Why? What are typical plot patterns involving tricksters?

UTOPIAS AND DYSTOPIAS

Short Stories

Grigoriev, Vladimir: "The Horn of Plenty"
Singer, Isaac Bashevis: "Fool's Paradise"
Vonnegut, Kurt, Jr.: "Harrison Bergeron"

Novels

Atwood, Margaret: *The Handmaid's Tale*

Bellamy, Edward: *Looking Backward*

Butler, Samuel: *Erewhon*

Dante: *The Divine Comedy*

Golding, William: *Lord of the Flies*

Graves, Robert: *Watch the North Wind Rise*

Hudson, W. H.: *A Crystal Age*

Huxley, Aldous: *Brave New World*

More, Sir Thomas: *Utopia*

Morris, William: *News from Nowhere*

Orwell, George: *1984*

Skinner, B. F.: *Walden Two*

Swift, Jonathan: *Gulliver's Travels*

Wells, H. G.: *A Modern Utopia*

Nonfiction

Erasmus: *The Praise of Folly*

The Federalist

Machiavelli: *The Prince*

Marx, Karl, and Engels, Friedrich: *Communist Manifesto*

Plato: *The Republic*

Plutarch: *Lycurgus*

Rousseau, Jean Jacques: *The Social Contract*

Tarde, Gabriel: *Underground Man*

Wooden, Kenneth: *The Children of Jonestown*

Xenophon: *Cyropedia*

Song

Mitchell, Joni: "Woodstock"

Key Concepts and Problems

How is this society different from our own? What are the assumptions behind the author's utopian or dystopian vision? What are the consequences of such a society? Is the society envisioned by the author possible? Why or why not? What is the relationship between human nature and utopia?

VALUES UNDER STRESS

Short Stories

Benet, Stephen Vincent: "By the Waters of Babylon"

du Maurier, Daphne: "The Birds"

Elder, Lauren, with Shirley Streshinsky: "Survival"

Kariara, Jonathan: "Her Warrior"

Kayira, Legson: "I Will Try"

Kelley, William Melvin: "Enemy Territory"

Kimenye, Barbara: "The Winner"

Matheson, Richard: "Duel"

Niland, D'Arcy: "The Parachutist"

Nzioki, J. Mutuko: "Not Meant for Young Ears"

Novels

Auel, Jean: *The Clan of the Cave Bear*

Bradbury, Ray: *The Martian Chronicles*

Cather, Willa: *O Pioneers!*

Childress, Alice: *A Hero Ain't Nothin' but a Sandwich*

Clarke, Arthur C.: *Childhood's End*

Farrell, James: *Studs Lonigan* trilogy

Jackson, Shirley: *We Have Always Lived in the Castle*

London, Jack: *The Call of the Wild*

Momaday, N. Scott: *House Made of Dawn*

Rolvaag, O. E.: *Giants in the Earth*

Solzhenitsyn, Alexander: *One Day in the Life of Ivan Denisovich*

Theroux, Paul: *The Mosquito Coast*

Wells, H. G.: *The War of the Worlds*

Nonfiction

Krakauer, Jon: *Into Thin Air*

Autobiographies

Brown, Claude: *Manchild in the Promised Land*

Films

School Daze

Seven Beauties

Key Concepts and Problems

What values are under stress? What factors are causing stress? How does the character respond to the stress? What is the outcome? How do the character's values withstand the stress? How does the character change during the story? What is the relationship between survival and values? When will values triumph? When will the need to survive triumph?

THE VICTORIANS
Poetry

Arnold, Matthew: "Dover Beach"

Brontë, Emily: "The Night Wind"

Browning, Elizabeth Barrett: "Sonnets from the Portuguese"

Browning, Robert: "My Last Duchess"

Meredith, George: "Modern Love"

Morris, William: "The Earthly Paradise"

Rossetti, Christina: "Shut Out"

Rossetti, Dante Gabriel: "The Blessed Damozel"

Swinburne, Algernon Charles: "Atalanta in Calydon"

Tennyson, Alfred, Lord: "Ulysses"

Short Stories

Eliot, George: "The Lifted Veil"

Novels

Brontë, Charlotte: *Jane Eyre*

Brontë, Emily: *Wuthering Heights*

Dickens, Charles: *Oliver Twist; Hard Times*

Eliot, George: *Middlemarch*

Meredith, George: *The Egoist*

Nonfiction (Essays)

Carlyle, Thomas: "The French Revolution"

Huxley, Thomas Henry: "A Liberal Education"

Mill, John Stuart: "What Is Poetry?"

Newman, John Henry Cardinal: "The Idea of a University"

Pater, Walter: "The Renaissance"

Ruskin, John: "Modern Painters"

Key Concepts and Problems

What literary precedents led to the Victorian Age? What historical events separated the Victorians from the romantics? What distinguishes the Victorians from other British writers in terms of (a) style and (b) themes?

WAR AND PEACE

Poetry

Berry, Jan: "Floating Petals"

Brooke, Rupert: "The Soldier"

Crane, Stephen: "War Is Kind"

Ehrhart, W. D.: "Fragment: 5 September 1967"

Floyd, Bryan Alec: "Private Rex Jones U.S.M.C."

Hardy, Thomas: "The Man He Killed"

Larsen, Wendy Wilder, and Tran, Thi Nga: "Deciding"

Melville, Herman: "Battle Pieces"

Owen, Wilfred: "Greater Love, Futility"; "Sonnet: On Seeing a Piece of Our Artillery Brought into Action"; "Anthem for a Doomed Youth"; "Strange Meeting"

Short Stories

Belin, Esther: "indigenous irony"

Bierce, Ambrose: "Parker Adderson, Philosopher"

D'J Pancake, Breece: "The Honored Dead"

Fowler, Karen Joy: "Letters from Home"

Grau, Shirley Ann: "Homecoming"

Heinemann, Larry: "The First Clean Act"

Mailer, Norman: "The Language of Men"

O'Brien, Tim: "Don't I Know You"

Robinson, Kim Stanley: "The Monument"

Roscoe, Judith: "Soldier, Soldier"

Rossman, Michael: "The Day We Named Our Child We Had Fish for Dinner"

Szilard, Leo: "Voice of the Dolphins"

Novels

Crane, Stephen: *The Red Badge of Courage*

Frazier, Charles: *Cold Mountain*

Heller, Joseph: *Catch-22*

Hemingway, Ernest: *A Farewell to Arms*

Jones, James: *From Here to Eternity*

Mahfouz, Naguib: *Love in the Rain*

Mailer, Norman: *The Naked and the Dead*

Mason, Bobbie Ann: *In Country*

O'Brien, Tim: *Going After Cacciato; The Things They Carried*

Remarque, Erich Maria: *All Quiet on the Western Front*

Shaara, Michael: *The Killer Angels*

Films

Apocalypse Now

The Bridge on the River Kwai

Coming Home

The Deerhunter

Platoon

Saving Private Ryan

The Thin Red Line

Songs

"Battle Hymn of the Republic"

"Caissons Go Rolling Along"

Creedence Clearwater Revival: "Fortunate Son"

The Fifth Dimension: "The Age of Aquarius"

Haggard, Merle: "The Fighting Side of Me"; "Okie from Muskogee"

Jefferson Airplane: "Volunteers"

Key, Francis Scott: "The Star Spangled Banner"

Kingston Trio: "Where Have All the Flowers Gone?"

Lennon, John: "Give Peace a Chance"; "Merry X-mas (The War Is Over)"

Lynn, Loretta: "Dear Uncle Sam"

"Marine's Hymn" (Halls of Montezuma)

Sadler, Barry: "Ballad of the Green Berets"

"When Johnny Comes Marching Home"

Wright, Johnny: "Hello Vietnam"

The Youngbloods: "Get Together"

Key Concepts and Problems

What are the characters' reasons for going to war? What do they learn from their experiences? How do they change? What are the reasons for the fighting? What are the characters' visions of peace, before and after their experience in war? How do the characters' attitudes toward war change?

THE WESTERN

Novels

Berger, Thomas: *Little Big Man*

Cather, Willa: *My Antonia*

Clark, Walter Van Tilburg: *The Ox-Bow Incident*

Faust, Frederick Schiller: *Destry Rides Again*

Ferber, Edna: *Cimarron*

Gann, Walter: *The Trail Boss*

Grey, Zane: *Riders of the Purple Sage*

Guthrie, A. B., Jr.: *The Way West*

L'Amour, Louis: *The Fergeson Rifle*

Le May, Alan: *The Searchers*

Sandoz, Mari: *Cheyenne Autumn*

Schaefer, Jack: *Shane*

Films

Cheyenne Autumn

High Noon

High Plains Drifter

The Searchers

The Unforgiven

Key Concepts and Problems

Describe the white characters' attitudes toward (a) nature, (b) Native Americans, and (c) the law. How does the author feel about the white characters' attitudes? How do the whites "settle" the land? What types of conflicts arise in the story? How are they resolved? With whom do your sympathies lie in the story? What are the common properties of Westerns?

WILDERNESS ADVENTURES

Short Stories

Buford, Jim: "Swam Justice"

Davidson, W. E.: "The Jaguar Sprang to Kill"

Freedman, Benedict and Nancy: "Fire in the Wilderness"

Judson, William: "Survival on Cold River"

McPhee, John: "A Postponed Death"

Vandercook, John W.: "The Man Who Loved Elephants"

Novels

Defoe, Daniel: *Robinson Crusoe*

Dickey, James: *Deliverance*

Stevenson, Robert Louis: *Treasure Island*

Theroux, Paul: *The Mosquito Coast*

Verne, Jules: *A Voyage to the Center of the Earth*

Nonfiction

Brown, Joseph E.: *The Mormon Trek West*

Curry, Jane: *The River's in My Blood: River Boat Pilots Tell Their Stories*

DeVoto, Bernard (Ed.): *The Journals of Lewis and Clark*

Graham, Robin Lee: *Home Is the Sailor*

Heyerdahl, Thor: *Kon-Tiki; Aku-Aku: The Secret of Easter Island; The Ra Expeditions*

Linedam, Hannes: *Alone at Sea*

Severin, Tim: *The Brendan Voyage*

Key Concepts and Problems

What are the obstacles that the characters face? How do they overcome them? What are the characters' goals? What characteristics enable the characters to triumph? How do the characters benefit from their adventures? How does the environment affect the characters?

APPENDIX B

Courtroom Case Study

One year while teaching high school English, I was summoned for jury duty. To my surprise, I found myself assigned to a jury for a murder that had taken place in Chicago. The murder had been committed by a street gang member who'd shot the cousin of a member of a rival gang. The experience of serving on the jury was remarkable. In addition to giving me the opportunity to take part in the judicial system, it raised a number of questions for me. What does it mean to commit a murder? On what evidence do you make that judgment? What is justice? Is justice a true form, as argued by Plato, or is it circumstantial, as argued by the defense lawyer?

As I often did while teaching, I looked for ways to bring my experience into my classroom. I decided to do so by recreating the court case for my students as a way to teach them about extended definition and as a way to introduce a thematic unit on the topic of justice. The definition instruction was appropriate because one of our duties on the jury was to match the defendant's actions to one of three classifications of action: murder, voluntary manslaughter, or self-defense. The question of justice was appropriate because the trial centered on the defendant's choice between following the code of justice specified by U.S. law and following the code of justice required by his street gang.

The following activity is based on the murder trial. I made a number of changes in the story to make it suitable for the classroom, changing some testimony to make the case more difficult to resolve. I created a few new characters and compressed several witnesses into one character to create different perspectives. The principal actors of the case were natives of Mexico, Puerto Rico, and Iraq. To avoid perpetuating stereotypes of inner-city minorities, I anglicized their names and reworked their language. Finally, I consolidated each witness's testimony into a single block rather than presenting testimony interspersed with lawyers' questions. Each witness's testimony appears as a single statement, and this better suits the limitations of the classroom. This form did not seem to affect my students' involvement in the activity.

THE MURDER TRIAL ACTIVITY

The following activity puts students in the position of being jury members judging a person accused of murder. It is based on a real murder trial that took place in a circuit court in Cook County, Illinois. The names of the individuals, gangs, and locations have been changed, and the testimony has been reconstructed to fit the purposes of this activity.

Students need to remember the following information:

- The legal terms that describe the three possible charges for taking a life—murder (which carries a very heavy sentence), voluntary manslaughter (which carries a moderate sentence), and self-defense (which absolves the killer of guilt and sets him or her free).
- A brief statement of certain facts concerning the incident.
- The testimony of several witnesses.

Reviewing the Case

Students, in groups of six to eight, examine the extended definitions of the three types of killing and then look at the facts and testimony from the case. They discuss the events of the case and try to determine what really happened. Was the testimony of the various witnesses consistent? Where did they differ? Which testimony was more credible? Why? Students should take notes as they discuss the case because they will write a composition after the deliberation.

Defining the Charge

To help jurors decide how to judge a defendant, the court provides descriptions of different charges for taking a life. In this court case, the students will classify the defendant's behavior as murder, voluntary manslaughter, or self-defense. In an actual court, the jurors are provided only with the description of each charge. For this activity, students receive additional information to help clarify the definition, an example of a situation that meets the criterion, a contrasting example that seems to meet the criterion but lacks some essential ingredient, and a warrant that explains why the example does or does not illustrate the criterion.

Murder

The charge for taking someone's life is murder if *one* of the following criteria is met.

1. A person intends either to kill or to injure another person critically or knows that the act he or she intends to commit could cause death.
   Example: Joe fires a gun at Bob with the intention of killing him. *Warrant:* The act is murder because it is intentional and the killer has knowledge that it could cause death.
   Contrasting Example: Joe believes his gun is not loaded. He playfully points it at Bob and pulls the trigger, killing him. *Warrant:* The act is unintentional and therefore not murder.

2. A person knows that the act he or she commits creates a strong probability of death or serious injury.
   Example: Bob puts arsenic in Joe's coffee, knowing that the poison will probably kill him. *Warrant:* Because the act is intentional and Bob is aware of the consequences, it satisfies the criterion.
   Contrasting Example: Bob puts sugar in Joe's coffee, not knowing that Joe has a lethal allergy to sugar. *Warrant:* Bob is unaware of the consequences of his act; therefore, his action is not murder.

3. A person attempting a forcible felony, such as kidnapping, hijacking, arson, armed robbery, or rape, kills a person in the process.
   Example: Joe, in robbing a bank with a loaded gun, shoots and kills a guard, who had shot first at Joe. *Warrant:* The act takes place during a felony and therefore is murder.
   Contrasting Example: Joe observes Bob shoplifting clothing from Joe's store and begins to chase him. When Joe catches him, Bob pushes him down, causing Joe to strike his head on the ground and die from a severe concussion. *Warrant:* Although Bob has killed Joe while Bob was committing a crime, the crime is not a felony and so the act that caused the death is not murder.

Voluntary Manslaughter

Taking someone's life is voluntary manslaughter if *one* of the following criteria is met.

1. A person acts with sudden and intense passion after being seriously provoked by the person killed.
   Example: Joe, in his car, is being followed and harassed by Bob, who is using his car to bump and swerve into Joe's car. Bob, angry because Joe has married his ex-wife Sally, forces Joe's car off the road. They both get out of their cars and argue heatedly. Bob makes lewd and obscene remarks about Sally's extramarital behavior and about Joe's mother's extramarital behavior. Joe punches Bob, killing him. *Warrant:* The combination of the threatening actions with the car and the insults to his wife and mother have provoked Joe to a sudden and intense passion, so the act is voluntary manslaughter.
   Contrasting Example: Bob's car runs into Joe's car at an intersection. They get out of their cars and argue about whose fault it is. When Bob accuses Joe of running a stop sign, Joe strikes and kills Bob with a tire iron. *Warrant:* The initial situation was not serious enough to be called "seriously provoked," so this is not voluntary manslaughter.

2. A person acts with a sudden and intense passion after being seriously provoked and tries to kill the person provoking him or her but accidentally kills someone else.
   Example: Joe breaks into Bob's house and begins to shatter Bob's collection of priceless Ming vases. Bob's mother tells him to stop, but he continues and then threatens her with bodily harm, calls her obscene names, and spits in her face. This enrages Bob, who pulls a gun and shoots at Joe. He misses, and the

bullet accidentally kills the butler. *Warrant:* Because the combination of destruction of precious property and the disrespect and threats to his mother had provoked Bob to a sudden and intense passion, the act is voluntary manslaughter.

Contrasting Example: Joe ridicules Bob's haircut. This enrages Bob, who pulls a gun, shoots at Joe, and misses. The bullet accidentally kills an innocent bystander. *Warrant:* The insult is about a minor issue; therefore, Bob has not been seriously provoked. This is not voluntary manslaughter.

3. A person incorrectly but honestly believes that if he or she does not kill the other person, his or her own life will be endangered.

Example: Joe shoots and kills Bob, who had been threatening him with a gun. Joe finds later that Bob's gun had not been loaded. *Warrant:* Because he honestly believed his life was in danger, Joe has committed voluntary manslaughter.

Contrasting Example: Bob owns a store. Joe enters, looking very suspicious and seeming to have a gun in his coat pocket. Bob, thinking that Joe might rob and kill him, pulls out a gun and kills Joe. *Warrant:* Because the threat is not certain, this is not voluntary manslaughter.

Self-Defense

Taking someone's life is done in self-defense if *one* of the following criteria is met.

1. A person reasonably believes that he or she is in imminent danger of death or great bodily harm and has exhausted every reasonable means to escape the danger other than by using deadly force.

Example: Sally is threatened with rape in a deserted part of a city. She first screams for help. The attacker tackles her and begins to pull off her clothing. She tries unsuccessfully to defend herself with physical resistance. She finally shoots her attacker when she has no other means of defending herself. *Warrant:* Because she has tried several means of escape and is still greatly threatened, this act is one of self-defense.

Contrasting Example: Joe asks Sally for the time when she is walking in a dangerous part of town. She walks faster and he follows. When he taps her on her shoulder, she turns and shoots him fatally. *Warrant:* Because she has only tried one means of escape, this act is not considered one of self-defense.

2. If two people are involved in physical confrontation and one person withdraws from physical contact with the other person and indicates clearly to the other person that he or she wishes to withdraw and stop the use of force, but the other person refuses and continues to use force, any action by the person wishing to withdraw is an act of self-defense.

Example: During a heated argument and knife fight, Joe offers to stop fighting, but Bob refuses and again attacks. Joe then stabs Bob to death. *Warrant:* Because Joe has done everything possible to end the conflict, his act of stabbing is one of self-defense.

Contrasting Example: During a heated argument and knife fight, Joe backs off to catch his breath. Bob then attacks and Joe stabs him to death. *Warrant:* Joe did not pause to end the conflict but only to rest, so Joe's act is not done in self-defense.

The Case

In the following case, students should classify the defendant's behavior as murder, voluntary manslaughter, or self-defense.

Facts of the Case

On Saturday, July 16, at 10:30 P.M., John Tyler, age 28, was shot with a handgun fired by Jeff "Ace" Johnson. Tyler died ten minutes later from the bullet wound. The shooting followed an argument and fistfight on the sidewalk in front of Hank's Tavern at the corner of 17th Street and Broad Street. The people involved in the argument and fistfight were Tyler's cousin, Jerry Knight, age 22, who was a member of the Jukers street gang, and Jeff "Ace" Johnson, age 20, a member of the Cobras street gang. The deceased was not a member of any street gang. At the trial eleven months after the incident, the accused is being defended by a successful private attorney, Baxter Newsome. The prosecutors are two attorneys for the state, James Lincoln and Hannah Grimes.

Testimony

The testimony of various witnesses called to the stand during the murder trial reflects the opinions and viewpoints of people involved in the case. Often the testimony of one is in conflict with that of another. The jury, and here the students, must decide which witnesses are the most believable. Students must remember that in a real court case, testimony does not come in neat paragraphs as it is presented here, but rather as responses to lawyers' questions. This questioning can be tedious and repetitive. The lawyers asked the same questions over and over again, trying to get many different witnesses to tell the same story for the jury to believe. To avoid the repetition of the actual interrogation process, each defendant's testimony here is condensed to a single account that includes information about his or her job and criminal record that would have been elicited by the lawyers' questions.

David Rodriguez, 42, detective, Gang Crimes Division, City Police: Every gang has its own hand signal, colors, and insignia. When gang members greet each other, they give their gang hand signal. When they want to insult the members of another gang, they use the word "killer" after a rival gang's name. In this case, if a Juker said 'Cobra killer' to a Cobra, it would be a great insult, one that a Cobra could not back down from. If a Cobra did not accept the challenge of someone who had said this to him and his fellow gang members found out about it, they would beat him to a pulp. This way, the gangs ensure loyalty, because they will beat one of their own if they feel he does not protect the gang's reputation. Gang members often fear retaliation from their own gang much more than they fear the other gangs. Gang members have a very special loyalty to one another, and if they don't stand up for the reputation of the gang, they commit an act of great betrayal.

Another way to insult a member of a rival gang is to make his gang's hand signal and point it towards the ground. This is known as "throwing down" the gang's sign and is an insult that a gang member must respond to or else he will be outcast by his own gang.

Every gang has its own neighborhood, called its turf, with very specific boundaries that it enforces. Each gang knows the boundaries of other gangs' turf. A gang owns its turf and controls all criminal activities within it, and members from other gangs who trespass anywhere within its boundaries are subject to harassment and whatever physical abuse, including murder, the gang can inflict upon them. This is part of the unwritten code followed by all of the city's street gangs: Each can protect its turf as vigorously as they think is necessary to retain their control over it.

Gang members rarely carry guns. Usually, their girlfriends carry the guns for them because the girls are less likely to be stopped by police for searches and questioning. The girls usually are part of an auxiliary gang and often have names based on the boys' gangs. The West Side Kings, for instance, are complemented by a girls' gang called the West Side Queens. The girls are usually in the vicinity of the boys, and when one of the boys needs a gun, he simply tells a girl to give him one.

Chau Vuong, 37, detective, Violent Crimes Division, City Police: The Jukers and Cobras occupy turfs that are adjacent to one another. The borderline between the two is Harrison Street; the Jukers are to the east, and the Cobras are to the west. The Cobras are a much bigger gang, with about forty members, plus about twenty Cobra Queens. The Jukers only have about fifteen members, plus about five or six girls that hang around with them. The Cobras have a much bigger turf and are involved in far more criminal activity.

Both Hank's Tavern and Frank's Hot Dog Stand are located on the Jukers' turf, at the corner of 17th and Broad. This is just a short block away from Harrison Street, so it's very close to the Cobras' turf. Gangs usually stay on their own turf, but the Cobras, because they're so big, will often travel in packs into the turf of neighboring gangs. This is usually where we have trouble, around the borderlines that separate gang turfs. This isn't the first time that these gangs have fought around this intersection.

Jerry Knight (cousin of the deceased), 22, unemployed Juker. Criminal record: assault and battery (6 months probation) and petty theft (30 days in county jail): That night a bunch of us were playing softball, and after we were done we went over to the bar to have some sandwiches and beers. We brought our gloves and bats into the bar with us because, you know, if we left them in the car they might get stolen. That's a pretty dangerous neighborhood, you know.

We started playing pool and having a good time. We were drinking beer, but none of us was drunk. Well, after a while I went to stand in the doorway because it was getting kind of stuffy in the bar with all that smoke and all, plus it was a hot night, you see, and I saw those Cobras walking on the street in front of the bar. So I yelled at them to get off our turf and go home. They yelled some stuff back at us, and me and Ace started to mix it up pretty good.

By this time a bunch of my boys were out in the street watching and making sure that none of the other Cobras joined in to help Ace. Well, then I'm not sure what happened, because, you see, I was still fighting. But I think my cousin John tried to break up the fight, because he doesn't like any trouble, see, he's not in the gang. He pushed us apart, and the next thing I know Ace has a gun and shoots John in the stomach. The Cobras all ran, and we called an ambulance for John, but it was too late. He was dead.

Michael "Speedy" Clark, 21, part-time attendant at Broadway Car Wash, Cobra. Criminal record: reckless driving ($150 fine), possession of cocaine (3 months probation), armed robbery (2 years, state penitentiary), possession of marijuana and amphetamines (6 months probation):

Testimony 1 (sworn statement after having been picked up by the police on the night of the killing): We were over at my place playing cards tonight. Me, Ace, Rosie, Bopper, and Slick. We stayed there all night, just having a little fun together.

Testimony 2 (sworn statement two days after the killing, when questioned by Detective Rodriguez at police headquarters): That night we were playing poker at my place, and then we went out for some hot dogs at about 10:00. We didn't want any trouble, because some of us got to report to our parole officers. We just wanted some dogs. So we went to Frank's, where the dogs are pretty good. Lots of times the Jukers hassle us if we go there, but we thought we'd be okay if we hurried. When we were leaving, a Juker started cussing us and telling us to leave, so we left. Like I said, we didn't want any trouble.

Testimony 3 (in the courtroom): Me and the boys were hungry, so we decided to go get some hot dogs. We went to Frank's because we like the food there. I didn't want to go because I just got out of jail and didn't want any trouble and those Jukers were always beating on us when we crossed their turf, but the boys said it's okay, we'll just get our dogs and go. We got our dogs and were heading back, when this Juker, him over there (pointing to Jerry Knight) comes out and starts calling on us. He was yelling "Cobra killer" and throwing down our sign and cussing us to get off their turf. Well, Ace, he didn't like that and started cussing him back. Then they started mixing. Then some other Jukers came out of the bar. They were carrying pool sticks and baseball bats. The one that got wasted had a pool stick and he came between Ace and him (pointing to Knight) and pushed them apart. Ace, he didn't waste any time. He got the gun from Rosie, because the Jukers all had bats and looked like they were going to kill us. Rosie was standing right behind him, so it only took a second. The guy with the stick looked pretty mad, like he was gonna come after us with the stick, so Ace, he shot him and we all ran.

Ace, man, he never shot anybody before. I've seen him handle a piece [gun], but that was just fooling around, you know, shooting bottles and a few rats. But he never shot any people before. We don't do that kind of stuff. Us Cobras, you know, we just like to have fun, you know, we don't like to hurt anybody. If they weren't coming at us with those bats, Ace wouldn't have shot anybody.

William "Beano" Rose, 19, part-time suit bagger at O'Rourke Cleaners, Juker. Criminal record: petty theft (90 days, juvenile detention center), auto theft (8 months, county jail), drunk and disorderly conduct (10 days, city jail): We were cooling off at the bar after a softball game. It was really hot, see, and after the game we were hungry and wanted a few beers. So we went over to Hank's because it's, like, our hangout, and had some sandwiches and drank a few beers. We weren't drunk, see, we just had a few beers to cool off because it was so hot. While we were there, some of us played some pool because that's what we like to do, see, we like to have a few beers and play some pool and just have a little fun. Most of us there were in the Jukers, but John [Tyler, the deceased], he wasn't in the gang. See, he's married and has got some kids, so he didn't want to be in a gang because he didn't want to get in trouble. He had this job, and he just wanted to work and make some money so he could take care of his family. But him and Jerry was cousins and were pretty tight, so he'd play softball with us sometimes and go out to the bar with us afterwards to have a few beers and cool off.

Well, that night we were inside the bar playing pool and Jerry went out to get some fresh air, because the air conditioner in the bar didn't work too good and it gets pretty smoky in there with everybody smoking cigarettes and all. So Jerry went to stand outside and get some air when he saw these Cobras on our turf, so he starts to cuss them and tell them to go home. They start cussing him back, so a few of us went outside to help Jerry just in case there was any trouble. I had been showing everybody in the bar my swing with the baseball bat, because you see I'd hit a couple of homers that night and everybody wanted to see my swing, and so I still had the bat in my hand when I went outside. John was playing pool, and when he heard Jerry arguing with the Cobras he ran outside because, you see, him and Jerry were pretty tight and he wanted to help him if there was any trouble. He went out so fast that he forgot to put his pool stick down. I know he must have forgot, because John, he never wanted any trouble. But then, he didn't want his cousin to get hurt either.

So when they started fighting he went to break them up. He still had the stick in his hands. He pushed them apart. He was so strong that he could push them apart while holding the pool stick in one hand. Then Ace, he reached around and got a gun from the girl and shot John in the stomach. We were afraid to go after them because he might shoot us, too. Then they ran and we called an ambulance. But John was dead before they got there.

Hank Evans, 46, owner and bartender at Hank's Tavern: The guys in the Jukers are regular customers of mine. Some of them come in almost every night, and on weekends, a lot of them stop in for a few beers. Some people in the neighborhood say that they're in a gang and are bad, but they never caused me any trouble. One time, they even stopped a guy who tried to hold me up. Right when he pulled his gun, a Juker threw a pool ball from one of the pool tables and cracked him in the head. The rest of the Jukers in the bar then jumped him and slapped him around a little, and threw him out in the street. They gave him a break, too, because they told me not to call the cops about it.

Anyhow, the night John got shot, a bunch of the Jukers were in having some beer, playing pool, and hanging out after their softball game. I remember I had to yell at Beano to quit swinging his bat in the bar, because he might kill someone. At about 10:30—I remember this, because it was right after they did the sports on the news—Jerry stepped out into the doorway, and the next thing I know he's in a fight with one of those Cobras. That's not such a big deal, because these boys like to get rowdy on the weekends, and lots of times they end up arguing and fighting even with each other, and anyhow they hate those Cobras. Well anyhow, just about everybody in the bar runs out onto the sidewalk. I had to stay inside to protect the cash register, plus there were some other customers in the bar who didn't care about the fight. The next thing I know I hear a shot, and everybody starts yelling to call an ambulance. I did, but John was dead when it got there.

John, he was a real sweet guy. He had himself a good job and a nice family. He was really strong, too, the best arm wrestler at the tavern, but he didn't like to fight or get in trouble. He'd usually have a few beers after a game, stay till maybe ten or eleven o'clock, and then go home to his wife and kids, while the other guys would stay till I closed, or go off and stay out all night. I sure hated to see a nice guy like that killed by those gang-bangers.

Jeff "Ace" Johnson, 21, unemployed, Cobra. Criminal record: Illegal possession of a handgun (30 days, juvenile detention center), possession of narcotics (6 months, juvenile detention center), carrying a concealed weapon (90 days, suspended sentence), armed robbery (1 year, state penitentiary), assault and battery (8 months probation): It was Saturday night, see, and it was really hot. We'd had a few beers and some wine up at Speedy's, and got hungry. We decided to go to Frank's. We got there and ate our food, and then started walking home. We didn't want any trouble, see, because some of the boys are on probation and didn't want to go back to jail. They aren't bad, you know, they'd just gotten into a little trouble.

But anyway, we were just minding our own business walking home, when this Juker (pointing to Jerry Knight) comes out of the bar and asks us what we're doing on his turf. We say we just come for some dogs and were going home. He starts cussing us and throwing down our sign like this (makes his gang hand signal and points it down). That's really bad, see, because he's saying our gang's no good. Then he starts saying "Cobra killer" and that's bad too, like he wants to kill our gang. We just wanted to leave, but he was saying all that stuff and we got in a fight. All these other Jukers are around then and they got bats and sticks like they're really gonna stomp us. I was fighting him (points to Knight), but there were all these guys with bats and I thought they were gonna waste us. See, it's their turf and we were really outnumbered. Well, this one guy steps in to help him (points to Knight) and he's got a stick. I thought that I was dead now if I didn't do something fast. I broke away and Rosie gave me the gun. I shot at the guy with the stick. I didn't mean to kill him, just to scare him and maybe slow him down and keep the rest of the Jukers from hitting us with those bats. I mean, I was really scared I was going to die. That's why I shot him. Then we ran home so they wouldn't beat on us.

I never shot anybody before. I'd handled a piece, sure, but I just shot at bottles and a few cats. Shooting at people, man, that's bad. I never did that before. I only shot that guy because I was so scared they were going to kill me.

Donna James, 31, X-ray technician at Good Shepherd Hospital: I'd just gotten off work—my hospital is just around the corner from the bar where all this happened—and was waiting for the bus at the stop at the intersection of 17th and Broad. I'd been there for a few minutes when these four guys and their girlfriend came out of the hot dog stand, acting like they owned the place, throwing their wrappers on the ground and talking loud and tough. I wait at that bus stop every night after work, and I see punks like that in there all the time. The food is almost as slimy as they are—I've eaten there a few times when I was starved after work.

Anyhow, they came out, as I said, acting real tough, and made some lewd remarks at me that they thought were very funny. Of course I ignored them, the way I always do—you can't let these bums think that you actually are listening to any of their talk. So they just laughed and cussed me and kept going. But then this other guy (points to Jerry Knight) came out of the bar and started to curse them in incredibly foul language. I mean, I've lived in the city for a long time now, and I'm used to hearing street talk, but this was ridiculous. And they were making gestures at each other and cussing away—I just stood there hoping that the bus would get there so I could just leave.

The next thing you know one of the guys from the hot dog stand was fighting the guy from the bar, and right away the whole bar emptied out into the street. One of the men from the bar—he looked a little older than the rest and had a pool stick in his hand—yelled something and tried to push them apart. Well, by this time people were crowded all around, and I couldn't see everything quite so clearly. Everyone was screaming things like "Hit him! Kill him!" but I couldn't tell who was shouting what. You see, the crowd had formed a kind of circle around the guys who were fighting, and I really couldn't tell who was on whose side. The man with the pool stick finally got them pushed apart, and he was holding that stick in his hand and looking very angry. I suppose he must have been 5 or 10 feet from the other guy (points to Jeff Johnson). I really couldn't say for sure. The next thing I knew that guy there (points to Johnson again) had a gun in his hand—I think he got it from that girl over there (points to Rosalyn Clay), but by now everything was happening so fast, and there were so many people shouting and moving about that I can't say for sure. He shot the man with the stick, and then everybody started screaming and running around more than ever. I think the group with the killer must have run away, but I was worried about the man who'd been shot and didn't notice. I stayed until the ambulance came, but there wasn't much I could do for him; I mean, he had a bullet wound, and all I do at the hospital is work with X rays. He was dead before the ambulance arrived.

THE ASSIGNMENT

After studying the case, students should try to determine what really happened. Then, they must make a decision about how to classify the killing. They must decide which of the three types of charges (murder, voluntary manslaughter, and self-defense) applies to this case and justify their choice.

Before the groups begin to evaluate the evidence, they should each select a jury foreperson. The foreperson acts as the group's leader and should have a strong, confident personality. The foreperson makes sure that all jury members voice their opinions, without any members being too dominant. He or she takes charge of all voting and insures that ballots are secret. The foreperson makes certain that the jurors argue reasonably and that the defendant is evaluated according to the law and not according to the jurors' feelings and prejudices. The foreperson sees that the jurors are attentive to all of the evidence and testimony in the case, and not just those segments that are convenient to their perspectives.

In a trial of this type, the verdict must be unanimous. The jury's decision will determine to a large extent how the rest of the defendant's life will proceed: He may go completely free, or he may spend the rest of his life in jail. (The state is not asking for the death penalty in this case.) The jury's job is to classify the action. The judge will then determine the sentence. The trial, however, will not end until the jury has reached a unanimous decision. The groups must remember that in order to judge someone guilty, he or she must be determined guilty beyond a reasonable doubt. A jury should not judge someone guilty of a crime unless the evidence against him or her is overwhelming.

When the jury has reached a decision, each member of the group is responsible for writing an essay explaining his or her judgment about the defendant and classification of this incident. Using examples, students should explain how their decision meets each of the criteria in the type of killing they decided on. Then, students should explain why they have not classified the action as either of the other two types. Because their decision determines the fate of another human being, students should strive to develop thoughtful, clear, and well-documented essays. Students should be aware of the need for thoroughness and responsibility, the hallmarks of good legal work.

ADAPTING THE ACTIVITY

At the time I developed this activity, I was teaching in a high school that bordered the west side of Chicago. Because a number of my students were familiar with gangs, the activity fascinated them and brought a part of their world into the classroom. My own experience on the jury was characterized by continual amazement as I learned of gang codes and practices. The defending lawyer maintained throughout the case that the jury ought to judge the defendant by gang standards rather than by society's standards because those were the "real" laws that governed his life. My students, too, were riveted by the accounts from the gang subculture that existed so close to them and whose values seemed so antithetical to mainstream American society's.

When I described this activity to teachers from rural Oklahoma, they felt that their students would not find the case nearly as intriguing as my more urban students had. I was heartened, however, to find that they considered the concept of using court cases as the basis of teaching argumentation to be valuable. Together we generated a number of possible scenarios from local court cases that could serve as vehicles for similar types of activities.

Teachers who are looking for cases to adapt should consider several issues. The most important issue would be how the case could tie in with the curriculum being taught. When I used the case I have described, it was in conjunction with a literary theme we were about to examine, the theme of justice in *Native Son*, and in the context of composition instruction on extended definition. Teachers should use court cases that relate to and illuminate curricular issues. A second consideration would involve the students' interest in the particular case. A case with some local connection would seem to be a logical choice. The case would also need to be problematic or amenable to rewriting in order to make it ambiguous. The case should be controversial, but should not suggest a political agenda on the teacher's part.

The activity I have outlined produced some of the most spirited discussions I have ever heard in a classroom and some of the clearest and most detailed writing. The jury discussions enabled the students to consider the case from a variety of angles, all of which they needed to account for in their essays. Usually in a jury of eight students, some students will argue strongly for at least two of the possible verdicts.

Students who are attentive during those discussions have a great deal of information from which to draw as they formulate reasons for their decision.

Beyond the quality of the discussions and the writing, the activity helps students develop an understanding of the judicial system in the United States, which is one of the most important features of our democracy. I always stress to my students how extraordinary I found my own experience and how important it is for them to participate when called to jury duty. I will never know how successful I am in promoting greater involvement in civic affairs by my students, but I do know that their participation in this activity heightened their awareness of civil procedures and sparked, at least temporarily, greater interest in service to their community.

Role-Playing Peer-Response Groups

A role-playing peer-response group is a mock situation in which students read from the perspective of a designated group of readers. Role-playing peer-response groups can help students develop a sense of how their writing will be read by particular audiences. In the process they can learn to think in the manner of their readers and thus understand the reasons behind audience demands. For instance, my own experience as a reviewer for journals and publishers has taught me to think the way editors think, helping me in the production of my own professional writing. By role-playing another reader's response, then, students can learn how others might evaluate their own writing.

The peer-response group can also provide feedback for other students' writing that can help them shape it up for whatever readers they're ultimately writing for. Role-playing peer-response groups, then, have the potential to serve students by giving them recommendations on how to improve their own texts and by giving them experience as critics who read from a particular point of view. Having this knowledge is especially useful in writing circumstances where the stakes are high.

Let me illustrate with a lesson I've used with high school juniors who are learning to write in response to essay questions that typically occur on college applications. In the school I taught in at the time, we were required to teach juniors how to write college-application essays, whether they intended to go to college or not. The applications often ask students to write on open-ended personal topics, with prompts like the following:

- Discuss your goals, values, or ideas
- Describe a special interest you have
- Evaluate one of your most important personal achievements
- Describe a significant experience in your life
- Describe a change you have noticed in yourself

Fortunately, writing on such topics could potentially benefit both college-bound and non-college-bound students. If written on a college application, the stakes are very high, with the quality of the essays having some bearing on admissions in many cases. Yet few high school students have any understanding of how these essays might be read by a college admissions committee. The assignment thus lends itself well to an activity in which students respond to one another's writing in role-playing peer-response groups. Each group could play the role of an admissions committee and return a judgment on whether the student would be admitted to the college.

The response of these mock admissions committees would come relatively late in the instruction. As in most writing instruction, attention to *form* would also come later in the process. The first order of business is to find a suitable topic and generate ideas. As I will outline next, you could plan an instructional sequence that begins with the students' need to explore a topic and ends with consideration for presenting those ideas with particular readers in mind.

FINDING A TOPIC

Students first need procedures for finding a topic. One effective method for topic discovery is through freewriting or clustering, an outlining technique that relies on free association rather than on a strict linear list of ideas. Students can use either technique to begin generating ideas, with the general set of essay topics as a stimulus for their thinking. A student identifying kung fu as an interest, for instance, would then either freewrite or begin a cluster that explored goals, significant achievements, personal changes, or other areas that could serve as the topic for a good college-admissions essay.

This exploratory thinking and writing could then serve as the basis for a first draft of an essay in which the goals, experiences, and so on are elaborated. At this point, the students are still focusing on getting their ideas out, without worrying about how others would read them. Consideration for readers' expectations would enter the picture after the students have generated the ideas that will serve as the substance of the paper. They should, however, be cautioned about focusing on topics that would be considered trivial, inappropriate, or otherwise work against the purpose of a college admissions essay (e.g., an essay about their partying ability, their bottlecap collection, etc.). When they have produced a draft of their essays that they are ready to have evaluated, you can introduce the idea of a mock admissions committee to review their application.

UNDERSTANDING READERS' EXPECTATIONS

Students need to have some idea of what colleges are looking for in candidates. Of course, this varies from college to college. School guidance departments provide materials that students can examine in small groups to infer the kinds of students colleges are looking for. One such document appeared in the alumni bulletin of my alma mater, Kenyon College. Entitled "Getting into Kenyon," it included a discussion of members of the admissions committee regarding the characteristics they look for in applicants. The following exchange was part of the discussion:

Anderson: Students at Kenyon are people who are very much involved in the life of the college and the community, through extracurricular activities, jobs, clubs and community service.

Morse: As students have those experiences, they tend to develop a tolerance for and interest in differences among people, and of course that benefits everybody in the community.

Monheim: We also want diversity in terms of students' interests, what they'll be involved in here. For example, if we had four hundred freshmen all interested in theater, how exciting would this place be?

Leftridge: We're not looking for certain opinions and interests in our students, but for students who do have opinions and aren't afraid to explore and express them.

Monheim: For those who don't interview, the essay part of the application is the only chance to say "This is me" and to talk about something that's important to them. My advice is to spend some time on them.

York: I remember an essay about growing up with a handicapped sister. That gave us information about the student's background and values. Through the essay we got to know that student a little better.

Anderson: We want students who took advantage of what's available to them in their schools and community. I like to see that students sought out a challenge or took an extra step to educate themselves. (Rosenberg, 1988)

John R. Hayes (1990) found that the attitudes of the Kenyon admissions committee are representative of many such committees. He examined readers' perceptions of writers' personality traits by studying the decisions of the admissions team at Carnegie-Mellon University. The admissions team appeared to make inferences about the applicants' personality traits based on their admissions essays. They included those inferences in their admissions considerations along with other, more familiar factors (e.g., grades, class rank, test scores, extracurriculars, etc.). Hayes found that the admissions team had six ranks of personality types, with each having implications for admissions decisions. The kinds of impressions students made, and the types of traits within each, were as follows:

Highly positive: positive, mature, sensitive to others, down-to-earth

Positive: socially adept, serious, determined/persistent, broad, self-sufficient

Mildly positive: hardworking, modest

Mildly negative: assertive, arrogant

Negative: socially awkward/nerdy, weird, negative, ambitious, immature

Highly negative: dull, narrow, naïve, or egocentric

Knowledge of these audience preferences can help students develop standards to guide both the production and evaluation of their essays. Many students, for instance, believe that being hardworking is a highly desirable trait. Hayes, however, found, that this is a questionable characteristic to highlight for this audience.

The teacher can use the small-group analyses of college documents and information from Hayes's research to conduct a whole-class study in which the class generates a set of criteria by which to evaluate the application essays. Each student should maintain a copy of these criteria and use it as a set of guidelines for preparing a final draft of his or her application essay. When these are ready, the class can move into the next stage in the sequence: the evaluation of the essays themselves.

ETHICAL QUESTIONS IN CONSIDERING READERS' EXPECTATIONS

I should pause here to say that I originally published a version of this activity in the *English Journal*. Some months later, a former colleague of mine wrote to the journal, accusing me of writing "the most unethical piece of crap" he'd ever seen in a professional journal. He felt that by encouraging students' to learn about their readers' expectations, I was promoting cynicism. He compared me to Clarence Thomas, who at the time had been accused (though was never proved guilty) of lying under oath during the hearings prior to his appointment to the Supreme Court. He also took exception to the idea that I referred to researchers who'd studied the problem, a breed of people he dismissed out of hand.

This letter, published in the National Council of Teachers of English's most widely read journal, stunned me for both the ferocity of the accusation and the naïveté of its assumptions. The letter's author bought wholly into the notion that writing is done purely for the sake of the writer, a view that I can easily dispute. My editor for this book, Linda McElhiney, has repeatedly advised me of the need to write for my readers and their needs. My attention to these readers has caused me to change my phrasing, syntax, and other aspects of my presentation so that they find these ideas more comprehensible. It seems silly to me to claim that there's anything cynical about considering the expectations of readers, especially when the stakes are high. In fact, I'd say that any writing teacher who focuses only on what writing accomplishes for the writer is doing students a great disservice. Throughout this book I've argued that writing should indeed serve the writer's purposes, yet should also function to communicate effectively. Overlooking this dimension of writing strikes me as irresponsible, uninformed, and egocentric.

Teacher-Led Analysis

Prior to forming committees, the class would benefit from evaluating a sample composition together to ensure that students understand their responsibilities. This group analysis would be the first step in an instructional scaffold and would take place under the teacher's guidance. It would include the following pieces.

Types of Decisions

One thing students should know about is the kinds of decisions that admissions committee members make. For our task, we will use the following four decisions:

- Admit to honors program—The writer shows exceptional skill in satisfying all standards
- Admit—The writer satisfies all standards
- Waiting list—The writer satisfies most standards
- Reject—The writer satisfies few or no standards

Admissions Standards

Each of the decision types is based on the degree to which a writer meets admissions standards. One way to introduce the idea of standards is to present the criteria used by Kenyon and Carnegie-Mellon. Another would be to have a guidance counselor come in and discuss college admissions essays. You could also consult with documents provided by colleges to see what they say about admissions essays and infer a set of standards from there.

These standards could then result in the development of a rubric for making the admissions decisions. You could accomplish this in one of two ways, depending on how much time you have. One is to develop one yourself; the other is to have the students generate one based on their analysis of available information.

Teacher-Led Admissions Decision

The teacher would then lead the class through an application of the admissions standards to at least one essay. If you use an essay written by a student, you would want to remove the name first. The students would first read the essay silently, and then would volunteer judgments based on the rubric. During this evaluation, you might find it necessary to adjust the rubric to take into account new bases for judgment that emerge from the discussion.

If students are ready, you could then move to the role-playing response groups. If you feel that they would benefit from additional group decisions first, lead them through a second (or more) analysis.

FORM ROLE-PLAYING PEER-RESPONSE GROUPS

The class then forms mock admissions committees to conduct their evaluations. I tried to have four students in each committee, though the number depends on the size of the class. This size enabled each student to read and evaluate about four essays.

Using pseudonyms, students submit their essays, and the teacher distributes about four to each committee. Teachers with two sections of the same course may even distribute the essays from one class to committees in the other. Each committee uses the rubric to evaluate the essays and judge the candidates, making one of the four decisions. The mock admissions committee provides a written justification for its decision on each essay evaluated, offering suggestions on how to change the writing. Thus, students play an important role in improving the writing of peers while developing critical standards to guide their own writing.

REVISE AND RESUBMIT

Students use their evaluations to guide a revision and then submit the revision to a different committee. The committees evaluate this second set in the same way, except this time their decisions stand. Teachers can use this final judgment to assign a grade, with the honors admission equaling an A, a regular admission receiving a B, and so on; or they can simply let the evaluations speak for themselves and not issue a formal grade. Assigning a grade based solely on the mock committees' evaluations can be problematic, for students can make highly idiosyncratic judgments in spite of their experience on the committees and use of the rubrics. Teachers may decide in such cases to issue their own evaluations along with those of the admissions groups or to use examples of unusual judgments as the basis for a class discussion on audience characteristics.

BENEFITS
To the Students as Critics

The mock admissions committees serve several purposes. They allow students to play the role of their audience, getting inside the minds of an admissions committee and reading from their perspective. The experience of playing the critic can help students learn evaluative skills to bring to their own writing. Through their role as committee member, they can become better critics of their own work. Here, for instance, are some remarks made by students in their evaluations of the lesson:

Student 1:   Evaluating other people's papers gave me insights into what college boards might be looking for in an applicant. It gave me the opportunity to objectively look at my own work. I felt that I even had to distance myself from the paper I was reading over. Even though it was a mock committee I still had to take my decision making serious. I learned what it is like to be on the other side of the issue. To see how my own paper looked. I saw what it was like to evaluate something close to my own essay. I kept thinking about my own paper and critiquing it like the four papers before me. It boosted a lesson I learned over the summer, and that is what it is like to be a teacher.

Student 2:   Looking at other papers I rejected most of them because they didn't contain the things I was looking for. I've learned that when I was the judge I was hard on the people who applied. I was able to explain the things that were wrong. I should be able to use these pointers in my essay.

To the Students as Writers

The activity also provides feedback that helps students improve writing for a particular audience. Here is a sequence one student went through in writing a first draft, getting peer responses, writing a revision, and getting a final peer response.

First Draft

Helping is, I think one of my greatest qualities. I love helping people out. In highschool I was in the Service club which was a club that did different things around the community. From the service club, I got started at the [community] Hospital where I served dinner trays to patients and did some work in the foodservice office. Working with people and helping them out is something I really enjoy I sometimes enjoy volunteering more than working for money.

The committee that evaluated this essay decided that the student should go on the waiting list. Their advice to the author:

Tell more about how you have helped individual lives. What did you exactly do in the service club. "helping" is soo broad. At the beginning you write Helping is; I think is my greatest qualities.

You need to be a little more sure of yourself. In your paper you continued to say helping helping helping use some syninims. Shows it hasn't been thought through well. How does all this effect you?

Based on these suggestions, the student produced the following final draft:

Final Draft

I'm not quite sure of what I want to study, but I do have some idea. Helping is one of my greatest qualities. Everyone says how good it is to have me around because I can always be counted on to help someone out in a time of trouble. In my school I am in the service club which is a club where students can choose what activity or event you want and volunteer your time.

In the service club, I helped [an office] that comforts and discusses with rape victims and/or their children, relocate to another office. It took about five hours, but it was worth it, because in one day we packed, loaded, traveled to the new location, unloaded and unpacked, cleaned the rooms and set all the offices up. I also bowled to raise money for handicapped children, and volunteered for a while at [a community school] playing with children. One day, a nearby hospital was having a "Children's Day" celebration, and they needed a few high school students to supervise some activities, so for a few hours, I face painted kids. At my school library, I used to volunteer my study hall time working with the librarians. I did light filing, labeling, or typing. I still do it, but now I get paid for the job. Every Friday, I volunteer at [a community] hospital filing and picking up menus, and passing out and picking up dinner trays to the patients. Working in the hospital is really a lot of fun, not that I want to be a nurse, or work in a hospital environment or anything, but it's nice to know that I can help them since they're short on nurses.

What I really want to do is manage an advertising agency. Whenever I watch a commercial I think to myself "Oh I can do better than that! I can think of a better commercial that will catch the eyes of the audience!" Because I'm pretty creative, I think I would succeed in this career. I want to be able to help consumers to buy what is best. I believe your college will help me with my career.

The mock admissions committee decided to admit the student, with the following feedback: "You seem pretty helpful, and care about other people, but you don't say what or how our facilities can help you."

This writer has clearly improved the quality of her essay, providing many more specific examples to illustrate the traits of being caring and helpful. The remarks of the mock admissions committee are supportive and constructive and seem to have helped her recognize the need for concrete support for her claim. The feedback, along with the experience of evaluating the essays of other students, appears to have pointed her in the right direction.

OTHER USES OF ROLE-PLAYING PEER-RESPONSE GROUPS

Students can form role-playing peer-response groups any time they may ultimately submit their work to an external audience. Students preparing creative writing for submission to a literary magazine or competition might form mock editorial boards to critique one another's work. Students learning argumentation could write essays in support of candidates for school elections and submit them to a mock electorate. Students writing letters to corporations could form mock corporate boards to evaluate the presentation of ideas. Students writing Advanced Placement exams could gather information about AP readers and form mock AP committees to evaluate one another's practice exams (an activity suggested by Pamela Fly [1991]).

Giving students an authoritative voice in the evaluation of other writers can help them develop a sense of control over their own writing. Provided that the impetus to write is important to them, activities such as these should help students achieve the balance among speaker, argument, and audience that rhetoricians find so important and make writing an important means of expression and growth.

INDEX

Activities, 8. *See also* Culminating
  texts/activities; In-process
  texts/activities
  introductory, 152–163
Activity theory, 344
Adventures of Huckleberry Finn, The
  (Twain), 292–295
Aesthetic awareness, 87, 93,
  95, 98
Affective response, 130
Affirmation, 275
AIDS education, 319
Alternative assessments, 121–134
  connected knowing, 130
  creative writing, 132–134
  exploratory expression/talk,
    123–128
  multimedia/multigenre
    productions, 130–131
  narrative knowing, 129–130
  unconventional genres,
    131–132
  Virtual Library of Conceptual
    Units, 121, 122
American Dream (thematic unit),
  361–363
Analytic essays, 95, 101–102
  for coming-of-age literature,
    198–201, 202
  conventional assessments
    and, 114, 115
  literary, 118–119
  on paradigmatic knowledge,
    75–76
Analytic process, teaching,
  239–240
Angelou, Maya, 299

Animals as symbols theme,
  363–364
Anthologies, 38–39, 291
Anti-affirmative action
  movement, 289
Apathy, 276, 279, 280
Applebee, Arthur, 2, 340
Appropriate instruction, 25, 30, 31
Arguing to learn, 9, 146
Arguing to win, 9
Argumentative writing, 115,
  119–120
Art as Experience (Dewey), 22
Artists of your state unit/
  theme, 41
Asking questions. *See* Questions
Assessments, 7, 25, 27. *See also*
  Course design;
  Knowledge, students';
  Unit design/goals
  alternative, 121–134
  analytic essays, 95,
    101–102
  assignment for individual,
    193–194
  conventional, 115–121
  course, 94–103
  diversity and, 68–69
  extended definition essays,
    95, 98–99
  multimedia projects, 95,
    99–100
  overarching concepts and,
    86–87
  portfolio, 95, 96–98
  prescribed curriculum
    and, 35

  as reflective practice, 32
  rubrics for, 134–137
  student-developed, 95,
    102–103
  teacher, 103–105
  of units, 114–115
Athletics, 336
Attitude problems, curricular
  change and, 296–297
Audio recordings, 263
Authoritative knowledge, 66
Authoritative ways of
  relating, 78
Authors' style characterization
  theme, 367
Authors unit/theme, 41, 56
Autobiographies
  American Dream theme, 363
  changing times
    theme, 365
  coming of age theme, 369
  courage theme, 373
  cultural conflict theme, 375
  discrimination theme, 377
  family theme, 380
  journey theme, 387
  justice theme, 388
  outcast theme, 396
  protest literature, 401
  sense of place theme, 410
  values under stress
    theme, 418

Banned books sampler, 39
Beauty concept, 93
Beginning of school year, 174
Berliner, David, 302, 319, 340

Bible
  animals as symbols theme, 364
  character as symbols
      theme, 366
  conflict with authority
      theme, 369
  epic hero theme, 378
  journey theme, 387
  loss of innocence theme, 390
  loyalty theme, 392
  rites of passage theme, 404
  romance theme, 405
  Trickster theme, 416
Biddle, Bruce, 302, 319, 340
Black Boy (Wright), 298–299
Bodily/kinesthetic
    intelligence, 81
Body biographies, 131, 214,
    258–284
  author's reflection on,
      258–259
  classroom environment for,
      261–262
  composing processes for,
      266–274
  composition of, 264–265
  establishing working
      relationships, 274–280
  Gertrude, 268–271
  goal congruency, 280–281
  Hamlet unit, 262–264
  journal articles on, 284
  Laertes, 272–274
  mainstream schools and,
      259–260
  Ophelia, 266–268, 271
  requirements, 265
  social dynamics of Gertrude
      group, 276–279
  social dynamics of Ophelia
      group, 275–276
  symbolic and inferential
      thinking using, 268
Body of knowledge, 87, 93
Book clubs, 50, 128, 146–147
Book reviews, 132
Books and journal articles
  banned/protested topics, 39
  body biographies, 284
  book clubs and literature
      circles, 50

censorship, 301
character education, 316
classroom discussions, 221, 241
critical literacy, 93
culturally appropriate
    teaching, 91
culture and education, 43
curricular additions of, 38–39
dramatic/artistic literature
    responses, 92
flow experiences, 228
gender and talk, 79
grammar use and language
    instruction, 170
human development, 45
ideal adult conceptions, 335
introductory activities, 163
literature curriculum, 301
moral education, 316
multicultural awareness
    stances, 94
multimedia composing, 257
multiple intelligences, 82
narrative perspective, 90
portfolio assessment, 97
progressive education, 261
reading workshops and
    independent reading, 51
small groups, 226
standards, 326, 330
on student learning
    assessments, 139
teacher research, 106
tools for learning, 166
tracking, 53
Vygotskian activity theory,
    342–343
Western culture emphasis, 94
workshops, 89
writing/speech as exploratory
    tools, 74
British literary characters,
    psychology of, 403
Britton, James, 74
Brown, Darlene, 38, 58
Bruner, Jerome, 19, 75
Bullying, rates of, 302

Canonical literature, 289–290, 292
Cartoons, political satire, 407
Case studies, 152, 154, 159–161

Catcher in the Rye (Salinger), 38
Centralized core curriculum, 321
Change, politics of, 40
Changing times theme, 365–366
Character
  definition of, 303–304
  location of, 303, 304–305
  relational traits of, 311–313
  as symbol theme, 366–367
Character education, 285,
    302–317. *See also* Character
  books about, 316
  constructivism and, 315
  didactic approach, 306
  Hatch Act (1984) and, 333
  how students learn and,
      305–308
  peer groups unit, 310–315
  reflective approach, 306–308
  success unit, 308–310
  thematic units on, 308–315
Character Education
    Partnership, 312
Characterizing an author's style
    theme, 367
Children's books/stories, 132,
    415–416
Citizenship
  multicultural education
      and, 295
  reflective approach to
      character education
      and, 307–308
  teaching, 290
Civic awareness rationale, 61
Claims, argumentation, 119, 120
Classrooms. *See also* Discussions;
    Small groups
  discussion-leading
      techniques, 220
  learning students' names,
      218–219
  life in, 213–214
  management of, 226–228
  seating/furniture
      arrangement, 217–218,
      263
  setting up, 216–229
  social context of, 341
  student-designed
      environments, 219

traditional arrangements for, 216–217

Clinton, Bill, 322

Cliques. *See* Peer-groups pressure unit

Clustering, 437

Coach, teacher as, 30

Co-constructed discussions, 146, 225

Codes, language, 168

Cognition, *versus* common sense, 245

Cognition taxonomies, 72–73

Cole, Michael, 108

Collaborative learning, 130

College preparation rationale, 62

Color Purple, The, 38, 58

Comedy theme, 367–368

Coming-of-age unit design, 141–151. *See also* Construction zone; Daily plan
    culminating texts/activities, 142–143, 147–151
    goals for, 142–147
    literary analysis, 149–150
    materials, 142
    multimedia projects, 150–151
    personal narratives, 148–149
    reading/response logs, 143–145, 181–182
    student-generated discussions, 145–147
    thematic texts on, 368–369
    time considerations for, 175
    writing about personal experiences, 157

Common sense, *versus* cognitive sophistication, 245

Communication. *See also* Constructivism
    constructivist, 71–72
    grammar and, 167–168
    theories on, 69–72
    transmission, 70–71, 73, 255, 305–308, 318, 319

Community
    character education and, 304–305
    context of school and, 172–173

ethnographies of, 42–43, 104–105

materials appropriateness and, 54–56

multiculturalism and, 290

understanding of, 46–47

Compare/contrast papers, 75

Compathy, 312–313

Composing, 8, 10, 214
    across the curriculum, 244–249
    English multimedia projects, 249–255
    generation of new meaning and, 271–272
    texts, 242

Conceptual units of instruction, 2, 5–10. *See also* Assessments; Themes; Unit design/goals
    activities, 8
    assessments, 7
    benefits, 15–16
    composing, 10
    definition of, 5–6
    discussions, 8–9
    drawback, 16
    genres, 13–15
    goals, 7
    integrated knowledge, 16–18
    inventories, 6
    lessons, 7–8
    movements, 13
    periods, 13
    principles of practice, 25–32
    rationale, 16–32
    regions, 13
    scaffolding learning, 19–22
    schemas and scripts, 18–19
    texts, 9
    themes, 11
    tools, 9–10
    transactional learning, 22–25
    types, 10–15

Confidentiality
    of reading logs, 144
    of student journals, 124–125

Conflict with authority theme, 369–370

Connected knowing, 78, 80
    assessment of, 130

Connected knowing talk, 78, 80

Connotation theme, 370–371

Construction zone. *See also* Daily plan
    approach to, 165–167
    classroom as, 108–109, 164–165
    final thoughts, 211–212
    outlining the unit, 170–172
    preliminaries, 167–172
    school/community context, 172–173
    setting up shop, 174–176
    starting the unit, 177–178
    teaching contexts, 172–174, 337
    teaching language, 167–170
    time considerations, 173–174

Constructivism, 66
    assessment of culminating projects, 134–137
    character education and, 305, 315
    culminating texts and, 86–87
    interpretive processes and, 252
    seating arrangements and, 218
    social context of, 341
    theory of, 71–72

Context
    classroom social, 341
    constructed knowledge and, 71–72
    discussions to generate interpretation, 233–237
    of instruction, 33
    for learning, 25, 29–30
    of school and community, 172–173
    teaching, 172–174, 337
    unit approach and, 15–16

Conventional assessments, 115–121
    argumentation, 119–120
    extended definitions, 115, 117–118

Conventional assessments,
Continued
literary analysis, 118–119
research reports, 120–121
Virtual Library of Conceptual
Units, 115, 116
Coping with loss theme,
371–373
Copying work concerns,
217–218
Cotner, Cindy, 104
Counterarguments, 99, 118,
119, 120
Counterexamples, 99, 117
Courage theme, 373–374
Course design, 84–107
analytic essays, 95, 101–102
assessment, 94–103
challenges, 84–85
curriculum planning
considerations, 87
extended definition essays,
95, 98–99
multimedia projects, 95, 99–100
negotiating thresholds theme,
88–90
overarching concepts and
assessments, 86–87
overarching concepts types,
87–88
portfolio, 95, 96–98
sophomore year English
curriculum, 85–94
student-developed, 95,
102–103
teacher, 103–105
unit distribution/sequencing,
89–90
Course-long portfolio
preparation, 123–124
Courtesy, 275, 305
Courtroom case study, 423–434
adaptation of, 433–434
case facts, 427
case review, 424
charge definition, 424–427
class assignment, 432–433
murder trial activity, 424–432
testimony, 427–432
Creative writing, assessment of,
132–134

Crime by minors, 302
Criteria, 99, 117
Critical literacy, 91–92, 93
Csikszentmihalyi, M., 17
Culminating texts/activities, 85, 86
assessment, 134–137
for coming of age unit,
142–143, 147–151
extended definitions, 117–118
identification, 103
setting goals for, 110
social action engagement for,
114
for teachers, 103–105
Cultural background, 72,
104–105. *See also*
Ethnographies,
community
Cultural conflict theme/unit, 41,
374–375
Cultural-historical activity
theory, 344
Cultural knowledge, 67–68
Cultural literacy, 93
Cultural modeling, 90–91
Cultural significance rationale, 60
Curriculum. *See also* Multicultural
curriculum
additions, 38–39
attitude problems and change
in, 296–297
centralized core, 321
composing across, 244–249
diversity in, 320
materials selection and, 49
planning, course design
and, 87
requirements, 39–40
restrictions, 37–39
rethinking, 285–286
sophomore year English,
85–94
student-determined, 34, 36,
153–154
teacher-determined, 34,
35–36, 47–48
as topic determinator, 34, 35

Daily plan, 178–211. *See also*
Coming-of-age unit design
day 2, transitions, 178–179

day 3, discussions, reading
logs, 179–182
day 4, reading log
maintenance, 182
day 5, homework
assignment, 182–183
day 6, quiz, freewrites,
portfolio assignment,
185–186
day 7, discussion, homework
assignment, 187–188
day 8, quiz, small groups, 188
day 9, whole-class
discussion, homework
assignment, 188–189
day 10, quiz, small groups,
collect reading logs, 190
day 11, return reading logs,
discussion, 191–192
day 12, finish discussion,
story choices, 192
day 13, small groups, 192
day 14, finish small groups,
192–193
day 15, individual assessment
assignment, 193
day 16, freewrites, peer
evaluation instruction,
rubric distribution,
195–201
day 17, goal reevaluation,
201–202
day 18, multimedia project
assignment, 202
day 19, student reading,
teacher grading, 202
day 20, student-led
discussions
responsibilities, 203–204
day 21, return essays, teach
open-ended question
formation, 205
day 22, teach open-ended
discussion formation,
206–208
day 23, small group
questions/formats
preparation, 208
day 24, small group
questions/formats
preparation, 209

day 25 to 30, student-led
    discussions, 209
week 1, 178–183
week 2, 183–191
week 3, 191–195
week 4, 195–204
week 5, 205–209
week 6, 209–211
Death of a Salesman, 310
Defensible instruction, 25, 26
Definitions. *See also* Extended
    definitions
    courtroom charges, 424–427
Delinquency rates, 302
*Designing and Sequencing Prewriting
    Activities* (Johannessen,
    Kahn, and Walter), 117
Detective theme, 375–376
Developmental level, 43–44, 45
Dewey, John, 22
Dialogic discussions, 146
Dialogue journals, 125–126
Didactic approach to character
    education, 306
Discipline, 226, 228, 305
Discourtesy, 276, 278–279
Discrimination unit/theme, 117,
    158, 376–378
Discussions, 8–9. *See also* Body
    biographies; Reading logs;
    Small groups; Student-
    generated discussions
    books on, 221, 241
    building on contributions to
        generate questions, 238
    co-constructed, 146, 225
    contrasting approaches to,
        232–238
    dialogic, 146
    making analysis process
        explicit, 239–240
    planning, 241
    prompting to elaborate on
        responses, 237
    prompting to generate
        context for
        interpretation, 233–237
    teacher-led, 232, 438–439
    techniques for teaching
        leading, 220
    whole-class, 187, 188, 189, 190

Distant themes rationale, 60
Diversity
    instructional goals and, 69,
        288–292
    knowledge/assessment and,
        68–69
Documentary films, 378, 401
Dramas
    American Dream theme, 363
    changing times theme, 365
    character as symbols
        theme, 366
    comedy theme, 368
    conflict with authority
        theme, 370
    coping with loss
        theme, 372
    courage theme, 374
    discrimination theme, 377
    family theme, 380
    friends and enemies
        theme, 382
    gender roles theme, 384
    justice theme, 389
    love theme, 391
    loyalty theme, 393
    new kid on the block
        theme, 395
    outcast theme, 396
    peer-group pressure
        theme, 383
    Puritan ethic, 402
    responsibility theme, 404
    romance theme, 406
    satire, 408
    social responsibility
        theme, 412
    success theme, 413
    tragic hero theme, 415
    Trickster theme, 416
Dramatic images
    books on, 92
    culminating texts/activities
        showing, 148
    multimedia project
        assessments, 95,
        99–100
    strategies, 91, 141
Drivers' education class,
    227–228
Drop-outs, 302

Dumbed-down instruction, 25,
    28, 85
*Dynamics of English Instruction,
    Grades 7–12, The* (Hillocks,
    McCabe, and
    McCampbell), 11
Dystopias themes, 416–417

Early-career teachers, 167, 187,
    201. *See also* Preservice
    teachers
Edmiston, Brian, 91
Educational standards. *See*
    Standards, educational
Eisner, Elliot, 98
Electronic conversations, 105
Electronic dialogue journals, 126
Elementary texts, on Puritan
    ethic, 401
Emotional response, teaching
    definition of, 206
Emotional response *versus*
    analysis, 293–294
Empathy, 311–313
End of class segment, 179
Engagement with content, 115
English, textbook, 168
English Coalition Conference, 52
English Journal, 264
Enlightenment goals, 295–297
Epic poetry
    epic hero theme, 378–379
    journey theme, 387
    picaresque hero theme, 397
    tragic hero theme, 415
    Trickster theme, 416
Ethnographies, community,
    42–43, 104–105. *See also*
    Cultural background
Evaluation. *See also* Assessments;
    Peer evaluation; Reading
    logs; Rubrics, assessment;
    Teacher evaluation
    teaching definition of, 205
Evidence, argumentation,
    119, 120
Evocation, literary work, 141
Examples, 99, 117
Exhibits, portfolio, 96–97,
    123–124, 185, 186, 195
Exorcist, The (film), 255

Expectations, teacher, 25, 27–28, 134–135

Experiences, typology of, 322

Exploratory expression/talk, 73–75, 214

 aesthetic awareness assessment and, 99

 asking questions, 127–128

 book clubs and literature circles, 128

 journals, 124–126

 portfolios, 123–124

 reading logs, 144–145

 for role-playing peer-response group topic decisions, 437

 rough drafts, 126–127

 for unit assessment, 121, 123–128

Exploratory learning, connected knowing and, 130

Extended definitions

 in conventional assessments, 115, 117–118

 in courtroom case study, 423

 essays on, 75, 95, 101–102

 of good literature, 98–99

 prompting to generate context for interpretation and, 235

 success unit, 308–309

Fables, 363–364, 407, 415–416

Facilitator, teacher as, 30

Factory, school as, 336

Fairy tales, 363–364, 383, 396, 405

Family theme, 379–380

"Fault Lines in the Contact Zone" (Miller), 282

Feedback, 180, 195–196, 247–248

Feminine conceptions of knowledge, 77–80

Field observations

 anthology cultural texts, 299

 classroom arrangement, 219

 classroom discussions, 240

 conventional to alternative assessments continuum, 113

disaffected/disengaged students, 283

English teachers' knowledge and transmission of, 249

expectations of students/teachers, 330

instructional planning, 167

introductory activities, 158

knowledge, learning, and flow, 249

NBPTS standards, 330

overarching curriculum concept, 85

peer groups characteristics, 311

small groups, 274

student backgrounds, 47

student conduct/safety, 304

student questions, 143

student shadowing, 231

transmission *versus* constructivist teaching, 73

unit goals, 211

Film reviews, 132

Films

 American Dream theme, 363

 changing times theme, 365

 character as symbols theme, 367

 coming of age theme, 369

 courage theme, 374

 discrimination theme, 377–378

 documentaries, 378, 401

 family theme, 380

 friends and enemies theme, 382

 gender roles theme, 384

 journey theme, 387

 leader theme, 389

 love theme, 392

 loyalty theme, 393

 outcast theme, 396

 peer-group pressure theme, 383

 progress theme, 399

 propaganda theme, 400

 protest literature, 401

 romance theme, 406

 satire, 408

 science fiction, 409

 self-reliance theme, 410

 sense of place theme, 411

 success theme, 413

 technology, nature, and society theme, 415

 values under stress theme, 418

 war and peace theme, 420

 Western theme, 421

Final draft speech, 73

Five-paragraph theme, 115

Flow experiences, 229

 books on, 228

 classroom management and, 227–228

 conceptual units and, 17

 field observation, 249

 in sewing class, 246

Fly, Pamela, 213, 442

Focused freewrites, 185

Folk hero theme, 380–381

Folktales, 363–364, 380, 415–416

Frame experiments, 105

Freedman, Sarah, 105

Free time, 188–189

Freewrites, 185, 195, 437

Freeze frames, group, 264

Friends and enemies theme, 381–382

Frontier literature, 41, 382

Frost, Robert, 154

Fulfillment, teacher's, 342–343

Funding, curriculum diversity and, 320

Future needs preparation rationale, 61–62

Gangs. *See* Peer-groups pressure unit

Gardener, teacher as, 337

Gardner, Howard, 80–81, 93, 246, 249

Gay, Lesbian, Bisexual Teachers of Speakers of Other Languages (GLESOL) listserve, 105

Gendered ways of knowing, 77–80, 154

 books on, 79

Gender roles unit/theme, 41, 383–384

Generalization, teaching
    definition of, 204
Genres, 13–15
    assessment of writing in
        literary, 133–134
    works by single author,
        14–15
Goals, instructional, 7. *See also*
    Unit design/goals
    congruency of, 280–281
    diversity and, 69, 288–292
    educational standards and,
        334–335
Goodness concept, 93
Grammar, 167–170
Griffin, Peg, 108
Groups, working in, 146. *See also*
    Small groups
Group task, 225
Growth model of education, 22,
    74–75
Guide books, 132

Hamlet, 262–264
    body biographies and, 258
    Claudius body biography,
        277, 279–280, 281
    Gertrude body biography,
        268–271, 276–279
    Ophelia body biography,
        266–268, 271, 275–276
Hansberry, Lorraine, 299
Happiness, human, 17
Hatch Act (1984), 333
Hayes, John R., 437, 438
Health care, school as, 336
Hillocks, George, 2, 3, 4, 105
Hirsch, E. D., 93
Homework, 147, 183, 187
Huebner, Dwayne, 76
Hurston, Zora Neale, 299
Hypertext libraries, 361

Imagery theme, 371
Inclusion, 275, 276
Independent reading, 51
Indirect talk, connected
    knowing and, 80
Individual application, 180
Inference/inferential thinking,
    204, 268

Influences on personality theme,
    384–385
Inherent knowledge, 67
In Our Time (Hemingway), 23
In-process texts/activities
    for coming of age unit,
        142–147
    response logs, 143–145
    student-generated
        discussions, 145–147
Inquiring stance, 144–145
*Inside City Schools: Investigating
    Literacy in Multicultural
    Classrooms* (Freedman, et
    al.), 105
Instructional emphasis,
    knowledge and, 69
Instructional scaffolds. *See*
    Scaffolding
Instructions
    context of, 33
    hard copy of, 178, 225
Integrated knowledge, 16–18
Interests, student, 44–45
Interests, teacher, 48
International Reading
    Association. *See* NCTE/IRA
    Standards for English
    Language Arts
Internet. *See also* Virtual Library
    of Conceptual Units
    communities, 260–261
    hypertext libraries, 361
Interpersonal intelligence, 81–82
Interpretation, 250–255
    of multimedia productions,
        131
    through body biographies,
        272–274
    through drama, 254–255
    through drawings, 253–254
    through music, 253
    using dance, 251–253
    using reading logs,
        144–145, 182
Interviews of literature
    characters, 264
Intrapersonal intelligence, 82
Introductory activities, 152–163
    opinionnaires/surveys,
        158–159

peer groups unit, 313–314
    for scaffolding, 152–155
    scenarios/case studies,
        159–161
    success unit, 309
    Virtual Library of Conceptual
        Units, 155–156
    writing about personal
        experiences,
        156–157
    writing about related
        problems, 161–162
Inventories, 6
    diagnostic, 176
    student interests/performance
        levels, 175
Irony themes, 385–387
i sing of Olaf glad and big
    (cummings), 55–56

James, Jasper, 138
Jefferson, Thomas, 306–307
Journal articles, professional. *See*
    Books and journal articles
Journals, personal, 124–126
Journey theme, 387–388
Justice theme, 388–389. *See also*
    Courtroom case study

Knowledge, students', 66–83
    assessment and, 68–69
    assumptions about, 66–69
    communication theories and,
        69–72
    exploratory talk and, 73–75
    field observation, 249
    final draft speech and, 73
    gendered, 77–80
    intelligences types and,
        80–83
    narrative, 75, 76–77
    paradigmatic, 75–76
Knowledge, teacher's, 48, 249
Knowledge construction, 71–72

Lab reports, parody theme
    and, 396
Language, instruction in,
    167–170
Larson, R., 17
Leader theme, 389

Learning. *See also* Multiple
    intelligences
  assumptions about, 3
  prior knowledge for, 25, 29
  recursive nature of, 154–155
  styles, 25, 27
  ways of talking and,
    230–241
Lee, Carol, 42, 90
Legends, with folk hero
    theme, 380
Lessons, definition of, 7–8
Letters to the editor, 132
Liberal perspective, of
    standards, 331
*Lies My Teacher Told Me: Everything
    Your American History
    Textbook Got Wrong*
    (Loewen), 70
Life in classrooms, 214–215
Linguistic intelligence, 80–81
Listserves, 105, 107
Literary analysis, 95, 118–119,
    149–150
Literary canon, 289–290, 292
Literary codes, 15, 71
Literary form and technique, 205
Literary narratives' retelling,
    129–130
Literary significance rationale,
    60–61
Literary value, 54
Literature as Exploration
    (Rosenblatt), 22
Literature circles, 50, 128,
    146–147
Literature response, 176, 315
Local themes rationale, 60
Loewen, James W., 70
Logical/mathematic
    intelligence, 81
Loss of innocence theme,
    390–391
Love theme, 391–392
Loyalty theme, 392–393

*Manufactured Crisis, The: Myths,
    Fraud, and the Attack on
    America's Public Schools*
    (Berliner and Biddle), 319
Marshall, James, 231

Masculine conceptions of
    knowledge, 77–80
Master teachers, 286
Materials selection, 48–57
  appropriateness, 54–56
  authorship variety, 56
  book clubs, 50
  considerations in, 51–57
  curriculum and, 49
  exercise, 57
  literary value, 54
  literature circles, 50
  menu choices, 50
  student choice and, 48–49,
    50–51
  teacher's role in, 49
  textual forms variety, 54
  tracking and, 51–53
  turf and, 56–57
Mathematics standards, 323
McCann, Tom, 161
McElhiney, Linda, 438
Meaning, interpretive processes
    and, 253–254, 271–272
Measurement means and
    focus, 68
Middle school security guards, 302
Miller, Richard E., 282
Mock college admissions
    committees, 436–438
  role-playing peer-response
    groups, 439–440
  teacher-led analysis, 438–439
Modeling. *See also* Growth model
    of education
  cultural, 90–91
  teacher, 180, 233–234
"Modest Proposal, A" (Swift), 14
Moll, Luis, 42, 104
Movements, 13
Movie reviews, 132
Multicultural awareness stances,
    92, 94
Multicultural curriculum, 285,
    288–301
  American cultural changes
    and, 288–290
  books and journal articles, 301
  for broad education, 295–297
  Huckleberry Finn and, 292–295
  issues in, 290–292

texts representing one group
    of people, 297–299
Multimedia projects, 214
  assessment of, 130–131
  background, 242–243
  books and journal
    articles, 257
  for coming of age unit,
    150–151
  composing across the
    curriculum, 244–249
  English compositions,
    249–255
  in mainstream schools,
    259–261
  rationale for, 243–244
  student, 95, 99–100
  teacher, 104
  tool kit for, 242–257
  unit design, 256
Multiple intelligences, 80–83
Murder, definition of, 424–425
Murders by unemployed
    teens, 302
Musical intelligence, 81
Mythology
  character as symbols
    theme, 366
  courage theme, 373
  loss of innocence theme, 390
  mythic hero theme, 393
  new kid on the block
    theme, 394
  rites of passage theme, 404
  romance theme, 405

Narrative
  knowledge/perspective,
    75, 76–77, 90, 129–130
National Board for Professional
    Teaching Standards
    (NBPTS), 286, 325–330
  Adolescence and Young
    Adulthood English
    Language Arts,
    328–329
  Early Adolescence English
    Language Arts,
    327–328
  ideology of, 331, 333–334
  readings on, 330

National Council of Teachers of English (NCTE), 107, 260, 326. *See also* NCTE/IRA Standards for English Language Arts

National Council of Teachers of Mathematics, 323

National themes rationale, 60

National Writing Project, 260

Naturalism, 402–403

Naturalistic intelligence, 82

NBPTS standards. *See* National Board for Professional Teaching Standards (NBPTS)

NCTE/IRA Standards for English Language Arts, 286, 322, 324–325, 331, 333–334

NCTE-talk (listserve), 105

Needs, student, 45–46

Negotiating thresholds theme, 88–90, 140–141, 148

New Criticism, 75

New kid on the block theme, 394–395

Newman, Dennis, 108

Nonfiction
American Dream theme, 362–363
coping with loss theme, 372
courage theme, 374
cultural conflict theme, 375
discrimination theme, 377
dystopias theme, 417
family theme, 380
journey theme, 387
justice theme, 388
loyalty theme, 393
mythic hero theme, 393
persuasion theme, 397
progress theme, 399
propaganda theme, 399–400
protest literature, 400–401
Puritan ethic, 402
rites of passage theme, 405
self-reliance theme, 410
sense of place theme, 411
social responsibility theme, 412
success theme, 413

technology, nature, and society theme, 414
utopias theme, 417
values under stress theme, 418
Victorians theme, 419
wilderness adventures theme, 422

Novels
American Dream theme, 362
animals as symbols theme, 364
author's style characterization theme, 367
changing times theme, 365
character as symbols theme, 366
comedy theme, 367–368
coming of age unit/theme, 142, 188, 201–202, 368–369
conflict with authority theme, 370
coping with loss theme, 372
courage theme, 373
cultural conflict theme, 374–375
detective theme, 375–376
discrimination theme, 376–377
discussions of, 203–204
dystopias theme, 417
epic hero theme, 378–379
exam on, 210
family theme, 379–380
friends and enemies theme, 381
frontier literature, 382
gender roles theme, 384
influences on personality theme, 384–385
irony themes, 385–386
journey theme, 387
justice theme, 388
leader theme, 389
loss of innocence theme, 390
love theme, 391
loyalty theme, 393
naturalism, 402
new kid on the block theme, 394
outcast theme, 395
peer-group pressure theme, 383

persuasion theme, 397
picaresque hero theme, 397–398
point of view theme, 398
progress theme, 399
propaganda theme, 399
protest literature, 400
Puritan ethic, 402
realism, 402
responsibility theme, 403–404
rites of passage theme, 405
romance theme, 406
satire, 407–408
science fiction, 408–409
self-reliance theme, 409
sense of place theme, 410
social responsibility theme, 412
success theme, 413
technology, nature, and society theme, 414
tragic hero theme, 415
Trickster theme, 416
utopias theme, 417
values under stress theme, 418
Victorians theme, 419
war and peace theme, 420
Western theme, 421
wilderness adventures theme, 422

Nurturing talk, connected knowing and, 80

O'Donnell-Allen, Cindy, 143–144, 219, 259–260. *See also* Body biographies

Official meaning, 67, 71

Of Mice and Men (Steinbeck), 294

Oklahoma Council of Teachers of English, 260

Open-ended questions, 145, 182, 218

Opinionnaires, 152, 154, 158–159

Oral interpretation, 243

Outcast theme, 395–396

Outline, unit, 170–172

Outsiders, The, 127–128, 161, 315

Overarching concepts, 17, 40–41, 84, 85, 87–88
  for coming of age unit, 140–141
Owners' manuals, 175

Paradigmatic knowledge, 75–76, 95
Parents, 156, 175
Parody theme, 396
Pathetic fallacy, 313
Peace theme. *See* War and peace theme
Peer evaluation, 118, 193–194, 201
Peer-groups pressure unit, 310–315, 383. *See also* Courtroom case study
  introductory activity, 313–314
  personal experience writing, 314
  relational character traits and, 311–313
  writing in response to literature, 315
Peer-response groups. *See* Peer evaluation; Role-playing peer-response groups
Performance, minimum level of, 322
Periods
  literary, 13
  marking, 173–174
Personal connection, teaching definition of, 206
Personal evaluation. *See* Reading logs
Personal experiences, 71
  journals, 124–126
  as narratives, 129
  unit theme and, 148–149
  writing as introductory activity, 152, 154, 156–157, 175
  writing for coming of age unit, 178
  writing for peer groups unit, 314
Personality influences theme, 384–385

Personal response. *See* Reading logs
Persuasion theme, 396–397
Picaresque hero theme, 397–398
Pigeonhole effect, 16
Planning, 138, 164. *See also* Course design; Unit design/goals
Poetry. *See also* Epic poetry
  American Dream theme, 361
  animals as symbols theme, 364
  author's style characterization theme, 367
  changing times theme, 365
  character as symbols theme, 366
  coming of age unit/theme, 142, 182, 210, 368
  conflict with authority theme, 370
  connotation theme, 370–371
  coping with loss theme, 371–372
  courage theme, 373
  cultural conflict theme, 374
  discrimination theme, 376
  epic hero theme, 378
  family theme, 379
  gender roles theme, 383
  imagery theme, 371
  irony themes, 385–386
  justice theme, 388
  loss of innocence theme, 390
  love theme, 391
  loyalty theme, 392
  naturalism, 402
  new kid on the block theme, 394
  outcast theme, 395
  persuasion theme, 396
  protest literature, 400
  psychology of British literary characters, 403
  Puritan ethic, 401
  realism, 402
  rites of passage theme, 404
  romance theme, 405
  satire, 407
  self-reliance theme, 409
  sense of place theme, 410

social responsibility theme, 411
  success theme, 412–413
  technology, nature, and society theme, 414
  Victorians theme, 418–419
  war and peace theme, 419
Point of view theme, 398
Political cartoons, 407
Politics of change, 40
Portfolios
  assessment of, 135–137
  assignment/introduction of, 185, 194
  books about, 97
  rubrics for, 197–198
  student, 95, 96–98
  synthesis paper, 97, 124, 186
  teacher, 103–104
  for unit assessment, 123–124
Prayers, for coping with loss theme, 371
Preservice teachers, 237
Primary research sources, 121
Principles of planning, 33
Principles of practice, 2–5, 25–32
  appropriate instruction, 25, 30, 31
  assessments, 25, 27
  context for learning, 25, 29–30
  defensible instruction, 25, 26
  dumbed-down instruction, 25, 28
  growth through teaching, 25, 30–32
  learning styles, 25, 27
  prior knowledge for learning, 25, 29
  purposeful instruction, 25, 26
  sequenced instruction, 25, 28–29
  teacher expectations, 25, 27–28
  teaching assessments, 25, 32
  theory in, 340–344
Prior knowledge for learning, 25, 29, 85
Prison, school as, 336
Process portfolio, 96–98, 123
Products, portfolio, 96
Progressive teaching, 261

Progress theme, 399
Propaganda theme, 399–400
Prose writers, 367, 396, 403
Prostitution, high school, 302
Protest literature, 40, 400–401
    banned books, 39
Provisional planning, 138
Psychology of British literary
    characters, 403
Public alternative school English
    classes, 214
Public school English classes,
    213–214
Punishment, 226
Pupil Rights Amendment to the
    General Education
    Provisions Act
    (1984), 333
Puritan ethic, 401–402
Puritan ethic unit, 41
Purposeful instruction, 25, 26

Questions
    categories of, 145–146
    exploratory, 127–128
    formation of, 143
    reading log, 125, 144–145
    student-generated
        discussions, 145–147
Quizzes, summary, 184–185,
    186, 188, 190
QWERTY typewriter
    keyboards, 111

Racism, 292–294, 298, 299
Random organization for small
    group formation,
    221–222
Ranking activity, success unit,
    309–310
Rationales, 57–65, 107, 151
    civic awareness, 61
    course design, 94
    cultural significance, 60
    evaluation exercise, 63
    for expanded tool kit,
        243–244
    future needs, 61–62
    literary significance, 60–61
    for multiple forms of
        composition, 243

planning exercise, 64
psychology/human
    development, 58, 60
social problems relevancy, 61
Virtual Library of Conceptual
    Units examples, 58, 59
writing, 62–63, 65
*Reader, the Text, the Poem, The: The
    Transactional Theory of the
    Literary Work* (Rosenblatt),
    22
Reading assignment quizzes,
    184–185
Reading a text, 11
    generative method for, 198
Reading logs, 125
    as class discussion starters,
        186, 187, 188, 189
    for coming of age unit,
        143–145, 181–182
    instruction in maintenance
        of, 182
    scaffolding use of, 179–180
    teacher evaluation of, 190
Reading workshops, 51
Realism, 402–403
Rebuttals, 99, 118, 119, 120
Recipes, parody theme, 396
Red Ribbon Week programs,
    319–320
Reflective approach, character
    education, 306–308
Reflective practice, 32, 171–172
Reflective thinking, 97, 310
Reflective writing, 104, 185,
    186, 195
Reflective writing prompt
    on character education, 303
    on classroom arrangements,
        217
    on construction
        metaphor, 110
    on grading schools, 318
    on grammar/language
        instruction, 170
    on invasive nature of
        journals, 125
    on literary discussions, 232
    on multicultural
        curriculum, 292
    on overarching concepts, 87

on personal experience in
    learning, 154
schooling metaphors, 337
on Shakespeare units, 262
on teachers teaching subject
    versus students, 57
on teaching skills for
    assessment, 145
on writing/speaking
    experiences, 74
Regions, geographic, 13
Related problems, writing about,
    152, 154, 161–162
Religion exam vignette, 69
Required curriculum, 39–40
Research reports, 120–121
Resistance to discourtesy, 276
Response logs. *See*
    Reading logs
Responsibilities
    student feedback, 195–196
    student-led discussions,
        203–204
    teaching, 170–171
Responsibility theme, 403–404
Retelling literary narratives,
    129–130
Risk-taking, reading logs and,
    144–145
Rites of passage theme,
    404–405
Role-playing peer-response
    groups, 435–442, 439
    ethical questions, 438–439
    finding a topic, 436
    revise/resubmit texts, 440
    for students as critics, 440
    for students as writers,
        441–442
    for understanding readers'
        expectations, 436–438
Romance theme, 405–407
Rosenblatt, Louise, 22, 141, 230
Rough drafts, 126–127
    architectural model, 248
    coming of age unit,
        149–150
    extended definition essay,
        118
    of individual assessment
        essays, 193–194

Rubrics, assessment, 134–137
  distribution/discussion of,
    197–198
  for essays analyzing coming-
    of-age literature,
    198–201
  for grading student-led
    discussions, 206–208
  introduction of, 185
  student-determined, 198

Satire, 14, 407–408
Scaffolding, 19–22, 25, 28
  classroom discussions and, 240
  criticism of, 21
  in *Hamlet* unit, 262–263
  introductory activities for,
    153–155
  on reading logs, 179–180
  weakness in, 152–153
Scenarios, 152, 154, 159–161
Schema theory, 18–19
Schooling metaphors, 335–337
Schools, polls on, 318–319
School socialization, 220
School uniforms, 305
Science fiction, 408–409
Scripts, 18–19
Seating arrangements, 217–218
Seating chart, 218–219
Secondary research sources, 121
Self-defense, definition of,
    426–427
Self-determination
  for coming of age unit, 143
  culminating texts/activities
    showing, 148
  portfolios assessments, 95
  stances, 92, 141
  student-developed
    assessments, 95
Self-reliance theme, 409–410
Sense of place theme, 410–411
Sequenced instruction, 25, 28–29
Sewing class, composing in,
    245–247
Shakespearean language
  instruction, 263
Short stories
  American Dream theme, 362
  analysis of, 189

animals as symbols theme,
    364
author's style characterization
    theme, 367
changing times theme, 365
character as symbols theme,
    366
choices for, 192
coming of age unit/theme,
    142, 183–184, 187, 368
coping with loss theme, 372
courage theme, 373
cultural conflict theme, 374
detective theme, 375
discrimination theme, 376
dystopias themes, 416
essays on, 191–192, 193–194,
    205, 206
family theme, 379
friends and enemies
    theme, 381
gender roles theme, 384
irony themes, 385–386
journey theme, 387
leader theme, 389
loss of innocence theme, 390
love theme, 391
loyalty theme, 392
naturalism, 402
outcast theme, 395
parody theme, 396
peer-group pressure
    theme, 383
persuasion theme, 396–397
point of view theme, 398
progress theme, 399
protest literature, 400
Puritan ethic, 401
realism, 402
rites of passage theme, 404
romance theme, 405
satire, 407
science fiction, 408
self-reliance theme, 409
sense of place theme, 410
social responsibility
    theme, 412
success theme, 413
summary quiz on, 186, 188
technology, nature, and
    society theme, 414

Trickster theme, 416
utopias theme, 416
values under stress theme,
    417–418
Victorians theme, 419
war and peace theme, 420
wilderness adventures
    theme, 422
Showcase portfolio, 96
Significant events, teaching
    definition of, 205
"Silken Tent, The" (Frost), 154
Single author works, 14–15
Situated practice, 164
Situational language, 168, 169
Small groups, 221–226. *See also*
    Body biographies;
    Student-generated
    discussions
  books on, 226
  discussions, 178–179,
    186–187, 188, 189, 192
  formation of, 221–223
  group task for, 225
  physical arrangement for,
    223, 224–225
  practice, 180
  size for, 225
  teacher role during,
    225–226
Smith, Michael W., 15, 90
Social context of reading, 71–72
Socialization, school, 220
Social needs rationale, 62
Social problems, current
    relevancy to, 61
Social responsibility theme,
    411–412
Sommers, Christina Hoff, 77
Songs
  changing times theme, 365
  coping with loss theme, 372
  cultural conflict theme, 375
  discrimination theme, 378
  dystopias theme, 417
  irony themes, 385–386
  journey theme, 387
  justice theme, 389
  loss of innocence theme, 390
  progress theme, 399
  sense of place theme, 411

social responsibility theme, 412

success theme, 414

utopias theme, 417

war and peace theme, 420–421

Soul on Ice (Cleaver), 54

Spatial intelligence, 81, 246

Special education, costs of, 319

Speech, 73–75. *See also* Exploratory expression/talk

Spiritual knowledge, 76–77

Sports writing, parody theme, 396

Sputnik, U.S. education and, 288

Stances

critical literacy, 91–92

inquiring, 144–145

multicultural awareness, 92, 94

as overarching concept, 87

self-determination, 92, 141

Standards, educational, 285–286, 318–339

books on, 326

definitions, 321–322

development considerations, 330–337

English discipline definition, 330–331

ideal adult conceptions, 334–335

ideological values of, 331–334

schooling metaphors, 335–337

standards for development of, 337–338

for students, 322, 323–324

for teachers, 322, 325–330

Standards for English Language Arts. *See* NCTE/IRA Standards for English Language Arts

Strategies, learning, 15

cultural modeling, 90–91

dramatic images, 91, 141

as overarching concept, 87

understanding narrative perspective, 90

Stratification, for small group formation, 222

Student(s), 41–47. *See also*

Student-generated discussions

assessments developed by, 95, 102–103

classroom environment design by, 219

copying other student's work, 217–218

cultivated expertise of, 240

culture of, 42–43

curriculum determinations by, 34, 36, 153–154

developmental level of, 43–44

educational standards for, 322, 323–324

emotional response of, 293–295

field observation of, 47

humiliation vignette, 205

interests of, 44–45

knowledgeable, 286

learning names of, 218–219

materials selection by, 48–49, 50–51

needs of, 45–46

rubric production by, 198

small group formation by, 222

teacher/unit evaluation by, 210–211

unit focus and, 110

Student-generated discussions, 145–147, 181, 209. *See also* Body biographies; Small groups; Student(s)

assigned reading for, 188

books on, 221

failure of, 231

preparation for small groups, 224

responsibilities in, 203–204

rubrics for grading, 206–208

student talking and, 232–233

techniques for, 220

Study guides, composition of, 263

Substance abuse programs, 319–320

Success unit/theme, 41, 308–310, 412–414

Suicide rates, 302

Summary quiz, 184–185, 186, 188, 190

Summary *versus* reflection, 195

Surveys, 152, 154, 158–159, 175–176

Swift, Jonathan, 14

Symbolic thinking, 268

Synthesis of ideas, small groups', 225

Synthesis paper, portfolio, 97, 124, 186

Talk/talking. *See also* Connected knowing talk; Exploratory expression/talk; Speech

architecture/interior design course, 247–248

books on gender and, 79

building on contributions to generate questions, 238

contrasting approaches to, 232–238

learning and, 230–241

making analysis process explicit, 239–240

prompting to elaborate on responses in discussions, 237

prompting to generate context for interpretation in discussions, 233–237

student, 218

Taxel, Joel, 304

Teacher(s). *See also* Teacher evaluation; Teaching

culminating texts for, 103–107

curriculum determined by, 34, 35–36, 47–48

discussions led by, 232, 438–439

domination by, 231

fulfillment of, 342–343

instructional theories and, 340–341

modeling by, 180, 233–234

personal narratives and, 148–149

research by, 38, 105, 106

role for, 230

Teacher(s). *See also* Teacher evaluation; Teaching (*Continued*)
 unit focus and, 109–110
 work for, 343–344
Teacher evaluation
 of individual essays, 202
 of individual vs. group essays, 192
 of reading logs, 190
 standards for, 322, 325–330
 by students, 210–211
 vignette, 321
Teachers Applying Whole Language (TAWL) listserve, 105
Teaching. *See also* Teacher(s); Teacher evaluation
 assessments and, 32
 assumptions about, 3–5
 growth through, 25, 30–32
 language, 167–170
 students *versus* subjects, 41–42
Teaching logs, 104
Teaching Writing as Reflective Practice (Hillocks), 105
Team teaching, 80
Technology, nature, and society theme, 414–415
Tentative talk, connected knowing and, 78
Textbook English, 168
Textbooks, mass-produced, 37, 70–71
Texts, 9. *See also* Themes
 architectural model, 247–248
 clothing as, 245–246
 composing, 242
 construction of, 108–109
 grading rubric effects on, 197–198
 horse ranch design, 247
 interior design, 248–249
 outside English department, 214
 process of planning/ constructing, 164
 production of, 164–165
 restrictions on, 37–39

scope of, 11
various forms of, 54
Themes, 11. *See also* Courtroom case study
 American Dream, 361–363
 animals as symbols, 363–364
 changing times, 365–366
 character as symbol, 366–367
 characterizing an author's style, 367
 comedy, 367–368
 coming of age, 368–369
 conflict with authority, 369–370
 connotation and imagery, 370
 coping with loss, 371–373
 courage, 373–374
 cultural conflict, 374–375
 detective, 375–376
 discrimination, 376–378
 dystopias, 416–417
 epic hero, 378–379
 extended definitions and, 117
 family, 379–380
 folk hero, 380–381
 friends and enemies, 381–382
 frontier literature, 382
 gender roles, 383–384
 influences on personality, 384–385
 irony, 385–387
 journey, 387–388
 justice, 388–389
 leader, 389
 loss of innocence, 390–391
 love, 391–392
 loyalty, 392–393
 mythic hero, 393
 naturalism, 402–403
 negotiating thresholds, 88–90, 140–141
 new kid on the block, 394–395
 outcast, 395–396
 as overarching concept, 87
 parody, 396
 peer-group pressure, 383
 persuasion, 396–397
 picaresque hero, 397–398
 point of view, 398
 progress, 399

propaganda, 399–400
protest literature, 400–401
psychology of British literary characters, 403
Puritan ethic, 401–402
realism, 402–403
responsibility, 403–404
rites of passage, 404–405
romance, 405–407
satire, 407–408
scaffolding and, 20–21
science fiction, 408–409
self-reliance, 409–410
sense of place, 410–411
social responsibility, 411–412
success, 412–414
technology, nature, and society, 414–415
tragic hero, 415
Trickster, 415–416
utopias, 416–417
values under stress, 417–418
Victorians, 418–419
war and peace, 419–421
Western, 421–422
wilderness adventures, 422
Theory as extended metaphor, 341
Thesis, argumentation, 119, 120
Three-point theme, 115
Time considerations, 173–174, 177, 190–191, 194–195
Tool kits, 165, 198, 243–244. *See also* Multimedia projects
Tools, 8, 9–10, 165, 169–170
Topic determination factors, 34–36
Topic identification, 36–48
 community and, 46–47
 curriculum requirements, 39–40
 curriculum restrictions, 37–39
 exercise, 49
 overarching concepts, 40–41
Tracking, 51–53
Tragic hero theme, 415
Transactional learning, 22–25
Transformation through literature, 295–297
Transitions, efficiency in, 179

Transmission communication theory, 70–71, 73, 255, 305–308, 318, 319. *See also* Constructivism
Trickster theme, 415–416
Truth concept, 93
Turner, Nat, 307
Twain, Mark, 41, 292
Typewriter keyboards, 111

Unconventional assessment genres, 131–132
Underground Railroad, 307
Understanding Unreliable Narrators (Smith), 15
Unit assessments. *See* Assessments
Unit design/goals, 108–139. *See also* Coming-of-age unit design; Construction zone; Course design
  alternative assessments for, 121–134
  alternatives and conventions, 111–113
  assessment elements, 114–115
  assessment rubrics, 134–137
  basics of, 34–65
  character education, 317
  classroom arrangement, 228
  conceptualization of, 109–110
  construction, 108–109
  conventional assessments for, 115–121
  conventions and alternatives, 111–113
  culminating texts identification, 103
  discussion plans, 241
  diversity issues, 300
  educational standards and, 339
  engagement, 282
  examine lessons in model units, 181
  goals identification, 134
  introductory activity design, 163
  materials selection, 48–57
  mid-term refinement of, 201–202
  multimedia composing, 256
  for planning week 1, 183
  for planning week 2, 191
  for planning week 3, 194
  for planning week 4, 204
  for planning week 5, 208
  portfolio preparation, 123–124
  preliminaries, 108–113
  principles of, 2
  provisional planning and, 138
  rationales, 57–65, 107, 151, 212, 283
  refinement of, 140–151
  rubric preparation, 137
  setting, 110
  success unit, 308–309
  topic determination, 34–36
  topic identification, 36–48
  whole course considerations, 140–141
United States, educational goals for, 288
University of Texas at Austin, Supreme Court case analysis at, 296
Unlocking Shakespeare's Language (Robinson), 263
"Use of Force, The" (Williams), 250
Utopias theme, 416–417

Values under stress theme, 417–418
Victorians theme, 418–419
Videotapes, 263. *See also* Documentary films; Films
Vignettes
  adding books to curriculum, 38
  appropriate instruction, 31
  character education, 307
  community needs, 47
  demands on good teachers, 203
  discipline methods, 337
  emotional responses to offensive literature, 294
  exam on religion, 69
  free time, 189
  on homework, 147
  information chunking, 113
  merit pay for teachers, 321
  offensive essays, 282
  politics of change, 40
  question formation, 128
  schedule challenges, 171
  on school socialization, 220
  student humiliation, 205
  student preparation for small group discussions, 224
  team-teaching, 80
  U.S. standard railroad gauge, 112
Violence, youth, 302, 311
Virtual Library of Conceptual Units, 11, 12
  alternative assessments, 121, 122
  conventional assessments, 115, 116
  introductory activities, 155–156
  rationale examples, 58, 59
Voices from the Middle (NCTE journal), 326
Voluntary manslaughter, definition of, 425–426
Vygotsky, Lev, 19, 344
  books on activity theory of, 342–343

Walking with Dinosaurs (Discovery Channel program), 138
War, school as, 336
War and peace theme, 419–421
Warrants, 99, 118
Weekly plan. *See* Daily plan
Wertsch, James, 111
Western culture, 94, 318, 319
Western theme, 421–422
Whole-group practice, 180
Wilderness adventures theme, 422
Wilhelm, Jeffrey, 91
Workshops
  books about, 89
  for overarching theme, 88–89
  reading, 51
  writing, 194, 209–210
Wright, Richard, 298

Writing
  analytic or argumentative, 115
  art and interpretive, 271
  creative, 132–134
  as exploratory tool, 73–75
  nature of reader and,
    197–198
  about personal experiences,
    152, 154, 156–157, 175
  rationales, 62–63, 65
  as reflective practice, 57
  about related problems, 152,
    154, 161–162
  related to unit concept, 133
  for teacher *versus* outside
    readerships, 198
  as tool, 8
  workshops, 194, 209–210

Zeffirelli's *Hamlet,* 263

Peter Smagorinsky teaches in the English Education program at The University of Georgia. He holds a B.A. from Kenyon College, an M.A.T. from the University of Chicago, and a Ph.D. from the University of Chicago. He taught English in public high schools in the Chicago area from 1976 to 1990. In 1999 he won the Raymond B. Cattell Early Career Award for Programmatic Research, presented by the American Educational Research Association to the person who has conducted the most distinguished program of research in any field of educational inquiry within the first decade of receiving his or her doctorate. He lives in Athens, Georgia, with his wife, Jane, daughter, Alysha, and son, David.